lonely

D0196847

Bali &
Lombok

WITHDRAWN

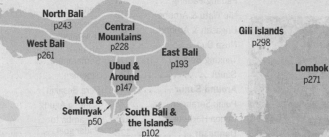

North Bali
p243

Central Mountains
p228

West Bali
p261

Ubud & Around
p147

East Bali
p193

Gili Islands
p298

Lombok
p271

Kuta & Seminyak
p50

South Bali & the Islands
p102

Kate Morgan, Ryan Ver Berkmoes

PLAN YOUR TRIP

ON THE ROAD

BARONG-STYLE TEMPLE DECORATION

TROPICAL STUDIO / SHUTTERSTOCK ©

GILI TRAWANGAN P300

DUDAREV MIKHAIL / SHUTTERSTOCK ©

Contents

Welcome to Bali & Lombok

The mere mention of Bali evokes thoughts of a paradise. It's more than a place; it's a mood, an aspiration, a tropical state of mind.

Island of the Gods

The rich and diverse culture of Bali plays out at all levels of life, from the exquisite flower-petal offerings placed everywhere, to the processions of joyfully garbed locals, shutting down major roads as they march to one of the myriad temple ceremonies, to the otherworldly traditional music and dance performed island-wide. Almost everything has spiritual meaning. The middle of Bali is dominated by the dramatic volcanoes of the central mountains and hillside temples such as Pura Luhur Batukau, while the tallest peak, Gunung Agung, is the island's spiritual centre.

One Island, Many Destinations

On Bali you can lose yourself in the chaos of Kuta or the sybaritic pleasures of Seminyak and Kerobokan, surf wild beaches in the south or just hang out on Nusa Lembongan. You can go family-friendly in Sanur or savour a lavish getaway on the Bukit Peninsula. Ubud is the heart of Bali, a place where the culture of the island is most accessible, and it shares the island's most beautiful rice fields and ancient monuments with east and west Bali. North and west Bali are thinly populated but have the kind of diving and surfing that make any journey worthwhile.

Bali's Essence

Yes, Bali has beaches, surfing, diving, and resorts great and small, but it's the essence of Bali – and the Balinese – that makes it so much more than just a fun-in-the-sun retreat. It is possible to take the cliché of the smiling Balinese too far, but in reality, the inhabitants of this small island are indeed a generous, genuinely warm people. There's also a fun, sly sense of humour. Upon seeing a bald tourist, many locals exclaim '*bung ujan*', which means today's rain is cancelled – it's their way of saying that the hairless head is like a clear sky.

Lombok & the Gilis

Almost as big as Bali, Lombok is the completely different island right next door. From its volcanic centre to idyllic beaches, it rewards travellers who want to explore. Many are drawn to mighty Gunung Rinjani, Indonesia's second-highest volcano. Rivers and waterfalls gush down its fissured slopes, while its summit – complete with hot springs and a dazzling crater lake – is the ultimate trekker's prize. In the south, you encounter one superb beach after another. The fabled Gili Islands are three exquisite droplets of white sand sprinkled with coconut palms and surrounded by coral reefs teeming with marine life.

Why I Love Bali & Lombok

By Ryan Ver Berkmoes, Writer

In 1993 I visited Bali for the first time. When I went through immigration, the officer glanced at my passport and said in the sweetest voice possible: 'Have a wonderful birthday on Bali.' Who wouldn't fall in love? I spent a lot of that trip slack-jawed with wonderment. I remember dancers and musicians materialising from across the rice fields to perform in Ubud, I remember driving little back roads of east Bali and being unable to comprehend all the green. Since then, these places – like me – have changed greatly, but their essence still evokes love.

For more about our writers, see p416

Above: Hindu procession in the lead up to Nyepi (p337)

Bali & Lombok

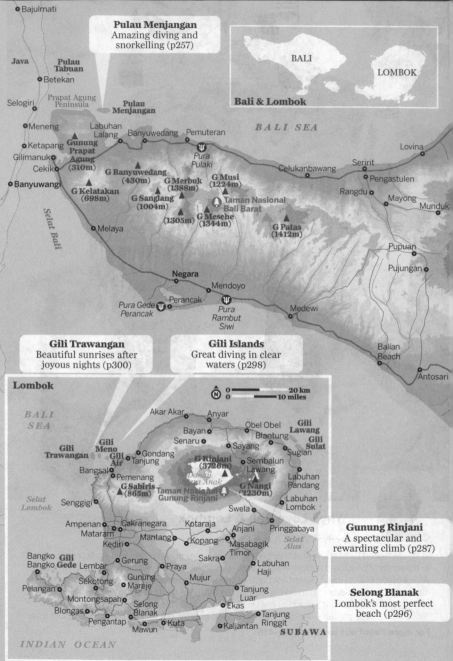

Pulau Menjangan
Amazing diving and
snorkelling (p257)

Bali & Lombok

BALI

LOMBOK

Bajulmati

Java

Pulan
Tabuan

Betekan

Selogiri

Meneng

Ketapang

Gilimanuk

Cekik

Banyuwangi

Prapat Agung
Peninsula

Labuhan
Lalang

Banyuwedang

Pemuteran

BALI SEA

Lovina

Seririt

Pengastulen

Celukanbawang

Rangdu

Mayong

Munduk

Gunung
Prapat
Agung
(310m)

Pura
Pulaki

G Banyuwedang
(430m)

G Merbuk
(1388m)

G Musi
(1224m)

G Kelatakan
(698m)

G Sanglang
(1004m)

Taman Nasional
Bali Barat

G Meseke
(1305m)

G Mesehe
(1344m)

G Patas
(1412m)

Pupuan

Pujungan

Melaya

Selat Bali

Negara

Mendoyo

Pura Gede
Perancak

Perancak

Pura
Rambut
Siwi

Medewi

Balian
Beach

Antosari

Gili Trawangan
Beautiful sunrises after
joyous nights (p300)

Gili Islands
Great diving in clear
waters (p298)

Lombok

BALI
SEA

Akar Akar

Anyar

Obel Obel

Gili
Lawang

0   20 km
0   10 miles

Bayan

Blantung

Senaru

Sayang

Sembulan
Lawang

Gili
Sulat

Gili
Trawangan

Gili
Meno

Gili
Air

Gondang

G Rinjani
(3726m)

Sugian

Tanjung

Danau
Sega Anak

Bangsal

Pemenang

G Sabiris
(865m)

Taman Nasional
Gunung Rinjani

G Nangi
(2230m)

Labuhan
Pandang

Labuhan
Lombok

Selat
Lombok

Senggigi

Swela

Ampenan

Cakranegara

Kotaraja

Anjani

Pringgabaya

Selat
Alas

Mataram

Mantang

Kopang

Masabagik
Timor

Kediri

Sakra

Labuhan
Haji

Bangko
Bangko

Gili
Gede

Lembar

Gerung

Praya

Mujur

Tanjung
Luar

Pelangan

Sekotong

Gunung
Mareje

Montongsapah

Selong
Blanak

Ekas

Tanjung
Ringgit

Blongas

Pengantap

Kuta

Mawun

Kalianton

SUBAWA

INDIAN OCEAN

Gunung Rinjani
A spectacular and
rewarding climb (p287)

Selong Blanak
Lombok's most perfect
beach (p296)

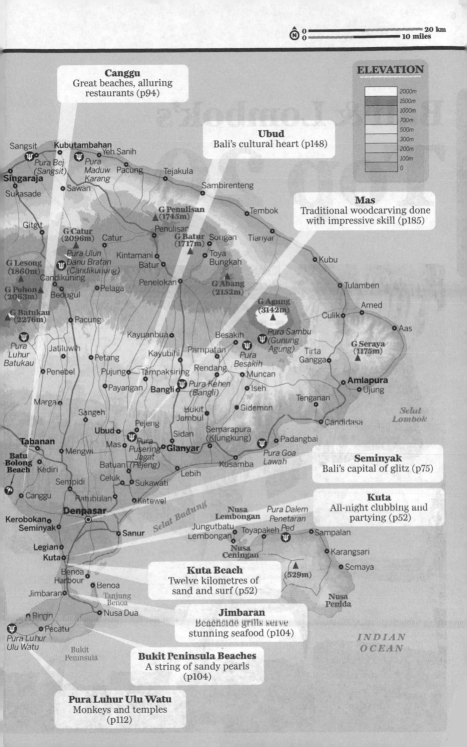

ELEVATION

	2000m
	1500m
	1000m
	700m
	500m
	300m
	200m
	100m
	0

N 0 ——— 20 km
   0 ——— 10 miles

Canggu
Great beaches, alluring
restaurants (p94)

Ubud
Bali's cultural heart (p148)

Mas
Traditional woodcarving done
with impressive skill (p185)

Seminyak
Bali's capital of glitz (p75)

Kuta
All-night clubbing and
partying (p52)

Kuta Beach
Twelve kilometres of
sand and surf (p52)

Jimbaran
Beachside grills serve
stunning seafood (p104)

Bukit Peninsula Beaches
A string of sandy pearls
(p104)

Pura Luhur Ulu Watu
Monkeys and temples
(p112)

Sangsit
Kubutambahan
Yeh Sanih
Pura Bej
(Sangsit)
Pura
Maduw
Karang
Pacung
Tejakula
Sambirenteng
Singaraja
Sukasade
Sawan
Tembok
Gitgit
G Penulisan
(1745m)
Penulisar
G Catur
(2096m)
Catur
G Batur
(1717m)
Songan
Tianyar
Pura Ulun
Danu Bratan
(Candikuning)
Kintamani
Batur
Toya
Bungkah
Kubu
G Lesong
(1860m)
Candikuning
Pelaga
Penelokan
G Abang
(2152m)
Tulamben
G Pohon
(2063m)
Bedugul
G Agung
(3142m)
Amed
G Batukau
(2276m)
Pacung
Kayuanbua
Besakih
Pura Sambu
(Gunung
Agung)
Culik
Aas
Pura
Luhur
Batukau
Jatiluwih
Kayubihi
Pampatan
Pura
Besakih
Tirta
Gangga
G Seraya
(1175m)
Petang
Pujung
Tampaksiring
Rendang
Muncan
Amlapura
Penebel
Payangan
Bangli
Pura Kehen
(Bangli)
Iseh
Ujung
Marga
Sangeh
Bukit
Jambul
Sideman
Tenganan
Selat
Lombok
Pejeng
Semarapura
(Klungkung)
Candidasa
Tabanan
Ubud
Mengwi
Mas
Pura
Pusering
Jagat
(Pejeng)
Sidan
Gianyar
Padangbai
Batu
Bolong
Beach
Kediri
Batuan
Celuk
Lebih
Kusamba
Pura Goa
Lawah
Marga
Sempidi
Sukawati
Ketewel
Ratubulan
Nusa
Lembongan
Pura Dalem
Penetaran
Ped
Canggu
Denpasar
Selat Badung
Jungutbatu
Lembongan
Toyapakeh
Sampalan
Kerobokan
Seminyak
Sanur
Nusa
Ceningan
Karangsari
Legian
Kuta
(529m)
Semaya
Benoa
Harbour
Benoa
Nusa
Penida
Jimbaran
Tanjung
Benoa
Nusa Dua
Bingin
Pecatu
Pura Luhur
Ulu Watu
Bukit
Peninsula
INDIAN
OCEAN

Bali & Lombok's
Top 20

Bali's Processions

1 There you are sipping a coffee at a cafe in, say, Seminyak or Ubud, when there's a crash of the gamelan and traffic screeches to a halt as a crowd of elegantly dressed people comes flying by bearing pyramids of fruit, tasselled parasols and a furred, masked Barong (mythical lion-dog creature) or two. It's a temple procession, disappearing as suddenly as it appeared, leaving no more than a fleeting sparkle of gold and white silk and hibiscus petals in its wake. Dozens occur daily across Bali.

Bukit Peninsula Beaches

2 A little plume of white sand rises out of the blue Indian Ocean and fills a cove below limestone cliffs clad in deep green tropical beauty. It sounds idyllic, and it is. The west coast of the Bukit Peninsula in south Bali is dotted with these very beaches, such as Balangan Beach (p107), Bingin and Padang Padang. Families run surfer bars built on bamboo stilts over the tide, where the only views are the breaks, just metres away. Grab a lounger and be lulled by the waves. Below: Balangan Beach

TROPICAL STUDIO / SHUTTERSTOCK ©

PANAREOFOTOGRAFIA / GETTY IMAGES ©

Serene Spas

3 Whether it's a total fix for the mind, body and spirit, or simply desire for serenity, visitors to Bali spend many happy hours (sometimes days) being massaged, scrubbed, bathed and blissed out. Sometimes all this attention to your well-being happens on the beach or in a garden – think Ubud's Taksu Spa (p157) – other times it's in stylish, even lavish, surroundings. The Balinese massage techniques of stretching, long strokes, skin rolling and palm-and-thumb pressure result in an all-over feeling of calm; it's the perfect holiday prescription.

Diving

4 Legendary Pulau Menjangan (p257) thrills, one tank after another. It offers multiple types of diving around a protected island renowned for its coral walls. And that's just one of Bali's great dive sites. Under the waves at Nusa Penida, you can feel small as a manta ray blocks out the sun's glow overhead, its fluid movement causing barely a disturbance in the surrounding waterst. And just when you think your dive can't get more dramatic, you turn to find a 2.5m sunfish motionlessly hovering, checking you out. Below bottom: Nusa Penida (p143)

PRISMA ARCHIVE / SHUTTERSTOCK ©

KRISTINA VACKOVA / SHUTTERSTOCK ©

MATTHEW MICAH WRIGHT / GETTY IMAGES ©

TUUL AND BRUNO MORANDI / GETTY IMAGES ©

Ubud

5 Famous in books and movies, the artistic heart of Bali exudes a compelling spiritual appeal. The streets are lined with galleries where artists, both humble and great, create. Beautiful performances showcasing the island's rich culture grace a dozen stages nightly. Museums honour the works of those inspired here over the years, while people walk the rice fields to find the perfect spot to sit in lotus position and ponder life's endless possibilities. Ubud (p148) is a state of mind and a beautiful state of being. *Above left: Ubud rice paddies*

Kuta's Never-Ending Nights

6 It starts with stylish cafes and bars in Seminyak, open-air places where everything seems just that bit more beautiful amid the post-sunset glow and pulsing house beats. Maybe you move down to action at Double Six beach. Later, the legendary clubs of Kuta draw you in, with international DJs spinning their legendary sets to packed dance floors. Some time before dawn, Kuta's harder, rawer clubs such as Sky Garden Lounge (p64) suck you in like black holes, spitting you out hours later into an unsteady daylight, shattered but happy. *Above right top: Kuta beach bar*

Selong Blanak

7 Southern Lombok's coastline has a wild savage beauty and few visitors, generating lots of talk about the vast tourism potential of the region. When you set eyes on pristine Selong Blanak beach (p296), you'll appreciate the hype. Enjoy a perfect swath of sand where the swimming in clear, turquoise-tinged water is superb. At the rear of the bay is a crescent of powdery white sand; a dream of a beach that now has the kinds of amenities that come with discovery. Other, as yet barely trod beaches, are nearby. *Above right bottom: Selong Blanak beach*

Surfing Bali

8 If it's a month containing the letter 'r', go east; during the other months, go west to fabled breaks like Padang Padang (p34). Simplicity itself. On Bali you have dozens of great breaks in each direction. This was the first place in Asia where surfing took off and, like the perfect set, it shows no signs of calming down. Surfers buzz around the island on motorbikes with board racks, looking for the next great break. Waves blown out? Another spot is just five minutes away. Don't miss classic surfer hang-out Balian Beach. Above top: Padang Padang

Underwater Gilis

9 Taking the plunge? There are few better places to dive than the Gilis, encircled by coral reefs teeming with life such as at Trawangan Wall (p301) and visited by pelagics such as cruising manta rays. Scuba diving is a huge draw – there are numerous professional schools and all kinds of courses taught (from absolute beginner to nitrox specialist). With easy access from beach to reef, snorkelling is also superb, and you're very likely to see turtles. Want to take snorkelling to the next level? Try freediving; it's sweeping the Gilis.

Luxe Stays

10 On an island that honours art and serenity, is it any wonder you'll find some of the world's finest hotels and resorts? From blissful retreats like Katamana (p89) on south Bali's beautiful beach in Kerobokan or Seminyak to perches on cliffs above the dazzling white sands that dot the Bukit Peninsula, these stylish hotels are as lovely outside as they are luxurious inside. Further resorts by vaunted architects can be found in Ubud's river valleys and in remote idyllic coastal locations right round the island.

Canggu's Beaches

11 Canggu is more of an idea and really less of a distinct place, given that the area was all rice fields just a few years ago. But now it's a label that denotes sandy fun and frolic on beaches such as Batu Bolong (p96), pounding surf offshore and nights you hope will never end at a fast-expanding collection of creative cafes and superb restaurants. Find your own faves and make Canggu your Canggu. See what cool new place opens just as you turn your back.

DAVIDNNP / SHUTTERSTOCK ©

HEDGEHOG111 / SHUTTERSTOCK ©

ARTUSH / SHUTTERSTOCK ©

Jimbaran Seafood

12 Enormous fresh prawns marinated in lime and garlic and grilled over coconut husks. Tick. A hint of post-sunset pink on the horizon. Tick. Stars twinkling overhead. Tick. A comfy teak chair settling into the beach while your toes play in the sand. Tick. An ice-cold beer. Tick. A strolling band playing the Macarena. OK, maybe not a tick. But the beachside seafood grills such as Warung Ramayana (p106) in Jimbaran are a don't-miss evening out, with platters of seafood that arrived fresh that morning to the market just up the beach.

Snorkelling

13 Bali has oodles of places where you can slip on fins and mask and enter another beautiful world. Swim a short distance from shore and see the eerie ghost of a sunken freighter at Tulamben (p224), or hover a few metres over the marine life teeming around the beautiful reef wall at Pulau Menjangan. The mangroves of Nusa Lembongan lure a rainbow of fish that gather in profusion. Or simply make your way into the calm waters off a beach such as Sanur and see what darts off into the distance.

Bali's Food

14 'Oh goody!' It's virtually impossible not to say this when you step into a classic warung like Warung Teges (p176) in Ubud for lunch to find dozens of freshly made dishes on the counter awaiting you. It shouldn't surprise that this fertile island provides a profusion of ingredients that combine to create fresh and aromatic dishes. Local specialities such as *babi guling* (roast suckling pig that's been marinated for hours in spices) will have you lining up again and again. Try lunch at one of the excellent Balinese cafes in Denpasar.

Kuta Beach

15 Tourism on Bali began here, and is there any question why? A sweeping arc of sand curves from Kuta into the misty horizon northwest to Echo Beach. Surf that started far out in the Indian Ocean crashes to shore in long symmetrical breaks. You can stroll the 12km of sand (p52), enjoying a foot massage and cold beer with thousands of your new best friends in the south, or find a hip hang-out or even a plot of sand to call your own up north.

Balinese Dance

16 The antithesis of Balinese mellow is Balinese dance, a discipline that demands methodical precision. A performer of the Legong, the most beautiful dance, spends years learning minutely choreographed movements from her eyeballs to her toes. Each movement has a meaning and the language flows with a grace that is hypnotic. Clad in silk and ikat, the dancers tell stories rich with the very essence of Balinese Hindu beliefs and lore. Every night there are multiple shows in Ubud at venues such as the Ubud Palace (p180).

IRYNA RASKO / SHUTTERSTOCK ©

MATTHEW MICAH WRIGHT / GETTY IMAGES ©

Pura Luhur Ulu Watu

17 Just watch out for the monkeys. One of Bali's holiest temples, Pura Luhur Ulu Watu (p112) is perched on tall cliffs in the southwest corner of the island. In the 11th century a Javanese priest first prayed here, and the site has only become holier since. Shrines and sacred sites are strung along the edge of the limestone precipice. Gaze across an ocean rippled by swells that arrive with metronomic precision. Sunset dance performances delight while those monkeys patiently await a banana – or maybe your sunglasses.

Sunrise over Trawangan

18 If you think Gili Trawangan is a stunner by daylight, you should see it at dawn after a night of partying – if you're still seeing. You won't find slick decor, flashy visuals, door staff and stiff entrance prices at venues like Tir na Nog (p309), where the parties started as raves on the beach and still have a raw, unorganised spirit. Local DJs normally spin hypnotic tribal beats and superstar DJs have been known to turn up and play unannounced sets.

Hiking Rinjani

19 Glance at a map of Lombok and you'll see that virtually the entire northern half of the island is dominated by the brooding, magnificent presence of Gunung Rinjani (p286), at 3726m Indonesia's second-highest volcano. Hiking Rinjani is no picnic, and involves planning, hiring a guide and porters, stamina and sweat. The route winds up the sides of the great peak until you reach the rim of a vast caldera, where there's a magnificent view of Rinjani's sacred crater lake (an important pilgrim site) and the smoking, highly active mini-cone of Gunung Baru below.

Seminyak

20 People wander around Seminyak (p75) and ask themselves if they are even in Bali. Of course! On an island that values creativity like few other places, the capital of glitz is where you'll find inventive boutiques run by local designers, the most eclectic and interesting collection of restaurants, and little boutique hotels that break with the island clichés. Expats, locals and visitors alike idle away the hours in its cafes, at ease with the world and secure in their enjoyment of life's pleasures.

JR-STOCK / SHUTTERSTOCK ©

20

Need to Know

For more information, see Survival Guide (p375)

Currency
Rupiah (Rp)

Language
Bahasa Indonesia and Balinese

Money
ATMs are easy to find throughout Bali and you'll find plenty of places to exchange money, also. Credit cards are accepted at more upmarket establishments.

Visas
It's easy to obtain visas but if you're hoping to stay longer than 30 days you may find it a hassle to arrange.

Mobile Phones
Any modern mobile phone will work here and you can buy cheap local SIM cards everywhere (from 5000Rp with no calling credit). Data speeds of 3G and faster are the norm right across Bali.

Time Zone
Indonesia Central Time (GMT/UTC plus eight hours)

When to Go

North Bali
GO year-round

Gili Islands
GO year-round

Ubud
• GO year-round

Lombok
GO year-round

South Bali
GO year-round

Tropical climate, wet & dry seasons
Tropical climate, rain year-round

High Season
(Jul, Aug & Dec)

➡ Accommodation rates increase by 50% or more.

➡ Many hotels are booked far ahead; the best restaurants need to be booked in advance.

➡ Christmas and New Year are equally expensive and crowded.

Shoulder
(May, Jun & Sep)

➡ Coincides with the best weather (drier, less humid).

➡ You may find a good room deal, and last-minute bookings are possible.

➡ Best time for many activities including diving.

Low Season
(Jan–Apr, Oct & Nov)

➡ Deals everywhere, good airfares.

➡ Rainy season – though rainfall is never excessive.

➡ Can do most activities except volcano treks.

Useful Websites

Bali Advertiser (www.baliadvertiser.biz) Bali's expat journal with insider tips and good columnists.

Bali Discovery (www.balidiscovery.com) Excellent weekly summary of news and features, plus hotel deals.

Bali Paradise (www.bali-paradise.com) Info and links.

The Beat Bali (http://thebeatbali.com) Comprehensive listings for nightlife, music and events.

Coconuts Bali (http://bali.coconuts.co) Local news and occasional features.

Lonely Planet (www.lonelyplanet.com/bali) Destination information, hotel bookings, traveller forum and more.

Lombok Guide (www.thelombokguide.com) Comprehensive site covering main areas of interest.

Important Numbers

The international access code can be any of three versions; try all three.

Indonesia country code	☏62
International call prefix	☏001/008/017
Police	☏110
Fire	☏113
Medical Emergency	☏119

Exchange Rates

Australia	A$1	9900Rp
Canada	C$1	10,000Rp
Japan	¥100	12,100Rp
New Zealand	NZ$1	9500Rp
UK	UK£1	16,800Rp
US	US$1	13,400Rp

For current exchange rates, see www.xe.com.

Daily Costs

Budget: Less than US$80

➡ Room at guesthouse or homestay: less than US$50

➡ Cheap food and drink, meals: under US$5

➡ Beaches: free

Midrange: US$80–250

➡ Room at midrange hotel: US$50–150

➡ Great night out eating and drinking: from US$20

➡ Spa treatment: US$10–40

Top end: More than US$250

➡ Room at top-end hotel or resort: over US$150

➡ Lavish evening out: over US$40

➡ Car and driver per day: US$60

Opening Hours

Typical opening hours are as follows:

Banks 8am to 2pm Monday to Thursday, 8am to noon Friday, 8am to 11am Saturday

Government offices 8am to 3pm Monday to Thursday, 8am to noon Friday (although these are not standardised)

Post offices 8am to 2pm Monday to Friday, longer in tourist centres

Restaurants & cafes 8am to 10pm daily

Shops & services catering to visitors 9am to 8pm or later daily

Arriving in Bali & Lombok

Ngurah Rai International Airport A taxi to Kuta is 80,000Rp, to Seminyak it's 130,000Rp and to Ubud it's 300,000Rp.

Lombok International Airport (LOP; www.lombok-airport.co.id) Near Praya, this airport is ever more busy. There is good service to Bali and Java, with fewer services going east into Nusa Tenggara. Flights also serve the international hubs of Singapore and Kuala Lumpur. You'll find travel agents for airline tickets in Kuta, Mataram and Senggigi.

Getting Around

The best way to get around is with your own transport, whether you drive, hire a driver or cycle. This gives you the flexibility to explore places that are otherwise inaccessible.

Car Small 4WDs can be rented for under US$30 a day. Otherwise you can hire a car with a driver for US$60 a day.

Motorbike Rent one for as little as US$5 a day.

Public transport Small vans called bemos are a cheap way of getting around on fixed routes, though most locals now just use motorbikes. In Lombok public transport is generally restricted to the main routes; away from these, you need a car or motorbike, or to charter an *ojek* (motorcycle taxi).

Tourist shuttle bus Both economical and convenient.

Taxi Fairly cheap, but only use Bluebird Taxis to avoid scams.

For much more on **getting around**, see p387

What's New

New Canggu Restaurants

Along the lanes snaking through the remaining rice fields of Canggu, hip and nifty new cafes are opening; typical is Shady Shack, with its uberfresh veggie fare. (p100)

Seminyak Village

Bali's shopping wonderland got its first enclosed air-con mall. It earns points for presenting a modest front to the street and for low-cost atrium stalls leased to young local designers. (p86)

Nusa Penida Tourism

Tourism to the most mysterious corner of Bali has really started to take off. New guesthouses and cool cafes are cropping up in coastal Ped. (p144)

Katamana

With its daring design and pure fun ethos, Potato Head beach club forever changed how people relate to Bali's beaches. Its companion resort, Katamana, now takes bold design even further. (p89)

Bukit Resorts

The Bukit Peninsula's southern limestone cliffs soar over luscious cove beaches near Ungasan. Now it seems each will have its own resort, such as the Kempinski set to open in 2017. (p114)

Bali Asli

Noted Oz chef Penelope Williams opened this fine restaurant and cooking school just outside of Amlapura. (p217)

Nonstop Action

Bali is drawing more and more airline services. Long-haul goliath Emirates now flies from Dubai, with worldwide connections. (p386)

Echo Beach Bars

Almost overnight, beer joints appeared west of Echo Beach towards Pererenan Beach. These barely there bamboo beach bars are perfect for sunset; Sand Bar sometimes goes till dawn. (p101)

Kura-Kura Bus

This Japanese-run tourist shuttle offers routes across south Bali and Ubud; some schedules run frequently enough to allow hop-on, hop-off exploring. (p389)

Boats from Serangan

Because of traffic to Padangbai on east Bali roads, more fast boats to Lombok and the Gilis are leaving from Serangan, midway between Kuta and Sanur. This is a real time-saver. (p128)

Mandapa, a Ritz-Carlton Reserve

After several years without new hotels, Ubud's lush Sungai Ayung river valley has a major addition in this stunning and daringly designed luxury resort. Watch out Four Seasons and Amandari. (p172)

South Lombok Beaches

As roads east and west from Kuta improve, the world-class beaches of south Lombok become ever-more accessible.

West Lombok Islands

Now routinely called the 'new Gilis', the tiny islands off the coast of southwest Lombok offer the low-key, white-sand experience that the *other* Gilis were once famous for.

For more recommendations and reviews, see lonelyplanet. com/Traveller Destination

If You Like...

Beaches

While there's no shortage of beaches, ones with white sand aren't as common as you'd think — most are some variation of tan or grey.

Seminyak Beach This wide stretch of sand boasts great surf for both swimmers and surfers. Don't miss sunset. (p78)

Balangan Beach This curving white-sand beach is ramshackle in an endearing way and perfect for a snooze or booze. (p107)

Padang Padang Beach Great white sands and some of the best surfer-watching you'll find anywhere. (p111)

Nusa Lembongan Beaches Little coves of dreamy sand you can walk between, plus fab swimming. (p136)

Gili Island beaches The beaches are uniformly gorgeous, with white sand, great snorkelling and a timeless traveller vibe. (p298)

Selong Blanak An idyllic Lombok bay and beach that astounds first time visitors. (p296)

Temples

With more than 10,000 temples, Bali has such a variety that you can't even categorise them.

Pura Luhur Batukau One of Bali's most important temples is a misty, remote place that's steeped in ancient spirituality. (p241)

Pura Taman Ayun A beautiful moated temple with a royal past; part of Unesco's recognition of Bali's rice traditions. (p263)

Pura Pusering Jagat One of the famous temples at Pejeng, which date to the 14th-century empire that once flourished here. (p185)

Pura Luhur Ulu Watu As important as it is popular, this temple has sweeping views, sunset dance performances and monkeys. (p112)

Nightlife

Nightclubs on Bali draw acolytes from across Southeast Asia.

Seminyak Beach clubs where the cocktails somehow taste better when you can hear the surf. (p75)

Kuta All raw energy and a mad mix of party-goers enjoying every aspect of Bali hedonism. (p52)

Legian Beach bars and beanbags on the sand where the glow of sunset segues into the twinkle of stars. (p52)

Echo Beach A necklace of ephemeral beach bars runs along the sand going west; some have raves. (p100)

Gili Trawangan The place for pounding beats and party vibes just about every night (and day!) of the week. (p300)

Culture

The island's creative heritage is everywhere you look and there's nothing manufactured about it. Dance and musical performances are the result of an ever-evolving culture with a legacy that's centuries long.

Dance Rigid choreography and discipline are hallmarks of beautiful, melodic Balinese dance, which no visitor should miss. (p352)

Gamelan The ensemble orchestra creates its unforgettable music with bamboo and bronze instruments at performances and celebrations. (p352)

Painting Balinese and Western styles merged in the 20th century and the results are often extraordinary. See some of the best in Ubud's museums. (p353)

Offerings Artful and ubiquitous, you'll discover them at your hotel room door and in huge stacks at temples. (p340)

Great Food

Enjoy superb dining on cuisines from around the world, or go local with the subtle flavours of Balinese cuisine.

Seminyak The spot with the greatest variety of top restaurants – on a 10-minute stroll you can wander the world. (p75)

Kerobokan The go-to area for the hottest and best restaurants, plus some superb Balinese warungs. (p88)

Canggu Bali's liveliest spot sees interesting cafes and restaurants opening every week. (p96)

Denpasar Local cafes serve exceptional Balinese and Indonesian food in simple surrounds. (p128)

Ubud A profusion of creative restaura nts and cafes, many organic and healthful, all delicious. (p148)

Shopping

Some consider Bali a great destination for shopping; for others it's their destiny.

Seminyak Sometimes it seems everyone in Seminyak is a designer; the reality is that many actually are. (p75)

Kerobokan A continuation of stores north of Seminyak sees places offering everything from housewares to fashion. (p88)

Canggu Soon to be Bali's shopping hot spot as low rents (at least for now!) and creative energy draw designers. (p96)

Ubud Excellent for handicrafts, art, books, yoga wear and more. (p148)

South of Ubud Artisan craft shops abound in towns like Mas; look for the don't-miss market in Sukawati. (p188)

Top: Revolver cafe in Seminyak (p85)
Bottom: Gili Meno (p310)

Month by Month

February

The rainy season pours on and the island start to hum again after the January pause following the holiday high season. Accommodation bargains abound.

☆☆ Nyale Festival

The ritual harvesting of *nyale* (wormlike sea fish) takes place on Seger Beach near Lombok's Kuta. The evening begins with poetry readings, continues with gamelan performances and carries on until dawn, when the *nyale* start appearing. Can also be held in March.

March

The rainy season is ending and there's a lull in the crowds – this is low season for tourism, especially around Nyepi when even many non-Balinese flee the silence.

☆☆ Nyepi (Day of Silence)

Bali's major Hindu festival, Nyepi celebrates the end of the old year and the start of the next. It's marked by inactivity – a strategy to convince evil spirits that Bali is uninhabited so they'll leave the island alone for another year. (p337)

April

The islands dry out after the rainy season and there's a small but noticeable uptick in visitors. This is another month when insiders recommend visiting.

☆☆ Bali Spirit Festival

A hugely popular yoga, dance and music festival from the people behind the Yoga Barn in Ubud. There are more than 100 workshops and concerts, plus a market and more. It's usually held in early April but may begin in late March. (p162)

◉ Malean Sampi

Yoked buffalo race over waterlogged earth in Narmada, near Mataram on Lombok, their jockeys clinging tight. It's as dangerous, muddy and fun as it sounds. Held early in the month.

June

The airport is getting busier, but much of what makes May a good month also applies in June. Crowds begin at the Bukit breaks.

☆☆ Bali Arts Festival

The premier event on Bali's cultural calendar. Based at the Taman Wedhi Budaya arts centre in Denpasar, the festival is a great way to see traditional Balinese dance and music, as village-based groups compete fiercely for local pride. Held mid-June to mid-July. (p131)

Lebaran Topat

Held during the seven days after the end of the fasting month (Idul Fitri; Ramadan) in the Islamic calendar, Lebaran Topat is a Sasak ceremony thought to be unique to west Lombok. Relatives gather in cemeteries to pour water over family graves, and add offerings of flowers, betel leaves and lime powder.

July

After August, July is the second-busiest month for visitors to Bali. Don't expect to have your pick of places to stay, but do plan to enjoy the energy of crowds on holiday.

🎎 Bali Kite Festival

In south Bali scores of kites soar overhead much of the year. Often huge (10m-plus), they fly at altitudes that worry pilots. There's a spiritual connection: the kites urge the gods to provide abundant harvests. During this festival the skies fill with huge creations.

August

The busiest time on Bali sees an ever-increasing number of visitors each year. Book your room and tables far in advance and expect crowds.

🎎 Indonesian Independence Day

Celebrated across Indonesia, 17 August is the day Indonesia's independence from the Dutch was declared in 1945. Legions of school kids march with great enthusiasm on Bali's main roads. Traffic is snarled (as it is days before for rehearsals) and lots of fireworks are shot off.

🏃 Surf Contests

The exact names and sponsorships change every year but you'll find top international surf contests being held throughout August down at Padang Padang Beach. Peak tourist season coincides with peak wave season.

GALUNGAN & KUNINGAN

One of Bali's major festivals, Galungan celebrates the death of a legendary tyrant called Mayadenawa. During this 10-day period, all the gods come down to earth for the festivities. Barong (mythical lion-dog creatures) prance from temple to temple and village to village, and locals rejoice with feasts and visits to families. The celebrations culminate with the Kuningan festival, when the Balinese say thanks and goodbye to the gods.

Every village in Bali celebrates Galungan and Kuningan in grand style, and visitors are welcome to join in.

The 210-day wuku (or Pawukon) calendar is used to determine festival dates. The calendar uses 10 types of weeks that are between one and 10 days long, which all run simultaneously, and the intersection of the various weeks determines auspicious days. Dates for future Galungan and Kuningan celebrations are as follows:

YEAR	GALUNGAN	KUNINGAN
2017	5 Apr & 1 Nov	15 Apr & 11 Nov
2018	30 May & 26 Dec	9 Jun
2019	22 Jul	5 Jan & 3 Aug

October

Skies darken more often with seasonal rains, but mostly the weather is pleasant. Outside of Ubud, crowds are few.

🎎 Ubud Writers & Readers Festival

Scores of writers and readers from around the world in a celebration of writing – especially that which touches on Bali. Each year there is a theme and famous authors whose works address the topic attend. (p162)

November

It's getting wetter, but not so wet that you can't enjoy the islands to the fullest. Usually a quiet month crowd-wise, you can find accommodation bargains.

🎎 Perang Topat

This 'rice war' on Lombok takes place at Pura Lingsar outside Mataram and involves a costumed parade, and Hindus and Wektu Telu pelting balls of ketupat (sticky rice) at each other. Can be held in December.

December

Visitors rain on Bali ahead of the Christmas and New Year holidays. Hotels and restaurants are booked out and everybody is busy.

⦿ Peresean

Martial arts, Lombok-style. Competitors, stripped to the waist, spar with sticks and cowhide shields. The winner is the first to draw blood. It's held annually in Mataram late in the month.

Top: Dancers in traditional costume at the Bali Arts Festival (p131)

Bottom: Bali Kite Festival (p124)

TROPICAL STUDIO / SHUTTERSTOCK ©

Itineraries

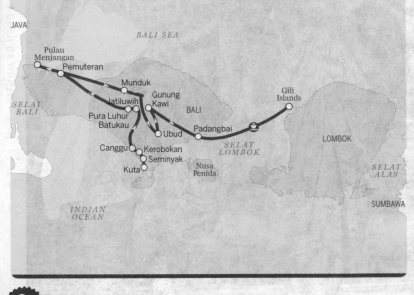

2 WEEKS Bali & the Gilis

See an incredible cross-section of Bali and enjoy the most popular parts of a Bali trip, including the Gili Islands.

Start your trip in **Seminyak**, which has the best places to go out for a meal or a drink or to buy a new frock. Allow at least three days to experience the refined charms of **Kerobokan**, the beachy pleasures of **Canggu** and the wild nights of **Kuta**. Once you're sated, head north, driving through the rice terraces of **Jatiluwih** and on to **Pura Luhur Batukau**, a holy temple up in the clouds. Head northwest to the mellow beach resorts at **Pemuteran**, from where you can snorkel or scuba Bali's best dive site at **Palau Menjangan**. Next, driving east inland, stop in **Munduk** for some hiking to remote waterfalls.

Carry on via Candikuning to **Ubud**, the cultural centre of Bali. Nights of dance and culture are offset by days of walking through the serene countryside. Do a day trip to the ancient monuments at **Gunung Kawi**. Then head down to the cute little port town of **Padangbai** and catch a fast boat to the **Gili Islands**. Wander the islands, enjoy the pulsing nightlife of Gili T and go snorkelling to spot a turtle.

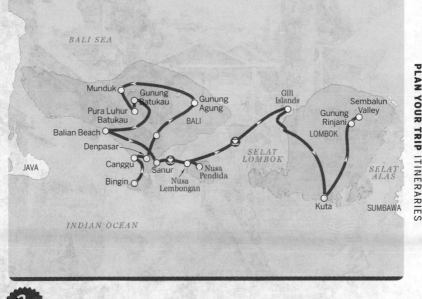

3 WEEKS Total Bali & Lombok

You'll visit six islands and countless beaches on a trip that takes you to the most interesting sites and places across Bali, Lombok and the Gilis.

Begin your trip at **Bingin**. Settle back in the sand and let the jet lag vanish. Then move to **Canggu** for Bali's hippest scene. Transit through **Denpasar** for a purely Balinese lunch and head up the hill to **Ubud** to get a full taste of Balinese culture. Next, tackle **Gunung Agung**, the spiritual centre of the island. Start early to reach the top, and take in the views before the daily onslaught of clouds and mist.

Having climbed Bali's most legendary peak, head west to the village of **Munduk**, which looks down to the north coast and the sea beyond. Go for a walk in the area and enjoy waterfalls, truly tiny villages, wild fruit trees and the sinuous ribbons of rice paddies lining the hills. Then head south to the wonderful temple of **Pura Luhur Batukau** and consider a trek up Bali's second-highest mountain, **Gunung Batukau**. Recover with some chill-out time on popular **Balian Beach**, just west.

Next, bounce across the waves from **Sanur** to **Nusa Lembongan**, the island hiding in the shadow of **Nusa Penida**. The latter is visible from much of the south and east – it's almost unpopulated and makes a good day trip. Take in the amazing vistas from its cliffs and dive under the waves to check out the marine life.

Head to the **Gili Islands** on the direct boat from Nusa Lembongan for more tranquil time circumnavigating the three islands above and below the idyllic sapphire waters fringing them. Take a boat to Senggigi, but ignore the resorts and head south. Still off the beaten path, the south coast near Lombok's **Kuta** has stunning beaches and surfing to reward the intrepid. The seldom-driven back roads of the interior will thrill the adventurous and curious, with tiny villages where you can learn about the amazing local handicrafts. Many of these roads lead up the flanks of **Gunung Rinjani**, the volcanic peak that shelters the lush and remote **Sembalun Valley**. Trekking from one village to the next on the rim can take days but is one of Bali and Lombok's great walks.

Top: Ubud (p148)

Bottom: Pura Tanah Lot (p263)

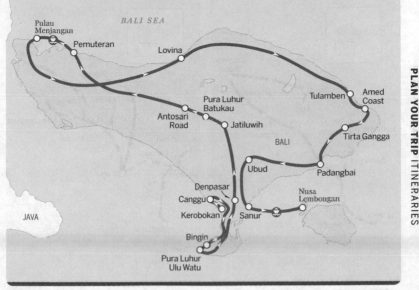

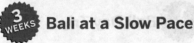

3 WEEKS Bali at a Slow Pace

Find accommodation close to the beach in **Kerobokan**. Be sure to get to the trendy restaurants and cafes of **Canggu** before you leave this part of south Bali behind. Maybe you can learn how to surf, or at least brush up on your skills, before you head south to **Bingin** and its groovy cliff-side inns overlooking fab surfing. Make the short drive down to Bukit Peninsula's spiritual centre (and monkey home) **Pura Luhur Ulu Watu**.

Take a trip through **Denpasar** and stop at the excellent local restaurants and museum. Next, Bali's ancient rice terraces will exhaust your abilities to describe green. Sample these in a drive up to the terraces of **Jatiluwih** followed by the lyrical **Pura Luhur Batukau**. Make your way over the mountains via the **Antosari Road**, pausing at a remote hotel on the way. Head west to **Pemuteran** where the hotels and resorts define relaxation. Dive or snorkel nearby **Pulau Menjangan** in Bali Barat National Park. It's renowned for its coral and sheer 30m wall.

Lovina is a good break on a route around the coast to **Tulamben**, where scores of people explore the shattered hulk of a WWII freighter underwater. Get some serious chill time on the **Amed Coast** before the short jaunt to **Tirta Gangga** and hikes through rice fields and up jungle-clad hills to remote temples. Continue to **Padangbai**. This enjoyable port town is an ideal place to hang out for a couple of days before you take back roads to **Ubud**. Find your favourite cafe and let the world wander past, or rid yourself of travel kinks at a spa. You might consider staying at one of the iconic family homestays, taking gentle walks through rice fields by day and marvelling at dance performances at night.

When you're ready and rested, get a fast boat from **Sanur** to **Nusa Lembongan**. This little island has its own buzz, with a string of hotels – from basic to semi-posh – lining its sands. It's a timeless travellers' scene with a backdrop of excellent surfing and splendid snorkelling and diving.

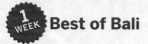

Best of Bali
1 WEEK

Seven days will fly by on this trip which covers Bali's best.

Start at a beachside hotel in **Seminyak**, **Kerobokan** or **Canggu**; shop the streets and spend time at the beach. Enjoy a seafood dinner on **Jimbaran Bay** as part of a day trip to the monkey-filled temple at **Ulu Watu**.

In the east, take the coast road to wild beaches like the one near **Pura Masceti**, followed by the well-mannered royal town of **Semarapura** with its ruins. Head north up to breathtaking **Sideman**, which combines rice terraces with lush river valleys and cloud-shrouded mountains. Then go west to **Ubud**, the crowning stop on any itinerary.

To spoil yourself, stay in one of Ubud's many hotels with views across rice fields and rivers. Sample the offerings at a spa before you try one of the myriad great restaurants. Bali's rich culture is most celebrated and most accessible in Ubud and you'll be captivated by nightly dance performances. Check out local craft studios, including the woodcarvers of **Mas**. Hike through the surrounding rice fields to river valleys, taking a break in museums bursting with paintings.

Bali Day Trips
1 WEEK

This is for the traveller who wants to unpack only once, seeing what's possible on Bali during a series of relaxed day trips. Base yourself at a beachside hotel in **Sanur**. In between your days out, soak up the mellow beach vibe and let your cares float away at a spa.

Day trip one starts with the short drive to the markets and museums of **Denpasar**, followed by a visit to the shops of **Seminyak** and **Kerobokan**. Finish up with a sunset seafood grill at **Jimbaran**.

Day trip two heads to **Ubud** for a half-day strolling the streets, looking at shops, galleries and museums. Take different routes there and back so you can enjoy the temples of **Pejeng**, the carvers of **Mas** and the village market at **Sukawati**.

Day trip three follows the wave-tossed volcanic beaches along the east coast. Stop at **Lebih**, which has a temple and mica-infused glittering sand. Go inland to the temple ruins and market at **Semarapura**, then head north along beautiful **Sideman**. Next, loop west and head back down through the tidy regional centre of **Gianyar**, where you can check out traditional fabric showrooms and feast at the night market.

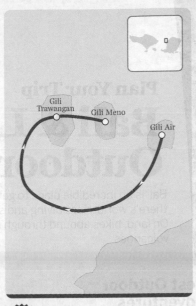

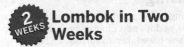

2 WEEKS Lombok in Two Weeks

Lombok is all about the great outdoors, from its incredible beaches to its iconic volcano.

Kick off in gorgeous **Kuta** and spend a day or two finding the perfect beach. East or west of town there are a dozen or so bays to choose from: magnificent **Selong Blanak** is just one. While you're here, it would be rude not to sample the fabled south Lombok surf – tiny **Gerupuk** is an excellent place to either take a lesson or hitch a boat ride to an epic break. Not far away, tranquil southwest Lombok is ideal for more aqua action; swim in sheltered waters or explore the dozen or so islands by boat. Tiny **Gili Gede** makes a perfect base.

Sacred **Gunung Rinjani** is up next. You can explore its foothills from the rustic base of **Tetebatu**, or go the whole hog and trek from **Senaru** to the crater rim, the sublime crater lake or the summit itself (depending on your time, energy and commitment level). Just don't miss the beautiful Sembalun Valley. Finish off with a stay at one of the quietly luxurious resorts on the white beaches of **Sire**.

1 WEEK Gili Islands in One Week

These three little dots of white sand off Lombok can easily occupy your entire trip, with their top-class options for diving, lazing, partying and hanging out on the beaches.

The ideal place to get to grips with island life is **Gili Air**, where the main beachfront strip is perfect tropical lounging territory. You can while away a day or two doing nothing but chilling with a book, taking a cooling dip, snorkelling the offshore coral and feasting on inexpensive fresh seafood.

Next up is **Trawangan**, where there's much more action. The perfect day here could start with a morning dive at a site such as Shark Point, followed by a healthy lunch and an afternoon snooze. Then take a gentle stroll round the sandy lanes of the island, slipping in a sunset cocktail on the west coast. After dinner, feel the beat at one of Trawangan's parties.

The final stop is **Gili Meno**, where, once you've secured the perfect place to stay (including at some new upscale choices), there's little to do except ponder the sheer desert-isle-ness of the place. If you can drag yourself away from the beach, you can go egret-spotting on the inland lake.

Plan Your Trip
Bali & Lombok Outdoors

Bali is an incredible place to get outside and play. In its waters there's world-class diving and some of the world's best surfing. On land, hikes abound through rice fields, mountain lakes and up volcanoes.

Best Outdoor Adventures

Top Surfing

World famous Ulu Watu, which every serious surfer needs to tackle once, and all-round great Batu Bolong.

Top Diving & Snorkelling

Spectacular Pulau Menjangan, whether you're just drifting or following a wall; Tulamben's sunken WWII freighter, and its snorkelling and diving from shore.

Top Hiking

Munduk's lush, spice-scented, waterfall-riven landscape; beautiful walks lasting from one hour to one day in Ubud and its rice-field surrounds; Tirta Gangg's emerald rice terraces, gorgeous views and temples.

Surfing

Surfing kick-started Bali tourism in the 1960s, and it's never looked back. Many Balinese have taken to surfing, and the grace of traditional dancing is said to influence their style.

Where to Surf: Bali

Swells come from the Indian Ocean, so the surf is on the southern side of the island and, strangely, on the northwest coast of Nusa Lembongan, where the swell funnels into the strait between there and the Bali coast.

In the dry season (around April to September), the west coast has the best breaks, with the trade winds coming in from the southeast; this is also when Nusa Lembongan is at its best. In the wet season, surf the eastern side of the island, from Nusa Dua around to Padangbai. If there's a north wind – or no wind at all – there are also a couple of breaks on the south coast of the Bukit Peninsula.

Note that the best breaks almost always have good beaches of the same name.

To reach the breaks, many will rent a motorbike with a surfboard rack while others will hire a surfboard-carrying-capable car with a driver. Either option is easily accomplished.

Balangan

Follow Jl Pantai Balangan and its surfer crash pads until you reach the parking area overlooking the Balangan beach cafes. Balangan (p107) is a fast left over a shallow reef, unsurfable at low tide, but good at mid-tide with anything over a 4ft swell; with an 8ft swell, it's magic.

Balian

There are a few peaks near the mouth of Sungai Balian (Balian River; p266) in western Bali. The best break here is an enjoyable and consistent left-hander that works well at mid- to high tide if there's no wind. Choose from guesthouses simple to luxe.

Batu Bolong

North of Kerobokan, on the northern extremity of the bay, Batu Bolong (often called Canggu; p96) has a nice beach with light-coloured sand, many surfers and a cool party scene. An optimum size for Batu Bolong is 5ft to 6ft. There's a good right-hander that you can really hook into, which works at high tide.

Bingin

Accessible down a cliff, this spot (p109) can get crowded. It's best at mid-tide with a 6ft swell, when it manufactures short but perfect left-hand barrels. The cliffs backing the beach are lined with plenty of accommodation options.

Impossibles

Just north of Padang Padang, this challenging outside reef break (p111) has three shifting peaks with fast left-hand tube sections that can join up if the conditions are perfect.

Keramas & Ketewel

These two beaches are northeast of Sanur. They're both right-hand beach breaks, which are dodgy at low tide and close out over 6ft. The surf is fairly consistent year-round and you can night surf at the Komune Bali surf resort.

Kuta Area

For your first plunge into the warm Indian Ocean, try the breaks at Kuta's beach. At full tide, go out near the life-saving club at the southern end of the beach road. At low tide, try the tubes around Halfway Kuta (p53), probably the best place in Bali for beginners to practise. Start at the beach breaks if you are a bit rusty, but treat even these breaks with respect.

Further north, the breaks at Legian Beach (p52) can be pretty powerful, with lefts and rights on the sandbars off Jl Melasti and Jl Padma.

For more serious stuff, go to the reefs south of the beach breaks, about a kilometre out to sea. Kuta Reef (p52), a vast stretch of coral, provides a variety of waves. You can paddle out in around 20 minutes, but the easiest way to get there is by boat. The main break is a classic left-hander, best at mid- to high tide, with a 5ft to 6ft swell, when it peels across the reef and has a beautiful inside tube section.

Medewi

Along the south coast of western Bali is a soft left called Medewi (p267). It's a point break that can give a long ride right into the river mouth. This wave has a big drop, which fills up then runs into a workable inside section. There's accommodation here.

Nusa Dua

During the wet season, there are some fine reef breaks on the eastern side of the island. The reef off Nusa Dua (p115) has very consistent swells. The main break is 1km off the beach to the south of Nusa Dua – go past the golf course and look for the remaining shred of Gegar Beach up against the huge Mulia resort, where there will be some boats to take you out. There are lefts and rights that work well on a small swell at low to mid-tide. Further north, in front of the Club Med, there is a fast, barrelling right reef break called **Sri Lanka**, which works best at mid-tide.

Nusa Lembongan

In the Nusa Penida group, this island is separated from the southeast coast of Bali by Selat Badung (Badung Strait).

The strait is very deep and generates huge swells that break over the reefs off the northwest coast of Lembongan. **Shipwrecks**, clearly visible from the beach, is the most popular break, a longish right that gets a good barrel at mid-tide with a 5ft swell.

A bit to the south, **Lacerations** is a very fast, hollow right breaking over a very shallow reef – hence the name. Still further south is a smaller, more user-friendly left-hander called **Playgrounds**. Remember that Lembongan is best with an easterly wind, so it's dry-season surfing.

Padang Padang

Just Padang (p111) for short, this super-shallow, left-hand reef break is off a very popular beach and just below some rickety accommodation joints where you can crash *and* watch the breaks. Check this place carefully before venturing out. It's a very demanding break that only works over about 6ft from mid- to high tide.

If you can't surf tubes, backhand or forehand, don't go out. After a ledgy take-off, you power along the bottom before pulling up into the barrel. Not a wave for the faint-hearted and definitely not one to surf when there's a crowd (such as you'll find during high-profile surf contests throughout the year).

Sanur

Sanur Reef has a hollow wave with excellent barrels. It's fickle and doesn't even start until there is a 6ft swell, but anything over 8ft will be world-class, and anything over 10ft will be brown-boardshorts mate-

rial. There are other reefs further offshore and most of them are surfable.

Hyatt Reef, over 2km from shore, has a shifty right peak that can give a great ride at full tide. The classic right is off the Grand Bali Beach Hotel.

Serangan

The development at Pulau Serangan (Turtle Island) has caused huge disruption on the southern and eastern sides of the island; paradoxically, these changes to the shape of the shore have made the surf here much more consistent. In addition, the causeway has made the island more accessible, and several warung (food stalls) face the water, where waves break right and left in anything over a 3ft swell.

South Coast

The extreme south coast, around the end of the Bukit Peninsula, can be surfed any time of the year provided there is a northerly wind, or no wind at all – get there very early to avoid onshore winds. The peninsula is fringed with reefs, and big swells are produced, but access is a problem; the shoreline is all cliff (getting down to **Nyang-Nyang** requires traversing more than 500 steps).

Bali & Lombok Surf Breaks

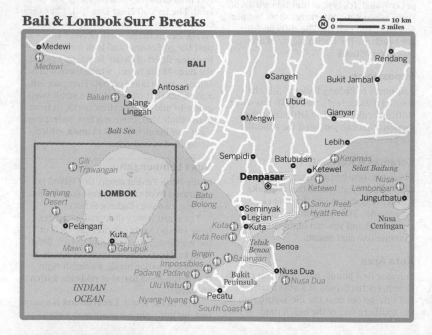

Ulu Watu

When Kuta Reef is 5ft to 6ft, Ulu Watu (p113), the most famous surfing break in Bali, will be 6ft to 8ft with bigger sets. It's way out on the southern extremity of the bay and consequently picks up more swell than Kuta.

Teluk Ulu Watu (Ulu Watu Bay) is a great set-up for surfers – local boys will wax your board, get drinks for you and carry the board down into the cave, which is the usual access to the waves. There are popular cafes, and accommodation for every budget.

Ulu Watu has about seven different breaks. The **Corner** is straight in front of you to the right. It's a fast-breaking, hollow left that holds about 6ft. The reef shelf under this break is extremely shallow, so try to avoid falling head first. At high tide, the **Peak** starts to work. This is good from 5ft to 8ft, with bigger waves occasionally right on the Peak itself. You can take off from this inside part or further down the line. It's a great wave.

Another left runs off the cliff that forms the southern flank of the bay. It breaks outside this in bigger swells, and once it's 7ft, a left-hander pitches right out in front of a temple on the southern extremity. Out behind the Peak, when it's big, is a *bombora* (submerged reef) appropriately called the **Bommie**. This is another big left-hander and it doesn't start operating until the swell is about 10ft. On a normal 5ft to 8ft day, there are also breaks south of the Peak.

Observe where other surfers paddle out and follow them. If you are in doubt, ask someone. It's better having some knowledge than none at all. Climb down into the cave and paddle out from there. When the swell is bigger you will be swept to your right. Don't panic – it is an easy matter to paddle around the white water from down along the cliff. Coming back in you have to aim for the cave. When the swell is bigger, come from the southern side of the cave because the current runs to the north.

Where to Surf: Lombok & Gili Islands

Lombok has some good surfing and the dearth of tourists means that breaks are generally uncrowded.

Gerupuk

This giant bay 6km east of Kuta boasts four surf breaks, so there's always some wave action no matter what the weather or tide. **Bumbang** is extremely dependable: best on an incoming tide, this right-hander over a flat reef is good for all levels and can be surfed year-round. **Gili Golong** excels at mid- to high tide between October and April. **Don-Don** needs a bigger swell to break but can be great at any time of year. Finally **Kid's Point** (or Pelawangan) only breaks with big swells, but when it does it's barrels all the way. You need to hitch a boat ride to each wave.

Gili Trawang

Much better known as a diving mecca, Trawangan (p300) also boasts a surf spot off the island's southwestern tip, offshore from, yes, the Surf Bar. It's a quick right-hander that breaks in two sections, one offering a steeper profile, over rounded coral. It can be surfed all year long and is best at high tide.

Mawi

About 18km west of Kuta, the stunning bay of Mawi has a fine barrelling left with a late take-off and a final tube. It's best in the dry season, from May to October, with easterly offshore winds and a southwest swell. As there are sharp rocks and coral underwater, and the rip tide is very fierce, take great care.

Tanjung Desert

Located in an extremely remote part of Lombok, Tanjung Desert is a legendary if elusive wave that has been voted the 'best wave in the world' by *Tracks* magazine. Only suitable for very experienced surfers, it's a fickle beast, in a region known for long, flat spells.

On its day this left-handed tube can offer a 300m ride, growing in size from take-off to close-out (which is over razor-sharp coral). Tanjung Desert only really performs when there's a serious ground swell – May to September offers the best chance. Wear a helmet and boots at low tide.

Equipment: Pack or Rent?

A small board is usually adequate for the smaller breaks, but a few extra inches on your usual board length won't go astray.

BEST DIVING & SNORKELLING SITES

Bali's most spectacular diving and snorkelling locations draw people from near and far. Skilled divers will enjoy the challenges of Nusa Penida (p143), as well as the schools of manta rays and 2.5m sunfish, but novices and snorkellers will be in over their heads. Spectacular 30m walls await off Pulau Menjangan (p257) and are good for divers and snokellers of all skills and ages. Tulamben (p224), with its sunken WWII freighter, is another site for both divers and snorkellers with good swimming skills.

For the bigger waves – 8ft and upwards – you'll need a 'gun'. For a surfer of average height and build, a board around the 7ft mark is perfect.

If you try to bring more than two or three boards into the country, you may have problems with customs officials, who might think you're going to try to sell them.

There are surf shops in Kuta and elsewhere in south Bali. You can rent boards of varying quality (from 50,000Rp to 100,000Rp per day) and get supplies at most popular surf breaks. If you need repairs, ask around: there are lots of places that can help.

Other recommended equipment you might bring:

➡ Solid luggage for airline travel

➡ Board-strap for carrying

➡ Tough shoes for walking down rocky cliffs

➡ Your favourite wax if you're picky

➡ Wetsuit (a spring suit or shorty will be fine) and reef booties

➡ Wetsuit vest, rashvest or other protective cover from the sun, reefs and rocks

➡ Surfing helmet for rugged conditions (and riding a motorbike)

Surf Operators

Surf schools operate right off Kuta Beach in Kuta and Legian and north to Batu Bolong Beach. Kuta and the Bukit Peninsula have long been where surfers ride waves and crash; the Canggu area is also popular now.

South Bali has some renowned board shapers, including Kuta's Luke Studer (p74) and Canggu's Dylan Longbottom, who runs Dylan Board Store (p99).

Rip Curl School of Surf (p121) Works out of Sanur, teaches windsurfing and also has standup paddle boards.

Surf Goddess (p80) Runs surf holidays for women that include lessons and lodging in a posh guesthouse in Seminyak.

Diving & Snorkelling

With its warm water, extensive coral reefs and abundant marine life, Bali offers excellent diving and snorkelling adventures. Reliable dive schools and operators all around Bali's coast can train complete beginners or arrange challenging trips that will satisfy the most experienced divers.

Snorkelling gear is available near all the most accessible spots but it's definitely worthwhile bringing your own and checking out some of the less-visited parts of the coasts.

Equipment

If you are not picky, you'll find all the equipment you need in Bali, the Gilis and Lombok (the quality, size and age of the equipment can vary). If you bring your own, you can usually get a discount on your dive. Some small, easy-to-carry things to bring from home include protective gloves, spare straps, silicone lubricant and extra globes/bulbs for your torch/flashlight. Other equipment to consider bringing:

Mask, snorkel & fins Many people bring these as they are not too big to pack and you can be sure they will fit you. Snorkelling gear rents from about 30,000Rp per day and is often shabby.

Tanks & weight belt Usually included with the cost of a dive.

Thin, full-length wetsuit For protection against stinging animals and possible coral abrasions. Bring your own if you are worried about size. If diving off Nusa Penida, you'll need a wetsuit thicker than 3mm, as up-swells bring up 18°C water from the deep.

Regulators & BCVs Most dive shops have decent ones. (BCVs are also known as BCDs or buoyancy control devices.)

Dive Operators

Major dive operators in tourist areas can arrange trips to the main dive sites all around the islands. Distances can be long, so it's better to sleep relatively close to your diving destination.

For a local trip, count on US$60 to US$100 per person for two dives, which includes all equipment. Note that it is becoming common to price in euros.

Wherever there is decent local diving on Bali there are dive shops. Usually you can count on some reefs in fair condition being reachable by boat. Recommended sites with shops include the following:

➡ Amed (p220)

➡ Candidasa (p212)

➡ Lovina (p247)

➡ Nusa Lembongan (p136)

➡ Nusa Penida (p143)

➡ Padangbai (p207)

➡ Pemuteran (p254)

➡ Sanur (p120)

➡ Tulamben (p224)

Learn to Dive

If you're not a qualified diver and you want to try scuba diving in Bali, you have several options, including packages that include lessons and cheap accommodation in a pretty place.

COURSE	DETAILS	COST
Introductory/ orientation	Perfect for novices to see if diving is for them	US$60-100
Basic certification	Three- or four-day limited courses for the basics; popular at resorts	US$300-400
Open Water certification	The international PADI standard, recognised everywhere	US$350-500

Responsible Diving

Bear in mind the following tips when diving and help preserve the ecology and beauty of reefs:

➡ Never use anchors on reefs, and take care not to run boats aground on coral.

➡ Avoid touching or standing on living marine organisms or dragging equipment across the reef.

➡ Be careful with your fins. Even without contact, the surge from fin strokes near the reef can damage delicate organisms. Don't kick up clouds of sand, which can smother organisms.

➡ Practise and maintain proper buoyancy control. Major damage can occur from reef collisions.

➡ Do not collect or buy coral or shells, or loot marine archaeological sites (mainly shipwrecks).

➡ Ensure that you take home all your rubbish and any other litter you may find as well. Plastics are a serious threat to marine life.

➡ Do not feed the fish.

➡ Minimise your involvement with marine animals. *Never* ride on the backs of turtles.

Hiking & Trekking

You could wander Bali for a year and still not see all the islands have to offer, but their small size means that you can nibble off a bit at a time, especially as day hikes and treks are easily arranged. Guides can help you surmount volcanoes, while tour companies will take you to remote regions and emerald-green valleys of rice terraces. In terms of what to pack, you'll need good boots for mountain treks and solid hiking sandals for walks.

Where to Hike: Bali

Bali is very walkable. No matter where you're staying, ask for recommendations and set off for discoveries and adventures. Ubud, the Sideman area and Munduk are obvious choices. The adjoining lakes of Danau Tamblingan and Danau Buyan are great places to explore and feature two different groups of great local guides. Even from busy Kuta or Seminyak, you can just head to the beach, turn right and walk north as far as you wish alongside the amazing surf while civilisation seems to evaporate.

For strenuous treks that verge on mountain climbing, consider Gunung Agung or Gunung Batur. There are varying routes, none of which take longer than a day. Bali does not offer remote wilderness treks beyond the volcano climbs and day trips within Bali Barat National Park. For the most part, you'll make day trips from the closest village, often leaving before dawn to avoid the clouds and mist that usually blanket the peaks by mid-morning. No treks require camping gear.

Where to Hike: Lombok

Gunung Rinjani draws trekkers from around the world. Besides being Indonesia's second-tallest volcano, it holds cultural and spiritual significance for the various people of the region. And then there's its stunning beauty: a 6km-wide cobalt blue lake some 600m below the rim of the vast caldera.

Expert advice is crucial on the mountain – people die on its slopes every year. You can organise explorations of Gunung Rinjani at Sembalun Valley, Senaru and Senggigi.

Equipment

You'll need to provide any gear you'll need for your hike. Guides may have a few bits of gear but don't count on it. Depending on the hike, consider bringing the following:

➔ Torch

➔ Warm clothes for higher altitudes (it can get pretty chilly up there)

➔ Waterproof clothes because rain can happen at any time and most of the mountains are misty at the least

➔ Good hiking sandals, shoes or boots – you definitely won't find these items locally

HIKING HIGHLIGHTS
Bali

One of Bali's great joys is hiking. You can have good experiences across the island, often starting right outside your hotel. Hikes can last from an hour to a day.

LOCATION	DETAILS
Bali Barat National Park	Remote, wilde scenery, wildlife
Danau Buyan & Danau Tamblingan	Natural mountain lakes, few people, great guides
Gunung Agung	Sunrises and isolated temples
Gunung Batukau	Misty climbs amid the clouds, with few people
Gunung Batur	Hassles but other-worldly scenery
Munduk	Lush, spice-scented waterfall-riven landscape
Sideman area	Rice terraces, lush hills and lonely temples; comfy lodging for walkers
Tirta Gangga	Rice terraces, gorgeous views, remote mountain temples
Ubud	Beautiful walks from one hour to one day; rice fields and terraces, river-valley jungles and ancient monuments

Lombok

Like the island itself, Lombok has walks and hikes that are often remote, challenging or both.

LOCATION	DETAILS
Air Terjun Sindang Gila	One of many waterfalls
Gilis	Beach-bum circumnavigations
Gunung Rinjani	Superb for trekking; climb the 3726m summit then drop into a crater with a sacred lake and hot springs
Sembalun Valley	Garlic-scented hikes on the slopes of Rinjani

Hiking Tour Operators

Guides and agencies are available in various areas such as Ubud, Gunung Agung and Tirta Gangga on Bali. In addition, there are Bali-wide agencies, including the following:

Adventure & Spirit (☑0853 3388 5598; www.adventureandspirit.com; from US$145) This professional operator offers popular canyoning day trips to central Bali involving abseiling, swimming, jumping, climbing and ziplining among scenic gorges and waterfalls.

Bali Nature Walk (p160) Walks in isolated areas in the Ubud region. Routes are customisable depending on your desires.

Bali Sunrise Trekking & Tours (☑0877 5342 1201; www.balisunrisetours.com; Gunung Agung treks from 1,000,000Rp) Leads treks throughout the central mountains.

Safety Guidelines for Trekking

Before embarking on a trekking trip, consider the following points to ensure a safe and enjoyable experience:

➡ Pay any fees and carry any permits required by local authorities; often these fees will be rolled into the guide's fee, meaning that it's all negotiable.

➡ Be sure you are healthy and feel comfortable walking for a sustained period.

➡ Obtain reliable information about environmental conditions along your intended route – the weather can get quite wet and cold in the upper reaches of the volcanoes.

➡ Confirm with your guide that you will only go on walks/treks within your realm of experience.

➡ Carry the proper equipment. Depending on the trek and time of year this can mean rain gear or extra water. Carry a torch; don't assume the guide will have one.

Cycling

Cyclists are becoming common on Bali's busy roads. The main advantage of touring Bali by bike is the quality of the experience – you can be totally immersed in the environment, hearing the wind rustling in the rice paddies or the sound of a gamelan practising while catching the scent of flowers. The island's back roads more than make up for the traffic-clogged streets of the south.

Some people are put off cycling in a tropical location, but when you're riding on level ground or downhill, the breeze really moderates the heat.

Where to Cycle: Bali

It's really much easier to tell you where *not* to ride in Bali: Denpasar south through Sanur in the east, and Kerobokan to Kuta in the west, suffer from lots of traffic and narrow roads. Across the rest of the island you can find many rides that reward with lush tropical beauty. For something really different, try the still-lonely lanes of Nusa Penida.

Where to Cycle: Lombok & Gili Islands

Lombok is good for touring by bicycle. In the populated areas the roads are flat, and the traffic across the island is less chaotic than on Bali.

East of Mataram are several attractions that would make a good day trip: south to Banyumulek via Gunung Pengsong and then back to Mataram, for example. Some coastal roads have hills and curves like a roller coaster. Try going north from Senggigi to Pemenang along the spectacular, recently improved, paved road, and then (if you feel energetic) return via the steep climb over the Pusuk Pass. The Gilis are good for riding only as a means to get around.

Equipment

Serious cyclists will want to pack personal gear they consider essential. For top-end gear, there's Bali Bike Hire (p94), which stocks top brands not found elsewhere. Casual riders can rent bikes and helmets in many locations; when in doubt ask at your accommodation.

Cycling Tour Operators

Popular tours start high in the central mountains at places such as Kintamani or Bedugul. The tour company takes you to the top and then you ride down relatively quiet mountain roads, soaking up the lush scenery, village culture and tropical scents.

The cost including bicycle, gear and lunch is US$40 to US$80. Transport to/ from south Bali and Ubud hotels is usually included; hotel pick-up in Kuta can be as early as 6.30am. Tours usually run from 8.30am to 4pm and involve a lot of coasting and stopping. Not all companies provide helmets, which is outrageous. Be sure yours does.

The following are companies to consider:

Archipelago Adventure (✆0361-808 1769, 0851 0208 1769; www.archipelago-adventure. com; adult/child from US$55/45) Offers a huge and interesting range of tours, including ones on Java. In Bali, there are rides around Jatiluwih and Danau Buyan, and mountain biking on trails from Kintamani.

Bali Bike-Baik Tours (✆0361-978052; www. balibike.com; tours from 450,000Rp) Tours run downhill from Kintamani. The emphasis is on cultural immersion and there are frequent stops in tiny villages and at rice farms.

Bali Eco Cycling (✆0361-975557; www.balieco-cycling.com; tours adult/child from US$40/30)

Tours start at Kintamani and take small roads through lush scenery south to Ubud; other options focus on rural culture.

Banyan Tree Cycling Tours (p159) Enjoy day-long tours of remote villages in the hills above Ubud. It's locally owned by Bagi and very popular. The tours emphasise interaction with villagers; there is also an extreme cycling tour.

Bung Bung Adventure Biking (p218) Based in Tirta Gangga, these tours follow back roads in fecund east Bali that are ignored by other tours.

C.Bali (p233) Offers excellent bike tours in and around Gunung Batur and the lake. The antidote to cookie-cutter bike tours.

Rafting

Rafting is popular, usually as a day trip from either south Bali or Ubud. Operators pick you up, take you to the put-in point, provide all the equipment and guides, and return you to your hotel at the end of the day. The best time is during the wet season

CYCLING SUGGESTIONS

You can't get too lost on an island as small as Bali. The following are areas good for exploring on two wheels:

LOCATION	DETAILS
Bukit Peninsula	Explore cliffs, coves and beaches along the west and south coasts; beach promenade at Nusa Dua; avoid the congested area by the airport
Central Mountains	Ambitious routes; explore Danau Bratan, Danau Buyan and Danau Tamblingan; ride downhill to the north coast via Munduk and to the south via small roads from Candikuning
East Bali	Coast road lined with beaches; north of the coast is uncrowded with serene rice terraces; the Sideman area has lodges good for cyclists
North Bali	Lovina is a good base for day trips to remote waterfalls and temples; the northeast coast has resorts popular with cyclists circumnavigating Bali
Nusa Lembongan	Small, with beaches that make good goals for each ride; cross the cool narrow suspension bridge and explore Nusa Ceningan
Nusa Penida	For serious cyclists who bring bikes; nearly traffic-free, with remote vistas of the sea, sheer cliffs, white beaches and lush jungle
Ubud	Many tour companies are based here; narrow mountain roads lead to ancient monuments and jaw-dropping rice-terrace views
West Bali	Rice fields and dense jungle rides in and around Tabanan, Kerambitan and Bajera; further west, small roads off the main road lead to mountain streams, deserted beaches and hidden temples

Manta Point, Nusa Penida (p143)

(November to March) or just after. At other times, water levels can be too low.

Some operators use the Sungai Ayung (Ayung River), near Ubud, where there are between 25 and 33 Class II to III rapids (ie potentially exciting but not perilous). The Sungai Telagawaja (Telagawaja River) near Muncan in east Bali is also popular. It's more rugged than the Ayung and the scenery is more wild.

Discounts on published prices are common, so do ask. Consider the following operators:

Bio (📞0361-270949; www.bioadventurer.com; adult/child from US$80/65) Get closer to the water on an individual river board or a tube. Tours go to west Bali.

Bali Adventure Tours (📞0361-721480; www.bali adventuretours.com; rafting trips from US$85) Sungai Ayung; also has kayak trips.

Mega Rafting (📞0361-246724; www.megaraft ingbali.com; adult/child from US$75/65) Sungai Ayung.

Sobek (📞0361-729016; www.balisobek.com; rafting from US$80) Trips on both the Sungai Ayung and Sungai Telagawaja.

Plan Your Trip
Travel with Children

Travelling with anak-anak (children) in Bali is an enriching experience. Locals consider kids part of the community, and everyone has a responsibility towards them. Children of all ages will enjoy both the attention and the many diversions that will make their holiday as special as that of the adults.

Highlights

Beaches

From surf schools at Kuta Beach to flying kites at Sanur Beach – kids of all ages will get their kicks.

Water Fun

Play in the ocean at Nusa Lembongan, or snorkel at Pulau Menjangan. For something different, walk across rice fields – who could resist the promise of muddy water filled with fun critters?

Animals

Meets the beasts at Ubud's Sacred Monkey Forest Sanctuary; the Bali Bird Park south of Ubud; the Elephant Safari Park north of Ubud; and the Bali Safari & Marine Park, in east Bali.

Bali & Lombok for Kids

Children are a social asset when you travel in Bali, and people will display great interest in any Western child they meet. You will have to learn your child's age and sex in Bahasa Indonesia – *bulau* is month, *tahun* is year, *laki-laki* is boy and *perempuan* is girl. You should also make polite enquiries about the other person's children, present or absent.

The obvious drawcards for kids are the loads of outdoor adventures available. But there are also many cultural treats that kids will love.

Dance

A guaranteed snooze right? Wrong. Check out an evening Barong dance at the Ubud Palace (p180) or Pura Dalem Ubud (p180), two venues that look like sets from Tomb Raider right down to the flaming torches. Sure, the Legong style of Balinese might be tough going for fidgety types, but the Barong has monkeys, monsters, a witch and more.

Markets

If young explorers are going to temples, they will need sarongs. Give them 100,000Rp at a traditional market and let 'em loose. Vendors will be truly charmed as the kids try to bargain and assemble the most colourful combo (and nothing is too loud for a Balinese temple).

Temples

Pick the fun ones. Goa Gajah (p184) in Bedulu has a deep cavern where hermits lived and which you enter through the mouth of a monster. Pura Luhur Batukau (p241) is in dense jungle in the Gunung Batukau area with a cool lake and a rushing stream.

Children's Highlights

Beaches

Kuta Beach (p52) Surf schools.

Sanur Beach (p121) Kids will get their kicks in the gentle surf.

Batu Bolong Beach (p96) Where the cool kids of all ages hang out.

Water

Pulau Menjangan (p257), **north Bali** The best snorkeling on the island.

Rice fields walks, Ubud For something different, walk amid muddy water filled with ducks, frogs and other fun critters.

Frolicking

Bali Treetop Adventure Park (p236), **Candikuning** Kids can make like monkeys.

Waterbom Park (p53), **Tuban** A huge aquatic playground.

Animals

Sacred Monkey Forest Sanctuary (p154), **Ubud** Monkeys and temples!

Bali Bird Park (p191), **south of Ubud** Amazing birds and reptiles.

Cool Old Things

Tirta Empul (p187), **north of Ubud** Kids will love the Indiana Jones–like pools at the ancient water palace and park.

Tirta Gangga (p218), **east Bali** Fun water palace where you can swim.

Pura Luhur Ulu Watu (p112), **south Bali** A beautiful temple with monkeys.

Planning

The critical decision is deciding where to base yourselves.

Where to Stay

There's a huge range of accommodation options for families.

➡ A hotel with a swimming pool, air-con and a beachfront location is fun for kids and very convenient, and still provides a good break for parents. Fortunately there are plenty of choices.

➡ Many larger resorts from Tuban north through Legian and also at Nusa Dua have special programs for kids that include lots of activities during the day and evening. Better ones have special supervised pool areas and other fun kids' zones.

➡ Many hotels and guesthouses, at whatever price range, have a 'family plan', which means that children up to about 12 years old can share a room with their parents free of charge. The catch is that hotels may charge for extra beds, although many offer family rooms which can accommodate four or more.

➡ A family might really enjoy a villa style unit in Seminyak, Kerobokan and the Canggu area. Within your own small private compound you'll have a pool and often more than one TV. Cooking facilities mean you can prepare familiar foods while the relative seclusion makes naps easy.

STAYING SAFE

The main danger to kids – and adults for that matter – is traffic and bad footpaths in busy areas.

The sorts of facilities, safeguards and services that Western parents regard as basic may not be present. Not many restaurants provide highchairs, places with great views might have nothing to stop your kids falling over the edge, and shops often have breakable things down low.

Given the ongoing rabies crisis in Bali, be sure to keep children away from stray dogs.

For any activity it's worth checking out conditions carefully. Just because that rafting company sells tickets to families doesn't mean they are well set up to cater to the safety needs of children.

➡ Many hotels can arrange a babysitter during the day or evening. In Kuta, Cheeky Monkeys (p53) offers drop-off childcare during the day.

➡ Hotel staff are usually very willing to help and improvise, so always ask if you need something for your children.

➡ At family homestays and guesthouses, especially in Ubud, young travellers might just feel part of the family as they watch offerings being made and people their own age going about their daily business.

What to Pack

Huge supermarkets and stores such as Carrefour in south Bali stock almost everything you'd find at similar shops at home, including many Western foods. Nappies (diapers), Western baby food, packaged UHT milk, infant formula and other supplies are easily purchased.

Babies & Toddlers

➡ A front or back sling or other baby carrier: Bali's barely walkable streets and paths are not suited to prams and pushchairs.

➡ A portable changing mat, hand-wash gel et al (baby changing facilities are a rarity).

➡ Kids' car seats: cars, whether rented or chartered with a driver, are unlikely to come with these.

Six to 12 Years

➡ Binoculars for young explorers to zoom in on wildlife, rice terraces, temples, dancers and so on.

➡ A camera or phone that shoots video to inject newfound fun into grown-up sights and walks.

Eating with Kids

Eating out as a family is one of the joys of visiting Bali. Kids are treated like deities by doting staff who will clamour to grab yours (especially young babies) while parents enjoy some quiet time together.

Bali, especially, is so relaxed that kids can just be kids. There are plenty of top-end eateries in Seminyak and elsewhere where kids romp nearby while their parents enjoy a fine meal.

If your children don't like spicy food, show caution in offering them the local cuisine. For older babies, bananas, eggs, peelable fruit and *bubur* (rice cooked to a mush in chicken stock) are all generally available. Many warungs (food stalls) will serve food without sauces upon request, such as plain white rice, fried tempeh or tofu, chicken, boiled vegetables and boiled egg. Otherwise, kid-pleasers like burgers, chicken fingers, pizza and pasta are widespread, as are fast-food chains in south Bali.

BEST REGIONS FOR KIDS

Ubud There are many things to see and do (walks, monkeys, markets and shops). Evenings may require greater creativity to keep younger kids amused, although many will be entranced by the dance performances.

Kuta & Legian Though crowded and crazy, and sometimes sleazy, beachfront resorts near the sand, surf lessons and all manner of cheap souvenirs will entice kids and teens.

Seminyak There's traffic and the surf is strong, but there's also large hotels on the beach and an appealing mix for all ages.

Lovina Modest, quiet hotels near the beach, limited traffic and a reef-protected beach make this place a good choice far from the rest of Bali.

Nusa Dua Huge beachside resorts with kids' programs, a reef-protected beach and modest traffic.

Sanur Beachside resorts, a reef-protected beach, light traffic and close to many kid-friendly activities.

Gili Air Small island so kids won't get lost; gentle surf; many tourist amenities and activities such as snorkelling.

Senggigi Modest, quiet hotels on the beach; limited traffic; reef-protected beach with gentle waves.

Top: Balinese children

Bottom: Long-tailed macaques in the Sacred Monkey Forest Sanctuary (p154), Ubud

FROLOVA_ELENA / SHUTTERSTOCK©

Regions at a Glance

Kuta and Seminyak are the main towns in the most touristed part of Bali, the part of the south that follows the magnificent stretch of sand from the airport northwest via Canggu to Pererenan Beach. The Bukit Peninsula combines remote surf breaks with vast resorts.

Ubud occupies the heart of Bali in many respects and shares some of the island's most beautiful rice fields with east Bali. The latter has no major centre but does have popular areas such as Padangbai and the Amed Coast.

Bali's centre is dominated by dramatic volcanoes. North and west Bali are thinly populated but have fine diving.

Kuta & Seminyak

Beaches
Nightlife
Shopping

Kuta Beach

Kuta's famous sweep of wave-pounded sand extends for 12km past Legian, Seminyak, Kerobokan and Canggu, before finally ending up on the rocks near Pererenan Beach. All along the sand are beach bars and vendors where the atmosphere is always merry.

Party 'Til Dawn

Restaurants and cafes in Seminyak, Kerobokan and Canggu are some of the best on Bali. Some have gorgeous sunset views, while bars and clubs have a vaguely sophisticated air. Nightlife becomes manic in Kuta, where the party goes all night.

Seminyak's Shops

Shopping in Seminyak and Kerobokan is reason enough to visit Bali – the choice is extraordinary.

p50

South Bali & the Islands

Beaches
Surfing
Diving

Balangan Beach

Beaches can be found right around south Bali: little coves of white sand like Balangan and Bingin are idyllic and inspire one to just plop down on a chair and watch the gorgeous surf.

Ulu Watu Breaks

You can't say enough about the surf breaks on the west coast of the Bukit Peninsula; Ulu Watu is famous the world over, and its multitude of breaks are world-renowned. Cool guesthouses let you stay near the action.

Underwater Nusa Penida

The best diving is at the islands. Nusa Penida has challenging conditions and deep-water cliffs, and you might even see large creatures, such as manta rays winging their way along.

p102

Ubud & Around

Culture
Indulgence
Walks

Dancers & Artists

Ubud is the nexus of Balinese culture. Each night there are a dozen performances of traditional dance, music, puppets and more. It's home to talented artists, including superb woodcarvers who make the masks for the shows.

Spas

Spas of every stripe, often with traditional medicine sessions and yoga classes, are the soul of Ubud indulgence. Services for mind and body abound, with near limitless options from bargain-priced massages to opulent all-day retreats.

Explore Nature

The rice fields surrounding Ubud are some of Bali's most picturesque. You can walk for an hour or a day, enjoying river valleys, small villages and enveloping natural beauty.

p147

East Bali

Beaches
Hikes
History

Pasir Putih

Beaches are found along much of the Bali's east coast. While you'll come across many a dark volcanic sand strand along the coast road, the real star is popular Pasir Putih, with its swimmable surf, lovely sand and mellow vendors.

Wandering Sideman

Some of Bali's most alluring rice fields and landscapes are found in the east. You're spoiled for choice around Sideman, which has walks aplenty through the verdant green hills and valleys. Or go all out, rise early and tackle Gunung Agung.

A Tragic Past

Taman Kertha Gosa has the moving remains of a palace lost when the royals committed ritual suicide rather than surrender to the Dutch in 1908.

p193

Central Mountains

Hikes
Culture
Solitude

Munduk Treks

The centre of the island offers hikes around volcanoes and lakes. Trails radiating from Munduk include these natural highlights along with misty walks through spice plantations and jungle to waterfalls.

Top Temple

Pura Luhur Batukau never fails to touch the spirit of those who find this temple on the slopes of Gunung Batukau. It is a mystical and misty – place to contemplate Bali's beliefs and to commune with nature.

Remote Walks

A solitary visit to Pura Luhur Batukau can be followed by retreats to nearby remote lodges, treks through the volcanic mountains and wanderings around the adjoining lakes Danau Buyan and Danau Tamblingan.

p228

North Bali

Resorts
Chilling
Diving

Pemuteran's Resorts

The crescent of beach hotels at Pemuteran is the real star of north Bali. Beautifully built, the hotels form a fine human-scale resort area, and they're close to Pulau Menjangan.

Lovina's Quiet

Settle onto a mat on Lovina's tan and grey sand, pick up a book and let the day drift past at your low-cost, quiet getaway. Even the surf is mellow: much of the north coast is protected by reefs.

Pulau Menjangan

Pulau Menjangan lives up to its many superlatives. A 30m coral wall close to shore delights both divers and snorkellers with a cast of fish and creatures that varies from sardines to whales.

p243

West Bali

Surfing
Beaches
Rice Fields

Medewi Breaks

The breaks at Balian Beach have a following, and a small surfer community has sprung up with simple guesthouses and somewhat posher retreats. Hang out with locals who know the waters well. Further west, Medewi is even more remote.

Balian Beach

Balian Beach is the main strand in the west, and it makes a good place to hang even if you're not surfing. Enjoy the range of accommodation, from hip to simple to posh.

Tabanan

Unesco has given Bali's *subak* system of rice-field irrigation World Heritage Site status. The area around Tabanan has some of the most beautiful rice fields, plus a nice little museum and the nearby temple of Pura Taman Ayun.

p261

Lombok

Hiking
Coastline
Tropical Chic

Gunung Rinjani

A majestic volcano, Gunung Rinjani's very presence overshadows all of northern Lombok. Hiking trails sneak up Rinjani's astonishing caldera, where you'll find a shimmering crater lake, hot springs and a smoking mini-cone.

South Coast

Lombok's southern coastline is nature in the raw. There's absolutely nothing genteel about the magnificent shoreline, which is pounded by oceanic waves that make it a surfer's mecca. Empty beaches allow exceptional swimming in azure waters.

Sire

For total immersion in tropical chic, the Sire area offers some gorgeous resorts that combine a bamboo and thatched motif with pampering.

p271

Gili Islands

Diving
Beaches
Chilling

Coral Reefs

Forming one of Indonesia's most species-rich environments, the Gilis' coral reefs teem with fascinating sea life. The islands are perfect for divers (including freedivers) and snorkellers, and you're almost guaranteed to see turtles.

Gili Air Beaches

Pack your sunscreen, mat, some water and a good book and head out in the morning to walk around Gili Air. Along the way stop at each and every beach that catches your fancy.

Gili Meno

We've all dreamed of finding the ultimate beach: a vision of palm trees, blinding white sands and a turquoise sea, plus a bamboo shack selling cool drinks and fresh fish. Yours might just be an obscure corner on Meno.

p298

On the Road

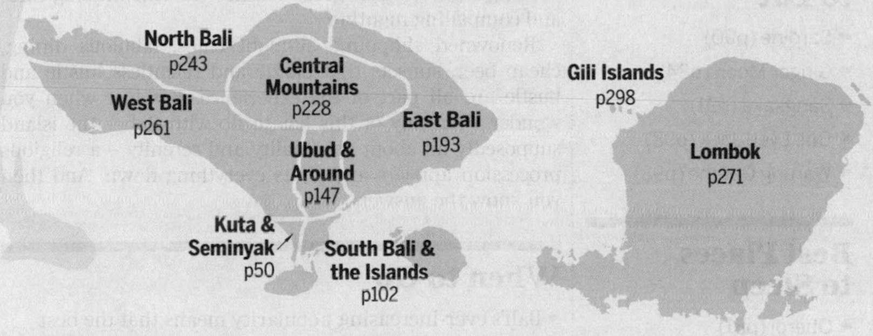

North Bali
p243

Central
Mountains
p228

West Bali
p261

East Bali
p193

Gili Islands
p298

Ubud &
Around
p147

Lombok
p271

Kuta &
Seminyak
p50

South Bali &
the Islands
p102

Kuta & Seminyak

Best Places to Eat

➡ Sardine (p90)

➡ Ginger Moon (p84)

➡ Sangsaka (p91)

➡ One Eyed Jack (p98)

➡ Warung Goûthé (p98)

Best Places to Sleep

➡ Oberoi (p81)

➡ Samaya (p81)

➡ Alila Seminyak (p89)

➡ Katamana (p89)

➡ Hotel Tugu Bali (p97)

Why Go?

Crowded and hectic, the swathe of south Bali hugging the amazing ribbon of beach that runs north almost from the airport is the place many travellers begin and end their visit to the island.

In Seminyak and Kerobokan there is a bounty of restaurants, cafes, designer boutiques, spas and the like that rivals anywhere in the world, while Kuta and Legian are the choice for rollicking all-night clubbing, cheap singlets and carefree family holidays. North around Canggu is Bali's most exciting region, where great beaches vie with enticing cafes and compelling nightlife.

Renowned shopping, all-night clubs, fabulous dining, cheap beer, sunsets that dazzle and relentless hustle and bustle are all part of the experience. But just when you wonder what any of this has to do with Bali – the island supposedly all about spirituality and serenity – a religious procession appears and shuts everything down. And then you know the answer.

When to Go

➡ Bali's ever-increasing popularity means that the best time to visit Kuta, Seminyak and their neighbours is outside high season (July, August and the weeks around Christmas and New Year). Holidays in other parts of the world mean that visitor numbers spike and it can require actual effort to organise tables in the best restaurants, navigate trendy shops and get a room with a view.

➡ Many prefer April to June and September, when the weather is drier and slightly cooler, and the crowds manageable.

➡ To surf this side of Bali, or just revel in the surf culture, visit during Bali's west coast surfing season: April to September.

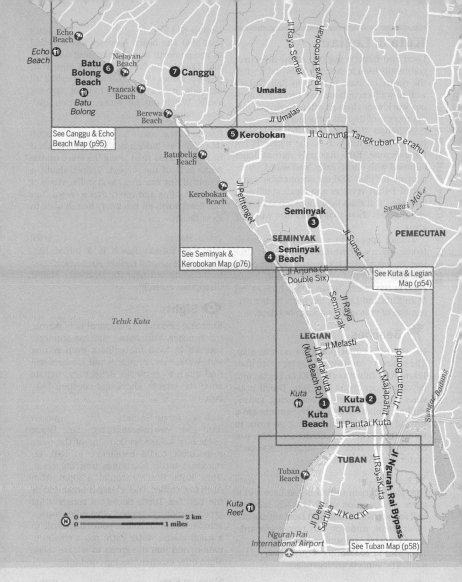

Kuta & Seminyak Highlights

1 Kuta Beach (p52) Lolling around on Bali's original tourist magnet.

2 Kuta Nightlife (p52) Raving through the night in the manic clubs and legendary nightlife scene of Kuta.

3 Seminyak (p75) Ignoring your resolve while shopping in the myriad boutiques and designer outlets.

4 Seminyak Sunsets (p85) Revelling in a technicolour sunset with a beer.

5 Kerobokan (p88) Savouring a meal at one of the many fabulous and world-class restaurants.

6 Batu Bolong Beach (p96) Joining the hip beach and surf scene, while debating where to have a refreshment.

7 Canggu (p96) Making a delightful discovery, be it food, drink or commerce, amid rice fields and villas on the twisting and confounding lanes.

Kuta & Legian

Loud and frenetic are two of the adjectives commonly used to describe Kuta and Legian, the centre of mass tourism in Bali. Today's wall-to-wall cacophony has become notorious worldwide through often overhyped media reports of tourists behaving badly.

Although this is often the first place many visitors hit in Bali, the region is not for everyone. Kuta has ugly narrow lanes jammed with cheap cafes, surf shops, incessant motorbikes and an uncountable number of T-shirt vendors and bleating offers of 'massage'. But flash new shopping malls and chain hotels show that Kuta's lure will only grow.

Legian appeals to a slightly older crowd (some say it's where fans of Kuta go after they're married). It's equally commercial and has a long row of family-friendly hotels close to the beach. Tuban differs little in feel from Kuta and Legian, but has a higher percentage of visitors on package holidays.

🏄 Beaches

It's the beach that put Kuta on the map. The strand of sand stretching for more than 12km from Tuban north to Kuta, Legian and beyond to Seminyak and Echo Beach is always a scene of surfing, massaging, games, chilling, imbibing and more. Sunsets are a time of gathering for just about everyone in south Bali. When conditions are right, you can enjoy an iridescent magenta spectacle better than fireworks.

★Kuta Beach   BEACH
(Map p55) Tourism in Bali began here and is there any question why? Low-key hawkers will sell you soft drinks and beer, snacks and other treats, and you can rent surfboards, lounge chairs and umbrellas (negotiable at 10,000Rp to 20,000Rp), or just crash on the sand. The sunsets are legendary.

★Legian Beach   BEACH
(Map p55) An extension north from Kuta Beach, Legian Beach is quieter thanks to the lack of a raucous road next to the sand and fewer people.

Kuta Reef Beach   BEACH
(Map p58; Pantai Segara) Some still call this beach 'Pantai Jerman', a legacy of some long-forgotten early surfing tourist. It's nicely low-key, with beer vendors and surfboard rentals.

Double Six Beach   BEACH
(Map p54) The beach becomes less crowded as you go north from Legian until very popular Double Six Beach, which is alive with pick-up games of football and volleyball all day long. It's a good place to meet partying locals. Watch out for water pollution after heavy rains.

Pantai Patra Jasa   BEACH
(Map p58) This hidden gem of sand is reached by a tiny access road along the fence on the north side of the airport. There's shade, a couple of tiny warungs (food stalls), views of planes landing and rarely ever a crowd. You can head north on the lovely beach walk to Kuta Beach.

Tuban Beach   BEACH
(Map p58) Tuban's beach is a mixed bag. There are wide and mellow stretches of sand to the south but near the Discovery Mall it disappears entirely.

⊙ Sights

Kuta and Legian's main appeal is, of course, the beaches. Otherwise, you can immerse yourself in local life without even getting wet. Wanderers, browsers and gawkers will find much to fascinate, delight and irritate amid the streets, alleys and constant hubbub.

Bali Sea Turtle Society   HATCHERY
(Map p54; www.baliseaturtle.org; Kuta Beach; ⊙site 24hr, 4.30pm Apr-Oct) One of the more responsible turtle hatcheries in Bali, re-releasing turtle hatchlings into the ocean from Kuta Beach, around 4.30pm from April to October. The release is organised by the Bali Sea Turtle Society, a conservation group working to protect olive ridley turtles. Join the queue to collect your baby turtle in a small plastic water bath; pay a small donation; and join the group to release them. Signs offer excellent background info.

Museum Kain   MUSEUM
(Map p54; ☏0361-846 5568; www.museumkain.org; Jl Pantai Kuta, Beachwalk; adult/child 100,000/50,000Rp; ⊙10am-8pm Tue-Sun) An unexpected haven of high culture in the heart of Kuta Beach, this air-con complex in the upper levels of the Beachwalk Mall celebrates indigenous textiles. Exhibits include beautiful displays of batik fabrics. You'll learn how batik is made and at times be offered a chance to make your own. Interactive screens deconstruct the patterns and designs.

Memorial Wall   MONUMENT
(Map p54; Jl Legian) This memorial wall reflects the international scope of the 2002 bombings, and people from many countries pay their respects. Listing the names of the 202 known victims, including 88 Australians and 35 Indonesians, it is starting to look quite weathered. Across the street, a parking lot is all that is left of the destroyed Sari Club.

Vihara Dharmayana Temple   BUDDHIST TEMPLE
(Map p54; Chinese Temple; Jl Blambangan; ⊙8am-8pm) Dating back nearly 200 years, this Buddhist temple is a colourful place of calm, slightly off the beaten path. Incense burns in the serene courtyard.

Site of Sari Club   HISTORIC SITE
(Map p54) Across the street from the Bali Memorial Wall is where the Sari Club stood before it was destroyed in the 2002 bombings. It's now a parking lot; plans to turn it into a memorial park have circulated for years.

🏃 Activities

From Kuta you can easily go surfing, sailing, diving or rafting anywhere in the southern part of Bali and still be back for the start of happy hour at sunset.

Surfing
The beach break called Halfway Kuta (Map p54), offshore near the Hotel Istana Rama, is popular with novices. More challenging breaks can be found on the shifting sandbars off Legian, around the end of Jl Padma, and at Kuta Reef, 1km out to sea off Kuta Reef Beach.

Surf culture is huge in Kuta. Shops large and small sell mega-brand surf gear and boards. Stalls on the side streets hire out surfboards (for a negotiable 30,000Rp per day) and boogie boards. They also repair dings and sell new and used boards. Some can arrange transport to nearby surfing spots. Used boards in good shape average US$200.

Pro Surf School   SURFING
(Map p54; ☑0361-751200; www.prosurfschool.com; Jl Pantai Kuta; lessons per day from 675,000Rp) Right along Kuta Beach, this well-regarded school has been getting beginners standing for years. It offers all levels of lessons, including semi-private ones, plus gear and board rental. There's a pool and cool cafe.

Rip Curl School of Surf   SURFING
(Map p54; ☑0361-735858; www.ripcurlschoolof surf.com; Jl Arjuna; lessons from 700,000Rp) Usually universities sell shirts with their logos; here it's the other way round: the beachwear company sponsors a school. Lessons at all levels are given across the south; there are special courses for kids. It has a location for kitesurfing, windsurfing and stand-up paddle boarding (SUP) in Sanur.

Massages & Spas

Jamu Traditional Spa   SPA
(Map p54; ☑0361-752520, 165; www.jamutradition alspa.com; Jl Pantai Kuta, Alam Kul Kul; 1hr massage from 350,000Rp; ⊙9am-7pm) In serene surrounds at a resort hotel you can enjoy massage in rooms that open on to a pretty garden courtyard. If you've ever wanted to be part of a fruit cocktail, here's your chance – treatments involve tropical nuts, coconuts, papayas and more, often in fragrant baths.

Garbugar   MASSAGE
(Map p54; ☑0361-769121; Istana Kuta Galleria, Blok OG 09; massage from 100,000Rp; ⊙10am-8pm) Blind masseurs here are experts in sensing

KUTA FOR KIDS

Besides cavorting on the beach all day, there are other activities in Kuta, Legian and Tuban that will delight kids, including special youth-oriented surf lessons at all the major surf shops.

Waterbom Park (Map p58; ☑0361-755676; www.waterbom-bali.com; Jl Kartika Plaza; adult/child 520,000/370,000Rp; ⊙9am-6pm) This watery amusement park covers 3.5 hectares of landscaped tropical gardens. It has assorted water slides, swimming pools and play areas, a supervised park for children under five years old, and a 'lazy river' ride. Other indulgences include the 'pleasure pool', a food court and bar, and a spa.

Cheeky Monkeys (Map p54; ☑0361-846 5610; www.cheekymonkeysbali.com; Jl Pantai Kuta, Beachwalk, level 3; half-day from 185,000Rp) Offers drop-in childcare for young children. There's a huge range of activities on offer; it's located in the back of the mall.

Kuta & Legian

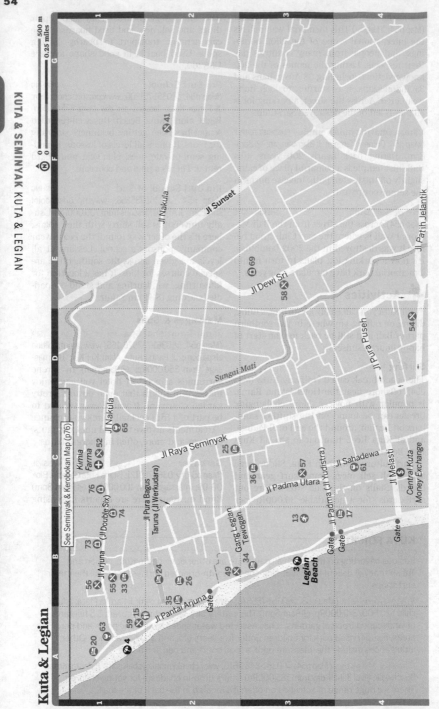

See Seminyak & Kerobokan Map (p76)

Jl Arjuna (Jl Double Six)

Kimia Farma

Jl Nakula

Jl Raya Seminyak

Jl Pura Bagus Taruna (Jl Werkudara)

Jl Padma Utara

Jl Padma (Jl Yudistra)

Gang Legian Tewoggh

Jl Pantai Arjuna

Legian Beach

Gate

Jl Sahadewa

Jl Melasti

Central Kuta Money Exchange

Sungai Mati

Jl Dewi Sri

Jl Nakula

Jl Sunset

Jl Pura Puseh

Jl Patih Jelantik

Gate

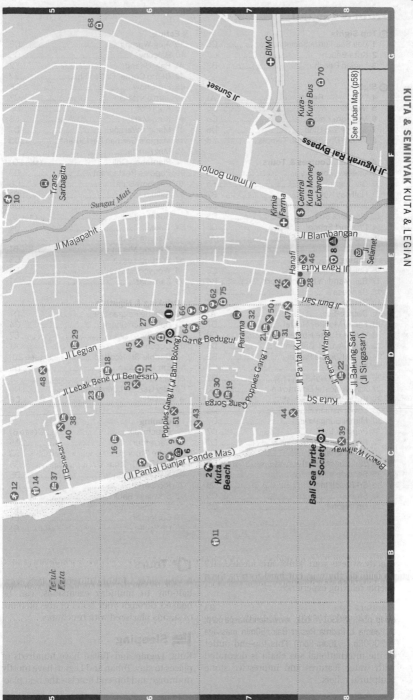

Kuta & Legian

exactly where your kinks are located. It's no-frills all the way, but hard to beat for a deeply relaxing experience.

Mandara Spa SPA
(Map p54; ☎0361-752111; www.mandaraspa.com; Jl Padma 1, Padma Resort Bali; 50min massage 795,000Rp; ☉10am-8pm) This top-end outlet of the international spa chain is decorated with water features and impressive stone sculptural reliefs.

☞ Tours

A vast range of tours all around Bali, from half-day to multiday excursions, can be booked through your hotel or the plethora of stands plastered with brochures.

🛏 Sleeping

Kuta, Legian and Tuban have hundreds of places to stay. Tuban and Legian have mostly midrange and top-end hotels – the best places for budget accommodation are Kuta and southern Legian. Almost every hotel has air-con and a pool. Dozens of generic midrange chain hotels are appearing throughout the area. Many are very inconveniently located.

Any place west of Jl Legian won't be more than a 10-minute walk to the beach.

Tuban

There is a string of large hotels along the sometimes-nonexistent Tuban Beach. These places are popular with groups; many have extensive activities geared to children.

Patra Jasa Bali Resort & Villas RESORT $$$
(Map p58; ☎ 0361-935 1161; www.thepatrabali.com; Jl Ir H Juanda; r incl breakfast 1,300,000-1,800,000Rp; ❄ ☎ ☎) At the far-south end of Tuban near Kuta Reef Beach, this low-key resort is very quiet, yet close to the action thanks to the beach walk. The spacious grounds have two pools and sprawling gardens. The 228 rooms have a standard charm; the villas have nice sea views from their terraces.

Kuta

Wandering the *gang* (alleys) looking for a cheap room is a rite of passage for many. Small and family-run options can still be found even as chains crowd in. Some of the hotels along Jl Legian are of the type that assume men booking a single actually aspire to a double.

ON THE BEACH

Note that hotels on Jl Pantai Kuta are sep-arated from the beach by a busy main road south of Jl Melasti.

Stones RESORT $$$
(Map p54; ☎ 0361-300 5888; www.stoneshotelbali.com; Jl Pantai Kuta; r incl breakfast from US$110; ❄ ☎ ☎) Looming across the road from Kuta Beach, this vast resort boasts a huge pool, a vertical garden and 308 rooms in five-storey blocks. The design is hip and contemporary, and high-tech features abound. It's one of the growing number of megahotels along this strip and affiliated with Marriott. Some rooms have bathtubs on the balcony.

CENTRAL KUTA

Good streets to shop for budget accommo-dation include Gang Sorga, Gang Bedugul and Jl Lebak Bene.

★**Hotel Ayu Lili Garden** HOTEL $
(Map p54; ☎ 0361-750557; ayuliligardenhotel@yahoo.com; off Jl Lebak Bene; r with fan/air-con from 195,000/250,000Rp; ❄ ☎ ☎) In a *relatively* quiet area near the beach, this vintage family-run hotel has 22 bungalow-style

---

KUTA: WHERE BALI TOURISM BEGAN

Mads Lange, a Danish copra trader and 19th-century adventurer, set up a successful trading enterprise near modern-day Kuta in 1839. He mediated profitably between local rajahs (lords or princes) and the Dutch, who were encroaching from the north. His busi-ness soured in the 1850s and he died suddenly, just as he was about to return to Den-mark. It's thought that his death may have been the result of poisoning by locals jealous of his wealth. His restored **tomb** (Map p58; Jl Tuan Langa) is at the site where he used to live in a quiet, tree-shaded area by the river. Lange bred Dalmatians and today locals assume that any dog with a hint of black and white has some of this blood.

Beach tourism got its start in Bali when Bob and Louise Koke – a globetrotting couple from the US – opened a small guesthouse on virtually deserted Kuta Beach in the 1930s. The guests, mostly from Europe and the US, were housed in thatched bungalows built in an idealised Balinese style. In a prescient move, Bob taught the locals to surf, something he'd learned in Hawaii.

Kuta really began to change in the late 1960s when it became a stop on the hippie trail between Australia and Europe. By the early 1970s it had relaxed losmen (small Balinese hotels) in pretty gardens, friendly places to eat, vendors peddling magic mushrooms and a delightfully laid-back atmosphere. Enterprising Balinese seized the opportunity to profit from the tourists and surfers, often in partnership with foreigners seeking a pretext to stay longer.

Legian, the village to the north, sprang up as an alternative to Kuta in the mid-1970s. At first it was a totally separate development, but these days you can't tell where one ends and the other begins.

Tuban

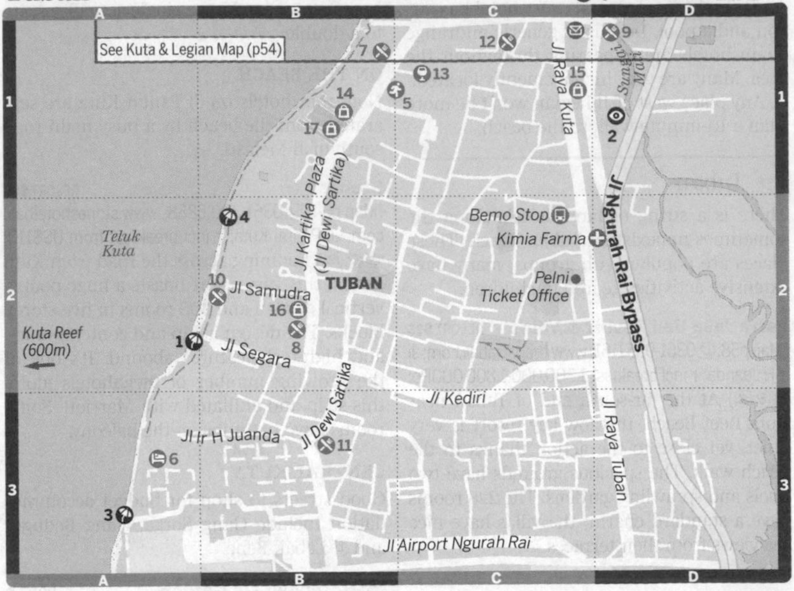

Tuban

Sights
- 1 Kuta Reef Beach ... A2
- 2 Mads Lange Tomb ... D1
- 3 Pantai Patra Jasa ... A3
- 4 Tuban Beach ... B2

Activities, Courses & Tours
- 5 Waterbom Park ... C1

Sleeping
- 6 Patra Jasa Bali Resort & Villas ... A3

Eating
- 7 B Couple Bar 'n' Grill ... B1
- 8 Kafe Batan Waru ... B2
- 9 Kuta Night Market ... D1
- 10 Pantai ... B2
- 11 Pisgor ... B3
- 12 Warung Nikmat ... C1

Drinking & Nightlife
- 13 DeeJay Cafe ... C1

Shopping
- 14 Discovery Mall ... B1
- 15 Joger ... C1
- 16 Lippo Mall Kuta ... B2
- 17 Periplus Bookshop ... B1
- Sogo ... (see 17)

rooms. Standards are high and for more dosh you can add amenities such as a fridge.

★ **Kuta Bed & Breakfast** GUESTHOUSE $
(Map p54; KBB; ☎0818 568 364, 0821 4538 9646; kutabnb@gmail.com; Jl Pantai Kuta 1E; r from 250,000Rp; ❄📶) There are nine comfortable rooms in this excellent guesthouse right across from Bemo Corner – it has all the basics. It's a 10-minute walk from the beach and a 10-minute ride from the airport. It has a wonderful rooftop with views over the Kuta skyline; nightlife is close too.

Mimpi Bungalows HOTEL $
(Map p54; ☎0361-751848; mimpibungalowkuta@gmail.com; Gang Sorga; r 200,000-500,000Rp; ❄📶🏊) The cheapest of the 12 bungalow-style rooms here are the best value (and are fan only). Private gardens boast orchids and shade, and the pool is a good size.

Funky Monkey Hostel HOSTEL $
(Map p54; ☎0812 4636 4386; www.funkymonkeybali.com; Poppies Lane 1; dm 60,000-120,000Rp, r 300,000Rp; ❄📶🏊) In a tourist-thronged location in the back alleys of Kuta, close to

Poppies Restaurant (p62), this homely and intimate Dutch-run hostel is a top place to meet fellow travellers. There's a small pool, free pancakes and cheap beer. The cheapest dorms are outdoor bunks.

Guess House Hostel   HOSTEL $

(Map p54; ☑ 0361-475 3199; www.guesshousehostel.com; Jl Tegal Wangi; dm from 80,000Rp; ☺ reception 24hr; ❀@�) Right in the heart of Kuta, this modern hostel has two very large dorm rooms. There's a kitchen, shared bathrooms, luggage storage and more.

Bendesa   HOTEL $

(Map p54; ☑ 0361-754366; www.bendesaaccommodation.com; off Poppies Gang II; r US$15-40; ❀�♨) The 42 rooms here are in a three-storey block overlooking a pleasant-enough pool area. The location manages to be quiet amid the greater hubbub. The cheapest rooms have cold water (some with bathtubs) and fan. There's wi-fi in some rooms near the lobby.

Kayun Hostel Downtown   HOSTEL $

(Map p54; ☑ 0361-758442; www.kayun-downtown.com; Jl Legian; dm incl breakfast from 120,000Rp; ❀�♨) In the heart of Kuta, close to all the nightlife, this hostel is the place to be if you're here to party. Set in an elegant colonial building, it has a sense of style and a small plunge pool. Dorm rooms have between four and 20 beds, with curtains for privacy.

Puri Agung Homestay   GUESTHOUSE $

(Map p54; ☑ 0361-750054; off Gang Bedugul; r with fan/air-con from 120,000/200,000Rp; ❀) Hungover travellers will appreciate the 12 dark, cold water-only rooms at this attractive little place that features a tiny grotto-like garden. Nonvampires can find more light on the top floor. Run by a charming family; a novelty as chains take over Kuta.

Berlian Inn   HOTEL $

(Map p54; ☑ 0361-751501; off Poppies Gang I; s/d from 135,000/210,000Rp; ❀) A stylish cut above other budget places, the 27 rooms in the two-storey buildings here are pleasingly quiet, with ikat bedspreads and an unusual open-air bathroom design. Pricier rooms have air-con and hot water.

★ Un's Hotel   HOTEL $$

(Map p54; ☑ 0361-757409; www.unshotel.com; Jl Benesari; r with fan/air-con 460,000-500,000Rp; ❀@�♨) A hidden entrance sets the tone for the secluded feel of Un's, a two-storey place with bougainvillea spilling over the pool-facing balconies. The 30 spacious rooms in a pair of blocks (the southern one is quieter) feature antiques and comfy cane loungers. It's close to the beach.

Love Fashion Hotel   HOTEL $$

(Map p54; ☑ 0361-849 6688; www.lovefhotel.com; Jl Legian 121; r incl breakfast US$45-90; ❀�♨) This gaudy hotel in the heart of the Kuta strip is an offshoot of the Fashion TV channel, featuring a design that's suitably over the top. Strut your stuff down the catwalk in the lobby, where mirrors and lighting effects are designed to make you feel like a model. There's a rooftop Jacuzzi and a bar with nightly parties.

Bali Bungalo   HOTEL $$

(Map p54; ☑ 0361-755109; www.bali-bungalo.com; off Jl Pantai Kuta; r 270,000-600,000Rp; ❀�♨) Large rooms close to the beach yet away from irritations are a big part of the appeal of this older 40-room hotel. It's well maintained and there are statues of prancing horses to inspire horseplay in the pool. Rooms are in two-storey buildings and have patios/porches; not all have wi-fi.

Poppies Bali   HOTEL $$$

(Map p54; ☑ 0361-751059; www.poppiesbali.com; Poppies Gang I; r 1,700,000-2,000,000Rp; ❀@�♨) This Kuta institution has a lush, green setting for its 20 thatch-roofed cottages with outdoor sunken baths. Bed choices include kings and twins. The pool is surrounded by stone sculptures and water fountains in a garden that almost makes you forget you are in the heart of Kuta.

🛏 Legian

ON THE BEACH
Part of the beach road north of Jl Melasti is protected by gates that exclude almost all vehicle traffic. Hotels here have what is in effect a quiet, paved beachfront promenade.

Sari Beach Hotel   HOTEL $$

(Map p54; ☑ 0361-751676; www.thesaribeach.com; off Jl Padma Utara; r incl breakfast US$65-80; ❀�♨) Follow your ears down a long *gang* to the roar of the surf at this good-value beachside hotel that defines mellow. It feels like a time warp from the 1980s but is perfect for a no-frills beach holiday. The 21 rooms have patios and the best have big soaking tubs. Grassy grounds boast many little statues and water features.

Bali Mandira Beach Resort HOTEL **$$$**
(Map p54; ☑0361-751381; www.balimandira.com; Jl Padma 2; r US$130-200; ❄️🤖🛜🏊) Gardens filled with bird-of-paradise flowers set the tone at this 191-room, full-service resort with four-storey blocks and individual garden units. Cottages have updated interiors, and the bathrooms are partly open-air. A dramatic pool at the peak of a stone ziggurat (which houses a spa) offers sweeping ocean views, as does the cafe.

Seaside Villas VILLA **$$$**
(Map p54; ☑0361-737138; www.seasidebali.com; Jl Pantai Arjuna 18; US$130-450; ❄️🛜🏊) Tucked into a popular stretch of sand just south of ever-so-happening Double Six Beach are these 28 rooms and villas set in lush gardens. Most of the rooms are in a sleek, curving four-storey block; the overall atmosphere is surprisingly intimate given the location. The beach is very close. Rooms come in many sizes, some with kitchens.

CENTRAL LEGIAN

Sri Beach Inn GUESTHOUSE **$**
(Map p54; ☑0361-755897; Gang Legian Tewngah; r with fan/air-con from 200,000/350,000Rp; ❄️🛜) Follow a series of paths into the heart of old Legian; when you hear the rustle of palms overhead, you're close to this guesthouse in a garden with five rooms. More money gets you hot water, air-con and a fridge. It offers cheap monthly rates.

Island GUESTHOUSE **$$**
(Map p54; ☑0361-762722; www.theislandhotel bali.com; Gang Abdi; dm/r incl breakfast from 220,000/500,000Rp; ❄️@🛜🏊) One of Bali's few flashpacker options, Island is a real find – literally. Hidden in the attractive maze of tiny lanes west of Jl Legian, this stylish place with a sparkling pool lies at the confluence of Gang 19, 21 and Abdi. It has a deluxe dorm room with eight beds.

DOUBLE SIX BEACH

★**Puri Damai** GUESTHOUSE **$$**
(Map p54; ☑0361-730665; www.puridamai.com; Jl Werkudara; apt 1-/2-bedroom US$70/140; ❄️🛜🏊) An elegant choice tucked away near Double Six Beach, this exquisite little hotel is run by Made, the doyen of the Made's Warung empire. The 12 units are sizeable apartments with full kitchens, dining and living areas, terraces and balconies. The compact compound is lush and the furniture is relaxed tropical.

Hotel Kumala Pantai HOTEL **$$**
(Map p54; ☑0361-755500; www.kumalapantai. com; Jl Werkudara; r incl breakfast 1,100,000-1,800,000Rp; ❄️@🛜🏊) The 173 rooms are large, with marble bathrooms featuring separate shower and tub. The three-storey blocks are set in lush grounds across from popular Double Six Beach. Many rooms have fridges and microwaves; ask for one.

Jayakarta Hotel RESORT **$$**
(Map p54; ☑0361-751433; www.jayakartahotels resorts.com; Jl Pura Bagus Taruna; r incl breakfast 1,100,000-2,400,000Rp; ❄️🤖🛜🏊) The Jayakarta fronts a long and shady stretch of beach. The palm-shaded grounds, several pools and various restaurants make it a favourite with groups and families. Hair-braiders by the pool give kids that holiday look. The 331 rooms are large and in two- and three-storey blocks. Wi-fi is not in every room.

Double-Six RESORT **$$$**
(Map p54; ☑0361-730466; www.double-six. com; Double Six Beach 66; r incl breakfast from 3,200,000Rp; ❄️🛜🏊) A colossus five-star resort, Double-Six takes a leaf out of the Vegas book of extravagance. Fronted by a luxurious 120m pool, the 146 spacious rooms all overlook the beach, and have 24-hour butlers and TVs in the bathrooms. Some have balcony hot tubs. It has an enormous rooftop bar (p73), plus several restaurants including the noted Plantation Grill (p64).

🍴 Eating

There's a profusion of places to eat here. Cheap tourist cafes with Indonesian standards, sandwiches and pizza are ubiquitous.

Find laid-back travellers' cafes by wandering the *gang* and looking for crowds. For quick snacks and 4am beers, 24-hour Circle K stores are everywhere.

Beware of big-box restaurants on Jl Sunset. Heavily promoted, they suffer from traffic noise and are aimed squarely at tourists who follow the bus.

🍴 Tuban

Tuban has oodles of chains and fast-food joints. The beachfront hotels all have restaurants or cafes, which are often good for nonguests to enjoy a snack or a sunset drink.

The south end of Jl Raya Kuta near the airport road is lined with good local warungs and cafes. Browse around and pick a favourite.

★ **Pisgor** INDONESIAN $

(Map p58; JI Dewi Sartika; treats from 2000Rp; ⊗10am-10pm) All sorts of goodness emerges from the ever-bubbling deep-fryers at this narrow storefront near the airport. The *pisang goreng* (banana fritters) are not to be missed and you can enjoy more esoteric fare such as *ote-ote* (vegetable cakes). Get a mixed bag and munch away with raw chillies for accent.

Warung Nikmat INDONESIAN $

(Map p58; ☑ 0361-764678; JI Banjar Sari; meals 15,000-30,000Rp; ⊗8am-9pm) This long-running Javanese favourite is known for its array of authentic Indonesian dishes, including beef rendang, *perkedel* (fritters), prawn cakes, *sop buntut* (oxtail soup) and various curries and vegetable dishes. Get there before 2pm for the best selection.

Pantai SEAFOOD $$

(Map p58; ☑ 0361-753196; JI Wana Segara; meals 50,000-150,000Rp; ⊗8am-11pm; 🛜) It's location, location, location at this beachside bar and grill. The food is stock tourist (seafood, Indo classics, pasta etc) but the setting overlooking the ocean is idyllic. Each year it gets a bit more stylish and upscale but still avoids pretence. It's on the beachfront walk, well behind the Lippo Mall Kuta (p74).

Kafe Batan Waru INDONESIAN $$

(Map p58; ☑ 0361-897 8074; www.baligoodfood. com; JI Kartika Plaza, Lippo Mall Kuta; meals 50,000-150,000Rp; ⊗11am-11pm) The Tuban branch of the noted Ubud restaurant is a slicked-up version of a warung, albeit with excellent and creative Asian and local fare.

There's also good coffee, baked goods and kid-friendly items. It has a high-profile spot in front of the glam Lippo Mall (p74).

B Couple Bar 'n' Grill SEAFOOD $$

(Map p58; ☑ 0361-761414; JI Kartika Plaza; meals 60,000-200,000Rp; ⊗11am-midnight) A vibrant mix of upscale local and international tourists tuck into Jimbaran-style grilled seafood at this slick operation. Pool tables, TV sports and live music add to the din while flames flare in the open kitchens.

✗ Kuta

Beach vendors are pretty much limited to drinks. Otherwise you'll find mostly surfer fare (pizzas, burgers, Indo classics) at myriad spots along the narrow streets.

CENTRAL KUTA

Ajeg Warung BALINESE $

(Map p54; ☑ 0822 3777 6766; Kuta Beach; mains from 20,000Rp; ⊗8am-10pm) This simple stall with shady tables is right on Kuta Beach. It dishes up some of the freshest local fare you'll find in a shady location near the sand, with views of the surf. Enter the beach where JI Pantai Kuta turns north and walk south 100m along the beach path.

Bemo Corner Coffee Shop CAFE $

(Map p54; ☑ 0361-755305; www.facebook.com/ bemocappucino; JI Pantai Kuta 10A; mains from 40,000Rp; ⊗8am-9pm) An attractive oasis just off the madness of JI Legian, this sweet little open-fronted cafe serves excellent coffee drinks, smoothies and casual fare such as sandwiches and huge trad breakfasts with eggs, bacon, sausage etc.

KUTA COWBOYS UNSADDLED

You see them all around Bali's southern beaches: young men who are buff, tattooed, long-haired and gregariously courtly. Long known as 'Kuta cowboys', they turn the Asian cliché of a younger local woman with an older Western man on its ear. For decades women from Japan, Australia and other nations have found companionship on Bali's beaches that meets a need, be it romantic, adventurous or otherwise.

The dynamic between these foreign women and Balinese men is more complex than a simple exchange of money for sexual services (which is illegal in Bali): although the Kuta cowboys do not receive money directly for sex, their female companions tend to pay for their meals, buy gifts, and may even pay other expenses such as rent.

This well-known Bali phenomenon is detailed in the entertaining documentary *Cowboys in Paradise* (stream it at www.cowboysinparadise.com). Director Amit Virmani says he got the idea for the film after he talked to a Balinese boy who said he wanted 'to sex-service Japanese girls' when he grew up. The result looks at the lives of the Kuta cowboys and explores the economics and emotional costs of having fleeting dalliances with female tourists on a schedule.

Kuta Night Market INDONESIAN $

(Map p58; Jl Blambangan; meals 15,000-25,000Rp; ⊙6pm-midnight) This is an enclave of stalls and plastic chairs. It bustles with locals and tourism workers chowing down on hot-off-the-wok treats, grilled goods and other fresh foods.

Kuta Market MARKET $

(Map p54; Jl Raya Kuta; ⊙6am-4pm) Not big but its popularity ensures constant turnover. Look for some of Bali's unusual fruits here, such as the mangosteen.

★ Poppies Restaurant INDONESIAN $$

(Map p54; ☑0361-751059; www.poppiesbali.com; Poppies Gang I; mains 40,000-130,000Rp; ⊙8am-11pm; 🐾) Opening its doors in 1973, Poppies was one of the first restaurants to be established in Kuta (Poppies Gang I is even named after it). It's popular for its elegant garden setting and a menu of upmarket Balinese, Western and Thai cuisine. The *rijstaffel* (selection of dishes served with rice) and seafood is popular.

Made's Warung INDONESIAN $$

(Map p54; ☑0361-755297; www.madeswarung. com; Jl Pantai Kuta; mains from 40,000Rp; ⊙8am-11pm) Made's was the original tourist warung in Kuta and its Westernised Indonesian menu has been much copied. Classic dishes such as *nasi campur* (rice with a choice of side dishes) are served in an open-fronted setting that harks back to when Kuta's tourist hot spots were lit by gas lantern.

Jamie's Italian ITALIAN $$$

(Map p54; ☑0361-762118; www.jamieoliver.com; Jl Pantai Kuta; ⊙noon-11pm) One of 40 worldwide, this outlet of Jamie Oliver's chain has the expected creative and seasonal menu. The dishes bust cliches and also, possibly, your wallet. Burgers are priced the same as you'd get in NYC. There are tables inside and out. Service and presentation is polished.

ALONG JL LEGIAN

The eating choices along Jl Legian seem endless; worthy choices are not.

Kopi Pot CAFE $$

(Map p54; ☑0361-752614; www.kopipot.com; Jl Legian; meals 60,000-150,000Rp; ⊙6am-11pm; 🐾) Shaded by trees, Kopi Pot is a favourite, popular for its coffees, milkshakes and myriad desserts. The multilevel, open-air dining area and bar sits back from noxious Jl Legian.

POPPIES GANG II & AROUND

Rainbow Cafe INTERNATIONAL $

(Map p54; ☑0361-765730; Poppies Gang II; mains from 40,000Rp) Join generations of Kuta denizens quaffing the afternoon away. The vibe at this deeply shaded spot has changed little over the years, even as malls have sprouted nearby. Many current customers are the offspring of backpackers who met at adjoining tables.

Fat Chow ASIAN $$

(Map p54; ☑0361-753516; www.fatchowbali.com; Poppies Gang II; mains from 60,000Rp; ⊙9am-11pm; 🐾) A stylish, modern take on the traditional open-fronted cafe, Fat Chow serves Asian-accented fare at long picnic tables, small tables and lounges. The food is creative, with lots of options for sharing. Among the favourites: crunchy Asian salad, pork buns, Tokyo prawns and authentic pad Thai.

Sushi Tei SUSHI $$

(Map p54; ☑0361-849 6496; Jl Pantai Kuta, Beachwalk, fl 2; mains 40,000-10,000Rp; ⊙11am-11pm) Let the beach breezes waft across your cheeks at this upscale sushi outlet with views of the surf. The menu is long on sushi and quality is high. Watch for incredible-value specials. There's a good drinks list and sunset happy hour.

Mama's German Restaurant GERMAN $$

(Map p54; ☑0361-761151; www.bali-mamas.com; Jl Legian; mains 50,000-150,000Rp; ⊙24hr) Once you get used to the local serving staff in full German dirndl, you might almost think you're in a sweatier version of Munich. The menu is authentic German, with a vast array of sausages, roasts and pork steaks from the restaurant's own private butcher. (Nonwurst options include burgers, noodles, pizza etc.) Quaff draught Bintang by the litre.

Balcony INTERNATIONAL $$

(Map p54; ☑0361-757409; Jl Benesari 16; meals 50,000-150,000Rp; ⊙6am-11pm) The Balcony has a breezy tropical design and sits above the din of Jl Benesari below. Get ready for the day with something from the long breakfast menu. At night choose from pasta, grilled meats and a few Indo classics. It's all nicely done and the perfect place for an impromptu date night.

Stakz Bar & Grill AUSTRALIAN $$

(Map p54; ☑0361-762129; www.stakzbarandgrill.com; Jl Benesari; mains 40,000-140,000Rp; ⊙8am-midnight; 🐾) From Vegemite on toast and a flat white for brekkie, a potato-cake roll or meat pie in the afternoon, and an Aussie burger with the lot (including beetroot, egg and pineapple) for dinner, Stakz is pure Aussie fare. Patrons mob the bar from the morning; the tattoo outpaces the clothing count.

EAST OF JL LEGIAN

Wooyoo ICE CREAM $

(Map p54; Jl Dewi Sri 18F; treats from 20,000Rp; ⊗10am-10pm) In a hot tropical place, what is better than ice cream? The soft-serve treats here come from a well-known Korean brand renowned for its rich, creamy swirls. Enjoy in a cup, cone or on sweet 'snail' bread. Toppings include sweet popcorn, chocolate bits and churros. The dining area has a woodsy, open style.

★ **Take** JAPANESE $$

(Map p54; ☑0361-759745; Jl Patih Jelantik; meals 70,000-300,000Rp; ⊗11am-midnight; 🛜) Flee Bali for a relaxed version of Tokyo just by ducking under the traditional fabric shield over the doorway at this ever-expanding restaurant. Hyper-fresh sushi, sashimi and more are prepared under the keen eyes of a team of chefs behind a long counter. The head chef is a stalwart at the Jimbaran fish market in the early hours.

✕ Legian

Along the streets of Legian, the ho-hum greatly outnumber the good, so browse before choosing.

Warung Murah INDONESIAN $

(Map p54; ☑0361-732082; Jl Arjuna; meals 20,000-35,000Rp; ⊗8am-11pm) Lunch goes swimmingly at this authentic warung specialising in seafood. An array of grilled fish awaits; if you prefer fowl over fin, the *sate ayam* is succulent *and* a bargain. Hugely popular at lunch; try to arrive right before noon. Don't miss the sambal.

Warung Asia ASIAN $

(Map p54; ☑0361-742 0202; Jl Werkudara; mains from 35,000Rp; ⊗11am late; 🛜) Staffed by waiters cheery even by Bali standards, this popular upstairs warung serves both Indo classics and Thai fare. It gets boozy and raucous at night.

Warung Yogya INDONESIAN $

(Map p54; ☑0361-750835; Jl Padma Utara; mains from 25,000Rp; ⊗8am-10pm) Hidden in the heart of Legian, this simple warung is spotless and has a bit of mod style. It serves up hearty portions of local food for prices that would almost tempt a local.

Saleko INDONESIAN $

(Map p54; Jl Nakula 4; meals from 15,000Rp; ⊗8am-11pm) If you haven't tried Masakan Padang food yet, you haven't eaten proper Indonesian. Saleko is a great place to sample this simple, delicious and cheap Sumatran street food. Spicy grilled chicken and fish dare you to ladle on the volcanic sambal – not de-spiced for timid tourist palates. All dishes are halal; there's no alcohol.

Balé Udang INDONESIAN $$

(Map p54; Mang Engking; ☑0361-894 7119; www.baleudang.com; Jl Nakula 88; mains 35,000-150,000Rp; ⊗11am-10pm) Serving the food of Indonesia, this large restaurant is a metaphor for the islands themselves, with various thatched dining pavilions set amid ponds and water features. The long menu focuses on fresh seafood. Service is snappy, but friendly.

ON THE BEACH

Mozzarella ITALIAN, SEAFOOD $$

(Map p54; ☑0361-751654; www.mozzarella-resto.com; Jl Padma Utara; mains 70,000-200,000Rp; ⊗7am-11pm; 🛜) The best of the beachfront restaurants on Legian's car-free strip, Mozzarella serves Italian fare that's more authentic than most. Fresh fish also features; service is rather polished and there are various open-air areas for moonlit dining, plus a more sheltered dining room. A great spot for a quiet beachfront breakfast.

DON'T MISS

SUNSET DRINKS IN KUTA & LEGIAN

Bali sunsets regularly explode in stunning displays of reds, oranges and purples. Sipping a cold one while watching this free show to the beat of the surf is the top activity at 6pm. Genial local guys offer plastic chairs on the sand and cheap, cold Bintang (20,000Rp).

In Kuta, head to the car-free south end of the beach; in Legian, the best place is the strip of beach that starts north of Jl Padma and runs to the south end of Jl Pantai Arjuna.

ℹ FOLLOW THE PARTY

Bali's most infamous clubs cluster in about a 300m radius of Sky Garden Lounge. The distinction between drinking and clubbing is blurry at best, with one morphing into another as the night wears on (or the morning comes up). Most bars are free to enter, and often have special drink promotions and 'happy hours' that run at various intervals until after midnight. Savvy partiers follow the specials from venue to venue and enjoy a massively discounted night out. Look for cut-price-drinks coupon fliers.

Bali club ambience ranges from the laid-back vibe of the surfer dives to high-concept nightclubs with long drink menus and hordes of prowling servers. Prostitutes have proliferated at some Kuta clubs.

Zanzibar   INTERNATIONAL $$
(Map p54; ☑0361-733529; www.zanzibarbali.com; Jl Arjuna; mains 50,000-120,000Rp; ☉7am-11pm) This popular patio fronts a busy strip at Double Six Beach. Sunset is prime time; the best views are from the tables on the 2nd-floor terrace. Dishes include the nasi family and the burger bunch. If it's crowded, the many nearby competitors will do just fine.

Plantation Grill   MODERN AUSTRALIAN $$$
(Map p54; ☑0361-734300; www.plantationgrill bali.com; Jl Arjuna, Double-Six Hotel, 4th fl; mains 220,000-420,000Rp; ☉6pm-midnight) The gaudy sign outside leaves no doubt that this posh hotel restaurant springs from the empire of Australian chef Robert Marchetti. Inside you'll find a luxurious tropical setting meant to evoke a 1920s fantasy. The menu features big steaks and seafood with some wildly priced specials such as lobster Thermidor (855K!). Sling bar is an intimate retreat for a fantasy cocktail.

🍸 Drinking & Nightlife

Sunset on the beach is popular, with a drink at a sea-view cafe or beachside beer vendor. Later, the legendary nightlife action heats up. Many ragers spend the early evening at a hipster joint in Seminyak before working their way south to oblivion.

Stylish Seminyak clubs are popular with gay and straight crowds, but you'll usually find a mixed crowd in Kuta and Legian.

The Beat (www.beatmag.com) has nightlife listings.

🍷 Tuban

DeeJay Cafe   CLUB
(Map p58; ☑0361-758880; Jl Kartika Plaza 8X, Kuta Station Hotel; ☉midnight-9am) The choice for closing out the night (or starting the day). House DJs play tribal, underground, progressive, trance, electro and more. Expect a hardcore crowd of ravers.

🍷 Kuta

Jl Legian is lined with interchangeable bars with bar stools moulded to the butts of hard-drinking regulars. Expect come-ons from pimps, Viagra sellers and lots of cries of 'we got bloody cold beer, mate!'

★ Velvet   BAR
(Map p54; ☑0361-846 4928; www.vhbali.com; Jl Pantai Kuta, Beachwalk, level 3; ☉11am-late) The sunset views can't be beat at this large terrace bar and cafe at the beach end of the Beachwalk mall. It morphs into a club after 10pm Wednesday to Sunday. Grab a lounger for two.

Sky Garden Lounge   CLUB
(Map p54; www.skygardenbali.com; Jl Legian 61; ☉24hr) This multilevel palace of flash flirts with height restrictions from its rooftop bar where all of Kuta twinkles around you. Look for top DJs, a ground-level cafe and paparazzi-wannabes. Possibly Kuta's most iconic club, with hourly drink specials. Gets backpackers, drunken teens, locals on the make etc.

Engine Room   CLUB
(Map p54; www.engineroombali.com; Jl Legian 89; ☉4pm-4am) Open to the street, this lurid club features go-go dancers in cages as a come-on. As the evening progresses almost everyone dances and clothing gets shed. It's a wild party, with four venues for hedonism and music that includes hip-hop, trap and rap.

Bounty   CLUB
(Map p54; www.bountydiscotheque.com; Jl Legian; ☉8pm-4am) Set on a faux sailing boat amid a mini-mall of food and drink, the Bounty is a vast open-air disco that pumps all night to hip-hop, techno, house and party tracks. Foam parties, go-go dancers, drag shows and cheap shots add to the rowdiness.

Bali & Lombok's Best Beaches

Bali and Lombok are ringed by beaches, with sand from white to black and surf from wild to tame. They draw visitors in droves for sunbathing, yoga, running, surfing, snorkelling, diving and good times aplenty. With so many to chose from, you'll find one – or several – for any mood.

➡ Beaches
➡ Surfing
➡ Diving
➡ Marine Life

Above: Green Bowl Beach (p114), Bukit Peninsula

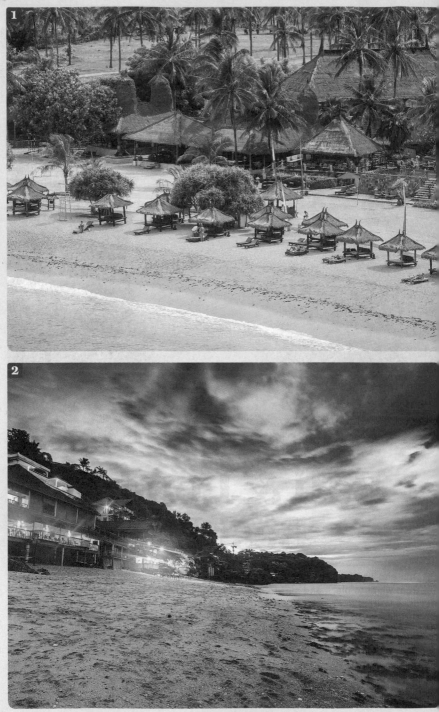

1. A Kuta beach resort (p290), South Lombok **2.** Dingin Beach (p109), Bukit Peninsula **3.** Dreamland, Bukit Peninsula (p104)

Beaches

There are so many great beaches on Bali and Lombok that it's best to just categorise them by region. Within each of these five areas, you'll find many different patches of sand to enjoy.

Tuban to Echo Beach

Stretching some 12km from just north of the airport all the way northwest to Pererenan Beach (p101), this is the beach that made Bali famous. This multifaceted playground has multiple personalities, including surfer, hip, family, lonely, boozy and more.

Bukit Beaches

The cliffs on the west coast of the Bukit Peninsula (p104) often shelter little coves of beautiful white sand, like that found at Balangan, Bingin and Padang Padang. It can be hard to reach these sands (and their neighbours) but the rewards include incredible views of the surf breaks, nameless little bamboo warungs with Bintang and sublimely beautiful water.

East Coast Beaches

A vast crescent of black sand that started up the volcanic slopes of Gunung Agung sweeps from north of Sanur to the east side of the island (p193). Some beaches here are empty, others have surfers, while still more have temples and slices of local Bali life.

South Lombok Beaches

The best Kuta Beach isn't on Bali. Along Lombok's south coast (p289) running east and west from *that* Kuta, you'll discover a dozen gorgeous bays ringed with white sand and, often, not much else.

Gili Beaches

The Gili Islands (p209) – Trawangan, Meno and Air – are each ringed by beautiful sands. Walk the big loop, sample at the beach buffets, try some offshore snorkelling and just enjoy.

Surfing

Surfing is the top reason many come to Bali and surf culture is part of the island's fabric. On Lombok, the lifestyle is more low key but the breaks are not.

Kuta Beach

Kuta Beach (p52), Bali's original surf beach, is still a winner. You can't help but be drawn to this vast sweep of sand, where surfers of all stripes are drawn to the nonstop breaks right offshore. And you can easily learn to surf here. Schools abound and there are classes all day long.

Echo Beach

Echo Beach (p100) has wild waves and plenty of spectators. It's really an extension of equally popular Batu Bolong. Both have cafes that are always brimming with a good mix of locals and visitors.

Ulu Watu

Ulu Watu (p112) is where you'll find Bali's most legendary surfing. It's really the climax of a string of breaks that march down the west coast of the Bukit Peninsula. The conditions are challenging and you can spend days just sussing out the scene.

1. Surfboards on Kuta Beach (p52), Bali 2. Suluban Beach (p113), Bali 3. Surfer, Bali

Nusa Lembongan

Nusa Lembongan (p136) off Bali is an excellent place for days of riding. Breaks – accessed by boat – are offshore, past the reefs. And there are cheap places to stay with good views of the action, so you can pick your moment to plunge in.

Tanjung Desert

Tanjung Desert (Desert Point; p277) on Lombok wins plaudits, and that's not just from surfers congratulating themselves for trekking out to this remote spot. Fickle (its season is a short one: May to September), this break is tough for even the most experienced and a reward for all.

Diving

The islands have great diving and a whole bunch of great dive shops to support your explorations. From simple wall dives to challenging open-water observations of massive creatures, you'll find something here to fit your skills and desires.

Tulamben

Tulamben (p224) seems like a mere village along the coast road of east Bali – until you notice all the dive shops. The big attraction here lies right offshore: an old ship, the *Liberty*, sunk during WWII. You can dive and snorkel the wreck from right offshore.

Gili Trawangan

Gili Trawangan is a fabulous centre for diving and snorkelling (p300). Great places to explore the depths abound in the waters around all three Gilis. Freediving is popular here, you can snorkel right off the beaches and there are reefs in all directions.

Nusa Penida

Seldom-visited Nusa Penida (p143) is surrounded by what could be an underwater theme park. Conditions can be challenging – the services of an excellent dive shop are essential – but you might see huge, placid sunfish and manta rays.

Nusa Lembongan

Nusa Lembongan (p136) is a good base for exploring dozens of sites here, in the surrounding mangroves and at the two neighbouring islands. With the guidance of a good operator, you can drift dive between the latter and Lembongan.

Pulau Menjangan

Pulau Menjangan (p257) is Bali's best-known dive and snorkel area and has a dozen superb dive sites. The diving is excellent – iconic tropical fish, soft corals, great visibility (usually), caves and a spectacular drop-off. It's best visited as part of an overnight jaunt to Pemuteran.

1. Diver at Pulau Menjangan (p257) 2. Snorkeller exploring the *Liberty* wreck, Tulamben (p224) 3. Nusa Penida (p143)

Sea turtle (p372), Nusa Penida

Marine Life

There is a rich variety of coral, seaweed, fish and other marine life in the coastal waters off the islands; in fact Indonesia's entire marine territory was declared a manta ray sanctuary in 2014. Much of the marine life can be appreciated by snorkellers, but you're only likely to see the larger marine animals while diving.

Dolphins

Dolphins can be found right around the islands and have been made into an attraction off Lovina (p247). But you're just as likely to see schools of dolphins if you take a fast boat between Bali and the Gilis.

Sharks

Sharks are always dramatic and there are very occasional reports of large ones, including great whites, throughout the region, although they are not considered a massive threat. In the Gilis, reef sharks are easily spotted at Shark Point (p308).

Sea Turtles

Sea turtles (p372) are common but greatly endangered. Long considered a delicacy by the Balinese, it is a constant struggle by environmentalists to protect them from poachers. Still, you can find them, especially in the Gilis.

Fish of All Kinds

Smaller fish and corals can be found at a plethora of spots around the islands. Everybody's favourite first stop is Bali's Menjangan (p257). Fish as large as whale sharks have been reported, but what thrills scores daily are the coloured beauty of an array of corals, sponges, lacy sea fans and much more. Starfish abound and you'll easily spot clownfish and other polychromatic characters.

Apache Reggae Bar BAR

(Map p54; Jl Legian 146; ⊙7pm-3am) One of the rowdier spots, Apache jams in locals and visitors, many of whom are on the make. The music is loud, but that pounding you feel the next day is from the free-flowing *arak* (distilled palm and cane alcohol) served in huge plastic jugs.

🍸 Legian & Double Six Beach

Most of Legian's bars are smaller and appeal to a more sedate crowd than those in Kuta. The very notable exception is the area at the end of Jl Arjuna/Jl Double Six where there are cafes and clubs. A string of beach bars runs north from here on the Seminyak beach walk.

★**Jenja** CLUB

(Map p54; ☑0361-882 7711; www.jenjabali.com; TS Suites, Jl Nakula 18; ⊙9pm-4am Wed-Sat) A very slick, high-concept nightclub in the TS Suites hotel. Spread over several levels, DJs rev it up with disco, R&B, funk, soul and techno. The crowd is a mix of well-heeled locals and expats. The restaurant serves upscale fare, good for sharing.

★**Double-Six Rooftop** BAR

(Map p54; ☑0361-734300; www.doublesixrooftop. com; Double Six Beach 66; ⊙3-11pm; 🐟) Sharks swimming in aquarium-lined walls, suave lounges, a commanding location and tiki torches: this ostentatious bar above the Double-Six hotel could be the villain's lair from a Bond film. Amazing sunset views are best enjoyed from the circular booths enclosed – the minimum 1,000,000Rp spend to reserve one is redeemable against food, and perfect for groups. Drinks here are pricey.

Bali Beach Shack BAR

(Map p54; ☑0819 3622 2010; www.balibeachshack. com; Jl Sahadewa; ⊙3-11pm Tue-Sun) A fab open-air bar, gets nightly crowds for live music and vivacious drag shows. Live music spans pop to country.

Cocoon CLUB

(Map p54; ☑0361-731266; www.cocoon-beach. com; Jl Arjuna; ⊙10am-late) A huge pool with a view of Double Six Beach anchors this sort of high-concept club (alcohol-branded singlets not allowed!), which has parties and events around the clock. Beds, loungers and VIP areas surround the pool; DJs spin theme nights.

🔒 Shopping

Kuta has a vast concentration of cheap tawdry shops, as well as huge, flashy surf-gear emporiums. As you head north along Jl Legian, the quality of the shops improves and you start finding cute little boutiques, especially near Jl Arjuna (which has wholesale fabric, clothing and craft stores, giving it a bazaar feel). Continue into Seminyak for absolutely fabulous shopping.

Large malls are also making inroads. Tuban has the Discovery Mall and the flashy Lippo Mall. The Beachwalk complex is a bouquet of gloss on Jl Pantai Kuta.

Stalls with T-shirts, souvenirs, beachwear and gaudy junk are virtually everywhere. Bali's top-selling souvenirs for those left at home are penis-shaped bottle openers in a range of colours and sizes.

UpCycle DESIGN

(Map p54; ☑0813 9674 9986; www.navehmilo. com; Jl Arjuna; ⊙10am-8pm) Old vinyl albums, drinking cans, biscuit wrappers and the like are turned into highly useful, everyday items such as purses, bags, bracelets and more. Exploring this shop feels like a treasure hunt; the goods are made in Indonesian villages.

Sriwijaya Batik TEXTILES

(Map p54; ☑0812 365 0939; Jl Arjuna; ⊙10am-6pm) Makes batik and other fabrics to order in myriad colours. Great browsing.

Summer Batik TEXTILES

(Map p54; ☑0361-735401; Jl Arjuna; ⊙10am-8pm) Although most other outlets have left, Jl Arjuna still has a few batik wholesalers hanging on amid the construction boom in chain hotels. This one is a riot of colour with thousands of samples in a tight little space.

Periplus Bookshop BOOKS

(Map p58; ☑0361-769757; Jl Kartika Plaza, Discovery Mall, 1st fl; ⊙10am-10pm) Large selection of new books.

Beachwear & Surf Shops

A huge range of surf shops sells big-name surf gear – including Mambo, Rip Curl, Billabong and Quiksilver. Local names include Surfer Girl and Drifter. Most have numerous locations in south Bali.

You'll also find local surf shops with some renowned board-shapers ready to make you a custom ride.

KUTA & SEMINYAK KUTA & LEGIAN

★**Luke Studer** SPORTS & OUTDOORS
(Map p54; ☑0361-894 7425; www.studersurf-boards.com; Jl Dewi Sri 7A; ☺9am-8pm) Legendary board-shaper Luke Studer works from this large and glossy shop. Short boards, retro fishes, single fins and classic longboards are sold ready-made or custom-built.

Rip Curl SPORTS & OUTDOORS
(Map p54; ☑0361-754238; www.ripcurl.com; Jl Legian 62; ☺9am-10pm) Cast that mopey black stuff aside and make a splash! Bali's largest arm of the surfwear giant has a huge range of beachwear, swimsuits and surfboards.

Surfer Girl CLOTHING
(Map p54; ☑0361-752693; www.surfer-girl.com; Jl Legian 138; ☺9.30am-11pm) A local legend, this vast store for girls of all ages has a winsome logo that says it all. Clothes, gear, bikinis and plenty of other stuff in every shade of bubblegum ever made.

Naruki Surf Shop SPORTS & OUTDOORS
(Map p54; ☑0361-765772; Jl Lebak Bene; ☺10am-8pm) One of dozens of surf shops lining the lanes of Kuta, sells a huge range of boards at popular prices.

Malls & Department Stores

Beachwalk MALL
(Map p54; www.beachwalkbali.com; Jl Pantai Kuta; ☺10am-midnight) This vast open-air mall, hotel and condo development across from Kuta Beach is filled with international chains: from Gap to Starbucks. Water features course amid the generic retail glitz. Dig deep for the odd interesting find.

Lippo Mall Kuta MALL
(Map p58; ☑0361-897 8000; www.lippomalls.com; Jl Kartika Plaza; ☺10am-10pm) The latest large

mall in south Bali only adds to the traffic chaos on Tuban's under-engineered streets. A huge Matahari department store is joined by scores of international chains, restaurants and a supermarket.

Sogo DEPARTMENT STORE
(Map p58; ☑0361-769555; Jl Kartika Plaza, Discovery Mall; ☺10am-10pm) Stylish Japanese department store that has an international cult following.

Discovery Mall MALL
(Map p58; ☑0361-755522; www.discoveryshop-pingmall.com; Jl Kartika Plaza; ☺9am-9pm) Swallowing up a significant section of the shoreline, this huge, hulking and popular enclosed Tuban mall is built on the water and filled with shops of every kind, including the large Centro and trendy Sogo department stores.

Carrefour MALL
(Map p54; ☑0361-847 7222; Jl Sunset; ☺8am-10pm) This large outlet of the French discount chain combines lots of small shops (books, computers, bikinis) with one huge hypermarket. It's the place to stock up on staples and there's a large ready-to-eat section and food court as well. The downside, however, is inescapable: it's a mall.

Mal Bali Galeria MALL
(Map p54; ☑0361-758875; www.malbaligaleria.co.id; Jl Ngurah Rai) Huge, uninspiring mall at the traffic-congested bypass construction site. The duty-free emporium is big with the group-tour set.

ℹ Information

DANGERS & ANNOYANCES
The streets and *gang* are usually safe but there are many annoyances. Touts offer prostitutes, Viagra and other tawdry diversions. You'll also grow weary of the cloying cries of 'massage?' and other dubious offers. But your biggest irritation will likely be the sclerotic traffic.

MEDICAL SERVICES
BIMC (pwww.bimcbali.com; ☑0361-300 0911, 0361-761263; Jl Ngurah Rai 100X; ☺24hr) On the bypass road just east of Kuta near the Bali Galeria shopping mall. It's a modern Australian-run clinic that can do tests, hotel visits and arrange medical evacuation. Visits can cost US$100 or more. It has a branch in Nusa Dua.

Kimia Farma (☑0361-755622; Jl Pantai Kuta 102; ☺24hr) Part of a local chain of pharmacies, this is well-stocked and carries hard-to-

---

KUTA'S FAVOURITE STORE
....

The mobs out the front look like they're making a run on a bank. Inside it's simply pandemonium. Welcome to **Joger** (Map p58; ☑0361-752523; Jl Raya Kuta; ☺10am-8pm), a Bali retail legend that is the most popular store in the south. No visitor from elsewhere in Indonesia would think of leaving the island without a doe-eyed plastic puppy (4000Rp) or one of the thousands of T-shirts bearing a wry, funny or simply inexplicable phrase (almost all are limited edition). Warning: conditions inside the cramped store are simply insane.

find items, such as that antidote for irksome revellers in the morning: earplugs. Also has branches at **Tuban** (☑ 0361-757472; Jl Raya Kuta; ☺ 24hr) and **Legian** (☑ 0361-734970; Jl Legian 504; ☺ 24hr).

MONEY

Central Kuta Money Exchange (☑ 0361-762970; www.centralkutabali.com; Jl Raya Kuta 168; ☺ 8am-6pm) This trustworthy place deals in numerous currencies. Has many locations, including a branch in **Legian** (Jl Melasti; ☺ 8.30am-9pm) and counters inside some Circle K convenience stores.

POLICE

Police Station (☑ 0361-751598; Jl Raya Kuta; ☺ 24hr) Ask to speak to the tourist police.

Tourist Police Post (☑ 0361-784 5988; Jl Pantai Kuta; ☺ 24hr) This is a branch of the main police station in Denpasar. It's right across from the beach; the officers have a gig that is sort of like a Balinese *Baywatch*.

POST

Postal agencies that can send mail are common. **Main Post Office** (☑ 0361-754012; Jl Selamet; ☺ 7am-2pm Mon-Thu, to 11am Fri, to 1pm Sat) On a little road east of Jl Raya Kuta, this small and efficient post office is well practised in shipping large packages.

TOURIST INFORMATION

There's no useful official tourist office. Places that advertise themselves as 'tourist information centres' are usually commercial travel agents, or worse: time-share condo sales operations.

TRAVEL AGENCIES

Hanafi (www.hanafi.net; ☑ 0821 4538 9646; Jl Pantai Kuta) This legendary tour guide operates from Kuta. Customises trips of all kinds whether for families or couples. Gay-friendly too.

❶ Getting There & Away

BEMO

Bemos (minibuses) regularly travel between Kuta and the Tegal terminal in Denpasar – the fare should be 8000Rp. The route goes from Jl Raya Kuta near Jl Pantai Kuta, looping past the beach, then on Jl Melasti and back past Bemo Corner for the trip back to Denpasar.

There's a **bemo stop** (off Jl Raya Kuta) for infrequent bemo service between Kuta and Tuban.

BUS

For public buses to anywhere in Bali, you'll have to go to the appropriate terminal in Denpasar first. Tourist shuttles are widely advertised on backstreets.

Perama (☑ 0361-751551; www.peramatour.com; Jl Legian 39; ☺ 7am-10pm) is the main tourist shuttle-bus operation in town; it may do hotel pickups and drop-offs for an extra 10,000Rp (confirm with staff when making arrangements). It usually has at least one bus a day to destinations, which include Lovina (100,000Rp, 4½ hours), Padangbai (60,000Rp, three hours) and Ubud (50,000Rp, 1½ hours).

Trans-Sarbagita (p389), Bali's nascent public bus service, has two routes that converge on the central parking area just south of Istana Kuta Galleria. Destinations include Denpasar, Sanur, Jimbaran and Nusa Dua.

Kuta is a hub for the highly useful Kura-Kura tourist bus (p389) service.

BOAT

Pelni Ticket Office (www.pelni.co.id; ☑ 0361-763963; Jl Raya Kuta 299; ☺ 8am-noon & 1-4pm Mon-Fri, 8am-1pm Sat) Source for schedules and tickets for the national shipping line.

❶ Getting Around

The hardest part about getting around south Bali is the traffic. Besides using taxis, you can rent a motorbike, often with a surfboard rack, or a bike – just ask at the place you're staying. One of the nicest ways to get around the area is by foot along the beach.

TO/FROM THE AIRPORT

An official taxi from the airport monopoly costs 55,000Rp to Tuban, 80,000Rp to Kuta and 95,000Rp to Legian. When travelling *to* the airport, get a metered taxi for savings.

TAXI

In traffic, a ride into Seminyak can top 80,000Rp and take more than 30 minutes; walking the beach will be quicker.

Seminyak

Seminyak is flash, brash and arguably a bit phoney. It's also the centre of life for hordes of the island's expats (many of whom own boutiques, design clothes, surf, or do seemingly nothing at all). It may be immediately north of Kuta and Legian, but in many respects, not the least of which is its intangible sense of style, Seminyak feels almost like it's on another island.

It's a very dynamic place, home to scores of restaurants and clubs and a wealth of creative, designer shops and galleries. World-class hotels line the beach, and what a beach it is – as wide and sandy as Kuta's but less crowded.

Seminyak & Kerobokan

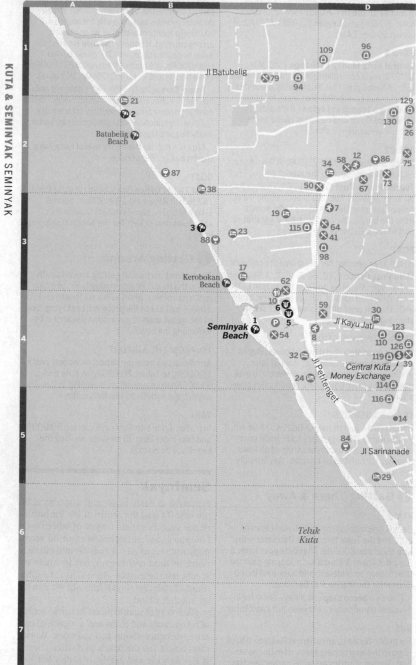

N
0   500 m
0   0.25 miles

Central Kuta
Money Exchange

18
113
43 66 16
76
35
40
107
Jl Gunung Tangkuban Perahu
61
Jl Petitenget
4
77
Sari Kembar (650m);
Blambangan Warung
Syariah (1km)

KEROBOKAN

Jl Raya Kerobokan

Jl Raya Mettanadi

Bali Bike
Rental
60
65
104
117
105
131
Jl Pangkung Sari
52
55
Kimia
56
120
Farma
100
ChannelOne
122
51
Jl Braban
127
27
68
72
118 89
45
46
Jl Sunset
92
49 70
47
125
111
15
Jl Kayu Aya (Jl Laksmana & Jl Oberoi)
85
121
74
90
99
102
95
112

11

SEMINYAK
Jl Basangkasa

108
48 44
20
124
Jl Sarinande
93
69
Jl Kunti
57
63 9 13
71
106
25 37
Jl Drupadi
128
33
53
36
83
103 101
Jl Sarinande
Jl Plawa
28
70
81
22
80
Jl Camplung Tanduk
42 97
(Jl Dhyana Pura & Jl Abimanyu)

Jl Raya Seminyak
Seminyak
Beach
31
82
See Kuta & Legian Map (p54)
91

Seminyak & Kerobokan

Seminyak seamlessly merges with Kerobokan, which is immediately north – in fact the exact border between the two is as fuzzy as most other geographic details in Bali. You could easily spend your entire holiday in Seminyak.

☂ Beaches

Kuta Beach morphs seamlessly into Legian, then Seminyak. Because of the limited road access, the sand in Seminyak tends to be less crowded than in Kuta. This also means that it's less patrolled and the water conditions are less monitored. The odds of encountering dangerous rip tides and other hazards are ever-present, especially as you head north.

★ **Seminyak Beach**   BEACH

A sunset lounger and an ice-cold Bintang on the beach at sunset is simply magical. A good stretch can be found near Pura Petitenget, and it tends to be less crowded than further south in Kuta.

◉ Sights

Seminyak's sights are almost entirely related to consumption. After the beach and its temples, simply strolling the main strips and pausing to people-watch can be richly rewarding – and entertaining.

Pura Petitenget   HINDU TEMPLE

(Jl Petitenget) This is an important temple and the scene of many ceremonies. It is one of a string of sea temples that stretches from

Pura Luhur Ulu Watu on the Bukit Peninsula north to Pura Tanah Lot in western Bali. Petitenget loosely translates as 'magic box'; it was a treasured belonging of the legendary 16th-century priest Nirartha, who refined the Balinese religion and visited this site often.

The temple is renowned for its anniversary celebrations on the Balinese 210-day calendar. It is right next to Pura Masceti.

Pura Masceti   HINDU TEMPLE
(Jl Petitenget) An agricultural temple where farmers pray for relief from rat infestations, and savvy builders make offerings of forgiveness before planting yet another villa in the rice fields.

🏃 Activities

Seminyak's spas (and those of Kerobokan) are among the best in Bali and offer a huge range of treatments, therapies and pleasures.

⭐ **Jari Menari**   SPA
(☎ 0361-736740; www.jarimenari.com; Jl Raya Basangkasa 47; sessions from 385,000Rp; ⊙ 9am-9pm) Jari Menari is true to its name, which means 'dancing fingers': your body will be one happy dance floor. The all-male staff use massage techniques that emphasise rhythm. They also offer classes in giving massage (from US$170).

SEMINYAK'S CURVING SPINE

The thriving heart of Seminyak is along meandering Jl Kayu Aya (aka Jl Oberoi/ Jl Laksmana). It heads towards the beach from bustling Jl Basangkasa and then turns north through a part of Seminyak along Jl Petitenget. The road is lined with a profusion of restaurants, upscale boutiques and hotels as it curves through Seminyak and into Kerobokan. Sidewalks have hugely improved window-shopping and cafe-hopping; now it's the drivers stuck in traffic who fume.

Prana SPA
(☑ 0361-730840; www.pranaspabali.com; Jl Kunti 118X; massages 1hr from 510,000Rp; ☺ 9am-10pm) A palatial Moorish fantasy that is easily the most lavishly decorated spa in Bali, Prana offers everything from basic hour-long massages to facials and all manner of beauty treatments.

Bodyworks SPA
(☑ 0361-733317; www.bodyworksbali.com; Jl Kayu Jati 2; massage from 295,000Rp; ☺ 9am-10pm) Get waxed, get your hair done, get the kinks rubbed out of your joints – all this and more is on the menu at this uber-popular spa in the heart of Seminyak.

Chill SPA
(☑ 0361-734701; www.chillreflexology.com; Jl Kunti; treatments per hour from 225,000Rp; ☺ 10am-10pm) The name says it all. This Zen place embraces reflexology; treatments include full-body pressure-point massage.

Seminyak Yoga Shala YOGA
(☑ 0361-730498; www.seminyakyogashala.com; Jl Basangkasa; classes from 120,000Rp) No-nonsense yoga studio with daily classes in several styles including ashtanga, Mysore and yin yang.

Surf Goddess SURFING
(☑ 0858 997 0808; www.surfgoddessretreats.com; per week package with r from US$3000) Surf holidays for women that include lessons, yoga, meals and lodging in a posh guesthouse in the backstreets of Seminyak.

Deluta Surf SURFING
(Jl Petitenget 40X; surfboard rental per day from 150,000Rp; ☺ 9am-7pm) Has board rental and surf gear near Seminyak Beach.

☕ Courses

Sate Bali COOKING
(☑ 0361-736734; Jl Kayu Aya 22; courses from 400,000Rp; ☺ 9.30am-1.30pm) Restaurant Sate Bali runs this excellent Balinese cooking course. Students learn to prepare Balinese spices and sambals, which are then used to flavour duck, fish and pork dishes.

🛏 Sleeping

Seminyak has a wide range of accommodation, from world-class resorts on the beach to humble hotels hidden on backstreets. This is also the start of villa-land, which runs north from here through the vanishing rice fields beyond Canggu. For many, a private villa with its own pool is a holiday dream.

Oodles of midrange chain hotels have popped up across south Bali that add Seminyak to their names even when they're as far away as Denpasar.

🛏 Jl Camplung Tanduk & Around

Raja Gardens GUESTHOUSE $
(☑ 0361-730494; www.jdw757.wixsite.com/rajagardens; off Jl Camplung Tanduk; r with fan/air-con from 400,000/600,000Rp; ❋ 🛜 ≋) Here since 1980, this old-school guesthouse has spacious, grassy grounds with fruit trees and a quiet spot located almost on the beach. The eight rooms are fairly basic but there are open-air bathrooms and plenty of potted plants. The large pool is a nice spot to lounge by, and it's generally a mellow place.

Inada Losmen GUESTHOUSE $
(☑ 0361-732269; putuinada@hotmail.com; Gang Bima 9; s/d from 150,000/180,000Rp) Buried in a *gang* behind Bintang Supermarket, this budget champ is a short walk from clubs, the beach and other Seminyak joy. The 12 rooms are small and somewhat dark.

Ned's Hide-Away GUESTHOUSE $
(☑ 0361-731270; waynekelly1978@gmail.com; Gang Bima 3; r with fan/air-con from 180,000/300,000Rp; ❋ 🛜) While its standards have slipped, Ned's remains a good budget choice with 16 rooms, some basic and others more plush. Wi-fi is only available in reception.

Sarinande Beach Inn HOTEL $$
(☑ 0361-730383; www.sarinandehotel.com; Jl Sarinande 15; r incl breakfast 550,000-800,000Rp; ❋ 🛜 ≋) The 26 excellent-value rooms here

are in older two-storey blocks set around a small pool; the decor is a bit dated but everything is well maintained. Amenities include fridges, satellite TV and DVD players, and there's a cafe. The beach is a three-minute walk away.

Villa Kresna   BOUTIQUE HOTEL **$$**
(📞0361-730317; www.villakresna.com; Jl Sarinande 17; r/villa from 690,000/920,000Rp; ❋ 🖥 ☎) The beach is only 50m from this cute, idiosyncratic property tucked away on a small *gang*. The 22 art-filled units are mostly suites, which have a nice flow-through design with both public and private patios. A small, sinuous pool wanders through the property.

Villa Karisa   HOTEL **$$$**
(📞0361-739395; www.villakarisabali.com; Jl Drupadi 100X; r 1,250,000-2,500,000Rp; ❋ 🖥 ☎) It's like visiting the gracious friends in Bali you wish you had. Ideally located on a little *gang* off busy Jl Drupadi, this large villa-style inn has a row of rooms filled with antiques and many comforts. Guests gather in the common room or around the luxurious 12m pool. Enjoy Javanese antique style in the 'Shiva' room.

Luna2 Studiotel   BOUTIQUE HOTEL **$$$**
(📞0361-730402; www.luna2.com; Jl Sarinande 20; r incl breakfast US$280-450; ❋ 🖥 ☎) Is it Mondrian? Is it Roy Lichtenstein? We're not sure which modern artists are the inspiration for this eye-popping hotel, but we can say the results astound. The 14 boldly decorated studio apartments feature kitchens, gadgetry, balconies and access to a rooftop bar looking over the ocean. A 16-seat cinema shows movies, and the pool is a full 25m.

Jl Kayu Aya & Around

Mutiara Bali   HOTEL **$$**
(📞0361-734966; www.mutiarabali.com; Jl Braban 77; r/villa from 860,000/2,100,000Rp; ❋ 🖥 ☎) The 17 private villas here are good value, each with an open lounge area looking out to a private plunge pool. The hotel-style rooms have all the usual amenities plus deep balconies for lounging.

Casa Artista   GUESTHOUSE **$$**
(📞0361-736749; www.casaartistabali.com; Jl Sari Dewi 17; r incl breakfast 750,000-1,400,000Rp; ❋ 🖥 ☎) You can literally dance for joy at this cultured guesthouse where the owner, a professional tango dancer, offers lessons. The eight compact rooms, with names such as Passion and Inspiration, are in an elegant two-storey house surrounding a pool. Some have crystal chandeliers; breakfast is served on your patio.

★**Oberoi**   HOTEL **$$$**
(📞0361-730361; www.oberoihotels.com; Jl Kayu Aya; r incl breakfast from 4,400,000Rp; ❋ @ 🖥 ☎) The beautifully understated Oberoi has been a refined Balinese-style beachside retreat since 1971. All accommodation options have private verandahs, and as you move up in price, additional features include walled villas, ocean views and private pools. From the cafe that overlooks the almost-private sweep of beach to the numerous luxuries, this is a place to spoil yourself.

★**Samaya**   VILLA **$$$**
(📞0361-731149; www.thesamayabali.com; Jl Kayu Aya; villa from US$625; ❋ 🖥 ☎) Understated yet cultured, the Samaya is one of the best bets for a villa right on the beach in south Bali. It boasts 52 villas in a luxurious contemporary style, each featuring a private pool. Some units are in a compound away from the water. The food, from breakfast onwards, is superb.

Legian   HOTEL **$$$**
(📞0361-730622; www.ghmhotels.com; Jl Pantai Kaya Aya; ste/villa incl breakfast from 6,900,000/11,600,000Rp; ❋ @ 🖥 ☎) The Legian is flash and brash – one of the reasons it's a fave with people who use their own jets to reach Bali. All 79 rooms claim to be suites, even if some are just large rooms (called 'studios'). On a little bluff right on the beach, the views are panoramic. The design mixes traditional materials with contemporary flair.

Pradha Villas   VILLA **$$$**
(📞0361-735446; www.pradhavillas.com; Jl Kayu Jati 5; villa from 3,100,000Rp; ❋ 🖥 ☎) Ground zero for Seminyak: the 11 villas are a short walk to some of the best restaurants and the beach. Units vary in size but each is a private walled compound with a swimming pool. Jacuzzis add an extra romantic touch; wake up to a custom-prepared breakfast by the gracious staff.

✗ Eating

Jl Kayu Aya is the focus of Seminyak eating (despite the hokey nickname 'Eat St') but there are great choices for every budget virtually everywhere. Note that some restaurants morph into clubs as the night wears on. Conversely, some bars and clubs also have good food. Meanwhile, you're never far from top-notch coffee as Seminyak has a thriving cafe culture.

Jl Camplung Tanduk & Around

Kreol Kitchen MODERN AUSTRALIAN $$
(📞0361-738514; www.kreolkitchen.com; Jl Drupadi 56; mains from 60,000Rp; ⊗8am-10pm) You won't find pralines here but you'll find modern Australian cuisine with ingredients sourced locally. It's a fusion of Asian and Western flavours with daily and seasonal specials. The Melbourne-style dim sum is a hit as are the savoury pies and South Asian mains. The decor is ubiquitous retro; avert your eyes from the hideous Harris Hotel across the street.

Jl Raya Seminyak & Jl Basangkasa

Warung Taman Bambu BALINESE $
(📞0361-888 1567; Jl Plawa 10; mains from 25,000Rp; ⊗9am-10pm; 🔊) This classic warung may look simple from the street but the comfy tables are – like the many fresh and spicy dishes on offer – a cut above the norm. There's a small stand for *babi guling* (suckling pig) right next door.

Warung Ibu Made INDONESIAN $
(Jl Basangkasa; mains from 15,000Rp; ⊗7am-7pm) The woks roar almost from dawn to dusk amid the constant hubbub on this busy corner of Jl Raya Seminyak, where several stalls cook food fresh under the shade of a huge banyan. Try refreshing with the juice of a young coconut.

Bintang Supermarket SUPERMARKET $
(📞0361-730552; Jl Raya Seminyak 17; ⊗8am-10.30pm) Always busy, this large supermarket is the grocery favourite among expats, who appreciate its good prices and broad range of food, including good fruit and veg. It sells affordable sunscreen, bug spray and other sundries as well.

Café Moka CAFE $
(📞0361-731424; www.cafemokabali.com; Jl Basangkasa; treats 15,000-35,000Rp; ⊗7am-10pm; ✳) Enjoy French-style baked goods (fresh baguettes!) at this popular bakery and cafe. Many escape the heat and linger here for hours over little French treats. The bulletin board spills over with notices for villa rentals.

PICK A NAME, ANY NAME

A small lane or alley is known as a *gang*, and most of those in Bali lack signs or even names. Some are referred to by the name of a connecting street, eg Jl Padma Utara is the *gang* going north of Jl Padma.

Meanwhile, some streets in Kuta, Legian and Seminyak have more than one name. Many streets were unofficially named after a well-known temple and/or business place. In recent years there has been an attempt to impose official – and usually more Balinese – names on the streets. But the old names are still common and some streets may have more than one.

Following are the old (unofficial) and current official names, from north to south:

OLD (UNOFFICIAL)	CURRENT (OFFICIAL)
Jl Oberoi/Jl Laksmana	Jl Kayu Aya
Jl Raya Seminyak	Northern stretch: Jl Basangkasa
Jl Dhyana Pura/Jl Abimanyu	Jl Camplung Tanduk
Jl Double Six	Jl Arjuna
Jl Pura Bagus Taruna	Jl Werkudara
Jl Padma	Jl Yudistra
Poppies Gang II	Jl Batu Bolong
Jl Pantai Kuta	Jl Pantai Banjar Pande Mas
Jl Kartika Plaza	Jl Dewi Sartika
Jl Segara	Jl Jenggala
Jl Satria	Jl Kediri

Café Seminyak CAFE $
(☎0361-736967; Jl Raya Seminyak 17; mains 40,000-70,000Rp; ☺7am-10pm) Right in front of the busy Bintang Supermarket, this cute and casual place has excellent smoothies and sandwiches made with freshly baked bread.

Mama San FUSION $$
(☎0361-730436; www.mamasanbali.com; Jl Raya Kerobokan 135; mains 90,000-200,000Rp; ☺noon-3pm & 6.30-11pm; ✳☎) One of Seminyak's most popular restaurants, this stylish warehouse-sized space is split into levels, with photographs hanging from exposed brick walls. The menu has an emphasis on creative dishes from across Southeast Asia. A long cocktail list provides liquid balm for the mojito set and has lots of tropical-flavoured pours.

Fat Gajah ASIAN $$
(☎0851 0168 8212; www.fatgajah.com; Jl Basangkasa 21; dumplings 52,000-110,000Rp; ☺11am-10.30pm; ☎) Fat Gajah is all about dumplings and noodles, prepared with mostly organic ingredients. They come fried or steamed with innovative fillings such as beef rendang, black-pepper crab, *kimchi* tuna or lemongrass lamb. There's a range of small Asian plates. The spare dining room is very appealing.

Rolling Fork ITALIAN $$
(☎0361-733 9633; Jl Kunti 1; mains from 80,000Rp; ☺8.30am-11pm; ☎) A gnocchi-sized little trattoria, Rolling Fork serves excellent Italian fare. Breakfast features gorgeous baked goods and excellent coffees. Lunch and dinner include authentic and tasty homemade pastas, salads, seafood and more. The open-air dining room has an alluring retro charm; the Italian owners provide just the right accent.

Divine Earth VEGAN $$
(☎0361-731964; www.divineearthbali.com; Jl Raya Basangkasa 1200A; mains 50,000-140,000Rp; ☺7am-11pm; ✳☎☑) 🍴 A sibling of the much-loved Earth Cafe (p84), this organic vegetarian restaurant also does tasty vegan and raw food. It's perhaps better known for its Upstairs Lounge Cinema Club (p86), where you can bring your food and drink to watch classic, art-house and documentary films.

Corner House CAFE $$
(☎0361-730276; www.cornerhousebali.com; Jl Laksmana 10A; dishes 35,000-125,000Rp; ☺7am-11pm; ☎) With polished concrete floors, dangling light bulbs, distressed walls and vintage-style furniture, this cavernous cafe is almost a Seminyak cliche. A popular brunch spot, it does great coffee, big breakfasts, homemade sausage rolls and steak sandwiches. There's also a small shady courtyard and a relaxed, breezy upstairs dining area.

Mannekepis BELGIAN $$
(☎0361-847 5784; Jl Raya Seminyak 2; mains 50,000-150,000Rp; ☺10am-midnight; ☎) That little icon of Brussels is permanently peeing out front at this delicious Belgian bistro. Tear your eyes away from the fish swimming in the ceiling tank to peruse a selection of excellent steaks, all served with top-notch *frites*. Sit on the upper-floor terrace away from the bedlam of the street. There is live jazz and blues many nights.

Taco Beach Grill MEXICAN $$
(☎0361-854 6262; www.tacobeachgrill.com; Jl Kunti 6; mains 50,000-80,000Rp; ☺10am-11pm; ☎) As sprightly as a chilli-accented salsa, this open-fronted casual cafe is known for its *babi guling* tacos. Obviously merging Bali's iconic suckling pig with Mexican flavours is a good thing. Expect the usual south-of-the-border standards plus good juices, smoothies and margaritas. Offers hotel and villa delivery.

✗ Jl Kayu Aya

Warung Aneka Rasa INDONESIAN $
(Jl Kayu Aya; meals from 20,000Rp; ☺7am-7pm) Keeping things real in the heart of Seminyak's upmarket retail strip, this humble warung cooks up all the Indo classics in an inviting open-front cafe. It's a refuge from the buzz.

Bali Bakery CAFE $
(☎0361-738033; www.balibakery.com; Jl Kayu Aya; mains 40,000-70,000Rp; ☺7.30am-10.30pm; ☎) The best feature of the Seminyak Sq open-air mall is this bakery with its shady tables and long menu of baked goods, salads, sandwiches and other fine fare. It's a good place to linger before heading back out to shop.

★ Sisterfields CAFE $$
(☎0361-738454; www.sisterfieldsbali.com; Jl Kayu Cendana 7; mains 70,000-150,000Rp; ☺7am-5pm; ☎) Trendy Sisterfields does classic Aussie breakfasts such as smashed avocado, and more-inventive dishes such as truffled oyster mushrooms with duck eggs and crispy pig

ears. There are also hipster faves like pulled-pork rolls and lobster sliders. Grab a seat at a booth, the counter or in the rear courtyard. Several other good coffee cafes are nearby.

★ **Ginger Moon** ASIAN $$
(☑0361-734533; www.gingermoonbali.com; Jl Kayu Aya 7; mains 70,000-160,000Rp; ⏰11am-midnight; 🛜🐾) Australian Dean Keddell is one of scores of young chefs lured to Bali to run restaurants. His creation is an appealing, airy space, with carved wood and palms. The menu features a 'Best of' list of favourites, served in portions designed for sharing and grazing. Top picks include cauliflower pizza and a special chicken curry. There's a good kids menu.

Petitenget MODERN AUSTRALIAN $$
(☑0361-473 3054; www.petitenget.net; Jl Petitenget 40X; mains breakfast 40,000-80,000Rp, lunch & dinner 60,000-200,000Rp; ⏰7am-10.30pm; 🛜) If it wasn't so hot, you could be in Paris. Soft jazz classics play at this very appealing bistro run by noted Australian chef Simon Blaby that mixes a casual terrace, bar and a more formal dining area. The menu has seasonal specials and features flavours of Europe and Asia. Everything is artfully prepared; there's a fun little kids menu.

Motel Mexicola MEXICAN $$
(☑0361-736688; www.motelmexicolabali.com; Jl Kayu Jati 9; mains from 60,000Rp; ⏰11am-1am) Not your average taqueria, Motel Mexicola is an extravaganza that channels a tropical version of a nightclub. The huge space is decked out in kitschy neon and palm trees. Food is secondary to drinks: soft corn tortilla tacos filled with tempura prawn or shredded pork, along with meaty mains. Cocktails, served in copper kettles, are a treat on a balmy evening.

Earth Cafe & Market VEGETARIAN $$
(☑0851 0304 4645; www.earthcafebali.com; Jl Kayu Aya; mains 40,000-100,000Rp; ⏰7am-11pm; 🛜🥄) 🌿 The good vibes are organic at this vegetarian cafe and store. Choose from creative salads, sandwiches or wholegrain vegan and raw-food goodies. It's most famous for its six-course 'Planet Platter'. The beverage menu includes fresh juices and detox mixes.

Wacko Burger BURGERS $$
(☑0821 4401 0888; www.wackoburger.com; Jl Drupadi 18; mains from 50,000Rp; ⏰noon-9.30pm) It's like you died and went to comfort-food heaven. The burgers here are beloved as

are the onion rings, fries, shakes and more. There are all manner of toppings and condiments to choose from. The tables are in an open-air covered patio with actual rice-field views.

Ultimo ITALIAN $$
(☑0361-738720; www.balinesia.co.id; Jl Kayu Aya 104; mains 70,000-180,000Rp; ⏰4pm-1am) This vast and always popular restaurant thrives in a part of Seminyak that's as thick as a good risotto with eateries. Choose a table overlooking the street action, out the back in one of the gardens or inside. Ponder the surprisingly authentic menu and then let the army of servers take charge.

Grocer & Grind CAFE $$
(☑0361-730418; www.grocerandgrind.com; Jl Kayu Jati 3X; mains from 60,000Rp; ⏰7am-10pm; ✹🛜) You might think you're at a sleek Sydney cafe, but look around and you're unmistakably in Bali. Classic sandwiches, homemade Aussie pies, salads and big breakfasts are popular at this south Bali chain.

La Lucciola FUSION $$$
(☑0361-730838; Jl Petitenget; mains 120,000-400,000Rp; ⏰9am-11pm) A sleek beachside restaurant with good views across a lovely lawn and sand to the surf from its 2nd-floor tables. The bar is popular with sunset-watchers, most of whom move on to dinner here. The menu is a creative melange of international fare with Italian flair.

🍸 Drinking & Nightlife

Like your vision at 2am, the division between restaurant, bar and club blurs in Seminyak. Although it lacks massive clubs where you can greet the dawn (or vice versa), stalwarts can head south to the rough edges of Kuta and Legian in the wee hours. Belgian bistro Mannekepis (p83) has live jazz some nights.

Numerous bars line Jl Camplung Tanduk, though noise-sensitive locals complain if things get too raucous.

Jl Camplung Tanduk & Around

Bali Joe GAY & LESBIAN
(☑0361-730931; www.balijoebar.com; Jl Camplung Tanduk; ⏰3pm-3am; 🛜) One of several lively LGBT venues along this strip. Drag queens and go-go dancers rock the house nightly.

Ryoshi Seminyak House of Jazz   BAR
(📞 0361-731152; www.facebook.com/ryoshibali; Jl Raya Seminyak 17; ⊙ noon-midnight, music from 9pm Mon, Wed & Fri) The Seminyak branch of the Bali chain of Japanese restaurants has live jazz three nights a week on an intimate stage under a traditionally thatched roof. Expect some of the best local and visiting talent.

Champlung Bar   BAR
(📞 0361-730603; off Jl Camplung Tanduk; ⊙ 11am-midnight) The most substantial of the beach bars along the beach walk south of Jl Camplung Tanduk, Champlung has its share of ubiquitous brightly coloured umbrellas and beanbags on the sand, plus a typical beach menu (pizzas, noodles etc). After sunset, expect DJs and beach parties.

Koh   CLUB
(📞 0812 3643 9919; www.facebook.com/kohbali; Jl Camplung Tanduk; ⊙ 11pm-5am Thu-Sat) Popular with locals and expats (as opposed to tourists), Koh can be quiet but it does have events with world-class DJs when it jams. Entry is through a shipping container.

Bottoms Up   GAY
(www.bottomsupseminyak.webs.com; Jl Camplung Tanduk; ⊙ 6pm-4am) Nightly drag shows, go-go dancers and general frivolity.

🍸 Jl Kayu Aya

★ La Favela   BAR
(📞 0361-730603; www.lafavela.com; Jl Kayu Aya 177X; ⊙ noon-3am; 🛜) An alluring, mysterious entry lures you into full bohemian flair at La Favela, one of Bali's coolest and most original nightspots. Themed rooms lead you on a confounding tour from dimly lit speakeasy cocktail lounges and antique dining rooms to graffiti-splashed bars. Tables are cleared after 11pm to make way for DJs and a dance floor.

It's equally popular for its garden **restaurant**, which has a Mediterranean-inspired menu.

★ Revolver   CAFE
(📞 0361-788 4968; off Jl Kayu Aya; coffee 20,000-30,000Rp; ⊙ 7am-6pm; 🛜) Wander down a tiny *gang* and push through narrow wooden doors to reach this matchbox of a coffee bar that does an excellent selection of brews. There are just a few tables in the creatively retro room that's styled like a Wild West sa-

SEMINYAK SUNSETS

At the beach end of Jl Camplung Tanduk you have a choice: turn left for a beachy frolic at the string of beach bars, both simple and plush; or turn right for trendy beach clubs such as Ku De Ta, or cheery vendors offering cheap Bintang, a plastic chair and maybe some bad guitar music.

loon; nab one and enjoy tasty fresh bites for breakfast and lunch.

Red Carpet Champagne Bar   BAR
(📞 0361-737889; www.redcarpetchampagnebar.com; Jl Kayu Aya 42; ⊙ noon-late) Choose from more than 200 types of champagne at this over-the-top glam bar on Seminyak's couture strip. Waltz the red carpet and toss back a few namesake flutes while contemplating a raw oyster and displays of frilly frocks. It's open to the street (but elevated, darling) so you can gaze down on the masses.

Ku De Ta   CLUB
(📞 0361-736969; www.kudeta.net; Jl Kayu Aya 9; ⊙ 8am-late; 🛜) Ku De Ta teems with Bali's beautiful people (including those whose status is purely aspirational). Scenesters perfect their 'bored' look over drinks during the day while gazing at the fine stretch of beach. Sunset brings out crowds, who dine on eclectic fare at tables. The music throbs with increasing intensity through the night. Special events are legendary.

Anomali Coffee   CAFE
(📞 0361-767119; www.anomalicoffee.com; Jl Kayu Aya 7B; coffee from 26,000Rp; ⊙ 6.30am-10pm; 🛜) A Jakarta-based chain, Anomali is a serious coffee drinker's standout. Single-origin beans are sourced from across the archipelago and roasted on-site. Take your pick of V-60 drip coffee, Aeropress, siphon or espresso made by expert baristas in cool warehouse-style surrounds. It also sells packaged ground beans.

Zappaz   BAR
(📞 0361-742 5534; Jl Kayu Aya 78; ⊙ 11am-midnight) Brit Norman Findlay tickles the ivories nightly at this cheerful piano bar, where he's been not-quite perfecting his enthusiastic playing for years and years. An enthusiastic cover band lures in gleeful crowds. Skip the food.

☆ Entertainment

Upstairs Lounge Cinema Club   CINEMA
(☑0361-731964; www.facebook.com/divineearth-bali; JL Raya Basangkasa 1200A; ⊙films 8pm)
State-of-the-art screenings of new, classic, art-house and unusual movies in a comfy and small cinema. Admission is free with any food purchase from the downstairs Divine Earth cafe (p83).

🛍 Shopping

Seminyak has it all: designer boutiques (Bali has a thriving fashion industry), retro-chic stores, slick galleries, wholesale emporiums and family-run workshops.

The best shopping starts on Jl Raya Seminyak at Bintang Supermarket and runs north through Jl Basangkasa. The retail strip branches off into Jl Kayu Aya and Jl Kayu Jati while continuing north on Jl Raya Kerobokan into Kerobokan. Try not to step into one of the yawning pavement caverns.

Seminyak Village   MALL
(☑0361-738097; www.seminyakvillage.com; Jl Kayu Jati 8; ⊙9am-10pm; 🛜) Rice fields just a few years ago, this new air-con mall deserves a compliment for being discreetly placed back from the street. The selection of shops is refreshingly local, with some notable names such as Lily Jean on the three levels. The small carts leased to up-and-coming Balinese designers is a nice touch.

Sandio   SHOES
(☑0361-737693; www.facebook.com/sandio.bali; Jl Basangkasa; ⊙10am-8pm) Shoes and sandals, from formal to casual, at great prices. Replace the one you lost riding your scooter.

Periplus Bookshop   BOOKS
(☑0361-736851; Jl Kayu Aya, Seminyak Sq; ⊙8am-10pm) A large outlet of the island-wide chain of lavishly fitted bookshops. In addition to design books numerous enough to have you fitting out even your garage with 'Bali Style', it stocks bestsellers, magazines and newspapers.

Cotton Line by St Isador   TEXTILES
(☑0361-738836; Jl Kaya Aya 44; ⊙9am-8pm)
The workshops upstairs spew forth lovely bed linens, pillows and other items made of fabrics imported from across Asia.

Clothing

Seminyak's surf shops rival those found in Kuta and you'll find branches of the big brands here as well.

★Drifter Surf Shop   FASHION & ACCESSORIES
(☑0361-733274; www.driftersurf.com; Jl Kayu Aya 50; ⊙7.30am-11pm) High-end surf fashion, surfboards, gear, cool books and brands such as Obey and Wegener. Started by two savvy surfer dudes, the shop stocks goods noted for their individuality and high quality. There's also a small cafe-bar and a patio.

★Bamboo Blonde   CLOTHING
(☑0361-731864; www.bambooblonde.com; Jl Kayu Aya 61; ⊙10am-10pm) Shop for frilly, sporty or sexy frocks and formal wear at this cheery designer boutique (one of 11 island-wide). All goods are designed and made in Bali.

★Milo's   CLOTHING
(☑0361-822 2008; www.milos-bali.com; Jl Kayu Aya 992; ⊙10am-8pm) The legendary local designer of silk finery has a lavish shop in the heart of designer row. Look for batik-bearing, eye-popping orchid patterns.

★Samsara   CLOTHING
(www.samsaraboutique.com; Jl Raya Seminyak; ⊙10am-10pm) Balinese-made textiles using global inspiration. This appealing shop displays hand-painted batik used in a range of exquisite casual wear by designer Coretta Hutson.

★Prisoners of St Petersburg   FASHION & ACCESSORIES
(☑0361-736653; Jl Kaya Aya 42B; ⊙10am-10pm) Some of Bali's hottest young designers are behind this eclectic and ever-evolving hip collection of women's wear and accessories.

Thaikila   CLOTHING
(☑0361-731130; www.blue-glue.com; Jl Kayu Aya; ⊙9am-9pm) 'The dream bikini of all women' is the motto of this local brand that makes a big statement with its tiny wear. The swimwear is French-designed and made right in Bali. If you need something stylish for the beach, come here.

Lily Jean   CLOTHING
(☑0811 398 272; www.lily-jean.com; Jl Kayu Jati 8, Seminyak Village, 1st fl; ⊙10am-10pm) Selling mostly Bali-made items, this designer shop combines international allure with local motifs.

Uma & Leopold CLOTHING
(☑0361-737697; www.umaandleopold.com; Jl Kayu Aya 77X) Luxe clothes and little frilly things to put on before slipping off... Designed in Bali by a French couple.

Paul Ropp CLOTHING
(☑0361-735613; www.paulropp.com; Jl Kayu Aya; ☺9am-9pm) The main shop of one of Bali's premier high-end fashion designers for men and women. Most goods are made in the hills above Denpasar. And what goods they are: rich silks and cottons, vivid to the point of gaudy, with hints of Ropp's roots in the tie-dyed 1960s.

Lucy's Batik TEXTILES, CLOTHING
(☑0361-736008; www.lucysbatikbali.com; Jl Raya Basangkasa 88; ☺9.30am-9pm) Great for both men and women, Lucy's is a good spot to shop for the finest batik. Shirts, dresses, sarongs and bags are mostly handwoven or hand-painted. It also sells material by the metre.

Biasa CLOTHING
(☑0361-730766; www.biasagroup.com; Jl Raya Seminyak 36; ☺9am-9pm) This is Bali-based designer Susanna Perini's premier shop. Her line of elegant tropical wear for men and women combines cottons, silks and embroidery.

Niconico CLOTHING
(☑0361-738875; www.niconicoswimwear.com; Jl Kayu Aya; ☺9am-9pm) German designer Nico Genge has a line of intimate clothing, resort wear and swimwear that eschews glitz for a slightly more subtle look. Among his many Seminyak shops this one has both the full collection and an art gallery upstairs.

Duzty CLOTHING
(Jl Raya Seminyak 67; ☺9am-10pm) Casual wear designed by Rahsun, an up-and-coming Balinese talent. Features edgy rock-and-roll and counterculture themes.

Quarzia Boutique CLOTHING
(☑0361-736644; Jl Kayu Aya; ☺10am-9pm) Casual cotton clothes designed with colour and flair; worn with attitude and authority.

Lulu Yasmine CLOTHING
(☑0361-736763; www.luluyasmine.com; Jl Kayu Aya; ☺9am-10pm) Designer Luiza Chang gets inspiration for her elegant line of women's clothes from her worldwide travels.

Divine Diva CLOTHING
(☑0361-732393; www.divinedivabali.com; Jl Kayu Aya 1A; ☺9am-7pm) A simple shop filled with Bali-made breezy styles for larger figures. You can custom order from the on-site tailors.

Arts & Crafts

★Indivie ARTS & CRAFTS
(☑0361-730927; www.indivie.com; Jl Raya Seminyak, Made's Warung; ☺9am-9pm) The works of young designers based in Bali are showcased at this intriguing and glossy boutique.

★Theatre Art Gallery ARTS & CRAFTS
(Jl Raya Seminyak; ☺9am-8pm) Specialises in vintage and reproduction *wayang* puppets used in traditional Balinese theatre. Just looking at the animated faces peering back at you is a delight.

★Ashitaba ARTS & CRAFTS
(☑0361-737054; Jl Raya Seminyak 6; ☺9am-9pm) Tenganan, the Aga village of east Bali, produces the intricate and beautiful rattan items sold here. Containers, bowls, purses and more (from 50,000Rp) display the very fine weaving.

Kody & Ko ART
(☑0361-737359; www.kodyandko.com; Jl Kayu Jati 4A; ☺9am-9pm) The polychromatic critters in the window set the tone for this vibrant shop of art and decorator items. There's a large attached gallery with regular exhibitions.

Kendra Gallery ART
(☑0361-736628; www.kendragallery.com; Jl Drupadi 88B; ☺10am-7pm) This high-end gallery regularly has shows that are thoughtfully and creatively curated. It has regular special events too.

Homewares

★Souq HOMEWARES
(☑0822 3780 1817; www.souqstore.co; Jl Basangkasa 10; ☺8.30am-8pm) The Middle East meets Asia at this glossy high-concept store with Bali designed housewares and clothing. It has a small cafe with healthy breakfast and lunch choices plus good coffee and cold-pressed juices.

White Peacock HOMEWARES
(☑0361-733238; Jl Kayu Jati 1; ☺9am-8pm) Styled like a country cottage, this is the place for cute cushions, throw rugs, table linens and more.

Samantha Robinson HOMEWARES
(📞0361-737295; www.samantharobinson.com.
au; Jl Kayu Jati 2; ⏰9am-8pm) The eponymous
Sydney porcelain designer offers her full
range of colourful and artful housewares at
this small boutique.

Domicil HOMEWARES
(📞0818 0569 8417; www.domicil-living.com; Jl
Raya Seminyak 56; ⏰10am-10pm) Facade meets
merchandise: everything is designed with
colonial flair at this appealing housewares
shop.

❶ Information

DANGERS & ANNOYANCES
Seminyak is generally more hassle-free than
Kuta and Legian. But it's worth reading up on the
warnings, especially those regarding surf and
water pollution.

MEDICAL SERVICES
Kimia Farma (📞0361-916 6509; Jl Raya
Kerobokan 140; ⏰24hr) Located at a major
crossroads, this outlet of Bali's best chain of
pharmacies has a full range of prescription
medications.

MONEY
ATMs can be found along all the main roads.
Central Kuta Money Exchange (www.cen-
tralkutabali.com; Jl Kaayu Aya, Seminyak
Sq; ⏰8.30am-9.30pm) Reliable currency
exchange.

POST
Post Office (📞0361-761592; Jl Raya Seminyak
17, Bintang Supermarket; ⏰8am-8pm) Convenient and friendly.

❶ Getting There & Away

The Kura-Kura tourist bus (p389) has a route
linking Seminyak with Umalas in the north and
Kuta in the south, however it runs infrequently.

Metered taxis are easily hailed. A trip from the
airport with the airport taxi cartel costs about
130,000Rp; a regular taxi to the airport, about
80,000Rp. You can beat the traffic, save the
ozone and have a good stroll by walking along
the beach; Legian is only about 15 minutes away.
Blue Bird (p392) has the most reliable service.

Kerobokan

Continuing seamlessly north from Seminyak, Kerobokan combines some of Bali's best restaurants and shopping, lavish
lifestyles and still more beach. Glossy new

resorts mix with villa developments. One
notable landmark is the notorious Kerobokan jail.

🏖 Beaches

Kerobokan Beach BEACH
Backed by flash resorts and trendy clubs,
Kerobokan's beach is surprisingly quiet. A
lack of access keeps away crowds because all
the roads running west from Jl Petitenget
dead-end in developments. You can reach
the sand from Seminyak Beach in the south
or by walking down from Batubelig Beach.
There are beach vendors and loungers just
north of the W Bali hotel.

The most direct access, however, is by
waltzing through the Potato Head (p92)
beach club or the W Bali hotel. The surf is
more thunderous here than to the south, so
be careful when swimming.

Batubelig Beach BEACH
The sand narrows here but there are some
good places for a drink, both grand and simple. Easily reached via Jl Batubelig, this is a
good place to start a walk along the curving
sands northwest to popular beaches as far
as Echo Beach.

About 500m north, a river and lagoon
flow into the ocean, sometimes up to 1m
deep – after rains it may be much deeper. In
this case, take the little footbridge over the
lagoon to La Laguna (p99) bar, where you
can call a taxi.

⊙ Sights

Kerobokan Jail LANDMARK
(Jl Gunung Tangkuban Perahu) The notorious
Kerobokan jail is home to prisoners both
infamous and unknown.

🏃 Activities

★Sundari Day Spa SPA
(📞0361-735073; www.sundari-dayspa.com; Jl
Petitenget 7; massages from 250,000Rp; ⏰10am-
10pm) This much-recommended spa strives
to offer the services of a five-star resort without the high prices. The massage oils and
other potions are organic, and there's a full
menu of therapies and treatments on offer.

Jiwa Bikram YOGA
(📞0361-841 3689; www.jiwabikram.com; Jl Petitenget 78; classes from 180,000Rp; ⏰9am-8pm)
In a convenient location, this no-frills place
offers several different types of yoga, including bikram, hot flow and yin.

Amo Beauty Spa
SPA

(☑0361-473 7943; www.amospa.com; Jl Petitenget 100X; massages from 220,000Rp; ⊘9am-9pm) With some of Asia's top models lounging about it feels like you've stumbled into a *Vogue* shoot. In addition to massages, services range from haircare to pedicures and unisex waxing. Book ahead.

🛏 Sleeping

Bali's blight of generic midrange chain hotels has also infected Kerobokan. Otherwise you'll find good-value choices amid sybaritic villa hotels plus some excellent beach resorts.

M Boutique Hostel
HOSTEL $

(☑0361-473 4142; www.mboutiquehostel.com; Jl Petitenget 8; dm 250,000-300,000Rp; ❄@🛜🏊) A contemporary choice for flashpackers, M Boutique's beds are capsule dorms, which come with the benefit of privacy. Each has shutter blinds, a drop-down chest table, a reading light and an electrical plug. The neatly trimmed lawn and small plunge pool add charm. Extras include free laundry.

Villa Bunga
HOTEL $

(☑0361-473 1666; www.villabunga.com; Jl Petitenget 18X; r 310,000-500,000Rp, apt from 400,000Rp; ❄🛜🏊) An excellent deal in the heart of Kerobokan, this 13-room hotel has rooms set in two-storey blocks around a small pool. Rooms are also small but are modern and have fridges.

Brown Feather
GUESTHOUSE $$

(☑0361-473 2165; www.brownfeather.com; Jl Batu Belig 100; r 630,000-900,000Rp; ❄🛜🏊) On the main road, but backing on to rice paddies, this small hotel exudes a Dutch-Javanese colonial charm. Rooms mix simplicity with old-world character, such as wooden writing desks and washbasins made from old Singer sewing machines. For rice-field views, go for room 205 or 206. There's a small, attractive pool and free bicycle rental, too.

Grand Balisani Suites
HOTEL $$

(☑0361-473 0550; www.balisanisuites.com; Jl Batubelig; r US$85-220; ❄🛜🏊) Location! This elaborately carved complex is right on popular Batubelig Beach. The 96 rooms are large and have standard teak furniture plus terraces (some also have great views). Wi-fi is limited to public areas.

Taman Ayu Cottage
HOTEL $$

(☑0361-473 0111; www.thetamanayu.com; Jl Petitenget; r incl breakfast 375,000-700,000Rp; ❄@🛜🏊) This great-value hotel has a fabulous location. Most of the 52 rooms are in two-storey blocks around a pool shaded by mature trees. Everything is a bit frayed around the edges, but all is forgotten when the bill comes. Family rooms and villas are available.

★Buah Bali Villas
VILLA $$$

(☑0361-847 6626; www.thebuahbali.com; Jl Petitenget, Gang Cempaka; villa from 2,600,000Rp; ❄🛜🏊) This small development has only seven villas, which range in size from one to two bedrooms. Like the many other nearby villa hotels, each unit has a private pool in a walled compound and a nice open-air living area. The location is superb: hot spots such as Biku (p90) and Potato Head (p92) are a five-minute walk.

★Katamana
BOUTIQUE HOTEL $$$

(☑0361-302 9999; www.katamama.com; Jl Petitenget 51; ❄🛜🏊) The same architectural derring-do that makes Potato Head much copied is on display at the club's hotel. However here the details are lavish and artful. Designed by Indonesian Andra Martin, it has 58 suites in a confection of Javanese bricks, Balinese stone and other indigenous materials. There are huge windows, lavish seating areas and private terraces and balconies.

★Alila Seminyak
RESORT $$$

(☑0361-302 1888; www.alilahotels.com; Jl Taman Ganesha 9; r from 4,000,000Rp; ❄🛜🏊) This sprawling resort (new in 2016) has a prime position right at the junction of Seminyak and Kerobokan beaches (and nightlife). A whopping 240 rooms come in various flavours. The cheapest have garden views, but as you rise up through the rate card you get beach views and more room. The colour scheme is a sandy palette of beige and tan.

W Bali – Seminyak
RESORT $$$

(☑0361-473 8106; www.wretreatbali.com; Jl Petitenget; r incl breakfast from 4,500,000Rp; ❄@🛜🏊) Like many W hotels, the usual too-cute-for-comfort vibe is at work here (how 'bout an 'extreme wow' suite?), but the location on a wave-tossed stretch of sand and the views are hard to quibble with. Stylish, hip bars, restaurants and smiling staff abound. The pricey rooms all have balconies, but not all have ocean views.

The Woobar is a great spot for a sundowner; happy-hour two-for-one cocktails come with a free pizza (from 4pm to 6pm).

✕ Eating

Kerobokan boasts some of Bali's best restaurants, whether budget or top end.

Jl Petitenget

★ Warung Eny   BALINESE $
(☑ 0361-473 6892; www.warungeny.blogspot.com; Jl Petitenget 97; mains from 35,000Rp; ☺ 8am-11pm) The eponymous Eny cooks everything herself at this tiny open-front warung nearly hidden behind various potted plants. Look for the roadside sign that captures the vibe: 'The love cooking'. The seafood, such as large prawns smothered in garlic, is delicious and most ingredients are organic. Ask about Eny's excellent cooking classes.

Pasar Kerobokan   MARKET $
(Fruit Market; cnr Jl Raya Kerobokan & Jl Gunung Tangkuban Perahu; ☺ 7am-10pm) Bali's numerous climate zones (hot and humid near the ocean, cool and dry up the volcano slopes) mean that pretty much any fruit or vegetable can be grown within the island's small confines. Vendors sell them all here, including unfamiliar fruits such as nubby mangosteens. A string of stalls prepare assorted tasty snacks and there's a small night market.

Gourmet Cafe   CAFE $
(☑ 0361-847 5115; www.balicateringcompany.com; Jl Petitenget 77A; snacks from 30,000Rp; ☺ 8am-9pm; ✻) Like a gem store of treats, this upscale deli-cafe run by the Bali Catering Company serves an array of fanciful little delights. Many spend all day battling the temptation of the mango ice cream; others succumb to the croissants from the in-house bakery.

★ Saigon Street   VIETNAMESE $$
(☑ 0361-897 4007; www.saigonstreetbali.com; Jl Petitenget 77; mains 50,000-175,000Rp; ☺ 11.30am-11pm; 🊷) Modern, vibrant and packed, this Vietnamese restaurant lures in the buzzing masses with its swanky neon decor. Creative Vietnamese dishes include peppery betel leaves filled with slow-cooked octopus, and there's an impressive rice-paper roll selection, along with curries, *pho*

(rice-noodle soup) and grilled meats cooked on aromatic coconut wood. Cocktails include the 'bang bang' martini, a chilled bit of boozy splendour. Book ahead.

Biku   FUSION $$
(☑ 0361-857 0888; www.bikubali.com; Jl Petitenget 888; meals 50,000-140,000Rp; ☺ 8am-11pm; 🊷🊮) Housed in a 150-year-old teak *joglo* (traditional Javanese house), wildly popular Biku retains the timeless vibe of its predecessor. The menu combines Indonesian and other Asian with Western influences in a cuisine Biku calls 'Asian comfort food'. The burgers get raves as do the desserts. Be sure to book ahead. There's a good kids menu.

It's also popular for high tea (from 11am to 5pm; 110,000Rp per person). It can be served Asian-style – with samosa, spring rolls etc, and green or oolong tea – or traditional – with cucumber sandwiches etc.

Cafe Degan   ASIAN $$
(☑ 0361-744 8622; www.facebook.com/cafedegan; Jl Petitenget 9; meals 90,000-180,000Rp; ☺ noon-11pm) The menu at this upscale warung veers towards Indonesian but features dishes from the region you don't often find, such as *daging sambal hijau* (spicy beef with green chillies). A small bakery produces an array of delectable desserts. The drinks list includes some interesting choices made with coconut water.

Merah Putih   INDONESIAN $$
(☑ 0361-846 5950; www.merahputihbali.com; Jl Petitenget 100X; mains 80,000-200,000Rp; ☺ noon-3pm & 6-11pm) Merah Putih means 'red and white', which are the colours of the Indonesian flag. That's perfect for this excellent restaurant, which celebrates food from across the archipelago. The short menu is divided between traditional and modern – the latter combining Indo flavours with diverse foods. The soaring dining room has a hip style and the service is excellent.

★ Sardine   SEAFOOD $$$
(☑ 0811 397 8111; www.sardinebali.com; Jl Petitenget 21; meals US$20-50; ☺ 11.30am-4pm & 6-11pm; 🊷) Seafood fresh from the famous Jimbaran market is the star at this elegant yet intimate, casual yet stylish restaurant. It's in a beautiful bamboo pavilion, with open-air tables overlooking a private rice field patrolled by Sardine's own flock of ducks. The inventive bar is a must and stays open until 1am. The menu changes to reflect what's fresh. Booking is vital.

Sarong FUSION $$$
(☑ 0361-473 7809; www.sarongbali.com; Jl Petitenget 19X; mains 120,000-180,000Rp; ⊙ 6.30-10.45pm; 🛜) Sarong is an elegant affair by the owners of Seminyak's excellent Mama San (p83). The cuisine spans Asia, and its small plates are popular with those wishing to pace an evening and enjoy the commodious bar. No children allowed. Dine outside under the stars.

Barbacoa BRAZILIAN $$$
(☑ 0361-739235; www.barbacoabali.com; Jl Petitenget 14; mains 110,000-250,000Rp; ⊙ noon-midnight; 🛜) Barbacoa is an impressive space with soaring timber ceilings, colourful mosaic-tiled floors and rice-field views (for now). The food is all about grilled meats; the restaurant's walls are lined with firewood to cook up its menu of Latin American dishes.

Elsewhere in Kerobokan

Gusto Gelato & Coffee GELATERIA $
(☑ 0361-552 2190; www.gusto-gelateria.com; Jl Raya Mertanadi 46; gelato from 22,000Rp; ⊙ 10am-10pm; ⊛🛜) Bali's best gelato is made fresh throughout the day, with unique flavours such as rich Oreo, surprising and delicious tamarind and *kamangi* (lemon basil). The classics are here as well. It gets mobbed in the afternoons.

Warung Sobat SEAFOOD $
(☑ 0361-731256; Jl Pengubengan Kauh 27; mains 37,000-100,000Rp; ⊙ 11am-10.30pm; 🛜) Sobat is set in a sort of bungalow-style large open-sided brick restaurant. Much bigger than the original on Jl Batu Belig, this old-fashioned restaurant excels at fresh Balinese seafood with an Italian accent (lots of garlic!). Prices are extraordinary, as you can see from the value-minded expats who pack the place every night.

★ **Sangsaka** INDONESIAN $$
(☑ 0812 3695 9895; www.sangsakabali.com; Jl Pangkung Sari 100; mains 80,000-180,000Rp; ⊙ 6pm-midnight Tue-Sun) On a Kerobokan backstreet, this casual restaurant serves well-nuanced versions of Indonesian dishes drawn from across the archipelago. Many are cooked over various types of charcoal, which vary depending on the origin of the dish. The dining area is done up in the usual vintage-wood motif, with just a touch more polish than usual. It has a good bar.

DON'T MISS

KEROBOKAN'S WARUNGS

Although seemingly upscale, Kerobokan is blessed with many a fine place for a truly authentic local meal. Top choices include the following:

Warung Sulawesi (Jl Petitenget; meals from 35,000Rp; ⊙ 7am-8pm) Here you'll find a table in a quiet family compound and enjoy fresh Balinese and Indonesian food served in classic warung style. Choose rice, then pick from a captivating array of dishes that are always at their peak at noon. The long beans – yum!

Warung Kolega (Jl Petitenget 98A; meals from 25,000Rp; ⊙ 9am-7.30pm Mon-Sat) A Javanese halal classic. Choose your rice (we prefer the fragrant yellow), then pick from a delectable array that includes tempeh in sweet chilli sauce, *sambal terung* (spicy eggplant), *ikan sambal* (spicy grilled fish) and other daily specials. Most of the labels are in English.

Sari Kembar (☑ 0361 847 6021; Jl Teuku Umar Barat/Jl Marlboro 99; mains from 15,000Rp; ⊙ 8am-10pm) One of Bali's best places for *babi guling* (spit-roast pig stuffed with chilli, turmeric, garlic, and ginger) is back on this busy street about 1.6km east of the junction with Jl Raya Kerobokan. Besides the succulent marinated pork, there's melt-in-your-mouth crackling, duck stuffed with cassava leaves, sausage and more. It's dead simple and amazingly good.

Blambangan Warung Syariah (Jl Gunung Salak; mains from 15,000Rp; ⊙ 24hr) The spicy foods of East Java are served around the clock at this simple roadside warung near some interesting shops. The chicken is free range and stars in the *ayam gulai,* a sort of chicken curry. When in doubt, have the *nasi campur* (rice with a choice of side dishes) and try a bit of everything.

KUTA & SEMINYAK KEROBOKAN

Naughty Nuri's INDONESIAN $$
(📞 0361-847 6783; www.naughtynurisseminyak.com; Jl Mertanadi 62; mains from 60,000Rp; ⊙ 11am-10pm) Inspired by the overhyped Ubud original, this Nuri's works to promote the concept. Relocated from Jl Batubelig, the current location has a much larger outdoor component. Remarkably, it has become a must-see stop for visitors from across Indonesia, who tuck into the not-especially tender pork ribs. The original's trademark kick-ass martinis remain.

Watercress CAFE $$
(📞 0851 0280 8030; www.watercressbali.com; Jl Batubelig 21A; mains from 65,000Rp; ⊙ 7.30am-11pm; 🅿🖥) A hit with the hipster set, this leafy roadside cafe does a roaring trade. As well as hearty breakfasts and gourmet burgers, it features healthy mains and salads. Excellent coffee, beer on tap and cocktails are other reasons to stop by. The small garden area out front is nice.

L'Assiette FRENCH $$
(📞 0361-735840; Jl Raya Mertanadi 29; meals 50,000-100,000Rp; ⊙ 10am-11pm Mon-Sat; 🖥) The huge quiet garden behind this airy cafe is the perfect place to enjoy a *salade niçoise* or any of the other fresh and tasty, classic French-cafe fare served here. Perhaps a *steak frites* or a terrine will strike your fancy. If not, there are Asian-accented dishes too. It shares space with Pourquoi Pas antique shop.

🍸 Drinking & Nightlife

Some of Kerobokan's trendier restaurants have stylish bar areas that stay open late.

★ Potato Head CLUB
(📞 0361-473 7979; www.ptthead.com; Jl Petitenget; ⊙ 11am-2am; 🖥) Bali's highest-profile beach club is one of the best. Wander up off the sand or follow a long drive off Jl Petitenget and you'll find much to amuse, from an enticing pool to a swanky restaurant, plus lots of lounges and patches of lawn for chillin' the night away under the stars.

Mirror CLUB
(📞 0811 399 3010; www.facebook.com/mirrorbali; Jl Petitenget 106; ⊙ 11pm-4am Wed-Sat) This newish club is big with south Bali expats, who may own those designer shops you were in a few hours before. The interior is sort of like a cathedral out of Harry Potter, albeit with an unholy amount of lighting effects. Mainstream electronica blares forth.

Pantai BAR
(Batubelig Beach; ⊙ 9am-9pm) The authorities regularly bulldoze away the impromptu drinking shacks that appear along this inviting stretch of beach just north of the W Bali hotel. But so far Pantai has had more lives than a cat – it stubbornly keeps offering up cheap drinks, mismatched tables and splendid surf and sunset views.

🔒 Shopping

You'll find boutiques interspersed with the trendy restaurants on Jl Petitenget. Jl Raya Kerobokan, extending north from Jl Sunset, has interesting shops primarily selling decorator items and housewares. Wander Jl Raya Mertanadi for an ever-changing line-up of homewares shops, many of them more factory than showroom.

★ Purpa Fine Art Gallery ART
(📞 0819 9940 8804; www.purpagallerybali.com; Jl Mertanadi 22; ⊙ 10am-6pm Tue-Sat) This long-time gallery has shown some of Bali's very best artists going back to the most notable names of the 1930s such as Spies, Snell and Lempad. It has regular special exhibits.

★ Bathe BEAUTY, HOMEWARES
(📞 0811 388 640; www.bathestore.com; Jl Batu Belig 88; ⊙ 7am-10pm) Double-down on your villa's romance with handmade candles, air diffusers, aromatherapy oils, bath salts and homewares that evoke the feel of a 19th-century French dispensary. It's in a cluster of upscale boutiques.

Tulola JEWELLERY
(📞 0361-473 0261; www.shoptulola.com; Jl Petitenget; ⊙ 10am-8pm) This is the jewellery shop of noted Balinese-American designer Sri Luce Rusna. High-end items are created in Bali and displayed in this exquisite boutique.

Ayun Tailor CLOTHING
(📞 0821 8996 5056; Jl Batubelig; ⊙ 10am-6pm) Ayun is an excellent tailor. Buy batik or other fabric at one of Bali's many textile emporiums and she'll turn it into a frock for a man, woman or child. Bring along a shirt you love and she can copy it. Great rates.

Mercredi HOMEWARES
(📞 0812 4634 0518; Jl Petitenget; ⊙ 9am-7pm) Fashionable cushions to turn your tired sofa into a spry fashion statement are but some of the goods on sale in this stylish shop of well-designed housewares.

SHOPPING SAFARI

East of Seminyak and Kerobokan, a series of streets is lined with all manner of interesting shops selling and manufacturing housewares, baubles, fabric and other intriguing items. Head east of Kerobokan jail for about 2km on Jl Gunung Tangkuban Perahu and then turn south on – get this – a street with the same name.

This particular *jalan* has been called 'the street of amazement' by a shopaholic friend; look for an array of stores with vintage seaman's gear and primitive art. South, it becomes Jl Gunung Athena, with housewares and art, and then heads east as Jl Kunti II where it ends at the busy intersection with Jl Sunset and Jl Kunti.

Yoga Batik (Jl Gunung Athena; ⊙9am-6pm) A huge variety of the iconic Indonesian fabric.

Rainbow Tulungagung (Jl Gunung Athena; ⊙9am-6pm) Handicrafts made from marble and stone. The soap dispensers are easily carried home.

My Basket Bali (☑0361-994 3683; Jl Gunung Athena 39B; ⊙9am-6pm) If it can be woven from fibre, it's here. Baskets that look as good as they're practical.

Victory Art (☑0817 569 631; Jl Gunung Tangkuban Perahu; ⊙9am-6pm) As much spectacle as store, this corner place is jammed with intriguing works of new art. All manner of primitive faces gaze out from the array of merchandise that's inspired by indigenous cultures from across Indonesia.

Kevala Home HOMEWARES
(☑0361-473 5869; www.kevalaceramics.com; Jl Batubelig; ⊙10am-8pm) Designed and made in Bali, the top-end ceramics here are exquisite examples of the art.

Geneva Handicraft Centre ARTS & CRAFTS
(☑0361-733582; www.genevahandicraft.com; Jl Raya Kerobokan 100; ⊙9am-8pm) Tourist vans flock to the big space out front of this multifloor emporium of Indonesian handicraft. And with good reason, quality is good and prices are fair and fixed.

Tribali JEWELLERY
(☑0818 0541 5453; Jl Petitenget 12B; ⊙10am-8pm) Rustic jewellery and accessories with a luxe hippy vibe are shown in earthy display cases.

Carga HOMEWARES
(☑0361-847 8180; Jl Petitenget 886; ⊙9am-9pm) This beautiful shop is set back from the cacophony of Jl Petitenget in a vintage house shaded by palm trees. The housewares are sourced across Indonesia and range from elegant to whimsical.

Pourquoi Pas ANTIQUES
(Jl Raya Mertanadi; ⊙9am-7pm) Owned by the French family behind the cafe L'Assiette (p92), this adjoining antique store is filled with treasures from across the archipelago and Southeast Asia.

Hobo HOMEWARES
(☑0361-733369; www.thehobostore.com; Jl Raya Kerobokan 105; ⊙9am-8pm) Elegance mixes with quirky at this enticing shop filled with gifts and housewares, most of which can slip right into your carry-on bag.

Namu CLOTHING
(☑0361-279 7524; www.namustore.com; Jl Petitenget 23X; ⊙9.30am-8pm) Designer Paola Zancanaro creates comfy and casual resort wear for men and women that doesn't take a holiday from style. The fabrics are lusciously tactile; many are hand-painted silk.

JJ Ball Button ARTS & CRAFTS
(Jl Gunung Tangkuban Perahu; ⊙9am-5pm) Zillions of beads and buttons made from shells, plastic, metal and more are displayed in what at first looks like a candy store. Elaborately carved wooden buttons cost 800Rp. Kids may have to be bribed to leave.

You Like Lamp HOMEWARES
(☑0361-733755; Jl Raya Mertanadi; ⊙9am-7pm) Why yes, we do. All manner of endearing little paper lamps – many good for tea lights – are sold here cheap by the bagful. Don't see what you want? The staff working away on the floor will rustle it up immediately.

Nôblis HOMEWARES
(☑0813 3767 2012; Jl Raya Mertanadi 54; ⊙9am-7pm) Feel like royalty here with regal bits of decor from around the globe. Has its own line of flamboyant furniture.

ℹ Information

Central Kuta Money Exchange (www.central-kutabali.com; Jl Raya Kerobokan 51; ⊙8.30am-9pm) Reliable currency exchange.

ChannelOne (📱0878 6204 3224; www.channel1.biz; Jl Sunset 100X) Offers full immigration services, visa renewals and more.

ℹ Getting There & Away

Although the beach may seem tantalisingly close, few roads or *gang* actually reach the sand from the east. Note also that Jl Raya Kerobokan can come to a fume-filled stop for extended periods.

The Kura-Kura tourist bus (p389) has a route linking Seminyak with Umalas in the north and Kuta in the south, however it runs infrequently.

Metered taxis are easily hailed. A trip from the airport with the airport taxi cartel costs about 160,000Rp; a regular taxi to the airport, about 100,000Rp. You can beat the traffic, save the ozone and have a good stroll by walking along the beach; Legian is only about 15 minutes away. Blue Bird (p392) has the most reliable service.

ℹ Getting Around

Bali Bike Rental (📱0361-300 3533; www.balibikerental.com; Jl Raya Kerobokan 71; rental per day from US$9; ⊙10am-10pm) An alternative to the thousands of freelance motorbike renters in Bali. For the extra money, you get a motorbike in prime shape along with extras such as extra-clean helmets, roadside assistance and more. Faster, more powerful motorcycles are also available.

Canggu & Around

The Canggu region, north and west of Kerobokan, is Bali's fastest-growing area. Much of the growth is centred along the coast, anchored by the endless swathe of beach, which, despite rampant development, remains fairly uncrowded. Kerobokan morphs into Umalas inland and Canggu to the west, while neighbouring Echo Beach is a big construction site.

Cloistered villas lure expats who whisk past the remaining rice farmers on motorbikes or in air-con comfort. Traffic may be the ultimate commoner's revenge: road building is a decade behind settlement. Amid this maze of too-narrow lanes you'll find creative cafes, trendy restaurants and appealing shops. Follow the sounds of the surf to great beaches such as the one at Batu Bolong.

To stay current with the constant flurry of new openings, check out www.cangguguide.com.

Umalas

Expat villas and Balinese compounds mix with rice fields north of Kerobokan. Look for surprises such as a cute warung or a delightfully oddball shop on the back roads.

☞ Tours

⭐**Bali Bike Hire**   CYCLING
(📱0361-202 0054; www.balibikehire.com; Jl Raya Semer 61; rental per day from 60,000Rp) Run by people passionate about bikes, here you can choose from a variety of top-quality rides. It offers plenty of advice for navigating Bali's often tortuous roads, and leads various excellent guided tours by bike.

✗ Eating

Go exploring the small roads east of Jl Raya Kerobokan and you'll discover lots of interesting warungs serving a variety of cuisines.

⭐**Nook**   INTERNATIONAL $$
(📱0813 3806 0060; www.facebook.com/nookbali; Jl Umalas I; mains 40,000-160,000Rp; ⊙8am-11pm; 🛜) Sublimely positioned among the rice fields, this casual, open-air cafe is popular for its creative takes on Asian and Western fare. It has a modern vibe mixed with tropical flavours, plus good breakfasts and burgers. Get a table on the back wooden terrace.

Bali Buda   CAFE $$
(📱0361-844 5935; www.balibuda.com; Jl Banjar Anyar 24; mains from 35,000Rp; ⊙8am-10pm; ❋🛜📱) This appealing outlet of the Ubud original has all the excellent baked goods and organic groceries you'd expect. The small cafe serves healthy juices and smoothies plus an array of mostly vegetarian fare. Stop in for breakfast on your way to visit Tanah Lot (sane people visit the temple before noon).

🛍 Shopping

Reza Art 2   ANTIQUES
(📱0821 9797 4309; Jl Mertasari 99; ⊙10am-6pm) Oodles of lamps in many sizes mix with nautical antiques and junk (think old ship telegraphs and rudder wheels) in this shop that's more treasure hunt than retail establishment.

Canggu & Echo Beach

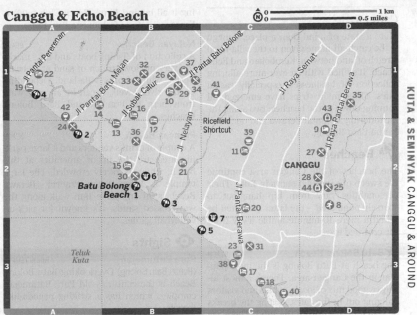

Canggu & Echo Beach

◎ Top Sights
1 Batu Bolong Beach.............................B2

◎ Sights
Berawa Beach..............................(see 17)
2 Echo Beach......................................A2
3 Nelayan Beach.................................B2
4 Pererenan Beach.............................A1
5 Prancak Beach.................................C3
6 Pura Batumejan...............................B2
7 Pura Dalem Prancak........................C3

🏃 Activities, Courses & Tours
8 Canggu Club.....................................D2

🛏 Sleeping
9 Big Brother Surf Inn.........................D2
10 Calmtree Bungalows.........................B1
11 Canggu Surf Hostel..........................C2
12 Coconuts Guesthouse Canggu..........B2
13 Echo Beach Resort...........................B2
14 Echoland...A1
15 Hotel Tugu Bali................................B2
16 Koming Guest House........................B1
17 Legong Keraton................................C3
18 Lv8 Resort Hotel..............................C3
19 Pondok Nyoman Bagus.....................A1
20 Sedasa..C2
21 Serenity Eco Guesthouse.................B2
22 Surfers Paradise...............................A1
23 Widi Homestay.................................C3

🍴 Eating
24 Beach House.....................................A2
Betelnut Cafe.............................(see 10)
25 Bungalow..D2
26 Deus Ex Machina..............................B1
Dian Cafe...................................(see 24)
27 Green Ginger....................................D2
28 Indotopia..D2
29 Monsieur Spoon................................B1
30 Old Man's..B2
31 One Eyed Jack...................................C3
32 Salumeria Tanah Bara.......................B1
33 Shady Shack......................................B1
34 Warung Bu Mi...................................B1
35 Warung Goûthé.................................D1
36 Warung Varuna.................................B2

🍸 Drinking & Nightlife
37 Black Shores.....................................B1
38 Finn's Beach Club.............................C3
39 Hungry Bird......................................C2
Ji...(see 15)
40 La Laguna..C3
41 Pretty Poison....................................C1
42 Sand Bar...A1

🛍 Shopping
Dylan Board Store.....................(see 29)
43 It Was All a Dream...........................D1
44 Ivy & Isabel......................................D2

Canggu

More a state of mind than a place, Canggu is the catch-all name given to the villa-filled stretch of land between Kerobokan and Echo Beach. It's filled with an ever-more alluring collection of businesses, especially casual cafes. Three main strips have emerged, all running down to the beaches: two along the meandering Jl Pantai Berawa and one on Jl Pantai Batu Bolong.

🏖 Beaches

The beaches of the Canggu area continue the sweep of sand that starts in Kuta. Their personalities vary from hip hang-out to sparsely populated – the latter can often be found a mere 10-minute amble away from the crowded areas.

★ Batu Bolong Beach   BEACH

The beach at Batu Bolong is the most popular in the Canggu area. There's almost always a good mix of locals, expats and visitors hanging out in the cafes, surfing the breaks or watching it all from the sand. There are rental loungers, umbrellas and beer vendors.

You can also rent surfboards (100,000Rp per day) and take lessons. Overlooking it all is the centuries-old Pura Batumejan complex.

Berawa Beach   BEACH

(parking motorbike/car 2000/3000Rp) Greyish Berawa Beach ('Brawa Beach' on many signs) has a couple of surfer cafes by the pounding sea. The grey volcanic sand here slopes steeply into foaming water. Overlook-

BEACH WALK

You can usually walk the 4km of sand between Batubelig Beach and Echo Beach in about one to two hours. It's a fascinating stroll and you'll see temples, tiny fishing encampments, crashing surf, lots of surfers, cool cafes and outcrops of upscale beach culture. The only catch is that after heavy rains, some of the rivers may be too deep to cross, especially the one just northwest of Batubelig. In any case, put your gear in waterproof bags in case you have to do some fording.

It's easy to find taxis at any of the larger beaches if you don't want to retrace your steps.

ing it all behind Finn's Beach Club (p99) is the vast estate of fashionista Paul Ropp.

Nelayan Beach   BEACH

A collection of fishing boats and huts marks the very mellow stretch of sand at Nelayan Beach, which fronts 'villa-land'. Depending on the river levels, it can be an easy walk from here to Prancak and Batu Bolong beaches.

Prancak Beach   BEACH

A couple of drinks vendors and a large parking area are the major amenities at this beach, which is rarely crowded. The large temple is Pura Dalem Prancak. Berawa Beach is an enjoyable 1km walk along the wave-tossed sands. It's known for pick-up volleyball games.

◉ Sights

Pura Batumejan   HINDU TEMPLE

(Pantai Batu Bolong) Overlooking Batu Bolong Beach is the centuries-old Pura Batumejan complex, which has a striking pagoda-like temple.

Pura Dalem Prancak   HINDU TEMPLE

(Pantai Prancak) This large temple is often the site of ceremonies.

🏃 Activities

Very popular for surfing, the Canggu area beaches draw a lot of locals and expat residents on weekends. Access to parking areas usually costs 5000Rp and there are cafes and warungs for those who work up an appetite in the water or watching others in the water.

Canggu Club   HEALTH & FITNESS

(📱0361-848 3939; www.cangguclub.com; Jl Pantai Berawa; adult/child day pass 300,000/180,000Rp; ⊙6am-10pm) Bali's expats shuttlecock themselves silly at the Canggu Club, a New Age version of something you'd expect to find during the Raj. The vast, perfectly virescent lawn is manicured for croquet. Get sweaty with tennis, squash, polo, cricket, bowling, the spa or the 25m pool. Many villa rentals include guest passes here. The garish Splash Waterpark is popular.

🛏 Sleeping

Canggu has all types of places to stay. Guesthouses self-billed as 'surf camps' have proliferated. For longer-term lodging, besides searching online, check the bulletin board at Warung Varuna (p98).

Serenity Eco Guesthouse
GUESTHOUSE $

(☑0361-846 9257; www.serenityecoguest-house.com; Jl Nelayan; dm/s/d incl breakfast 200,000/230,000/490,000Rp; ❄️🛜🏊) ✎ This hotel is an oasis among the sterility of walled villas. Rooms range from shared-bath singles to quite nice doubles with bathrooms (some with fans, others with air-con). The grounds are appealingly eccentric; Nelayan Beach is a five-minute walk. There are yoga classes (from 100,000Rp) and you can rent surfboards, bikes and more.

This place makes an effort to minimise its carbon footprint.

Big Brother Surf Inn
GUESTHOUSE $

(☑0812 3838 0385; www.bigbrotherbali.com; Jl Pantai Berawa 20; r 540,000-700,000Rp; ❄️🛜🏊) This sleek take on a traditional Balinese guesthouse has clean lines and plenty of minimalist white. The six rooms are airy and have outdoor sitting areas overlooking a garden with barbecue facilities and a pool. It's in a quiet location back off the road; despite the name, your high jinks are unlikely to end up on a reality TV show.

Canggu Surf Hostel
HOSTEL $

(☑0813 5303 1293; www.canggusurfhostels.com; Jl Raya Semat; dm 120,000-150,000Rp; r 400,000Rp; ❄️🛜🏊) This well-equipped hostel has a split personality: two locations, with the other just around the corner on Jl Pantai Berawa. There are six- and four-bed rooms plus private rooms. Enjoy multiple public spaces, pools, kitchens and lockable surfboard storage.

Widi Homestay
HOMESTAY $

(☑0819 3626 0860; widihomestay@yahoo.co.id; Jl Pantai Berawa; r from 250,000Rp; ❄️🛜) There's no faux-hipster vibe here with fake nihilist bromides, just a spotless, friendly family-run homestay. The four rooms have hot water and air-con; the beach is barely 100m away.

★ Sedasa
BOUTIQUE HOTEL $$

(☑0361 844 6666; www.sedasa.com; Jl Pantai Berawa; r incl breakfast 450,000-850,000Rp; ❄️🛜🏊) Both intimate and stylish, Sedasa has an understated Balinese elegance. The 10 large rooms overlook a small pool and have designer furniture. The beanbags on the rooftop make a good place to relax with a book. Downstairs there's an organic cafe. It's a five-minute walk to the beach, and

there's free bike rental and a shuttle into Seminyak.

Calmtree Bungalows
GUESTHOUSE $$

(☑0851 0074 7009; www.thecalmtreebungalows.com; Jl Pantai Batu Bolong; r from 600,000Rp; 🛜🏊) Right in the middle of the emerging heart of Batu Bolong, this family-run compound has eight traditional-style units around a pool. Inside the thatched walls you'll find rustic style fused with a touch of modern. The bathrooms are open-air. There's no air-con but there are nets and fans – think of it as atmospheric. Great staff.

Coconuts Guesthouse Canggu
GUESTHOUSE $$

(☑0878 6192 7150; www.coconutsguesthouse.com; Jl Pantai Batu Bolong; r from 750,000Rp; ❄️🛜🏊) The five breezy rooms at this contemporary guesthouse are very comfortable. Some have lovely views of the (surviving) rice fields, and all have fridges and a relaxed motif. Enjoy sunsets from the rooftop lounge area or take a dip in the 10m pool. Batu Bolong Beach is a 700m walk.

Legong Keraton
HOTEL $$

(☑0361-473 0280; www.legongkeratonhotel.com; Jl Pantai Berawa; r 820,000-1,400,000Rp; ❄️@🛜🏊) The Canggu boom has caught up with this well run 40-room beachfront resort. The grounds are shaded by palms and the pool borders the beach. The best rooms are in bungalow units facing the surf. Long isolated, the hotel is now in the centre of the action.

★ Hotel Tugu Bali
HOTEL $$$

(☑0361-473 1701; www.tuguhotels.com; Jl Pantai Batu Bolong; r incl breakfast from US$400; ❄️@🛜🏊) Right at Batu Bolong Beach, this exquisite hotel blurs the boundaries between accommodation and a museum-gallery, especially the Walter Spies and Le Mayeur Pavilions, where memorabilia from the artists' lives decorates the rooms. There's a spa and a high-style beachfront bar, Ji. The stunning collection of antiques and artwork begins in the lobby and extends throughout the hotel.

Lv8 Resort Hotel
RESORT $$$

(☑0361-894 8888; www.lv8bali.com; Jl Discovery 8; r 1,300,000-3,200,000Rp; ❄️🛜🏊) Right on a bend in the lagoon and fronting Berawa Beach, this light and airy resort makes the most of its long and narrow location. Even the smallest of the 124 rooms are large, with balconies and sitting areas. Some have sweeping ocean views while others have private plunge pools.

✖ Eating

Canggu is where you'll find some of Bali's most innovative and affordable places to eat. Look along the main strips, as new cafes and restaurants seem to open daily.

Warung Varuna INDONESIAN $
(📞0818 0551 8790; Jl Pantai Batu Bolong 89A; mains 20,000-40,000Rp; ⊙8am-10pm) The best deal for great local fare close to the beach, Varuna combines excellent Balinese fare with a surfer sensibility. The nasi goreng (fried rice) comes in several creative variations; there are also juices, smoothies and jaffles. It has good, hearty Western breakfasts. The bulletin board has many listings for villa and room rentals.

Warung Bu Mi INDONESIAN $
(📞0857 3741 1115; Jl Pantai Batu Bolong 52; meals 25,000-40,000Rp; ⊙8am-10pm) Classic Balinese warung-style food. Choose your style of rice (we like the local fave: nutty red) and then go down the line picking from various dishes. Don't pass up the corn fritters. It has long tables amid a simple, clean interior.

Bungalow CAFE $
(📞0361-844 6567; www.bungalowlivingbali.com; Jl Pantai Berawa; mains from 30,000Rp; ⊙8am-6pm Mon-Sat; ✱) Set just far enough back from the road to avoid the fumes, this cafe reflects the retro-chic design sensibilities of its parent housewares emporium. Relax amid distressed-wood surrounds on the verandah and choose from a vast range of coffee drinks, juices, smoothies, sandwiches, salads and desserts.

Indotopia ASIAN $
(📞0822 3773 7760; Jl Pantai Berawa 34; mains from 30,000Rp; ⊙8am-10pm; 🤙) Otherwise known as 'Warung Vietnam', this place serves bowls of *pho* that are simply superb. Lots of rich beefy goodness contrasting with perfect noodles and fragrant greens. Prefer something sweeter? Go for the Saigon banana crepes.

Betelnut Cafe CAFE $
(📞0821 4680 7233; Jl Pantai Batu Bolong; mains from 45,000Rp; ⊙7am-10pm; ✱🤙) There's a hippy-chic vibe at this thatched cafe with a mellow open-air dining room upstairs. The menu leans towards healthy, but not too

healthy – you can get fries. There are juices and lots of mains featuring veggies. It has good baked goods and nice shakes.

Monsieur Spoon CAFE $
(Jl Pantai Batu Bolong; snacks from 20,000Rp; ⊙6am-9pm; ✱) Beautiful French-style baked goods (the almond croissant, wow!) are the speciality at this small Bali chain of cafes. Enjoy pastries, sandwiches on picture-perfect bread and fine coffees at a table in the garden or inside.

Green Ginger ASIAN $
(📞0878 6211 2729; Jl Pantai Berawa; meals from 40,000Rp; ⊙8am-9pm; 🤙📞) An attractive little restaurant on the fast-changing strip in Canggu, Green Ginger specialises in fresh and tasty vegetarian and noodle dishes from across Asia.

★One Eyed Jack JAPANESE $$
(📞0819 9929 1888; www.oneeyedjackbali.com; Jl Pantai Berawa; ⊙5pm-midnight) *Izakaya,* the style of Japanese dining that encourages groups of friends to enjoy drinks and shared plates of food, is exemplified by this wonderful small restaurant. The chef is a veteran of internationally acclaimed Nomu; the dishes are superb. Tiny taco-style appetisers, chicken *tsukune* sliders and barbecue-pork buns will have you ordering seconds. Don't miss the tea-based cocktails.

★Warung Goûthé BISTRO $$
(📞0878 8947 0638; www.facebook.com/warung-gouthe; Jl Pantai Berawa 7A; mains from 60,000Rp; ⊙9am-5pm Mon-Sat) Superbly prepared and presented casual meals are the hallmark of this open-front cafe. The very short menu changes each day depending on what's fresh. The French owners can take a simple chicken sandwich and elevate it to magnificent and memorable. The desserts alone should cause you to stop in whenever you are nearby.

★Deus Ex Machina CAFE $$
(Temple of Enthusiasm; 📞0811 388 150; www.deuscustoms.com; Jl Batu Mejan 8; mains 60,000-170,000Rp; ⊙7am-11pm; 🤙) This surreal venue amid Canggu's rice fields has many personas. If you're hungry it's a restaurant-cafe-bar; for shoppers it's a fashion label; if you're into culture it's a contemporary-art gallery; for music lovers it's a live-gig venue (Sunday afternoons) for local punk bands; for bikers it's a custom-made motorcycle

shop; if you want your beard trimmed, it's a barber...

★**Old Man's**   INTERNATIONAL **$$**
(☑0361-846 9158; www.oldmans.net; Jl Pantai Batu Bolong; mains from 50,000Rp; ◎8am-midnight) You'll have a tough time deciding just where to sit down to enjoy your drink at this popular coastal beer garden overlooking Batu Bolong Beach. The self-serve menu is aimed at surfers and surfer-wannabes: burgers, pizza, fish and chips, salads. Wednesday nights are an institution, while Fridays (live rock and roll) and Sundays (DJs) are also big.

🍷 Drinking & Nightlife

Grab a beer from a vendor on the beach or hit one of the beach clubs or eating venues nearby. The party doesn't go late yet; you'll still need to head south for that.

★**Black Shores**   BAR
(☑0813 3987 4055; Jl Batu Bolong; ◎4pm-midnight) A laid-back bar with a pure Canggu vibe. Creative bartenders concoct drinks that are boozy, fresh and often fruity. Regular live acts (usually Friday nights) feature top visiting bands. When crowded it feels like a big house party by the beach, which it sort of is.

Ji   BAR
(☑0361-473 1701; www.jiatbalesutra.com; Jl Pantai Batu Bolong, Hotel Tugu Bali; ◎5-11pm) Easily Canggu's most alluring bar, Ji is a fantasy of historic Chinese and Balinese wood carving and rich decor. From the terrace on the 1st floor, there are fine views you can enjoy with exotic cocktails, sake and Japanese bites.

Pretty Poison   BAR
(☑0812 4622 9340; Jl Subak Canggu; ◎4pm-midnight) Pretty Poison's bar overlooks an old-school '80s skate bowl, so a surfboard isn't the only board you to need to pack. Run by longtime Aussie expat and surfer Maree Suteja, it's a great place to hang out, with cheap beers and bands. Being Canggu, there's logo'd wear for sale. It's close to the chaotic comedy of the rice-field shortcut.

Hungry Bird   CAFE
(☑0898 619 1008; www.facebook.com/hungrybirdcoffee; Jl Raya Semat 86; ◎8am-5pm Mon-Sat; 🔊) One of the few genuine third-wave coffee roasters in Bali, Hungry Bird does superb single-origin brews. The Javanese owner is incredibly knowledgeable on the subject, and roasts beans on-site from all over Indonesia; cupping sessions are possible if you call ahead. The food's also excellent (organic eggs and baked goods) and perfect for brunch.

Finn's Beach Club   BAR
(☑0361-844 6327; www.finnsbeachclub.com; Jl Pantai Berawa; ◎7am-midnight; 🔊) An enormous spectacle built from soaring bamboo, Finn's dominates the beachfront. There's a huge pool and driving sound system. Hipster types fill seating areas and groups seeking tans frame the pool. Day loungers cost a pricey 250,000Rp, which includes a towel. There's a big bar and various treats like 'nitro ice cream'. Food spans the casual gamut (mains from 130,000Rp).

Note that the grilled corn on the menu for 60,000Rp inside can be had from the cheery vendor on the sand for the (already inflated) tourist price of 10,000Rp.

La Laguna   COCKTAIL BAR
(☑0812 3638 2272; www.facebook.com/hungrybirdcoffee; Jl Pantai Kayu Putih; ◎11am-midnight; 🔊) A sibling of Seminyak's La Favela (p85), La Laguna is one of Bali's most alluring bars. It combines a beatnik look with Moorish trappings and sparkling tiny lights. Explore the eclectic layout, and sit on a couch, a sofa bed, at a table inside or a picnic table in the garden. The drinks are good, the food is fair (mains from 75,000Rp).

To arrive in style, walk along the beach and then take the footbridge right over the lagoon.

🛍 Shopping

★**It Was All A Dream**   FASHION & ACCESSORIES
(☑0811 388 3322; Jl Pantai Berawa 14B; ◎10am-7pm) Great-quality leather bags, fun sunglasses, vintage jeans, jersey basics, embroidered kaftans and more. This hip boutique has original pieces at reasonable prices. It's run by a French-American pair of expat designers.

Dylan Board Store   SPORTS & OUTDOORS
(☑0819 9982 5654; www.dylansurfboards.com; Jl Pantai Batu Bolong; ◎10am-8pm) Famed big-wave rider Dylan Longbottom runs this custom surfboard shop. A talented shaper, he creates boards for novices and pros alike. He also stocks plenty of his own designs that are ready to go.

Ivy & Isabel CLOTHING
(www.ivyandisabel.com; Jl Pantai Berawa; ⊙9am-6pm) From a popular designer in Western Australia, this shop has a full line of light-weight women's wear designed for a beachy frolic.

Echo Beach

One of Bali's most popular surf breaks, Echo Beach has reached critical mass in popularity; surf shops abound. Construction has not been kind to the area and there's an unsightly dormant resort complex just to the east. If it seems too crowded here, walk along the sands 200m east for quietude.

Sunsets – and big waves – draw crowds who enjoy drinks coloured by the rosy glow.

☂ Beaches

Echo Beach BEACH
(Pantai Batu Mejan) Surfers and those who like to watch them flock here for the high-tide left-hander that regularly tops 2m. The greyish sand right in front of the developments can vanish at high tide, but you'll find wide strands east and west. Batu Bolong Beach is 500m east.

🛏 Sleeping

Most places to stay here are villas or large villas with various apartments. Beware of low-calibre cheapies along Jl Pantai Batu Mejan.

Echo Beach Resort APARTMENT $$
(⊉021-781 8558; www.echobeach.co.id; Jl Mundu Catu; apt from 900,000Rp; ❋☎❄) Soaring above nearby villas, this apartment complex has nine one-bedroom units that come in various flavours. Some have ocean views, others have private pools. All have kitchen facilities. The compound is quiet and the decor is light-coloured and spartan. There is a good roof deck with sweeping water views. The beach is a 300m walk.

Koming Guest House GUESTHOUSE $$
(⊉0819 9920 0996; www.komingguesthouse.com; Jl Munduk Catu; r from 500,000Rp; ❋☎❄) Surrounded by other villas, this one has four rooms on two floors. The bottom ones have direct access to the pool. The upstairs pair have terraces with glimpses of the ocean. All have fridges and basic furnishings. Watch out for some tiled bathrooms that are not recommended after a night out.

Echoland GUESTHOUSE $$
(⊉0361-887 0628; www.echolandbali.com; Jl Pantai Batu Mejan; dm from 180,000Rp, r with fan/air-con from 435,000/500,000Rp; ❋☎❄) There are 17 private rooms plus dorms in this compact two-storey compound about 300m from the beach. The rooftop lounge has a nice cover for shade and predictably good views. **Yoga classes** are offered from 80,000Rp per hour.

✗ Eating

Cafes from basic to vaunted front the surf break. Some exceptional new eateries are appearing back from the beach.

Dian Cafe INDONESIAN $
(⊉0813 3875 4305; Jl Pantai Batu Mejan; mains from 30,000Rp; ⊙8am-10pm) Old-school Indonesian and Western standards are served up cheap at this open-air cafe just a few metres from the beach.

Shady Shack VEGETARIAN $$
(⊉0819 1639 5087; www.facebook.com/the-shadyshackbali; Jl Tanah Barak 53; mains 40,000-120,000Rp; ⊙7.30am-11pm; ✍) ✿ Under big trees, this charming cafe evokes the feel of a simple colonial country house in the Caribbean. There are tables in the garden as well as the woodsy dining room with huge open windows. The menu is a long list of bowls, wraps and juices. Most are vegan and/or veggie. Try the blueberry muesli, beautiful halloumi burger or gorgeous desserts.

Salumeria Tanah Bara ITALIAN $$
(⊉0361-300 3463; www.salumeria.asia; Jl Tanah Barak 47; mains 60,000-140,000Rp; ⊙4-11pm) Exceptionally authentic Italian meats, cheeses and antipasti are served in small portions and on platters at this cafe that could be lifted directly from Florence. Share plates of perfection on sofas, tables and stools, with views of the rice fields so you don't forget where you are. The bar menu is long, with excellent wines, martinis and drinks with Campari.

Beach House CAFE $$
(Echo Beach Club; ⊉0361-747 4604; www.echobeachhouse.com; Jl Pura Batu Mejan; mains 40,000-120,000Rp; ⊙7am-11pm; ☎) An Echo Beach icon, this seafront restaurant-bar has front-row seats (tables, sofas, picnic tables) to enjoy the surf action. There's an impressive display of skewered meats and seafood ready to grill, as well as a tasty breakfast and lunch menu. Evening barbecues are popu-

lar, especially on Sundays when there's live music.

🍷 Drinking & Nightlife

Enjoying a drink while watching the surf break is an Echo Beach tradition. Just west of the main cafe cluster, a string of ephemeral beach bars have appeared that are little more than bamboo shacks. They offer beanbags on the sand and cold beer. Note that an upscale development could sweep them away overnight.

Sand Bar
BAR

(Echo Beach; ⊘10am-late) This barely there bar is just west of the main cluster of Echo Beach businesses such as the Beach House. It serves cold beer and cheap drinks until predawn on many nights. Sit on beanbags, chairs or sand. On some nights bands play until after midnight.

Going west along the beach you'll find a long series of bamboo beach bars with simple food and cheap beer.

ℹ️ Getting There & Away

A local taxi cooperative will shuttle you to Seminyak and the south for 120,000Rp or more.

Pererenan Beach

The bookend of the vast sweep of sand that begins near the airport, Pererenan Beach is rapidly changing as villas and other buildings appear amid the vanishing rice fields, all the way back to the Tanah Lot road. Before long it will be indistinguishable from the Echo Beach area.

🏖️ Beaches

Pererenan Beach
BEACH

The most northern of the Canggu-area beaches, laid-back Pererenan is next in the sights of developers. Villas, guesthouses and beach bars are found near the dark tanned sands and decent waves. It's an easy 300m walk west from Echo Beach across sand and rock formations (or about 1km by road). Vendors sell beer and rent loungers and surfboards.

🛏️ Sleeping

Surfers Paradise
BUNGALOW $$

(📱0818 567 538; www.andysurfvilla.com; Jl Pantai Pererenan; r 450,000-700,000Rp; ✳🛜☒) Five small bungalows surround a compact courtyard and are watched over by a charming Balinese family; 12 people can rent the entire complex and throw a nonstop party. The beach is 200m away.

Pondok Nyoman Bagus
GUESTHOUSE $$

(📱0361-848 2925; www.pondoknyoman.com; Jl Pantai Pererenan; r 500,000-700,000Rp; ✳🛜☒) Just behind Pererenan Beach, this popular guesthouse has 14 rooms with terraces and balconies, all set in a modern two-storey building that boasts a rooftop infinity pool and a restaurant with average food and sensational sea views.

ℹ️ Getting There & Away

With traffic on the Tanah Lot road, it can take well over an hour to reach Seminyak from here. Taxis will cost upwards of 150,000Rp.

South Bali & the Islands

Best Places to Eat

➜ Bumbu Bali (p120)

➜ Depot Cak Asmo (p132)

➜ Men Gabrug (p132)

➜ Deck Cafe & Bar (p140)

Best Places to Sleep

➜ Temple Lodge (p110)

➜ Four Seasons Jimbaran Bay (p105)

➜ Sofitel Bali Nusa Dua Beach Resort (p116)

➜ Rock'n Reef (p111)

➜ Alila Villas Uluwatu (p114)

➜ Tandjung Sari (p123)

Why Go?

You won't have seen Bali if you haven't fully explored south Bali. The island's capital, Denpasar, sprawls in all directions from the centre with traditional markets, busy malls, great eating and lashings of Balinese history and culture, even as it threatens to absorb Seminyak, Kuta and Sanur.

The Bukit Peninsula (the southern part of south Bali) has multiple personalities. In the east, Tanjung Benoa is a beach-fronted playground of package resorts while Nusa Dua attempts to bring order out of chaos with an insulated pasture of five-star hotels. The south coast sees posh cliff-side resorts, but the west side is where the real action is. Small coves and beaches dotted with edgy guesthouses and luxe eco-resorts enjoy a cool vibe and fab surfing.

To the east, Nusa Penida dominates the horizon, but in its lee you'll find Nusa Lembongan, the ultimate island escape from the island of Bali.

When to Go

➜ The best time to visit south Bali is outside high season, which is July, August and the weeks around Christmas and New Year's Day. Visitor numbers spike and rooms from Bingin to Tanjung Benoa and Sanur to Nusa Lembongan may be filled. Many prefer April to June and September when crowds are manageable.

➜ Surfing is best at the world-class breaks along the west coast of the Bukit Peninsula from February to November, with May to August being especially good.

➜ To surf at the breaks in Nusa Lembongan, aim for October to March.

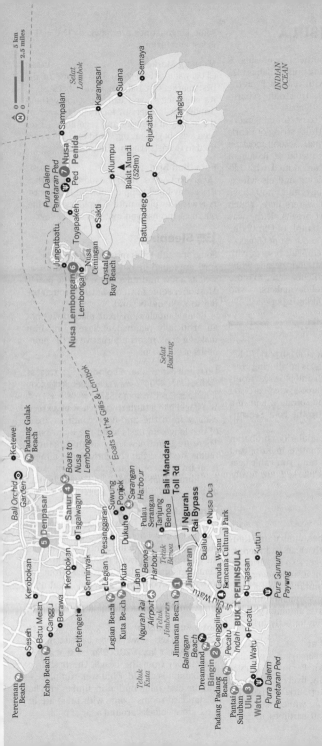

South Bali & the Islands Highlights

1 Jimbaran (p104) Picking a lobster for the grill at one of the many beachfront seafood joints.

2 Bingin (p109) Finding a perfectly retro-chic place to stay the night in the back lanes.

3 Ulu Watu (p113) Surfing Bali's ultimate breaks and an internationally revered swell magnet.

4 Sanur (p120) Watching as a full moon climbs over Nusa Penida.

5 Denpasar (p128) Savouring the best US$2 meal you've ever had.

6 Nusa Lembongan (p136) Escaping one island (Bali) for a more peaceful smaller one, with an ideal mix of fun and frolic.

7 Diving Nusa Penida (p143) Swimming with manta rays and other large fish in the challenging waters off this mysterious island.

0 | 5 km
0 | 2.5 miles

BUKIT PENINSULA

📍 0361

Hot and arid, the southern peninsula is known as Bukit (meaning 'hill' in Bahasa Indonesia). It's popular with visitors, from the cloistered climes of Nusa Dua to the sybaritic retreats along the south coast.

The booming west coast (often generically called Pecatu) with its string-of-pearls beaches is a real hotspot. Accommodation sits precariously on the sand at Balangan Beach while the cliffs are dotted with idiosyncratic lodges at Bingin and elsewhere. New places sprout daily and most have views of the turbulent waters here, which have world-famous surf breaks all the way south to the important temple of Ulu Watu.

The south coast east and west of Ungasan is the site of some huge cliff-side resorts, with serene views of the limitless ocean, while Nusa Dua and Tanjung Benoa cater to more traditional package-holidaymakers, who want a homogenised holiday experience.

Jimbaran

Just south of Kuta and the airport, Teluk Jimbaran (Jimbaran Bay) is an alluring crescent of white-sand beach and blue sea, fronted by a long string of seafood warungs (food stalls) and ending at the southern end in a bushy headland, home to the Four Seasons Jimbaran Bay.

Despite increased popularity, Jimbaran remains a relaxed alternative to Kuta and Seminyak to the north (and you can't beat the airport access!). Its markets are fun to visit too.

◎ Sights

★ Jimbaran Beach BEACH

One of Bali's best beaches, Jimbaran's 4km-long arc of sand is mostly clean and there is no shortage of places to get a snack, drink or seafood dinner, or to rent a sunlounger. The bay is protected by an unbroken coral reef, which keeps the surf more mellow than at popular Kuta further north, although you can still get breaks that are fun for bodysurfing.

★ Jimbaran Fish Market MARKET

(Jimbaran Beach; ⊙6am-3pm) A popular morning stop on a Bukit Peninsula amble, this fish market is smelly, lively and frenetic – watch where you step. Brightly painted boats bob along the shore while huge cases of everything from small sardines to fearsome langoustines are hawked. The action is fast and furious.

Morning Market MARKET

(Jl Ulu Watu; ⊙6am-noon) This is one of the best markets in Bali for a visit because a) it's compact so you can see a lot without wandering forever; b) local chefs swear by the quality of the fruit and vegetables – ever seen a cabbage that big?; and c) vendors are used to tourists trudging about.

Pura Ulun Siwi HINDU TEMPLE

(Jl Ulu Watu) Across from the morning market, this ebony-hued temple from the 18th century is a snoozy place until it explodes with life, offerings, incense and more on a holy day.

🛏 Sleeping

Some of south Bali's most luxurious large resorts are found in and around Jimbaran, as well as a few midrange places off the beach. Most offer some form of shuttle through the day to Kuta and beyond.

Being a much more 'real' place (ie it's not an artificially planned enclave), Jimbaran makes a good resort alternative to the monoliths of Nusa Dua.

Udayana Kingfisher Ecolodge LODGE $$

(📍0361-747 4204; www.udayanaecolodge.com; Jl Kampus Bukit; r from US$85; ❋@🛜☀) 🌿 You'll feel like a butterfly perched in a green canopy from the 2nd-floor common areas of this lodge, an oasis amid the Bukit buzz. There are grand views over south Bali; the 15 rooms are basic but comfortable; and there is an inviting common area, with an excellent library that includes copies of a butterfly book written by the managers.

Keraton Jimbaran Resort HOTEL $$

(📍0361-701961; www.keratonjimbaranresort.com; Jl Mrajapati; r from 1,100,000Rp; ❋@🛜☀) Sharing the same idyllic Jimbaran beach as the neighbouring pricier resorts, the low-key Keraton is great value for a beachfront resort. Its 102 rooms are scattered about one- and two-storey bungalow-style units. The grounds are spacious and typically Bali-lush.

Hotel Puri Bambu HOTEL $$

(📍0361-701468; www.hotelpuribambu.com; Jl Pengeracikan; r from 720,000Rp; ❋@🛜☀) A mere 200m from the beach, the flash-free Puri Bambu is an older but well-run place – and the best-value option in Jimbaran. The 48 standard rooms (some with tubs) are in three-storey blocks around a large pool.

★ **Belmond Jimbaran Puri**   RESORT **$$$**

(☏0361-701605; www.belmond.com; off Jl Ulu Watu; cottages from 4,200,000Rp; 🗶@🛜🌊) This luxurious beachside retreat is set in nice grounds complete with a maze-like pool that looks on to open ocean. The 64 cottages and villas have private gardens, large terraces and a stylish room design with sunken tubs. It's a lavish yet low-key escape.

Four Seasons Jimbaran Bay   RESORT **$$$**

(☏0361-701010; www.fourseasons.com; Jl Bukit Permai; villas from US$600; 🗶@🛜🌊) Each of the 147 villas here are designed in a traditional Balinese manner, complete with a carved entranceway, which opens on to an open-air living pavilion overlooking a plunge pool. The site is a hillside overlooking Jimbaran Beach, which is a short walk away; most villas have sweeping views across the bay.

Hotel Intercontinental Bali   RESORT **$$$**

(☏0361-701888; www.bali.intercontinental.com; Jl Ulu Watu; r US$170-400; 🗶@🛜🌊) With 419 rooms, the Intercontinental is really a little city on the beach. Decorated with Balinese arts and handicrafts, it tries to meld local style to a huge resort. The plethora of pools feed each other and meander through the grounds. There is a good kids' club and it's on a prime swathe of beach.

✗ Eating

Jimbaran's three groups of seafood restaurants cook fresh barbecued seafood every evening (and lunch at many), drawing tourists from across the south. The open-sided affairs are right by the beach and perfect for enjoying sea breezes and sunsets. Tables and chairs are set up on the sand almost to the water's edge. Arrive before sunset, so you can get a good table and enjoy the solar show over a couple of beers before you dine.

Fixed prices for seafood platters in a plethora of varieties have become common and allow you to avoid the sport of choosing your fish and then paying for it by weight on scales that cause locals to break out in laughter. However, be sure to agree on costs first. Generally, you can enjoy a seafood feast, sides and a couple of beers for less than US$20 per person. Lobster (from US$30) will bump that figure up considerably.

The best kitchens marinate the fish in garlic and lime, then douse it with chilli and oil while grilling over coconut husks. Thick clouds of smoke from the coals are part of the atmosphere, as are roaming bands,

who perform cheery cover tunes (think the *Macarena*). Almost all take credit cards. Expect mixed seafood grills to cost 90,000Rp to 350,000Rp.

SOUTH BALI & THE ISLANDS JIMBARAN

Northern Seafood Restaurants

The northern seafood restaurants run south from the fish market along Jl Kedonganan and Jl Pantai Jimbaran. This is the area you will likely be taken to by a taxi if you don't specify otherwise. Most of these places are restaurant-like, with tables inside and out on the raked sand. However, the area lacks the fun atmosphere of the two areas to the south.

Jimbaran Bay Seafood   SEAFOOD $$
(JBS; ☑ 0361-701517; Jl Pantai Kedonganan; mains from 100,000Rp; ☺ 11am-10pm) The menu assures patrons that seeing the prices means 'Don't be worry!' Part of the rather staid northern group, JBS is especially welcoming with a huge variety of tables: inside under cover, on the concrete terrace or out where your toes can tickle the sand.

Middle Seafood Restaurants

The middle seafood restaurants are in a compact and atmospheric group just south of Jl Pantai Jimbaran and Jl Pemelisan Agung. These are the simplest affairs, with old-fashioned thatched roofs and wide-open sides. The beach is a little less manicured, with the fishing boats resting up on the sand. Huge piles of coconut husks await their turn on the fires.

Warung Bamboo   SEAFOOD $$
(off Jl Pantai Jimbaran; meals 80,000-200,000Rp; ☺ noon-10pm) Warung Bamboo is slightly more appealing than its neighbours, all of which have a certain raffish charm. The menu is dead simple: choose your seafood and the sides and sauces are included.

Warung Ramayana   SEAFOOD $$
(☑ 0361-702859; off Jl Pantai Jimbaran; mains from 80,000Rp; ☺ 11am-10pm) Fishing boats dot the beach in front of this long-running favourite. The seafood marinates from the early morning and grills smoke all evening. The menu has useful fixed prices so you can avoid bargaining.

Southern Seafood Restaurants

The southern seafood restaurants (also called the Muaya group) are a compact and festive collection of about a dozen places at the south end of the beach. There's a parking area off Jl Bukit Permai, and the beach here is well groomed, with nice trees.

Made Bagus Cafe   SEAFOOD $$
(☑ 0361-701858; off Jl Bukit Permai; meals 80,000-200,000Rp; ☺ noon-10pm) Tucked away at the north end of the southern group; the staff serving their narrow patch of tables on the beach here radiate charm. Go for one of the mixed platters and ask for extra sauce, it's that good.

🍷 Drinking & Nightlife

Jimbaran Beach Club   CAFE
(☑ 0361-709959; Jl Pantai Muaya; minimum spend 200,000Rp; ☺ 8am-11pm; 🛜) Just in case Jimbaran Bay wasn't alluring enough, this beach bar has a long pool bordering the sand. It's rather upscale; you can rent a comfy lounger and umbrella and enjoy ordering from a long drinks and food menu.

Rock Bar   BAR
(☑ 0361-702222; www.ayanaresort.com/rockbar-bali; Jl Karang Mas Sejahtera, Ayana Resort; ☺ 4pm-1am; 🛜) Star of a thousand glossy articles written about Bali, this bar perched 14m above the crashing Indian Ocean is very popular. In fact, at sunset the wait to ride the lift down to the bar can top one hour. There's a no-backpacks, no-singlets dress code. The food is Med-flavoured bar snacks.

🔒 Shopping

Jenggala Keramik
Bali Ceramics   CERAMICS
(☑ 0361-703311; www.jenggala.com; Jl Ulu Watu II; ☺ 8am-8pm) This modern warehouse showcases beautiful ceramic homewares that are a favourite Balinese purchase. There's a viewing area where you can watch production, as well as a cafe. Ceramic courses are available for adults and children; a paint-a-pot scheme lets you create your own work of art (ready five days later after a trip through the kiln).

ℹ Getting There & Away

Plenty of taxis wait around the beachfront warungs in the evening to take diners home (about 140,000Rp to Seminyak). Some of the seafood warungs provide free transport if you call first.

The Kura-Kura tourist bus (p389) has a route linking Jimbaran with its Kuta hub. Buses run every 75 minutes and cost 40,000Rp.

Around Jimbaran

Folding around limestone bluffs, **Tegalwangi Beach**, 4.5km southwest of Jimbaran, is the first of cove after cove holding patches of alluring sand all down the west coast of the peninsula. A small parking area lies in front of **Pura Segara Tegalwangi** temple, a popular place for addressing the ocean gods. There's usually a lone drinks vendor offering refreshment before – or after – you make the short but challenging trip over the bad paths down to the beach. Immediately south, the vast Ayana Resort sprawls over the cliffs.

From Jimbaran, take Jl Bukit Permai for 3km until the gates of the Ayana, where it veers west 1.5km to the temple.

Central Bukit

Jl Ulu Watu goes south of Jimbaran, climbing 200m up the peninsula's namesake hill, affording views over southern Bali. As the region has surged in popularity, traffic has become a major problem.

About 2km south of Garuda Wisnu Kencana Cultural Park is a vital crossroads with a useful landmark, the **Nirmala Supermarket** (Jl Ulu Watu; ⊘8am-10pm). There are ATMs and cafes, and you can reach all points on the Bukit from here.

◎ Sights

**Garuda Wisnu
Kencana Cultural Park** VIEWPOINT
(GWK; ☑0361-703603; www.gwk-culturalpark.com; Jl Raya Ulu Watu; 100,000Rp; ⊘9am-10pm; ⚑) After years of false starts, the gigantic Garuda Wisnu Kencana Cultural Park is under construction. When finished, the centrepiece will be a 120m-tall monument that includes a 66m-high statue of Garuda (you can already see the basic structure from across south Bali). This Brobdingnagian dream is meant to be on top of a shopping and gallery complex. For now, the sweeping views from the parking area don't justify the entrance fee.

✗ Eating

Bali Buda CAFE $
(☑0361-701980; Jl Ulu Watu; treats from 20,000Rp; ⊘8am-8pm) A small outlet of the excellent island-wide bakery/cafe chain.

Balangan Beach

Balangan Beach is a long, low strand at the base of rocky cliffs. It's covered with palm trees and fronted by a ribbon of near-white sand, picturesquely dotted with sun umbrellas. Surfer bars, cafes in shacks and even slightly more permanent guesthouses precariously line the shore where buffed First World bods soak up rays amid Third World sanitation. Think of it as a bit of the Wild West not far from Bali's glitz.

◎ Sights & Activities

At the northern end of the beach is a small temple, **Pura Dalem Balangan**. Bamboo beach shacks line the southern end; visitors laze away with one eye cast on the action at the fast-left surf break here.

You can access the beach via rough tracks from two parking areas: the north end is near the uncrowded temple, the south end is above and back from the beach bars.

🛏 Sleeping

Balangan Beach has some established guesthouses up on the bluff, five minutes from the surf. Down on the sand, things are much more ad hoc, with everything seeming to be one pass of a bulldozer from oblivion. At the latter option you can negotiate for small, windowless thatched rooms in bars next to cases of Bintang. Don't pay more than 180,000Rp.

Numerous guesthouses are appearing on the access road from Jl Ulu Watu, but many are far from the beach.

Santai Bali Homestay BUNGALOW $
(☑0338-695942; www.facebook.com/santai-warungbalihomestay; from 220,000Rp) Right on the sands of Balangan Beach, the 12 bare-bones rooms at this shack bungalow are perfect for surfers and beach bums wanting easy access to the water. Its restaurant has tables and chairs plonked on the beach.

Balangan Sea View Bungalow GUESTHOUSE $
(☑0851 0080 0499; www.balanganseaview-bungalow.com; off Jl Pantai Balangan; r with fan/air-con from 350,000/450,000Rp; bungalow from 700,000Rp; ❉ 🛜 ☒) A cluster of thatched bungalows (some with multiple rooms) are the pick here. The 25 rooms surround a 14m pool in an attractive compound; some have sea views.

La Joya HOTEL $$
(☑0811 399 0048; www.la-joya.com; Jl Pantai Balangan; r US$95-120; ❉ 🛜 ☒) The pick of the Balangan bunch, these two luxe compounds have hotel rooms, bungalows and villas. There are 21 different units, but all enjoy their position on the lush grounds. Sinuous curves dominate from the lines of the rooms to the infinity pool. The beach is a short walk.

Balangan Beach & Ulu Watu

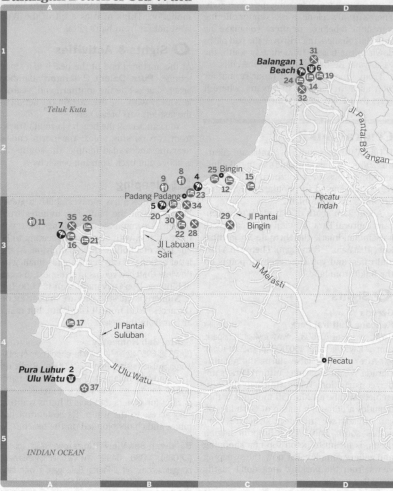

Flower Bud Bungalows GUESTHOUSE **$$**
(☑ 0816 472 2310, 0828 367 2772; www.flowerbud-balangan.com; off Jl Pantai Balangan; r incl breakfast from 550,000Rp; ☞☒) On top of a knoll, 14 bamboo bungalows are set on spacious, pretty grounds near a classic kidney-shaped pool. There's a certain Crusoe-esque motif, and a small spa.

✗ Eating

Nerni Warung INDONESIAN **$**
(☑0813 5381 4090; mains from 30,000Rp) Down on the sand at the south end of the beach, this simple place has great views from its cafe.

Nerni keeps a close watch on things; simple sleeping rooms (from 200,000Rp) are cleaner than the competition. She may seem dour but is smiling on the inside. We think.

Nasa Café CAFE **$**
(meals from 30,000Rp; ⊘8am-11pm) Inside the shady bamboo bar built on stilts above the sand, the wraparound view through the drooping thatched roof is of a vibrant azure ribbon of crashing surf. The simple Indo meals set the tone for the four very basic rooms (about 200,000Rp) off the bar. It's one of several similar choices.

Getting There & Away

Balangan Beach is 6.2km off Jl Ulu Watu on Jl Pantai Balangan. Turn west at the crossroads at Nirmala Supermarket (p107).

Taxis from the Kuta area cost at least 70,000Rp per hour for the round trip and waiting time.

Bingin

An ever-evolving scene, Bingin comprises scores of unconventionally stylish lodgings scattered across cliffs and on the strip of white-sand Bingin Beach below. Smooth Jl Pantai Bingin runs 1km off Jl Melasti (look for the thicket of accommodation signs) and then branches off into a tangle of lanes.

The scenery here is simply superb, with sylvan cliffs dropping down to surfer cafes and the foaming edge of the azure sea. The beach is a five-minute walk down fairly steep paths. The surf here is often savage but the boulder-strewn sands are serene and the roaring breakers mesmerising.

An elderly resident collects 5000Rp at a T-junction near where you park for the trail down to the beach.

Sleeping

This is one of the Bukit's coolest places to stay. Numerous individual places are scattered along and near the cliffs, well off the main road. You can also get basic accommodation down the cliff at a string of bamboo and thatch surfer crash pads near the water.

Adi's Homestay BUNGALOW $
(0816 297 106, 0815 5838 8524; Jl Pantai Bingin; r with fan/air-con from US$22/39; ❄ 🛜) The nine bungalow-style rooms facing a nice garden are comfy. It's down a very small lane, near the beach parking. It has a small cafe.

Chocky's Place GUESTHOUSE $
(0818 0530 7105; www.chockysplace.com; Bingin Beach; r 100,000-400,000Rp; 🛜) Down the bottom of the stairs and right on Bingin Beach, this classic surfer hang-out has cosy rooms varying from charming with awesome views to rudimentary with shared bathrooms. Its bamboo restaurant looks out to the beach; it's a great place to meet fellow travellers over a few cold ones.

Kembang Kuning Bungalows GUESTHOUSE $
(0361-743 4424; www.binginbungalows.com; off Jl Pantai Bingin; r from US$60; 🛜❄) The best-value cliff-side option has 12 rooms in modern two-storey bungalow-style blocks. The grounds are thickly landscaped but the real appeal is the infinity swimming pool on the edge of the limestone and the various nearby loungers, all with sensational views.

Bingin Garden GUESTHOUSE $
(0816 472 2002; tommybarrell76@yahoo.com; off Jl Pantai Bingin; r with fan/air-con 280,000/400,000Rp; ❄🛜❄) There's a relaxed hacienda feel to Bingin Garden, where six bungalow-style rooms are set among an arid garden and a large pool. It's back off the cliffs and about 300m from the path down to the beach. It's run by gun local surfer Tommy Barrell and his lovely wife.

Balangan Beach & Ulu Watu

★ **Temple Lodge**   BOUTIQUE HOTEL **$$**
(☏0857 3901 1572; www.thetemplelodge.com; off Jl Pantai Bingin; r incl breakfast US$80-230; ☞☎) 'Artsy and beautiful' just begins to describe this collection of huts and cottages made from thatch, driftwood and other natural materials. Each sits on the cliffs above the surf breaks, and there are superb views from the infinity pool and some of the units. You can arrange meals, and there are yoga classes.

Mick's Place   BOUTIQUE HOTEL **$$**
(☏0812 391 3337; www.micksplacebali.com; off Jl Pantai Bingin; r from US$100, villa from US$300; ✳☞☎) A hippy-chic playground where you rough it in style, Mick's never has more than 16 guests. Five artful bungalows and one luxe villa are set in lush grounds. The turquoise water in the postage-stamp-sized infinity pool matches the turquoise sea below. By day there's a 180-degree view of the world-famous surf breaks.

Mu   GUESTHOUSE **$$**
(☏0361-895 7442; www.mu-bali.com; off Jl Pantai Bingin; r US$80-220; ✳☞☎) ⌀ The 12 very individual bungalows with thatched roofs are scattered about a compound dominated by a cliff-side infinity pool. All have open-air living spaces; some have air-con bedrooms and hot tubs with a view. Two units have multiple bedrooms. There's an excellent cafe as well as a yoga studio.

Secret Garden   GUESTHOUSE **$$**
(☏0816 474 7255; r from 450,000Rp; ☞) Tasteful and ultra laid-back, this guesthouse has open-plan bamboo bungalows with futon beds, and a design that incorporates its natural environment. It's run by a Japanese surfer-photographer who has good knowledge of local waves. It's at the top of the hill near the path leading down to the beach.

✖ Eating

★ **Cashew Tree**   CAFE **$**
(☏0813 5321 8157; www.facebook.com/the-cashew-tree; Jl Pantai Bingin; meals from 40,000Rp; ☻8am-10pm; ☞☏) *The* place to hang out in Bingin. Surfers and beachgoers gather in this large garden for tasty vegetarian

meals. Expect the likes of burritos, salads, sandwiches and smoothies. It's also a good spot for a drink; Thursday nights especially go off, attracting folk from up and down the coast with live bands.

Drifter
CAFE $

(http://driftersurf.com; Jl Labuan Sait; mains from 50,000Rp; ⊙10am-10pm) Right at the turn to Bingin, this new outlet of the awesome Seminyak surf shop has a great cafe that will tempt anyone driving past. All the Drifter surf goods are on offer, plus you can settle back at a table inside or out for some of the Bukit's best coffee and a range of snacks, healthy lunches and alluring cakes.

ⓘ Getting There & Away

A metered taxi from Kuta will cost about 200,000Rp and take at least an hour, depending on traffic.

Padang Padang

The namesake beach here is near Jl Labuan Sait. It's fairly easily reached. Immediately east, Impossibles Beach is more of a challenge. Rocks and tide may prevent you from coming over from Padang Padang.

Both, however, are the stuff tropical surf dreams are made of. The backdrop of rocky cliff faces gives them an isolated feel you won't get in Kuta or Seminyak. A very cool scene has developed, with groovy cafes, oddball sleeps and iconoclastic surf shops.

On Saturdays and full-moon nights there's a party on the beach at Padang Padang, with grilled seafood and tunes until dawn.

⊙ Sights

Parking is easy at Padang Padang and it's a short walk through a temple and down a well-paved trail where you'll be hit up for bananas by monkeys. There are patches of shade near the sand plus a couple of simple warungs. The beach-bar scene of *Eat Pray Love* was filmed here (using a bar set that's long gone).

If you're feeling adventurous, you can enjoy a much longer stretch of nearly deserted white sand that begins on the west side of the river. Ask locals how to get there or take the precipitous stairs by Thomas Homestay off the main road.

Padang Padang Beach
BEACH

Slight in size but not in perfection, this little cove is near the main Ulu Watu road where a stream flows into the sea. Parking is easy and it is a short walk to the beach. Experienced surfers flock here for the tubes.

Impossibles Beach
BEACH

About 100m west of Jl Pantai Bingin on Jl Melasti, you'll see another turn towards the ocean. Follow this paved road for 700m and look for a scrawled sign on a wall reading Impossibles Beach. Follow the treacherous path and you'll soon understand the name. It's a tortuous trek but you'll be rewarded with an empty cove with splotches of creamy sand between boulders.

✱ Activities

You can rent surfboards to hit the breaks right offshore. It can get very crowded in high season. Many surf competitions are held here.

★ Padang Padang
SURFING

Padang for short, this super-shallow, left-hand reef break is off a very popular beach and just below some rickety accommodation joints where you can crash and watch the breaks. Check carefully before venturing out. It's a very demanding break that only works if it's over about 6ft from mid- to high tide. The best times for a good swell here are June to August.

Impossibles
SURFING

Just north of Padang Padang, this challenging outside reef break has three shifting peaks with fast left-hand tube sections that can join up if the conditions are perfect.

🛌 Sleeping

To get really close to the waves, consider one of the cliff-side guesthouses that are reached by a steep path down from the bluff. The trail starts at the end of a twisting lane that runs for 200m from Jl Labuan Sait just west of Om Burger. Note, however, that a fire destroyed and damaged some of these places in 2016. Rebuilding is ongoing so check the latest situation before you book.

★ Rock'n Reef
BOUTIQUE HOTEL $$

(☑ 0813 5336 3507; www.rock-n-reef.com; Impossibles Beach; r incl breakfast US$105-125; ❋ 🛜) Six individualistic bungalows are built into the rocks on Impossibles Beach. All share the stunning views of the ocean directly in front. Each has a rustic, artful design with natural materials such as stucco and driftwood. There are private balconies and sunny decks. An all-day cafe offers simple

PILLAGING BUKIT PENINSULA

Many environmentalists consider the always-arid Bukit Peninsula a harbinger for the challenges that face the rest of Bali, as land use far outpaces the water supply. The small guesthouses that once perched above and on the string of pearls that are the beaches on the west side are being supplanted by large water-sucking developments. Besides the vast Pecatu Indah complex, many more projects such as the controversial Kempinski Hotel near Nusa Dua are carving away the beautiful limestone cliffs to make way for huge concrete structures housing resorts.

There are few controls to regulate the growth; many of the vehicles stuck with you in traffic jams on Jl Ulu Watu will be water trucks that service the area's thirst by the hundreds daily. Meanwhile, a road-building frenzy on the southern coast has sparked a villa building boom, most with private pools.

Grassroots efforts to control growth have been diverted to an effort to save the vast Benoa Bay mangroves at the base of Bukit from that vast development.

Indonesian meals. During peak surf season, staying here is a fantasy.

PinkCoco Bali HOTEL $$
(☎ 0361-895 7371; http://pnkhotels.com; Jl Labuan Sait; r US$75-135; ❉ 🔊 🖉 ⚏) One of the pools at this romantic hotel is suitably tiled pink. The 12 rooms have terraces and balconies, plus artistic touches. There is a lush Mexican motif throughout, with an appealing mix of white walls accented with bold, tropical colours. Surfers are catered to and you can rent bikes and other gear.

Le Sabot BUNGALOW $$
(☎ 0812 3768 0414; www.lesabotbali.com; r from 700,000Rp) This collection of cliff-face bungalows was damaged in the 2016 fire. Confirm their status before trying to stay here. The location itself is superb – you cannot sleep closer to one of the world's best surf breaks. When open, the bungalows are a steep descent from the bluff.

✖ Eating

Mango Tree Cafe CAFE $$
(☎ 0813 5309 8748; Jl Labuan Sait 17; mains 50,000-120,000Rp; ☺ 7am-10pm) This two-level cafe has a long menu of healthy options. Sandwiches and the tasty burgers have amazing buns. The salads, soups, breakfast burritos and more are fresh and interesting. There are good juices and a decent drinks list. Try for a table under the namesake tree. The owner, Maria, is a generous delight.

Buddha Soul CAFE $$
(☎ 0361-897338; www.facebook.com/buddha-soul; Jl Labuan Sait; mains 50,000-150,000Rp; ☺ 7.30am-10pm; 🔊 🖉) This chilled-out roadside cafe has an outdoor deck where you can enjoy healthy, organic meals such as grilled calamari, chicken salad and lentil burgers.

Om Burger BURGERS $$
(☎ 0812 391 3617; Jl Labuan Sait; mains from 55,000Rp; ☺ 7am-10pm; 🔊) 'Superfood burgers' – that's the come-on at this joint with nice 2nd-floor views. The burgers are indeed super and supersized. The wagyu burger is the speciality, but the nasi goreng veggie burger is unique. There are intimations of health across the menu: baked sweet-potato fries, vitamin-filled juices and more. It's very popular; expect to wait for a table at night.

🔒 Shopping

White Monkey Surf Shop SPORTS & OUTDOORS
(☎ 0853 3816 7729; www.instagram.com/white-monkey_surfshop; Jl Labuan Sait 63; surfboard rental used/new 150,000/250,000Rp; ☺ 10am-10pm) Great little surf shop offers board sales and rental, plus gear.

Ulu Watu & Around

Ulu Watu has become the generic name for the southwestern tip of the Bukit Peninsula. It includes the much-revered temple and the fabled namesake surf breaks.

About 2km north of the temple there is a dramatic cliff with steps leading to the water and Suluban Beach. All manner of cafes and surf shops spill down the nearly sheer face to the water below. Views are stellar and it's quite the scene.

⊙ Sights & Activities

⭐ **Pura Luhur Ulu Watu** HINDU TEMPLE
(off Jl Ulu Watu; adult/child 30,000/20,000Rp, parking 2000Rp; ☺ 8am-7pm) This important temple

is perched precipitously on the southwestern tip of the peninsula, atop sheer cliffs that drop straight into the ceaseless surf. You enter through an unusual arched gateway flanked by statues of Ganesha. Inside, the walls of coral bricks are covered with intricate carvings of Bali's mythological menagerie.

Only Hindu worshippers can enter the small inner temple that is built on to the jutting tip of land. However, the views of the endless swells of the Indian Ocean from the cliffs are almost spiritual. At sunset, walk around the clifftop to the left (south) of the temple to lose some of the crowd.

Ulu Watu is one of several important temples to the spirits of the sea along the south coast of Bali. In the 11th century the Javanese priest Empu Kuturan first established a temple here. The complex was added to by Nirartha, another Javanese priest who is known for the seafront temples at Tanah Lot, Rambut Siwi and Pura Sakenan. Nirartha retreated to Ulu Watu for his final days when he attained *moksa* (freedom from earthly desires).

A popular Kecak dance is held in the temple grounds at sunset.

Suluban Beach BEACH

While others paddle out to the Ulu Watu surf breaks, you can linger on this strip of sand in an uberdramatic setting: limestone cliffs and caves surround the beach. Check the tides before making the steep climb down.

★**Ulu Watu** SURFING

On its day Ulu Watu is Bali's biggest and most powerful wave. It's the stuff of dreams and nightmares, and definitely not one for beginners! Since the early 1970s when it featured in the legendary surf flick *Morning of the Earth*, Ulu Watu has drawn surfers from around the world for left breaks that seem to go on forever.

⌶ Sleeping

The cliffs above the main Ulu Watu breaks are lined with cafes and bars. There are various midrange places to stay; since most people are here for the view, quality inside the rooms is not assured.

Gong GUESTHOUSE $

(☑0361-769976; www.thegonguluwatubali.com; Jl Pantai Suluban; r from 250,000Rp; @🔊🛜🏊) The 12 tidy rooms here have good ventilation and hot water, and face a small compound with a lovely pool. Some 2nd-floor units have distant ocean views. It's about 1km south of the Ulu Watu cliff-side cafes; the host family is lovely. Ongoing renovations should improve conditions and raise rates.

Delpi Uluwatu GUESTHOUSE $

(☑0361-769863; Ulu Watu; r with fan/air-con from 400,000/450,000Rp) Four very basic cliff-side rooms rattle to the beat of the surf day and night. Set in the rocks amid the various bars, this is the place if all you want is a 24-hour view of the breaks.

★**Uluwatu Cottages** BUNGALOW $$

(☑0857 9268 1715; www.facebook.com/uluwatucottages/about; off Jl Labuan Sait; r US$68-130; 🌀🛜🏊) Fourteen bungalows are spread across a large site right on the cliff, just 400m east of the Ulu Watu cafes (about 200m off Jl Labuan Sait). The units are comfortable, have individual terraces and enjoy views that are simply stunning. The pool is large and a great place to lose a day.

Mamo Hotel HOTEL $$

(☑0361-769882; www.mamohoteluluwatu.com; Jl Labuan Sait; r US$35-90; 🌀🛜🏊) Right at the entrance to the area above the Ulu Watu breaks, this modern 30-room hotel is a good mainstream choice. The three-storey main building surrounds a pool and there's a breezy basic cafe. The rooftop parties on Friday nights are a major event.

✕ Eating & Drinking

Delpi CAFE

(🕑7am-8pm; 🛜) A relaxed cafe-bar sitting on a cliff away from other cafe spots, with stunning views. One area is perched on a gigantic mushroom of concrete atop a rock out above the surf. The food is basic.

Single Fin CAFE $$

(☑0361-769941; www.singlefinbali.com; Jl Mamo; mains 65,000-150,000Rp; 🕑8am-11pm; 🛜) The views of the surf action from this triple-level cafe are breathtaking. Watch the never-ending swells march in across the Indian Ocean from this cliff-side perch; it's a great spot to watch surfers carving it up when the waves are big. Drinks here aren't cheap (or very good) and the food is merely passable, but come sunset, who cares?

☆ Entertainment

★**Kecak Dance** DANCE

(Pura Luhur Ulu Watu, off Jl Ulu Watu; 100,000Rp; 🕑sunset) Although the performance obviously caters for tourists, the gorgeous setting at Pura Luhur Ulu Watu in a small amphitheatre in a leafy part of the grounds makes it one of the more evocative on the island. The views out to sea are as inspiring as the dance. It's very popular in high season; expect crowds.

① Getting There & Away

The best way to see the Ulu Watu region is with your own wheels. Note that the cops often set up checkpoints near Pecatu Indah for checks on motorcycle-riding Westerners. Be aware you may pay a fine for offences such as a 'loose' chin strap.

Coming to the Ulu Watu cliff-side cafes from the east on Jl Labuan Sait you will first encounter an access road to parking near the cliffs. Continuing over a bridge, there is a side road that leads to another parking area, from where it is a pretty 200m walk north to the cliff-side cafes.

A taxi ride out here will cost at least 200,000Rp from Seminyak and take more than an hour in the coagulated traffic.

Ungasan & Around

If Ulu Watu is all about celebrating surf culture, Ungasan is all about celebrating yourself. From crossroads near this otherwise nondescript village, roads radiate to the south coast where some of Bali's most exclusive oceanside resorts can be found. With the infinite turquoise waters of the Indian Ocean rolling hypnotically in the distance it's hard not to think you've reached the end of the world, albeit a very comfortable one.

The scalloped cliff faces hide many a tiny cove beach with white sand. Some are now crowded with top-end resorts, others await discovery down perilous cliff-side stairs.

◉ Sights & Activities

Green Bowl Beach   BEACH
(Jl Pura Batu Pageh; parking 5000Rp) One of the Bukit's southern-facing cove beaches, Green Bowl is reached by a pretty and strenuous walk down 300 concrete steps that begin near the Pura Batu Pageh temple and the failed Bali Cliff Resort. This splotch of sand is uncrowded during the week but draws many at weekends (including a few persistent vendors). There are caves, bats and monkeys. The water is deep turquoise.

Pura Mas Suka   HINDU TEMPLE
This diminutive temple (one of seven devoted to the sea gods) is reached by a twisting narrow road through a mostly barren red-rock landscape that changes dramatically when you reach the Karma Kandara resort, which surrounds the temple. It's a perfect example of a Balinese seaside temple. It is often closed, so consider that before setting off on the rough track to the temple.

Sundays Beach Club   BEACH CLUB
(☑0361-848 2111; www.sundaysbeachclub. com; Jl Pantai Selatan Gau; day pass adult/child 300,000/50,000Rp; ⊙9am-10pm) Located on a pocket of powdery white sand at the base of a cliff, this private beach club offers a full day's worth of activities and pampering. Admission includes a 150,000Rp credit, which will go quickly in the bars, beachside spa pavilions etc. There are weekend afternoon DJs, sunset bonfires and, crucially, an elevator up and down the cliff.

🛏 Sleeping

Several luxurious resorts already have views out over the Indian Ocean from the high limestone cliffs on the southern coast of the Bukit. Many more are mooted, including a newly opened Ritz-Carlton, a Kempinski (which has been assailed for breaking Bali's height limitations) and a Waldorf Astoria.

★**Alila Villas Uluwatu**   RESORT $$$
(☑0361-848 2166; www.alilahotels.com/uluwatu; Jl Belimbing Sari; r incl breakfast from US$800; ✳@🛜☒) Visually stunning, this vast resort has an artful contemporary style that is at once light and airy while still conveying a sense of luxury. The 85-unit Alila offers gracious service in a setting where the blue of the ocean contrasts with the green of the surrounding (hotel-tended) rice fields. It's 2km off Jl Ulu Watu.

Karma Kandara   RESORT $$$
(☑0361-848 2200; www.karmaresorts.com; Jl Villa Kandara Banjar; villa from US$450; ✳@🛜☒) This beautiful resort clings to the side of hills that roll down to the sea. Stone paths lead between walled villas draped in bougainvillea and punctuated by painted doors, creating the mood of a tropical hill town. The restaurant, **Di Mare** (meals US$15 to $30), is linked to the bifurcated property by a little bridge; there's a beach elevator.

Nusa Dua

Nusa Dua translates literally as 'Two Islands' – although they are actually small raised headlands, each with a small temple. But Nusa Dua is much better known as Bali's gated compound of resort hotels. It's a vast and manicured place where you leave the rest of the island behind as you pass the guards. Gone is the chaos of the rest of the island.

Built in the 1970s, Nusa Dua was designed to compete with international beach resorts the world over. Balinese 'culture', in the form of condensed cultural displays, is literally trucked in nightly in an effort to make it seem like less of a generic beach resort.

With more than 20 large resorts and thousands of hotel rooms, Nusa Dua can live up to some of its promise when full, but during slack times it's desolate.

◉ Sights

★ Pasifika Museum
MUSEUM

(☑ 0361-774559; www.museum-pasifika.com; Bali Collection shopping centre, block P; 70,000Rp; ⊙ 10am-6pm) When groups from nearby resorts aren't around, you'll probably have this large museum to yourself. A collection of art from Pacific Ocean cultures spans several centuries and includes more than 600 paintings (don't miss the tikis). The influential wave of European artists who thrived in Bali in the early 20th century is well represented. Look for works by Arie Smit, Adrien-Jean Le Mayeur de Merpres and Theo Meier. There are also works by Matisse and Gauguin.

Pura Gegar
HINDU TEMPLE

(road toll 2500Rp) Just south of Gegar Beach is a bluff with a good cafe and a path that leads up to Pura Gegar, a compact temple shaded by gnarled old trees. Views are great and you can spot swimmers who've come south in the shallow, placid waters around the bluff for a little frolic. There's a pleasant walkway up to the temple from the Nusa Dua beach promenade.

⚡ Activities

Nusa Dua's beaches are clean and raked; offshore reefs catch the swells, so the surf is almost nil.

All the resort hotels have pricey spas that provide a broad range of therapies, treatments and just plain, simple relaxation. The most lauded of the spas are at the Amanusa, Westin and St Regis hotels. All are open to nonguests; expect fees for a massage to start at US$100.

★ Beach Promenade
WALKING

One of the nicest features of Nusa Dua is the 5km-long beach promenade that stretches the length of the resort from Pura Gegar in the south and north along much of the beach through Tanjung Benoa.

Nusa Dua
SURFING

During wet season, the reef off Nusa Dua has very consistent swells. The main break is 1km off the beach to the south of Nusa Dua – off Gegar Beach (where you can get a boat out to the break). There are lefts and rights that work well on a small swell at low to midtide.

Bali National Golf Resort
GOLF

(☑ 0361-771791; www.balinationalgolf.com; Kawasan Wisata; course fees from 1,800,000Rp; ⊙ 6.30am-6.30pm) This 18-hole links meanders through Nusa Dua and boasts a grand clubhouse. The course plays to over 6500m.

Gegar Beach
BEACH

(off Jl Nusa Dua Selatan; 3000Rp; ⊞) The once gemlike Gegar Beach is now gem-sized with the addition of a 700-room Mulia resort. The public area has some cafes, rental loungers and water activities (kayak/SUP rental 100,000Rp per hour); it gets jammed on weekends. Boats to Nusa Dua surf break beyond the reef cost 200,000Rp. You can also

SOUTH BALI & THE ISLANDS NUSA DUA

PANDAWA BEACH

An old quarry on the remote southern coast of the Bukit Peninsula has been transformed into a Hindu-shrine cum-beach-attraction. Pay a steep admission price (10,000Rp) to guards (who were swilling Bintang when we were there) and then descend on a road through dramatically cut limestone cliffs. Large statues of Hindu deities are carved into niches in the stone. At the base, you'll find a long swathe of sand known as Pandawa Beach, which is all but deserted weekdays except for a few village seaweed farmers. But come weekends this makes for a major day trip for the Balinese.

Some warungs (food stalls) provide refreshments and sunlounger rental, and the reef-protected waters are good for swimming. Look for Pandawa Beach signs on the main road between Ungasan and Nusa Dua – Jl Dharmawangsa. It's 2km down to the village where you can park by the sand.

SOUTH BALI & THE ISLANDS NUSA DUA

Nusa Dua

use the immaculate public sands in front of the resorts.

🛏 Sleeping

Nusa Dua resorts are similar in several ways: they are big (some are huge) with most major international brands represented. Many are right on the placid beach.

Major international brands such as Westin and Hyatt have invested heavily, adding loads of the amenities (such as elaborate pools and kids' day camps). Other hotels seem little changed from when they were built in the 1970s heyday of the Suharto era.

⭐ **Sofitel Bali Nusa Dua Beach Resort**   RESORT $$$
(☏ 0361-849 2888; www.sofitelbalinusadua.com; Jl Nusa Dua; r from US$200; ❋ @ 🛜 ⚊) Making up a part of the resort strip, the Sofitel has a vast pool that meanders past the 415 rooms, some of which have terraces with direct pool access. The room blocks are huge;

many rooms have at least a glimpse of the water. The Sofitel's lavish Sunday brunch (11am to 3pm) is one of Bali's best; it costs from 400,000Rp.

Grand Hyatt Bali   RESORT $$$
(☑0361-771234; www.bali.grand.hyatt.com; r from US$200; ❄@◈☲) A little city, of sorts, the 636-room Hyatt has areas that are better than others. Some rooms in the West Village face the taxi parking lot (of the four Villages, East and South are the best located). The riverlike pool (one of six) is huge and has a fun slide. The children's club will keep 'em busy for days.

St Regis Bali Resort   RESORT $$$
(☑0361-847 8111; www.stregisbali.com; Kawasan Pariwisata; ste from US$650; ❄@◈☲) This lavish Nusa Dua resort leaves most of the others in the sand. Every conceivable luxury is provided, from electronics to furnishings, the marble and the personal butler. Pools abound and the 123 units are huge. Go for the pool suite with ocean views if you want to relax in style.

Westin Resort   RESORT $$$
(☑0361-771906; www.westin.com/bali; r from US$200; ❄@◈☲) Attached to a large convention centre, the Westin has an air-conditioned lobby (a rarity) and vast public spaces. Guests in the 433 rooms enjoy the best pools in Nusa, with waterfalls and other features forming an aquatic playground. The Kids Club has extensive activities and facilities. It has a mall and is connected to the **Bali International Convention Centre** (☑0361 771906; www.baliconvention.com).

🍴 Eating

There are dozens of restaurants charging resort prices in the huge hotels. For nonguests, venture in if you want a bounteous Sunday brunch, such as the Sofitel's.

Good warungs cluster at the corner of Jl Srikandi and Jl Pantai Mengiat. Also along the latter street, just outside the central gate, open-air eateries offer an unpretentious dining alternative. None will win culinary awards, but most provide transport.

Warungs   INDONESIAN $
(off Jl Terompong; meals from 20,000Rp; ⊘8am-10pm) Your best bet for fresh and delicious local fare in the Nusa Dua area.

Warung Dobiel   BALINESE $
(☑0361-771633; Jl Srikandi 9; meals from 40,000Rp; ⊘10am-3pm) A bit of authentic food action amid the bland streets of Nusa, this is a good stop for *babi guling* (spit-roast pig). Pork soup is the perfect taste-bud awakener, while the jackfruit is redolent with spices. Diners perch on stools and share tables; service can be slow and tours may mob the place. Watch out for 'foreigner' pricing.

Nusa Dua Beach Grill   INTERNATIONAL $$
(☑0851 0043 4779; Jl Pura Gegar; mains from 80,000Rp; ⊘8am-10.30pm) A good spot for day trippers, this warm-hued cafe (hidden by the Mulia resort) is just south of Gegar Beach. The drinks menu is long, the seafood fresh and the relaxed beachy vibe intoxicating.

Hardy's   SUPERMARKET
(☑0361-774639; Jl Ngurah Rai; ⊘8am-9pm) This huge outlet of the local chain of supermarkets is about 1km west of the main gate. Besides groceries it has most other goods you might need and at real (ie not inflated resort) prices.

☆ Entertainment

Many of the hotels offer attenuated Balinese dances on one or more nights, usually as part of a buffet deal. Hotel lounges also often have live music, from crooners to mellow rock bands.

ℹ Information

ATMs can be found at the **Bali Collection** (☑0361-771662; www.bali-collection.com; off Jl Nusa Dua; ⊘8am-10pm) shopping centre, some hotel lobbies and at the huge Hardy's Department Store out on the Jl Ngurah Rai Bypass.

ℹ Getting There & Away

The Bali Mandara Toll Rd (motorbike/car 4000/11,000Rp) greatly speeds journeys between Nusa Dua and the airport and Sanur.

BUS

The Kura-Kura tourist bus (p389) has two routes linking Nusa Dua with its Kuta hub. Buses run every two hours and cost 50,000Rp.

Bali's Trans-Sarbagita Bus System serves Nusa Dua on a route that follows the Jl Ngurah Rai Bypass up and around past Sanur to Batubulan.

SHUTTLE

Find out what shuttle-bus services your hotel provides before you start hailing taxis. A free **shuttle bus** (☑0361-771662; www.bali-collection.com/shuttle-bus; ⊘9am-10pm) connects all Nusa Dua and Tanjung Benoa resort hotels with the Bali Collection shopping centre about every hour. Better still, walk the delightful beach promenade.

TAXI

The taxi from the airport cartel is 150,000Rp; a metered taxi to the airport will be much less. Taxis to/from Seminyak average 150,000Rp for the 45-minute trip, although traffic can double this time.

Tanjung Benoa

The peninsula of Tanjung Benoa extends about 4km north from Nusa Dua to Benoa village. It's flat and lined with family-friendly resort hotels, most of midrange calibre. By day the waters buzz with the roar of dozens of motorised water-sports craft. Group tours arrive by the busload for a day's aquatic excitement, straddling a banana boat among other thrills.

Overall, Tanjung Benoa is a fairly sedate place, although the Bali Mandara Toll Rd speeds access to the nightlife diversions of Kuta and Seminyak.

Tanjung Benoa 0 500 m / 0 0.25 miles

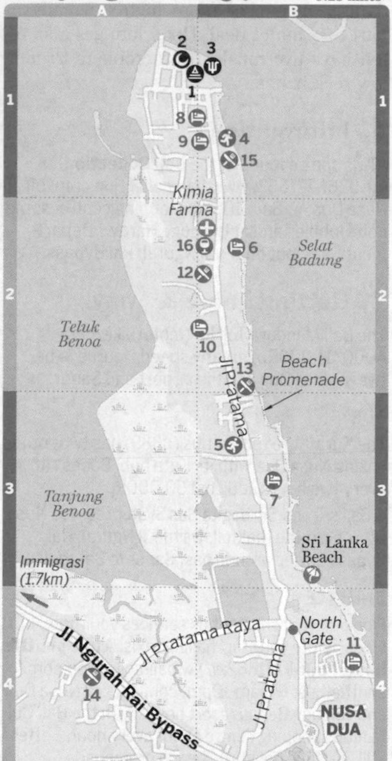

Sights

The village of Benoa is a fascinating little fishing settlement that makes for a good stroll. Amble the narrow lanes of the peninsula's tip for a multicultural feast. Within 100m of each other are a brightly coloured **Chinese Buddhist temple** (Jl Segara Lor) , a domed **mosque** (Jl Segara Lor) and a **Hindu temple** (Jl Segara Lor) with a nicely carved triple entrance. Enjoy views of the busy channel to the port. On the dark side, Benoa's backstreets hide Bali's illegal trade in turtles, although police raids are helping to limit it.

Activities

★**Jari Menari** SPA
(☎0361-778084; www.jarimenarinusadua.com; Jl Pratama; massage from 385,000Rp; ⏰9am-9pm) This branch of the famed Seminyak original offers all the same exquisite massages by the expert all-male staff. Call for transport.

★**Bumbu Bali Cooking School** COOKING
(☎0361-774502; www.balifoods.com; Jl Pratama; course without/with market visit US$105/118; ⏰6am-3pm Mon, Wed & Fri) This much-lauded cooking school at the eponymous restaurant strives to get to the roots of Balinese cooking. Courses start with a 6am visit to Jim-

Tanjung Benoa

Sights
1 Caow Eng Bio A1
2 Mosque A1
3 Pura Dalem Ning Lan Taman Beji B1

Activities, Courses & Tours
4 Benoa Marine Recreation B1
Bumbu Bali Cooking School .... (see 13)
5 Jari Menari B3

Sleeping
6 Bali Khama B2
7 Conrad Bali B3
8 Pondok Benoa A1
9 Pondok Hasan Inn B1
10 Rumah Bali B2
11 Sofitel Bali Nusa Dua Beach Resort B4

Eating
12 Bali Cardamon B2
13 Bumbu Bali B2
14 Hardy's A4
15 Tao B1

Drinking & Nightlife
16 Atlichnaya Bar B2

WATER SPORTS

Water-sports centres along Jl Pratama offer daytime diving, cruises, windsurfing and waterskiing. Each morning convoys of buses arrive with day trippers from all over south Bali, and by 10am parasailers float over the water.

All feature unctuous salespeople whose job it is to sell you the banana-boat ride of your dreams while you sit glassy-eyed in a thatched-roof sales centre and cafe. Check equipment and credentials before you sign up, as a few tourists have died in accidents.

Among the established water-sports operators is **Benoa Marine Recreation** (BMR; ☑ 0361-772438; www.bmrbali.com; Jl Pratama; ⊙ 8am-4pm). As if by magic, all operators have similar prices. Note that 'official' price lists are just the starting point for bargaining. Activities here include the following (with average prices):

Banana-boat rides Wild rides for two as you try to maintain your grasp on the inflatable fruit moving over the waves (US$20 per 15 minutes).

Glass-bottomed boat trips The non-wet way to see the denizens of the shallows (US$50 per hour).

Jet-skiing Go fast and belch smoke (US$25 per 15 minutes).

Parasailing Iconic; you float above the water while being towed by a speedboat (US$20 per 15-minute trip).

Snorkelling Trips include equipment and a boat ride to a reef (US$35 per hour).

One nice way to use the beach here is at Tao restaurant, where for the price of a drink, you can enjoy resort-quality loungers and a pool.

baran's fish and morning markets, continue in the large kitchen and finish with lunch.

🛏 Sleeping

Tanjung Benoa's east shore is lined with midrange low-key resorts aimed at groups. They are family-friendly, offer kids' programs and enjoy repeat business by holidaymakers who are greeted with banners such as 'Welcome Back Underhills!' There are also a couple of simple guesthouses.

Pondok Hasan Inn GUESTHOUSE $
(☑ 0361-772456; hasanhomestay@yahoo.com; Jl Pratama; r incl breakfast from 250,000Rp; ❄ 🛜) Back 20m off the main road, this friendly family-run homestay has 11 immaculate hot-water rooms that include breakfast. The tiles on the outdoor verandah gleam; it's shared by the rooms, and there is a small garden.

Pondok Benoa GUESTHOUSE $
(☑ 0812 384 9640; www.pondok-benoa.com; Jl Pratama 99; r incl breakfast 350,000-550,000Rp; ❄ 🛜) The nine airy rooms (most with tubs) in a large, houselike building are spotless. Higher-priced rooms come with small kitchens. The gardens are large, shady and attractive.

Rumah Bali GUESTHOUSE $$
(☑ 0361-771256; www.balifoods.com; off Jl Pratama; r incl breakfast from US$90, villa from US$250;
❄ @ 🛜 🏊) Rumah Bali is a luxurious interpretation of a Balinese village by cookbook author Heinz von Holzen, who also runs local restaurant Bumbu Bali. Guests choose from large family rooms or individual villas (some have three bedrooms) with their own plunge pools and kitchens. There's a large communal pool and a tennis court. The beach is a short walk away.

Conrad Bali RESORT $$$
(☑ 0361-778788; www.conradbali.com; Jl Pratama 168; r incl breakfast US$200; ❄ @ 🛜 🏊) The top-end choice of Tanjung Benoa, the huge Conrad combines a modern Bali look with a refreshing, casual style. The 353 rooms are large and thoughtfully designed. Some units have patios with steps right down into the 33m pool, easing the morning dip. Bungalows have their own private lagoon and there is a large kids' club.

Bali Khama RESORT $$$
(☑ 0361-774912; www.thebalikhama.com; Jl Pratama; villas US$110-250; ❄ @ 🛜 🏊) Bali Khama is set on its own crescent of sand at the northern end of the beach promenade. The 60 mostly individual walled villas are large, tasteful and – obviously – private. More expensive ones have plunge pools; there are also honeymoon and multiroom villas.

✕ Eating & Drinking

★ Bumbu Bali
BALINESE $$

(✆ 0361-774502; www.balifoods.com; Jl Pratama; mains from 100,000Rp, set menus from 295,000Rp; ⊙ noon-9pm) Long-time resident and cookbook author Heinz von Holzen, his wife Puji, and their well-trained and enthusiastic staff serve exquisitely flavoured dishes at this superb restaurant. Many diners opt for one of several lavish set menus. Cooking classes (p118) on Mondays, Wednesdays and Fridays (from US$103) are highly recommended.

Bali Cardamon
ASIAN $$

(✆ 0361-773745; www.balicardamon.com; Jl Pratama 97; mains 55,000-120,000Rp; ⊙ 8am-10pm) A cut above most of the other restaurants on the Jl Pratama strip, this ambitious spot has a creative kitchen that takes influences from across Asia. It has some excellent dishes including pork belly seasoned with star anise. Sit under the frangipani trees or in the dining room.

Tao
ASIAN $$

(✆ 0361-772902; www.taobali.com; Jl Pratama 96; mains 60,000-100,000Rp; ⊙ 8am-10pm; 🐾) On its own swathe of pure-white sand, Tao has a large curling pool that wends between the tables. The food is an eclectic mix of Asian (but a club sandwich awaits philistines).

Atlichnaya Bar
BAR

(✆ 0813 3818 9675; www.atlichnaya.com; Jl Pratama 88; ⊙ 8am-late; 🐾) The lively and convivial alternative to the stiff hotel bars, this rollicking place serves a long list of cheap mixed drinks and even offers **massages** (from 50,000Rp). There are cheap and cheery Indo and Western menu items as well.

ℹ Information

Kimia Farma (✆ 0361-916 6509; Jl Pratama 87; ⊙ 8am-10pm) Reliable chain of pharmacies.

ℹ Getting There & Away

Taxis from the airport cartel cost 175,000Rp. Bemos (mini-buses) shuttle up and down Jl Pratama (5000Rp) – although after about 3pm they become scarce.

A free **shuttle bus** (✆ 0361-771662; www.bali-collection.com/shuttle-bus; ⊙ 9am-10pm) connects Nusa Dua and Tanjung Benoa resort hotels with the Bali Collection shopping centre about every hour. Or stroll the Beach Promenade and enjoy the view in lieu of the bus. Many restaurants will provide transport from Nusa Dua and Tanjung Benoa hotels.

SANUR
📱 0361

Many consider Sanur 'just right', as it lacks most of the hassles found to the west while maintaining a good mix of restaurants and bars that aren't all owned by resorts.

The beach, while thin, is protected by a reef and breakwaters, so families appreciate the limpid waves. Sanur has a good range of places to stay and it's well placed for day trips. Really, it doesn't deserve its local moniker, 'Snore'.

Sanur stretches for about 5km along an east-facing coastline, with the lush and green landscaped grounds of resorts fronting right on to the sandy beach. West of the beachfront hotels is the busy main drag, Jl Danau Tamblingan, with hotel entrances and oodles of tourist shops, restaurants and cafes.

Noxious, traffic-choked Jl Ngurah Rai Bypass skirts the western side of the resort area, and is the main link to Kuta and the airport. Don't stay out here.

◉ Sights

★ Museum Le Mayeur
MUSEUM

(✆ 0361-286201; Jl Hang Tuah; adult/child 20,000/10,000Rp; ⊙ 8am-3.30pm Sat-Thu, 8.30am-12.30pm Fri) Artist Adrien-Jean Le Mayeur de Merpres (1880–1958) arrived in Bali in 1932, and married the beautiful Legong dancer Ni Polok three years later, when she was just 15. They lived in this compound back when Sanur was still a quiet fishing village. After the artist's death, Ni Polok lived in the house until she died in 1985. Despite security (some of Le Mayeur's paintings have sold for US$150,000) and conservation problems, almost 90 of Le Mayeur's paintings are displayed.

The house is an interesting example of Balinese-style architecture – notice the beautifully carved window shutters that recount the story of Rama and Sita from the Ramayana. The museum has a naturalistic Balinese interior of woven fibres. Some of Le Mayeur's early works are impressionist paintings from his travels in Africa, India, the Mediterranean and the South Pacific. Paintings from his early period in Bali are romantic depictions of daily life and beautiful Balinese women – often Ni Polok. The works from the 1950s are in much better condition, displaying the vibrant colours that later became popular with young Balinese artists. Look for the haunting black-and- white photos of Ni Polok.

Sanur Beach BEACH

Sanur Beach curves in a southwesterly direction and stretches for more than 5km. It is mostly clean and overall quite serene – much like the town itself. Offshore reefs mean that the surf is reduced to tiny waves lapping the shore. With a couple of unfortunate exceptions, the resorts along the sand are low-key, leaving the beach uncrowded.

Bali Orchid Garden GARDENS

(📞0361-701988; www.baliorchidgardens.com; Coast Rd; 100,000Rp; ⊙8am-6pm) Orchids thrive in Bali's warm weather and rich volcanic soil. At this garden you can see thousands of orchids in a variety of settings. It's 3km north of Sanur along Jl Ngurah Rai just past the major intersection with the coast road, and is an easy stop on the way to Ubud.

Stone Pillar MONUMENT

(off Jl Danau Poso) The pillar, down a narrow lane to the left as you face Pura Belangjong, is Bali's oldest dated artefact and has ancient inscriptions recounting military victories from more than a thousand years ago. These inscriptions are in Sanskrit and are evidence of Hindu influence 300 years before the arrival of the Majapahit court.

🏃 Activities

Water Sports

Sanur's calm water and steady breeze make it a natural centre for wind- and kitesurfing.

Sanur's fickle breaks (tide conditions often don't produce waves) are offshore along the reef. The best area is called **Sanur Reef**, a right break in front of the Grand Bali Beach Hotel. Another good spot is known as the **Hyatt Reef**, in front of, you guessed it, the old Bali Hyatt.

You can get a boat out to the breaks from **Surya Water Sports** (📞0361-287956; www.balisuryadivecenter.com; Jl Duyung 10; ⊙9am-5pm; 🖐) or a fishing boat (from 200,000Rp to 400,000Rp).

★ Rip Curl School of Surf KITESURFING

(📞0361-287749; www.ripcurlschoolofsurf.com; Beachfront Walk, Sanur Beach Hotel; kitesurfing lessons from 1,100,000Rp, rental per hr from 550,000Rp; ⊙8am-5pm) Sanur's reef-protected waters and regular offshore breezes make for good kitesurfing. The season runs from June to October. Rip Curl also rents boards for windsurfing and stand-up paddle boarding (including SUP yoga for 450,000Rp per hour) as well as kayaks.

Bali Stand Up Paddle WATER SPORTS

(📞0813 3823 5082; www.bali-standuppaddle.org; Jl Cemara 4B; rental per day 350,000Rp, lessons

---

DON'T MISS

SANUR'S BEACHFRONT WALK

Sanur's beachfront walk has been delighting locals and visitors alike from day one. Over 4km long, it curves past resorts, beachfront cafes, wooden fishing boats under repair and quite a few elegant old villas built decades ago by the wealthy expats who fell under Bali's spell. While you stroll, look out across the water to Nusa Penida.

Even if you're not staying in Sanur, the beach walk makes a good day trip or stop on the way to someplace else. A few highlights north to south:

Grand Bali Beach Hotel (Jl Hang Tuah) Built in the Sukarno era, this vast hotel is now slowly fading away. Local leaders, properly horrified at its outsized bulk, imposed the famous rule that no building could be higher than a coconut palm.

Turtle Tanks An engaging display about Bali's endangered sea turtles that usually includes some young hatchlings.

Small Temple Amid the tourist bustle, this little shrine is shaded by huge trees.

Batu Jimbar (www.villabatujimbar.com; Beachfront Walk) Just north of the old Hyatt, this villa compound has a colourful history: it was redesigned by the famous Sri Lankan architect Geoffrey Bawa in 1975, Mick Jagger and Jerry Hall were unofficially married here in 1990, and it has accommodated celebrities from Yoko Ono to Sting to Fergie. If your income approaches theirs, you too can stay here.

Fishing Boats Just south of the old Hyatt is a long area where multihued fishing boats are pulled ashore and repaired under the trees.

per 90min 350,000Rp) This specialist store offers great advice, gear sales and rental, and lessons. It also offers windsurfing and kiteboarding.

Yoga & Spas

★ Power of Now Oasis — YOGA

(☑ 0813 3831 5032; www.powerofnowoasis.com; Beachfront Walk, Hotel Mercure; classes from 100,000Rp) Enjoy a yoga class in this atmospheric bamboo pavilion looking out to Sanur Beach. Several levels are offered. Sunrise yoga is a popular choice.

★ Jamu Wellness — SPA

(☑ 0811 389 9930; www.jamutraditionalspa.com; Jl Danau Tamblingan 140; 1hr massage 350,000Rp; ☺ 9am-9pm) This gracious spa has classy new digs and offers a range of treatments including a popular Earth and Flower Body Mask and a Kemiri Nut Scrub.

Glo Day Spa & Salon — SPA

(☑ 0361-282826; www.glo-day-spa.com; Jl Danau Poso 57, Gopa Town Centre; massage 1hr from 195,000Rp; ☺ 8am-6pm) An insider pick by the many local Sanur expats, Glo eschews a fancy setting for a clean-lined storefront. Services and treatments run the gamut, from skin and nail care to massages and spa therapies.

🎓 Courses

Balinese Cooking Class — COOKING

(☑ 0361-288009; www.santrian.com; Puri Santrian, Beachfront Walk; 90min class from US$60; ☺ Wed & Fri) With a kitchen that's set on the beachfront, this is a memorable spot to learn to cook Balinese food. For a bit extra you can visit the market to source ingredients.

Crystal Divers — DIVING

(☑ 0361-286737; www.crystal-divers.com; Jl Danau Tamblingan 168; dives from US$65) This slick diving operation has its own hotel (the Santai) and a large diving pool. Recommended for beginners, the shop offers a long list of courses, including PADI open-water (US$500).

🛏 Sleeping

🏠 Beachfront

Amid the larger resorts you'll find some smaller beachfront hotels that are surprisingly affordable.

Kesumasari — GUESTHOUSE $

(☑ 0361-287824; villa_kesumasari@yahoo.com; Jl Kesumasari 6; r with fan/air-con from 400,000/450,000Rp; ❄️ 🛜 🏊) The only thing

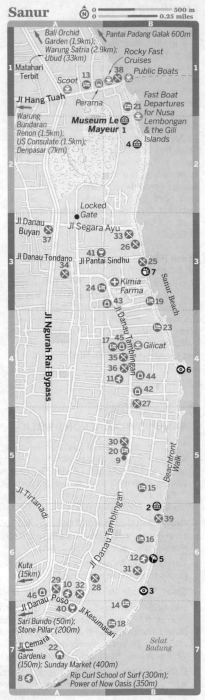

Sanur

Sanur

between you and the beach is a small shrine. Beyond the lounging porches, the multihued carved Balinese doors don't prepare you for the riot of colour inside the 15 idiosyncratic rooms at this family-run homestay.

Pollok & Le Mayeur Inn HOMESTAY $
(☎0361-289847; pollokinn@yahoo.com; Jl Hang Tuah, Museum Le Mayeur; r with fan/air-con from 250,000/350,000Rp; ❄☎) The grandchildren of the late artist Le Mayeur de Merpres and his wife Ni Polok run this small homestay. It's within the Le Mayeur museum compound (p120), and offers a good budget option on the beachfront. The 15 rooms vary in size.

La Taverna Suites HOTEL $$
(☎0361-288497; http://latavernasuites.com; Jl Danau Tamblingan 29; r US$90-160; ❄@☎▩) One of Sanur's first hotels, La Taverna has been reconstructed as an all-suites property while retaining its artful, simple charm. The pretty grounds and paths that link the buildings hum with a creative energy, infusing the 38 vintage bungalow-style units with an air of understated luxury.

Hotel Peneeda View HOTEL $$
(☎0361-288425; www.peneedaview.com; Jl Danau Tamblingan 89; r from US$45; ❄@☎▩) Another basic, small beachfront hotel, the Peneeda (which is *not* phonetically accurate for Penida) is a good choice for sun, sand and room service at a very affordable price. The 56 rooms are somewhat dated but you simply can't beat the (narrow) beach frontage and the price. There's free wi-fi in common areas.

★**Tandjung Sari** HOTEL $$$
(☎0361-288441; www.tandjungsarihotel.com; Jl Danau Tamblingan 41; bungalows incl breakfast from US$215; ❄@☎▩) One of Bali's first boutique hotels, Tandjung Sari has flourished since it opened in 1967 and continues to be lauded for its style. The 28 traditional-style bungalows are beautifully decorated with crafts and antiques. The gracious staff is a delight. Local children practise Balinese dance by the pool at 3pm Friday and Sunday.

Fairmont Sanur Beach Bali RESORT $$$
(☎0361-3011888; www.fairmont.com; Jl Kesumasari 8; r from US$215; ❄@☎▩) Looming

KITE-FLYING OVER SANUR

Travelling through south Bali you can't help but notice scores of kites overhead much of the year. These creations are often huge (10m or more wide, with tails stretching up to an astonishing 160m) and fly at altitudes that worry pilots. Many have noisemakers called *gaganguan* producing eerie humming and buzzing noises that are unique to each kite. Like much in Bali there are spiritual roots: the kites are meant to whisper figuratively into the ears of the gods suggestions that abundant harvests might be nice. But for many Balinese, these high-fliers are simply a really fun hobby (although it has its serious side as if one of these monsters crashes to earth it can kill and injure).

Each July, hundreds of Balinese and international teams descend – as it were – on open spaces north of Sanur for the **Bali Kite Festival**. They compete for an array of honours in categories such as original design and flight endurance. The action is centred around flat land behind the sand at **Pantai Padang Galak**, about 1km up the coast from Sanur. You can catch kite-flying Balinese-style here from May to September.

over Sanur's beachfront, this massive hotel has 120 elegant suites and villas on a sprawling site that includes a 50m infinity pool. The design is strikingly modern, and high-tech pleasures abound. There are also lavish spas and restaurants, and a state-of-the-art gym. Kids get their own pool and play area.

Hyatt Regency Bali   RESORT **$$$**
(www.bali.regency.hyatt.com; Jl Danau Tamblingan) *The* landmark Sanur beachfront resort, the former Bali Hyatt is getting a slightly grander name and a much grander makeover for a late-2017 reopening.

Puri Santrian   HUT, BUNGALOW **$$$**
(☎0361-288009; www.santrian.com; Jl Cemara 35; r US$110-300; ❄ 🖥 ⛱) Lush gardens, three large pools with fountains, a tennis court and beach frontage, as well as 199 comfortable, well-equipped rooms, make this a popular choice. Many rooms are in older-style bungalows, others in two- and three-storey blocks. It offers a recommended Balinese cooking class (p122).

🛏 Off the Beach

Hotels near Jl Danau Tamblingan are a short walk from the beach, cafes and shopping. Lacking sand as a feature, many try a bit harder than their beachfront brethren (as well as being more affordable).

Keke Homestay   GUESTHOUSE **$**
(☎0361-287282; www.keke-homestay.com; Jl Danau Tamblingan 100; r with fan/air-con from 150,000/250,000Rp; ❄ 🖥) Set 150m down a *gang* from the noisy road, Keke welcomes backpackers into its genial family (who are often busy making offerings). The five quiet, clean rooms vary from fan-only to air-con cool.

Agung & Sue Watering Hole I   GUESTHOUSE **$**
(☎0361-288289; www.wateringholesanurbali.com; Jl Hang Tuah 35; r 275,000-400,000Rp; ❄ 🖥) Ideally located for an early fast boat to Nusa Lembongan or the Gilis, this long-running guesthouse has a veteran conviviality. Rooms are standard, but the beer is indeed cold and Sanur Beach is a five-minute walk. A good place if you have that early fast boat to catch.

Yulia 1 Homestay   GUESTHOUSE **$**
(☎0361-288089; yulia1homestay@gmail.com; Jl Danau Tamblingan 38; r incl breakfast with fan/air-con from 180,000/300,000Rp; ❄ 🖥 ⛱) Run by a friendly family, this mellow guesthouse is set in a lovely bird-filled garden full of palms and flowers. Rooms vary in standards (some cold water, fan only), but all come with fridges. The plunge pool is a nice area for relaxing.

Maison Aurelia Sanur   HOTEL **$$**
(☎0361-472 1111; http://preferencehotels.com/maison-aurelia; Jl Danau Tamblingan 140; r US$75-150; ❄ 🖥 ⛱) High-style on the far side from the beach, this four-storey hotel is a dramatic addition to Sanur's main drag. The 54 rooms are capacious, have balconies and boast a richly restful decor. Details are plush and comforts include fridges.

Gardenia   GUESTHOUSE **$$**
(☎0361-286301; www.gardeniaguesthousebali.com; Jl Mertasari 2; r 600,000-700,000Rp; ❄ 🖥 ⛱) Like its many-petalled namesake, the Gardenia has many facets. The seven rooms are visions in white and sit well back from the road. Nice verandas face a plunge pool in a pretty courtyard. Up front there is a good cafe.

✗ Eating

Dine on the beach in a traditional open-air pavilion or in a genial bar. Although there are plenty of uninspired places on Jl Danau Tamblingan, there are also some gems.

For groceries, try the large **Hardy's Supermarket** (☑ 0361-285806; Jl Danau Tamblingan 136; ⊗ 8am-10pm). Nearby is the gourmet market of Cafe Batu Jimbar. The Mercure Hotel hosts a Sunday **organic market** (www.facebook.com/sundaymarketsanur; Jl Mertasari, Mercure Resort Sanur; ⊗ 10am-5pm last Sun of month). The **Pasar Sindhu night market** (off Jl Danau Tamblingan; ⊗ 6am-midnight) sells fresh vegetables, dried fish, spices and good Balinese meals.

✗ Beachfront

The beach path offers restaurants, cafes and bars where you can catch a meal, a drink or a sea breeze. Sunset drink specials are common (though the beach faces east, so you'll need to enjoy the reflected glow off Nusa Penida).

Nasi Bali Men Weti   BALINESE $
(Jl Segara Ayu; meals from 20,000Rp; ⊗ 7am-1pm) This simple stall prepares excellent *nasi campur*, the classic Balinese lunch plate of mixed dishes. Everything is very fresh and prepared while you wait in the inevitable queue. Enjoy your meal perched on a small plastic stool.

Byrdhouse Beach Club   INTERNATIONAL $$
(☑ 0361-288407; www.facebook.com/byrdhouse-beachclubbali; Segara Village, Sanur Beach; mains from 60,000Rp; ⊗ 6am-midnight; 🗟) With loungers, a swimming pool, a restaurant, bar and table tennis on-site, you could happily spend an entire day here by the beach. Check the club's Facebook page for upcoming events, including outdoor-cinema screenings and street-food stalls.

Minami   JAPANESE $$
(☑ 0812 8613 4471; Beachfront Walk; mains from 60,000Rp; ⊗ 10am-11pm) With its minimalist white decor, bright open-air atmosphere and a vast range of uberfresh fish, this authentic Japanese place is a great find on Sanur Beach.

Warung Pantai Indah   CAFE $$
(Beachfront Walk; mains 30,000-110,000Rp; ⊗ 9am-9pm) Sit at battered tables and chairs with your toes in the sand at this timeless beach cafe. It specialises in fresh barbecue-grilled seafood and cheap local dishes.

Beach Café   INTERNATIONAL $$
(☑ 0361-282875; Beachfront Walk; meals 50,000-100,000Rp; ⊗ 8am-10pm; 🗟) Brings a bit of flashy Med style to the Sanur Beach cliché of palm fronds and plastic chairs. Zone out on wicker sofas or hang on a low cushion on the sand. Enjoy salads and seafood. There is a good drinks list, just the reason to stop.

✗ Jl Danau Tamblingan

Warung Mak Beng   BALINESE $
(☑ 0361-282633; Jl Hang Tuah 45; meals 35,000Rp; ⊗ 8am-9pm) You don't need a menu at this local favourite: all you can order is its legendary barbecued fish (*ikan laut goreng*), which comes with various sides and some tasty soup. Service is quick, the air fragrant and diners of all stripes very happy.

ROYALTY & EXPATS

Sanur was one of the places favoured by Westerners during their pre-WWII discovery of Bali. Artists Miguel Covarrubias, Adrien-Jean Le Mayeur de Merpres and Walter Spies, anthropologist Jane Belo and choreographer Katharane Mershon all spent time here. The first tourist bungalows appeared in Sanur in the 1940s and '50s, and more artists, including Australian Donald Friend (whose antics earned him the nickname Lord Devil Donald), made their homes in Sanur.

During this period Sanur was ruled by insightful priests and scholars, who recognised both the opportunities and the threats presented by expanding tourism. They established village cooperatives that owned land and ran tourist businesses, ensuring that a good share of the economic benefits remained in the community.

The priestly influence remains strong, and Sanur is one of the few communities still ruled by members of the Brahmana caste. It is known as a home of sorcerers and healers, and a centre for both black and white magic. The black-and-white chequered cloth known as *kain poleng*, which symbolises the balance of good and evil, is emblematic of Sanur.

Warung Babi Guling Sanur BALINESE $

(☑ 0361-287308; Jl Ngurah Rai Bypass; mains from 25,000Rp; ⊙ 10am-10pm) Unlike many of Bali's *babi guling* places, which buy their suckling pigs precooked from large suppliers, this small outlet does all its cooking right out back. The meat is succulent and shows the benefits of personal attention.

Porch CAFE $

(☑ 0361-281682; www.flashbacks-chb.com; Jl Danau Tamblingan 111, Flashbacks; mains from 40,000Rp; ⊙ 7am-10pm; ✺ ⓢ) Housed in a traditional wooden building, this cafe offers a tasty mix of comfort food like burgers and freshly baked goods such as ciabatta. Snuggle up to a table on the porch or shut it all out in the air-con inside. Popular for breakfast; there's a long list of fresh juices. High tea is popular too (149,000Rp for two).

A cute guesthouse, **Flashbacks**, is in the rear.

★ Char Ming ASIAN $$

(☑ 0361-288029; www.charming-bali.com; Jl Danau Tamblingan N97; meals 60,000-250,000Rp; ⊙ 5-11pm) Asian fusion with a French accent. A daily menu board lists the fresh seafood available for grilling. Look for regional dishes, many with modern flair. The highly stylised location features lush plantings and carved-wood details from vintage Javanese and Balinese structures.

★ Three Monkeys Cafe ASIAN $$

(☑ 0361-286002; www.threemonkeyscafebali.com; Jl Danau Tamblingan; meals 58,000-105,000Rp; ⊙ 11am-11pm; ⓢ) This branch of the splendid Ubud original is no mere knock-off. Spread over two floors, there's cool jazz playing in the background and live performances some nights. Set well back from the road, you can enjoy excellent coffee drinks on sofas or chairs. The creative menu mixes Western fare with pan-Asian creations.

Pregina Warung BALINESE $$

(☑ 0361-283353; Jl Danau Tamblingan 106; mains 40,000-80,000Rp; ⊙ 11am-11pm) Classic Balinese duck dishes and crowd-pleasers such as *sate* are mainstays of the interesting menu here. It serves local foods several cuts above the all-too-common bland tourist versions (try anything with duck). The dining room has spare, stylish wooden decor and features vintage photos of Bali.

Café Smorgås CAFE $$

(☑ 0361-289361; www.cafesmorgas.com; Jl Danau Tamblingan; meals 58,000-100,000Rp; ⊙ 7am-10pm; ✺ ⓢ ⌨) A popular place with nice wicker chairs on a large terrace outside and cool air-con inside. The menu has a healthy range of fresh detox juices and salads, plus comfort food such as burgers and sandwiches. Good breakfasts and desserts as well.

Spice INDONESIAN $$

(☑ 0361-449 0411; http://spicebali.com; Jl Danau Tamblingan 140, Maison Aurelia Sanur; mains from 80,000Rp; ⊙ noon-11pm) The second edition of the buzzy new restaurant chain started by Ubud chef Chris Salans has a commanding position on the ground floor of the new Maison Aurelia Sanur hotel. The short menu of fresh and unusual Indonesian dishes is here and prepared in an open kitchen. The drinks are creative and can be enjoyed on the terrace outside.

La Playa Cafe SEAFOOD $$

(☑ 0821 4794 4514; Jl Duyung, Sanur Beach; meals 60,000-160,000Rp; ⊙ 8am-10pm) You can hear the surf and see the moonlight reflected on the water at this welcoming beachside seafood grill, set on the sand amid palm trees and fishing boats. The grilled seafood platter is packed with garlic - yum!

Massimo ITALIAN $$

(☑ 0361-288942; www.massimobali.com; Jl Danau Tamblingan 206; meals 80,000-200,000Rp; ⊙ 11am-11pm) The interior is like an open-air Milan cafe; the outside is like a Balinese garden – it's a combo that goes together like spaghetti and meatballs. Pasta, pizza and more are prepared with authentic Italian flair. No time for a meal? Nab some excellent gelato from the counter up front.

✖ South Sanur

Sari Bundo INDONESIAN $

(☑ 0361-281389; Jl Danau Poso; mains from 25,000Rp; ⊙ 24hr) This spotless Padang-style shopfront is one of several at the south end of Sanur. Choose from an array of fresh and very spicy food. The curry chicken is a fiery treat that will have your tongue alternatively loving and hating you.

Denata Minang INDONESIAN $

(Jl Danau Poso; meals from 20,000Rp; ⊙ 8am-10pm) One of the better Padang-style warungs, it's located just west of Cafe Billiard, the rollicking expat bar. Like its brethren, it has tender *ayam* (chicken) in myriad spicy forms – only better.

♟ Drinking & Nightlife

Fire Station
PUB

(☑ 0361-285675; Jl Danau Poso 108; mains from 80,000Rp; ☺ 4pm-late) There's some old Hollywood style here at this open-fronted pub. Vaguely 1960s Hollywood-esque portraits line walls; you expect to see a young Dennis Hopper lurking in the rear. Enjoy pitchers of sangria and other interesting drinks along with a varied menu of good pub food that features many specials. Order the fine Belgian beer, Duvel.

Kalimantan
BAR

(Borneo Bob's; ☑ 0361-289291; Jl Pantai Sindhu 11; mains from 40,000Rp; ☺ 7.30am-11pm) This veteran boozer has an old *South Pacific* thatched charm and is one of several casual bars on this street. Enjoy cheap drinks under the palms in the large, shady garden. The Mexican-style food features homegrown chilli peppers.

🔒 Shopping

★ Ganesha Bookshop
BOOKS

(www.ganeshabooksbali.com; Jl Danau Tamblingan 42; ☺ 8am-9pm) A branch of Bali's best bookshop for serious readers.

To~ko
CLOTHING

(☑ 0812 3624 0049; Jl Danau Poso 51A; ☺ 9am-7pm) This fascinating store in a small complex of shared workspaces showcases local designers. Look for the ecologically designed clothing of Maya Nursari. Her goods are edgy and simple, black and white.

Goddess on the Go
CLOTHING

(☑ 0361-270174; www.goddessonthego.net; Jl Danau Tamblingan; ☺ 9am-8pm) Supercomfortable clothes for women who, like the name says, travel a lot. Many of the items are made with organic fibres.

A-Krea
CLOTHING

(☑ 0361-286101; Jl Danau Tamblingan 51; ☺ 9am-9pm) An excellent spot for souvenirs, A-Krea has a range of items designed and made in Bali in its attractive store. Clothes, accessories, homewares and more are all hand made.

Nogo
TEXTILES

(☑ 0361-288765; www.nogobali.com; Jl Danau Tamblingan 104; ☺ 9am-8pm) Look for the wooden loom out front of this classy store, which bills itself as the 'Bali Ikat Centre'. The goods are gorgeous and easy to enjoy in the air-con comfort.

ⓘ Information

MEDICAL SERVICES
Kimia Farma (☑ 0361-271611; Jl Danau Tamblingan 20; ☺ 8am-10pm) Reliable local pharmacy chain.

MONEY
Moneychangers here have a dubious reputation. There are numerous ATMs along Jl Danau Tamblingan and several banks.

ⓘ Getting There & Away

BEMO
Green bemos go along Jl Hang Tuah to the Kereneng bemo terminal in Denpasar (7000Rp).

BOAT
The myriad fast boats to Nusa Lembongan, Nusa Penida, Lombok and the Gilis depart from a strip of beach south of Jl Hang Tuah. None of these services use a dock – be prepared to wade to the boat. Most companies have shady waiting areas facing the beach.

Gilicat (☑ 0361-271680; www.gilicat.com; Jl Danau Tamblingan 51) Ticket office for a fast boat service to the Gili Islands from Padangbai.

Public boats Regular boats to Nusa Lembongan and Nusa Penida depart from the beach at the end of Jl Hang Tuah.

Rocky Fast Cruises (☑ 0361-283624; www.rockyfastcruise.com; Jl Hang Tuah 41; ☺ 8am-8pm) Has an office for its services to Nusa Lembongan.

Scoot (☑ 0361-285522; www.scootcruise.com; Jl Hang Tuah; ☺ 8am-8pm) Has an office for its network of services to Nusa Lembongan, Lombok and the Gilis.

TOURIST SHUTTLE BUS
The Kura-Kura tourist bus (p389) has a route linking Sanur with its Kuta hub. Buses run every two hours and cost 40,000Rp.

The **Perama office** (☑ 0361-285592; www.peramatour.com; Jl Hang Tuah 39; ☺ 7am-10pm) is at Warung Pojok at the northern end of town. Its destinations include Ubud (40,000Rp, one hour), Padangbai (60,000Rp, two hours) and Lovina (125,000Rp, four hours).

ⓘ Getting Around

Taxis from the airport cartel cost 125000Rp.

Bemos go up and down Jl Danau Tamblingan and Jl Danau Poso for 5000Rp, offering a greener way to shuttle about the strip than a taxi.

AROUND SANUR

Pulau Serangan

Otherwise known as Turtle Island, Pulau Serangan is an example of all that can go wrong with Bali's environment. Originally it was a small (100-hectare) island offshore of the mangroves to the south of Sanur. However, in the 1990s it was selected by Suharto's son Tommy as a site for new development. More than half of the original island was obliterated while a new landfill area over 300 hectares in size was grafted on. The Asian economic crisis pulled the plug on the scheme. Nothing has happened since.

Meanwhile, on the original part of the island, the two small and poor fishing villages, **Ponjok** and **Dukuh**, remain, as does one of Bali's holiest temples, **Pura Sakenan**, just east of the causeway. Architecturally it is insignificant, but major festivals attract huge crowds of devotees, especially during the Kuningan festival.

Some fast boats to the Gili Islands and Lombok leave from here.

Benoa Harbour

Bali's main port is at the entrance of Teluk Benoa (Benoa Bay), the wide but shallow body of water east of the airport runway. Benoa Harbour is on the northern side of the bay – a square of docks and port buildings on reclaimed land. It is linked to mainland Bali by a 2km causeway which is now also part of the Bali Mandara Toll Rd. It's referred to as Benoa port or Benoa Harbour to distinguish it from Benoa village, on the southern side of the bay.

Benoa Harbour is the port for some tourist day-trip boats to Nusa Lembongan and for Pelni ships to other parts of Indonesia; however, its shallow depth prevents large cruise ships from calling.

DENPASAR

POP 1.1 MILLION / ☑ 0361

Sprawling, hectic and ever-growing, Bali's capital has been the focus of a lot of the island's growth and wealth over the last five decades. It can seem a daunting and chaotic place, but spend a little time on its tree-lined streets in the relatively affluent government and business district of Renon and you'll discover a more genteel side.

Denpasar might not be a tropical paradise, but it's as much a part of 'the real Bali' as the rice paddies and clifftop temples. This is the hub of the island for more than one million locals and here you will find their shopping malls and parks. Most enticing, however, are the authentic restaurants and cafes aimed at the burgeoning middle class.

History

Denpasar, which means 'next to the market', was an important trading centre and the seat of local rajahs (lords or princes) before the colonial period. The Dutch gained control of northern Bali in the mid-19th century, but their takeover of the south didn't start until 1906. After the three Balinese princes destroyed their own palaces in Denpasar and made a suicidal last stand – a ritual *puputan* – the Dutch made Denpasar an important colonial centre. As Bali's tourism industry expanded in the 1930s, most visitors stayed at one or two government hotels in the city.

The northern town of Singaraja remained the Dutch administrative capital until after WWII, when it was moved to Denpasar; in 1958, some years after Indonesian independence, the city became the official capital of the province of Bali. Recent immigrants have come from Java and all over Indonesia, attracted by opportunities in schools, business, construction and the enormous tourist economy. Denpasar's edges have merged with Sanur, Kuta, Seminyak and Kerobokan.

◉ Sights

★ **Museum Negeri**
Propinsi Bali   MUSEUM
(☑ 0361-222680; adult/child 20,000/10,000Rp; ⊗ 8am-4pm Sat-Thu, 8.30am-12.30pm Fri) Think of this as the British Museum or the Smithsonian of Balinese culture. It's all here, but unlike those world-class institutions, you have to work at sorting it out – the museum could use a dose of curatorial energy (and some new light bulbs). Most displays are labelled in English. The museum comprises several buildings and pavilions, including many examples of Balinese architecture, housing prehistoric pieces, traditional artefacts, Barong (mythical lion-dog creature), ceremonial objects and rich displays of textiles.

Museum staff members often play music on a bamboo gamelan to magical effect; visit in the afternoons when it's uncrowded. Ignore 'guides' who offer little except a chance to part with US$5 or US$10.

The **main building** has a collection of prehistoric pieces downstairs, including stone sarcophagi, and stone and bronze implements. Upstairs there are examples of traditional artefacts, including items still in everyday use. Look for the intricate wood-and-cane carrying cases for transporting fighting cocks, and tiny carrying cases for fighting crickets.

The **Northern Pavilion** is built in the style of a Tabanan palace. It houses dance costumes and masks, including a sinister *rangda* (widow-witch), a healthy-looking Barong and a towering Barong Landung (tall Barong) figure.

The spacious verandah of the **Central Pavilion** is inspired by the palace pavilions of the Karangasem kingdom (based in Amlapura), where rajahs held audiences. The exhibits are related to Balinese religion, and include ceremonial objects, calendars and priests' clothing.

In the **Southern Pavilion** there are rich displays of textiles, including *endek* (a Balinese method of weaving with predyed threads), double ikat, *songket* (silver- and gold-threaded cloth, handwoven using a floating weft technique) and *prada* (the application of gold leaf or gold or silver thread on traditional Balinese clothes).

★**Bajra Sandhi Monument**   MONUMENT
(Monument to the Struggle of the People of Bali; ☑0361-264517; Jl Raya Puputan, Renon; adult/child 20,000/10,000Rp; ☺9am-6pm) The centrepiece to a popular park, this huge monument is as big as its name. Inside the vaguely Borobudur-like structure are dioramas tracing Bali's history. Note that in the portrayal of the 1906 battle with the Dutch, the King of Badung is literally a sitting target. Take the spiral stairs to the top for 360-degree views.

Pura Maospahit   TEMPLE
(off Jl Sutomo) Established in the 14th century, at the time the Majapahit arrived from Java, this temple was damaged in a 1917 earthquake and has been heavily restored since. The oldest structures are at the back of the temple, but the most interesting features are the large statues of Garuda and the giant Batara Bayu.

Puputan Square   PARK
(Jl Gajah Mada) This bit of urban open space commemorates the heroic but suicidal stand of the rajahs of Badung against the invading Dutch in 1906. A monument depicts a Balinese family in heroic pose, brandishing the weapons that were so ineffective against the Dutch guns. The woman also has jewels in her left hand, as the women of the Badung court reputedly flung their jewellery at the Dutch soldiers to taunt them.

Pura Jagatnatha   HINDU TEMPLE
(Jl Surapati) FREE The state temple, built in 1953, is dedicated to the supreme god, Sanghyang Widi. Part of its significance is its statement of monotheism. Although the Balinese recognise many gods, the belief in one supreme god (who can have many manifestations) brings Balinese Hinduism into conformity with the first principle of Pancasila – the 'Belief in One God'.

The *padmasana* (temple shrine) is made of white coral, and consists of an empty throne (symbolic of heaven) on top of the cosmic turtle and two *naga* (mythical snake-like creatures), which symbolise the foundation of the world. The walls are decorated with carvings of scenes from the Ramayana and Mahabharata.

Two major festivals are held here every month, during the full moon and new moon, and feature *wayang kulit* (leather shadow puppet) performances.

Taman Wedhi Budaya   CULTURAL CENTRE
(☑0361-222776; off Jl Nusa Indah; ☺8am-3pm Mon-Thu, to 1pm Fri-Sun) This arts centre is a sprawling complex in the eastern part of Denpasar. Its lavish architecture houses an art gallery with an interesting collection. However, it's only worth dropping by if there's an event on. From mid-June to mid-July, the centre comes alive for the Bali Arts Festival, with dances, music and craft displays from all over Bali. Book tickets at the centre for more popular events.

🏃 Activities

Kube Dharma Bakti   MASSAGE
(☑0361-749 9440; Jl Serma Mendara 3; massage per hr 80,000Rp; ☺9am 10pm) Many Balinese wouldn't think of having a massage from anyone but a blind person. Government-sponsored schools offer lengthy courses to certify blind people in reflexology, shiatsu massage, anatomy and much more. In this

Denpasar

Ubung Bus & Bemo Terminal (1.5km)

Wangaya Bemo Terminal

Jl Pattimura

Jl Setiabudi

Jl Sutomo

Jl Kartini

Jl Nakula

⊗17

⊕9

Jl Kedondong

Jl Werkudara

Jl Sahedawa

Jl Veteran

Jl Belimbing

Jl Melati

Jl Kambola

Jl Plawa

◎5

Jl Karna

Jl Durian

Gunung Agung
Bemo Terminal
(200m);
Poltabes
Denpasar
(1km)

Jl Gajah Mada

18

Jl Arjuna

8

⊕

Jl Surapati

♨4

14
⊗

Kereneng
Bemo
Terminal

Jl Surapati

Jl Imam Bonjol

Jl Thamrin

22
🔒

23 🔒

20 🔒

Jl Sumatra

🕉3

🏛2
Museum
Negeri
Propinsi
Bali

Jl Sugianyar

19
🔒

Jl Hasanudin

Jl Udayana

Jl Kapten Agung

Tegal Bemo
Terminal

Jl Nusakambangan

Jl Diponegoro

Jl Udayana

Jl Ki Hajar Dewantara

Jl Jayagiri

Letda Tantular

24
🔒

Jl Teuku Umar

RENON

State
Railway
Company

Kimia
Farma

21 🔒

SANGLAH

Damri
Office

7
⊕

Australian
Consulate

Nasi Uduk
Kebon Kacang
(1.2km)

RSUP Sanglah
Hospital

15
⊗

Paviliun
Amerta Wing
International

Jl Nias

12 ⊗

Jl Tukad Gangga

Jl Pulau Kanrata

Jl Diponegoro

Jepun Bali (750m);
Benoa Harbour (6km)

airy building redolent with liniments you can choose from a range of therapies.

⚓ Courses

Indonesia Australia Language Foundation   LANGUAGE
(IALF; ☎ 0361-225243; www.ialf.edu; Jl Raya Sesetan 190) The best place for serious courses in Bahasa Indonesia.

✨ Festivals & Events

★**Bali Arts Festival**   PERFORMING ARTS
(www.baliartsfestival.com; Taman Wedhi Budaya; ⊙ mid-Jun–mid-Jul) This annual festival, based at the Taman Wedhi Budaya arts centre, is an easy way to see a wide variety of traditional dance, music and crafts. The productions of the Ramayana and Mahabharata ballets are grand, and the opening ceremony and parade in Denpasar are spectacles. Tick-

Denpasar

ets are usually available before performances; schedules are available online and at the Denpasar tourist office.

The festival is the main event of the year for scores of village dance and musical groups. Competition is fierce, with local pride on the line at each performance ('our Kecak is better than your Kecak', etc). To do well here sets a village on a good course for the year. Some events are held in a 6000-seat amphitheatre, a venue that allows you to realise the mass appeal of traditional Balinese culture.

🛏 Sleeping

Denpasar has many new midpriced chain hotels, but it's hard to think of a compelling reason to stay here unless you want to revel in the city's bright lights. Most visitors stay in the tourist towns of the south and visit Denpasar as a day trip.

Nakula Familiar Inn   GUESTHOUSE $
(☑ 0361-226446; www.nakulafamiliarinn.com; JI Nakula 4; r 150,000-250,000Rp; ❋ ☏) The eight rooms at this sprightly urban family compound, a longtime traveller favourite, are clean and have small balconies. There is a nice courtyard and cafe in the middle. Tegal–Kereneng bemos go along JI Nakula.

Inna Bali   HOTEL $$
(☑ 0361-225681; www.innabali.com; JI Veteran 3; r 400,000-1,000,000Rp; ❋ ☏ ☀) The Inna Bali has simple gardens, a huge banyan tree and a certain nostalgic charm; it dates from 1927 and was once the main tourist hotel on the island. Room interiors are standard, but many have deeply shaded verandahs. Ongoing renovations have added an attractive colonial facade, including a decent sidewalk cafe.

🍴 Eating

Denpasar has the island's best range of Indonesian and Balinese food. Savvy locals and expats each have their own favourite warungs and restaurants.

New places open regularly on JI Teuku Umar, while in Renon there is a phenomenal strip of eating places on JI Cok Agung Tresna between JI Ramayana and JI Dewi Madri and along Letda Tantular. See what you can discover.

★ Depot Cak Asmo   INDONESIAN $
(☑ 0361-798 9388; JI Tukad Gangga; mains from 15,000Rp; ❂ 9.30am-10.30pm) Join the government workers and students from the nearby university for superb dishes cooked to order in the bustling kitchen. Order the buttery and crispy *cumi cumi* (calamari) battered in *telor asin* (a heavenly mixture of eggs and garlic). Fruity ice drinks are a cooling treat. An English-language menu makes ordering a breeze. It's halal, so there's no alcohol.

★ Men Gabrug   BALINESE $
(JI Drupadi; snacks from 10,000Rp; ❂ 8am-6pm) A favourite sweet treat for Balinese of all ages is *jaje laklak* – disks of rice flour cooked in an open-air cast-iron pan, and redolent of coconut. One of the best places to get them is at this family-run outlet where the cooking takes place right on the street.

Bakso Supra Dinasty   BALINESE $
(JI Cok Agung Tresna; mains from 15,000Rp; ❂ 8am-10pm) One taste of the soup assembled to order out of the steaming vats at this small stall and you'll agree that the name (translated: Meatball Super Dynasty) is fully deserved. The broth is rich and the meatballs are filled with flavour.

Warung Wardani   INDONESIAN $
(☑ 0361-224398; JI Yudistira 2; nasi campur from 35,000Rp; ❂ 8am-4pm) Don't be deceived by the small dining room at the entrance: there's another vastly larger one out the back. The top-notch *nasi campur* (rice with side dishes) draws in the masses for lunch daily.

Warung Bundaran Renon   BALINESE $
(☑ 0361-234208; JI Raya Puputan 212; meals from 40,000Rp; ❂ 9am-5pm) A slightly upscale *babi guling* place with excellent plate lunches of same. It feels a bit like a suburban house and there's a shady patio.

Pondok Kuring   INDONESIAN $
(☑ 0361-234122; JI Raya Puputan 56; meals from 20,000Rp; ❂ 10am-9.30pm) The foods of the Sundanese people of west Java are the speciality here. Highly spiced vegetables, meat and seafood draw flavours from an array of herbs. Deceptively simple, the *lalapan* (fresh green salad) is excellent. This glossy restaurant has an arty dining room and a lovely and quiet garden out back.

Warung Lembongan   INDONESIAN $
(☑ 0361-236885; JI Cok Agung Tresna 6C; meals 17,000-25,000Rp; ❂ 8am-10pm) Silver folding chairs at long tables, shaded by a garish green awning out front. These are details

you will quickly forget after you have the house speciality: chicken lightly fried yet delicately crispy like the top of a perfect crème brûlée. The other speciality is a spicy *sop kepala ikan* (fish soup).

Ayam Goreng Kalasan INDONESIAN $
(☏0813 3950 5150; Jl Cok Agung Tresna 6; mains 12,000-25,000Rp; ⊙8am-10pm) The name here says it all: fried chicken (*ayam goreng*) named for a Javanese temple (Kalasan) in a region renowned for its fiery, crispy chicken. Note the hint of lemongrass imbued by a long marination before cooking.

Nasi Uduk Kebon Kacang INDONESIAN $
(☏0812 466 6828; Jl Teuku Umar 230; meals 12,000-25,000Rp; ⊙8am-midnight) Open to the street, this spotless cafe serves up Javanese treats such as *nasi uduk* (sweetly scented coconut rice with fresh peanut sauce) and *lalapan* (a simple salad of fresh lemon basil leaves). Chicken dishes win raves.

Pasar Malam Kereneng MARKET $
(Kereneng Night Market; Jl Kamboja; meals from 10,000Rp; ⊙6pm-5am) At this excellent night market dozens of vendors dish up food until dawn.

🍷 Drinking & Nightlife

★ Bhineka Djaja COFFEE
(☏0361-224016; Jl Gajah Mada 80; coffee 7000Rp; ⊙9am-4pm Mon-Sat) Home to Bali's Coffee Co, this storefront sells locally grown beans and makes a mean espresso, which you can enjoy at the two tiny tables while watching the bustle of Denpasar's old main drag.

🔒 Shopping

Markets
Denpasar's largest traditional markets are in a fairly compact area that makes visiting them easy, even if navigating their crowded aisles across multiple floors is not. Like other aspects of Balinese life, the big markets are in flux. Large chain supermarkets are biting into their trade and the evolving middle class say they prefer the likes of Carrefour because it has more imported goods. But the public markets aren't down yet. This is where you come for purely Balinese goods, such as temple offerings, ceremonial clothes and a range of foodstuffs unique to the island, including numerous types of mangosteen.

Pasar Badung MARKET
(Jl Gajah Mada; ⊙6am-5pm) Bali's largest food market is recovering from a 2016 fire. While rebuilding continues, there are ad hoc stalls in the surrounding area. Busy in the mornings and evenings, it's a great place to browse and bargain. You'll find produce and food from all over the island, and will revel in the range of fruits and spices on offer.

Pasar Kumbasari MARKET
(Jl Gajah Mada; ⊙8am-6pm) Handicrafts, a plethora of vibrant fabrics and costumes decorated with gold are just some of the goods at this huge market across the river from Pasar Badung. Note that the malls have taken their toll and there are a lot of empty stalls.

Kampung Arab MARKET
(Jl Hasanudin & Jl Sulawesi) Has jewellery and precious-metal stores run by scores of Middle Eastern and Indian merchants.

Textiles
Follow Jl Sulawesi north and, just as the glitter of Kampung Arab fades, the street glows anew as you come upon a strip of fabric stores. The textiles here – batiks, cottons, silks – come in colours that make Barbie look like an old purse. It's immediately east of Pasar Badung. Many shops are closed Sunday.

★ Jepun Bali TEXTILES
(☏0361-726526; Jl Raya Sesetan, Gang Ikan Mas 11; ⊙call for appointment) It's like your own private version of the Museum Negeri Propinsi Bali: Gusti Ayu Made Mardiani is locally famous for her *endek* and *songket* clothes woven using traditional techniques. You can visit her gracious home and workshop and see the old machines in action, then ponder her beautiful polychromatic selections in silk and cotton. She's in south Denpasar.

Maju TEXTILES
(☏0361-224003; Jl Sulawesi 19; ⊙9am-6pm) Jammed into a string of fabric stores just east of Pasar Badung, this narrow shop stands out for its huge selection of genuine Balinese batik. The colours and patterns are bewildering, while the clearly marked reasonable prices are not.

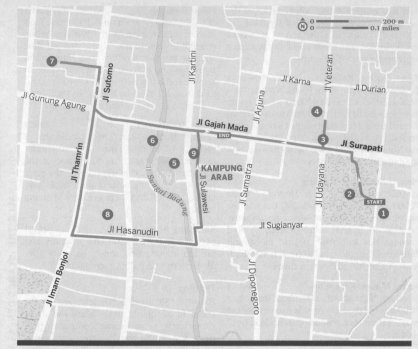

🏃 City Walk
Strolling Denpasar

START MUSEUM NEGERI PROPINSI BALI
END JL GAJAH MADA
LENGTH 2.5KM; TWO HOURS

While Denpasar can seem formidable and traf-fic-choked, it rewards those who explore on foot. This walk includes most attractions in the historic centre of town and a few vestiges of when Bali moved at a slower pace. Allow extra time for visiting the museum or for shopping.

Start the walk at **1 Museum Negeri Propinsi Bali** (p128). Opposite is large and green **2 Puputan Square** (p129).

Back on the corner of Jl Surapati and Jl Veteran is the towering **3 Catur Muka statue**, which represents Batara Guru, Lord of the Four Directions. The four-faced, eight-armed figure keeps a close eye (or eight) on the traffic swirling around him. Head 100m north on Jl Veteran to the **4 Inna Bali hotel** (p131), a favourite of longtime Indonesian dictator Sukarno.

Return to the Catur Muka statue and head west on Jl Gajah Mada (named after the

14th-century Majapahit prime minister). Go past banks, shops and a cafe towards the bridge over the grubby Sungai Badung (Ba-dung River). Just before the bridge, on the left, is the renovated **5 Pasar Badung** (p133), the main produce market, which is recovering from a fire. On the left, just after the bridge, is **6 Pasar Kumbasari** (p133), where you will find handicrafts, fabrics and costumes.

At the next main intersection, detour north up Jl Sutomo, and turn left along a small *gang* (alley) leading to the **7 Pura Maospa-hit temple** (p129).

Turn back, and continue south along Jl Thamrin to the junction of Jl Hasanudin. On this corner is the **8 Puri Pemecutan**, a pal-ace destroyed in the 1906 Dutch invasion. It's long since been rebuilt; you can look inside the compound, but don't expect anything palatial.

Go east on Jl Hasanudin, then north on to **9 Jl Sulawesi**, past its markets. Continue north past Pasar Badung market to return to Jl Gajah Mada. You could save your visit to the Museum Negeri Propinsi Bali for the end, when you'll just want to move slowly.

Malls

Western-style shopping malls are jammed on Sundays with locals shopping and teens flirting; the brand-name goods are genuine.

Most malls have a food court with stalls serving fresh Asian fare, as well as fast-food joints.

Matahari   MALL
(Jl Teuku Umar; ⊙10am-10pm) Main branch of the department store plus numerous other shops.

Robinson's   MALL
(cnr Jl Teuku Umar & Jl Sudirman) Matahari's arch-competitor has a large selection of mid-range goods.

ⓘ Information

MEDICAL SERVICES
Denpasar has many medical providers that serve the entire island.
BaliMed Hospital (p394) On the Kerobokan side of Denpasar.
RSUP Sanglah Hospital (p395) The city's general hospital has English-speaking staff and an ER. It has a special wing for well-insured foreigners.
Kimia Farma (☑0361-227811; Jl Diponegoro 125; ⊙24hr) The main outlet of the island-wide pharmacy chain has the largest selection of prescription medications in Bali.

POLICE
Call ☑0361-224111 for the tourist police.
Police Station (☑0361-424346; Jl Pattimura) The place for any general problems.

POST
Main Post Office (☑0361-223565; Jl Raya Puputan; ⊙8am-9pm Mon-Fri, to 8pm Sat) Your best option for unusual postal needs. Has a photocopy centre and ATMs.

ⓘ Getting There & Away

Denpasar is a hub of public transport in Bali – you'll find buses and minibuses bound for all corners of the island.

AIR
Sometimes called 'Denpasar' in airline schedules, Bali's Ngurah Rai International Airport is 12km south in Kuta.

BEMO & MINIBUS
The city has several bemo and bus terminals – if you're travelling by bemo around Bali you'll often have to go via Denpasar, and transfer from one terminal to another by bemo (7000Rp).

Note that the bemo network is sputtering and fares are approximate and at times completely subjective. Drivers often try to charge nonlocals at least 25% more.

Ubung
Well north of the town, on the road to Gilimanuk, the **Ubung Bus & Bemo Terminal** is the hub for northern and western Bali. It also has long-distance buses in addition to the ones serving the terminal 12km northwest in Mengwi.

DESTINATION	FARE
Gilimanuk (for the ferry to Java)	45,000Rp
Mengwi bus terminal	15,000Rp
Munduk	20,000Rp
Singaraja (via Pupuan or Bedugul)	40,000Rp

Batubulan
Located a very inconvenient 6km northeast of Denpasar on a road to Ubud, this terminal is for destinations in eastern and central Bali.

DESTINATION	FARE
Amlapura	25,000Rp
Padangbai (for the Lombok ferry)	18,000Rp
Sanur	7000Rp
Ubud	13,000Rp

Tegal
On the western side of town on Jl Iman Bonjol, Tegal Bemo Terminal is the terminal for Kuta and the Bukit Peninsula.

DESTINATION	FARE
Airport	15,000Rp
Jimbaran	17,000Rp
Kuta	13,000Rp

Kereneng
East of the town centre, Kereneng Bemo Terminal has bemos to Sanur (7000Rp).

Wangaya
Near the centre of town, this small terminal is the departure point for bemo services to northern Denpasar and the outlying Ubung bus terminal (8000Rp).

Gunung Agung
This **terminal** (Jl Gunung Agung), at the northwestern corner of town (look for orange bemo), is on Jl Gunung Agung, and has bemos to Kerobokan and Canggu (10,000Rp).

BUS

Long-distance bus services use the Ubung Bus & Bemo Terminal, well north of town. Most long-distance services also stop at the Mengwi terminal.

Damri office (☑ 0361-232793; Jl Diponegoro) Ticket office for long-distance buses.

TRAIN

Bali doesn't have trains but the state railway company does have an office (p387) in Denpasar. Buses leave from the nearby Damri office and travel to eastern Java where they link with trains at Banyuwangi for Surabaya, Yogyakarta and Jakarta among others. Fares and times are comparable to the bus but the air-conditioned trains are more comfortable, even in economy class.

❶ Getting Around

BEMO

Bemos take various circuitous routes from and between Denpasar's many bus/bemo terminals. They line up for various destinations at each terminal, or you can try and hail them from anywhere along the main roads – look for the destination sign above the driver's window.

TAXI

As always, the cabs of Blue Bird Taxi (p392) are the most reliable choice.

NUSA LEMBONGAN & ISLANDS

Look towards the open ocean southeast of Bali and the hazy bulk of Nusa Penida dominates the view. But for many visitors the real focus is Nusa Lembongan, which lurks in the shadow of its vastly larger neighbour. Here, there's great surfing, amazing diving, languorous beaches and the kind of laid-back vibe travellers cherish.

Once ignored, Nusa Penida is now attracting visitors, but its dramatic vistas and unchanged village life are still yours to explore. Tiny Nusa Ceningan huddles between the larger islands. It's a quick and popular jaunt from Lembongan.

The islands have been a poor region for many years. Thin soils and a lack of fresh water do not permit the cultivation of rice, but other crops such as maize, cassava and beans are staples grown here. The main cash crop has been seaweed, although the big harvest now comes on two legs.

Nusa Lembongan

☑ 0366

Once the domain of shack-staying surfers, Nusa Lembongan has hit the big time. Yes, you can still get a simple room with a view of the surf breaks and the gorgeous sunsets but now you can also stay in a boutique hotel and have a fabulous meal.

But even as Nusa Lembongan's popularity grows, it keeps a mellow vibe. The new-found wealth is bringing changes though: you'll see boys riding motorcycles 300m to school, temples being expensively renovated, multistorey hotels being built and time being marked by the arrival of tourist boats (which still lack any kind of dock). While you can still cock your ear to the crow of a rooster or the fall of a coconut, you may also need to be ready to get stuck in traffic.

◉ Sights

Jungutbatu Beach   BEACH

The beach here, a mostly lovely arc of white sand with clear blue water, has views across to Gunung Agung in Bali. The pleasant **sea-wall walkway** is ideal for strolling, especially – as you'd guess – at sunset. Floating boats save the scene from being clichéd idyllic. The once redolent odour of drying farmed seaweed is fading away as all available land is turned over to tourism.

Pantai Tanjung Sanghyang   BEACH

(Mushroom Bay) This beautiful bay, unofficially named Mushroom Bay after the mushroom corals offshore, has a crescent of bright white beach. By day, the tranquillity can be disturbed by banana-boat riders or parasailers. At other hours, this is a beach of dreams.

The most interesting way to get here from Jungutbatu is to walk along the trail that starts from the southern end of the main beach and follows the coastline for a kilometre or so. Alternatively, get a boat from Jungutbatu.

Pantai Selegimpak   BEACH

The long, straight beach is usually lapped by small waves at this remote-feeling spot where unfortunately some guesthouses have built seawalls below the low-tide line. This makes an easy traverse at high tide tough. About 200m east along the shoreline path where it goes up and over a knoll is a minute cove with a nub of sand, good swimming and a tiny warung.

Dream Beach   BEACH

Down a lane, on the southwestern side of the island, Dream Beach is a 150m deep pocket of white sand with pounding surf and pretty azure waters. From the right angle it looks lovely – until you see the ugly hotel that's been built over one end. It also gets unpleasantly crowded with day trippers.

⊙ Jungutbatu

The village itself is mellow, although lanes buzz with motorcycles and the rumble of trucks. **Pura Segara** and its enormous **sacred tree** are the site of frequent ceremonies.

The northern end of town holds the metal-legged **lighthouse**. Follow the road

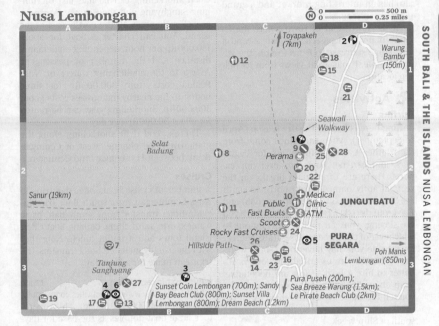

Nusa Lembongan

0 — 500 m
0 — 0.25 miles

SOUTH BALI & THE ISLANDS NUSA LEMBONGAN

Nusa Lembongan

around east for about 1km to **Pura Sakenan**.

Lembongan

The main town on the island looks across the seaweed-farm-filled channel to Nusa Ceningan. It's a beautiful scene of clear water and green hills. A few cafes have sprung up to take advantage of the view. The town also has an interesting **market** and a grand old **banyan tree**.

At the north end of town where the island's main road passes, you can ascend a long stone staircase to **Pura Puseh**, the village temple. It has great views from its hilltop location.

Activities

Surfing

Surfing here is best in the dry season (April to September), when the winds come from the southeast. It's definitely not for beginners, and can be dangerous even for experts. There are three main breaks on the reef, all aptly named. From north to south are Shipwrecks (p33), Lacerations (p33) and Playgrounds (p34). Depending on where you are staying, you can paddle directly out to whichever of the three is closest (although at lowest tide you may have to do some walking so booties are essential); for others it's better to hire a boat. Prices are negotiable, from about 70,000Rp for a one-way trip – you tell the owner when to return. A fourth break – **Racecourses** – sometimes emerges south of Shipwreck.

The surf can be crowded here even when the island isn't – charter boats from Bali sometimes bring groups of surfers for day trips from the mainland for a minimum of 1,000,000Rp.

Monkey Surfing   SURFING
(☑ 0821 4614 7683; www.monkeysurfing.com; Jungutbatu Beach; surfboard rental per day 110,000Rp, lessons from 550,000Rp; ☺ 8am-7pm) Rent surfboards and stand-up paddle boards from this shop on the beach, which offers guiding services.

Diving

★ **World Diving**   DIVING
(☑ 0812 390 0686; www.world-diving.com; Jungutbatu Beach; introductory dive 940,000Rp, open-water course 5,500,000Rp) World Diving, based at Pondok Baruna, is very well regarded. It offers a complete range of courses, plus div-

ing trips to dive sites all around the three islands. Equipment is first-rate.

Lembongan Dive Center   DIVING
(☑ 0821 4535 2666; www.lembongandivecenter. com; Jungubatu Beach; s dive from 500,000Rp, open-water course 4,950,000Rp) A recommended local dive centre.

Snorkelling

Good snorkelling can be had just off Tanjung Sanghyang and the **Bounty Pontoon**, as well as in areas off the north coast of the island. You can charter a boat for about 150,000Rp per hour, depending on demand, distance and the number of passengers. A trip to the challenging waters of Nusa Penida costs from 300,000Rp for three hours; to the nearby mangroves costs about 300,000Rp. Snorkelling gear can be rented for about 30,000Rp per day.

There's good drift snorkelling along the mangrove-filled channel west of Ceningan Point, between Lembongan and Ceningan.

Cruises

A number of cruise boats offer day trips to Nusa Lembongan from south Bali. Trips include hotel transfer from south Bali, basic water sports, snorkelling, banana-boat rides, island tours and a buffet lunch. Note that with the usually included hotel transfers, the trips can make for a long day.

Island Explorer Cruise   CRUISE
(☑ 0361-728088; www.bali-activities.com; adult/child from 1,400,000/700,000Rp) This operator's large boat doubles as the base for daytrip aquatic fun. It also has a sailing ship and fast boats for transfers. Boats leave from Benoa Harbour. It's affiliated with Coconuts Beach Resort.

Bounty Cruise   CRUISE
(☑ 0361-726666; www.balibountycruises.com; adult/child US$119/59.50) Boats dock at the garish yellow offshore Bounty pontoon with water slides and other amusements. The boat departs from Benoa Harbour.

Hiking & Biking

You can circumnavigate the island in a day on foot, or less on a bike. It's a fascinating journey into the small island's surprisingly diverse scenery. Start on the hillside path from **Jungutbatu** and overcome whatever obstacles developers have put on the path to **Tanjung Sanghyang**; with a little Tarzan spirit you can stay with the faint trail (you can't do this segment by bike: use the roads inland).

DIVING THE ISLANDS

There are great diving possibilities around the islands, from shallow and sheltered reefs, mainly on the northern side of Lembongan and Penida, to very demanding drift dives in the channel between Penida and the other two islands. Vigilant locals have protected their waters from dynamite bombing by renegade fishing boats, so the reefs are relatively intact. And a side benefit of tourism is that locals no longer rely so much on fishing. In 2012 the islands were designated the Nusa Penida Marine Protected Area, which encompasses more than 20,000 hectares of the surrounding waters.

If you arrange a dive trip from Padangbai or south Bali, stick with the most reputable operators, as conditions here can be tricky and local knowledge is essential. Diving accidents regularly happen and people die diving in the waters around the islands every year.

Using one of the recommended operators on Nusa Lembongan puts you close to the action from the start. The large marine animals are a particular attraction, including turtles, sharks and manta rays. The large (3m fin-to-fin) and unusual *mola mola* (sunfish) is sometimes seen around the islands between mid-July and October, while manta rays are often seen south of Nusa Penida from June to October.

The best dive sites include **Blue Corner** and **Jackfish Point** off Nusa Lembongan and **Ceningan Point** at the tip of that island. The channel between Ceningan and Penida is renowned for drift diving, but it is essential you have a good operator who can judge fast-changing currents and other conditions. Upswells can bring cold water from the open ocean to sites such as **Ceningan Wall**. This is one of the world's deepest natural channels and attracts all manner and sizes of fish.

Sites close to Nusa Penida include **Crystal Bay, SD, Pura Ped, Manta Point** and **Batu Aba**. Of these, Crystal Bay, SD and Pura Ped are suitable for novice divers and are good for snorkelling. Note that the open waters around Penida are challenging, even for experienced divers.

SOUTH BALI & THE ISLANDS NUSA LEMBONGAN

Next head to **Lembongan** village. Once the bridge has been rebuilt, you can follow it to **Nusa Ceningen**. Alternatively, from Lembongan village you take a gentle uphill walk along the sealed road to the killer hill that leads *down* to Jungutbatu, which cuts the circuit to about half a day.

To fully explore the island by foot, stick to the paved road that follows the channel between Nusa Lembongan and Nusa Ceningen. After a rugged uphill detour, curve back down and go north along the mangroves all the way to the **lighthouse**.

Bikes are easily rented for about 30,000Rp per day.

🛏 Sleeping & Eating

Rooms and amenities generally become increasingly posh as you head south and west along the water to Mushroom Bay.

🛏 Jungutbatu

Many lodgings in Jungutbatu have shed the surfer-shack cliché and are moving upmarket. But you can still find cheapies with cold water and fans.

★ Pondok Baruna
GUESTHOUSE **$**

(📱0812 394 0992; www.pondokbaruna.com; Jungutbatu Beach; r 350,000-650,000Rp; ❄🤶📶) Associated with World Diving, a local dive operator, this place offers fantastic rooms with terraces facing the ocean. Plusher rooms surround a dive pool behind the beach. There are another eight rooms at sister site Pondok Baruna Frangipani, set back in the palm trees around a large pool. Staff members, led by Putu, are charmers.

Secret Garden Bungalows
GUESTHOUSE **$**

(📱0813 5313 6861; www.bigfishdiving.com; Jungutbatu Beach; r with fan/air-con 250,000/400,000Rp; ❄🤶📶) 🏊 Affiliated with Big Fish Diving, there are nine bungalow-style cold-water and fan rooms in this palm-shaded compound back off the beach. Nearby there are also some newer air-con bungalows. It has on-site yoga classes for 100,000Rp. Marine Mega Fauna gives regular talks here about the amazing marine ecology around the islands.

★ Pemedal Beach
GUESTHOUSE **$$**

(📱0366-559 6394; www.pemedalbeach.com; Jungutbatu Beach; r from 500,000Rp; ❄🤶📶) A lovely affordable option if you want to be near a sandy beach; the 11 bungalows are set back a bit with an infinity pool.

Pondok Baruna Frangipani   GUESTHOUSE $$
(📲 0812 394 0992; www.pondokbaruna.com; Jungutbatu; r incl breakfast 750,000-850,000Rp; ❋ 🛜 🏊) The more upmarket sister guesthouse to Ponduk Baruna on the waterfront, Frangipani has spacious, luxurious rooms and a good-sized pool.

★**Indiana Kenanga**   BOUTIQUE HOTEL $$$
(📲 0828 9708 4367; www.indiana-kenanga-villas. com; Jungutbatu Beach; r US$150-650; ❋ 🛜 🏊) Two posh villas and 16 stylish suites shelter near a pool behind the beach at Lembongan's most upscale digs. The French designer-owner has decorated the place with Buddhist statues, purple armchairs and other whimsical touches. The restaurant has an all-day menu of seafood and various surprises cooked up by the skilled chef, plus there's a poolside creperie!

Bali Eco Deli   CAFE $
(📲 0812 3704 9234; www.baliecodeli.net; Jungutbatu; mains from 35,000Rp; ⏰ 7am-10pm) 🌿 This irresistible cafe has great green cred and is noted for giving back to the community. But what it gives customers is also good: fresh and creative breakfasts, healthy snacks, delicious baked goods, good coffees and juices plus an array of salads, all served in a garden setting.

Pondok Baruna Warung   INDONESIAN $
(Jungutbatu; mains from 40,000Rp; ⏰ 8am-10pm) The dining part of the Baruna empire boasts some of the best food on the island. Look for excellent Balinese dishes as well as a range of fine curries. Many order not one but two chocolate brownies.

★**Warung Bambu**   SEAFOOD $$
(📲 0813 3867 5451; Jungutbatu; mains 60,000-100,000Rp; ⏰ 9am-10pm) On the road to the mangroves, past the lighthouse, this family-run restaurant serves excellent seafood meals. The menu depends on what's caught offshore. Tables are on a large covered terrace with a sandy floor. By day you may luck out with Gunung Agung views, by night the lights of Bali twinkle.

99 Meals House   INDONESIAN, CHINESE $
(Jungutbatu Beach; mains from 15,000Rp; ⏰ 8am-10pm) An absolute bargain. Fried rice, omelettes, Chinese stir-fries and more prepared by a family at this great open-air spot overlooking the beach.

🛏 Hillside

The steep hillside just south of Jungutbatu offers great views and an ever-increasing number of luxurious rooms. The uppermost rooms at some places have gorgeous views across the water to Bali (on a clear day say hello to Gunung Agung), but such thrills come at a cost: upwards of 120 steep concrete steps. A motorcycle-friendly path runs along the top of the hill, good for leg-saving drop-offs.

Ware Ware Surf Bungalows   GUESTHOUSE $$
(📲 0812 397 0572, 0812 380 3321; www.warewaresurfbungalows.com; r incl breakfast from 750,000Rp; ❋ 🛜 🏊) The nine units at this hillside place are a mix of square and circular numbers with thatched roofs and balconies. The large rooms (some with fan only) have rattan couches and big bathrooms. The cafe scores with its spectacular, breezy location on a large cliff-side wooden deck.

Batu Karang   HOTEL $$$
(📲 0366-559 6376; www.batukaranglembongan.com; r incl breakfast from 2,200,000Rp; ❋ @ 🛜 🏊) This upmarket resort perched on a terraced hillside has a large infinity pool. Some of its 25 luxury units are villa-style and have multiple rooms and private plunge pools. All have open-air bathrooms and wooden terraces with sweeping views. Right on the hillside path, The hotel's Deck Cafe & Bar is a good pause for a gourmet snack or a drink.

Lembongan Island Beach Villas   VILLA $$$
(📲 0366-559 6398; www.lembonganbeachvillas. com; villa US$170-220; ❋ 🛜 🏊) Eleven luxe villas climb a hillside from a lobby right by the corner of Jungutbatu Beach. Units have comfy wicker loungers and hammocks as well as large kitchens. The covered balconies have great views across to Bali.

★**Deck Cafe & Bar**   CAFE $
(http://thedecklembongan.com; mains from 85,000Rp; ⏰ 7.30am-11pm; 🛜) Straddling the main hillside walkway, the stylish bar and cafe of the Batu Karang hotel offers creative drinks from a long list, gorgeous views and interesting snacks (it has a good bakery) plus upscale pub fare. On Sunday there's a DJ.

AQUATIC ALLIANCE

The waters around Nusa Lembongan, Ceningan and Penida are filled with some truly spectacular creatures: huge manta rays, the ponderous *mola mola* and more. Yet while they are regularly spotted by flocks of divers who explore these rich waters, little is known about the actual ecology of the area – except that it's remarkable.

A group called **Marine Mega Fauna** (www.marinemegafauna.org) is working to change that. Through extensive field studies they are beginning to understand just what's swimming around out there. One early discovery: like whales, manta rays have markings that make it easy to identify individuals. The group's website is filled with fascinating information and you can learn more at their regular public talks at the Secret Garden Bungalows (p139).

Tanjung Sanghyang

It's your own treasure island. Also known as Mushroom Bay, there is a nice beach, plenty of overhanging trees and some of the most atmospheric lodging on Lembongan. Get here from Jungutbatu by foot or with a ride (15,000Rp) or boat (70,000Rp).

Alam Nusa Huts   GUESTHOUSE $
(0819 1662 6336; www.alamnusahuts.com; r from 475,000Rp; ❇🛜) This small property is less than 100m from the beach. Four bungalows sit in a small, lush garden; each has an open-air bathroom and a secluded terrace. The interiors feature a lot of rich wood and bamboo. The staff are especially welcoming.

Nusa Bay Lembongan   HOTEL $$$
(0361-484085; www.wakahotelsandresorts.com; bungalow from US$200; ❇🛜🏊) A primitive motif blends with creature comforts at this low-key resort run by the Waka group. The 10 thatch-roofed bungalows are set on sandy grounds at the shore. The beachside restaurant and bar are shaded by coconut palms and you can dine on the sand.

★**Hai Bar & Grill**   INTERNATIONAL $$
(0361-720331; www.haitidebeachresort.com/hai-bar-and-grill; Hai Tide Beach Resort; mains 60,000-150,000Rp; ☺7am-10pm; 🛜) This wide-open bar with wide-open views of the bay and sunsets is the most stylish restaurant bar along Tanjung Sanghyang. The menu mixes Asian and Western dishes, and there are comforts such as fresh-baked muffins. You can use the pool if you eat here, and open-air movies screen some nights. Call for pickup from Jungutbatu.

Elsewhere on Lembongan

Poh Manis Lembongan   GUESTHOUSE $
(0821 4746 2726; www.pohmanislembongan.com; r US$32-50; ❇🛜🏊) If Nusa Lembongan is a getaway, this is the getaway from Nusa Lembongan. Perched on a bluff on the southeast corner of the island, there are sweeping views of the other two Nusas. The pool area is lovely and the 10 rooms are light and airy with a woodsy charm.

Sunset Coin Lembongan   GUESTHOUSE $$
(0812 364 0799; www.sunsetcoinlembongan.com; Sunset Bay; r incl breakfast from 1,100,000Rp; ❇🛜🏊) Run by an awesome family, this collection of 10 cottages is everything an island escape should be. It's near the sweet little spot of sand called Sunset Bay. The *lumbung*-style units (thatched rice barn) have terraces and fridges.

Sunset Villa Lembongan   GUESTHOUSE $$
(0812 381 9023; www.sunsetvillaslembongan.com; Sunset Bay; r US$40-70; ❇🛜🏊) Twelve modern-style bungalows are arrayed around a large pool in a newish compound with fast-growing vegetation. The units have terraces and sitting areas; some have fridges. The large open-air bathrooms have natural stone details.

Point Resort Lembongan   INN $$$
(www.thepointlembongan.com; ste from US$160; ❇🛜🏊) About 500m west of Tanjung Sanghyang is this eponymously named property with four plush suites. The views are sweeping, and should pirates sail in you can watch them get dashed on the rocks below the infinity pool. The units are bright and airy, with lovely sitting areas.

Sandy Bay Beach Club INTERNATIONAL $$
(0828 9700 5656; www.sandybaylembongan.com; Sunset Bay; mains from 55,000Rp; 8.30am-10.30pm;) Pushing the distressed bleached-wood look for all it's worth, this appealing beach club occupies a fine position on a sweet pocket of sand most call Sunset Beach (unless you're this place and call it Sandy Bay...). The menu spans Asia and Europe, with a detour to Burgerville. The evening seafood barbecues are popular. The beach here is less crowded than Dream Beach.

❶ Information

MEDICAL SERVICES

Medical Clinic (consultation from 250,000Rp; 8am-6pm) The medical clinic in the village has a modern building and is well versed in treating minor surfing injuries and ear ailments.

MONEY

It's vital that you bring sufficient cash in rupiah for your stay, as there is only one ATM and it won't accept most foreign cards, even when it actually has cash to dispense.

❶ Getting There & Away

Getting to/from Nusa Lembongan offers numerous choices, some quite fast. Note: anyone with money for a speedboat is getting into the fast-boat act; be wary of fly-by-night operators with fly-by-night safety.

Boats anchor offshore, so be prepared to get your feet wet. And travel light – wheeled bags are comically inappropriate in the water and on the beach and dirt tracks. Porters will shoulder your steamer trunk for 20,000Rp (and don't be like some low-lifes we've seen who have stiffed them for their service).

Perama (www.peramatour.com; Jungutbatu Beach; one-way 140,000Rp) Runs one good-value boat to Sanur daily. It takes less than an hour.

Public Fast Boats (one-way 150,000Rp) Leave from the northern end of Sanur Beach for Nusa Lembongan three times daily and take 40 minutes.

---

❶ BOAT SAFETY

There have been accidents involving boats between Bali and the surrounding islands. These services are unregulated and there is no safety authority should trouble arise. Take precautions (p388).

Rocky Fast Cruises (0361-283624; www.rockyfastcruise.com; Jungubatu Beach; one-way/return US$30/50) Runs four large boats daily that take 30 minutes.

Scoot (0361-285522; www.scootcruise.com; one-way adult/child 400,000/280,000Rp) Makes four trips daily; each takes 30 minutes.

❶ Getting Around

The island is fairly small and you can walk to most places. There are no cars (although pick-up trucks are proliferating); bicycles (30,000Rp per day) and small motorcycles (50,000Rp per day) are widely available for hire. One-way rides on motorcycles or trucks cost 15,000Rp and up. One unwelcome development is the SUV-sized golf carts that seem to be mostly rented by tourists who find a big cigar to be the perfect driving companion.

Nusa Ceningan

Tiny Nusa Ceningan is usually connected to Nusa Lembongan by an atmospheric – and rickety – narrow **suspension bridge** crossing the lagoon. However, in 2016 the bridge failed and nine people were killed. It remains to be seen if a replacement will be more substantial.

Normally the bridge makes it quite easy to explore the island. Besides the lagoon filled with frames for seaweed farming, you'll see several small agricultural plots and a fishing village. Nusa Ceningan is quite hilly and, if you're up for it, you can get glimpses of great scenery while wandering or cycling around. Key roads have been paved, which is opening up the island, although it is still very rural.

There's a **surf break**, named for its location at Ceningan Point, in the southwest; it's an exposed left-hander.

🏃 Activities

★ JED TOUR

(Village Ecotourism Network; 0361-366 9951, 0813 3842 7197; www.jed.or.id; per person US$150) To really savour Nusa Ceningan, take an overnight tour of the island with JED, a cultural organisation that gives people an in-depth look at village and cultural life. Trips include family accommodation in a village, local meals, a fascinating tour with seaweed workers and transport to/from mainland Bali.

FORSAKING SEAWEED

Few ice-cream fans know this but they owe big thanks to the seaweed growers of Nusa Lembongan, Nusa Ceningan and Nusa Penida. Carrageenan, an emulsifying agent that is used to thicken ice cream as well as cheese and many other products, is derived from the seaweed grown here.

As you walk around the villages, you'll see – and smell – vast areas used for drying seaweed. Looking down into the water, you'll see the patchwork of cultivated seaweed plots. The islands are especially good for production, as the waters are shallow and rich in nutrients. The dried red and green seaweed is exported around the world for final processing.

But for how much longer is the real question. Farming seaweed is back-breaking work with tiny returns. Where just a decade ago 85% of Lembongan's people farmed seaweed, today that number is quickly diminishing as the population gets caught up in the tourist boom, with its comparatively better wages and much easier work.

And Nusa Penida is just a little way behind. We asked one former seaweed farmer who now works as a guide if he missed the work. His response was comically unprintable.

🛏 Sleeping & Eating

Le Pirate Beach Club   GUESTHOUSE $$
(☑0811 388 3701, reservations 0361-733493; www.lepirate-beachclub.com; r incl breakfast from 700,000Rp; ❄🛜🏊) With a colour scheme of sprightly white and blue, the theme here is retro-chic island kitsch. The accommodation consists of air-conditioned beach boxes, which range from bunk beds that sleep four to doubles. The popular restaurant looks over the small kidney-shaped pool and has broad views of the channel. Two-night minimum.

Secret Point Huts   GUESTHOUSE $$
(☑0819 9937 0826; www.secretpointhuts.com; r from US$80; ❄🛜🏊) In the southwest corner of the island overlooking the Ceningan Point surf break, this cute little resort has a tiny beach and clifftop bar. The rooms are in *lumbung* (rice barn) style bungalows with open-air bathrooms.

Sea Breeze Warung   INDONESIAN $
(mains 30,000-70,000Rp; ☺8am-10pm) The charming Sea Breeze has a great location overlooking the channel and the seaweed harvest, and an attractive open-air setting decorated with plants. It offers an excellent seafood selection, and does a tasty *nasi campur*. And the Bintang is always cold.

Nusa Penida

Just beginning to appear on visitor itineraries, Nusa Penida still awaits discovery. It's an untrammelled place that answers the question: what would Bali be like if tourists never came? There are not a lot of formal activities or sights; rather, you go to Nusa Penida to explore and relax, to adapt to the slow rhythm of life here.

The island is a limestone plateau with a strip of sand on its north coast, and views over the water to the volcanoes in Bali. The south coast has 300m-high limestone cliffs dropping straight down to the sea and a row of offshore islets – it's rugged and spectacular scenery. The interior is hilly, with sparse-looking crops and old-fashioned villages. Rainfall is low and parts of the island are arid, although you can see traces of ancient rice terraces.

Beaches are very few although some are spectacular.

The population of around 60,000 is predominantly Hindu, although there is a Muslim community in Toyapakeh. It's an unforgiving area: Nusa Penida was once used as a place of banishment for criminals and other undesirables from the kingdom of Klungkung (now Semarapura), and still has a somewhat sinister reputation. Yet it's also a centre of rebirth: the iconic Bali starling is being reintroduced here after being thought nearly extinct in the wild. And there's a growing visitor scene near Ped.

🏃 Activities

Nusa Penida has world-class **diving**. Most people make arrangements through a dive shop on Nusa Lembongan. Between Toyapakeh and Sampalan there is excellent **cycling** on the beautiful, flat coastal road. The roads elsewhere are good for mountain bikes. Ask

PENIDA'S DEMON

Nusa Penida is the legendary home of Jero Gede Macaling, the demon who inspired the Barong Landung dance. Many Balinese believe the island is a place of enchantment and *angker* (evil power) – paradoxically, this is an attraction. Thousands of Balinese come every year for religious observances aimed at placating the evil spirits.

around to rent a bike, which should cost about 30,000Rp per day.

Quicksilver WATER SPORTS
(☎0361-721521; www.quicksilver-bali.com; adult/child US$110/55) Has day trips from Bali (that leave from Benoa Harbour). A large barge anchored off Toyapakeh is the base for all sorts of water sports. There are also village tours.

Sampalan

Sampalan, the main town on Penida, is quiet and pleasant and strung out along the curving coast road. The interesting **market** is in the middle of town. It's a good place to absorb village life.

Sleeping

MaeMae Beach House GUESTHOUSE $
(☎0817 479 4176; maemaebeachhouse2015@gmail.com; Kutampi; r with fan/air-con 250,000/300,000Rp; ❄📶) In the town of Kutampi just outside Sampalan, this guesthouse is convenient for the main harbour. The manager Agus speaks excellent English and is a wealth of knowledge about everything Penida. Rooms are modern, but with a few rough edges. The chilled-out warung does decent food and is close to the water.

Nusa Garden Bungalows GUESTHOUSE $
(☎0812 3990 1421, 0813 3812 0660; r from 200,000Rp; 📶) Crushed-coral pathways running between animal statuary link the 10 very basic rooms here. Turn on Jl Nusa Indah just east of the centre.

Ped & Bodong

Ped is home to a very important Balinese temple. Just 600m west, the tiny subvillage of Bodong is the appealing centre of Penida's nascent tourist scene.

Sights & Activities

This entire area has a narrow strip of **beach** along the sea.

★**Pura Dalem Penetaran Ped** HINDU TEMPLE
FREE The important temple of Pura Dalem Penetaran Ped is near the beach at Ped, 3.5km east of Toyapakeh. It houses a shrine for the demon Jero Gede Macaling that is a source of power for practitioners of black magic, and a place of pilgrimage for those seeking protection from sickness and evil. The temple structure is sprawling and you will see people making offerings for safe sea voyages from Nusa Penida; you may wish to join them.

★**Penida Tours** TOUR
(☎0852 0587 1291; www.penidatours.com; Jl Raya Bodong; tours from 750,000Rp; ⏰9am-6pm) A great local operation that arranges cultural tours around Penida, covering anything from black magic to seaweed farming. The office is located next door to Gallery cafe.

Octopus Dive DIVING
(☎0819 77677677, 0878 6268 0888; www.octopusdiveindonesia.com; Bodong; 2-tank dives from 1,000,000Rp) A small and enthusiastic local dive operator.

Sleeping

Several establishments aimed at visitors have set up shop in Bodong.

Full Moon Bungalows BUNGALOW $
(☎0852 0587 1291; www.facebook.com/fullmoonbungalows; Bodong; dm from 125,000Rp, r 300,000-350,000Rp; ❄📶) A well-run compound with 15 bungalows. Each is basic but comfortable with thatched walls. You're mere steps from Ped's small but delightful nightlife.

Jero Rawa HOMESTAY $
(☎0852 0586 6886; www.jerorawa.com; Jl Raya Ped; r incl breakfast with fan/air-con from 200,000/300,000Rp) Run by a delightful family, this laid-back guesthouse has clean bungalow-style rooms just across the street from the beach.

Ring Sameton Inn GUESTHOUSE $$
(☎0813 798 5141; www.ringsameton-nusapenida.com; Bodong; r incl breakfast 400,000-500,000Rp; ❄📶🏊) If you're seeking comfort, this is easily the best place to stay on Penida. As well as spiffy business-style rooms, there's a pool, an atmospheric restaurant and quick beach access.

✗ Eating

★ Gallery CAFE $

(🖉 0819 9988 7205; Bodong; mains from 25,000Rp;
⊘ 7.30am-9pm) A popular spot for volunteers
at the NGOs, this small cafe and shop is run
by the ever-charming Mike, a Brit who is
a font of Penida knowledge. There's art on
the walls, hand-roasted filter coffee, house-
made rosella tea and a Western menu of
breakfast items and sandwiches.

★ Penida Colada CAFE $

(🖉 0821 4676 3627; www.facebook.com/penidaco-
lada; Bodong; mains 35,000-60,000Rp; ⊘ 9am-
late; 🕾) The cocktails at this charming sea-
side-shack cafe, run by an Indo-Aussie couple, are a must. Fresh, creative concoctions
include mojitos and daiquiris to go with a
menu of grilled fish, BLTs and chips with
aioli. There's often a seafood barbecue in the
evenings. Enjoy the soothing sound of the
ocean lapping at the narrow beach. *This* is
Penida's nightlife!

Warung Pondok Nusa Penida INDONESIAN $
(Bodong; mains from 30,000Rp; ⊘ 9am-9pm) A
cute little breezy place right on the beach.
Enjoy well-prepared Indo classics and seafood (plus the odd international item) while
taking in the views to Bali. Try the 'seaweed
mocktail' dessert.

Toyapakeh

If you come by boat from Nusa Lembongan,
you'll probably be dropped at the beach at
Toyapakeh, a pretty village with lots of shady
trees. The beach has clean white sand, clear
blue water, a neat line of boats, and Gunung
Agung as a backdrop. There are usually people ready to help you sort transport.

Crystal Bay Beach

South of Toyapakeh, a paved 10km road
through the village of Sakti leads to idyllic
Crystal Bay Beach, which fronts the popular
dive spot. The sand here is light; palm trees
add a *South Pacific* motif.

The beach is popular with Bali day trippers who arrive in boats (one operator is
Bali Hai Cruises; www.balihaicruises.com),
but mostly the beach remains blessedly rural. At busy times, however, up to 60 boats
might arrive at once, so conditions can get
very crowded. Come after 3pm to avoid the
crowds. A couple of warungs and beach cafes sell drinks and snacks and rent snorkel-

ling gear. The temple, **Segara Sakti**, adds
the perfect touch.

🛏 Sleeping

Namaste GUESTHOUSE $

(🖉 0819 1793 3418; www.namaste-bungalows.
com; r with fan/air-con from 425,000/550,000Rp;
❄🕾❄) A very steep 1km back from the
beach, on the road to Toyapakeh, French-
owned Namaste is a high-concept guesthouse with 10 rustic-style bungalows made
with recycled materials and set around a
large pool. It has a good cafe.

Around the Island

A trip around the island, following the
north and east coasts and crossing the hilly
interior, can be completed in half a day by
motorcycle or in a day by bicycle if you're in
good shape. You could spend much longer,
lingering at the temples and the small villages, and walking to less accessible areas, but
there's no accommodation outside the two
main towns. The following description goes
clockwise from Sampalan.

The coastal road from Sampalan curves
and dips past bays with rows of fishing boats
and offshore seaweed gardens. After about
6km, just before the village of Karangsari,
steps go up on the right side of the road
to the narrow entrance of **Goa Karangsari** caves. There are usually people who can
guide you through one of the caves for a
small negotiable fee of around 20,000Rp
each. The limestone cave is more than 15m
tall in some sections. It extends more than
200m through the hill and emerges on the
other side to overlook a verdant valley.

Continue south past a naval station and
several temples to **Suana**. Here the main
road swings inland and climbs up into the
hills, while a very rough side track goes
southeast, past more interesting temples to
Semaya, a fishing village with a sheltered
beach and one of Bali's best dive sites offshore, **Batu Aba**.

About 9km southwest of Suana, **Tanglad**
is a very old-fashioned village and a centre
for traditional weaving. Rough roads south
and east lead to isolated parts of the coast.

A scenic ridgetop road goes northwest
from Tanglad. At Batukandik, a rough road
and 1.5km track leads to a spectacular **waterfall** *(air terjun)* that crashes on to a small
beach. Get a guide (20,000Rp) in Tanglad.

Limestone cliffs drop hundreds of feet
into the sea, surrounded by crashing surf. At

their base, underground streams discharge fresh water into the sea – a pipeline was made to bring the water up to the top.

Back on the main road, continue to Batumadeg, past **Bukit Mundi** (the highest point on the island at 529m; on a clear day you can see Lombok), through Klumpu to **Sakti**, which has traditional stone buildings. Return to the north coast at Toyapakeh, about one hour after Bukit Mundi.

The road between Sampalan and Toyapakeh follows the craggy and lush coast through Ped.

ℹ Information

MONEY
The one ATM accepts few foreign cards, so bring cash.

TOURIST INFORMATION
Penida Tours (p144) is an excellent contact for island-wide info.

VOLUNTEERING
Various environmental and aid groups are active on Nusa Penida, with volunteers needed for a variety of projects. They normally pay a fee (about US$20 per day) that includes accommodation and contributes to the cause. Two organisations with programs you can join:

Friends of the National Parks Foundation (FNPF; ☎ 0361-479 2286; www.fnpf.org) This group has a centre near Ped on the island's north coast. Volunteer work includes aid in the restoration of the native Bali starling and teaching in local schools. Accommodation is in simple but comfortable rooms with fans and cold water.

Green Lion Bali (☎ 0813 3775 7179, 0812 4643 4964; www.greenlionbali.com) Has an award-winning program to breed and protect turtles along Penida's north shore. Volunteers sign on for at least two weeks and work in the turtle compound as well as teaching in local schools. There is a nearby guesthouse.

ℹ Getting There & Away

The strait between Nusa Penida and southern Bali is deep and subject to heavy swells – if there is a strong tide, boats often have to wait. Charter boats to/from Kusamba are not recommended due to their small size and the potential for heavy seas.

SANUR
Various speedboats leave from the same part of the beach as the fast boats to Nusa Lembongan, and make the run in less than an hour.
Maruti Express (☎ 0852 6861 7972, 0812 4689 2524; www.facebook.com/marutiexpresspeedboat; one way adult/child from 300,000/150,000Rp) One of several fast boats making the Penida run.

PADANGBAI
Fast boats run across the strait from Padangbai to Buyuk, 1km west of Sampalan on Nusa Penida (110,000Rp, 45 minutes, four daily). The boats run between 7am and noon. A large car ferry also operates daily (passenger/motorcycle 50,000/41,000Rp, two hours).

NUSA LEMBONGAN
Nusa Penida public boats run between Lembongan town by the bridge and Toyapakeh (50,000Rp, 20 minutes). Boats depart about every 30 minutes and wait for a crowd of at least six passengers. Chartering a boat costs a negotiable 300,000Rp to 400,000Rp.

ℹ Getting Around

Bemos are rare after 10am. There are often people who can set you up for transport where boats arrive. Options for getting around:
Car & driver From 350,000Rp for a half-day.
Motorcycle Easily hired for 60,000Rp per day.
Ojek Not common but when you find a ride on the back of a motorcycle, expect to pay about 40,000Rp per hour.

Ubud & Around

Best Places to Eat

➜ Locavore (p174)
➜ Moksa (p177)
➜ Mozaic (p177)
➜ Warung Teges (p176)
➜ Hujon Locale (p173)

Best Places to Sleep

➜ Swasti Eco Cottages (p169)
➜ Padma Ubud (p164)
➜ Mandapa, a Ritz-Carlton Reserve (p172)
➜ Maya Ubud (p170)
➜ Como Uma Ubud (p170)

Why Go?

A dancer moves her hand just so and 200 pairs of entranced eyes follow the exact movement. A gamelan player hits a melodic riff and 200 pairs of feet tap along with it. The Legong goes into its second hour as the bumblebee dance unfolds with its sprightly flair and 200 butts forget they're stuck in rickety plastic chairs.

So another dance performance works its magic on a crowd in Ubud, the town amid a collection of villages where all that is magical about Bali comes together in one very popular package. From nightly cultural performances to museums showing the works of artists whose creativity flowered here to the unbelievably green rice fields that spill down lush hillsides to rushing rivers below, Ubud is a feast for the soul. Personal pleasures like fine dining, shopping, spas, yoga and nearby villages of artisans and ancient sites only add to the appeal.

When to Go

➜ From October to April the weather is slightly cooler but much wetter than in the south; expect it to rain at any time. At night, mountain breezes make air-con unnecessary and let you hear the symphony of frogs, bugs and distant gamelan practices echoing over the rice fields through your screened window.

➜ Temperatures during the day average 30°C and at night 20°C, although extremes are possible. Seasonal variation is muted.

➜ Peak season: July, August and the Christmas holidays bring a huge influx of visitors and lodgings and restaurants are booked.

➜ In October, the Ubud Writers & Readers Festival is hugely popular.

Ubud & Around Highlights

1 **Dance Performance** (p180) Feeling the rhythm of a traditional Balinese cultural event, one of Ubud's great night-time pageants.

2 **Ubud Cafes** (p178) Whiling away the hours among new friends at a breezy idyll with excellent locally roasted coffee.

3 **Cultural Courses** (p160) Refining your batik technique and sambal recipes by taking instruction from one of Ubud's talented locals.

4 **Gunung Kawi** (p188) Making like Indiana Jones at these towering ancient wonders.

5 **Traditional Villages** (p185) Exploring hamlets around Ubud, such as Mas, for artworks, crafts, ceremonial objects and other treasures.

6 **Yoga** (p157) Finding your inner balance at one of Ubud's famous yoga centres.

7 **Fine Dining** (p172) Enjoying the remarkable variety of restaurants in Ubud, where creativity and great taste are hallmarks.

UBUD

Ubud is culture, yes. It's also home to good restaurants, cafes and streets of shops, many selling goods from the region's artisans. There's somewhere to stay for every budget, and no matter what the price you can enjoy lodgings that reflect the local Zeitgeist: artful, creative and serene.

Ubud's popularity continues to grow, adding on the hoopla created by the bestselling *Eat, Pray, Love*. Tour buses with day trippers can choke the main streets and cause traffic chaos. Fortunately, Ubud adapts and a stroll away from the intersection of Jl Raya Ubud and Monkey Forest Rd, through the nearby verdant rice fields, can quickly make all right with the world.

Spend a few days in Ubud to appreciate it properly. It's one of those places where days can become weeks and weeks become months, as the noticeable expat community demonstrates.

History

Late in the 19th century, Cokorda Gede Agung Sukawati established a branch of the Sukawati royal family in Ubud and began a series of alliances and confrontations with neighbouring kingdoms. In 1900, with the kingdom of Gianyar, Ubud became (at its own request) a Dutch protectorate and was able to concentrate on its religious and cultural life.

The Cokorda descendants encouraged Western artists and intellectuals to visit the area in the 1930s, most notably Walter Spies, Colin McPhee and Rudolf Bonnet. They provided an enormous stimulus to local art, introduced new ideas and techniques, and began a process of displaying and promoting Balinese culture worldwide. As mass tourism arrived in Bali, Ubud became an attraction not for beaches or bars, but for the arts.

The royal family is still much a part of Ubud life, helping to fund huge cultural and religious displays such as memorable cremation ceremonies.

⊙ Sights

⊙ Central Ubud

Temples, art galleries, museums and markets dot the middle of Ubud. Some of the most important sit close to the main intersection at Jl Raya Ubud and Monkey Forest Rd.

★ **Pura Taman Saraswati**   HINDU TEMPLE
(Map p150; Jl Raya Ubud) FREE Waters from the temple at the rear of this site feed the pond in the front, which overflows with pretty lotus blossoms. There are carvings that honour Dewi Saraswati, the goddess of wisdom and the arts, who has clearly given her blessing to Ubud. There are regular dance performances by night.

Ubud Palace   PALACE
(Map p150; cnr Jl Raya Ubud & Jl Suweta; ⊙8am-7pm) FREE The palace and its temple, **Puri Saren Agung**, share a space in the heart of Ubud. The compound was mostly built after the 1917 earthquake and the local royal family still lives here. You can wander around most of the large compound and explore the many traditional, though not excessively ornate, buildings.

Take time to appreciate the stone carvings, many by noted local artists such as I Gusti Nyoman Lempad. On many nights you can watch a dance performance here.

Just north, **Pura Marajan Agung** (Jl Suweta) is the private temple for the royal family. The compound across from the palace has a magnificent banyan tree, and is also used as a residence for the family.

★ **Museum Puri Lukisan**   MUSEUM
(Map p150; Museum of Fine Arts; ☎0361-975136; www.museumpurilukisan.com; off Jl Raya Ubud; adult/child 85,000Rp/free; ⊙9am-5pm) It was in Ubud that the modern Balinese art movement started, when artists first began to abandon purely religious themes and court subjects for scenes of everyday life. This museum displays fine examples of all schools of Balinese art, and all are well labelled in English. It was set up by Rudolf Bonnet, with Cokorda Gede Agung Sukawati (a prince of Ubud's royal family) and Walter Spies.

East Building to the right upon entry has a collection of early works from Ubud and surrounding villages. These include examples of classical 16th-century cloth *wayang*-style paintings (art influenced by shadow puppetry).

North Building features fine ink drawings by I Gusti Nyoman Lempad and paintings by Pita Maha artists. Notice the level of detail in Lempad's *The Dream of Dharmawangsa*. Classic works from the 1930s heyday of expats are also here.

West Building has vibrant postwar modern art by Balinese painters. **South Building** is used for special exhibitions.

The museum has a good bookshop and a cafe. The lush, garden-like grounds alone are worth a visit.

Pura Desa Ubud   HINDU TEMPLE
(Map p150; Jl Raya Ubud) FREE The main temple for the Ubud community. It is often closed but comes alive for ceremonies.

Neka Gallery   GALLERY
(Map p150; ☎0361-975034; Jl Raya Ubud; ⊙8am-5pm) FREE Operated by Suteja Neka since

UBUD & AROUND UBUD

UBUD IN...

One Day

Stroll the streets of Ubud by starting with the classic loop of Monkey Forest Rd down to the namesake **park** (p154) and then coming back up along Jl Hanoman. You can spend hours browsing **shops** and **galleries** and stopping into characterful **cafes**. Wander side streets and *gang* (alleys), exploring Jl Dewi Sita and Jl Goutama, and venture a little further afield through the verdant **rice fields**, for a great introduction to Ubud. Follow it up with an evening **dance performance** (p180).

Three Days

During the mornings, take longer walks in the countryside, exploring the **Campuan Ridge** and **Sayan Valley**. Consider a guided walking tour. In the afternoons visit the **Museum Puri Lukisan**, **Neka Art Museum** (p152) and **Agung Rai Museum of Art** (p154). By night, catch more dramatic dance performances (p180) in Ubud and the nearby villages. Indulge at a local **spa** (p157).

One Week

Do everything we've listed in the one- and three-day itineraries but take time to simply chill out. Get in tune with Ubud's rhythm: take naps, read books, wander about. Think about a **course** (p160) in Balinese culture. Compare and choose your favourite cafe, get out to craft villages and explore ancient sites.

Central Ubud

UBUD & AROUND

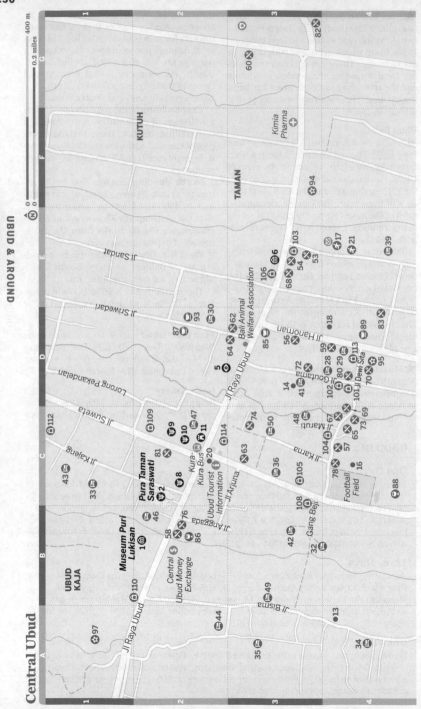

400 m
0.2 miles

KUTUH

TAMAN

Kimia Pharma

Bali Animal Welfare Association

Jl Sandat

Jl Sriwedari

Lorong Pekandelan

Jl Suweta

Jl Kajeng

Jl Raya Ubud

Museum Puri Lukisan

UBUD KAJA

Pura Taman Saraswati

Central Ubud Money Exchange

Ubud Tourist Information

Kura-Kura Bus

Jl Anggada

Jl Arjuna

Jl Bisma

Gang Beji

Football Field

Jl Hanoman

Jl Goutama

Jl Dewi Sita

Jl Maruti

Jl Karna

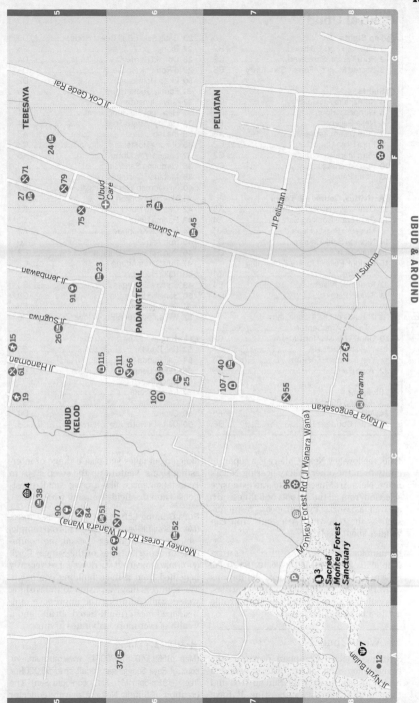

TEBESAYA

PELIATAN

Jl Cok Gede Rai

24

71

79

27

Ubud
Care

75

31

45

Jl Sukma

Jl Peliatan I

99

Jl Sukma

Jl Jembawan

23

91

PADANGTEGAL

Jl Sugriwa

26

15

19

Jl Hanoman

19

115

111

66

38

100

25

107

40

22

55

Perama

Jl Raya Pengosekan

UBUD
KELOD

Monkey Forest Rd (Jl Wanara Wana)

96

4

38

90

84

51

77

92

26

52

Monkey Forest Rd (Jl Wanara Wana)

3

Sacred
Monkey Forest
Sanctuary

P

37

7

12

Jl Nyuh Bulan

Central Ubud

1966, the low-key Neka Gallery is a separate entity from the other gallery bearing Neka's name, Neka Art Museum. It has an extensive selection from all the schools of Balinese art, as well as works by European residents, such as the renowned Arie Smit. You can wander about freely.

Komaneka Art Gallery　　　　　GALLERY
(Map p150; ☑0361-401 2217; Monkey Forest Rd; ⊙8am-9pm) FREE With special exhibitions of works from established Balinese artists, this gallery is a good place to see high-profile art, in a large and lofty space.

◉ West Ubud

Strolling Jl Raya Campuan down to the bridge (note the older historic wooden bridge just south) over the Sungai Wos and then up the busy and interesting Jl Raya Sanggingan takes you past a range of interesting sights. Venture up the steep steps to Penestanan for walks among small guesthouses and rice fields coursing with water.

Pura Gunung Lebah　　　　HINDU TEMPLE
(Map p156; off Jl Raya Campuan) This old temple, which sits on a jutting rock at the confluence of two tributaries of the Sungai Cerik (*campuan* means 'two rivers'), has recently benefited from a huge building campaign. The setting is magical; listen to the rushing waters while admiring the impressive multi-stepped *meru* (multi-tiered shrine) and a wealth of ever-more elaborate carvings.

★**Neka Art Museum**　　　　　GALLERY
(Map p156; ☑0361-975074; www.museumneka. com; Jl Raya Sanggingan; adult/child 50,000Rp/ free; ⊙9am-5pm Mon-Sat, noon-5pm Sun) The creation of Suteja Neka, a private collector

UBUD & AROUND UBUD

and dealer in Balinese art, Neka Art Museum has an excellent and diverse collection. It's a good place to learn about the development of painting in Bali. You can get an overview of the myriad local painting styles in the **Balinese Painting Hall**. Look for the *wayang* works.

The **Arie Smit Pavilion** features Smit's works on the upper level, and examples of the Young Artist school, which he inspired, on the lower level. Look for the Bruegel-like *The Wedding Ceremony* by I Nyoman Tjarka.

The **Lempad Pavilion** houses Bali's largest collection of works by the master I Gusti Nyoman Lempad.

The **Contemporary Indonesian Art Hall** has paintings by artists from other parts of Indonesia, including stunning works by Affandi. The upper floor of the **East-West Art Annexe** is devoted to the work of foreign artists, such as Louise Koke, Miguel Covarrubias, Rudolf Bonnet, Han Snel, Donald Friend and Antonio Blanco.

The temporary exhibition hall has changing displays, while the **Photography Archive Centre** features black-and-white photography of Bali in the early 1930s and '40s. Head upstairs in the lobby to see the large collection of ceremonial kris (daggers). The bookshop is noteworthy and there's a cafe.

Blanco Renaissance Museum MUSEUM
(Map p156; ☏ 0361-975502; www.blancomuseum. com; Jl Raya Campuan; adult/child 80,000Rp/ free; ⏰ 9am-5pm) The picture of Antonio Blanco (1912–99) mugging with Michael Jackson says it all. His surreal palatial neo-renaissance home and namesake museum captures the artist's theatrical spirit. Blanco came to Bali from Spain via the Philippines. Playing the role of an eccentric

UBUD'S FAMOUS ARTISTS

Spies House, home of German artist **Walter Spies**, is now part of Hotel Tjampuhan (p170); aficionados can stay if they book well in advance (if unoccupied, staff will give you a tour; be sure to tip). Spies played an important part in promoting Bali's artistic culture in the 1930s.

Dutch-born artist **Han Snel** lived in Ubud from the 1950s until his death in 1999, and his family runs his namesake bungalows (p164) on Jl Kajeng.

Lempad's House (Map p150; Jl Raya Ubud; ⊘daylight) FREE, the home of **I Gusti Nyoman Lempad**, is open to visitors but it's mainly used as a gallery for a group of artists that includes Lempad's grandchildren. The Puri Lukisan and Neka museums have more extensive collections of Lempad's drawings.

Music scholar **Colin McPhee** is well known thanks to his evocative book about his time in Ubud, the perennial favourite *A House in Bali*. Although the actual 1930s house is long gone, you can visit the riverside site (which shows up in photographs in the book) at the **Sayan Terrace** (Map p156; www.sayanterraceresort.com; Jl Raya Sayan; ☑0361-974384). The hotel's Wayan Ruma, whose mother was McPhee's cook, is good for a few stories.

Arie Smit (1916–2016) was the best-known and longest-surviving Western artist in Ubud. He worked in the Dutch colonial administration in the 1930s, was imprisoned during WWII, and came to Bali in 1956. In the 1960s his influence sparked the Young Artists school of painting in Penestanan, earning him an enduring place in the history of Balinese art. His home is not open to the public.

artist à la Dalí, he is known for his expressionist art and illustrated poetry that incorporates a mix of styles and mediums. Enjoy the waterfall and exotic birds on the way in, and good views over the river.

👁 South Ubud

You can reach some of Ubud's best sights via walks along Jl Hanoman and Monkey Forest Rd, which are both lined with interesting shops and cafes. Duck down narrow paths to find hidden rice fields.

⭐**Sacred Monkey Forest Sanctuary** PARK
(Map p150; Mandala Wisata Wanara Wana; ☑0361-971304; www.monkeyforestubud.com; Monkey Forest Rd; adult/child 40,000/30,000Rp; ⊘8.30am-6pm) This cool and dense swath of jungle, officially called Mandala Wisata Wanara Wana, houses three holy temples. The sanctuary is inhabited by a band of over 600 grey-haired and greedy long-tailed Balinese macaques who are nothing like the innocent-looking doe-eyed monkeys on the brochures. Nestled in the forest is the interesting **Pura Dalem Agung** FREE.

Enter the monkey forest through one of three gates: the main one at the southern end of Monkey Forest Rd; from 100m further east, near the car park; or from the southern side, on the lane from Nyuhkuning. Useful brochures about the forest, macaques and temples are available.

Note that the monkeys keep a keen eye on passing tourists in hope of handouts (or an opportunity to help themselves). Irritating recorded warnings (and signs) list of all the ways monkeys can cause trouble: avoid eye contact and showing your teeth, including smiling, which is deemed a sign of aggression. Also, don't try to take bananas from the moneys or feed them. Despite this, you will be harangued to buy bananas to feed the monkeys; there is no need for this as most are already pudgy.

⭐**Agung Rai Museum of Art** GALLERY
(ARMA; Map p156; ☑0361-976659; www.armabali.com; Jl Raya Pengosekan; adult/child incl drink 60,000Rp/free; ⊘9am-6pm, Balinese dancing 3-5pm Mon-Fri, classes 10am Sun) Founded by Agung Rai as a museum, gallery and cultural centre, the impressive ARMA is the only place in Bali to see haunting works by influential German artist Walter Spies, alongside many more masterpieces. The museum is housed in several traditional buildings set in gardens with water coursing through channels. The collection is well labelled in English.

Highlights include works by 19th-century Javanese artist Raden Saleh, including his enigmatic *Portrait of a Javanese Nobleman and His Wife*, which predates the similar American Gothic by decades. Exhibits also include classical Kamasan paintings, Batuan-style work from the 1930s and '40s, and works by Lempad, Affandi, Sadali, Hofker, Bonnet and Le Mayeur.

It's fun to visit ARMA when local children practise **Balinese dancing** and during **gamelan practice**. There are regular Legong and Kecak performances and myriad cultural courses offered here.

Enter the museum grounds from Kafe Arma on Jl Raya Pengosekan or around the corner at the ARMA Resort entrance.

Pranoto's Art Gallery   GALLERY
(📞0361-970827; Jl Raya Goa Gajah, Teges; ⊗9am-5pm) Pranoto, a long-time Ubud artist, displays his works at this gallery/studio/home which backs up to beautiful rice fields southwest of Ubud. The scenes of Indonesian life are lovely. The studio is about 1km east of Jl Peliatan. Ask about an atmospheric walking path you can take back to central Ubud. There are figure modelling sessions (30,000Rp) Wednesday and Saturday at 10am.

Museum Rudana   GALLERY
(Map p156; 📞0361-975779; www.museumrudana.com; Jl Raya Mas; 50,000Rp, ⊗9.30am-5pm) This imposing museum overlooking rice fields is the creation of local politician and art lover Nyoman Rudana and his wife, Ni Wayan Olasthini. The three floors contain more than 400 traditional paintings, including a calendar dated to the 1840s, some Lempad drawings and more modern pieces. The museum is beside the Rudana Gallery, which has a large selection of paintings for sale.

Ketut Rudi Gallery   GALLERY
(📞0361-974122; Pengosekan; ⊗9am-7pm) These sprawling galleries showcase the works of more than 50 Ubud artists with techniques as varied as primitive and new realism. The gallery's namesake is on display as well; he favours an entertaining style best described as 'comical realism'. It's about 2km south of Ubud.

Agung Rai Gallery   GALLERY
(Map p156; 📞0361-975449; Jl Peliatan; ⊗9am-6pm) This gallery is in a pretty compound and its collection covers the full range of Balinese styles. It functions as a cooperative, with the work priced by the artist and the gallery adding a percentage.

◉ **North Ubud**

Wandering on the many lanes running north from Jl Raya Ubud takes you past sweet little homestays. As the buildings thin out you are rewarded with beautiful views of rice fields and river valleys.

Petulu   NATURAL FEATURE
(village admission 20,000Rp) Every evening beginning after 5pm, up to 20,000 big **herons** fly in to Petulu, a village about 2.5km north of Jl Raya Ubud, squabbling over prime perching places before settling into the trees beside the road and becoming a tourist attraction.

The herons, mainly the striped Java pond species, started their visits to Petulu in 1965 for no apparent reason. Villagers believe they bring good luck (as well as tourists), despite the smell and the mess. A few warung (food stalls) have been set up in the paddy fields, where you can have a drink while enjoying the spectacle. Walk quickly under the trees if the herons are already roosting. Nesting and egg-laying begins in November, with the fledglings taking flight in March.

Petulu is a pleasant walk or bicycle ride on any of several routes north of Ubud, but if you stay for the birds you'll be heading back in the dark.

🏃 **Activities**

Made Surya   HEALTH & FITNESS
(📞0361-788 0822; www.balihealers.com) One of Bali's top *balian* (traditional healers). He is an excellent resource if you'd like to try Balinese therapies.

Wayan Nuriasih   HEALTH & FITNESS
(Map p150; 📞0361-917 5991, 0361-884 3042; balihealer@hotmail.com; Jl Jembawan 5; ⊗9am-5pm) Wayan Nuriasih, one of the stars of *Eat, Pray, Love,* can work wonders with medicinal plants (many are for sale out front) as well as massage and other treatments. The 'vitamin lunch' is the antidote to a Bintang dinner.

ⓘ **REFILL YOUR WATER BOTTLE**

The number of plastic water bottles emptied in Bali's tropical heat daily and then tossed in the trash is colossal. In Ubud there are a few places where you can refill your water bottle (plastic or reusable) for a small fee, usually 3000Rp. The water is the same Aqua brand that is preferred locally and you'll be helping to preserve Bali's beauty, one plastic bottle at a time. A good central location is Pondok Pekak Library & Learning Centre (p160).

Ubud Area

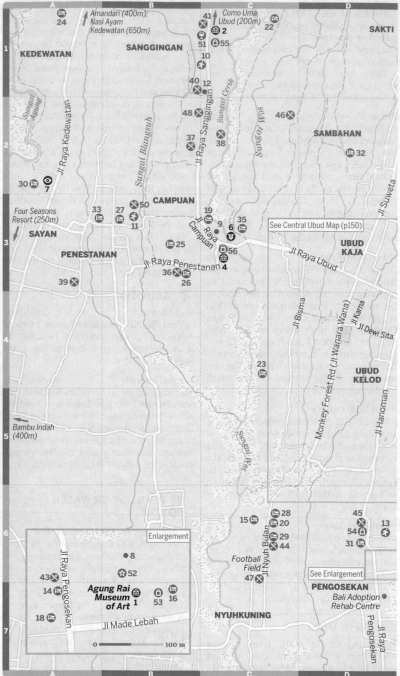

Amandari (400m);
Nasi Ayam
Kedewatan (650m)

Como Uma
Ubud (200m)

KEDEWATAN

SAKTI

SANGGINGAN

SAMBAHAN

CAMPUAN

See Central Ubud Map (p150)

Four Seasons
Resort (250m)

SAYAN

UBUD
KAJA

PENESTANAN

Jl Raya Ubud

Jl Raya Penestanan

UBUD
KELOD

Bambu Indah
(400m)

PENGOSEKAN

Bali Adoption
Rehab Centre

NYUHKUNING

Football
Field

See Enlargement

Enlargement

Jl Raya Pengosekan

Agung Rai
Museum
of Art

Jl Made Lebah

0   100 m

Jl Raya Pengosekan

Jl Raya Kedewatan
Sungai Ayung
Sungai Blangsuh
Jl Raya Sanggingan
Sungai Cerik
Sungai Wos
Jl Suweta
Jl Raya Campuan
Jl Bisma
Monkey Forest Rd (Jl Wanara Wana)
Jl Kajeng
Jl Dewi Sita
Jl Hanoman
Sungai Wos
Jl Nyuh Bulan

Massages, Spas & Yoga

Ubud brims with salons and spas where you can heal, pamper, rejuvenate or otherwise focus on your personal needs, physical and mental. Visiting a spa is at the top of many a traveller's itinerary and the business of spas, yoga and other treatments grows each year. Expect the latest trends from any of many practitioners (the bulletin board outside Bali Buddha is bewildering) and prepare to try some new therapies, such as 'pawing'. If you have to ask you don't want to know. You may also wish to seek out a *balian*.

Many spas also offer courses in therapies, treatments and activities such as yoga.

★Taksu Spa   SPA

(Map p150; ☑ 0361-479 2525; www.taksuspa.com; Jl Goutama; massage from 375,000Rp; ⊙ 9am-9pm) Taksu has a long and rather lavish menu of treatments, as well as a strong focus on yoga. There are private rooms for couples massages; a breezy, healthy cafe; and a range of classes. Very popular, Taksu is expanding to additional locations.

★Yoga Barn   YOGA

(Map p150; ☑ 0361-971236; www.theyogabarn.com; off Jl Raya Pengosekan; classes from 130,000Rp; ⊙ 7am-8pm) The chakra for the yoga revolution in Ubud, the life force that is the Yoga Barn sits in its own lotus position amid trees back near a river valley. The name exactly describes what you'll find: a huge range of classes in yoga, Pilates, dance and life-affirming offshoots are held through the week. Owner Meghan Pappenheim also organises the popular Bali Spirit Festival.

Ubud Sari Health Resort   SPA

(Map p156; ☑ 0361-974393; www.ubudsari.com; Jl Kajeng 35; 1hr massage from 200,000Rp; ⊙ 9am-8pm) A spa and hotel in one. It is a serious place with extensive organic treatments bearing such names as 'total tissue cleansing'. Beside a long list of daytime spa and salon services, there are packages that include stays at the hotel. Many treatments focus on cleaning out your colon.

Bali Botanica Day Spa   SPA

(Map p156; ☑ 0361-976739; www.balibotanica.com; Jl Raya Sanggingan; massage from 180,000Rp; ⊙ 9am-9pm) Set beautifully on a lush hillside past little fields of rice and ducks, this spa offers a range of treatments, including Ayurvedic. The herbal massage is popular. Transport is provided if needed.

Ubud Area

Top Sights

1	Agung Rai Museum of Art	B7
2	Neka Art Museum	C1

Sights

3	Agung Rai Gallery	E6
4	Blanco Renaissance Museum	C3
5	Museum Rudana	F7
6	Pura Gunung Lebah	C3
7	Sayan Terrace	A2
	Spies House	(see 19)

Activities, Courses & Tours

8	ARMA	B6
9	Bali Bird Walks	C3
10	Bali Botanica Day Spa	C1
11	Intuitive Flow	B3
12	Mozaic Cooking Classes	C1
	Ubud Sari Health Resort	(see 32)
13	Ubud Wellness Spa	D6
	Wayan Karja Painting	(see 27)

Sleeping

14	Agung Raka	A7
15	Alam Indah	C6
16	ARMA Resort	B7
17	Bali Asli Lodge	E2
18	Casa Ganesha Hotel	A7
19	Hotel Tjampuhan	C3
20	Kertiyasa Bungalows	C6
21	Ketut's Place	E2
22	Klub Kokos	C1
23	Komaneka at Bisma	C4
24	Mandapa, a Ritz-Carlton Reserve	A1
25	Melati Cottages	B3
26	Roam	B3
27	Santra Putra	B3
28	Saren Indah Hotel	C6
29	Swasti Eco Cottages	C6
30	Taman Bebek	A2
31	Tegal Sari	D6
32	Ubud Sari Health Resort	D2
33	Villa Nirvana	A3
34	Wapa di Ume	E1
35	Warwick Ibah Luxury Villas	C3

Eating

36	Alchemy	B3
37	Bintang Supermarket	B2
38	Elephant	C2
	Kubu	(see 24)
39	Moksa	A3
40	Mozaic	B1
41	Naughty Nuri's	C1
42	Pitri Minang	E6
43	Pizza Bagus	A6
44	Swasti Beloved Cafe	C6
45	Taco Casa	D6
46	Warung Bodag Maliah	C2
47	Warung Pojok	C6
48	Warung Pulau Kelapa	B2
49	Warung Teges	F7
50	Yellow Flower Cafe	B3

Drinking & Nightlife

	Bridges	(see 4)
51	Room 4 Dessert	C1

Entertainment

52	Arma Open Stage	B6

Shopping

53	ARMA	B7
54	Goddess on the Go!	D6
55	Neka Art Museum	C1
56	Rumble	C3

Radiantly Alive YOGA

(Map p150; ☎0361-978055; www.radiantlyalive.com; Jl Jembawan 3; per class/day/week 125,000/170,000/550,000Rp) This school will appeal to those looking for an intimate space, and offers a mix of drop-in and long-term yoga classes in a number of disciplines.

Intuitive Flow YOGA

(Map p156; ☎0361-977824; www.intuitiveflow.com; Penestanan; yoga from 120,000Rp; ⊙classes daily) A lovely yoga studio up amid the rice fields – although just climbing the concrete stairs to get here from Campuan may leave you too spent for a round of asanas. Wide range of workshops in healing arts.

Ubud Wellness Spa SPA

(Map p156; ☎0361-970493; www.ubudwellness.com; off Jl Pengosekan; massage from 150,000Rp; ⊙9am-10pm) A spa that concentrates on what counts, not the fru-fru. A favourite among Ubud's creative community.

Nur Salon SPA

(Map p150; ☎0361-975352; www.nursalonubud.com; Jl Hanoman 28; 1hr massage 175,000Rp; ⊙9am-9pm) In a traditional Balinese compound filled with labelled medicinal plants; offers a long menu of straightforward spa and salon services.

Cycling

Many shops and hotels in central Ubud display mountain bikes for hire. The price is usually a negotiable 35,000Rp per day. If in doubt about where to rent, ask at your hotel and someone with a bike is likely to appear.

In general, the land is dissected by rivers running south, so any east–west route will involve a lot of ups and downs as you cross the river valleys. North–south routes run between the rivers, and are much easier going, but can have heavy traffic. Most of the sites in Ubud are reachable by bike.

Riding a bike is an excellent way to visit the many museums and cultural sites located around Ubud, although you'll need to consider your comfort level with traffic south of Ubud.

Banyan Tree Cycling Tours   CYCLING
(☑0813 3879 8516; www.banyantreebiketours. com; tours adult/child from US$55/35) Enjoy day-long tours of remote villages in the hills above Ubud. The tours are very popular, and emphasise interaction with villagers. Hiking and rafting trips are also available.

Rafting
The **Sungai Ayung** (Ayung River) is the most popular river in Bali for white-water rafting. You start north of Ubud and end near the Amandari hotel in the west. Note

that depending on rainfall the run can range from sedate to thrilling.

Tours

Ubud Tourist Information   CULTURAL
(Map p150; Fabulous Ubud; ☑0361-973285; www. fabulousubud.com; Jl Raya Ubud; tours 185,000-300,000Rp; ⊗8am-8pm) Runs interesting and affordable half- and full-day trips to a range of places, including Besakih and Kintamani.

Dhyana Putri Adventures   CULTURAL
(☑0812 380 5623; www.balispirit.com/tours/ bali_tour_dhyana.html; tours per hr from US$25) Bi-cultural and trilingual, author and Balinese dance expert Rucina Ballinger offers custom tours, with an emphasis on Balinese performing arts and in-depth cultural experiences.

Bali Nature Herbal Walks   WALKING
(☑0812 381 6024; www.baliherbalwalk.com; walks per person 200,000Rp; ⊗8.30am) Three-hour

---

BALI'S TRADITIONAL HEALERS

Bali's traditional healers, known as *balian* (*dukun* on Lombok), play an important part in Bali's culture by treating physical and mental illness, removing spells and channelling information from the ancestors. Numbering about 8000, *balian* are the ultimate in community medicine, making a commitment to serve their communities and turning no one away.

Lately, however, this system has come under stress in some areas due to the attention brought by *Eat, Pray, Love* and other media coverage of Bali's healers. Curious tourists are turning up in village compounds, taking the *balian*'s time and attention from the genuinely ill. However, that doesn't mean you shouldn't visit a *balian* if you're genuinely curious. Just do so in a manner that befits the experience: gently.

Consider the following before a visit:

➡ Make an appointment before visiting a *balian*.

➡ Know that English is rarely spoken.

➡ Dress respectfully (long trousers and a shirt, better yet a sarong and sash).

➡ Women should not be menstruating.

➡ Never point your feet at the healer.

➡ Bring an offering into which you have tucked the consulting fee, which will average about 250,000Rp per person.

➡ Understand what you're getting into: your treatment will be very public and probably painful. It may include deep-tissue massage, being poked with sharp sticks or having chewed herbs spat on you.

Finding a *balian* can take some work. Ask at your hotel, which can probably help with making an appointment and providing a suitable offering for stashing your fee. Or consider getting a referral from Made Surya (p155), who is an authority on Bali's traditional healers and offers one- and two-day intensive workshops on healing, magic, traditional systems and history, which include visits to authentic *balian*. His website is an excellent resource on visiting healers in Bali and he can also select an appropriate *balian* for you to visit and accompany you there as liaison and translator.

Some Western medical professionals question whether serious medical issues can be resolved by this type of healing, and patients should see a traditional healer in conjunction with a Western doctor if their ailment is serious.

walks through lush Bali landscape include identifiying and explaining medicinal and cooking herbs and plants in their natural environment. Includes herbal drinks.

Bali Nature Walk WALKING
(☑0817 973 5914; https://balinaturewalks.net; tour from US$25) Walks in isolated areas in the Ubud region. Routes are customisable depending on your desires.

Bali Bird Walks BIRDWATCHING
(Map p156; ☑0361-975009; www.balibirdwalk. com; Jl Raya Campuan; tour incl lunch US$37; ⊙9am-12.30pm Tue, Fri, Sat & Sun) Started by Victor Mason more than three decades ago, this tour, ideal for keen birders, is still going strong. On a gentle morning's walk (from the long-closed Beggar's Bush Bar) you may see up to 30 of the 100-odd local species.

☙ Courses

Ubud is the perfect place to develop your artistic or language skills, or learn about Balinese culture and cuisine. The range of courses offered could keep you busy for a year. With most classes you must book in advance.

★**ARMA** CULTURAL TOUR
(Map p156; ☑0361-976659; www.armabali.com; Jl Raya Pengosekan; classes from US$25; ⊙9am-6pm) A cultural powerhouse offering classes in painting, woodcarving, gamelan and batik. Other courses include Balinese history, Hinduism and architecture.

★**Museum Puri Lukisan** ART
(Map p150; www.museumpurilukisan.com; off Jl Raya Ubud; classes from 145,000Rp) One of Ubud's best museums teaches courses in puppet-making, gamelan, offering-making, Balinese dance, mask painting and much more. Classes are taught on demand; make arrangements at the museum ticket office.

Threads of Life Indonesian Textile Arts Center TEXTILE
(Map p150; ☑0361-972187; www.threadsoflife.com; Jl Kajeng 24; classes from 75,000Rp; ⊙10am-7pm) Textile appreciation courses in the gallery and educational studio last from one to eight days. Some classes involve extensive travel around Bali and should be considered graduate level.

Studio Perak JEWELLERY
(Map p150; ☑081 2365 1809, 0361-974244; www. studioperak.com; Jl Hanoman; lessons per 3hr

400,000Rp) Specialises in Balinese-style silversmithing courses. In one three-hour lesson you'll make a finished piece. Classes can be geared to children.

Pondok Pekak Library & Learning Centre LANGUAGE
(Map p150; ☑0361-976194; www.pondokpekakli brary.com; Monkey Forest Rd; classes per hr from 100,000Rp; ⊙9am-5pm Mon-Sat, 1-5pm Sun) On the far side of the football field, this centre offers painting, dance, music and woodcarving classes; some are geared to kids.

Wayan Pasek Sucipta MUSIC
(Map p150; ☑0361-970550; Eka's Homestay, Jl Sriwedari 8; classes per hr 100,000Rp) Learn the gamelan and bamboo drums from a master.

Wayan Karja Painting ART
(☑0361-977810; Jl Pacekan 18, Penestanan, off Jl Raya Campuan; classes from 300,000Rp) Intensive painting and drawing classes are run by abstract artist Karja, whose studio is behind his guesthouse, the Santra Putra (p170).

Nirvana Batik Course ART
(Map p150; ☑0361-975415; www.nirvanaku.com; Jl Goutama 10, Nirvana Pension; classes from 485,000Rp; ⊙classes 10am-2pm Mon-Sat) Nyoman Suradnya teaches these highly regarded batik courses.

Cooking

★**Balinese Farm Cooking School** COOKING
(☑0812 3953 4446; http://balinesecooking. net; Banjar Patas, Taro; 1-day course 400,000Rp) Spend a day out in untrammelled countryside 18km north of Ubud *and* learn how to cook Balinese food. This highly recommended cooking course is held in a village of lush gardens. Run by villagers passionate about organic farming, students learn about local produce and foods. It's all cleverly designed for tourists: herbs are grown in raised beds so there's no stooping etc.

★**Casa Luna Cooking School** COOKING
(Map p150; ☑0361-973282; www.casalunabali.com; Honeymoon Guesthouse, Jl Bisma; classes from 450,000Rp) Regular cooking courses are offered at Honeymoon Guesthouse and/or Casa Luna restaurant (p173). Half-day courses cover ingredients, cooking techniques and the cultural background of the Balinese kitchen (note, not all courses include a visit to the market). Each day has a different focus so you can return for many days of instruction. Tours are also offered, including a good one to the Gianyar night market.

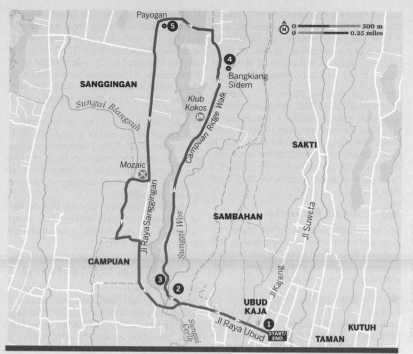

🏃 Walking Tour
Campuan Ridge

START UBUD PALACE
END UBUD PALACE
LENGTH 8.5KM; 3½ HOURS

This walk passes over the lush river valley of Sungai Wos (Wos River), offering views of Gunung Agung and glimpses of small village communities and rice fields.

Start at ❶ **Ubud Palace** (p149) and walk west on Jl Raya Ubud. At the confluence of Sungai Wos and Sungai Cerik (Cerik River) is ❷ **Campuan**, which means 'Where Two Rivers Meet'. This area was among the first to attract Western painters in the 1930s and you'll understand why from the still-lush foliage and the soothing roar of the rivers. The walk leaves Jl Raya Campuan here at the Warwick Ibah Luxury Villas. Enter the hotel driveway and take the path to the left, where a walkway crosses the river to the high-profile yet serene ❸ **Pura Gunung Lebah** (p152). From there follow the concrete path north, climbing up onto the ridge between the two rivers. Fields of elephant grass, traditionally

used for thatched roofs, slope away on either side. You can see the rice fields above Ubud folding over the hills in all directions.

Continuing north along Campuan ridge past the Klub Kokos lodging, the road improves as it passes through paddy fields and the village of ❹ **Bangkiang Sidem**; from its outskirts, an unsigned road heads west, winding down to Sungai Cerik, then climbing steeply up to ❺ **Payogan**. From here you can walk south to the main road, and continue along Jl Raya Sanggingan, which seems to boast one or two more small boutiques and galleries every week. At Mozaic restaurant, veer to the west onto trails that stay level with the rice fields as the main road drops away. It's a fantasyland of coursing waterways and good views among the rice and villas. If you're entranced with Ubud and want to linger longer, many of the small bungalows are for rent by the month. When you come to the steep concrete steps, take them down to Campuan and back to Ubud.

Mozaic Cooking Classes COOKING
(Map p156; ☑0361-975768; www.mozaic-bali.com; Jl Raya Sanggingan; classes from 900,000Rp) Learn cooking techniques at one of Bali's best restaurants. A full menu of classes is taught, from casual to professional.

Cafe Wayan Cooking Class COOKING
(Map p150; ☑0361-977565; www.lakaleke.com; Jl Nyuh Bulan; lesson 350,000Rp; ☺classes 10am & 4pm) Near the south entrance to the Monkey Forest, the setting for this cooking class is lush and lovely. During the two-hour session, students will learn how to prepare a basic Balinese meal. Afterwards, they'll eat their work.

⚜️ Festivals & Events

One of the best places to see the many religious and cultural events celebrated in Bali each year is the Ubud area. The tourist office is unmatched for its comprehensive information on events each week.

★**Ubud Writers & Readers Festival** LITERATURE
(www.ubudwritersfestival.com; 1-day pass 1,200,000Rp; ☺late Oct/early Nov) Brings together scores of writers and readers from around the world in a five-day celebration of writing – especially writing that touches on Bali. A major event on the Ubud calendar.

Bali Spirit Festival DANCE, MUSIC
(www.balispiritfestival.com; day pass US$150; ☺Mar/early Apr) A popular yoga, dance and music festival from the people behind the Yoga Barn, a local yoga hub. There are hundreds of workshops and concerts, plus a market and more.

🛏️ Sleeping

Ubud has the best and most appealing range of places to stay on Bali, including fabled resorts, artful guesthouses and charming, simple homestays. Choices can be bewildering, so give some thought to where you want to stay (p171), especially if you are renting private accommodation via the web.

Generally, Ubud offers good value for money at any price level. Simple accommodation within a family home compound is a cultural experience and costs around US$25 per night. Ubud enjoys cool mountain air at night, so air-con isn't necessary, and with your windows open, you'll hear the symphony of sounds off the rice fields and river valleys.

Guesthouses may be a bit larger and have amenities like swimming pools but are still likely to be fairly intimate, often nestled amid rice fields and rivers. The best hotels are often perched on the edges of the deep river valleys, with superb views (although even some budget places have amazing views). Some provide shuttle service around the area.

Addresses in Ubud can be imprecise – but signage at the end of a road will often list the names of all the places to stay. Away from the main thoroughfares there are few streetlights and it can be challenging to find your way after dark. If walking, you'll want a torch (flashlight).

Due to its popularity and the lack (so far) of an invasion of chain hotels, Ubud is the one place on Bali where accommodation prices are rising sharply.

🛏️ Jalan Raya Ubud & Around

Nirvana Pension GUESTHOUSE $
(Map p150; ☑0361-975415; www.nirvanaku.com; Jl Goutama 10; s with fan/air-con 250,000/350,000Rp, d with fan/air-con 350,000/450,000Rp; ❄️📶) Nirvana has *alang-alang* (thatched roofs), a plethora of paintings, ornate doorways and six rooms with modern bathrooms, all set in a shady, secluded locale next to a large family temple. Batik courses are also held here. It's a great location, back off popular Goutama.

Sania's House GUESTHOUSE $
(Map p150; ☑0361-975535; sania_house@yahoo.com; Jl Karna 7; r 300,000-600,000Rp; @📶🏊) Pets wander about this family-run place, where the large, clear pool, huge terrace and spacious rooms will have you howling at the moon. The 29 rooms are basic but clean; the market is nearly next door, and souvenir stands crowd the entrance.

d'Rompok House GUESTHOUSE $
(Map p150; ☑0353-344837; drompokhouse@yahoo.com; Jl Hanoman 39; r incl breakfast 250,000-350,000Rp; ❄️📶) Tucked down a tight *gang* (alley), the well-priced d'Rompok is more suave than your usual homestay, with five large, modern rooms decorated with contemporary art. Go for one of the top-floor rooms with views of the rice fields.

Raka House GUESTHOUSE $
(Map p150; ☑0361-976081; Jl Maruti; r 300,000-450,000Rp; ❄️📶🏊) Six bungalow-style rooms cluster at the back of a compact family compound. You can soak your toes in a

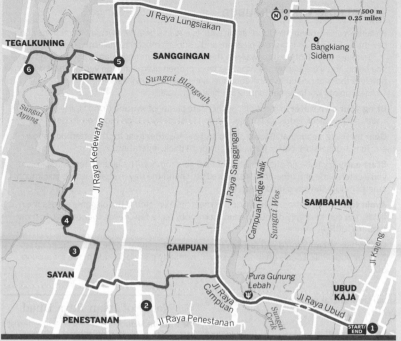

🏃 Walking Tour
Sungai Ayung Valley

START UBUD PALACE
END UBUD PALACE
LENGTH 6.5KM; FOUR HOURS

The wonders of Sungai Ayung (Ayung River) are the focus of this outing, where you will walk below the luxury hotels built to take advantage of the lush, tropical river valley.

From ❶ **Ubud Palace** (p149), head west on Jl Raya Ubud, over the Campuan bridge (noting the picturesque old bridge), past the expanded Pura Gunung Lebah below. Take the steep steps opposite the Hotel Tjampuhan up to a road that bends left and winds across the forested gully of Sungai Blangsuh (Blangsuh River) to the artists' village of ❷ **Penestanan**. West of Penestanan, head north on the small road (before the busy main road) that curves around to Sayan. The ❸ **Sayan Terrace** (p154) was Colin McPhee's home in the 1930s, as chronicled in his classic book *A House in Bali*. The views over the valley of the magnificent ❹ **Sungai Ayung** are superb. The best place to get to the riverside is just north of the Sayan Terrace hotel – look for the downhill path before the gate to the rooms and follow the increasingly narrow tracks down. Locals will ask you for a tip of about 10,000Rp to show you the way. As you follow the river, you'll encounter farmers asking for money to cross their land; 5000Rp is a reasonable amount to give. There is no need to give money to any 'guides'.

Following the rough trails north, along the eastern side of the Ayung, you traverse steep slopes, cross paddy fields and pass irrigation canals and tunnels. This is a highlight for many people, as we're talking about serious tropical jungle here. You don't need to follow any specific trail as you head north along the river; instead just wander and see where your mood takes you. After 1.5km you'll reach the finishing point for many white-water rafting trips – a good but steep trail goes from there up to the main road at ❺ **Kedewatan**, where you can walk back to Ubud. Alternatively, cross the river on the nearby bridge and take a steep, 1km loop through tropical forest to the untouristy village of ❻ **Tegalkuning**. Return to Ubud on Jl Raya Sanggingan.

ⓘ WALKING WISELY IN UBUD

Walking in and around the Ubud region with its endless beauty, myriad fascinations and delightful discoveries is a great pleasure and a superb reason to visit the area.

There are lots of interesting walks in the area to surrounding villages and through the rice fields. You'll frequently see artists at work in open rooms and on verandahs, and the timeless tasks of rice cultivation continue alongside luxury villas.

A few points worth remembering to enjoy your walk:

Bring your own water In most places there are plenty of warung (food stalls) or small shops selling snack foods and drinks but don't risk dehydration between stops.

Gear up Bring a good hat, decent shoes and wet-weather gear for the afternoon showers; long trousers are better for walking through thick vegetation.

Start early Try to begin at daybreak, before it gets too hot. The air also feels crisper and you'll catch birds and other wildlife before they spend the day in shadows. It's also much quieter before the day's buzz begins.

Avoid tolls Some entrepreneurial rice farmers have erected little toll gates across their fields. You can a) simply detour around them, or b) pay a fee (never, ever accede to more than 10,000Rp).

Quit while ahead Should you tire don't worry about reaching some goal – the point is to enjoy your walk. Locals on motorbikes will invariably give you a ride home for around 30,000Rp.

small trapezoidal plunge pool. More choices nearby.

Donald Homestay
HOMESTAY $

(Map p150; ☑ 0361-977156; Jl Goutama; r 250,000-300,000Rp; ❄️🔊) The four rooms – some fan-only – are in a nice back corner of this well-located family compound. Even in the heart of today's madcap Ubud, you can still get to know a Balinese family and experience their life's rhythms.

Puri Saraswati Bungalows
HOTEL $$

(Map p150; ☑ 0361-975164; www.purisaraswati-ubud.com; Jl Raya Ubud; r US$60-80; ❄️🔊🏊) Very central and pleasant with lovely gardens that open onto the Ubud Water Palace. The 18 bungalow-style rooms are well back from Jl Raya Ubud, so it's quiet. Some rooms are fan-only; interiors are simply furnished but have richly carved details.

Puri Saren Agung
GUESTHOUSE $$

(Map p150; ☑ 0361-975057; Jl Suweta 1; r US$65-80; ❄️) Part of the Ubud royal family's historic palace, seven rooms are tucked behind the courtyard where the dance performances are held. Accommodation is in traditional Balinese pavilions, with big verandahs, four-poster beds, antique furnishings and hot water. Give a royal wave to wandering tourists from your patio.

📷 North of Jalan Raya Ubud

★ Padma Ubud
GUESTHOUSE $

(Map p150; ☑ 0823 4008 4680; www.padmaubud.com; Jl Kajeng 13; r 300,000-550,000Rp; 🔊🏊) There are 12 very private bungalows in a tropical garden with a pool here. Rooms are decorated with local crafts and the modern outdoor bathrooms have hot water. Nyoman Sudiarsa, a painter and family member, has a studio here and often shares his knowledge with guests.

Eka's Homestay
HOMESTAY $

(Map p150; ☑ 0361-970550; eka_sutawan@yahoo.com; Jl Sriwedari 8; r incl breakfast 150,000-250,000Rp; 🔊) Follow your ears to this nice little family compound with seven basic rooms. Eka's is the home of Wayan Pasek Sucipta, a teacher of Balinese music. It's in a nice sunny spot on a quiet road (well, except during practice times).

Han Snel Siti Bungalows
GUESTHOUSE $

(Map p150; ☑ 0361-975699; www.sitibungalow.com; Jl Kajeng 3; r incl breakfast with fan/air-con from 250,000/350,000Rp; ❄️🔊🏊) Owned by the family of the late Han Snel, a well-known Dutch painter, Siti Bungalows is one of Ubud's original guesthouses. While its standards have slipped, it remains excellent value and a wonderful choice for those seeking somewhere with character, a delightful garden and eight spacious bungalows – some of which overlook the river gorge.

Monkey Forest Road

Jukung Hostel HOSTEL $
(Map p150; ☑0812 3633 9998; www.jukunghostel.
com; Jl Monkey Forest 14; dm incl breakfast from
100,000Rp; ☉check-in 1-10pm) You can't get
more central than this hostel. Beds are in
six- and eight-bed dorms. The decor, which
looks like the leftovers from a fake distressed
wood factory, extends to the kitchen.

★Oka Wati Hotel HOTEL $$
(Map p150; ☑0361-973386; www.okawatihotel.
com; off Monkey Forest Rd; r incl breakfast US$65-
120; ❋☎≋) Owner Oka Wati is a lovely lady
who grew up near the Ubud Palace. Go for a
room in the original wing, where the decor
features vintage detail and some rooms have
views over a small rice field and river val-
ley. All of the 20 rooms have large verandas,
where you'll enjoy your choice of breakfast
(don't miss the house-made yoghurt).

Griya Jungutan GUESTHOUSE $$
(Map p150; ☑0361-975752; www.griyajungutan.com;
off Monkey Forest Rd; r 300,000-600,000Rp; ❋☎
≋) Overlooking a small river valley in the
very heart of Ubud, Griya Jungutan has good-
value rooms well away from the traffic of central Ubud down a small *gang*. Rooms come
in several flavours: the cheapest are fan-only,
the best have terraces with lush views.

Warsa's Garden Bungalows GUESTHOUSE $$
(Map p150; ☑0361 971548; http://warsagarden-
bungalows.com; Monkey Forest Rd; r 400,000-
550,000Rp; ❋☎≋) A good-sized pool with
fountains enlivens this comfy but simple
place in the heart of Monkey Forest action.
The 23 rooms are reached through a tradi-
tional family-compound entrance. Some
have tubs; some are fan-only.

Sri Bungalows GUESTHOUSE $$
(Map p150; ☑0361-975394; www.sribungalowsub
ud.com; Monkey Forest Rd; r 500,000-1,200,000Rp;
❋@☎≋) Popular for its iconic views of rice
fields (you think you hear it growing but
really it's the sound of your soul decom-
pressing). Be sure to get one of the comfy
rooms (choose from 34) with relaxing loung
ers that command the views.

Lumbung Sari GUESTHOUSE $$
(Map p150; ☑0361-976396; www.lumbungsari.com;
Monkey Forest Rd; r 700,000-1,300,000Rp; ❋@
☎≋) Artwork decorates the walls at the styl-
ish Sari, which has a nice breakfast *bale* (tra-
ditional pavilion) by the pool. The 14 rooms
have tubs in elegant bathrooms.

Jalan Bisma

Batik Sekar Bali Guest House GUESTHOUSE $
(Map p150; ☑0361-975351; Jl Sugriwa 32; ☉r incl
breakfast from 300,000Rp; ❋☎) In a primo loca-
tion, this family homestay offers the timeless
Ubud experience. Come and go past a charm-
ing family as they make offerings. The four
rooms have the basics plus cleanly tiled bath-
rooms and terraces. The hosts offer classes in
batik painting (300,000Rp per day).

Pondok Krishna GUESTHOUSE $
(Map p150; ☑0361-977126; kriz_tie@yahoo.com; Jl
Bisma; r from 250,000Rp; ❋☎) This light and
airy family compound has seven rooms set
among the frog-filled rice fields west of Jl
Bisma. The open common area with its sun-
ny location is good for nailing that tan.

Happy Mango Tree HOSTEL $
(Map p150; ☑0812 3844 5498; www.thehappy
mangotree.com; Jl Bisma 27; dm/d from
100,000/250,000Rp; ☎) This bright and bubbly
hostel revels in its hippie vibe. Bright colours
abound inside the rooms and out on the var-
ious terraces, some of which have rice-field
views. Mixed dorms have four or five beds;
doubles come with names (and matching de-
cor) such as Love Shack and Ceiling Museum.
There's a social bar and a restaurant, too.

Ni Nyoman Warini Bungalows HOMESTAY $
(Map p150; ☑0361-978364; Jl Hanoman; r
200,000-350,000Rp; ❋☎) There's a whole
pod of simple family compounds with
rooms for rent back on a little footpath off Jl
Hanoman. It's quiet, and without even try-
ing you'll find yourself enjoying the rhythms
of family life. The eight rooms here have hot
water and traditional bamboo furniture.

Puri Asri 2 GUESTHOUSE $
(Map p150; ☑0361-973210; Jl Sukma 59; r 200,000-
350,000Rp; ❋☎≋) Work your way through
a classic family compound and you'll find
seven bungalow-style rooms with views of a
ravine. It's a fabulous deal and rooms come
with hot water. Cool off in the nice pool.

Biangs HOMESTAY $
(Map p150; ☑0361-976520; wah_oeboed@ya
hoo.com; Jl Sukma 28; r with fan/air-con from
100,000/300,000Rp; ❋☎) In a little garden,
Biangs (meaning 'mama') homestay has
six well-maintained rooms, with hot water.
Three generations of the family make this a
genuine family homestay. Jl Sukma is one of
Ubud's most atmospheric streets.

IVOHA / SHUTTERSTOCK ©

1. Sacred Monkey Forest Sanctuary
Home to over 600 grey-haired and light-fingered long-tailed macaques - watch your possessions! (p154)

2. Yoga Retreats
Ubud has a number of famous yoga centres and spas offering yoga classes. (p157)

3. Balinese Dancers
There are more than a dozen different dances in Bali. Temple performances can last several hours. (p350)

4. Pura Taman Saraswati
Hindu temple decorated with carvings honouring Dewi Saraswati, goddess of wisdom and the arts. (p149)

① FINDING LONG-TERM ACCOMMODATION

There are many houses and flats you can rent or share in the Ubud area. For local information about options, check the noticeboards at Pondok Pekak Library (p160) and Bali Bunda (p173). Also look in the free *Bali Advertiser* (www.baliadvertiser.biz) newspaper and the local website www.banjartamu.org. Prices start at about US$300 a month and climb rapidly as you add amenities.

Ina Inn   GUESTHOUSE $
(Map p150; ☑0361-971093; http://inainnubud. com; Jl Bisma; r 300,000-400,000Rp; 🛜🛖) Stroll the thickly planted grounds and enjoy views across Ubud and the rice fields. The 12 rooms (some fan-cooled) are basic but clean and comfy. The pool is ideal after a day of walking. If you want to take the plunge closer to your bed, rooms have tubs.

Adipana Bungalow   GUESTHOUSE $$
(Map p150; ☑0817 978 8934; www.adipanabunga low.com; Jl Jembawan 27; r incl breakfast 600,000Rp; ❄🛜🛖) An appealing two-storey guesthouse, the six rooms here give you a choice of having a terrace with direct access to the pool or a balcony with airy views of bamboo-bedecked Ubud. There are some flashes of style and kitchen facilities in each unit.

Sama's Cottages   GUESTHOUSE $$
(Map p150; ☑0361-973481; www.samascottages ubud.com; Jl Bisma; s with fan/air-con 520,000/ 630,000Rp, d with fan/air-con 575,000/700,000Rp; ❄🛜🛖) Terraced down a hill, this lovely little hideaway has 12 bungalow-style rooms with lashings of Balinese style layered on absolute simplicity. The oval pool feels like a jungle oasis. Ask for low-season discounts.

Komaneka at Bisma   BOUTIQUE HOTEL $$$
(Map p156; ☑0361-971933; http://bisma.komane ka.com; Jl Bisma; r from US$220; ❄@🛜🛖) Set well back in the rice fields near the river valley, this newish resort defines posh with a heavy overlay of Bali style. Accommodation ranges from suites to large three-bedroom villas for 17 units total. The compound exudes grace, along with thoughtful touches ranging from Apple TVs loaded with movies to freshly baked cookies.

Ladera Villa Ubud   HOTEL $$$
(Map p150; ☑0361-978127; http://laderavillaubud. com; Jl Bisma; villa from 1,500,000Rp; ❄🛜🛖)

With the bottom of Jl Bisma now linked to Monkey Forest Rd, there is a lot of development near the pretty river valley. This comfortable hotel gets all the details right. The eight villas have alluring private pools, full kitchens and gleaming hardwood floors. Service is good and the value is excellent.

🛏 Padangtegal & Tebesaya

★Family Guest House   HOMESTAY $
(Map p150; ☑0361-974054; www.familyubud.com; Jl Sukma 39; r incl breakfast with fan/air-con from 250,000/300,000Rp; ❄🛜) There's a bit of bustle from the busy family at this charming homestay. The eight rooms have modern comforts in a traditional shell. Some also include tubs; and at the top, they have a balcony with a valley view.

Aji Lodge   HOMESTAY $
(Map p150; ☑0361-973255; ajilodge11@yahoo.com; off Jl Sukma; r 200,000-300,000Rp; 🛜) A group of comfortable family compounds lines a footpath east of Jl Sukma. Enjoy one of six rooms here that are down the hill by the river for the full bedtime symphony of birds, bugs and critters. All rooms have terraces.

Artini Cottages 1   HOMESTAY $
(Map p150; ☑0361-975348; www.artinibaligroups. com; Jl Hanoman; r from 400,000Rp; 🛜) The Artini family runs a small empire of good-value guesthouses on Jl Hanoman. This, the original, is in an ornate family compound with many flowers. The three bungalows have hot water and large bathtubs. The more upscale Artini 2, with views and a pool, is opposite.

★Matahari Cottages   GUESTHOUSE $$
(Map p150; ☑0361-975459; www.matahariubud. com; Jl Jembawan; r 400,000-800,000Rp; ❄🛜🛖) 🍃 This whimsical place has 15 flamboyant, themed rooms, including the 'Batavia Princess' and the 'Indian Pasha'. The library is a vision out of a 1920s fantasy. It also boasts a self-proclaimed 'jungle jacuzzi', an upscale way to replicate the old Bali tradition of river-bathing. There's a multicourse breakfast and high tea elaborately served on silver.

🛏 Sambahan & Sakti

Bali Asli Lodge   HOMESTAY $
(Map p156; ☑0361-970537; www.baliaslilodge.com; Jl Suweta; r incl breakfast from 300,000Rp; 🛜) Escape the central Ubud hubbub here. Made is your friendly host, and her five rooms are in traditional Balinese stone-and-brick houses

set in verdant gardens. There are terraces where you can let the hours pass; interiors are clean and comfy. Town is a 15-minute walk away.

Ketut's Place
GUESTHOUSE $$

(Map p156; ☎ 0361-975304; www.ketutsplace. com; Jl Suweta 40; r incl breakfast with fan/air-con from 500,000/600,000Rp; ✹@🛜🏊) A step up from the usual temple compound homestays, here the 16 rooms all have artful accents and river-valley views. A dramatic pool shimmers down the hillside. Rooms range from basic with fans to deluxe versions with air-con and bathtubs.

Ubud Sari Health Resort
GUESTHOUSE $$

(Map p156; ☎ 0361-974393; www.ubudsari.com; Jl Kajeng; r from US$45; ✹🛜🏊) Overlooking a bubbling stream and surrounded by forest, the 21 rooms at this noted health spa have a name that says it all: Zen Village. The plants in the gardens are labelled for their medicinal qualities, and the cafe serves organic, vegetarian fare. Guests can use the health facilities, including the sauna and whirlpool.

Klub Kokos
GUESTHOUSE $$

(Map p156; ☎ 0361-849 3502; www.klubkokos.com; r incl breakfast US$54-100; ✹@🛜🏊) A beautiful 1.5km walk north along the Campuan ridge, Klub Kokos is a ridge-top hideaway with a big pool and eight appealing bungalow-style rooms. It's reachable by car from the north; call for directions. There's a cafe with rice-field views.

Wapa di Ume
RESORT $$$

(Map p156; ☎ 0361-973178; www.wapadiume.com; Jl Suweta; r incl breakfast from US$170, villas from US$260; ✹@🛜🏊) Located a gentle 2.5km uphill from the centre, this elegant compound enjoys engrossing verdant views across rice fields. New and old styles mix in the 33 large units; go for a villa with a view. Service is superb yet relaxed. Listening to gamelan practice echoing across the fields at night is quite magical. There's a shuttle bus on the hour to central Ubud.

🛏 Nyuhkuning

★ Swasti Eco Cottages
GUESTHOUSE $$

(Map p156; ☎ 0361-974079; www.baliswasti.com; Jl Nyuh Bulan; r incl breakfast with fan/air-con from 650,000/750,000Rp; ✹@🛜) 🍴 A five-minute walk from the south entrance to the Monkey Forest, this compound has large grounds that feature an organic garden (produce is used in the cafe). Some rooms are in simple two-storey blocks; others are in vintage traditional houses brought here from across Indonesia. Swasti offers a mix of Balinese classes and workshops. Its green cred out-Ubud's Ubud.

Alam Indah
HOTEL $$

(Map p156; ☎ 0361-974629; www.alamindahbali. com; Jl Nyuh Bulan; r incl breakfast US$65-140; ✹🛜🏊) Just south of the Monkey Forest, this isolated and spacious resort has 16 rooms that are beautifully finished in natural materials to traditional designs. The Wos Valley views are entrancing, especially from the multilevel pool area. There's a free shuttle into central Ubud.

Kertiyasa Bungalows
GUESTHOUSE $$

(Map p156; ☎ 0361-971377; www.kertiyasabungalow.com; Jl Nyuh Bulan; r US$38-80; ✹🛜🏊) Set in a quiet location, this recently renovated place has 15 rooms ranging from garden-view standards to private, very large rooms. The meandering pool is surrounded by beautiful plantings.

Saren Indah Hotel
HOTEL $$

(Map p156; ☎ 0361-971471; www.sarenhotel.com; Jl Nyuh Bulan; r US$55-85; ✹🛜🏊) South of the Monkey Forest, this 15-room hotel sits in the middle of rice fields – be sure to get a 2nd-floor room to enjoy the views. Rooms have classic Balinese charm; better ones have fridges and stylish tubs.

🛏 Pengosekan

Casa Ganesha Hotel
HOTEL $

(Map p156; ☎ 0361-971488; www.casaganesha. com; Jl Raya Pengosekan; r US$30; ✹🛜🏊) A great-value budget choice in a great location just south of Ubud's centre, this 24-room hotel has two-storey blocks built around a pool. Rooms are straightforward and have terraces or balconies. There are pretty rice fields nearby.

★ Agung Raka
BOUTIQUE HOTEL $$

(Map p156; ☎ 0361-975757; www.baliagungrakaresort.com; Jl Raya Pengosekan; r from US$50, bungalow from US$80; ✹🛜🏊) This 43-room hotel sprawls out across picture perfect rice fields just south of the centre of Ubud. Rooms are large and suitably Balinese in motif but the real stars are the bungalows set back on a rice terrace amid palm trees. You can live the life of a duck as you hear the nighttime symphony of bugs and birds.

Tegal Sari   HOTEL **$$**

(Map p156; ☑0361-973318; www.tegalsari-ubud.
com; Jl Raya Pengosekan; r 330,000-990,000Rp;
✴@🛜🏊) Though literally a stone's throw
from the hectic main road, here rice
fields (along with ducks) miraculously
materialise. Go for a superdeluxe cottage
(770,000Rp) with bathtub looking out to
soul-calming bucolic views. Units in the
new brick buildings, on the other hand, are
stark. It has two pools, including one on the
rooftop, and a yoga space.

ARMA Resort   HOTEL **$$$**

(Map p156; ☑0361-976659; www.armabali.com;
Jl Raya Pengosekan; r from US$120, villas from
US$250; ✴@🛜🏊) Get full Balinese cultural
immersion at the hotel enclave of the ARMA
compound. The expansive property has a
large library and elegant gardens. The 10
villas come with private pools. The fabulous
namesake museum is on the grounds.

🛏 Peliatan

★**Maya Ubud**   HOTEL **$$$**

(☑0361-977888; www.mayaubud.com; Jl
Gunung Sari, Peliatan; r/villa incl breakfast
US$280/440; ✴@🛜🏊) One of the most
beautiful large hotels around Ubud, this
massive 10-hectare property is superbly inte-
grated into its surrounding river valley and
rice fields. The 108 rooms and villas have
the sort of open and light feeling combined
with traditional materials that defines the
concept of 'Bali style'. The infinity pool over-
looking the jungle is dramatic, as is the spa.

🛏 Campuan & Sanggingan

Hotel Tjampuhan   HOTEL **$$**

(Map p156; ☑0361-975368; www.tjampuhan-bali.
com; Jl Raya Campuan; r incl breakfast US$110-
180; ✴@🛜🏊) This venerable 67-room place
overlooks the confluence of Sungai Wos and
Campuan. The influential German artist
Walter Spies lived here in the 1930s, and his
former home, which sleeps four people, is
part of the hotel. Bungalow-style units spill
down the hill and enjoy mesmerising valley
and temple views.

The historic house where Spies lived can
be rented for 3,000,000Rp a night.

★**Warwick Ibah Luxury Villas**   HOTEL **$$$**

(Map p156; ☑0361-974466; www.warwickibah.com;
off Jl Raya Campuan; ste/villa incl breakfast from
US$170/275; ✴🛜🏊) Overlooking the rushing

waters and rice-clad hills of the Wos Valley,
the Ibah offers refined luxury in 17 spacious,
stylish, individual suites and villas that com-
bine ancient and modern details. Each could
be a feature in an interior-design magazine.
The swimming pool is set into the hillside
amid gardens and lavish stone carvings.

★**Como Uma Ubud**   BOUTIQUE HOTEL **$$$**

(☑0361-972448; www.comohotels.com; Jl Raya
Sanggingan; r from US$290, villa from US$390;
✴🛜🏊) One of Ubud's most attractive properties, the 46 rooms here come in a variety of
sizes but all have a relaxed naturalistic style
that goes well with the gorgeous views over
the gardens and the river valley beyond. Service and amenities like the restaurant are
superb.

🛏 Penestanan

Santra Putra   GUESTHOUSE **$**

(Map p156; ☑0361-977810; www.facebook.com/
santraputraKAS; Jl Pacekan 18, off Jl Raya Campuan; r incl breakfast 300,000-400,000Rp; 🛜)
Run by internationally exhibited abstract
artist I Wayan Karja – whose studio-gal-
lery (p160) is also on-site – this place has 11
big, open, airy rooms with hot water. Enjoy
paddy-field views from all vantage points.
Painting and drawing classes are offered by
the artist.

Roam   DESIGN HOTEL **$$**

(Map p156; ☑0361-479 2884; www.roam.co/
places/ubud; Jl Raya Penestanan; r per week from
US$500; ✴🛜) Set in an old renovated apart-
ment, this hipster co-living hotel has your
classic motel configuration but with rock-
and-roll panache. The 24 rooms are com-
fortable and include fridges and fast wi-fi.
The rooftop deck has sunloungers, a healthy
cafe and a yoga space. The target market are
'global nomads', who set up shop in Ubud
and design an app or two.

Melati Cottages   HOTEL **$$**

(Map p156; ☑0361-974650; www.melati-cottages.
com; Jl Raya Penestanan; r US$35-60; ✴🛜) Set
back among the rice fields, the deeply shaded Melati has 22 simple rooms in two-storey,
bungalow-style buildings. All have porches
for listening to the sounds of the fields and
taking in the cool night air. Top-floor guests
enjoy good views.

Villa Nirvana   BOUTIQUE HOTEL **$$**

(Map p156; ☑0361-979419; www.villanirvanabali.
com; Penestanan; r incl breakfast US$120-200;

WHERE TO STAY IN UBUD

Do you want to be in the centre or the quiet countryside? Have a rice-field view or enjoy a room with stylish design? Choices are myriad, especially on sites like airbnb.com and homeaway.com where everything seems to be 'close to Ubud', even when the '10-minute drive' actually takes half an hour. The main areas of accommodation in Ubud are as follows.

Central Ubud
This original heart of Ubud has a vast range of places to rest your weary head and you'll enjoy a location that will cut down on the need for long walks or 'transport'. If you're near **Jl Raya Ubud**, don't settle for a room with noise from the main drag. Small and quiet streets to the east of the main crossroads, including Jl Karna, Jl Maruti and Jl Goutama, have numerous family-style homestays. **North of Jl Raya Ubud**, streets like Jl Kajeng and Jl Suweta offer a timeless tableau, with kids playing in the streets and many fine homestays. **Monkey Forest Rd** has a high concentration of lodgings: go for one well off the traffic-choked road. **Jl Bisma** runs into a plateau of rice fields. New places are popping up all the time, especially down at the south end where a path links to Monkey Forest Rd.

Padangtegal & Tebesaya
A good place to browse. East of central Ubud, but still conveniently located, Padangtegal has several budget lodgings along Jl Hanoman. A little further east, the quiet village of Tebesaya comprises little more than its main street, Jl Sukma, which runs between two streams. Cute homestays can be found down small footpaths. Also check out Jl Sugriwa and Jl Jembawan.

Sambahan & Sakti
Going north from Jl Raya Ubud, you are soon in rolling terraces of rice fields. Tucked away here you'll find interesting and often luxurious hotels, yet you can have a beautiful walk to the centre in well under an hour.

Nyuhkuning
A popular area just south of the Monkey Forest, Nyuhkuning has some creative guesthouses and hotels, yet is not a long walk to the centre.

Pengosekan
Immediately south of the centre, Pengosekan is good for shopping, dining and activities like yoga.

Campuan & Sanggingan
The long sloping road that takes its names from these two communities west of the centre has a number of posh properties on its east side that overlook a lush river valley.

Penestanan
Just west of the Campuan bridge, steep Jl Raya Penestanan branches off to the left, and climbs up and around to Penestanan, a large plateau of (fast disappearing) rice fields and lodgings. Rooms and bungalows amid the rice are pitched at those seeking longer-term lodgings. Stroll the narrow paths and you'll find options at all prices. You can also get here via a steep climb up a set of concrete stairs off Jl Raya Campuan.

Sayan & Ayung Valley
Two kilometres west of Ubud, the fast-flowing Sungai Ayung has carved out a deep valley, its sides sculpted into terraced paddy fields or draped in thick rainforest. Overlooking this verdant valley are some of Bali's best resorts.

❊ ❈ ❊) You may find nirvana reaching Villa Nirvana: access is along a 150m path through a small river valley from the west or along a rice-field path from the top of steep steps from the east. The six-villa compound, designed by local architect Awan Sukhro Edhi, is a serene retreat. Rates include shuttle service and free loan of a mobile phone.

Sayan & Ayung Valley

Taman Bebek   HOTEL $$

(Map p156; ☑0361-975385; www.tamanbebek-bali.com; Jl Raya Sayan; r 750,000-1,600,000Rp; ✸✿🖨🏊) A spectacular, verdant location overlooking the Sayan Valley may keep you glued to your terrace throughout the day. Four suites and seven villas here wrap around the Sayan Terrace (p154) and enjoy a stylish common area. All have understated yet classic Balinese wood-and-thatch architecture as designed by the late Made Wijaya, the legendary garden designer.

Bambu Indah   BOUTIQUE HOTEL $$$

(☑0361-977922; www.bambuindah.com; Banjar Baung; r incl breakfast US$200-500; 🖨🏊) Famed expat entrepreneur John Hardy sold his jewellery company in 2007 and became a hotelier. On a ridge near Sayan and his beloved Sungai Ayung, he's assembled a compound of 100-year-old royal Javanese houses and a stunning Sumbanese thatched house; each space is furnished with style and flair. Several outbuildings create a timeless village with underpinnings of luxury. Free shuttle into central Ubud.

Amandari   HOTEL $$$

(☑0361-975333; www.amanresorts.com; Kedewatan; ste incl breakfast from US$850; ✸@🖨🏊) In Kedewatan village, the storied Amandari does everything with the charm and grace of a classical Balinese dancer. Superb views over the jungle and down to the river – the 30m green-tiled swimming pool seems to drop right over the edge – are just some of the inducements. The 30 private pavilions may prove inescapable.

Four Seasons Resort   HOTEL $$$

(☑0361-977577; www.fourseasons.com; Sayan; ste from US$700, villas from US$900; ✸@🖨🏊) Set below the valley rim, the curved open-air reception area looks like a Cinerama screen of Ubud beauty. Many villas have private pools and all share the same amazing views and striking modern design. At night you hear just the water rushing below from any of the 60 units (each of which is very sizeable).

Kedewatan

★Mandapa,
a Ritz-Carlton Reserve   VILLA $$$

(Map p156; ☑0361-4792777; www.ritzcarlton.com; Jl Kedewatan; ste/villa incl breakfast from US$580/800; ✸🖨) Epic doesn't even begin to describe the extent to which this stunning new resort soars. Sprawling over 5.5 hectares, it's the size of a small village, and set in a spectacular valley enclosed by rice fields. The stars of the show are the villas on the riverfront, but you can't go wrong in any of the villas or suites.

Kubu (p177) restaurant is worth a visit even if you're not staying here, both for its scenic riverfront location and its five-course degustation menu.

🍴 Eating

Ubud's cafes and restaurants are some of the best in Bali. Local and expat chefs produce a bounty of authentic Balinese dishes, as well as inventive Asian and other international cuisines. Healthy menus abound. Cafes with good coffee seem almost as common as frangipani blossoms. Be sure to be seated by 9pm or your options will narrow rapidly. Book dinner tables in high season.

🍴 Jalan Raya Ubud & Around

Gelato Secrets   GELATERIA $

(Map p150; www.gelatosecrets.com; Monkey Forest Rd; from 20,000Rp; ⊙10am-10.30pm) This temple to frozen goodness has fresh flavours made from local fruits and spices, such as dragonfruit cinnamon or cashew black sesame.

Bali Bunda Shop   MARKET $

(Map p150; www.balibuda.com; Jl Raya Ubud; ⊙8am-8pm) The prepared food and grocery shop for Bali Bunda is a great source for organic produce and groceries; its baked goods are excellent.

Anomali Coffee   COFFEE $

(Map p150; Jl Raya Ubud; snacks from 20,000Rp; ⊙7am-11pm; 🖨) Local hipsters get their java from this place which is, well, from Java. Indonesia's answer to Starbucks takes its (excellent) coffee seriously and so does the young crowd that gathers here. .

Kué   CAFE $

(Map p150; ☑976 7040; Jl Raya Ubud; meals 30,000-80,000Rp; ⊙8am-9pm; ✸🖨) A top organic chocolate shop with a couple of stools downstairs; climb the side stairs for a lovely cafe that sits above the road chaos. Good baked items as well as juices, coffees, sandwiches, organic wraps and Indo mains make it a great casual stop.

★**Hujon Locale** INDONESIAN **$$**
(Map p150; ☑0361-849 3092; www.hujanlocale.
com; Jl Sriwedari 5; mains 110,000-200,000Rp;
☺noon-10pm; 🛜) From the team of the criti-
cally acclaimed Mama San in Seminyak, Hu-
jon Locale is one of Ubud's most enjoyable
restaurants. The menu mixes traditional In-
donesian dishes with modern, creative flair,
from Achenese prawn curry to slow-braised
Sumatran lamb curry. The setting within a
chic colonial-style two-storey bungalow is
made for a balmy evening. Great cocktails.

Bali Bunda CAFE **$$**
(Map p150; ☑0361-976324; www.balibuda.com; Jl
Jembawan 1; mains 45,000-80,000Rp; ☺7.30am-
10pm; ☑) This breezy upper-floor place offers a full range of vegetarian *jamu* (health
tonics), salads, sandwiches, savoury crepes,
excellent thin-crust pizzas and gelato. The
bulletin board downstairs is packed with
idiosyncratic Ubud notices.

Casa Luna INDONESIAN **$$**
(Map p150; ☑0361-977409; www.casalunabali.
com; Jl Raya Ubud; meals from 50,000Rp; ☺8am-
10pm) Enjoy creative Indonesian-focused
dishes such as addictive bamboo skewers
of minced seafood satay (try to pick out the
dozen or so spices). Goods from its well-
known bakery are also a must. The owner,
Janet deNeefe, is the force behind the laud-
ed Ubud Writers & Readers Festival (p162).

Spice INDONESIAN **$$**
(Map p150; ☑0361-479 2420; www.spicebali.
com; Jl Raya Ubud 23; mains 60,000-125,000Rp;
☺noon-11pm) Coming to a mall near you, this
high-concept cafe is the prototype for a new
dining concept by Ubud chef Chris Salans.
No matter, the open kitchen cooks up tasty
takes on uncommon Indonesian dishes on a
changing menu. It's very casual and there's a
big emphasis on the bar.

Il Giardino ITALIAN **$$**
(Map p150; ☑0361-974271; www.ilgiardinobali.
com; Jl Kajeng 3, Han Snel Siti Bungalows; mains
60,000-150,000Rp; ☺5-10.30pm; 🛜) This ro-
mantic outdoor Italian restaurant has a
beautiful setting overlooking a lily pond. It's
at the studio/gallery and namesake bunga-
lows of the late Dutch painter Han Snel. It
does *aperitivo*, wood-fired pizzas, home-
made pastas and hearty Italian mains.

Clear FUSION **$$**
(Map p150; ☑0361-889 4437; www.facebook.com/
ClearCafeUbud/; Jl Hanoman 8; meals US$4-15;
☺8am-10pm; 🖉🛜) 🖉 This high-concept restaurant brings a bit of Hollywood to Ubud.
The dishes are relentlessly healthy but also
creative; served artfully and sourced locally.
Tables are now on two levels after a post-fire
reconstruction. It has a deli counter for pic-
nics and fresh snacks. BYOB; kids menu.

Fair Warung Balé INTERNATIONAL **$$**
(Map p150; ☑0361-975370; www.fairfuturefounda-
tion.org; Jl Sriwedari 6; mains 50,000-110,000Rp;
☺11am-10pm) 🖉 Mellow by day, hot spot by
night; there are often queues in the evenings
to get a table at this attractive upstairs res-
taurant. It's run by the Swiss-based NGO,
Fair Future Foundation, and 100% of pro-
ceeds go to healthcare in the local communi-
ty. Food ranges from local curries to freshly
baked baguettes with tuna tartare.

Black Beach ITALIAN **$$**
(Map p150; ☑0361-971353; www.blackbeach.asia;
Jl Hanoman; mains 50,000-120,000Rp; ☺11am-
10pm) They beat their own dough and then
let it slowly rise before turning it into good
thin-crust pizza. If that doesn't sway you, the
tasty pasta might. Views from the upstairs
dining area are nice but what really draws
in the intelligentsia is the regular showing
of art-house movies on the terrace.

🍴 North of Jalan Raya Ubud

Warung Ibu Oka BALINESE **$$**
(Map p150; ☑0361-976345; Jl Suweta; mains
from 55,000Rp; ☺11am-6pm) Opposite Ubud
Palace, lunchtime crowds are waiting for
one thing: Balinese-style roast *babi guling*
(suckling pig). Order a *spesial* to get the best
cut. Plenty of tourist hype means that prices
are more than double the norm.

🍴 Monkey Forest Road

★**Three Monkeys** FUSION **$$**
(Map p150; ☑0361-975554; www.threemonkey-
scafebali.com; Monkey Forest Rd; mains 60,000-
185,000Rp; ☺8am-10pm; 🛜) Order a kaf-
fir-lime mojito and settle back amid the frog
symphony of the rice fields. Add the glow of
tiki torches for a magical effect. By day there
are sandwiches, salads and gelato. At night
there's a fusion menu of Asian classics.

Watercress CAFE **$$**
(Map p150; ☑0361-976127; www.watercressubud.
com; Monkey Forest Rd; mains 90,000-150,000Rp;
☺7.30am-11pm; 🛜) The Ubud version of the
Canggu original attracts a young fashion-

able crowd for quality Western food. It has a stylish double-level open-air setting, does creative all-day breakfasts, and offers a menu leaning towards modern Australian. Fresh salads, awesome fish burgers with crispy chat potatoes, king prawn linguine and charred lamb chops.

✖ Jalan Dewi Sita & Jalan Goutama

East of Monkey Forest Rd, a short stroll takes you into Ubud's best selection of restaurants.

Juice Ja Cafe   CAFE $
(Map p150; ☑0361-971056; Jl Dewi Sita; mains from 30,000Rp; ☺8am-11pm; 🕏) 🍴 Glass of spirulina? Dash of wheat grass with your papaya juice? Organic fruits and vegetables go into the food at this funky bakery-cafe. Little brochures explain the provenance of items such as the organic cashew nuts. Enjoy the patio.

Tutmak Cafe   CAFE $
(Map p150; ☑0361-975754; Jl Dewi Sita; mains 40,000-100,000Rp; ☺8am-11pm; 🕏) This smart, breezy multilevel terrace restaurant is a popular place for a refreshing drink or something to munch on from the menu of Indo classics. The *nasi campur* (rice with a choice of side dishes) with fresh tuna is one of Ubud's finest.

Dewa Warung   INDONESIAN $
(Map p150; Jl Goutama; meals 20,000-30,000Rp; ☺8am-11pm) When it rains, the tin roof sounds like a tap-dance convention and the bare lightbulbs sway in the breeze. A little garden surrounds tables a few steps above the road where diners tuck into plates of sizzling fresh Indo fare. Cheap Bintang.

Waroeng Bernadette   INDONESIAN $$
(Map p150; ☑0821 4742 4779; Jl Goutama; mains from 60,000Rp; ☺11am-11pm; 🕏) It's not called the 'Home of Rendang' for nothing. The west Sumatran classic dish of long-marinated meats (beef is the true classic, but here there's also a veggie jackfruit variety) is pulled off with colour and flair. Other dishes have a zesty zing missing from lacklustre versions served elsewhere. The elevated dining room is a vision of kitsch.

Locavore to Go   CAFE $$
(Map p150; ☑0361-977733; Jl Dewi Sita; mains 50,000-120,000Rp; ☺8.30am-6pm; 🕏) From the same team as critically acclaimed Locavore down the road, this much simpler affair uses

their famous charcuterie for tasty brunches ranging from breakfast burgers and banh mi to pulled-pork brioche, all in an open-fronted cafe. A mandatory Slow Food stop.

Melting Wok   ASIAN $$
(Map p150; ☑0821 5366 6087; Jl Goutama; mains from 50,000Rp; ☺10am-11pm Tue-Sun) Pan-Asian fare pleases the masses at this very popular open-air restaurant on the Goutama strip. Curries, noodle dishes, tempeh and a lot more fill a menu that makes decisions tough. Desserts take on a bit of colonial flavour: French accents abound. The service is relaxed but efficient. Booking advised.

Cafe Havana   LATIN AMERICAN $$
(Map p150; ☑0361-972973; Jl Dewi Sita; mains from 60,000Rp; ☺8am-11pm) All that's missing is Fidel. Actually, the decrepitude of its namesake city is also missing from this smart and stylish cafe. Dishes exude Latin flair, such as the tasty pork numbers, but expect surprises such as the fab crème brûlée oatmeal in the mornings. There's nightly live music 7pm to 10pm (salsa dancing Wednesdays).

Kafe Batan Waru   INDONESIAN $$
(Map p150; ☑0361-977528; Jl Dewi Sita; mains from 60,000Rp) This cafe serves consistently good Indonesian food. Tired of *mie goreng* made from instant noodles? With noodles made fresh daily, this version celebrates a lost art. Western dishes include sandwiches and salads. *Bebek betutu* (smoked duck) and *babi guling* can be ordered in advance.

★Locavore   FUSION $$$
(Map p150; ☑0361-977733; www.restaurant-locavore.com; Jl Dewi Sita; 5-/7-course menu 675,000/775,000Rp; ☺noon-2pm & 6-10pm; 🅿✳🕏) *The* foodie haven in Ubud, this temple to locally sourced foods is the town's toughest table. Book weeks in advance. Meals are degustation and can top out at nine courses; expect the joy to last three hours. Chefs Eelke Plasmeijer and Ray Adriansyah in the open kitchen are magicians; enjoy the show (and go for the wine pairings). Up the hill, try Locavore to Go, which serves a great brunch, with the likes of breakfast burgers and banh mi. It has excellent picnic fare.

★Pica   SOUTH AMERICAN $$$
(Map p150; ☑0361-971660; Jl Dewi Sita; mains 160,000-300,000Rp; ☺11am-10pm Tue-Sun) Much-acclaimed, the South American cuisine here is one of Ubud's culinary high-

lights thanks to the young couple behind this excellent restaurant. From the open kitchen, dishes making creative use of beef, pork, fish, potatoes and more issue forth in a diner-pleasing stream. The house sourdough bread is superb.

✗ Padangtegal & Tebesaya

Warung Sopa   VEGETARIAN $
(Map p150; ☎0361-276 5897; Jl Sugriwa 36; mains 30,000-60,000Rp; ⊙8am-9.30pm; 🛜🍴) This popular open-air place in a residential street captures the Ubud vibe with creative and tasty vegetarian fare with a Balinese twist. Look for specials of the day on display; the ever-changing *nasi campur* is a treat.

Earth Cafe & Market   VEGETARIAN $
(Map p150; www.dtebali.com/earth-cafe-market-ubud; Jl Gotama Selatan; meals from 30,000Rp; 🛜🍴) 'Eliminate free radicals' is but one of many healthy drinks at this hard-core outpost for vegetarian organic dining and drinking. The seemingly endless menu has a plethora of soups, salads and platters that are heavy on Med flavours. There's a market on the main floor.

Warung Mangga Madu   INDONESIAN $
(Map p150; ☎ 0361-977334; Jl Gunung Sari; mains from 15,000Rp; ⊙8am-10pm) The slightly elevated dining terrace here is a fine place to enjoy excellent versions of Indo classics like *nasi campur*. That's your driver at the next table reading the *Bali Pos* newspaper. Load up on road snacks to go.

Mama's Warung   INDONESIAN $
(Map p150; ☎0361-977047, Jl Sukma; mains 25,000-50,000Rp; ⊙8am-10pm) A real budget find among the bargain homestays of Tebesaya. Mama and her retinue cook up Indo classics that are spicy and redolent with garlic (the avocado salad, yum!). The freshly made peanut sauce for the satay is silky smooth, the fried sambal superb.

Ubud Organic Market   MARKET $
(Map p150; www.ubudorganicmarket.com; off Jl Sukma; ⊙9am-2pm Wed & Sat) Operates twice a week: Wednesdays at the UBC Tebesaya, the village *wantilan* (open pavilion), and Saturdays at Pizza Bagus (p176) on Jl Raya Pengosekan.

Kafe   CAFE $
(Map p150; ☎0361-780 3802; Jl Hanoman 44; mains 15,000-50,000Rp; ⊙8am-11pm; 🍴) 🌱 Kafe has a huge organic menu great for veg-

WALKING FOR ORGANIC TREATS
....

Looking for a fun walk of an hour or so? Set in a beautiful location on a plateau overlooking rice terraces and river valleys, the small cafe Warung Bodag Maliah (p177) sits in the middle of a big organic farm belonging to the locally popular Sari Organic brand.

Yes the food's healthy, but more importantly, given that some of the pleasure is getting here, the drinks are cool and refreshing. Look for a little track heading north off Jl Raya Ubud that goes past Abangan Bungalows, then follow the signs along footpaths for another 800m. Beware, however, that Ubud's furious development is happening here as well; you may be run down by a motorbike carrying building supplies.

Keep walking north through the rice fields, as long as your interest or endurance lasts, because the surroundings will get more natural. Look for little offshoot trails to either side that lead to small rivers.

gie grazing or just having a coffee, juice or house-made natural soft drink. Breakfasts are healthy while lunch meals feature excellent salads, bowls and burritos, with many raw items. It's always busy.

Kebun   MEDITERRANEAN $$
(Map p150; ☎ 0361-780 3801; www.kebunbistro.com; Jl Hanoman 44; mains from 60,000Rp; ⊙11am-11pm) Napa meets Ubud at this cute little bistro and it's a good match. A long wine list (with specials) can be paired with French- and Italian-accented dishes large and small. There are daily specials including pastas and risottos. Dine inside or out on the appealing terrace.

Bebek Bengil   INDONESIAN $$
(Map p150; Dirty Duck Diner; ☎0361-975489; www.bebekbengil.com; Jl Hanoman; mains 70,000-220,000Rp; ⊙10am-11pm) This famous place is hugely popular for one reason: its crispy Balinese duck, which is marinated for 36 hours in spices and then fried. The ducks on one of the few surviving rice fields outside the huge open-air dining pavilions look worried.

Siti's Warung Little India   INDIAN $$
(Map p150; ☎ 0819 9962 4555; Jl Sukma 36; mains from 45,000Rp; ⊙10am-10pm) Run by the

delightful Siti, this character-filled Indian restaurant is decked out in vintage Bollywood posters and accompanied by a soundtrack of Hindi pop. Its thalis, samosas and masala chai are all delicious and authentic. Also delivers tiffins.

Teges

Jl Cok Rai Pudak – which turns into Jl Raya Mas, which runs due south to Mas from Peliatan – has an excellent choice for Balinese food.

★**Warung Teges** BALINESE $
(Map p156; Jl Cok Rai Pudak; mains from 25,000Rp; ☺8am-6pm) The *nasi campur* is better here than almost anywhere else around Ubud. The restaurant gets just about everything right, from the pork sausage to the chicken, the *babi guling* and even the tempeh. The sambal is legendary: fresh, tangy, with a perfect amount of heat.

Nyuhkuning

Warung Pojok INDONESIAN $
(Map p156; ☎0361-749 4535; Jl Nyuh Bulan; mains 20,000-40,000Rp; ☺8am-10pm; ☎) This buzzing corner cafe has a serene spot overlooking Ubud's other football field. Besides plenty of rice and noodle dishes, there are lots of veggie options, lassies and juices.

Swasti Beloved Cafe INTERNATIONAL $$
(Map p156; ☎0361-974079; www.baliswasti.com; Jl Nyuh Bulan; meals 40,000-80,000Rp; ☺8am-10pm; ☎) ✿ This cafe attached to the excellent guesthouse of the same name is reason enough to take a stroll through the Monkey Forest. Indonesian and Western dishes prepared from the large in-house organic garden are fresh and tasty. Have a glass of fresh juice with the beloved fondant au chocolat or raw mango cheesecake. Watch for children's evening dance performances.

Pengosekan

Many highly regarded restaurants are found along the curves of Jl Raya Pengosekan. It's always worth seeing what's new.

Pitri Minang INDONESIAN $
(Map p156; Jl Cok Gede Rai; meals from 15,000Rp; ☺10am-10pm) In the heart of the unadorned neighbourhood of Peliatan, this open-fronted restaurant serves up fresh and tasty Padang-style meals. Choose from the variety of prepared mains and settle down for a fine local meal in the view of a historic old banyan tree.

Pizza Bagus PIZZA $$
(Map p156; ☎0361-978520; www.pizzabagus.com; Jl Raya Pengosekan; mains 40,000-100,000Rp; ☺9am-10pm; ☀☎) First-rate pizza with a crispy thin crust is baked here. Besides the long list of pizza options, there's pasta and sandwiches – all mostly organic. Tables are in and out, there's a play area, and it delivers.

Taco Casa MEXICAN $$
(Map p156; ☎0812 2422 2357; www.tacocasabali.com; Jl Raya Pengosekan; mains from 50,000Rp; ☺11am-10pm) Sure, Mexico is almost exactly on the opposite side of the globe (get one and check!), but the flavours have found their way to Bali. Tasty versions of burritos, tacos and more have just the right mix of heat and spice. It delivers.

FOOD SHOPPING IN UBUD

Ubud Organic Market Operates two times a week: Wednesday at Tebesaya *wantilan* (open pavilion used to stage cockfights) and Saturday at **Pizza Bagus** (p176). It attracts top vendors from around the region.

BundaMart (p172) A top-quality outlet of Bali Bunda; it's a good source for organic produce and superb baked goods.

Delta Dewata Supermarket (Map p150; ☎0361-973049; Jl Raya Andong; ☺8am-10pm) and **Bintang Supermarket** (Map p156; Jl Raya Sanggingan; ☺7am-10pm) Both have a large range of food and other essentials.

Produce market (Map p150; Jl Raya Ubud; ☺6am-1pm) The traditional produce market is a multilevel carnival of tropical foods and worth exploring despite the clamouring tourist hordes. It's in the back corner of the Pasar Seni.

Delta Mart convenience stores are common but, in our experience, so is the store's pricing variability. The ubiquitous Circle Ks are reliable and sell Bintang around the clock.

✕ Campuan & Sanggingan

Warung Bodag Maliah HEALTH FOOD $
(Map p156; Sari Organik; ☑ 0361-972087; Subak Sok Wayah; mains from 40,000Rp; ☺ 8am-8pm) ⌀ In a beautiful location on a plateau overlooking rice terraces and river valleys, this attractive cafe is in the middle of a big organic farm. The food's healthy and the drinks are cool and refreshing. The walk (p175) through the rice fields means half the fun is getting here.

Warung Pulau Kelapa INDONESIAN $$
(Map p156; ☑ 0361-971872; http://warungpu-laukelapa.com; Jl Raya Sanggingan; mains 50,000-75,000Rp; ☺ 10am-10pm) Kelapa has stylish takes on Indonesian classics plus more unusual dishes from around the archipelago. The surrounds are stylish as well: plenty of whitewash and antiques. Terrace tables across the wide expanse of grass are best. Sample the seven kinds of satay.

Elephant VEGETARIAN $$
(Map p156; ☑ 0361-716 1907; www.elephantbali. com; Jl Raya Sanggingan, Hotel Taman Indrakila; mains 60,000-150,000Rp; ☺ 8am-9.30pm; 🛜🖉) ⌀ High-concept vegetarian dining with gorgeous views across the Sungai Cerik valley. Foods are well seasoned, interesting and topped off with an especially good dessert menu. A stop on Ubud's Slow Food trail, the food is organic and ethically sourced.

Naughty Nuri's BARBECUE $$
(Map p156; ☑ 0361 977547; Jl Raya Sanggingan; meals from 80,000Rp; ☺ 11am-11pm) This overhyped expat hang-out now has queues waiting for food and tourist cars double parked out front through the day and night. The grilled steaks, ribs and burgers are popular – proof that a little media hype helps – even if all the chewing needed gets in the way of chatting. Potent martinis, the original lures, are as large as ever.

★ Mozaic FUSION $$$
(Map p156; ☑ 0361-975768; www.mozaic-bali.com; Jl Raya Sanggingan; 6-course menu 700,000Rp; ☺ 6-10pm; 🛜) Chef Chris Salans oversees this much-lauded top-end restaurant. Fine French fusion cuisine features on a constantly changing seasonal menu that takes its influences from tropical Asia. Dine in an elegant garden twinkling with romantic lights or an ornate pavilion. Choose from four tasting menus, one of which is a surprise.

✕ Penestanan

Yellow Flower Cafe INDONESIAN $
(Map p156; ☑ 0361-889 9865; off Jl Raya Campuan; mains from 30,000Rp; ☺ 8am-9pm; 🛜) New Age Indonesian right up in Penestanan along a little path through the rice fields. Organic mains such as *nasi campur* or rice pancakes are good; snackers will delight in the decent coffees, cakes and smoothies. From 5.30pm Sunday evenings there's an excellent Balinese buffet (85,000Rp). Great views.

★ Moksa VEGETARIAN $$
(Map p156; ☑ 0361-479 2479; www.moksaubud. com; Gang Damai, Sayan; mains 40,000-80,000Rp; ☺ 10am-9pm Tue-Sun) Forget that farm-to-table stuff, at Moksa it's farm-to-fork-to-farm. Based at their own permaculture farm, the restaurant shows the extraordinary meals that can be made with vegetables prepared simply. Half the dishes are raw, half cooked. The changing menu usually features the popular 'Lasagne Love', which includes nut cheese and pesto. The setting is rustic with polish amid the farm.

It's a bucolic 400m walk from the nearest street along coursing rice-field waterways.

Alchemy VEGAN $$
(Map p156; ☑ 0361-971981; www.alchemybali. com; Jl Raya Penestanan 75; mains from 50,000Rp; ☺ 7am-9pm; 🛜🖉) ⌀ A prototypical 100% vegan Ubud restaurant, Alchemy features a vast customised salad menu as well as cashew-milk drinks, durian smoothies, ice cream, fennel juice and a lot more. The raw-chocolate desserts are addictive.

✕ Kedewatan

★ Nasi Ayam Kedewatan BALINESE $
(☑ 0361-742 7168, Jl Raya Kedewatan; meals from 25,000Rp; ☺ 9am-6pm) Few locals making the trek up the hill through Sayan pass this Bali version of a roadhouse without stopping. The star is *sate lilit*: chicken is minced, combined with an array of spices including lemongrass, then moulded onto bamboo skewers and grilled. Stock up on traditional Balinese road snacks: fried chips combined with nuts and spices.

Kubu MEDITERRANEAN $$$
(Map p156; ☑ 0361-4792777; www.ritzcarlton.com; Jl Kedewatan, Mandapa, a Ritz-Carlton Reserve; set menu from 750,000Rp; ☺ 6-10pm) A vision in bamboo, Kubu is the premier restaurant of the Mandapa resort and offers intimate

EAT, PRAY, LOVE & UBUD

'That damn book' is a common reaction by many Ubud residents, who fear the town's popularity is driven in part by *Eat, Pray, Love* fans. *Eat, Pray, Love* is the Elizabeth Gilbert book (and not-so-successful movie) that chronicles the American author's search for self-fulfilment (and fulfilment of a book contract) across Italy, India and, yes, Ubud.

Some criticise Gilbert for not offering a more complete picture of Ubud's locals, dance, art, expats and walks, warts and all. And they decry basic factual errors such as the evocative prose about surf spots on the north coast (there are none), which lead you to suspect things might have been embellished for the plot.

Then there are the genuine fans, those who found a message in *EPL* that resonated, validating and/or challenging aspects of their lives. For some an ultimately self-fulfilling journey to Ubud wouldn't have happened without *EPL*.

dining in just nine private cocoons overlooking the Ayung river. Talk about romantic, you may not notice the exquisite Mediterranean-European cuisine. With guests receiving booking preference, nonguests will need to book well in advance.

🍷 Drinking & Nightlife

No one comes to Ubud for wild nightlife, although that may be changing. A few bars get lively around sunset and later in the night; still, the venues don't aspire to the extremes of boozy debauchery and clubbing found in Kuta and Seminyak. Most bars close early in Ubud, often by 11pm.

★**Freak Coffee**　　　COFFEE
(Map p150; ☎0361-898 7124; JI Hanoman 1; ⊗8am-8pm; 🍴) The name is appropriate here as these people are coffee fanatics. The best Bali beans are hand-selected and then roasted with precision before being brewed with an attention to detail that would please a persnickety mad scientist. Overlaying this is a quest to produce fantastic coffee with the lowest carbon footprint possible. Enjoy the results at this simple, open-fronted shop.

★**Room 4 Dessert**　　　LOUNGE
(Map p156; ☎0821 4429 3452; www.room4dessert. asia; JI Raya Sanggingan; treats from 100,000Rp; ⊗6pm-late) Celebrity chef Will Goldfarb, who gained fame as *the* dessert chef in Manhattan, runs what could be a nightclub except that it just serves dessert. Get some friends and order the sampler. Pair everything with his line-up of classic and extraordinary cocktails and wines, then let the night pass by in a sugary glow.

★**Coffee Studio Seniman**　　　CAFE
(Map p150; ☎0812 3607 6640; www.seniman-coffee.com; JI Sriwedari 5; coffee from 30,000Rp;

⊗8am-10pm; 🍴) That 'coffee studio' moniker isn't for show; all the equipment is on display at this temple of single-origin coffee. Take a seat on the designer rocker chairs and choose from an array of pourovers, siphon, Aeropress or espresso using a range of quality Indonesian beans. It's also popular for food (mains from 50,000Rp) and drinks in the evening. Across the road is the studio's cold brew bar.

★**Laughing Buddha**　　　LOUNGE
(Map p150; ☎0361-970928; www.facebook.com/ laughingbuddhabali; Monkey Forest Rd; ⊗9am-late; 🍴) People crowd the street at night in front of this small cafe with live music Monday through Saturday nights. Rock, blues, vocals, acoustic, jazz and more. The kitchen is open until 1am for Asian bites (mains 40,000Rp to 70,000Rp).

Bar Luna　　　LOUNGE
(Map p150; ☎0361-977409; www.facebook.com/ barlunaubud; JI Raya Ubud; ⊗3-11pm) Deep in the basement of Casa Luna, you can enjoy relaxed drinks as well as regular live music and literary events. Drink specials include Margarita Monday.

Rio Helmi Gallery & Cafe　　　CAFE
(Map p150; ☎0361-972304; http://riohelmi.com; JI Suweta 5; mains from 60,000Rp; ⊗7am-7pm) As tasty as one of their famous cupcakes, this cafe in the eponymous gallery is the perfect place to pause for a coffee and/or an all-day breakfast and to soak up some Ubud vibe. Settle back with a fine beverage and take in Helmi's renowned photography.

Bridges　　　LOUNGE
(Map p156; ☎0361-970095; www.bridgesbali.com; JI Raya Campuan; ⊗11am-11.30pm, happy hour 4-7pm) The namesake bridges are right out-

side this multilevel restaurant with sweeping views of the gorgeous river gorge. You'll hear the rush of the water over rocks far below while you indulge in a top-end cocktail *on* the rocks. There are gourmet bites for sharing and a long wine list for exploring. Popular happy-hour drink specials.

Noma's   BAR
(Map p150; ☑0361-908 0800; Monkey Forest Rd; ⊙4pm-1am) Intentionally looking like the oddly appealing amalgam of several failed bars from the 1950s, Noma's touts its mediocrity, boasting about its untalented staff, bad drinks etc. Of course it's all a meme and in reality the cocktails at this open-sided two-storey bar are interesting and the servers all charmers.

Seniman Cold Brew Bar   COFFEE
(Map p150; www.senimancoffee.com; Jl Sriwedari; ⊙11am-7pm; 🖥) Across the road from the main cafe, Coffee Studio Seniman, this cool little hang-out specialises in slow-drip cold-brew coffee and iced teas. A wonderful pit stop in the heat of the day.

Napi Orti   BAR
(Map p150; Jl Jembawan; ⊙noon-late) Let rasta season your cheap cocktails and pizzas at this open-front streetside bar. Get boozy under the hazy gaze of Jim Morrison and Sid Vicious.

CP Lounge   BAR, CLUB
(Map p150; ☑0361-978954; www.cp-lounge.com; Monkey Forest Rd; ⊙11am-4am) Open til early morning, CP is the place to kick on once everything else has closed. It has garden seating, live bands and a club with a DJ. Never once will you think you're in Kuta.

☆ Entertainment
Few travel experiences can be more magical than attending a Balinese dance performance, especially in Ubud. Cultural entertainment keeps people returning and sets Bali apart from other tropical destinations. Ubud is the perfect base for the nightly array of performances and for accessing events in surrounding villages.

In a week in and around Ubud, you can see Kecak, Legong and Barong dances, Mahabharata and Ramayana ballets, *wayang kulit* (shadow-puppet plays) and gamelan (traditional Javanese and Balinese orchestras). There are eight or more performances to choose from each night.

★ Paradiso   CINEMA
(Map p150; ☑0361-783 5545; www.paradisoubud.com; Jl Gautama Selatan; 50,000Rp incl food or drinks; ⊙films from 5pm) This organic vegetarian restuarant also screens two or three nightly movies at its surprisingly plush

UBUD & AROUND UBUD

DANCE TROUPES: GOOD & BAD

All dance groups on Ubud's stages are not created equal. You've got true artists with international reputations and then you've got some who really shouldn't quit their day jobs. If you're a Balinese dance novice, you shouldn't worry too much about this; just pick a venue and go.

But after a few performances, you'll start to appreciate the differences in talent, and that's part of the enjoyment. Clue: If the costumes are dirty, the orchestra seems particularly uninterested, performers break character to tell stale jokes (really!) and you find yourself watching a dancer and saying 'I could do that', then the group is B-level.

Excellent troupes who regularly perform in Ubud include the following:

Semara Ratih High-energy, creative Legong interpretations. The best local troupe musically.

Gunung Sari Legong dance; one of Bali's oldest and most respected troupes.

Semara Madya Kecak dance; especially good for the hypnotic chants. A mystical experience for some.

Tirta Sari Legong and Barong dance.

Cudamani One of Bali's best gamelan troupes. They rehearse in Pengosekan.

Finally, watch for temple ceremonies (which are frequent). Go around 8pm and you'll see Balinese dance and music in its full cultural context. You'll need to be appropriately dressed – your hotel or a local can tell you what to do.

The website Ubud Now & Then (www.ubudnowandthen.com) has schedules of special events and performances. Also check with Ubud Tourist Information (p183).

150-seat cinema. The price of admission is redeemable against items from the Earth Cafe menu – so a great deal. During the day it hosts regular talks and events; check the website for schedule.

Dance

Dances performed for visitors are usually adapted and abbreviated to some extent to make them more enjoyable, but usually have appreciative locals in the audience (or peering around the screen!). It's also common to combine the features of more than one traditional dance in a single performance.

Ubud Tourist Information (p183) has performance information and sells tickets (usually 75,000Rp to 125,000Rp). For performances outside Ubud, transport is often included in the price. Tickets are also sold at many hotels, at the venues and by street vendors – all charge the same price.

Vendors often sell drinks at the performances, which typically last about 1½ hours. Before the show, you might notice the musicians checking out the size of the crowd – ticket sales fund the troupes.

One note about your phone: nobody wants to hear it; nor do the performers want flash in their eyes. And don't be rude and walk out loudly in the middle.

Pura Dalem Ubud DANCE
(Map p150; Jl Raya Ubud) At the west end of Jl Raya Ubud, this open-air venue has a flame-lit carved-stone backdrop and is one of the most evocative places to see a dance performance.

Puri Agung Peliatan DANCE
(Map p150; Jl Peliatan) A simple setting backed by a large carved wall. Has some excellent performances.

Padangtegal Kaja DANCE
(Map p150; Jl Hanoman) A simple, open terrace in a convenient location. In many ways this location hints at what dance performances have looked like in Ubud for generations.

Pura Taman Saraswati DANCE
(Map p150; Ubud Water Palace; Jl Raya Ubud) The beauty of the setting may distract you from the dancers, although at night you can't see the lily pads and lotus flowers that are such an attraction by day.

Pura Padang Kerta DANCE
(Map p150; Jl Hanoman) Attractive dance venue in front of a temple but well off the street.

Ubud Palace DANCE
(Map p150; Jl Raya Ubud) Performances are held here almost nightly against a beautiful backdrop.

Arma Open Stage DANCE
(Map p156; ☑0361-976659; Jl Raya Pengosekan) Has some of the best troupes performing Kecak and Legong dance.

Shadow Puppets

Shadow-puppet shows are greatly attenuated from traditional performances, which often last the entire night. Regular performances are held at **Oka Kartini** (Map p150; ☑0361-975193; Jl Raya Ubud; adult/child 100,000/50,000Rp; ☺8pm Wed, Fri & Sun), which has bungalows and a gallery.

Pondok Bamboo Music Shop PUPPET THEATRE
(Map p150; ☑0361-974807; Monkey Forest Rd; tickets 75,000Rp; ☺performances 8pm Mon & Thu) Short-attention-span-friendly shadow-puppet shows are performed here by noted experts.

🔒 Shopping

Ubud has myriad art shops, boutiques and galleries. Many offer clever and unique items made in and around the area. Ubud is the ideal base for exploring the enormous number of craft galleries, studios and workshops in villages north and south.

With so much of central Ubud now devoted to visitors, the area's main shopping strip has moved over to Jl Peliatan in Tebesaya and Peliatan. Here you'll find all the stores and shops that supply locals with their daily needs.

What to Buy

You can spend days in and around Ubud shopping. The upper part of Jl Hanoman and Jl Dewi Sita have the most interesting local shops. Look for jewellery, homewares and clothing. Monkey Forest Rd is becoming the domain of upmarket chains. Arts and crafts and yoga goods are found everywhere and at every price point and quality.

Ubud is the best place in Bali for books. Selections are wide and varied, especially for tomes on Balinese art and culture.

🏠 Jalan Raya Ubud & Around

★**Ganesha Bookshop** BOOKS
(Map p150; www.ganeshabooksbali.com; Jl Raya Ubud; ☺9am-8pm) A quality bookshop with an excellent selection of titles on Indonesian studies, travel, arts, music, fiction (in-

cluding used books) and maps. Great staff recommendations.

★ **Threads of Life Indonesian Textile Arts Center** TEXTILES
(Map p150; ☑0361-972187; www.threadsoflife.com; Jl Kajeng 24; ◷10am-7pm) This small, professional textile gallery and shop sponsors the production of naturally dyed, handmade ritual textiles from around Indonesia. It exists to help recover skills in danger of being lost to modern dyeing and weaving methods. Commissioned pieces are displayed in the gallery, which has good explanatory material. Also runs regular textile-appreciation courses (p160).

Smile Shop ARTS & CRAFTS
(Map p150; ☑0361-233758; www.senyumbali.org; Jl Sriwedari; ◷10am-4pm Tue-Sun) All manner of secondhand, donated goods are for sale in a charity shop to benefit the Smile Foundation of Bali.

Rio Helmi Gallery & Cafe PHOTOGRAPHY
(Map p150; ☑0361-978773; www.riohelmi.com; Jl Suweta 06B; ◷7am-7pm) Noted photographer and Ubud resident Rio Helmi has a small commercial gallery and cafe where you can admire or purchase his journalistic and artistic work.

Moari MUSIC
(Map p150; ☑0361-977367; Jl Raya Ubud; ◷10am-8pm) New and restored Balinese musical instruments are sold here. Splurge on a cute little bamboo flute for 30,000Rp.

Street 278 FASHION & ACCESSORIES
(Map p150; ☑0812 3815 0310; www.street278.com.au; Jl Raya Ubud; ◷10am-8pm) 🏷 Recycled goods are used for handbags and a full range of other accessories that exude a confident, colourful style.

Neka Art Museum BOOKS
(Map p150; ☑0361-975074; www.museumneka.com; Jl Raya Sanggingan; ◷9am-5pm) This museum shop in Sanggingan has a good range of books on art and Bali.

Ubud Market GIFTS & SOUVENIRS
(Map p150; Pasar Seni; Jl Raya Ubud; ◷7am-8pm) The large Ubud Market is your one-stop shop for kitschy souvenirs, clothing and presents for back home. It's inside a large complex; stallholders set up across several buildings, and also along Jl Karna. Push to the far southeast corner for the produce market (p176), which still serves the daily needs of locals.

181

🔒 Monkey Forest Road

Kou Cuisine HOMEWARES
(Map p150; ☑0361-972319; Monkey Forest Rd; ◷10am-8pm) A repository of small and exquisite gifts, including beautiful little jars of jam made with Balinese fruit or containers of sea salt harvested from along Bali's shores.

Goddess on the Go! CLOTHING
(Map p156; ☑0361-976084; www.goddessonthego.net; Jl Raya Pengosekan; ◷9am-8pm) A large selection of women's clothes designed for adventure, made to be super-comfortable, easy-to-pack and eco-friendly.

Pondok Bamboo Music Shop MUSICAL INSTRUMENTS
(Map p150; ☑0361-974807; Monkey Forest Rd; ◷10am-8pm) Hear the music of a thousand bamboo wind chimes at this store owned by noted gamelan musician Nyoman Warsa, who offers music lessons and stages shadow-puppet shows.

Periplus BOOKS
(Map p150; ☑0361-975178; Monkey Forest Rd; ◷10am-10pm) A typically glossy outlet of the popular Indonesian chain.

🔒 Jalan Dewi Sita

★ **Kou** COSMETICS
(Map p150; ☑0361-971905; Jl Dewi Sita; ◷9am-8pm) The perfume of luxurious locally handmade organic soaps wafts as you enter. Put some in your undies drawer and it'll smell fine for weeks. The range is unlike that found in chain stores selling luxe soap. It also operates Kou Cuisine.

Tn Parrot CLOTHING
(Map p150; www.tnparrot.com; Jl Dewi Sita; ◷10am-8pm) The trademark parrot of this T-shirt shop is a characterful bird who appears in many guises on this shop's line of custom T-shirts. Designs range from cool to groovy to offbeat. Everything is made from high-quality cotton that's been pre-shrunk.

Confiture Michèle FOOD
(Map p150; Jl Goutama; ◷10am-9pm) Preserves made from Bali's fruit are the, er, preserve of this cute – and sweet-smelling – shop.

CreArt Story ARTS & CRAFTS
(Map p150; ☑0813 3881 8829; www.facebook.com/creartstoryshop; Jl Goutama 20; ◷11am-8pm) A shop for readers of *Adbusters:* a no-brand brand store. The store's ethos is

selling goods that aren't made by faceless poorly paid people. The handicrafts here are responsibly sourced and come with their own stories of their origin.

Padangtegal & Pengosekan

★ Rumble
CLOTHING

(Rmbl; Map p156; www.xrmblx.co; Jl Raya Campuhan; ⊗9am-10pm) Owned by the drummer of the famous Balinese punk act Superman is Dead, Rumble stocks a cool selection of locally designed streetwear. It's right at the entrance to the madcap Blanco Renaissance Museum.

Tegun Galeri
HOMEWARES

(Map p150; ☑0361-973361; Jl Hanoman 44; ⊗10am-8pm) It's everything the souvenir stores are not, with beautiful handmade items from around the island plus ancient art.

Ashitaba
HOMEWARES

(Map p150; ☑0361-464922; Jl Hanoman; ⊗10am-8pm) Tenganan, the Aga village of east Bali, is where the beautiful rattan items sold here are produced. Containers, bowls, purses and more (from US$5) display the fine and intricate weaving.

Namaste
GIFTS & SOUVENIRS

(☑0361-970528; Jl Hanoman 64; ⊗9am-7pm) Just the place to buy a crystal to get your spiritual house in order, Namaste is a gem of a little store with a top range of New Age supplies. Incense, yoga mats, moody instrumental music – it's all here.

ARMA
BOOKS

(Map p156; ☑0361-976659; www.armabali.com; Jl Raya Pengosekan; ⊗9am-6pm) Large selection of cultural titles.

Ubud Yoga Shop
CLOTHING

(Map p150; ☑0361-973361; Jl Hanoman 44B; ⊗8am-8pm) Huge range of quality yoga gear and wear.

ℹ Information

INTERNET ACCESS

Wi-fi is near universal in places to stay as well as most cafes. Mobile data speeds are fast.

Hubud (☑0361-978073; www.hubud.org; Monkey Forest Rd; per month from US$60; ⊗24hr Mon-Fri, 9am-midnight Sat & Sun; 🛜) is for the digital nomads; this co-work space and digital hub has ultrafast web connections, developer seminars and much more. Take in rice-field views as you create a billion-dollar app.

MEDICAL SERVICES

Kimia Pharma (Jl Raya Ubud; ⊗7am-10pm) Convenient location of the respected pharmacy chain.

Ubud Care (☑24hr 0821 8888 2273; www.ubudcare.com; Jl Sukma 37; ⊗office 9am-10pm) A modern clinic that provides examina-

---

SAVING BALI'S DOGS

Mangy curs. That's the only label you can apply to many of Bali's dogs. As you travel the island – especially by foot – you can't help but notice dogs that are sick, ill-tempered, uncared for and victims to a litany of other maladies.

How can such a seemingly gentle island have Asia's worst dog population (which now has a serious rabies problem)? The answers are complex, but benign neglect has a lot to do with it. Dogs are at the bottom of the social strata: few have owners and local interest in them is next to nil.

Some nonprofits in Ubud are hoping to change the fortunes of Bali's maligned best friends through rabies vaccinations, spaying and neutering, and public education. Donations are always greatly needed.

Bali Adoption Rehab Centre (BARC; ☑0361-975038; https://barc4balidogs.org.au; Jl Raya Pengosekan; ⊗10am-5pm) Cares for dogs, places strays with sponsors and operates a mobile clinic for sterilisation.

Bali Animal Welfare Association (BAWA; ☑0811 389 004; www.bawabali.com; Jl Ubud Raya 10; ⊗9am-8pm Mon-Fri, 9am-5pm Sat & Sun) Runs lauded mobile rabies vaccination teams, organises adoption, promotes population control.

Yudisthira Swarga Foundation (☑0361-900 3043; www.yudisthiraswarga.org) Based in Denpasar, cares for thousands of Bali strays a year and has vaccination and population-control programs.

tions and consultations, house and hotel calls, and prescriptions.

MONEY
Ubud has numerous banks and ATMs.

Central Ubud Money Exchange (www.central kutabali.com; Jl Raya Ubud; ⊙8am-9pm) is a respected Bali-wide chain of currency exchanges.

POLICE
Police Station (📋0361 975316; Jl Raya Andong; ⊙24hr) Located east, at Andong.

POST
Main Post Office (Jl Jembawan; ⊙8am-5pm) Handles parcels and has a desk for airline ticketing.

TOURIST INFORMATION
Visitors will find every service they need and then some along Ubud's main roads. Bulletin boards at Bali Buda and Kafe have info on housing, jobs, classes and much more.

Ubud is home to many nonprofit and volunteer groups.

Ubud Tourist Information (Fabulous Ubud; 📋0361-973285; www.fabulousubud.com; Jl Raya Ubud; ⊙8am-8pm; 🛜) is run by the Ubud royal family and is the one really useful tourist office in Bali. It has a good range of information and a noticeboard listing current happenings and activities. The staff can answer most regional questions and it has up-to-date information on ceremonies and traditional dances held in the area; dance tickets and tours are sold here.

❶ Getting There & Away

BEMO
Ubud is on two bemo routes. Bemo travel to Gianyar (10,000Rp) and Batubulan terminal in Denpasar (13,000Rp). Ubud doesn't have a bemo terminal; there are bemo stops on Jl Suweta near the market in the centre of town.

TOURIST SHUTTLE BUS
You'll see ads all around town for economical shared cars and buses to destinations across Bali.

Perama (📋0361-973316; www.peramatours.com; Jl Raya Pengosekan; ⊙9am-9pm) is the major tourist shuttle operator, but its terminal is inconveniently located in Padangtegal; to get to/from your destination in Ubud will cost another 15,000Rp. Destinations include Sanur (50,000Rp, one hour), Padangbai (75,000Rp, two hours) and Kuta (60,000Rp, two hours).

Kura-Kura Bus (www.kura2bus.com) runs from near the Ubud Palace to its hub in Kuta five times daily (80,000Rp, two hours).

❶ Getting Around
Many high-end spas, hotels and restaurants offer free local transport for guests and customers.

TO/FROM THE AIRPORT
Taxis with the cartel from the airport to Ubud cost 300,000Rp. A hired car with driver *to* the airport will cost about the same.

BEMO
Bemos to Gianyar travel along eastern Jl Raya Ubud, down Jl Peliatan and east to Bedulu. The fare for a ride within the Ubud area shouldn't be more than 7000Rp.

CAR & MOTORCYCLE
With numerous nearby attractions, many of which are difficult to reach by bemo, renting a vehicle is sensible. Ask at your accommodation or hire a car and driver.

Most drivers are very fair; a few – often from out of the area – not so much. If you find a driver you like, get his number and call him for rides during your stay. From central Ubud to, say, Sanggingan should cost about 40,000Rp – rather steep actually. A ride from the palace to the end of Jl Hanoman should cost about 20,000Rp.

It's easy to get a ride on the back of a motorbike; rates are half those of cars.

TAXI
There are no metered taxis based in Ubud – those that honk their horns at you have usually dropped off passengers from southern Bali in Ubud and are hoping for a fare back. Instead, you'll use one of the ubiquitous drivers with private vehicles hanging around on the streets hectoring passers-by (the better drivers politely hold up signs that say 'transport').

AROUND UBUD

Bedulu
Bedulu was once the capital of a great kingdom. The legendary Dalem Bedaulu ruled the Pejeng dynasty from here, and was the last Balinese king to withstand the onslaught of the powerful Majapahit from Java. He was defeated by Gajah Mada in 1343. The capital shifted several times after this, to Gelgel and then later to Semarapura (Klungkung). Today Bedulu is absorbed into the greater Ubud sprawl.

◉ Sights

★ Yeh Pulu
HISTORIC SITE

(adult/child 15,000/7500Rp; ⊘8am-5.30pm) Amid beautiful rice-terrace vistas, a man having his hand munched by a boar is one of the scenes on the 25m-long carved cliff face known as Yeh Pulu, believed to be a hermitage from the late 14th century. Even if your interest in carved Hindu art is minor, this site is quite lovely and rarely will you have much company. From the entrance, it's a 300m lush, tropical walk to Yeh Pulu.

Apart from the figure of Ganesha, the elephant-headed son of Shiva, most of the scenes deal with everyday life, although the position and movement of the figures suggests that it could be read from left to right as a story. One theory is that they are events from the life of Krishna, the Hindu god.

You can walk between the sites, following small paths through the paddy fields, but you might need to pay a local to guide you. By car or bicycle, look for the signs to 'Relief Yeh Pulu' or 'Villa Yeh Pulu', east of Goa Gajah.

★ Goa Gajah
CAVE

(Elephant Cave; Jl Raya Goa Gajah; adult/child 15,000/7500Rp, parking motorcycle/car 2000/5000Rp; ⊘8am-5.30pm) Some 2km southeast of Ubud on the road to Bedulu, Goa Gajah is carved into a rock face and you enter through the cavernous mouth of a demon. Inside the T-shaped cave you can see fragmentary remains of the lingam, the phallic symbol of the Hindu god Shiva, and its female counterpart the yoni, plus a statue of Shiva's son, the elephant-headed god Ganesha. In front of the cave are two square bathing pools with waterspouts held by six female figures.

There were never any elephants in Bali (until tourist attractions changed that); ancient Goa Gajah probably takes its name from the nearby Sungai Petanu, which at one time was known as Elephant River, or perhaps because the face over the cave entrance might resemble an elephant.

The origins of the cave are uncertain; one tale relates that it was created by the fingernail of the legendary giant Kebo Iwa. It probably dates to the 11th century, and was certainly in existence during the Majapahit takeover of Bali. The cave was rediscovered by Dutch archaeologists in 1923, but the fountains and pool were not found until 1954.

From Goa Gajah you can clamber down through the rice paddies to Sungai Petanu, where there are crumbling rock carvings of stupas (domes for housing Buddhist relics) on a cliff face, and a small cave.

A popular stop for tours, try to get to Goa Gajah before 10am, which is when the big tourist buses begin lumbering into the large souvenir-stall-filled parking lot like, well, elephants. Breeze past the 'Coffee Luwak' stalls and other irritants in the parking area.

Pura Samuan Tiga
HINDU TEMPLE

(10,000Rp; ⊘7am-5pm) The majestic Pura Samuan Tiga (Temple of the Meeting of the Three) is on a small lane about 200m east of the Bedulu junction. The name is possibly a reference to the Hindu trinity, or it may refer to meetings held here in the early 11th century. Despite these early associations, all the temple buildings have been rebuilt since a 1917 earthquake. It's an impressive, beautiful site.

❶ Getting There & Away

About 3km east of Teges, the road from Ubud reaches a junction where you can turn south to Gianyar or north to Pejeng, Tampaksiring and Penelokan. Ubud–Gianyar bemos will drop you off at this junction, from where you can walk to the sights. The road from Ubud is reasonably flat, so coming by bicycle is a good option.

Pejeng

On the road towards Tampaksiring you come to Pejeng and its famous temples. Like Bedulu, this was once an important seat of power, as it was the capital of the Pejeng

---

THE LEGEND OF DALEM BEDAULU

A legend relates how Dalem Bedaulu possessed magical powers that allowed him to have his head chopped off and then replaced. Performing this unique party trick one day, the servant entrusted with lopping off the king's head and then replacing it unfortunately dropped it in a river and, to his horror, watched it float away. Looking around in panic for a replacement, he grabbed a pig, cut off its head and popped it upon the king's shoulders. Thereafter, the king was forced to sit on a high throne and forbade his subjects to look up at him; Bedaulu means 'he who changed heads'.

kingdom, which fell to the Majapahit invaders in 1343. Give yourself a few hours to explore this untouristed area, close to Ubud.

◎ Sights

Pura Penataran Sasih   HINDU TEMPLE
(Jl Raya Tampaksiring; admission by donation; ☺7am-5pm) This was once the state temple of the Pejeng kingdom. In the inner courtyard, high up in a pavilion and difficult to see, is the huge bronze drum known as the **Fallen Moon of Pejeng**. The hourglass-shaped drum is 186cm long, the largest single-piece cast drum in the world. Estimates of its age vary from 1000 to 2000 years.

It is not certain whether the drum was made locally or imported – the intricate geometric decorations are said to resemble patterns from places as far apart as West Papua and Vietnam.

Balinese legend relates that the drum came to earth as a fallen moon, landing in a tree and shining so brightly that it prevented a band of thieves from going about their unlawful purpose. One of the thieves decided to put the light out by urinating on it, but the moon exploded and fell to earth as a drum, with a crack across its base as a result of the fall.

Although the big noise here is all about the drum, be sure to notice the **statuary** in the temple courtyard that dates from the 10th to the 12th century. There are simple food stalls in the parking area.

Pura Pusering Jagat   HINDU TEMPLE
(Jl Raya Tampaksiring) So that's what it looks like? The large Pura Pusering Jagat is said to be the centre of the old Pejeng kingdom. Dating from 1329, this temple is visited by young couples who pray at the stone lingam and yoni. The temple is on a small paved lane running west of the main road.

Museum Arca   MUSEUM
(Archaeology Museum; ☎0361-942354; I Raya Tampaksiring; admission by donation; ☺8am-4pm) This archaeological museum has a reasonable collection of artefacts from all over Bali, and most displays are in English. The exhibits in several small buildings include some of Bali's first pottery from near Gilimanuk, and sarcophagi dating from as early as 300 BC. The museum is about 500m north of the Bedulu junction, and is easy to reach by bemo or bicycle. It's a sleepy place and you'll get the most out of it if you come with a knowledgeable guide.

WORTH A TRIP

FIVE ELEMENTS

Bamboo soars overhead at the impressive and vast retreat and healing centre **Fivelements** (☎0361-469260; www.fivelements.org; Mambal; massage from 900,000Rp, r from 5,000,000Rp), about 10km west of Ubud near Mambal. It's an intensive health retreat that draws on myriad therapies and includes luxe guest rooms (think posh tree houses with hot tubs) and a large public space, which is the site of TEDx Ubud.

Pura Kebo Edan   HINDU TEMPLE
(Jl Raya Tampaksiring) Who can resist a sight called Crazy Buffalo Temple? Although not an imposing structure, it's famous for its 3m-high statue, known as the **Giant of Pejeng**, thought to be approximately 700 years old. Details are sketchy, but it may represent Bima, a hero of the Mahabharata, dancing on a dead body, as in a myth related to the Hindu Shiva cult. Note the large storage area for village kites.

ⓘ Getting There & Away

You can easily bike from Ubud to the sights in and around Pejeng. Otherwise you'll want your own wheels.

Mas

Just south of Ubud, Mas means 'gold' in Bahasa Indonesia, but woodcarving is the principal craft in this village. Carving was a traditional art of the priestly Brahmana caste, and the skills are said to have been a gift of the gods. Historically, carving was limited to temple decorations, dance masks and musical instruments, but in the 1930s carvers began to depict people and animals in a naturalistic way. Today it's hard to resist the oodles of winsome creatures produced here.

This is the place to come if you want something custom-made in sandalwood – just be prepared to pay well (and check the wood's authenticity carefully). Mas is also part of Bali's booming furniture industry, producing chairs, tables and antiques ('made to order!'), mainly from teak imported from other Indonesian islands.

BALI'S VILLAGE ARTISTS

In small villages throughout the Ubud region, from Sebatu to Mas and beyond across Bali, you'll see small signs for artists and craftspeople, often near the local temple. As one local told us, 'we are only as rich of a village as our art', so the people who create the ceremonial costumes, masks, kris (traditional dagger), musical instruments and all the other beautiful aspects of Balinese life and religion are accorded great honour. It's a symbiotic relationship, with the artist never charging the village for the work and the village in turn seeing to the welfare of the artist. Often there are many artists in residence because few events would bring more shame to a village than having to go to another village to procure a needed sacred object.

⊙ Sights

★**Setia Darma House of Masks & Puppets**　MUSEUM
(📞0361-898 7493; Jl Tegal Bingin; suggested donation 35,000Rp; ☺8am-4pm) FREE This is one of the best museums in the Ubud area, home to more than 7000 ceremonial masks and puppets from Bali, Indonesia, Asia and beyond. All are beautifully displayed in a series of historic buildings. Among the many treasures, look for the golden Jero Luh Mask and the faces of royalty, mythical monsters and even common people. The museum is about 2km northeast of the main Mas crossroads.

Tonyraka Art Gallery　GALLERY
(📞0361-781 6785; www.tonyrakaartgallery.com; Jl Raya Mas; ☺9am-5pm) One of the premier galleries in the Ubud area, look for exhibitions here with some of Bali's best contemporary artists such as Made Djirna.

Pura Taman Pule Mas　HINDU TEMPLE
(off Jl Raya Mas) The great Majapahit priest Nirartha once lived here, and Pura Taman Pule is said to be built on the site of his home. During the three-day Kuningan festival (p24), a performance of *wayang wong* (an older version of the Ramayana ballet) is held in the temple's courtyard.

⇄ Courses

Ida Bagus Anom Suryawan　ART
(📞0813 3844 8444; www.balimaskmaking.com; Jl Raya Mas; 2hr class 200,000Rp; ☺varies) Three

generations of some of Bali's best mask-carvers will show you their secrets in a family compound right off the main road; in two weeks you might have something. They are just north of the Mas soccer field.

🛏 Sleeping & Eating

★**Taman Harum Cottages**　HOTEL $
(📞0361-975567; www.tamanharumcottages.com; Jl Raya Mas; r from US$45, 2-bedroom villas from US$100; ❉@🛜⛱) Along the main road in Mas, this lushly landscaped hotel has 17 rooms and villas – some quite large. By all means get one overlooking the rice fields. It's behind a gallery, which is also a venue for a huge range of recommended art and cultural courses. Ubud shuttles are free.

Suly Resort　HOTEL $$
(📞0361-976186; www.sulyresort.com; Jl Raya Mas; r from 400,000Rp; ❉🛜⛱) This excellent hotel has 48 rooms in a four-storey main building and another 17 in cottages with lovely rice-field views. Balinese architecture details abound; there are yoga classes and spa treatments on offer. It's at the north end of Mas.

If the staff here seems both young and enthusiastic, it's because the Suly is run by a foundation that trains students from poor parts of Bali in the hospitality industry. Given the massive growth in tourism, graduates go on to great jobs across the island and beyond. Only a few applicants are accepted and tuition is free.

Semar Warung　BALINESE $$
(📞0878 8883 3348; Jl Raya Mas 165; mains from 50,000Rp; ☺9am-10pm) It doesn't look all that promising from the front, but step through to the breezy dining area and you'll be wrapped up in a green vista of rice fields stretching off to palm trees. It's a beautiful view and the Balinese food lives up to it. It's 1km south of where Jl Raya Mas meets Jl Raya Pengosekan.

NORTH OF UBUD

North of Ubud, Bali becomes cooler and more lush. Ancient sites and natural beauty abound.

The usual road from Ubud north to Batur is through Tampaksiring with Bali's own bit of Angkor at Gunung Kawi. But there are other lesser roads up the gentle mountain slope. One of the most attractive goes north from Peliatan, past Petulu and its birds, and through the rice terraces between Tegallalang and Ceking, to bring you out on the crater rim between Penelokan and Batur. It's a decent road all the way and you also pass through **Sebatu**, which has all manner of artisans tucked away in tiny villages.

The one off-note will be **Cekingan**, where the rice terraces are beautiful but have attracted a strip of ugly tourist traps overlooking them.

❶ Getting There & Away

North of Ubud, you'll need your own wheels. Plan on half a day for these sights.

Tegallalang

There are lots of shops and stalls in this busy market town you're likely to pass through on your visit to the area's temples. Stop for a stroll and you may be rewarded by hearing the practice of one of the local noted gamelan orchestras. Otherwise, plenty of carvers stand ready to sell you a carved fertility doll or the like. In **Ceking**, scores of carvers produce works from albesia wood, which is easily turned into simplistic, cartoonish figures. The wood is also a favourite of wind-chime makers.

🛏 Sleeping & Eating

Kampung Resort   RESORT **$$**
(✆0361-901201; www.thekampungresortubud.com; r from US$70; 🛜🗙) Staying in any of the nine rooms here is like having your own tree house. You're surrounded by soaring palms and rice terraces. The only break in the green is the blue sky spotted through the fronds. Rooms are solidly comfortable. Ubud is a 20-minute ride away.

Alam Sari   HOTEL **$$**
(✆0361-240308; www.alamsari.com; Keliki; r from 600,000Rp; ♿🛜🗙) 🌿 Go about 3km west of Tegallalang on the very green road to Keliki, and you'll pass Alam Sari, a small hotel in a wonderfully isolated location where the bamboo grows like grass. There are 10 luxurious yet rustic rooms, a pool and a great view. The hotel treats its own wastewater, among other environmental initiatives.

Kampung Resort   CAFE **$$**
(✆0361-901201; www.thekampungresortubud.com; Ceking; mains 40,000-80,000Rp; ⏱8am-9pm; 🛜) You can pause at Kampung Resort in the village of Ceking, an attractive cafe (perfect for lunch) and upmarket guesthouse with jaw-dropping rice-terrace views. The design makes great use of natural rock. The menu is pan-Asian with a big dose of pasta.

Tampaksiring

Tampaksiring is a small village about 18km northeast of Ubud with a large and important temple, Tirta Empul, and the most impressive ancient site in Bali, Gunung Kawi. It sits in the Pakerisan Valley; the entire area has been nominated for Unesco recognition.

◎ Sights

★**Tirta Empul**   MONUMENT
(adult/child 15,000/7500Rp, parking 2000Rp; ⏱7am-6pm) Discovered in AD 962 and believed to have magical powers, the holy springs here bubble up into a large, crystal-clear pool within the temple and gush out through waterspouts into a bathing pool. A well-signposted fork in the road north of Tampaksiring leads to these very popular springs. Selfies while in one of the pools are a cliché; priests come here for holy water.

The waters here are the main source of Sungai Pakerisan (Pakerisan River), the river that rushes by Gunung Kawi only 1km or so away. Next to the springs, **Pura Tirta Empul** is one of Bali's most important temples. Come in the early morning or late afternoon to avoid the tourist buses. You can also use the clean, segregated and free public baths here.

★**Gunung Kawi**   MONUMENT
(adult/child incl sarong 15,000/7500Rp, parking 2000Rp; ⏱7am-6pm) At the bottom of a lush

❶ BEST TIME TO VISIT GUNUNG KAWI

Get to Gunung Kawi as early as possible for the best experience. If you start down the steps by 7.30am, you'll avoid all the vendors and you'll still see residents going about their morning business in the swift-flowing streams such as ablutions and cleaning ceremonial offerings. You can hear the birds, the flowing water and your own voice going 'ooh' and 'aah' without the distractions that come later when large groups arrive. In addition, you'll still have cool air when you start back up the endless steps. Be sure to have a sarong in case there is nobody yet offering them for use. If the ticket office is closed, you can pay on your way out.

BALI'S CHOCOLATE FACTORY

You might think Swiss or Belgian when you think of chocolate, but soon you could be thinking Bali. **Big Tree Farms** (☑ 0361-846 3327; www.bigtreefarms. com; Sibang; tours with/without bookings 40,000/60,000Rp; ⊙ tours 2pm Mon-Fri), a local producer of quality foodstuffs that has made a big splash internationally, has built a chocolate factory about 10km southwest of Ubud in the village of Sibang. The chocolate made here comes from cocoa beans grown by over 13,000 farmers across Indonesia. The result is a very high-quality chocolate that you can watch being made on tours.

This is not just any factory: rather it is a huge and architecturally stunning creation made sustainably from bamboo – an ethos that extends to the company's very philosophy. Just seeing one of the world's largest bamboo structures is an attraction in itself; toss in fabulous chocolate and you've landed an all-round delectable experience.

Reaching the factory is easy as Sibang is on one of the roads linking Ubud to south Bali.

green river valley lies one of Bali's oldest and largest ancient monuments. Gunung Kawi consists of 10 *candi* (shrines) – memorials cut out of the rock face in imitation of actual statues. They stand in awe-inspiring 8m-high sheltered niches cut into the sheer cliff face. On the northern outskirts of Tampaksiring, a sign points east off the main road to Gunung Kawi. The views as you walk through ancient terraced rice fields are as fine as any in Bali.

Each *candi* is believed to be a memorial to a member of the 11th-century Balinese royalty, but little is known for certain.

Legends relate that the whole group of memorials was carved out of the rock face in one hard-working night by the mighty fingernails of Kebo Iwa.

The five monuments on the eastern bank are probably dedicated to King Udayana, Queen Mahendradatta and their sons Airlangga, Anak Wungsu and Marakata. While Airlangga ruled eastern Java, Anak Wungsu ruled Bali. The four monuments on the western side are, by this theory, to Anak

Wungsu's chief concubines. Another theory is that the whole complex is dedicated to Anak Wungsu, his wives, concubines and, in the case of the remote 10th *candi*, to a royal minister.

As you wander between monuments, temples, offerings, streams and fountains, you can't help but feel a certain ancient majesty here.

From the end of the access road, a steep, stone stairway leads down to the river, at one point cutting through an embankment of solid rock. Be prepared for long climbs – there are more than 270 steps. The sarong is necessary as parts of the site are considered holy.

SOUTH OF UBUD

The roads between Ubud and south Bali are lined with little shops making and selling handicrafts. Many visitors shop along the route as they head to and from Ubud, sometimes by the busload, but much of the craftwork is actually done in small workshops and family compounds on quiet back roads.

The roads form a real patchwork and you'll be rewarded with surprises if you take some time to wander the lesser routes. Look for temples, atmospheric villages and family-friendly attractions.

❶ Getting There & Away

South of Ubud, the roads are mostly flat so cyclists will be pleased, although the main roads can be busy. Otherwise you'll want your own wheels in this region. The back roads are great for cycling and walking.

For serious shopping and real flexibility in exploring these villages, it's worth arranging your own transport so you can follow the back roads and carry your purchases without any hassles. Note that your driver may receive a commission from any place you spend your money – this can add 10% or more to the cost of purchases (think of it as his tip). Also, a driver may try to steer you to workshops or artisans that he favours, rather than those of most interest to you.

Blahbatuh & Around

Blahbatuh has a small and interesting market in its centre and it has some good attractions nearby. Further west, there are sensational views of rice terraces off the main road near the village of Kemenuh.

⊙ Sights

Pura Gaduh
HINDU TEMPLE

(Jl Kebo Iwa) The temple of Pura Gaduh, 200m east of the Blahbatuh market, has a 1m-high stone head, believed to be a portrait of Kebo Iwa, the legendary strongman and minister to the last king of the Bedulu kingdom. The head possibly predates the Javanese 11th-century influence in Bali.

Gajah Mada – the Majapahit strongman – realised that it wouldn't be possible to conquer Bedulu (Bali's strongest kingdom) while Kebo Iwa was there. So Gajah Mada lured him away to Java (with promises of women and song) and had him murdered.

🛍 Shopping

Putri Ayu
TEXTILES

(📞 0361-942658; Jl Lapangan Astina 3, off Jl Wisma Gajah Mada; ⊗ 8am-5pm) See looms busily making ikat and batik fabrics at Putri Ayu. The workshops and showroom are a good complement to the textile shops in Gianyar and are just south of the main road and just east of the temple.

Kutri

Heading north from Blahbatuh, Kutri has the interesting **Pura Kedarman** aka Pura Bukit Dharma. If you climb up Bukit Dharma behind the temple, there's a great panoramic view and a **hilltop shrine**, with

---

COFFEE LUWAK

Coffee luwak, also known locally as *kopi luwak*, has become as much a part of the tourist shopping experience on Bali as the ubiquitous penis-shaped bottle openers. Only it's much more costly.

The supposed allure of coffee luwak is that civets (small and winsome nocturnal critters that are distant relatives of cats) eat only the best coffee beans off coffee bushes. Then as the beans pass through the civet, various enzymes and digestive juices affect the chemistry of the bean. Once liberated from the civet turds, the beans are roasted and brewed, producing a somehow superior cup of coffee.

In the last few years the hype around coffee luwak has become shrill and as more and more tourists are willing to plop down cash for 'the world's most expensive cup of coffee' the number of people selling the same has exploded. As you drive around Bali you will see come-ons everywhere for coffee luwak, especially along major roads in the hills. Besides the great opportunity for fraud, there are also real concerns about the treatment of the civets displayed as coffee luwak producers. Consider the following:

➡ There is no agreed-upon flavour profile for coffee luwak, thus no one can say definitively what a cup should – or does – taste like.

➡ The only way you know you are drinking a cup of coffee luwak is because the person selling you this brewed beverage for US$10 or more says so.

➡ Despite the potential for outright fakery, huge factory farms for coffee luwak have sprung up. Here civets captured in the wild are kept caged and force fed a diet of coffee beans, not unlike a foie gras goose. In the wild, civets roam widely and coffee is but a tiny part of their diet.

➡ You may well see a caged civet at a Bali coffee luwak attraction where the nocturnal creature is kept awake to amuse tourists. At one we listened while a guide explained that the sad-looking civet in the very small cage before us would only be on luwak duty for a few days. It would then spend its days and nights at a sort of civet fantasy farm where it would cavort with other civets.

For more on the controversies around coffee luwak, visit the website Project Luwak Singapore (projectluwaksg.wordpress.com). The BBC reported on the conditions of captive civets in 2013 (search for 'BBC coffee luwak') while National Geographic did the same in 2016 (go to nationalgeographic.com, search for 'coffee luwak'). Balinese journalist Cat Wheeler investigated the situation locally in the *Bali Advertiser* (http://baliadvertiser.biz/ethics/).

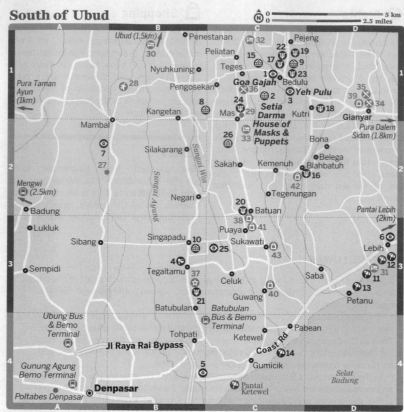

a stone statue of the six-armed goddess of death and destruction, Durga, killing a demon-possessed water buffalo.

Bona & Belega

On the back road between Blahbatuh and Gianyar, Bona is a basket-weaving centre and features many articles made from *lontar* (specially prepared palm leaves). It is also known for fire dances. (Note: most road signs in the area read 'Bone' instead of Bona, so if you get lost, you'll have to ask: 'Do you know the way to Bone?') Nearby, the village of Belega is a centre for bamboo-furniture production.

Batuan

Batuan's recorded history goes back 1000 years, and in the 17th century its royal fam-

ily controlled most of southern Bali. The decline of its power is attributed to a priest's curse, which scattered the royal family to different parts of the island.

☉ Sights

**Pura Puseh Batuan &
Pura Dasar Batuan** HINDU TEMPLE
(Jl Raya Batuan; donation 10,000Rp; ⊘7am-5pm) Just west of the centre, these twin temples are among Bali's oldest. They're accessible studies in classic Balinese temple architecture. The carvings are elaborate and visitors are given the use of vermilion sarongs. There are regular daytime dance performances aimed at visitors.

Sukawati & Puaya

Once a royal capital, Sukawati is now known for its market and for its specialised artisans, who busily work in small shops along

South of Ubud

UBUD & AROUND SINGAPADU

the roads. Puaya, about 1km northwest of Sukawati, is also known for its artisans.

🛍 Shopping

★ Sukawati Market   MARKET
(Jl Raya Sukawati, Sukawati; ⊙6am-8pm) Sukawati Market is a highlight of any visit to the area. Always lively, this large market is a major source of the flowers, baskets, fruits, knick-knacks and other items used in temple offerings. It's a riot of colour.

Nyoman Ruka   MUSICAL INSTRUMENTS
(Kubu Duah; ⊙10am-6pm) One of the first workshops, coming from the south, is Nyoman Ruka, a slick shop with Barong and masks.

Guwang Pasar Seni   GIFTS & SOUVENIRS
(craft market; Guwang; ⊙8am-6pm) About 2km south of Sukawati, this much hyped and very touristy market has every type of knick-knack and trinket on sale.

Baruna Art Shop   ARTS & CRAFTS
(☎0361-299490; Kubu Duah; ⊙10am-5pm) Has many Barong masks in stock for you to ponder.

Singapadu

The centre of Singapadu is dominated by a huge banyan tree. In the past, these were community meeting places; even today the local meeting hall is just across the road. The surrounding village has a traditional appearance, with walled family compounds and shady trees.

◎ Sights

Bali Bird Park   BIRD SANCTUARY
(☎0361-299352; www.bali-bird-park.com; Jl Serma Cok Ngurah Gambir; adult/child 432,000/216,000Rp; ⊙9am-5.30pm; 🅿) More than 1000 birds from 250 species flit about here, including rare cendrawasih (birds of paradise) from West Papua and the all but vanished Bali starlings. Many are housed in special walk-through aviaries; in one of the aviaries you follow a walk at tree-level, or what some with feathers might say is bird-level. A reptile section includes a Komodo dragon. It's popular with kids; allow at least two hours. It's located in the village of

Singapadu within the greater area of Batabulan, halfway between Ubud and Denpasar.

Nyoman Suaka Home HISTORIC BUILDING
(Singapadu; requested donation 30,000Rp; ⊘9am-5pm) This home, which is 50m off the main road, is just south of Singapadu's huge banyan tree. Pass through the old carved entrance to the walled family compound and you'll discover a classic Balinese home, which you can explore while the family goes about its daily business.

Celuk

Celuk is the silver and gold centre of Bali. The flashier showrooms are on the main road, and have marked prices that are quite high, although you can always bargain.

Hundreds of **silversmiths** and **goldsmiths** work in their homes on the backstreets north and east of the main road. Most of these artisans are from *pande* families, members of a sub-caste of blacksmiths whose knowledge of fire and metal has traditionally put them outside the usual caste hierarchy. Their small workshops are interesting to visit, and have the lowest prices, but they don't keep a large stock of finished work. They will make something to order if you bring a sample or sketch.

Batubulan

The start of the main road to Ubud from south Bali is lined with outlets for stone sculptures – **stone carving** is the main craft of Batubulan (moonstone). Workshops are found right along the road to Tegaltamu, with another batch further north around Silakarang. Batubulan is the source of the stunning temple-gate guardians seen all over Bali. The stone used for these sculptures is a porous grey volcanic rock called *paras,* which resembles pumice; it's soft and surprisingly light. It also ages quickly, so that 'ancient' work may be years rather than centuries old.

Batubulan is also a centre for making 'antiques', textiles and woodwork, and has numerous craft shops.

◉ Sights

Pura Puseh Batubulan HINDU TEMPLE
(admission by donation; ⊘8am-6pm) The temples around Batubulan are, naturally, noted for their fine stonework. Just 200m to the east of the busy main road, Pura Puseh Batubulan is worth a visit for its moat filled with lotus flowers and perfectly balanced overall composition. Statues draw on ancient Hindu and Buddhist iconography and Balinese mythology; however, they are not old – many are copied from books on archaeology.

☆ Entertainment

Barong Dance Show DANCE
(Pura Puseh Batubulan; admission 110,000Rp; ⊘9.30am) An attenuated Barong dance show about the iconic lion-dog creature is performed in an ugly hall; it's a bus-tour-friendly one-hour-long show. Note that Pura Puseh means 'central temple' – you'll find many around Bali. Some translations have 'Puseh' meaning 'navel', which is apt.

East Bali

Best Places to Eat

➡ Bali Asli (p217)

➡ Vincent's (p215)

➡ Gianyar Night Market (p198)

➡ Amankila Restaurant (p212)

➡ Warung Ida (p203)

➡ Warung Enak (p224)

Best Places to Sleep

➡ Meditasi (p224)

➡ Anini Amed Resort (p223)

➡ Alam Anda (p227)

➡ Villa Arjuna (p217)

➡ Komune Bali (p197)

➡ Amankila (p211)

Why Go?

Wandering the roads of east Bali is one of the island's great pleasures. Rice terraces spill down hillsides under swaying palms, wild volcanic beaches are washed by pounding surf and age-old villages soldier on with barely a trace of modernity. Watching over this region is Gunung Agung, the 3142m volcano known as the 'navel of the world' and 'Mother Mountain', which has a perfect conical shape.

You can find Bali's past amid evocative ruins in the former royal city of Semarapura. Follow the rivers coursing down the slopes on the Sideman road to find vistas and valleys where you can try to invent new words for 'green'. Down at the coast is groovy Padangbai and relaxed Candidasa.

Resorts and hidden beaches dot the seashore and cluster on the Amed coast. Just north of there, Tulamben is all about external exploration: the entire town is geared for diving.

When to Go

➡ The best time to visit east Bali is during the dry season – April to September – although recent weather patterns have made the dry season wetter and the wet season drier. Hiking in the lush hills from Gunung Agung over to Tirta Gangga is much easier when it isn't muddy.

➡ Along the coast there's little reason to pick one month over another; it's usually just tropical.

➡ Top-end resorts may book up in peak season (July, August and Christmas), but it's never jammed like south Bali.

➡ To surf the breaks off the beaches northeast of Sanur, aim for October to March.

East Bali Highlights

① Kertha Gosa (p200) Sensing Bali's violent past and proud traditions of sacrifice at Semarapura's historical site.

② Sideman (p202) Trekking this picture-perfect valley.

③ Padangbai (p207) Chilling with new friends at the mellow cafes and laid-back beaches of this port town.

④ Amed Coast (p220) Finding your perfect lotus position at an inn perched along the little villages of this beautiful coast.

⑤ Tulamben (p224) Diving into the blue waters to explore the famous shipwreck right off the beach.

⑥ Pura Lempuyang (p219) Counting the shades of green on one of the longest and best uphill treks of your life.

⑦ Pantai Klotek (p196) Marvelling at the combination of the sacred and the sublime amidst lots of black sand.

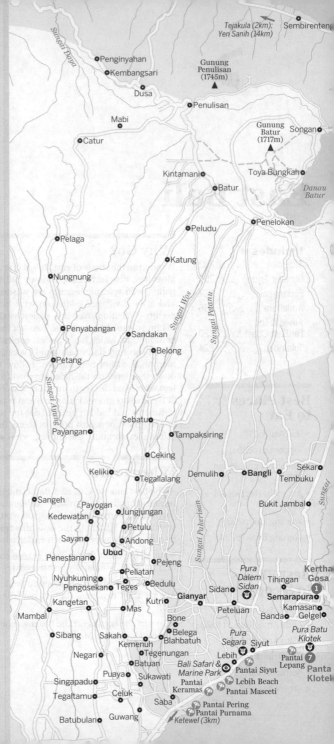

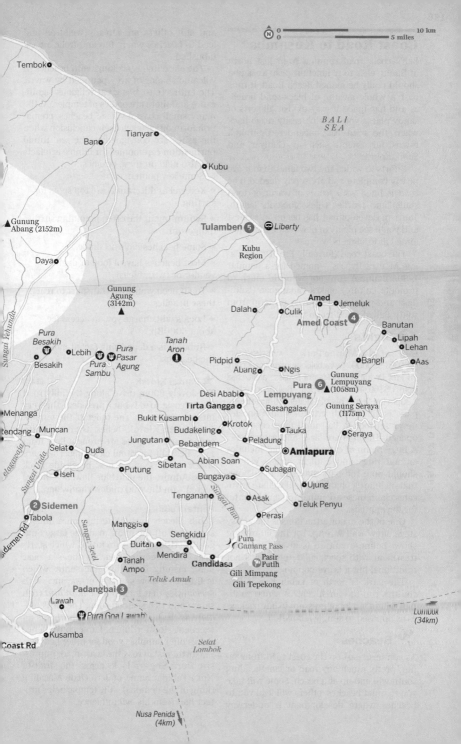

Coast Road to Kusamba

Bali's coast road running from just north of Sanur east to a junction past Kusamba should really be named Beach Road. It runs past a whole swathe of black-sand beaches and has made it easy to visit all sorts of sandy places you couldn't easily reach back when the road east meandered through towns far inland such as Gianyar and Semarapura.

Efforts to widen the two lanes to four are nearly complete and are sorely needed. The road is lined with scores of warungs (food stalls) and trucker cafes along its length. Tourism development has begun in earnest and you'll see plenty of new residential villas aimed at foreigners.

The coast road (formally Prof Dr Ida Bagus Mantra Bypass – named for a popular 1980s Balinese governor who did much to promote culture) makes Padangbai, Candidasa and points east an easy day trip from south Bali, depending on traffic.

◉ Sights

Bali Safari & Marine Park   AMUSEMENT PARK
(☏ 0361-950000; www.balisafarimarinepark.com; off Prof Dr Ida Bagus Mantra Bypass; adult/child from US$60/40; ⊙ 9am-5pm, Bali Agung show 2.30pm Tue-Sun) This big-ticket animal-theme park is filled with critters whose species never set foot in Bali until their cage door opened. Displays are large and naturalistic. A huge menu of extra-cost options includes animal rides and a night safari. Visitors should note the park stages animal shows that include elephants: animal welfare advocates claim these are unnatural and harmful for the animals.

One of the major attractions is the glossy stage show **Bali Agung**. For the 60-minute show, Balinese culture is given the Vegas treatment with spectacular results. It's not traditional but it is eye-popping.

The park is north of Lebih Beach; free shuttles run to tourist centres across south Bali. There is a lot of pressure to buy packages as opposed to simple admission.

🏖 Beaches

As you head east on the coast road from Sanur, pretty much any road or lane heading south will end up at a beach. Some will take you to quiet beaches, others will lead you to beaches where development is underway and still others are already well-trod and lead to beaches where fun and frolic are established.

The shoreline is striking, with beaches in volcanic shades of grey pounded by waves. The entire coast has great religious significance and there are oodles of temples. At the many small coastal-village beaches, cremation formalities reach their conclusion when the ashes are consigned to the sea. Ritual purification ceremonies for temple artefacts are also held on these beaches.

Some key points:

➡ Ketewel and Keramas are top spots for surfing.

➡ Swimming in the often pounding surf is dangerous.

➡ Some beaches have no shade.

➡ Most beaches have a food or drinks vendor or two, at least.

➡ You'll need your own transport to reach these beaches.

➡ Locals will charge you an access fee – about 5000Rp.

➡ Rubbish is a depressing fact at most of the beaches.

★**Pantai Klotek**   BEACH
The lovely 800m drive along the hilly road off the coast road is but a prelude to this very interesting beach. The quiet at the temple, **Pura Watu Klotok**, belies its great significance: sacred statues are brought here from Pura Besakih for ritual cleansing. There are snack vendors and a new beachside brick walk. Admire the pale blue flowers – they're sacred – on the wild midori shrubs here.

Pantai Lebih   BEACH
Lebih Beach has glittering mica-infused sand. Just off the main road, the large Sungai Pakerisan (Pakerisan River), which starts near Tampaksiring, reaches the sea near here. Fishing boats line the shore, which is fitting as there's a strip of warungs with specialities that include *sate ikan laut* (fish satay) and rich seafood soup. The air is redolent with the smell of BBQ fish; this is an excellent stop for lunch. Large convenience stores offer supplies good for other beaches.

North, just across the coast road, impressive **Pura Segara** looks across the strait to Nusa Penida, home of Jero Gede Macaling (king of the demons) – the temple helps protect Bali from his evil influence.

Pantai Lepang
BEACH

Worth visiting just for the threatened slice of rural Bali you pass through on the 600m drive from the main road. Down at the carbon-coloured sand you'll find small dunes, no shade, a couple of vendors and a lot of reasons to snap some pics. A sign explains that this is a sea turtle sanctuary. Just west, however, is the enormous new Wyndham Tamansari Jivva Resort, which is a harbinger of things to come.

Pantai Purnama
BEACH

(Purnama) Small, but has the blackest sand, reflecting billions of sparkles in the sunlight. Religion is big here: the temple, **Pura Erjeruk**, is important for irrigation of rice fields, while some of Bali's most elaborate full-moon purification ceremonies are held here each month. Villas are appearing as are vendors.

Pantai Keramas
BEACH

(Keramas) Villa and hotel projects are sprouting here. The surf is consistent and world-class. Unfortunately, an attraction here, Wake Bali, has a pool with captive dolphins.

Pantai Siyut
BEACH

A mere 300m off the road, and often deserted, this beach is a good place for a parasol: there's no shade otherwise. It remains development-free.

Pantai Masceti
BEACH

'What a strange place', our friend said. And indeed Masceti beach is a study in contrasts. Some 15km east of Sanur, it has a few drinks vendors and one of Bali's nine sacred directional temples, **Pura Masceti**. Right on the beach, the temple is built in the shape of a *garuda* (a large mythical bird) and enlivened with gaudy statuary.

There's a certain irony to the bird-shape as both the temple grounds and a huge building nearby are used for cockfights. The feathers of losing birds are everywhere. On days with no cockfights or ceremonies, the large pavilion is used for other gambling activities. A brick beachwalk is good for strolling.

Pantai Ketewel
BEACH

One of the first beaches you'll encounter off the coast road, Ketewel is known for its surfing, which demands advanced skills; it's a tricky reef-rocky right. Come here to surf – or watch, although there are no vendors.

Pantai Pering
BEACH

Choose your access: a twisting and jungle-like 1.1km drive from the coast road or a short and direct road just east. About 12km from Sanur, this beach has a few drinks vendors on the burnt-umber-hued sand and there is a small temple, covered shelters and a palm-shaded parking area.

🛏 Sleeping

★ Komune Bali
BOUTIQUE HOTEL **$$**

(📞 0361-301 8888; www.komuneresorts.com; Jl Pantai Keramas, Keramas; r from US$100; ❋ 🛜 ☎) This high-profile surf resort has erected light towers for night surfing, which has proven hugely popular. Despite this, the hotel has actually done a good job of trying to blend into the existing landscape. It has a very attractive pool area and a cafe in the dune up from the high-tide line.

Wyndham Tamansari Jivva Resort
RESORT **$$**

(📞 0366-543 7988; www.wyndhamjivvabali.com; Pantai Lepang; r US$70-150; ❋ 🛜 ☎) A bit of a revolution in the east: this new resort has 222 rooms and sports a daring, striking design. The stark lines contrast well with the dark sand here. The rooms are average size and not all have ocean/beach views.

Gianyar

This is the affluent administrative capital and main market town of the Gianyar district, which also includes Ubud. The town has a number of factories producing batik and ikat fabrics and a compact centre with some excellent food, especially at the famous night market.

◉ Sights

Pura Dalem Sidan
TEMPLE

When driving east from Gianyar you come to the turn-off to Bangli about 2km out of Peteluan. Follow this road for about 1km until you reach a sharp bend, where you'll find Sidan's Pura Dalem Sidan. This good example of a temple of the dead has very fine carvings. In particular, note the sculptures of Durga with children by the gate and the separate enclosure in one corner of the temple – this is dedicated to Merajapati, the guardian spirit of the dead.

🍴 Eating

People come to Gianyar to sample the market food, like *babi guling* (spit-roast pig stuffed with chilli, turmeric, garlic and ginger – delicious), for which the town is noted.

Near the night market are numerous stands selling fresh food, including delectable *piseng goreng* (banana fritters). The **food market** (Jl Ngurah Rai; ⊙11am-2pm), which lines both sides of the main section of Jl Ngurah Rai, is also good for sampling.

★**Gianyar Night Market** MARKET $
(Jl Ngurah Rai; dishes from 15,000Rp; ⊙5-11pm) The sound of scores of cooking pots and the glare of bright lights add a frenetic and festive clamour to Gianyar's delicious night market, which any local will tell you has some of the best food in Bali. Scores of stalls set up each night in the centre and cook up a mouthwatering and jaw-dropping range of dishes.

Much of the fun is just strolling, browsing and choosing. There's everything from *babi guling* to succulent combinations of vegetables that defy description. The average cost of a dish is 15,000Rp; with a group you can sample a lot and be the happier for it. Peak time is the two hours after sunset. Best of all, the night market is only a 20-minute drive from Ubud: a driver will bring you here for 140,000Rp, including waiting time.

🛍 Shopping

At the western end of town on the main Ubud road are textile factories that are beloved by connoisseurs of handwoven fabrics. You'll see weavers at work and observe how the thread is dyed before being woven to produce the vibrantly patterned weft ikat, which is called *endek* in Bali.

Cap Togog TEXTILES
(☏0361-943046; Jl Astina Utara 11; ⊙8am-5pm) This place is on the main drag west of the centre. Cap Togog has a fascinating production area below; follow the sounds of dozens of clacking wooden looms.

ℹ BUYING FABRIC

You can buy fabric by the metre or have it tailored. Prices are 50,000Rp to 120,000Rp per metre for handwoven ikat, depending on how fine the weaving is – costs will rise if it contains silk. You can get a top-quality batik sarong for about 600,000Rp (double that if you include gold accents for your wedding). The industry is struggling from competition with machine-made Javanese fabric, so your arrival will be welcomed.

Tenun Ikat Setia Cili TEXTILES
(☏0361-943409; Jl Astina Utara; ⊙9am-5pm) Located at the western end of town on the main Ubud road, 500m apart from its competitor Cap Togog, is this large textile factory. Connoisseurs of handwoven fabrics will be fit to be tied (dyed?). This place has a showroom where you can buy material by the metre or have it tailored.

ℹ Getting There & Away

Regular bemos run between Batubulan terminal near Denpasar and Gianyar's main terminal (15,000Rp), which is behind the main market. Bemo to/from Ubud (10,000Rp) use the bemo stop across the road from the main market.

Bangli

Halfway up the slope to Penelokan, Bangli, once the capital of a kingdom, is a humble market town noteworthy for its sprawling temple, Pura Kehen, which is on a beautiful jungle road that runs east past rice terraces and connects at Sekar with roads to Rendang and Sideman.

History

Bangli dates from the early 13th century. In the Majapahit era it broke away from Gelgel to become a separate kingdom, even though it was landlocked, poor and involved in long-running conflicts with neighbouring states.

In 1849 Bangli made a treaty with the Dutch that gave it control over the defeated north-coast kingdom of Buleleng, but Buleleng then rebelled and the Dutch imposed direct rule there. In 1909 the rajah (lord or prince) of Bangli chose for it to become a Dutch protectorate rather than face suicidal *puputan* (a warrior's fight to the death) or complete conquest by the neighbouring kingdoms or the colonial power.

◎ Sights

★**Pura Kehen** HINDU TEMPLE
(Jl Sriwijaya; adult/child incl sarong 30,000Rp/free; ⊙9am-5pm) The state temple of the Bangli kingdom, Pura Kehen is one of the finest temples in eastern Bali; it is a miniature version of Pura Besakih, Bali's most important temple. It's terraced up the hillside, with a flight of steps leading to the beautifully decorated entrance. The first courtyard has a huge banyan tree with a *kulkul* (hollow

tree-trunk drum used to sound a warning) entwined in its branches.

The inner courtyard has an 11-roof *meru* (multitiered shrine) and there are other shrines with thrones for the Hindu trinity: Brahma, Shiva and Vishnu. The carvings are particularly intricate. See if you can count all 43 altars.

Pura Dalem Penunggekan HINDU TEMPLE
(Jl Merdeka) FREE The exterior wall of this fascinating temple of the dead features vivid relief carvings of evil-doers getting their just desserts in the afterlife. One panel addresses the lurid fate of adulterers (men in particular may find the viewing uncomfortable). Other panels portray sinners as monkeys, while another is a good representation of sinners begging to be spared the fires of hell. It's 3km south of the centre of Bangli.

✖ Eating

The *pasar malam* (night market), on Jl Merdeka beside the bemo terminal, has some excellent traditional warungs (food stalls) and you'll also find fresh and tasty food stalls here in the shambolic **market** during the day. Temple-offering supplies are sold here 24 hours a day.

❶ Getting There & Away

Bangli is located on the main road between Denpasar's Batubulan terminal (17,000Rp) and Gunung Batur, via Penelokan. Most people visit with their own wheels on jaunts involving Pura Besakih.

Semarapura (Klungkung)

🗾 0366

A tidy regional capital, Semarapura is a must-see for its fascinating Kertha Gosa complex, a relic of Bali from the time before the Dutch. Once the centre of Bali's most important kingdom, Semarapura is still commonly called by its old name, Klungkung.

It's a good place to stroll and get a feel for modern Balinese life. The markets are large, the shops many and the streets are reasonably calm. Park in the car park across from the Taman Kertha Gosa entrance, ignore the vendors and enjoy!

History

Successors to the Majapahit conquerors of Bali established themselves at Gelgel (just south of modern Semarapura) around 1400,

---

EAST BALI'S BEST MARKET

Semarapura's sprawling **market** (Jl Diponegoro; ⊘ 6am-5pm) is a vibrant hub of commerce and a meeting place for people of the region. You can easily spend an hour wandering about the warren of stalls on three levels. It's grimy, yes, but also endlessly fascinating. Huge straw baskets of lemons, limes, tomatoes and other produce are islands of colour amid the chaos. A plethora of locally made snacks are offered in profusion; try several.

Glittering jewellery stalls crowd up against shops selling nothing but plastic buckets. Look for ikat vendors selling authentic fabric for a third of what you'd pay elsewhere. On breezeways out the back, climb to the top for views of multicultural Semarapura, where mosque minarets crowd the sky along with Balinese temples. Mornings are the best time to visit.

---

with the Gelgel dynasty strengthening the growing Majapahit presence on the island. During the 17th century the successors of the Gelgel line established separate kingdoms and the dominance of the Gelgel court was lost. The court moved to Klungkung in 1710, but never regained a pre-eminent position.

In 1849 the rulers of Klungkung and Gianyar defeated a Dutch invasion force at Kusamba. Before the Dutch could launch a counter-attack, a force from Tabanan arrived and the trader Mads Lange was able to broker a peace settlement.

For the next 50 years, the south Bali kingdoms squabbled, until the rajah of Gianyar petitioned the Dutch for support. When the Dutch finally invaded the south, the king of Klungkung had a choice between a suicidal *puputan*, like the rajah of Denpasar, or an ignominious surrender, as Tabanan's rajah had done (or cutting a deal like the rajah did up the road in Bangli). He chose the first. In April 1908, as the Dutch surrounded his palace, the Dewa Agung and hundreds of his relatives and followers marched out to certain death from Dutch gunfire or the blades of their own kris (traditional daggers). The sacrifice is commemorated in the towering Puputan Monument.

Sights

⭐Klungkung Palace
HISTORIC BUILDING

(Jl Puputan; adult/child 12,000/6000Rp; ⊙6am-6pm) When the Dewa Agung dynasty moved here in 1710, the Semara Pura was established. The palace was laid out as a large square, believed to be in the form of a mandala, with courtyards, gardens, pavilions and moats. Most of the original palace and grounds were destroyed by the 1908 Dutch attacks; the **Pemedal Agung**, the gateway on the south side of the square, is all that remains of the palace itself – check out its carvings.

Two important buildings are preserved in a restored section of the grounds and, along with a museum, they comprise the remains of the palace complex. The complex is sometimes referred to as Taman Gili (Island Garden).

➡ **Kertha Gosa**

(Hall of Justice) In the northeastern corner of the Klungkung Palace complex, the Kertha Gosa was effectively the supreme court of the Klungkung kingdom, where disputes and cases that could not be settled at the village level were eventually brought. This open-sided pavilion is a superb example of Klungkung architecture. The ceiling is completely covered with fine paintings in the Klungkung style. These paintings, done on asbestos sheeting, were installed in the 1940s, replacing cloth paintings that had deteriorated.

➡ **Bale Kambang**

(Floating Pavilion; Taman Kertha Gosa) Within Klungkung Palace, the ceiling of the beautiful Bale Kambang is painted in Klungkung

style. The different rows of paintings deal with various subjects. The first row is based on the astrological calendar, the second on the folk tale of Pan and Men Brayut and their 18 children, and the upper rows on the adventures of the hero Sutasona.

Museum Semarajaya
MUSEUM

(Klungkung Palace) This diverting museum in the Klungkung Palace compound has an interesting collection of archaeological and other pieces. There are exhibits of *songket* (silver- or gold-threaded cloth) weaving and palm toddy (palm wine) and palm-sugar extraction. Don't miss the moving display about the 1908 *puputan*, along with some interesting old photos of the royal court. The exhibit on salt-making gives you a good idea of the hard work involved.

Puputan Monument
MONUMENT

Klungkung was the last Balinese kingdom to succumb to the Dutch (1908) and the sacrifice is commemorated in the towering Puputan Monument, just across Jl Serapati from the Klungkung Palace.

Pura Taman Sari HINDU TEMPLE
(Jl Gunung Merapi) The quiet lawns and ponds around this temple, northeast of the Taman Kertha Gosa complex, make it a relaxing stop and make it live up to the translation of its name: Flower Garden Temple. The towering, 11-roofed *meru* indicates that this was a temple built for royalty; today it seems built for the geese who wander the grounds.

✖ Eating

The best bet for food is browsing the many choices in and around the market. There's a small stall selling good coffee at the Taman Kertha Gosa car park. For lunch, consider the choices east of nearby Kusamba on the coast.

Bali Indah CHINESE, INDONESIAN $
(☑ 0366-21056; Jl Nakula 1; dishes 15,000-25,000Rp) A veteran and an affable Chinese sit-down place with simple meals; you'll swear it's 1943. Sumber Rasa (almost) next door is similar.

Pasar Senggol MARKET $
(off Jl Besakih; ☺ 5pm-midnight) A night market, this is by far the best spot to eat if you're in town late. It's the usual flurry of woks, customers and noise.

❶ Information

Jl Nakula and the main street, Jl Diponegoro, have several ATMs.

❶ Getting There & Away

The best way to visit Semarapura is with your own transport and as part of a circuit taking in other sites up the mountains and along the coast.

Bemos from Denpasar (Batubulan terminal) pass through Semarapura (14,000Rp) on the way to points further east. They can be hailed from near the Puputan Monument.

Around Semarapura

Around Semarapura, there are dozens of small villages. Many specialise in various traditional crafts.

The road north of Semarapura climbs steeply into the hills via **Bukit Jambal**, which is understandably popular for its magnificent views. This road continues to Rendang and Pura Besakih.

GEGEL

Situated about 2.5km south of Semarapura on the way to the coast road and 500m south of Kamasan, Gelgel was once the seat of Bali's most powerful dynasty. The town's decline started in 1710, when the court moved to present-day Semarapura, and finished when the Dutch bombarded the place in 1908.

Today the wide streets and the surviving temples are only faintly evocative of past grandeur. **Pura Dasar Bhuana** has huge banyan trees shading grassy grounds where you may feel the urge for a quiet contemplative stroll. The vast courtyards are a clue to its former importance, and festivals here attract large numbers of people from all over Bali.

About 500m to the east, the **Masjid Gelgel** is Bali's oldest mosque. Although modern-looking, it was established in the late 16th century for the benefit of Muslim missionaries from Java who were unwilling to return home after failing to make any converts.

East of Semarapura, the old main road dramatically crosses Sungai Unda (Unda River), then swings south towards Kusamba and the sea. Lava from the 1963 eruption of Gunung Agung destroyed villages here, but the lava flows are now overgrown.

Tihingan

Several workshops in Tihingan are dedicated to producing gamelan instruments. Small foundries make the resonating bronze bars and bowl-shaped gongs, which are then carefully filed and polished until they produce the correct tone.

A few workshops with signs out front are good for visits. The often hot work is usually done very early in the morning when it's cool, but at other times you'll still likely see something going on.

From Semarapura, head west along Jl Diponegoro and look for the signs.

◉ Sights

Nyoman Gunarsa Museum MUSEUM
(☑ 0366-22256; Pertigaan Banda/Banda Intersection, Takmung; adult/child 50,000Rp/free; ☺ 9am-4pm Mon-Sat) Dedicated to classical and contemporary Balinese painting, this

slightly melancholy museum complex was established by Nyoman Gunarsa, one of the most respected and successful modern artists in Indonesia. A vast three-storey building exhibits an impressive variety of older pieces, including stone carvings, woodcarvings, architectural antiques, masks, puppets and textiles.

Many of the classical paintings are on bark paper and are some of the oldest surviving examples. Check out the many old puppets, still seemingly animated even in retirement. The top floor is devoted to Gunarsa's own bold, expressionistic depictions of traditional life. Look for *Offering*.

The museum is about 4km west from Semarapura, near a bend on the Gianyar road – look for the dummy policemen at the base of a large statue nearby.

Sideman

📍0366

The Sideman region is getting more popular as a verdant escape every year, where a walk in any direction is a communion with nature. Winding through one of Bali's most beautiful river valleys, the road to Sideman offers marvellous paddy-field scenery, a delightful rural character and extraordinary views of Gunung Agung (when the clouds permit).

German artist Walter Spies lived in Iseh for some time from 1932 in order to escape the perpetual party of his own making in Ubud. Later the Swiss painter Theo Meier, nearly as famous as Spies for his influence on Balinese art, lived in the same house.

⊙ Sights

The village of Sideman has a spectacular location and is a centre for culture and arts, particularly *endek* cloth (used for traditional sarongs) and *songket* (silver- or gold-threaded cloth). **Pelangi Weaving** (📍0366-23012; Jl Soka 67; ⊙8am-6pm) has a couple dozen employees busily creating downstairs, while upstairs you can relax with the Sideman views from comfy chairs outside the showroom.

🏃 Activities

There are many **walks** through the rice and chilli fields and streams in the multihued green valley. One involves a spectacular three-hour, round-trip climb up to **Pura Bukit Tageh**, a small temple with big views.

No matter where you stay, you'll be able to arrange guides for in-depth trekking (about 80,000Rp per hour) or just set out on your own exploration.

🛏 Sleeping

There is a good range of guesthouses at various budget levels in Sideman. Views throughout the area are sweeping, from terraced green hills to Gunung Agung, although the area's popularity means that new guesthouses have obstructed some views. It can get cool and misty at night, so pack an extra layer.

⭐**Khrisna Home Stay** HOMESTAY $
(📍0815 5832 1543; pinpinaryadi@yahoo.com; Jl Tebola; r incl breakfast from 300,000Rp; 🛜) Why go to a market for fruit when you can sleep in an orchard? This wonderful seven-room homestay is surrounded by organic trees and plants growing guava, bananas, passionfruit, papaya, oranges and more. Needless to say, breakfasts are excellent. The rooms are comfortable (with terraces) and the owners lovely.

Lihat Sawah GUESTHOUSE $
(📍0366-530 0516; www.lihatsawah.com; r incl breakfast 300,000-500,000Rp; 🛜🍽) Translating as 'see the rice fields', this guesthouse lives up to its name: all 12 rooms have views of the surrounding rice fields, valley and mountain. All have hot water – nice after a morning hike – and the best have lovely wooden verandahs. There are also three bungalows. The cafe has wi-fi and serves Thai and Indo dishes (mains from 15,000Rp). From near the centre of Sideman, take the right fork in the road to this guesthouse

⭐**Samanvaya** INN $$
(📍0821 4710 3884; www.samanvaya-bali.com; r incl breakfast US$70-185; 🛜🍽) An attractive boutique inn with sweeping views over rice fields to the ocean. The Brit owners are steadily expanding the complex: it has a stunning bamboo yoga space, spa pavilion and restaurant. Bamboo bungalows are the pick, but units with thatched roofs and deep, wooden terraces are also nice. The landscaped garden, infinity pool and hot tub are a dream. It's on the main lane of accommodation.

Giri Carik GUESTHOUSE $$
(📍0819 3666 5821; www.giricariksidemenbali.com; r incl breakfast from 475,000Rp; 🛜🍽) Great

budget quarters, good views and a central location (it's an easy walk to the emerging heart of Sideman tourism on the main lane of accommodation). The five rooms are simple but have comfortable basics. The pool terrace has rice terrace vistas.

Darmada　　　　　　GUESTHOUSE $$
(☑0853 3803 2100; www.darmadabali.com; r incl breakfast from 650,000Rp; 🛜❄) Beautifully set in a small river valley on spacious, lush grounds, this seven-room guesthouse has a large pool lined with tiles in gentle shades of green. Rooms have hammocks on the patio near the babbling waters and there's a natural-water swimming pool. The small warung has food made with vegetables and fruit grown on the grounds.

Darmada serves cake and coffee for walkers in the afternoons (40,000Rp). It's down the hill from the main lane of accommodation.

Nirarta Centre　　　　　HOTEL $$
(☑0366-530 0636; www.awareness-bali.com; r €25-60) Guests here partake in serious programs for personal and spiritual development, including meditation intensives and yoga. The motto: 'centre for living awareness'. The 11 comfortable rooms are split among six bungalows, some right on the river. It's on the main lane of accommodation.

Subak Tabola　　　　　HOTEL $$
(☑0811 386 6197; www.subaktabolavilla.com; r from 500,000Rp; ❄🛜❄) Set in an impossibly green amphitheatre of rice terraces, the 11 rooms have open-air bathrooms; two very large bungalows are especially appealing. Verandahs have mesmerising views down the valley to the ocean. The grounds are spacious and there's a cool pool with frog fountains. It's nearly 2km from the hotel signpost on the main lane with accommodation.

The high published rates have no bearing on reality; real prices online and in person are much less.

✕ Eating

Most inns have restaurants and there are cafes along the roads, with more appearing all the time. Meals can be arranged at guesthouses and villas that lack cafes.

★ Warung Ida　　　　　BALINESE $
(☑0812 364 7384; mains from 40,000Rp) There's an actual Ida here and boy can she cook. The rest of the family serve up her special Indo-

ROAD TO TEMBUKU

Travelling from the flatlands of the east up the slopes for Gunung Batur, Pura Besakih or even as part of a round-trip in combination with the Sideman road, you have several choices.

One of the best is the road that begins about 5km east of Gianyar on the main road to Semarapura. It runs north for about 12km to the village of Tembuku and is paved. It's narrow, which keeps the truck count down, and passes through a score of tiny, traditional villages. There are **rice terrace** and **river valley views** along its length.

You'll also see huge beams of yellow wood by the road. These are from jackfruit trees and are prized for their long-lasting qualities. They are used in temple construction.

nesian dishes in a relaxed open-air setting. Come for a sunset Bintang and stay for a fine meal made with produce from the surrounding fields. It's on the main lane with accommodation.

Joglo d'Uma　　　　　BALINESE $
(☑0819 1566 6456; mains from 45,000Rp; ⏱11am-8pm; 🛜) This restaurant is an ideal spot to sit back and take in stunning views of rice fields and verdant hills. It's just across from the Samanvaya inn and has a drinks menu.

ℹ Information

There is an excellent website (www.sidemen-bali.com) for the Sideman area that details accommodation options and the many activities in the region.

ℹ Getting There & Away

The Sideman road can be a beautiful part of any day trip from south Bali or Ubud. It connects in the north with the Rendang–Amlapura road just west of Duda. Unfortunately the road is busy due to huge trucks hauling rocks for Bali's incessant construction.

A less-travelled route to Pura Besakih goes northeast from Semarapura, via Sideman and Iseh, to another scenic treat: the Rendang–Amlapura road.

Near the centre of Sideman, a small road heads west for 500m to a fork where signs will direct you to various guesthouses.

Pura Besakih

Perched nearly 1000m up the side of Gunung Agung is Bali's most important temple, Pura Besakih. In fact it is an extensive complex of 23 separate but related temples, with the largest and most important being Pura Penataran Agung. Unfortunately, many people find it a disappointing (and dispiriting) experience due to the avarice of various local characters.

The multitude of hassles aside, the complex comes alive during frequent ceremonies.

History

The precise origins of Pura Besakih are not totally clear, but it almost certainly dates from prehistoric times. The stone bases of Pura Penataran Agung and several other temples resemble megalithic stepped pyramids and date back at least 2000 years. It was certainly used as a Hindu place of worship from 1284, when the first Javanese conquerors settled in Bali. By the 15th century Besakih had become a state temple of the Gelgel dynasty.

⊙ Sights

The largest and most important temple is Pura Penataran Agung. The other Besakih temples – all with individual significance and often closed to visitors – are markedly less scenic. When it's mist-free, the view down to the coast is sublime.

Pura Penataran Agung HINDU TEMPLE

Pura Penataran Agung is built on six levels, terraced up the slope, with the entrance approached from below, up a flight of steps. This entrance is an imposing *candi bentar* (split gateway) and, beyond it, the even more impressive *kori agung* is the gateway to the second courtyard.

You will find that it's most enjoyable during one of the frequent festivals, when hundreds or even thousands of gorgeously dressed devotees turn up with beautifully arranged offerings. Note that tourists are not allowed inside this temple.

❶ Information

There are ticket booths on the roads that access the site. Admission is 15,000Rp per person plus 5000Rp per vehicle.

When you reach the site there are two parking areas:

Parkir Bawa This is the main parking area and the first you'll encounter coming from the south. Avoid this one as it leaves you at the bottom of a hill with a long climb to the temples. During this 500m walk, you will be assailed by touts and persistent offers of a ride to the top.

Parkir Atas This preferred parking area is a very short walk from the base of the temple complex.

You'll need sarongs and sashes as you roam the temples. Vendors in the parking areas will sell you sets or bring your own.

---

❶ AN UNHOLY EXPERIENCE: VISITING PURA BESAKIH

So intrusive are the scams and irritations faced by visitors to Besakih that many wish they had skipped the complex altogether. In 2015 a top Bali tourist official complained that more than 50% of tourists commenting about Besakih on social media complained about having a bad experience. What follows are some of the ploys you should be aware of before a visit:

➡ Near both parking areas are 'guide' offices where touts hang around looking for visitors. They may emphatically tell you that you need their services, tell you that temples are 'closed for a ceremony' and quote a ridiculously high price of US$25 for a short visit. This is not true: you may always walk among the temples and no 'guide' can get you into a closed temple.

➡ Other 'guides' may foist their services on you throughout your visit. There have been reports of people agreeing to a guide's services only to be hit with a huge fee at the end. Again, refuse their entreaties.

➡ Once inside the complex, you may receive offers to 'come pray with me'. Visitors who seize this chance to get into a forbidden temple can face demands of 100,000Rp or more.

➡ Do not ever allow anyone to keep the ticket you were issued on the drive in. It's just an excuse for someone else to sell you another.

Pura Besakih Complex

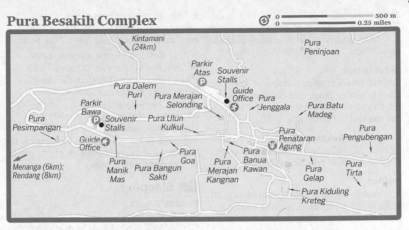

ℹ️ Getting There & Away

The best way to visit is with your own transport, which allows you to explore the many gorgeous drives in the area.

Gunung Agung

Bali's highest and most revered mountain, Gunung Agung is an imposing peak seen from most of south and east Bali, although it's often obscured by cloud and mist. Many sources say it's 3142m high, but some say it lost its summit in the 1963 eruption. The summit is an oval crater, about 700m across, with its highest point on the western edge above Besakih.

As it's the spiritual centre of Bali, traditional houses are laid out on an axis in line with Agung and many locals always know where they are in relation to the peak, which is thought to house ancestral spirits. Climbing the mountain takes you through verdant forest in the clouds and rewards with sweeping (dawn) views. More than 3000 tourists make the ascent each year.

🏃 Activities

It's best to climb during the dry season (April to September). July to November are the most reliable months. At other times the paths can be slippery and dangerous and the views are clouded over (especially true in January and February). Climbing Gunung Agung is not permitted when major religious events are being held at Pura Besakih, which generally includes most of April.

Points to consider for a climb:

➡ Use a guide.

➡ Respect your guide's pauses at shrines for prayers on the sacred mountain.

➡ Get to the top before 8am – the clouds that often obscure the view of Agung also obscure the view *from* Agung.

➡ Take a strong torch (flashlight), extra batteries, plenty of water (2L per person), snack food, waterproof clothing and a warm jumper (sweater).

➡ Wear strong shoes or boots and have manicured toes – the trail is very steep and the descent is especially hard on your feet.

➡ This is a hard climb, don't fool yourself.

➡ Take frequent rests and don't be afraid to ask your guide to slow down.

Guides

Trips with guides on either of the routes up Gunung Agung generally include breakfast and other meals as well as a place to stay, but be sure to confirm all details in advance. Guides are also able to arrange transport.

Most of the places to stay in the region, including those at Selat, along the Sideman road and at Tirta Gangga, will recommend guides for Gunung Agung climbs. Expect to pay a negotiable 1,000,000Rp to 1,200,000Rp for one to four people for your climb.

Yande   HIKING
(📞 0852 3025 3672, 0857 3988 5569) Affiliated with the Pondok Wisata Puri Agung Inn (p206) in Selat, which is a good place to stay for an early start.

Wayan Tegteg HIKING
(📱 0813 3852 5677; tegtegwayan@yahoo.co.id)
A recommended guide who wins plaudits
from hikers.

Ketut Uriada HIKING
(📱 0812 364 6426; ketut.uriada@gmail.com) This
knowledgeable guide can arrange transport
for an extra fee. Look for his small sign on
the road east of Muncan.

Gung Bawa Trekking HIKING
(📱 0812 387 8168; www.gungbawatrekking.com)
Experienced and reliable trekking guide.

Routes
It's possible to climb Agung from various directions. The two most popular routes are
from the following places:

➡ Pura Pasar Agung (on the southern
slopes; about eight hours) – this route
involves the least walking because Pura
Pasar Agung (Agung Market Temple)

is high on the southern slopes of the
mountain (around 1500m) and can be
reached by a good road north from Selat.

➡ Pura Besakih (on the southwest side
of the mountain; about 12 hours) – this
climb is much tougher than the already
demanding southern approach and is
only for the very physically fit; for the best
chance of a clear view before the clouds
close in you should start at midnight.
Either route can take you to the summit, although most people on the shorter route go
to the crater rim (2866m).

🛏 Sleeping

**Pondok Wisata
Puri Agung Inn** GUESTHOUSE **$**
(📱 0857 3857 4850; Jl Raya Selat; r incl breakfast
250,000-300,000Rp; 🛜) Located in relaxed
Selat, convenient for climbs up Gunung
Agung or rice-field walks, this attractive inn
has comfortable budget rooms. Room 2 is

SCENIC ROUTE: RENDANG TO AMLAPURA

A fascinating road goes around the southern slopes of Gunung Agung from Rendang almost to Amlapura. It runs through some superb countryside, descending more or less gradually as it goes east. Water flows everywhere and there are rice fields, orchards and temple-stone carvers most of the way.

You can get to the start of the road in Rendang from Bangli in the west on a very pretty road through rice terraces and thick jungle vegetation. **Rendang** itself is an attractive mountain village; the crossroads are dominated by a huge and historic banyan tree. After going east for about 3km, you'll come into a beautiful small valley of rice terraces. At the bottom is **Sungai Telagawaja**, a popular river for white-water rafting.

The old-fashioned village of **Muncan** has quaint shingle roofs. It's approximately 4km along the winding road. Note the statues at the west entrance to town showing two boys: one a scholar and one showing the naked stupidity of skipping class. Nearby are scores of open-air factories where the soft lava rock is carved into temple decorations.

The road then passes through some of the most attractive rice country in Bali before reaching **Selat**, where you turn north to get to **Pura Pasar Agung**, a starting point for climbing Gunung Agung.

Just before **Duda**, the very scenic Sideman road branches southwest via Sideman to Semarapura. Further east, a side road (about 800m) leads to **Putung**. This area is superb for hiking: there's an easy-to-follow track from Putung to Manggis, about 8km down the hill.

Continuing east, **Sibetan** is famous for growing salak, the delicious fruit with a curious 'snakeskin' covering, which you can buy from roadside stalls. This is one of the villages you can visit on tours and homestays organised by **JED** (📱 0851 0066 9951; www.jed.or.id; tour US$75), the nonprofit group that promotes rural tourism.

Northeast of Sibetan, a poorly signposted road leads north to **Jungutan**, with its **Tirta Telaga Tista** – a decorative pool and garden complex built for the water-loving old rajah of Karangasem.

The scenic road finishes at **Bebandem**, which has a cattle market every three days and plenty of other stuff for sale as well. Bebandem and several nearby villages are home to members of the traditional metal-worker caste, which includes silversmiths and blacksmiths.

the pick for both size and views of the rice fields. A pool was being built at the time of research.

Kusamba to Padangbai

The coast road from Sanur crosses the traditional route to the east at the fishing town of Kusamba before joining the road near Pura Goa Lawah.

Kusamba & Around

A side road leaves the main road and goes south to the fishing and salt-making village of Kusamba, where you will see rows of colourful *prahu* (outrigger fishing boats) lined up all along the grey-sand beach. The fishing is usually done at night and the 'eyes' on the front of the boats help navigate through the darkness. The fish market in Kusamba displays the night's catch.

Small local boats travel to Nusa Penida and Nusa Lembongan, which are clearly visible from Kusamba (boats from Padangbai are faster and safer, the modern Kusamba car ferry being the exception). Both east and west of Kusamba there are small salt-making huts lined up in rows along the beach.

Follow the crowds of Balinese to the open-air pavilion, Merta Sari, 300m north of the coast road in the village of Bingin (look for the signs). It's famous for its *nasi campur*. This version of the island's plate lunch includes juicy, pounded fish satay, a slightly sour, fragrant fish broth, fish steamed in banana leaves, snake beans in a fragrant tomato-peanut sauce and a fiery red sambal.

Another great eating option is **Sari Baruna** (Jl Raya Goa Lawa; meals 25,000Rp; ⊙10am-6pm), where they grill fish with attitude and authority. The fish satay is a melange of fragrant spices. It's in a solid, open-air building about 200m west of Pura Goa Lawah on the Coast road.

Pura Goa Lawah

Three kilometres east of Kusamba, **Pura Goa Lawah** (Bat Cave Temple; Jl Raya Goa Lawah; adult/child 10,000/5000Rp, car park 2000Rp; ⊙7am-6pm) is one of nine directional temples in Bali. The cave in the cliff face is packed, crammed and jammed full of bats, and the complex is equally overcrowded with worshippers and tour groups. Ceremonies are regularly held here, making it a good spot to observe Balinese Hindu rituals;

however, be sure to maintain a respectful distance and read any etiquette guidelines before entering.

Padangbai

☑ 0363

There's a real traveller vibe about this little beach town that is also the port for the public ferry connecting Bali with Lombok and many of the fast boats to the Gilis.

Padangbai is an attractive stop: it sits on a small bay and has a nice little curve of beach. A compact seaside backpacker hub offers cheap places to stay and some fun cafes.

The pace is slow, but should ambition strike there's good snorkelling and diving plus some easy walks and a couple of great beaches. Meanwhile you can soak up the languid air punctuated by the occasional arrival and departure of a ferry.

🏖 Beaches

With its protected bay, Padangbai has clear waters and a good beach right in front. Others are nearby.

Blue Lagoon Beach   BEACH
On the far side of Padangbai's eastern headland, about a 500m walk, is the small, light-sand Blue Lagoon Beach, an idyllic place with a couple of cafes and gentle, family-friendly surf.

Bias Tugal   BEACH
Walk southwest from the ferry terminal and follow the trail up the hill for about 1.3km to idyllic Bias Tugal, also known as Pantai Kecil (Little Beach), on the exposed coast outside the bay. Be careful in the water as it is subject to strong currents. There are a couple of daytime warung here.

⊙ Sights

Padangbai is interesting for a stroll. At the west end of town near the post office there's a small **mosque** (Jl Penataran Agung) and a temple, **Pura Desa** (Jl Polabuhan). Towards the middle of town are two more temples, **Pura Dalem** (Gang Segara II) FREE and **Pura Segara** (off Jl Silayukti) FREE.

On a headland at the northeast corner of the bay, a path leads uphill to three temples, including **Pura Silayukti**, where Empu Kuturan – who introduced the caste system to Bali in the 11th century – is said to have lived. It is one of the four oldest in Bali.

Padangbai

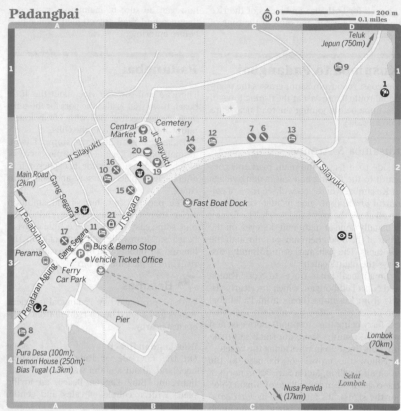

0   200 m
0   0.1 miles

🏃 Activities

Diving

There is good diving on the coral reefs around Padangbai, but the water can be a bit cold and visibility is not always ideal. The most popular local dives are **Blue Lagoon** and **Teluk Jepun** (Jepun Bay), both in Teluk Amuk, the bay just east of Padangbai. There's a good range of soft and hard corals and varied marine life, including sharks, turtles and wrasse, and a 40m wall at Blue Lagoon.

Many local outfits offer diving trips in the area, including to Gili Tepekong and Gili Biaha and on to Tulamben and Nusa Penida. All dive prices are competitive, costing from US$65 for dives in the area to US$110 for trips out to Nusa Penida.

Geko Dive   DIVING
(☑ 0363-41516; www.gekodivebali.com; Jl Silayukti; 2-tank dives from 1,100,000Rp) Geko is the longest-established operator in town. Its base is

just across from the beach and has a sandy-floored cafe.

Water Worx   DIVING
(☑ 0363-41220; www.waterworxbali.com; Jl Silayukti; 2-dank dives with/without equipment rental from US$80/60) A well-regarded dive operator offering trips to surrounding areas, plus PADI and SSI courses. Can also arrange dives for travellers with disabilities.

Snorkelling

One of the best and most accessible walk-in snorkel sites is off **Blue Lagoon Beach**. Note that it is subject to strong currents when the tide is out. Other sites such as **Teluk Jepun** can be reached by local boat (or check with the dive operators to see if they have any room on their dive boats; the cost is around 350,000Rp). Snorkel sets cost about 30,000Rp per day.

Local *jukung* (boats) offer snorkelling trips (bring your own gear) around Padang-

Padangbai

◎ Sights
1	Blue Lagoon Beach	D1
2	Mosque	A3
3	Pura Dalem	A2
4	Pura Segara	B2
5	Pura Silayukti	D3

◎ Activities, Courses & Tours
6	Geko Dive	C2
7	Water Worx	C2

◎ Sleeping
8	Bamboo Paradise	A4
9	Bloo Lagoon Village	D1
10	Darma Homestay	B2
11	Fat Barracuda	A3
12	Hotel Puri Rai	C2
13	Topi Inn	C2

◎ Eating
14	Colonial Restaurant	B2
15	Depot Segara	B2
16	Ozone Café	B2
	Topi Inn	(see 13)
17	Zen Inn	A3

◎ Drinking & Nightlife
18	Babylon Bar	B2
19	Sunshine	B2
20	Wareong Bloo	B2

◎ Shopping
21	Ryan Shop	B3

bai (90,000Rp per person per hour) and as far away as Nusa Lembongan (500,000Rp for two passengers).

🛏 Sleeping

Accommodation in Padangbai – like the town itself – is pretty laid-back. Prices are fairly cheap and it's pleasant enough here that there's no need to hurry through to or from Lombok. It's easy to wander the town comparing rooms before choosing one.

In the village there are several tiny places in the alleys, some with a choice of small, cheap downstairs rooms or bigger, brighter upstairs rooms.

Darma Homestay   HOMESTAY $
(🗗0363-41394; pondokwisata_dharma@yahoo. com; Gang Segara III; r 150,000-600,000Rp; ❊@🛜) A classic Balinese family homestay. The more expensive of the 12 rooms have hot showers and air-con; go for the room on the top floor. There are family rooms as well.

Topi Inn   GUESTHOUSE $
(🗗0363-41424; www.topiinn.nl; Jl Silayukti; dm/r from 60,000/150,000Rp; @🛜) Sitting at the east end of the strip in a serene location, Topi has six charming but rudimentary cold-water rooms. Some share bathrooms, others are literally a mattress on the outdoor deck. There's a popular restaurant downstairs, plus various cultural workshops on offer.

Bamboo Paradise   GUESTHOUSE $
(🗗0822 6630 4330; www.bambooparadisebali.com; Jl Penataran Agung; dm incl breakfast 95,000Rp, r incl breakfast 250,000-300,000Rp; ❊🛜) Away

from the main strip, 200m up a gentle hill from the ferry port, this popular backpackers has the cheapest crash in town (in four-bed, air-con dorms). Regular rooms are comfortable (some fan only) and it has a nice, large lounging area with hammocks and beanbags.

Fat Barracuda   GUESTHOUSE $
(🗗0822 3797 1212; www.facebook.com/fatbarracuda; Jl Segara; dm/r from 115,000/300,000Rp; ❊🛜) Run by the same owner from nearby Bamboo Paradise, this popular backpacker pad next to the harbour overlooks the water. It has 10 beds; some rooms are fan-only.

Lemon House   GUESTHOUSE $
(🗗0812 4637 1575; www.lemonhousebali.com; Gang Melanting 5; incl breakfast dm 90,000Rp, r 200,000-350,000Rp; 🛜) This house on the hill beside town has two rooms with sweeping views. On a clear day you can see Lombok. Other rooms are good deals and share bathrooms. Of course, a good view means a good climb. It's about 300m and 70 steps up from the ferry port. They'll come down and help with your bags.

Hotel Puri Rai   HOTEL $$
(🗗0363-41439, 0363-41385; www.puriraihotel. com; Jl Silayukti 3; r from 300,000Rp; ❊🛜❊) The Puri Rai has 34 rooms in a two-storey stone building pleasantly facing the good-sized pool. Other rooms enjoy harbour views or overlook a yucky parking area. Ask to see a couple. The cafe has a good view.

★ Bloo Lagoon Village   HOTEL $$
(🗗0363-41211; www.bloolagoon.com; Jl Silayukti; r incl breakfast US$125-230; ❊🛜❊) 🌿 While

far from five-star, the 25 open-air bunga-lows that overlook Blue Lagoon Beach are appealing. Designed in traditional thatched style, they're full of character. Stylish units come with one, two or three bedrooms. Yoga classes (inclusive in rates) are held in a space with inspiring ocean views, and good-value diving packages are available. Good recycling schemes.

✕ Eating

Beach fare and backpacker staples are mostly what's on offer in Padangbai – lots of fresh seafood, Indonesian classics, pizza and, yes, banana pancakes. You can easily laze away a few hours soaking up the scene at the places along Jl Segara and Jl Silayukti, which have harbour views during the day and cool breezes in the evening.

★ Topi Inn
CAFE $

(☑ 0363-41424; Jl Silayukti; mains from 50,000Rp; ⊘ 7.30am-10pm) 🍴 Juices, shakes and good coffees are served up throughout the day. Breakfasts are big and whatever is landed by the fishing boats outside the front door during the day is grilled by night. Refill your water bottle here for 2000Rp. It also has an atmospheric bamboo bar selling cheap beers.

Zen Inn
INTERNATIONAL $

(☑ 0363-41418; Gang Segara; dishes 18,000-30,000Rp; ⊘ 8am-11pm; 🛜) Burgers and BBQ mains are served in this airy cafe that goes late by local standards – often until 11pm. Lose yourself on the loungers amid vintage movie posters.

Colonial Restaurant
CAFE $

(☑ 0811 385 8821; www.divingbali.cz; Jl Silayukti 6, OK Divers; mains from 40,000Rp; ⊘ 7am-11pm; 🛜) This large cafe on the beach strip is the best place to while away time waiting for your boat. Lounge on beanbags, sofas or at actual tables and enjoy the harbour view. Food spans the burger–Indo gamut. Patrons can use the pool.

Depot Segara
SEAFOOD $

(☑ 0363-41443; Jl Segara; dishes 10,000-30,000Rp; ⊘ 8am-10pm) Fresh seafood, such as barracuda, marlin and snapper, is prepared in a variety of ways at this slightly stylish cafe (which also does good burgers). Soak up the harbour views from the elevated terrace. In a town where casual is the byword, this is the slightly nicer option.

Ozone Café
INTERNATIONAL $

(☑ 0817 470 8597; off Jl Silayukti; mains from 20,000Rp; ⊘ 8am-late) This popular travellers' gathering spot has low tables with pillows for lounging. It also has pizza, BBQ fish and live music, sometimes by patrons.

🍸 Drinking & Nightlife

Sunshine
BAR

(off Jl Silayukti; ⊘ 4pm-late) In keeping with the local vibe, this barely there bar (most seats are outside on the pavement) serves simple grilled fish at night along with cold beer. The motto is 'light up our soul', which can be defined many ways, possibly through the impromptu jam sessions.

Wareong Bloo
CAFE

(off Jl Silayukti; ⊘ 7am-3pm) The in-town cafe of the Bloo Lagoon Village hotel offers an upscale place for people waiting for their fast-boat departure. Excellent coffee, drinks and fresh juices are served in a breezy, shady setting.

Babylon Bar
BAR

(Jl Silayukti; ⊘ 5pm-late) A tiny all-open-air bar in the souvenir stall area back off the beach; a few chairs, tables and pillows scattered about are perfect for whiling away the evening with new friends.

🛍 Shopping

Ryan Shop
MARKET

(☑ 0363-41215; Jl Segara 38; ⊘ 8am-8pm) The mercantile pleasures of the Ryan Shop can't be underestimated. It has good used paperbacks and sundries. They note that 'postcards still sell well'.

❶ Getting There & Away

BEMO
Padangbai is 2km south of the main Semarapura–Amlapura road. Bemos leave from the car park in front of the port: some go east via Candidasa to Amlapura (10,000Rp), others go west to Semarapura (10,000Rp).

BOAT
Anyone who carries your luggage on or off the ferries or fast boats will expect to be paid, so agree on the price first or carry your own stuff. Also, watch out for scams where the porter may try to sell you a ticket you've already bought.

Ignore touts who meet all arriving boats and departing passengers. Only buy public ferry tickets from the official window in the ferry building.

EAST BALI PADANGBAI

Lombok & Gili Islands

There are many ways to travel between Bali and Lombok and the Gilis. Be sure to consider important safety information.

Fast Boats Several companies link Padangbai to the Gilis and Lombok. They have offices on the waterfront. Fares are negotiable and average 300,000Rp to 600,000Rp one way. Travel times will be more than the 90 minutes advertised.

Public Ferries (adult/child/motorbike/car 44 ,000/29,000/123,000/879,000Rp, five to six hours) Travel nonstop between Padangbai and Lembar on Lombok. Passenger tickets are sold near the pier. Boats supposedly run 24 hours and leave about every 90 minutes, but the service can be unreliable – boats have caught on fire and run aground.

Nusa Penida

Fast boats to Nusa Penida leave from just off the beach. The car ferry leaves from the ferry port.

BUS

To connect with Denpasar, catch a bemo out to the main road and hail a minibus to the Batubulan terminal (18,000Rp).

TOURIST BUS

Perama (Jl Pelabuhan; 0363-41419; 7am-8pm) has a stop here for its services around the east coast. Destinations include Kuta (75,000Rp, three hours), Sanur (75,000Rp, two hours) and Ubud (75,000Rp, 1½ hours).

Padangbai to Candidasa

It's 11km along the main road from the Padangbai turn-off to the tourist town of Candidasa. Between the two towns is an attractive stretch of coast, which has some tourist development and a large oil-storage depot in Teluk Amuk.

A short way beyond Padangbai, a cruise-ship port at Tanah Ampo has proved a flop. Visions of mega-ships docking and spewing 5000 free-spending tourists into east Bali became fantasies after it was discovered that the new dock had been built in water too shallow for cruise ships. Blame is going around and around (Benoa Harbour is also too shallow for large cruise ships.)

Manggis

A small village just inland from the coast, Manggis is the address used by luxury resorts hidden along the water off the main road.

WORTH A TRIP

MANGGIS TO PUTUNG ROAD

Winding up a lush hillside scented with cloves, the little-used road linking Manggis on the coast with the mountain village of Putung is worth a detour no matter which way you are heading: east or west, up or down. Heading up you'll round curves to see east Bali and the islands unfolding before you. After stopping for photos, you'll feel good until you round another curve and the views are even better. At some scenic points, adorable families will appear offering beautiful handmade baskets from about 30,000Rp. It's hard not to exceed your basket-buying quota.

Coming from Manggis the road is in good shape for the first half but then deteriorates the rest of the way. It remains just OK for cars but you'll want to go slow for the views anyway; give it an hour.

Sleeping & Eating

★ **Amankila** RESORT $$$
(0363-41333; www.amankila.com; villas from US$800;) One of Bali's best resorts, the Amankila is perched along the jutting cliffs. About 5.6km beyond the Padangbai turn-off and 500m past the road to Manggis, a discreetly marked side road leads to the hotel. It features an isolated seaside location with views to Nusa Penida.

The renowned architecture includes three swimming pools that step down to the sea in matching shades. The dining venue here, the obviously named Restaurant, has a creative and varied menu with global and local influences.

Alila Manggis RESORT $$$
(0363-41011; www.alilahotels.com; r from US$160;) The Alila Manggis has elegant, white, thatch-roofed buildings in spacious lawn gardens facing a beautiful stretch of secluded beach. The 55 large rooms have minimalist interiors heavy on creams with muted wood accents; go for deluxe ones on the upper floor to enjoy the best views. Activities include a kids camp, a spa and cooking courses.

Amankila Restaurant FUSION $$$
(☑0363-41333; www.amankila.com; Amankila, Manggis; lunch mains US$12-30; ☺8am-9pm) The vaunted Restaurant is the Amankila's casual, open-air cafe and it has a creative menu showing global and local influences. The view rivals the flavours.

Tenganan

Step back several centuries with a visit to Tenganan, home of the Bali Aga people – the descendants of the original Balinese who inhabited Bali before the Majapahit arrival in the 11th century. A visit here is one of Bali's most unusual – and authentic – cultural outings.

◉ Sights & Activities

The Bali Aga are reputed to be exceptionally conservative and resistant to change. Well, that's only partially true: TVs and other modern conveniences are hidden away in the traditional houses. But it is fair to say that the village has a much more traditional feel than most other villages in Bali. Cars and motorcycles are forbidden from entering. It should also be noted that this is a real village, not a creation for tourists.

The most striking feature of Tenganan is its postcard-like beauty, with the hills providing a photogenic backdrop to its setting. The compact 500m by 250m village is surrounded by a wall and consists basically of two rows of identical houses stretching up the gentle slope of a hill. As you enter the village (10,000Rp donation) through one of only three gates, you'll likely be greeted by a guide who will take you on a tour – and generally lead you back to his family compound to look at textiles and *lontar* (specially prepared palm leaves) strips. However, there's no pressure to buy anything.

A peculiar, old-fashioned version of the gamelan known as the *gamelan selunding* is still played here and girls dance an equally ancient dance known as the Rejang. There are other Bali Aga villages nearby, including **Tenganan Dauh Tenkad**, 1.5km west off the Tenganan road, with a charming old-fashioned ambience and several weaving workshops.

✨ Festivals & Events

Tenganan has customs and festivals different from the Balinese norm.

Usaba Sambah Festival CULTURAL
(☺May/Jun) At the month-long Usaba Sambah Festival, which usually starts in May or June, men fight with sticks wrapped in thorny pandanus leaves. At this same festival, small, hand-powered Ferris wheels are brought out and the village girls are ceremonially twirled around.

🛍 Shopping

A magical cloth known as *kamben gringsing* is woven here – a person wearing it is said to be protected against black magic. Traditionally this has been made using the 'double ikat' technique, in which both the warp and weft threads are 'resist dyed' before being woven. MBAs would be thrilled to study the integrated production of the cloth: everything, from growing the cotton to producing the dyes from local plants to the actual production, is accomplished here. It's very time-consuming and the exquisite pieces are costly (from 600,000Rp). You'll see cheaper cloth for sale but it usually comes from elsewhere in Bali or beyond.

Many baskets from across the region, made from *ata* palm, are on sale. Another local craft is traditional Balinese calligraphy, with the script inscribed onto *lontar* in the same way that the ancient *lontar* books were created. Most of these books are Balinese calendars or depictions of the Ramayana. They cost 150,000Rp to 300,000Rp, depending on quality.

Tenganan crafts are also sold in Ashitaba shops in Seminyak and Ubud.

ℹ Getting There & Away

Tenganan is 3.2km up a side road just west of Candidasa. At the turn-off where bemos stop, motorcycle riders offer rides on *ojeks* (motorcycles that take passengers) to the village for about 15,000Rp one way. A nice option is to take an *ojek* up to Tenganan and enjoy a shady downhill walk back to the main road, which has a Bali rarity: wide footpaths.

Candidasa

Candidasa is a relaxed spot on the route east, with hotels and some decent restaurants. However, it also has problems stemming from decisions made almost four decades ago that destroyed the local beach – and should serve as a cautionary note to any previously undiscovered place that suddenly finds itself on the map.

Candidasa

Candidasa

🏃 Activities

Gili Tepekong, which has a series of coral heads at the top of a sheer drop-off, is perhaps the best local dive site. It offers the chance to see lots of fish, including some larger marine life, but it's recommended for experienced divers only. Most hotels can arrange dive trips.

Alam Asmara Spa   SPA

(☎0363-41929; Alam Asmara Dive Resort; massage from 200,000Rp; ⊙9am-9pm) Candidasa's posh option is the Alam Asmara Spa at the hotel of the same name. Organic and natural products are used for a variety of traditional massages and treatments in a gently restful setting.

🧭 Tours

⭐ **Trekking Candidasa**   WALKING

(☎0878 6145 2001; www.trekkingcandidasa.com; walks from 250,000Rp) The delightful Somat leads walks through the verdant hills behind Candidasa. One popular route takes 90 minutes and follows rice-field paths to Tenganan.

Bali Conservancy   WALKING

(☎0822 3739 8415; www.bali-conservancy.com; Eastern Bali tour adult/child from US$85/55) Offers good cultural and nature walks around east Bali, including the lush rice fields and the hills around beautiful Pasir Putih.

🛏 Sleeping

Candidasa's busy main drag is well supplied with seaside accommodation, as well as restaurants and other tourist facilities. Quieter places can be found east of the centre along Jl Pantai Indah. These are nicely relaxed and often have a sliver of beach. West of town also offers quiet lodging amid the flaccid lapping of the waves. Even quieter are the hotels 2km west in Mendira.

West of Candidasa

Lotus Bungalows   HOTEL $$

(☎0363-41104; www.lotusbungalows.com; off Jl Raya Candidasa; r US$105-130; ❋@☀) Managed by earnest Europeans, the 20 rooms here (some with air-con) are in well-spaced, bungalow-style units. Four are right on the ocean. The decor is bright and airy and there is a large and inviting pool area. It offers diving packages.

Nirwana Resort
HOTEL **$$**

(📞0363-41136; www.thenirwana.com; off Jl Raya Candidasa; r US$90-125, villa from US$150; 🅿@ 🛜🏊) A dramatic walk across a lotus pond sets the tone at this intimate older resort that's been given a thorough update. The 18 units are near the infinity pool by the ocean. Go for one of the units right on the water.

Central Candidasa

Ari Home Stay
GUESTHOUSE **$**

(📞0817 970 7339; www.arihomestaycandidasa. com; Jl Raya Candidasa; r with fan/air-con 150,000/300,000Rp; 🅿🛜) Run by the ebullient Gary and his family, Ari Home Stay has rooms that ramble over the compound and range from cold-water with fans to air-con with hot water. Its position on the main road across from the water isn't ideal, but very cold beer is always available and there's a cheap and cheerful hot dog stand (p215).

Seaside Cottages
GUESTHOUSE **$**

(📞0363-41629; www.balibeachfront-cottages.com; Jl Raya Candidasa; cottages 250,000-560,000Rp; 🅿@🛜) A well-established, popular choice, the 15 rooms here are in cottages and span the gamut from cold-water basics with ineffectual fans to restful units with air-con and tropical bathrooms. The seafront has loungers right along the breakwater. The Temple Café is well-regarded; eat there or dine on tables set along the water.

Ashram Gandhi Chandi
GUESTHOUSE **$**

(📞0363-41108; www.ashramgandhi.com; Jl Raya Candidasa; s/d from 350,000/450,000Rp) This lagoon-side Hindu community follows the pacifist teachings of Mahatma Gandhi. Guests may stay for short or extended periods, but are expected to participate in community life. Simple guest cottages by the ocean are handy after a long day of yoga here.

★Rama Shinta Hotel
HOTEL **$$**

(📞0363-41778; www.ramashintahotel.com; off Jl Raya Candidasa; r incl breakfast 500,000-900,000Rp; 🅿🛜🏊) On a little lane near the lagoon and ocean, Rama Shinta's 15 rooms are split between a two-storey stone structure and bungalows. They've been nicely updated with outdoor bathrooms. It's worth upgrading to an upstairs room for views of the lagoon and its birdlife. The pool area is an inviting spot for lounging.

Bilik Bali
HOTEL **$$**

(📞0363-41538; www.ashyanacandidasa.com; Jl Raya Candidasa; r from US$70; 🅿🛜🏊) This well-managed waterside hotel has 12 older but immaculate bungalow-style units plus a spa. Most are far enough from the road to escape the noise. The waterfront cafe **Lezat** has standard Indonesian fare (mains from 50,000Rp; open 8am to 10pm) and fabulous views.

Watergarden
HOTEL **$$**

(📞0363-41540; www.watergardenhotel.com; Jl Raya Candidasa; r incl breakfast from US$90; 🅿🛜🏊) The Watergarden boasts a swimming pool and fish-filled ponds that wind around the buildings. The gardens are lush and worth exploring. Each of the 12 rooms has a verandah projecting over the lily ponds, which are fresher than the somewhat dated interiors. The good cafe has water views. Massages in the pretty spa are a mere 50,000Rp.

East of the Centre

A small road winds through banana trees passing several low-key lodgings that span the budget categories. This is the nicest area for lodging in Candidasa as you are less than 10 minutes by foot from the centre yet there is no traffic noise.

Puri Oka Beach Bungalows
GUESTHOUSE **$**

(📞0363-41092; www.purioka.com; Jl Pantai Indah; r US$23-70; 🅿🛜🏊) Hidden by a banana grove east of town, the cheapest of the 17 rooms here are fan-cooled and compact, while the better ones have water views. The beachside pool is small and is next to a cafe; at low tide there's a little beach out front. Two roomy bungalows are the pick here.

Puri Bagus Candidasa
HOTEL **$$$**

(📞0363-41131; www.puribaguscandidasa.com; Jl Pantai Indah; r from US$140; 🅿🛜🏊) At the eastern end of the shore near an outcropping of outriggers, this mainstream resort is hidden away in the palm trees. The large pool and restaurant have good sea views; the beach is illusory (and often missing). The 48 rooms have open-air bathrooms. Look for deals.

Mendira

Coming from the west, there are hotels and guesthouses well off the main road at Mendira, before you reach Candidasa. Although the beach has all but vanished and unsightly sea walls have been constructed, this area is a good choice for a getaway if you have your own transport. Think views, breezes and a good book.

The hotels are reached via narrow roads from a single turn-off from the main road. Look for a sign listing places to stay, a school and a huge banyan tree. A footpath along the main road greatly improves the 2km walk east to Candidasa proper.

Amarta Beach Cottages · HOTEL $$

(📞0363-41230; www.amartabeachcottages. com; Jl Raya Mendira; r incl breakfast 400,0000-800,000Rp; ❈@🛜🏊) In a panoramic and isolated seaside setting, the 16 rooms here are right on the water and are good value (the cheapest are fan only). The more expensive ones have modern style and open-air bathrooms. The delightful Sea Side restaurant looks out to Nusa Penida. The serene views are addictive.

Anom Beach Inn · HOTEL $$

(📞0363-419024; www.anom-beach.com; Jl Raya Mendira; r US$40-80; ❈❈🏊) This older resort from a simpler time has 24 rooms in a variety of configurations. The cheapest are fan only – not a problem given the constant offshore breezes. The best are bungalow-style. Many loyal customers have been coming for years, ageing gracefully right along with the staff.

Candi Beach Resort & Spa · RESORT $$$

(📞0363-41234; www.candibeachbali.com; Jl Raya Mendira; r incl breakfast $US95-270; ❈🛜🏊) This large beach resort has 84 comfortable rooms and cute individual bungalows. The pool has a nice beige-stone look, framed by the sea view and palm trees, and is located just up from a semidecent beach. The much-lauded Bali Conservancy (p213) runs nature tours in conjunction with the hotel.

✗ Eating

The cafes and restaurants along Jl Raya Candidasa are mostly simple and family-run, but beware of traffic noise (which does abate after dark). If you're out of town, some places provide transport.

Sea Side · INDONESIAN $

(📞0363-41230; Jl Raya Mendira, Amarta Beach Cottages; mains from 40,000Rp; ⏱8am-10pm; 🛜) Within the Amarta Beach Cottage (p215)

resort, this delightful open-air restaurant looks out to Nusa Penida – it's a great choice for lunch whether you are staying here or not.

Ari Hot Dog Shop · FAST FOOD $

(📞0817 975 5231; Jl Raya Candidasa, Ari Home Stay; mains 25,000-50,000Rp; ⏱11am-8pm; 🛜) The sign 'rice-free zone' says it all about this menu of hot dogs, sandwiches and loaded burgers. Served up by Aussie Gary and his cheery cohorts, the food is hot and the beer is cold, ice cold.

★ Vincent's · INTERNATIONAL $$

(📞0363-41368; www.vincentsbali.com; Jl Raya Candidasa; meals 60,000-150,000Rp; ⏱8am-11pm; 🛜) One of east Bali's best restaurants, Vincent's has several distinct open-air rooms and a large and lovely rear garden with rattan furniture. The bar is an oasis of jazz. The menu combines excellent and inventive Balinese, fresh seafood and European dishes – don't miss the sambal selection. Thursday evenings there's live music.

Crazy Kangaroo · PUB FOOD $$

(📞0363-41996; www.crazy-kangaroo.com; Jl Raya Candidasa; mains 40,000-120,000Rp; ⏱10am-late; 🛜) Wild by local standards, this pub is full of characters propped up at the bar to watch sports or shooting pool. The food is good, cooked in an open kitchen that mixes Western and local dishes with tasty seafood specials. There are often performances in the evening, from fire dancing to live music. A glass wall muffles road noise.

❶ Getting There & Away

Candidasa is on the main road between Amlapura and south Bali, but there's no terminal, so hail bemos as buses probably won't stop. You'll need to change in either Padangbai or Semarapura going west.

You can hire a ride to Amed in the far east for about 250,000Rp and to Kuta and the airport for 300,000Rp. A driver, **I Nengah Suasih** (📞0819 3310 5020), does day trips to Pasir Putih for 300,000Rp.

Ask at your accommodation about vehicle and bicycle rental.

Perama (📞0363-41114; Jl Raya Candidasa; ⏱7am-7pm) is at the western end of the strip. Destinations include Kuta (75,000Rp, three hours), Sanur (75,000Rp, 2½ hours) and Ubud (75,000Rp, two hours).

Candidasa to Amlapura

The main road east of Candidasa curves up to **Pura Gamang Pass** (*gamang* means 'to get dizzy' – an overstatement), from where you'll find fine views down to the coast and lots of greedy-faced monkeys (who have become so prolific that they have stripped crops bare from here up the mountain to Tenganan). If you walk along the coastline from Candidasa towards Amlapura, a trail climbs up over the headland, with fine views over the rocky islets off the coast and a good swathe of the region. Beyond this headland there's a long sweep of wide, exposed black-sand beach.

Pasir Putih

The most popular 'secret' beach on Bali, Pasir Putih (aka Dream Beach or Virgin Beach) is an idyllic white-sand beach whose name indeed means 'White Sand'. When we first visited in 2004, it was empty, save for a row of fishing boats at one end. Now it's an on-going lab in seaside economic development.

A dozen thatched beach warungs and cafes now line the sand. You can get nasi goreng (fried rice) or grilled fish. Bintang is, of course, on ice and loungers await bikini-clad bottoms. The beach itself is truly lovely: a long crescent of white sand backed by coconut trees. At one end cliffs provide shade. The surf is often mellow; you can rent snorkelling gear to explore the waters. Despite the 'secret' reputation, Pasir Puti can get very crowded.

Look for crude signs with the various monikers near the village of Perasi. Turn off the main road (5.6km east of Candidasa) and follow a paved track for about 1.5km to a large dirt parking area. Locals will collect an access fee (10,000Rp per person).

Cars and motorbikes are barred from driving any closer to the beach. There's a somewhat steep track down to the sand from the parking area. Ojek rides cost 10,000Rp each way.

Teluk Penyu

A little bend in the coast has earned the nickname Teluk Penyu, or Turtle Bay. The shelled critters do indeed come here to nest and there have been some efforts made to protect them. If you see a turtle or nest be sure to keep your distance; never attempt to touch or pick up a wild sea turtle. About 5km south of Amlapura, the area has attracted some expats and villas.

🛏 Sleeping

⭐**Turtle Bay Hideaway**   VILLA $$$
(☎ 0363-23611; www.turtlebayhideaway.com; Jl Raya Pura Mascima; cottages from 1,600,000Rp; 🔊🏠) Turtle Bay Hideaway comprises a compound built from old wooden tribal houses brought over from Sulawesi. Three buildings together have five ocean-view rooms near a large tiled pool. Interiors combine exotic details and modern comforts – there are fridges and organic food is served. There are enough shady verandahs, decks and loungers to keep you busy doing nothing for a week.

Amlapura

Amlapura is the tidy capital of Karangasem district, and the main town and transport junction in eastern Bali. The smallest of Bali's district capitals, it's a multicultural place with Chinese shophouses, several mosques and confusing one-way streets. The royal palaces are a compelling reason to stop.

⊙ Sights

Amlapura's atmospheric palaces, on Jl Teuku Umar, are vintage reminders of Karangasem's period as a kingdom – at its most important when supported by Dutch colonial power in the late 19th and early 20th centuries.

⭐**Puri Agung Karangasem**   PALACE
(Jl Teuku Umar; adult/child 10,000/5000Rp; ⊙8am-5pm) Outside the orderly Puri Agung Karangasem, there are beautifully sculpted panels and an impressive multitiered **entry gate**. After passing through the entry courtyard (all entrances point towards the rising sun in the east), a left turn takes you to the main building, known as the **Maskerdam** (Amsterdam) because it was built by the Dutch as a reward for the Karangasem kingdom's acquiescence to Dutch rule. This submission allowed the kingdom to continue long after the demise of other Balinese kingdoms.

Inside you'll see several rooms, including the royal bedroom and a living room with furniture that was a gift from the Dutch royal family. The Maskerdam faces the ornately decorated **Bale Pemandesan**, which was used for royal tooth-filing ceremonies.

Beyond this, surrounded by a pond, is the **Bale Kambang**, still used for family meetings and for dance practice.

Borrow one of the handy English-language info sheets and think about what this compound must have been like when the Karangasem dynasty was at its peak in the 19th century, having conquered Lombok. Don't miss the vintage photos. Various royal relatives can usually be found in the compound making offerings.

Puri Gede   PALACE
(Jl Teuku Umar; ⊙8am-6pm; FREE) Puri Gede is still used by the royal family. Surrounded by long walls, the palace grounds feature many brick buildings dating from the Dutch colonial period. Look for 19th-century stone carvings and woodcarvings. The **Rangki**, the main palace building, has been returned to its glory and is surrounded by fish ponds.

✘ Eating

Options are few in Amlapura; there is a good **night market** (Jl Kesatrian; ⊙5pm-midnight).

Hardy's Supermarket   SUPERMARKET $
(☑0363-22363; Jl Diponegoro; ⊙8am-10pm) This large supermarket has groceries, sundries of all kinds, ATMs and a row of stalls cooking up good, fresh, Asian food fast. It has the best range of supplies, such as sunscreen, east of Semarapura and south of Singaraja.

★ **Bali Asli**   BALINESE $$
(☑0822 3690 9215; www.baliasli.com.au; Jl Raya Glumpang, Glumpang; set menus 160,000-220,000Rp; ⊙10am-7pm; 🔊) The green hills around Amlapura are some of east Bali's most beautiful and Australian chef Penelope Williams takes full advantage of the vistas at this elegant restaurant and cooking school (1,000,000Rp). Produce sourced from her own garden is used for meals that explore the vibrancy of Balinese and Indonesian flavours. This may be the best *nasi campur* you'll ever have.

❶ Getting There & Away

Amlapura is a major transport hub. Minibuses and bemos regularly ply the main road towards Denpasar's Batubulan terminal (35,000Rp, roughly three hours) via Candidasa (10,000Rp), Padangbai and Gianyar. Plenty of minibuses also go around the north coast to Singaraja (about 30,000Rp) via Tirta Gangga, Amed and Tulamben.

Around Amlapura

Taman Ujung, 5km south of Amlapura, dates to 1921, when the last king of Karangasem completed the construction of a grand water palace here. Unfortunately it was mostly destroyed by a 1979 earthquake. The vast and bland replacement may leave you limp, as it somehow fails to impress despite its size.

OFF THE BEATEN TRACK

AMED, THE LONG WAY

Typically, travellers bound for the coast of **Amed** travel the inland route through Tirta Gangga. However, there is a longer, twistier and more adventurous road much less travelled that runs from **Ujung** right around the coast to the Amed area. The road climbs up the side of the twin peaks of Seraya and Lempuyang, and the views out to sea are breathtaking. Along the way it passes through numerous small villages where people are carving fishing boats, bathing in streams or simply standing a bit slack-jawed at the appearance of *tamu* (visitors or foreigners). Don't be surprised to see a pig, goat or boulder on the road. After the lush east, it's noticeably drier here and the people's existence thinner, corn replaces rice as the staple.

About 10km east of Amalapura, you'll pass **Villa Arjuna** (☑0813 3897 7140; www.villa-bali.nl; r from €55; ☒), a seaside guesthouse with great ocean views.

Near **Seraya** (which has a cute market) look for weavers and cotton-fabric-makers. For long stretches, you'll drive through fruit-filled orchards and thick greenery. About 4km south of **Aas** there's a lighthouse.

The road is narrow but paved and covering the 35km to Aas will take about one hour without stops. Combine this with the inland road through Tirta Gangga for a good circular visit to Amed from the west.

However, it is worth pushing on just a bit further past Taman Ujung to **Pantai Ujung** (Edge Beach), a rocky shoreline covered with boats from the nearby fishing village. Here you'll find one of the most exciting discoveries made in Bali recently: a 2m-long **penis-shaped rock** (*lingga*) that was exposed on the beach after a hard spell of storms. Locals attribute great power to the rock and it's now the scene of regular ceremonies. Experts have speculated that the stone is an ancient fertility symbol as there are signs of carving. And this has spawned additional speculation that a nearby large stone which somewhat resembles a *yoni* (the female counterpart of a *lingga*) may be a companion piece.

From Ujung, you can continue on the alternative road to Amed.

Tours

★ **Uforia**   FOOD & DRINK
(☑ 0363-21687; www.uforiachocolate.com; Jl Pura Mastima, Amlapura; ☺ 9am-5pm daily, production tours 10am-4pm Mon-Wed Jun-Aug) Uforia (12km east of Candidasa) produces its own range of single-origin chocolate on-site using elements of permaculture and organic ingredients. The tours (held June to August) offer fascinating insight into the production process; call ahead for bookings and directions. Each Saturday you can join a workshop and make your own personalised chocolate bars from scratch using a choice of ingredients.

Tirta Gangga & Around

Tirta Gangga (Water of the Ganges) is the site of a holy temple, some great water features and some of the best views of rice fields and the sea beyond in east Bali. Capping a sweep of green flowing down to the distant sea, it is a relaxing place to stop for an hour. With more time you can hike the surrounding terraced countryside, which ripples with coursing water and is dotted with temples. A small valley of rice terraces runs up the hill behind the parking area. It is a majestic vision of emerald steps receding into the distance.

Sights

★ **Taman Tirta Gangga**   PALACE
(adult/child 20,000/10,000Rp, parking 2000Rp; ☺ site 24hr, ticket office 7am-6pm) Amlapura's water-loving rajah, after completing his

lost masterpiece at Ujung, had another go at building the water palace of his dreams in 1948. He succeeded at Taman Tirta Gangga, which has a stunning crescent of rice-terrace-lined hills for a backdrop.

This multilevel aquatic fantasy features two swimming ponds that are popular on weekends and ornamental water features filled with huge koi and lotus blossoms, which serve as a fascinating reminder of the old days of the Balinese rajahs. Look for the 11-tiered *meru* fountain and plop down under the huge old banyans and enjoy the views. Best of all, it's one of the best-maintained sights in east Bali.

Activities

Hiking in the surrounding hills transports you far from your memories of frenetic south Bali. This far east corner of Bali is alive with coursing streams through rice fields and tropical forests that suddenly open to reveal vistas taking in Lombok, Nusa Penida and the lush green surrounding lands stretching down to the sea. The rice terraces around Tirta Gangga are some of the most beautiful in Bali. Back roads and walking paths take you to many picturesque traditional villages.

Sights that make a perfect excuse for a day trek are scattered in the surrounding hills. Or for the full Bali experience, ascend the side of Gunung Agung. Among the possible treks is a six-hour loop to Tenganan village, plus shorter ones across the local hills, which include visits to remote temples and all the stunning vistas you can handle.

Guides for the more complex hikes are a good idea as they help you plan routes and see things you simply would never find otherwise. Ask at any of the various accommodation options, especially Homestay Rijasa where I Ketut Sarjana is one of several experienced guides. Another local who comes with good marks is Komang Gede Sutama. Rates average about 80,000Rp per hour for one or two people.

Komang Gede Sutama   HIKING
(☑ 0813 3877 0893) A local Tirta Gangga guide who comes with good marks.

Tours

★ **Bung Bung Adventure Biking**   CYCLING
(☑ 0813 3840 2132, 0363-21873; bungbungbikeadventure@gmail.com; Homestay Rijasa, Tirta Gangga; half-/full-day tours from 250,000/300,000Rp) Ride downhill through the simply gorgeous

rice fields, terraces and river valleys around Tirta Gangga with this grassroots tour company. Itineraries last from two to four hours and include use of a mountain bike and helmet, water and plenty of local encounters. The office is at Homestay Rijasa, across from the Taman Tirta Gangga entrance. Book in advance.

🛏 Sleeping & Eating

🛏 Tirta Gangga

Homestay Rijasa HOMESTAY $
(📞 0363-21873; Jl Tirta Gangga; r incl breakfast from 175,000-250,000Rp; 🛜) With elaborately planted grounds, this well-run, nine-room homestay is located opposite the water palace entrance. Expect to pay around double the price for rooms with hot water, which is good for the large soaking tubs. It has a fantastic little warung at the front.

Good Karma HOMESTAY $
(📞 0363-22445; goodkarma.tirtagangga@gmail.com; Jl Tirta Gangga; r incl breakfast 300,000-400,000Rp; 🛜) A classic homestay, Good Karma has four very clean and simple bungalows and a good vibe derived from the surrounding pastoral rice field. The recommended cafe has gazebos that are the setting for fine meals (mains from 35,000Rp; open 7am to 9pm), including good tempe *sate* (satay).

Pondok Lembah Dukah GUESTHOUSE $
(📞 0813 3829 5142; dukuhstay@gmail.com; s/d from 150,000/200,000Rp; 🛜) Atop a hill with divine views over the rice fields, this guesthouse has charming bungalows. Rooms are basic but a stay here is a good chance to get close to local life.

It's a 10-minute walk from the palace, down the path to the right of Good Karma guesthouse; follow the signs for 300m along the rice field and then up a steep set of steps.

★Tirta Ayu Hotel HOTEL $$$
(📞 0363-22503; www.hoteltirtagangga.com; Pura Tirta Gangga; villas incl breakfast US$125-180; ❄🛜☀) Right in the palace compound, this hotel has two pleasant villas and three rooms that have plenty of royal decor. Enjoy the hotel's private pool or use the vast palace facilities. The restaurant (mains from 65,000Rp) has touches of style and serves creative takes on local classics, which come with great water-palace views.

Tirta Gangga Villas VILLA $$$
(📞 0363-21383; www.tirtagangga-villas.com; Pura Tirta Gangga; villas US$120-250; ☀) Built on the same terrace as the Tirta Ayu Hotel, the two villas here are part of the old royal palace. Thoroughly updated – but still possessing that classic Bali-style motif – they look out over the water palace from large shady porches. You can rent the entire complex and preside over your own court under a 500-year-old banyan tree.

Genta Bali INDONESIAN $
(📞 0363-22436; Jl Tirta Gangga; meals 15,000-25,000Rp; ⊙8am-9pm) You can find a fine homemade yoghurt lassi here, as well as pasta and Indonesian food. Try out the house-made black-rice wine. It's across the road from Tirta Gangga's parking area.

EAST BALI TIRTA GANGGA & AROUND

> **WORTH A TRIP**
>
> ### PURA LEMPUYANG
>
> One of Bali's nine directional temples and the one responsible for the east, Pura Lempuyang is perched on a hilltop on the side of 1058m Gunung Lempuyang, a twin of neighbouring 1175m Gunung Seraya. Together, the pair form the distinctive double peaks of basalt that loom over Amlapura to the south and Amed to the north. The Lempuyang temple is part of a compact complex that looks across the mottled green patchwork that is east Bali. Its significance means there are always faithful Balinese in meditative contemplation and you may wish to join them as you recover from the one key detail of reaching the temple: the 1700-step climb up the side of the 768m hill.
>
> Reaching the base of the stairs is about a 30-minute walk from Tirta Gangga. Take the turn south off the Amlapura–Tulamben road to Ngis (2km), a palm-sugar and coffee-growing area, and follow the signs another 2km to Kemuda (ask for directions if the signs confuse you). From Kemuda, climb those steps to Pura Lempuyang, allowing at least two hours, one way. If you want to continue to the peaks of Lempuyang or Seraya, you should take a guide.

Around Tirta Gangga

★ **Side by Side Organic Farm** HOMESTAY $
(☑ 0812 3623 3427; www.sites.google.com/site/
sidebysidefarmorg; Dausa; r from 150,000Rp, minimum 2 nights) Set amid lush rice fields near
Tirta Gangga in the tiny village of Dausa,
Side by Side Organic Farm serves bounteous and delicious buffet lunches (from
125,000Rp). Meals use organic foods grown
in the village farms. Call at least one day before for directions and to book lunch.

You can also arrange to stay in one of
the serene and traditional private Balinese
bale (open-sided pavilions) overlooking fish
ponds. The farm is a unique enterprise that
works with the local community to increase
incomes in what has always been one of Bali's poorer areas.

❶ Getting There & Away

Bemos and minibuses making the east-coast
haul between Amlapura (7000Rp) and Singaraja
stop at Tirta Gangga, which is 6km northwest of
Amlapura.

Amed & the Far East Coast

Stretching from Amed to Bali's far eastern
tip, this semiarid coast draws visitors with
its succession of small, scalloped, grey-sand
beaches (some more rocks than sand), relaxed atmosphere and excellent diving and
snorkelling.

The region here is often called simply
'Amed', but this is a misnomer as the coast
is a series of seaside *dusun* (small villages)
that starts with the actual Amed in the north
and then runs southeast to Aas. If you're
looking to get away from crowds, this is the
place to come and try some yoga. Everything
is spread out, so you never feel like you're in
the middle of anything much except maybe
one of the small fishing villages.

⚡ Activities

Diving & Snorkelling

Snorkelling is excellent along the coast.
Jemeluk is a protected area where you can
admire live coral and plentiful fish within
100m of the beach. A highlight are the coral gardens and colourful marine life at Selang. Snorkelling equipment rents for about
30,000Rp per day.

Diving is also good, with dive sites off
Jemeluk, Lipah and Selang featuring coral

slopes and drop-offs with soft and hard corals and abundant fish. Some are accessible
from the beach, while others require a short
boat ride. The *Liberty* wreck (p226) at Tulamben is only a 20-minute drive away.

Several dive operators have shown a commitment to the communities by organising
regular beach clean-ups and educating locals on the need for conservation. All have
similar prices for a long list of offerings (eg
local dives start from around US$80 and
open-water dive courses are about US$400).

Eco-Dive DIVING
(☑ 0363-23482; www.ecodivebali.com; Jemeluk
Beach) ⚓ Full-service dive operator with
simple, cheap accommodation (from
250,000Rp) for clients. Has led the way on
environmental issues.

Apneista DIVING
(☑ 0812 3826 7356; www.apneista.com; Green Leaf
Cafe, Jemeluk; 2-day courses US$200; ⊙ 8.30am–
10pm) Set up in Jemeluk's Green Leaf Cafe
(p224), Apneista runs freediving courses
and trips. There is a wide choice of courses:
most people learn to freedive to at least 10m.

Jukung Dive DIVING
(☑ 0363-23469; www.jukungdivebali.com; Amed)
⚓ Pushes its eco credentials and has a dive
pool. Also has bungalows for dive packages.

Euro Dive DIVING
(☑ 0363-23605; www.eurodivebali.com; Lipah) ⚓
Has a large facility and offers packages with
hotels. It wins praise for its guided trips.
Offers shore diving to the sunken Japanese
fishing boat for US$40.

Hiking

Quite a few trails go inland from the coast,
up the slopes of **Gunung Seraya** (1175m)
and to some little-visited villages. The countryside is sparsely vegetated and most trails
are well defined, so you won't need a guide
for shorter walks – if you get lost, just follow a ridge-top back down to the coast road.
Allow a good three hours to get to the top
of Seraya, starting from the rocky ridge just
east of Jemeluk Bay. Sunrise is spectacular
and requires a climb in the dark; ask at your
hotel about a guide.

⌘ Sleeping

The Amed region is very spread out, so
take this into consideration when choosing
accommodation. You'll need to choose be-

Amed & the Far East Coast

Amed & the Far East Coast

tween staying in the little beachside villages or on the sunny and dry headlands connecting the inlets. The former puts you right on the sand and offers a small amount of community life while the latter gives you broad, sweeping vistas and isolation.

Accommodation can be found in every price category.

🛏 Amed Village

Several recently opened budget guesthouses give this buzzy area the feel of a backpackers' scene.

Amed Stop Inn　　　　HOMESTAY $
(☏ 0817 473 8059; im.stop@yahoo.co.id; r from 250,000Rp) Right in Amed village, this

homestay has two simple rooms that are close to the beach. There are numerous walks in the surrounding rice fields and into the temple-dotted hills. The owners are charmers and experienced guides.

Hotel Uyah Amed　　　　HOTEL $$
(☏ 0363-23462; www.hoteluyah.com; r incl breakfast with fan/air con from 620,000/670,000Rp; ✳ 🛜 ☀) 🍃 This cute place features four-poster beds set in stylish, conical interiors bathed in light. From all 17 rooms (some with air-con) you can see the saltworks on the beach. The hotel has a strong green ethos, starting with the solar-powered hot water. The tasty Cafe Garam (p224) is appropriately named for salt.

ℹ️ DECODING AMED

The entire 10km stretch of far east coast is often called 'Amed' by both tourists and marketing-minded locals. Most development at first was around three bays with fishing villages: **Amed Village**, big with backpackers; **Jemeluk**, which has a buzzy travellers strip; **Banutan**, with both a beach and headlands; and **Lipah**, which has a lively mix of cafes and commerce.

Development has marched onwards through tiny **Lehan**, **Selang**, **Banyuning** and **Aas**, each a small and chilled-out oasis at the base of the dry, brown hills. To appreciate the narrow band of the coast, stop at the **lookout** (parking 10,000Rp) at Jemeluk, where you can see fishing boats lined up like a riot of multihued sardines on the beach.

Besides the main road via Tirta Gangga, you can also approach the Amed area from the Aas end in the south from Amlapura (p217).

🛏 Jemeluk

Hoky Home Stay & Cafe HOMESTAY $
(📞 0819 1646 3701; madejoro@yahoo.com; r incl breakfast 145,000-350,000Rp; 🛜) This place near the beach offers great cheap rooms with fans and hot water. The owner, Made, is tuned in to budget travellers' needs. The cafe (p224) has fresh and creative local foods, especially seafood. Bikes for rent (30,000Rp per day).

Sama Sama Cafe & Bungalows HOMESTAY $
(📞 0813 3738 2945; samasama_amed@yahoo. co.id; r 300,000-400,000Rp; ❄️🛜) Choose from a cold-water room with fan or something more posh (hot water and air-con) in one of six bungalows here; there's also a good seafood cafe (mains from 50,000Rp; open 8am to 9pm) across from the beach. The family here is often busy making offerings.

Galang Kangin Bungalows GUESTHOUSE $
(📞 0363-23480; bali_amed_gk@yahoo. co.jp; r incl breakfast with fan/air-con from 300,000/600,000Rp; ❄️🛜) Straddling the road amidst nice gardens, the 10 rooms here mix and match fans, cold water, hot water and air-con. The modern air-con rooms open to the beach, while the fan rooms

across the road have a more traditional, or-nate Balinese style.

🛏 Banutan Beach

This is a classic little village with a swathe of sand and fishing boats between arid headlands.

Aiona Garden of Health GUESTHOUSE $
(📞 0813 3816 1730; www.aionabali.com; s/d from €20/25) 🌿 This characterful place has enough signs outside that it qualifies as a roadside attraction. The simple bungalows are shaded by mango trees, which contribute to the uberhealthy menu. You can partake of organic potions and lotions and classes in yoga, meditation, tarot reading etc. Your inner peace might improve with the high-fibre diet.

Santai HOTEL $$
(📞 0363-23487; www.santaibali.com; r incl breakfast US$95-150; ❄️🛜🏊) This lovely option is set on a slight hill down to the beach. The name means 'relax' and that's just what you'll do here. A series of authentic, traditional thatched bungalows gathered from around the archipelago hosts 10 rooms with four-poster beds, open-air bathrooms and big balcony sofas. A swimming pool, fringed by purple bougainvillea, snakes through the property.

🛏 Banutan

These places are on a sun-drenched, arid stretch of highland. Most are on sloping hill-sides and spill down to the water.

Wawa-Wewe II HOTEL $$
(📞 0363-23522; www.bali-wawawewe.com; r incl breakfast 500,000-800,000Rp; ❄️🛜🏊) This restful place has 10 bungalow-style rooms on lush grounds that shamble down to the water's edge. The natural-stone infinity pool is shaped like a Buddha and is near the sea, as are two rooms with fine ocean views.

Apa Kabar Villas VILLA $$
(📞 0363-23492; www.apakabarvillas.com; cottage/ villa incl breakfast from 1,100,000/1,500,000Rp; 🛜🏊) Twelve cottages and villas are built into a compact compound. All are private, with views of the lush gardens. Some units have up to two bedrooms. There is an alluring terrace right on the shore where you can relax and read to sounds of the lapping water.

Puri Wirata
HOTEL $$

(📞 0363-23523; www.puriwirata.com; r from 750,000Rp, villa from 1,100,000Rp; ✳🛜🏊) The most mainstream Amed choice, this 30-room resort with two pools has rooms ambling down the hill to the rocky ribbon at the waterline. Choices include rooms, bungalows and villas. Service is professional and there are many dive packages on offer.

Anda Amed Resort
HOTEL $$$

(📞 0363-23498; www.andaamedresort.com; villa incl breakfast from 1,400,000Rp; ✳🛜🏊) This whitewashed hillside hotel contrasts with its lushly green grounds. The infinity pool is an ahhh-inducing classic of the genre and has sweeping views of the sea from well above the road. There are 11 rooms in four villas and lots of posh details such as deep soaking tubs, fridges and other niceties.

🛏 Lipah

Double One Villas
GUESTHOUSE $

(📞 0363-22427; www.doubleonevillasamed.com; r 400,000-850,000Rp; ✳🛜🏊) This charming 10-room guesthouse is split in two: cheaper rooms are on the hill side of the road, nicer ones are on the ocean side and run down a fairly steep hill to the pebbly shore. The waterfront rooms are a good deal and near the pool, although you'll get to know the stairs.

★ Coral View Villas
HOTEL $$

(📞 0363-23493; www.coralviewvillas.com; r US$60-150; ✳🛜🏊) Lush grounds surrounding a naturalistic pool set this tidy property apart from other more arid places. The 19 rooms are in bungalow-style units and have nice terraces outside; inside, the rooms are large and there are stone lined, open-air bathrooms. It has a great oceanfront location.

🛏 Lehan

Quiet, beachy Lehan has some of Amed's nicest boutique-style accommodation.

Palm Garden
HOTEL $$

(📞 0828 9700 1050; www.palmgardenamod.com; r incl breakfast US$100-240; ✳@🛜🏊) This oceanfront villa hotel verges on elegant. Certainly it has the best beach in Amed. The 10 units have large patios and the grounds are lined with palm trees, including one growing from its own island in the pool. There's a two-night minimum stay in high season.

Life in Amed
INN $$$

(📞 0363-23152, 0813 3850 1555; www.lifebali.com; r/villa incl breakfast r from 1,200,000/2,000,000Rp; ✳🛜🏊) Life here is posh. Six bungalow-style units are in a compact compound around a sinuous pool; two two-bedroom villas are directly on the beach. Bathrooms are open-air works of art, created from beach stones.

🛏 Selang

Aquaterrace
HOTEL $$

(📞 0813 3791 1096; www.aquaterrace-amed.com; r 800,000-1,300,000Rp; ✳🛜🏊) Perched on the headland right above the water, this dramatic seven-unit, whitewashed hotel has balconies and beautiful views. The units are light-toned, which makes the deep blue waters outside all the more striking. There are sitting areas and fridges.

Blue Moon Villas
GUESTHOUSE $$

(📞 0817 4738 100; www.bluemoonvilla.com; r €65-160; ✳🛜🏊) On the hillside across the road from the cliffs, Blue Moon is a small and upmarket place, complete with three pools. The rooms are set in villa-style buildings and have open-air stone bathrooms. Rooms can be combined into larger multi-bedroom suites. The restaurant (mains from 50,000Rp; open 8am to 10pm) serves good Balinese classics and grilled seafood.

🛏 Banyuning

Nalini Resort
HOTEL $$

(📞 0828 9761 1793; www.naliniresort.com; r from 1,100,000Rp; ✳🛜🏊) Clean geometric lines frame the six units at this beachfront compound. The infinity pool picks up the shades of blue from the ocean. Each room is large, with big beds and indoor and outdoor sitting areas. Some glimpse the sea, others have garden and mountain views.

Baliku
HOTEL $$

(📞 0828 372 2601; www.amedbaliresort.com; r 800,000-1,100,000Rp; ✳🛜🏊) Large villa-style units are among the attractions at this hillside resort overlooking a pretty bit of the Amed coast, where you often see fishing boats flying their brightly coloured sails. King-size beds and separate dressing areas and terraces primed for meals make for good retreats. There are Mediterranean accents throughout, including on the restaurant's menu.

🛏 Aas

★ Meditasi
GUESTHOUSE $

(☑ 0828 372 2738; www.meditasibungalows.blog spot.com; r 300,000-600,000Rp) 🏄 Get off the grid at this chilled-out and charming hideaway. Meditation and yoga help you relax and the eight rooms are well situated for good swimming and snorkelling. By far the best bet are the villa-style bungalows, complete with private garden, open-air bathrooms and balconies with superb sea views. Elizabeth Gilbert, author of *Eat, Pray, Love,* stayed in room 7.

🍴 Eating & Drinking

★ Warung Enak
BALINESE $

(☑ 0819 1567 9019; Jemeluk; mains from 50,000Rp; ⊗ 9am-11pm) Black rice pudding and other less-common local treats are the specialties of this dead-simple and super-tasty little eatery. It also does a fresh catch of the day and homemade ice cream.

Smiling Buddha Restaurant
BALINESE $

(☑ 0828 372 2738; Meditasi, Aas; mains from 30,000Rp; ⊗ 8am-10pm; 🍴) The restaurant at Meditasi (p224), the highly recommended guesthouse, has excellent organic fare, much of it sourced from its own garden. The Balinese and Western dishes are excellent and original and there are good views out to sea. The place even manages some full-moon fun. Happy hour is from 7pm to 8pm.

Hoky Home Cafe
CAFE $

(Jemeluk; mains from 25,000Rp; ⊗ 8am-10pm) The cafe at the Hoky Home Stay (p222) has fresh and creative local foods, especially seafood.

Green Leaf Cafe
CAFE $

(☑ 0812 3826 7356; www.apneista.com; Jemeluk; mains from 35,000Rp; ⊗ 8.30am-6.30pm; 🍴) 🏄 After you've chilled out, chill out some more. This excellent cafe has a good vegetarian menu, with many specials. There's a wide range of coffees, teas and juices. Sit at a table inside or on loungers outside. This is also a hub for yoga and freediving — Apneista (p220) is associated with the cafe.

Cafe Garam
INDONESIAN $

(☑ 0363-23462; Hotel Uyah Amed, Amed; mains 30,000-60,000Rp; ⊗ 8am-10pm) There's a relaxed feel here, with pool tables and Balinese food plus the lyrical and haunting melodies of live *genjek* music at 8pm on Wednesday and Saturday. *Garam* means 'salt' and the cafe honours the local salt-making industry (p225). Try the *salada ayam,* an addictive mix of cabbage, grilled chicken, shallots and tiny peppers.

Wawa-Wewe I
BAR

(☑ 0363-23506; Lipah; ⊗ 8am-late; 🛜) You won't know your wawas from your wewes if you spend the evening here trying the local *arak* (distilled palm wine) made from palm fronds. This is the coast's most raucous bar – which by local standards means that sometimes it gets sorta loud. Local bands jam on Wednesday and Saturday nights.

ℹ Getting There & Away

Most people drive here via the main highway from Amlapura and Culik. The spectacular road going all the way around the twin peaks from Aas to Ujung makes a good circle.

You can arrange for a driver and car to/from south Bali and the airport for about 500,000Rp.

Public transport is difficult. Minibuses and bemos between Singaraja and Amlapura pass through Culik, the turn-off for the coast. Infrequent bemos go from Culik to Amed (3.5km) and some continue to Seraya until 1pm. Fares average 7000Rp.

You can also charter transport from Culik for a negotiable 50,000Rp (by *ojek* is half). Specify which hotel you wish to go to – agree on 'Amed' and you could come up short in Amed village.

Amed Sea Express (☑ 0853 3925 3944; www.gili-sea-express.com; Jemeluk; one way from 300,000Rp) makes crossings to Gili Trawangan on an 80-person speedboat in under an hour.

Kuda Hitam Express (☑ 0852 3869 2853; www.kudahitamexpress.com; Jemeluk; one way from 300,000Rp) serves Gili Trawangan and Gili Air.

Tulamben

The big attraction here sunk over 60 years ago. The wreck of the US cargo ship *Liberty* is among the best and most popular dive sites in Bali and this has given rise to an entire town based on scuba diving. Even snorkellers can easily swim out and enjoy the wreck and the coral.

But if you don't plan to explore the briny waves, don't expect to hang out on the beach either. The shore is made up of rather beautiful, large washed stones – the kind that cost a fortune at a DIY store.

WORKING IN THE SALT BRINE

For a different day at the beach, try making some salt. You start by carrying, say, 500L of ocean water across the sand to bamboo and wood funnels, which filter the water after it is poured in. Next the water goes into a *palungan* (shallow trough), made of palm-tree trunks split in half and hollowed out, or cement canisters where it evaporates, leaving salt behind. And that's just the start – and just what you might see in Kusamba or on the beach in Amed.

In the volcanic areas around the east coast between Sanur and Yeh Sanih in the north, a range of salt-making methods is used. What is universal is that the work is hard, but is also an essential source of income for many families.

In some places the first step is drying sand that has been saturated with sea water. It's then taken inside a hut, where more sea water is strained through it to wash out the salt. This very salty water is then poured into a *palungan*. Hundreds of these troughs are lined up in rows along the beaches during salt-making season (the dry season) and as the sun evaporates the water, the almost-dry salt is scraped out and put in baskets. There are good exhibits on this method at the Museum Semarajaya (p200) in Semarapura.

Most salt produced on the coast of Bali is used for processing dried fish. And that's where Amed has an advantage: although its method of making salt results in a lower yield than that using sand, its salt is prized for its flavour. In fact there is a fast-growing market for this 'artisan salt' worldwide.

Visitors to the Amed area can sometimes learn about this fascinating process at Cafe Garam (p224). Many of the staff here also work in salt production (ask about tours from June to December during the salt season) and you can buy small bags of the precious stuff (10,000Rp) for a tiny fraction of what it costs once it reaches your local gourmet market.

EAST BALI TULAMBEN

For nonaquatic delights, check out the **morning market** in Tulamben village, 1.5km north of the dive site.

🏃 Activities

Diving and snorkelling are the reason Tulamben exists.

The **shipwreck** *Liberty* is about 50m directly offshore from Puri Madha Beach Bungalows (where you can park); look for the schools of black snorkels. Swim straight out and you'll see the stern rearing up from the depths, heavily encrusted with coral and swarming with dozens of species of colourful fish – and with scuba divers most of the day. The ship is more than 100m long, but the hull is broken into sections and it's easy for divers to get inside. The bow is in quite good shape, the midship's region is badly mangled and the stern is almost intact – the best parts are between 15m and 30m deep. You will want at least two dives to really explore the wreck.

Many divers commute to Tulamben from Candidasa or Lovina, and in busy times it can get quite crowded between 11am and 4pm, with 50 or more divers at a time around the wreck. Stay the night in Tulamben or in nearby Amed and get an early start.

Most hotels have their own diving centre and some offer good-value packages for guests.

Expect to pay from US$80 for two dives at Tulamben and a little more for night dives around Amed. Snorkelling gear is rented everywhere for 30,000Rp.

Note the privately run parking area (10,000Rp) behind Tauch Terminal where there are gear-rental stands, vendors, porters and more ready to get your attention. There are also pay-showers and toilets.

The local dive guide group, Organisasi Dive Guide Tulamben, wins praise for its efforts at reef clean up and restoration.

Apnea Bali DIVING
(☎ 0822 6612 5814; www.apneabali.com; Jl Kubu-Abang; lessons from US$30) This polished operator on Tulamben's main strip specialises in freediving courses and trips for all skill levels, including down to the *Liberty* wreck.

Tauch Terminal DIVING
(☎ 0363-774504, 0363-772920; www.tauch-terminal.com; 2 dives €55) Among the many dive operators, Tauch Terminal is one of the longest-established in Bali. It offers a large range of diving packages and has good-quality rental gear. A four-day SSI open-water

THE WRECK OF THE LIBERTY

In January 1942 the small US Navy cargo ship USAT *Liberty* was torpedoed by a Japanese submarine near Lombok. Taken in tow, it was beached at Tulamben so that its cargo of rubber and railway parts could be saved. The Japanese invasion prevented this and the ship sat on the beach until the 1963 eruption of Gunung Agung broke it in two and left it just off the shoreline, much to the delight of divers ever since. (And just for the record, it was *not* a Liberty-class WWII freighter.)

certificate course costs €450. It also runs its own dive resort.

🛏 Sleeping

Tulamben is a quiet place and is essentially built around the wreck – the hotels, all with cafes and many with dive shops, are spread along a 4km stretch either side of the main road. You have your choice of roadside (cheaper) or by the water (nicer). At high tide even the rocky shore vanishes.

Matahari Tulamben Resort　　HOTEL $
(🌐0859 3835 4762, 0813 3863 6670; www.divet-ulamben.com; r from 280,000Rp; 🅿️🛜🏊) This modest 34-room hotel has a very loyal following of divers, many of whom stay for weeks at a time, only coming up for air to crash in one of the very clean rooms. It has a narrow section of waterfront south of the wreck. There's a spa and small cafe with ocean views.

Dive Concepts　　GUESTHOUSE $
(🌐0812 3684 5440; www.diveconcepts.com; dm 50,000Rp, r 125,000-300,000Rp; 🅿️🛜) A great place to meet other divers, this busy French-run dive shop has an old-school guesthouse with 12 rooms in a variety of flavours (from cold water and fan to hot water and air-con), including six-bed dorms. The dive shop offers many excellent-value packages. It's on the hill side of the main road.

Deep Blue Studio　　GUESTHOUSE $
(🌐0363-22919; www.diving-bali.com; s/d incl breakfast US$28/44; 🛜🏊) Owned by Czechs, this dive operation has 10 rooms in two-storey buildings on the hill side of the main road. It's an attractive place and is well set up for dive classes and chilling out after a

day in the depths. Rooms have fans and balconies. A variety of packages are available with the affiliated dive shop.

★**Liberty Dive Resort**　　HOTEL $$
(🌐0812 3684 5440; www.libertydiveresort.com; r incl breakfast US$50-90; 🅿️🛜🏊) Just 100m up the hill from the rocky shore in front of the wreck, this 20-room resort has a great open feel and a very nice pool. Rooms come in various levels of comfort but all are modern, clean and large. Some 2nd-floor rooms have sea views.

★**Puri Madha Beach Bungalows**　　HOTEL $$
(🌐0363-22921; www.purimadhabeachhotel.weebly.com; r 200,000-600,000Rp; 🅿️🛜🏊) Reimagined bungalow-style units lying directly opposite the *Liberty* wreck dive site offshore. The best of the 21 rooms have air-con and hot water. The spacious grounds feel like a public park and there is a swish pool area overlooking the ocean. You can't beat getting out of bed and swimming right out to a famous shipwreck.

Tauch Terminal Resort　　HOTEL $$
(🌐0361-774504, 0363-22911; www.tauch-terminal.com; r incl breakfast from 1,200,000Rp; 🅿️🛜🏊) Down a side road, this sprawling waterfront hotel run by the popular dive operator has 27 rooms in several categories. Many of the rooms are recently built and all are comfortable in a modern, motel-style way. Expect amenities like satellite TV and fridges. Of the two waterfront pools, one is reserved for swimming only. The cafe serves a fine breakfast.

❶ Getting There & Away

Plenty of buses and bemos travel between Amlapura and Singaraja and will stop anywhere along the Tulamben road, but they're infrequent after 2pm. Expect to pay 30,000Rp to either town.

If you are driving to Lovina for the night, be sure to leave by about 3pm so you'll still have a little light when you get there.

If you're just going to snorkel the wreck and are day-tripping with a driver, don't let them park at a dive shop away from the wreck where you'll get a commission-paying sales pitch.

Tulamben to Yeh Sanih

North of Tulamben, the road continues to skirt the slopes of Gunung Agung, with frequent evidence of lava flows from the 1963 eruption throughout the Kubu region. Further north, the outer crater of Gunung Batur slopes steeply down to the sea. The rainfall is low and you can generally count on sunny weather. The scenery is very stark in the dry season and it's a thinly populated area.

There are regular markets in **Kubu**, a roadside village 5km northwest of Tulamben.

At **Les**, a road goes inland to the impressive **Air Terjun Yeh Mampeh** (Yeh Mampeh Waterfall; adult/child 20,000/10,000Rp) waterfall, at 40m one of Bali's highest and least visited. Look for a large sign on the main road, then turn inland for about 2.5km over a road that is steadily being improved. Walk the last 600m or so on a good path by the stream, shaded by rambutan and various other fruit trees. The best time to visit is during the peak rainy season December to February. Guides – not needed for Yeh Mampeh – can take you to even more remote waterfalls.

The next main town is **Tejakula**, famous for its stream-fed public bathing area, said to have been built for washing horses and often called the 'horse bath'. The renovated bathing areas (separate for men and women) are behind walls topped by rows of elaborately decorated arches; they are regarded as a sacred area. The baths are 100m inland on a narrow road with lots of small shops – it's a quaint village, with some finely carved *kulkul* (alarm drum) towers. Take a stroll above the baths, past irrigation channels flowing in all directions.

At Pacung, about 10km before Yeh Sanih, you can turn inland 4km to **Sembiran**, a Bali Aga village, although it doesn't promote itself as such. The most striking thing about the place is its hillside location and brilliant coastal views.

🛏 Sleeping

Bali's remote northeast coast has a growing number of resorts where you can indeed get away from it all. These are places to settle in for a few days and revive your senses. Getting here from the airport or south Bali can take three hours or more via two routes:

one up and over the mountains via Kintamani and then down a rustic, scenic road to the sea near Tejakula; the other going right round east Bali on the coast road via Candidasa and Tulamben.

Segara Lestari Villa GUESTHOUSE $
(☏0815 5806 8811; www.facebook.com/lesvillagevilla; Les; r from 350,000Rp; ✴) It doesn't get any simpler than this: six simple bungalows right on the ocean. There's hot water and air-con, though the shore breezes obviate the need to use the air-con. Use the kitchen or they can cook you meals.

★ Alam Anda HOTEL $$
(☏0812 465 6485; www.alamanda.de; Sambirenteng; r incl breakfast US$60-140; ✴ 🤖 🛱) The striking tropical architecture at this oceanside resort, near Sambirenteng, is the creation of the German architect-owner. A reef just offshore keeps the dive shop busy. The 34 units come in various sizes, from losmen rooms to cottages with views. All have artful thatch-and-bamboo motifs. The resort is 1km north of Poinciana Resort, roughly between Kubu and Tejakula.

Bali Sandat Guest House GUESTHOUSE $$
(☏0813 3772 8680; www.bali-sandat.com; Bondalem; s/d incl breakfast from 460,000/650,000Rp; 🤖) You'll feel like you're staying with friends at this low-key guesthouse located deep in a waterfront palm forest in a remote part of east Bali. The four rooms have open-air, cold-water bathrooms and deep and shady verandahs. Balinese dinners are available. The village of Bondalem is a 1km walk away and has a simple morning market and a weaving workshop.

Spa Village Resort Tembok HOTEL $$$
(☏0362-32033; www.spavillageresort.com; Tembok; full board d from US$260; 🛱 🤖 🤖 🤖) When you arrive at this posh 31-room oceanfront resort, you sign up for extensive spa treatments and daily activities geared to your inner rejuvenation. The full-board meals are healthful and focus on simple, local ingredients. It's northwest of Tembok

EAST BALI TULAMBEN TO YEH SANIH

Central Mountains

Best Places to Eat

➡ Pulu Mujung Warung (p232)

➡ Strawberry Hill (p235)

➡ Terrasse du Lac (p239)

➡ Puri Lumbung Cottages (p239)

Best Places to Sleep

➡ Puri Lumbung Cottages (p239)

➡ Sarinbuana Eco Lodge (p242)

➡ Bali Mountain Retreat (p242)

➡ Sanda Boutique Villas (p242)

Why Go?

Bali has a hot soul. The volcanoes stretching along the island's spine are seemingly cones of silence but their active spirits are just below the surface, eager for expression.

Gunung Batur (1717m) is constantly letting off steam; this place has an other-worldly beauty that may overwhelm the attendant hassles of a visit. At Danau Bratan there are sacred Hindu temples while the village of Candikuning has an engrossing botanic garden.

The old colonial village of Munduk, a hiking centre, has views down the hills to the coast of north Bali, which match the beauty of the many nearby waterfalls, and Danaus Tamblingan and Buyan. In the shadow of Gunung Batukau (2276m) you'll find one of Bali's most mystic temples. And, just south, the Unesco-listed ancient rice terraces around Jatiluwih bedazzle.

Amid it all, little roads lead to untouched villages. Start driving north from Antosari for one surprise after another.

When to Go

➡ Bali's central mountains can be cool and misty throughout the year. They also get a lot of rain and this is the starting point for the water that courses through rice terraces and fields all the way south. Temperatures show few seasonal variations but can drop to 10°C at night at high elevations.

➡ It rains most from October through April, but can pour at any time during the year.

➡ There's no peak tourist season, except when the group-tour hordes hit the Kintamani area during the peak visitor months of July and August. It's a good idea to book ahead for Munduk too at this time.

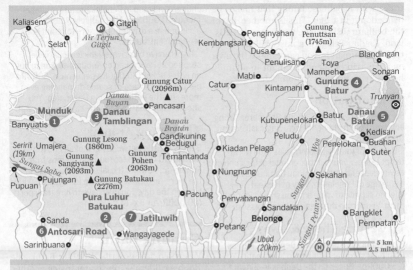

Central Mountains Highlights

1 Munduk (p239)
Claiming your own waterfall while trekking around this mountain idyll.

2 Pura Luhur Batukau (p241) Hearing the chant of priests at one of Bali's holiest temples.

3 Danau Tamblingan (p238) Taking a guided hike above and around the natural beauty and ancient

temples of this ancient volcanic lake.

4 Gunung Batur (p229) Beholding the other-worldly, lava-strewn side of a still-active volcano.

5 Danau Batur (p233) Discovering one stunning feature after another on the beautifully scenic road to Trunyan via Buahan and Abang.

6 Antosari Road (p242) Exploring the region's maze of rural drives, such as this one that runs through jade-green rice terraces.

7 Jatiluwih (p241) Identifying each ancient variety of rice grown at these magnificent Unesco-recognised terraces.

GUNUNG BATUR AREA

📍 0366

The Gunung Batur area is like a giant bowl, with its bottom half covered by water and a set of volcanic cones jutting out of the middle. Sound a bit spectacular? It is. On clear days – vital to appreciating the spectacle – the turquoise waters wrap around the newer volcanoes, which have old lava flows oozing down their sides.

In 2012 Unesco honoured the area by adding it to a list of more than 90 geologic wonders worldwide and naming it the Batur Caldera Geopark (www.globalgeopark. org, www.baturglobalgeopark.com). Some interesting signs detailing the unique geology of the area are posted along roads in the region; the Batur Geopark Museum (p232) in Penelokan has full details.

The road around the southwestern rim of the Gunung Batur crater is one of Bali's most important north–south routes and has one of its most stunning vistas.

Day trippers should bring some sort of wrap in case the mist closes in and the temperature drops (it can get to 16°C).

The villages around the Gunung Batur crater rim have grown into one continuous untidy strip. Kintamani is the main village, though the whole area is often referred to by that name. Coming from the south, the first village is Penelokan, where tour groups first stop to gasp at the view.

👉 Tours

⭐ JED   CULTURAL
(Village Ecotourism Network; 📞 0851 0066 9951; www.jed.or.id; day/overnight trip US$75/105) Learn everything about growing and producing

coffee with a Balinese family that makes its living doing just that. This is another one of the brilliant JED village tours across the island. Kiadan Pelaga is a misty village in the temperate uplands. You can explore the area on a day trip or spend the night in a family house. Trips are very customisable.

ⓘ Information

Services are few in the Gunung Batur area. Bring anything you might need, including cash, from the lowlands.

Be wary of touts on motorcycles, who will attempt to steer you to a tour or hotel of *their* choice as you descend into the Danau Batur area from the village of Penelokan. Very persistent, they offer no service of value and you should ignore them. Vendors in the area can be aggressive.

ⓘ Getting There & Away

From Batubulan terminal in Denpasar, bemos (minibuses) travel regularly to Kintamani (25,000Rp). Buses on the Denpasar–Singaraja route (via Batubulan, where you may need to

change) will stop in Penelokan and Kintamani (about 20,000Rp). Alternatively, you can hire a car or use a driver but be sure to rebuff buffet-lunch entreaties.

If you arrive by private vehicle, you will be stopped at Penelokan or Kubupenelokan to buy an entry ticket (30,000Rp per vehicle, 5000Rp per person, beware of scams demanding even more) for the entire Gunung Batur area. You shouldn't be charged again – save your receipt.

ⓘ Getting Around

Bemos shuttle between Penelokan and Kintamani (10,000Rp for tourists). Bemos from Penelokan down to the lakeside villages go in the morning (about 10,000Rp to Toya Bungkah). Later in the day, you may have to hire transport (40,000Rp or more).

Gunung Batur

Vulcanologists describe Gunung Batur as a 'double caldera', ie one crater inside another. The outer crater is an oval about 14km long,

Gunung Batur Area

with its western rim about 1500m above sea level. The inner is a classic volcano-shaped peak that reaches 1717m. Geological activity occurs regularly, and activity over the last decade has spawned several smaller cones on its western flank. There were major eruptions in 1917, 1926 and 1963.

One look at this other-worldly spectacle and you'll understand why people want to go through the many hassles and expenses of a trek. Note that the odds of clouds obscuring your reason for coming are greater from July to December, but at any time of year you should check conditions before committing to a trip, or even coming up the mountain.

🏃 Activities

The cartel of local guides known as **PPPGB** (formerly HPPGB) has a monopoly on guided climbs up Gunung Batur. It requires all trekking agencies to hire at least one of its guides for trips up the mountain, and has a reputation for tough tactics in requiring climbers to use its guides and in negotiations for its services.

That said, many people use the services of PPPGB guides without incident, and some of the guides win plaudits from visitors due to their ideas for customising trips.

The following strategies should help you have a good climb:

➡ Be absolutely clear in your agreement with the PPPGB about the terms you're agreeing to, such as whether fees are per person or group, whether they include breakfast, and exactly where you will go.

➡ Deal with one of the trekking agencies. There will still be a PPPGB guide along, but all arrangements will be done through the agency.

PPPGB rates and times are posted at its main **Toya Bungkah office** (Mt Batur Tour Guides Association; ☑ 0366-52362; ☉ 3am-6pm) and its second **access road office** (☉ 3am-3pm). Treks on offer include the following:

Mt Batur Sunrise A simple ascent and return; from 4am to 8am, 350,000Rp per person.

Mt Batur Main Crater Includes sunrise from the summit and time around the rim; from 4am to 9.30am, 500,000Rp per person.

Mt Batur Exploration Sunrise, caldera and some of the volcanic cones; from 4am to 10am, 650,000Rp per person.

Trekking Agencies

Even reputable and highly competent adventure-tour operators and trekking agencies cannot take their customers up Gunung Batur without paying to have one of the PPPGB guys tag along. However, they are useful for planning trips off well-trodden trails.

Most of the accommodation in the area can match you with guides and trekking agencies, which will add about 250,000Rp to 500,000Rp to the cost of a trek/climb.

Equipment

If you're climbing before sunrise, take a torch (flashlight) or be absolutely sure that your guide provides you with one. You'll need good sturdy footwear, a hat, a jumper (sweater) and drinking water.

Trekking Routes

The climb to see the sunrise from Gunung Batur is still the most popular trek. In high season 100 or more people will arrive at the top for dawn. Guides will provide breakfast on the summit for a fee (50,000Rp), which often includes the novelty of cooking an egg

CENTRAL MOUNTAINS GUNUNG BATUR

or banana in the steaming holes at the top of the volcano. There are pricey refreshment stops along the way.

Most travellers use one of two trails that start near Toya Bungkah. The shorter one is straight up (three to four hours return), while a longer trek (five to six hours return) links the summit climb with the other craters. Climbers have reported that they have easily made this journey without a PPPGB guide, although it shouldn't be tried while it's dark because people have fallen to their deaths. The major obstacle is actually avoiding any hassle from the guides.

There are a few separate paths at first, but they all rejoin sooner or later and after about 30 minutes you'll be on a ridge with quite a well-defined track. It gets pretty steep towards the top and it can be hard walking over the loose volcanic sand – you'll climb up three steps only to slide back two. Allow about two hours to get to the top.

There's also a track that enables you to use private transport to within about 45 minutes' walk of the top. From Toya Bungkah, take the road northeast towards Songan and take the left fork after about 3.5km at Serongga, just before Songan. Follow this inner-rim road for another 1.7km to a well-signposted track on the left, which climbs another 1km or so to a car park. From here, the walking track is easy to follow to the top.

Around Gunung Batur Crater

Penelokan

Appropriately, Penelokan means 'place to look' and you'll be stunned by the view across to Gunung Batur and down to the lake at the bottom of the crater (check out the large lava flow on Gunung Batur). The area is often generically called Kintamani.

Although the huge tourist places on the road from Penelokan to Kintamani disappoint, there are a few acceptable choices, including humble places where you can sit on a plastic chair and have a simple, freshly cooked meal while enjoying a priceless view. Look for ikan mujair signs, near which small sweet fish that are caught in the lake below are barbecued to a crisp with onion, garlic and bamboo sprouts.

◉ Sights

★ **Batur Geopark Museum**   MUSEUM
(☑0366-51186; www.baturglobalgeopark.com; ⊗9am-1pm) FREE The extraordinary geology of the Gunung Batur area is explained in fascinating detail in this new museum right near the crater rim. Using interactive displays. models and rock samples, the enormous forces that continue to shape this area are made real. Expect to spend about an hour and thank the Unesco Geopark designation for funding this complex. Note that you have to pay the region's access fees before you reach the museum.

🛏 Sleeping & Eating

Lakeview Hotel   HOTEL $$
(☑0366-52525; www.facebook.com/LakeviewBali; r incl breakfast from 750,000Rp; ⊗restaurant 7.30am-3.30pm; 🛜) This venerable hotel complex was recently revitalised by the family who've owned it for three generations. Twelve comfortable rooms have amazing views and access to a private lounge with snacks and meals until 10pm. The terrace cafe here has sweeping views.

★ **Pulu Mujung Warung**   INDONESIAN $$
(☑0813 3864 4037; mains 38,000-65,000Rp; ⊗9am-6pm) 🍲 Easily the best option for a meal in the area, this fantastic cafe has epic volcano views. It's affiliated with the much-loved Sari Organik (p177) restaurant in Ubud. Soups are enjoyable in the cool mountain air, and you can also choose from salads, pizzas, Indo specials, homemade wines, juices, smoothies and more. Accommodation is available in three simple rooms (from 250,000Rp) but book ahead.

Kintamani & Batur

The villages of Kintamani and Batur now virtually run together. Kintamani is famed for its large and colourful market, which is held every three days. The town is like a string bean: long, with pods of development. Activity starts early, and by 11am everything is all packed up. If you don't want to go on a trek, the sunrise view from the road here is good.

The original village of Batur was in the crater, but was wiped out by a violent eruption in 1917. It killed thousands of people before the lava flow stopped at the entrance to the village's main temple. Taking this as a good omen, the villagers rebuilt, but Gunung Batur erupted again in 1926. This time the lava flow covered everything except the loftiest temple shrine. Fortunately, few lives were lost. The village was then relocated up onto the crater rim.

Spiritually, Gunung Batur is the second-most-important mountain in Bali (only Gunung Agung outranks it), so its temple, the ever-more-flamboyant **Pura Batur** (Batur, 10,000Rp, sarong & sash rental 3000Rp), is of considerable importance. It's a great stop for the architectural spectacle. Within the complex is a Taoist shrine.

Penulisan

The road gradually climbs along the crater rim beyond Kintamani, and is often shrouded in clouds, mist or rain. Penulisan is where the road bends sharply and splits: the main branch runs down towards the north coast while the other leads to the remote scenic drive to Bedugul. A **viewpoint** about 400m south of here offers an amazing panorama over three mountains: Gunung Batur, Gunung Abang and Gunung Agung.

Near the Penilusan road junction, several steep flights of steps lead to Bali's highest temple, **Pura Puncak Penulisan** `FREE` (1745m). Inside the highest courtyard are rows of old statues and fragments of sculptures in the open bale (pavilion with steeply pitched thatch roof). Some of the sculptures date back to the 11th century. The temple views are superb: facing north you can see over the rice terraces clear to the Singaraja coast (weather permitting)

Around Danau Batur

The little villages around Danau Batur have a crisp lakeside setting and views up to the surrounding peaks. There's a lot of fish farming, and the air is pungent with the smell of onions from the myriad tiny vegetable farms. Don't miss the trip along the east coast to Trunyan.

A road hairpins its way down from Penelokan to the shore of Danau Batur. At the lakeside you can go left along the road that twists through lava fields to Toya Bungkah. Watch out for huge sand trucks battering the road into dust as they haul materials for construction across Bali.

ℹ **TOUR BUS RESTAURANTS**

Avoid the ugly monolithic restaurants lining the Gunung Batur crater rim (many have closed anyway, their carcasses littering the view like the forgotten egg rolls inside). They offer lacklustre buffet lunches costing from 100,000Rp (your guide usually gets at least 25% of the bill as a commission) and offer uninspired food by the bucket. Drivers also get in on the action: the most crowded restaurants often have driver's lounges with gyms, TVs, beds and free food.

Kedisan & Buahan

You can spend a day exploring the villages around Danau Batur. It's a pleasant 15-minute stroll between the villages of Buahan and Kedisan; market gardens grow right down to the lakeshore.

🏃 Activities

Hot springs bubble in a couple of spots, and have long been used for bathing pools. Cycling around the lake is an ideal way to explore the villages.

Lake Boats   BOATING
(Kedisan; rides 1/2 people from 515,000/545,000Rp) These boats leave from a jetty with gift shops. The price for a two-hour return trip (Kedisan–Trunyan–Kuban–Toya Bungkah–Kedisan) depends on the number of passengers, with a maximum of seven people. Our advice: to spend time out on the lake, take one of the canoe trips with C.Bali.

🧭 Tours

★ **C.Bali**   ADVENTURE
(☑ info only 0813 5342 0541; www.c-bali.com; Hotel Segara, Kedisan; tours adult/child from 500,000/400,000Rp) Operated by an Australian-Dutch couple, C.Bali offers cultural bike tours around the region and canoe tours on Danau Batur. Prices include pick-up across south Bali. Packages also include multiday trips. Note: these tours often fill up far in advance, so book ahead through the website.

🛏 Sleeping & Eating

A few guesthouses with lake views dot the shore. Beware of the motorcycle touts, who will follow you down the hill from Penelokan trying to nab a hotel commission. Local hotels ask that you call ahead and reserve so that they have your name on record and thus can avoid paying the touts.

Baruna Cottages GUESTHOUSE $
(📱 0813 5322 2896; www.barunacottage.com; Buahan; r/bungalow from 400,000/550,000Rp) The nine rooms at this small and tidy compound vary greatly in design and size; the middle grade have the best views. It's right across the Trunyan road from the lake, and there's a cute cafe.

Hotel Segara GUESTHOUSE $
(📱 0366-51136; www.batur-segarahotel.com; Kedisan; r incl breakfast 250,000-600,000Rp; 🛜) The popular Segara has bungalows set around a cafe and courtyard. The cheapest of the 32 rooms have cold water; the best rooms have hot water and bathtubs – perfect for soaking after an early trek.

Kedisan Floating Hotel BALINESE $
(📱 0366-51627, 0813 3775 5411; Kedisan; meals from 25,000Rp; ⏰ 8am-8pm; 🛜) This hotel on the shores of Danau Batur is hugely popular for its daily lunches. On weekends tourists vie with day-trippers from Denpasar for tables out on the piers over the lake. The Balinese food, which features fresh lake fish, is excellent. You can also stay here: the best rooms are cottages at the water's edge (from 400,000Rp).

Trunyan

The village of Trunyan is squeezed between the lake and the outer crater rim. It is inhabited by Bali Aga people and is the kind of place that can make you feel like you've left Bali altogether. Smiles are less common in this isolated corner of Danau Batur but the setting is beautiful. Stop and picnic on the road outside town.

Trunyan is known for the **Pura Pancering Jagat**, which is very impressive with its seven-roofed *meru*. Inside the temple is a 4m-high statue of the village's guardian spirit, although tourists are not usually allowed in. Ignore the touts and guides lurking about and know that 5000Rp is the absolute maximum you should pay to park here.

Kuban

About 500m beyond Trunyan, and accessible only by a hiking trail or boat, is the cemetery at Kuban (aka Kuburan). Locals don't cremate or bury their dead – they lay them out in bamboo cages to decompose. If you do decide to visit the cemetery, you'll be met by characters demanding huge fees. Our advice is to enjoy the views on the road to Trunyan and skip this ghoulish spectacle.

You can get here on one of the lake boats from Kedisan or on a very short and expensive boat ride from Trunyan (about 450,000Rp plus 150,000Rp for a 'guide' who will insist on coming along).

Toya Bungkah

The main lakeside tourist centre is Toya Bungkah (also known as Tirta), which boasts hot springs (*tirta* and *toya* both mean water). It's a very small village and one of the places people stay before climbing Gunung Batur early in the morning.

🏃 Activities

Batur Natural Hot Spring HOT SPRINGS
(📱 0813 3832 5552; adult/child from 150,000/75,000Rp; ⏰ 8am-6pm) This ever-expanding complex is on the edge of Danau Batur. The three pools have different temperatures, so you can simmer yourself successively. The overall feel of the hot springs matches the slightly shabby feel of the entire region. The simple cafe has good views.

Toya Devasya HOT SPRINGS
(📱 0366-51204; www.toyadevasya.com; adult/child 150,000/100,000Rp; ⏰ 8am-8pm) This glossy retreat is built around springs. One huge hot pool is 38°C, while a comparatively brisk lake-fed pool is 20°C. Admission includes refreshments, and there is a cafe with illusions of grandeur as well as lodging options.

CYCLING THE VILLAGES

The tiny lakeside villages have recently been busy building bicycle paths that make it easy to enjoy the incredible views across to Gunung Batur from along the lake's east side.

From the T-junction of the access road down from Penelokan near Kedisan, it's 9km to Trunyan via Abang. Whether walking, cycling or riding a motorbike, this is a very rewarding adventure. Cyclists will need to dismount for a few short and steep stretches north of Abang. Besides the views, there is a magnificent **banyan tree** east of Buahan and some good Geopark-sponsored panels with information on the area's wild geology at the Abang pier.

It also offers good **bike tours** (350,000Rp) and **canoe trips** (1,000,000Rp).

🛌 Sleeping

Avoid rooms near the noisy main road through Toya Bungkah: opt instead for placid ones with lake views.

Under the Volcano III   GUESTHOUSE **$**
(📞0813 3860 0081; s/d incl breakfast from 150,000/200,000Rp; 🛜) Featuring a lovely, quiet lakeside location opposite chilli plots, this inn has six clean and simple rooms; go for room 1 right on the water. There are two other nearby inns in the Volcano empire, all run by the same lovely family.

Songan

Around the lake, 2km from Toya Bungkah, Songan is a large and interesting village with market gardens extending to the water's edge. At the lakeside road end is **Pura Ulun Danu Batur**, under the edge of the crater rim.

A turn-off in Songan takes you on a rough but passable road around the crater floor. On the northwestern side of the volcano, the village of Toya Mampeh (Yeh Mampeh) is surrounded by a vast field of chunky black lava – a legacy of the 1974 eruption. Further on, is **Pura Bukit Mentik**, which was completely surrounded by molten lava from the 1974 eruption. The temple itself and its impressive banyan tree were quite untouched by the lava – it's called the 'Lucky Temple'.

DANAU BRATAN AREA

Approaching from south Bali, you gradually leave the rice terraces behind and ascend into the cool, often misty mountain country around Danau Bratan. Candikuning is the main village in the area, and has the important and picturesque temple Pura Ulun Danu Bratan. Munduk anchors the region with fine trekking to waterfalls and cloud-cloaked forests and at nearby Danau Tamblingan.

The choice of accommodation near the lake is limited because much of the area is geared towards domestic, not foreign, tourists. On Sundays and public holidays the lakeside can be crowded with courting couples and Toyotas bursting with day-tripping families. But Munduk has many excellent inns.

Wherever you go, you are likely to see the tasty local strawberries on offer. Note that it is often misty and can get chilly up here.

Bedugul
📞 0368

'Bedugul' is sometimes used to refer to the whole lakeside area, but strictly speaking it's just the first place you reach at the top of the hill when coming from south Bali, and even then you might not pause long because it's small.

🛌 Sleeping

Avoid the string of rundown places up at the ridge around Bedugul.

★ Strawberry Hill   GUESTHOUSE **$$**
(📞0368-21265; www.strawberryhillbali.com; Jl Raya Denpasar-Singaraja; r incl breakfast from 550,000Rp; 🛜) Just outside Candikuning you'll find 17 small conical woodsy cottages arrayed on a hill. Each has a deep soaking tub and nice views down to south Bali (some have better views than others, so compare). The cafe's Indo menu (mains from 40,000Rp) includes soul-healing *soto ayam* (chicken soup) and *gudeg yogya* (jackfruit stew). Pick your own strawberries for free from the hotel's patch.

Bali Ecovillage   BOUTIQUE HOTEL **$$**
(📞0819 9988 6035, reservations 0813 5338 2797; www.baliecovillage.com; Dinas Lawak; r/bungalow from US$45/80) 🖋 A vision in bamboo and set in a remote corner of Bali near coffee plantations, this idiosyncratic lodge is so green that just about the only other colour you'll see is the blue sky. The restaurant serves organic local and Western fare and there are numerous cultural activities plus a spa and yoga.

It's located in a hidden valley near the village of Kiadan Pelaga, about 25km from Bedugul.

ℹ Getting There & Away

Any bemo or minibus between south Bali and Singaraja will stop at Bedugul on request.

Candikuning
📞 0368

Often misty, Candikuning is home to a good botanic garden as well as one of Bali's most photographed temples. There's also the simple beauty of Danau Bratan amid the bowl of lushly forested mountains.

Danau Bratan Area

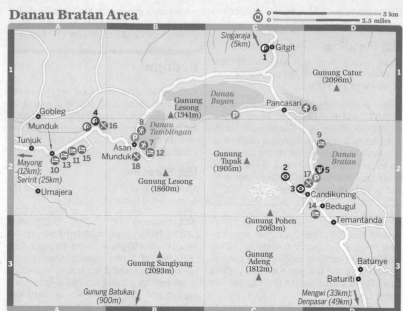

Danau Bratan Area

◉ Sights

Bali Botanic Garden   GARDENS
(☑ 0368-203 3211; Jl Kebun Raya Eka Karya Bali;
18,000Rp, parking 3000Rp; ☺ 7am-6pm) This
garden is a showplace. Established in 1959 as
a branch of the national botanic gardens at
Bogor, near Jakarta, it covers more than 154
hectares on the lower slopes of Gunung Po-
hen. Don't miss the **Panca Yadnya Garden**
(Garden of Five Offerings), which preserves
plants used in ancient Hindu ceremonies.

For an extra 10,500Rp you can drive your
own car (no motorbikes) about the gardens.

Some plants are labelled with their botanical names, and a booklet of self-guided
walks (20,000Rp) is helpful. The gorgeous
orchid area is often locked to foil flower
filchers; you can ask for it to be unlocked.
Look for the 'roton' or rattan bush to see the
unlikely source of so much furniture.

Within the park, you can cavort like an
ape at the Bali Treetop Adventure Park.

Pura Ulun Danu Bratan
HINDU TEMPLE

(off Jl Raya Denpasar-Singaraja; adult/child 30,000/15,000Rp, parking 5000Rp; ⊘6am-6pm) An iconic image of Bali, depicted on the 50,000Rp note, this important Hindu-Buddhist temple was founded in the 17th century. It is dedicated to Dewi Danu, the goddess of the waters, and is built on small islands. Pilgrimages and ceremonies are held here to ensure that there is a supply of water for farmers all over Bali as part of the Unesco-recognised *subak* system. Incredibly popular, you'll dodge selfie sticks as you search out your own quiet corner. The tableau includes classical Hindu thatch-roofed *meru* (multi-tiered shrines) reflected in the water and silhouetted against the often cloudy mountain backdrop.

Unfortunately, there's a bit of a sideshow atmosphere here: animals, including some very sad-eyed owls, are squashed into small cages and punters stop to caress snakes or hold huge bats, while the parking lot is lined with souvenir stalls. You can escape the masses by renting a pedalboat shaped like a deformed swan (75,000Rp). There are also speedboats available.

Candikuning Market
MARKET

(Jl Raya Denpasar-Singaraja; parking 2000Rp) This roadside market is very touristy, but among the eager vendors of tat, you'll find locals shopping for fruit, veg, herbs, spices and potted plants.

🏃 Activities

Bali Treetop Adventure Park
OUTDOORS

(☑0361-934 0009; www.balitreetop.com; Jl Kebun Raya Eka Karya Bali, Bali Botanic Garden; adult/child from US$25/16; ⊘9.30am-6pm) Within the Bali Botanic Garden, you can cavort like a bird or a squirrel at the Bali Treetop Adventure Park. Winches, ropes, nets and more let you explore the forest well above the ground. And it's not passive: you hoist, jump, balance and otherwise circumnavigate the park. Special programs are geared to different ages.

🛏 Sleeping

You'll find some simple guesthouses on the road to the botanic garden.

Kebun Raya Bali
GUESTHOUSE $$

(☑0368-2033211; www.kebunrayabali.com; Jl Kebun Raya Eka Karya Bali, Bali Botanic Garden; r incl breakfast 450,000-650,000Rp) Wake up and smell the roses. The Bali Botanic Garden has 14 comfortable hotel-style rooms in the heart of the botanic gardens.

SUNRISE JOY

For an almost surreal experience, take a quiet paddle across Danau Bratan and see Pura Ulun Danu Bratan at sunrise – arrange it with a boatman at the temple the night before. The mobs see it by day, but you'll see something entirely different – and magical – in the mists of dawn.

Enjung Beji Resort
HOTEL $$

(☑0852 8521; www.enjungbejiresort.com; Candikuning; cottages incl breakfast 400,000-700,000Rp) Just north of the temple and overlooking Danau Bratan is this peaceful pleasant option. The 23 cottages are modern and clean, the nicest with outdoor showers and sunken baths.

🍴 Eating

For an excellent bowl of chicken soup (*bakso ayam*), stop at one of the roadside stands where the road from Candikuning reaches Danau Bratan and turns north. Otherwise there are numerous mediocre restaurants with parking lots suitable for tour buses along the main road near the temple.

Roti Bedugul
BAKERY $

(☑0368-21838; Jl Raya Denpasar-Singaraja; snacks from 5000Rp; ⊘8am-4pm) Just north of the market, this bakery produces fine versions of its namesake, as well as croissants and other baked goods.

Pancasari

The broad green valley northwest of Danau Bratan is actually the crater of an extinct volcano. In the middle of the valley, on the main road, Pancasari is a nontourist town with a bustling market that happens every three days.

Just south of Pancasari, you will see the entrance to **Handara Golf & Country Club Resort** (☑0362-22646; www.halihandara countryclub.com; greens fees from 2,000,000Rp; club rental from US$25; r from US$100), a well-situated (compared with south Bali courses, there's plenty of water here) 18-hole golf course. It also offers comfortable accommodation in the sterile atmosphere of a 1970s resort (that could pass for Drax's Lair in a Bond movie. Online greens fees are often under US$40.

Danau Buyan & Danau Tamblingan

Northwest of Danau Bratan are two less-visited lakes, Danau Buyan and Danau Tamblingan, where some excellent guided hikes are on offer. There are several tiny villages and old temples along the shores of both lakes that reward those who take the time to explore. You'll leave crowded Bali behind and enjoy a tropical hike in nature, with few of the hassles so prevalent elsewhere.

🏃 Activities

The Munduk road on the hill above the lakes has sweeping views.

Danau Buyan has parking right at the lake, a pretty 1.5km drive off the main road. The entire area is home to market gardens growing strawberries and other high-value crops, such as the orange and blue flowers used in offerings.

A 4km **hiking trail** goes around the southern side of Danau Buyan from the car park, then over the saddle to Danau Tamblingan, and on to Asan Munduk. It combines forest and lake views. If you have a driver, walk this path in one direction and get the driver to meet you at the other end.

Danau Tamblingan has parking at the end of the road from the village of Asan Munduk. Trails start here.

★ **Organisasi Pramuwisata Bangkit Bersama** HIKING
(Guides Organization Standing Together; ☑ 0852 3867 8092; Danau Tambligan, Asan Munduk; guided hikes from 200,000Rp; ⊙ 8.30am-4pm) This great group of guys is based in a hut near the parking lot for Danau Tamblingan. Like the guiding group along the Munduk road, they offer a range of trips around the lakes, temples and mountains. You can ascend nearby Gunung Lesong for 600,000Rp (they have walking sticks for you to use).

★ **Pramuwisata Amerta Jati** HIKING
(☑ 0857 3715 4849; Munduk Rd; guided hikes 100,000-350,000Rp; ⊙ 8am-5pm) Located in a hut along the road above Danau Tamblingan, this group of excellent guides offers several different trips down and around the lakes. A popular two-hour trip includes ancient temples and a canoe trip on the lake (per person 250,000Rp). Trips can be as short as an hour or last all day.

🛏 Sleeping & Eating

Pondok Kesuma Wisata GUESTHOUSE $
(☑ 0812 3791 5865; Asan Munduk; r from 350,000Rp) This useful 12-room guesthouse features clean rooms with hot water and a pleasant cafe (meals 15,000Rp to 30,000Rp, confirm in advance). It's just up from the Danau Tamblingan parking lot. Note at times there will be very little service beyond getting you checked in or out.

THE ROAD LESS TRAVELLED

A series of narrow roads links the Danau Bratan area and the Gunung Batur region. Few locals outside this area even know that the roads exist, and your driver (if you have one) may need some convincing. Over a 30km route you not only step back to a simpler time, but also leave Bali altogether for something resembling less-developed islands such as Timor. The scenery is beautiful and may make you forget you had a destination.

South of Bedugul, turn east at Temantanda and take a small and winding road down the hillside into some lush ravines cut by rivers. After about 6km you'll come to a T-junction: turn north and travel about 5km to reach the pretty village of **Kiadan Pelaga**. This area is known for its organic coffee and cinnamon plantations, which you'll both see and smell. Consider a tour and homestay in Pelaga organised by JED (p229), a nonprofit group that offers rural tourism experiences.

From Pelaga, ascend the mountain, following terrain that alternates between jungle and rice fields. Continue north to Catur, then veer east to the junction with the road down to north Bali and drive east again for 1km to Penulisan.

A fun detour on *this* detour is the **Tukad Bangkung Bridge** at Petang: at 71m it is reputed to be the tallest bridge in Asia. It is a local tourist attraction and the roads are lined with vendors on weekends.

★ **Terrasse du Lac**   CAFE **$$**
(☑ 0819 0330 1917; Jl Danau Tamblingan; mains 40,000-120,000Rp; ☺ 9am-8pm; ☑) There's a French accent and excellent food at this cafe, which has lovely lake views. Breakfast features pancakes, while later in the day there are meaty mains, pasta and veggie specials. Excellent fresh juices, plus beer, coffee etc. Try the turmeric tea. You can rent two modern, tidy rooms that have sunset views from the balconies (from 600,000Rp).

Munduk & Around

☑ 0362

The simple village of Munduk is one of Bali's most appealing mountain retreats. It has a cool misty ambience set among lush hillsides covered with jungle, rice fields, fruit trees and pretty much anything else that grows on the island. Waterfalls tumble off precipices by the dozen. There are hikes and treks galore and a number of really nice places to stay, from old Dutch colonial summer homes to retreats where you can plunge full-on into local culture. Many people come for a day and stay for a week.

Archaeological evidence suggests there was a developed community in the Munduk region between the 10th and 14th centuries. When the Dutch took control of north Bali in the 1890s, they experimented with commercial crops, establishing plantations for coffee, vanilla, cloves and cocoa.

◉ Sights & Activities

Heading to Munduk from Pancasari, the main road climbs steeply up the rim of the old volcanic crater. It's worth stopping to enjoy the views back over the valley and lake – show a banana and the swarms of monkeys will get so excited they'll start spanking themselves with joy. Turning right (east) at the top will take you on a scenic descent to Singaraja. Taking a sharp left turn (west), you follow a ridge-top road with Danau Buyan on one side and a slope to the sea on the other.

At Asah Munduk, you'll find another T-junction. The left turn will take you down a road leading to Danau Tamblingan. Turning right takes you along beautiful winding roads to the main village of Munduk. Watch for superb panoramas of north Bali and the ocean.

Wherever you stay, staff will fill you in on walking and hiking options. There are numerous trails suitable for hikes of varying lengths to destinations as diverse as coffee plantations, rice paddies, waterfalls or villages. You could even hike around both Danau Tamblingan and Danau Buyan. Most are easy to do on your own, but guides will take you far off the beaten path to waterfalls and other delights that are hard to find.

Ask about the walking path linking Munduk's guesthouses, which saves you from traversing the perilous road.

⊨ Sleeping

Enjoy simple old Dutch houses in the village or more naturalistic places in the countryside. Most have cafes, usually serving good local fare.

Puri Alam Bali   GUESTHOUSE **$**
(☑ 0812 465 9815; www.purialambali.com; r 300,000-600,000Rp; ☜❄) Perched on a precipice at the east end of the village, the 15 rooms (all with hot water and balconies) have better views the higher you go. The rooftop cafe is worth a visit for its huge views. Think of the long concrete stairs down from the road as trekking practice.

Guru Ratna   GUESTHOUSE **$**
(☑ 0813 3719 4398; www.guru-ratna.com; r 225,000-400,000Rp; ☜) The cheapest place in the village has seven comfortable hot-water rooms (some share bathrooms). The best rooms have some style, carved wood details and nice porches, and are in a colonial Dutch house.

★ **Puri Lumbung Cottages**   GUESTHOUSE **$$**
(☑ 0812 387 4042; www.purilumbung.com; cottages incl breakfast US$80-175; @☜) ⌀ Founded by Nyoman Bagiarta to develop sustainable tourism, this lovely hotel has 43 bright two-storey thatched cottages and rooms set among rice fields. Enjoy intoxicating views (units 32 to 35 have the best) from the upstairs balconies. Dozens of trekking options and courses are offered.

The hotel's restaurant is very good, with dishes created and presented with attention to detail (mains 50,000Rp to 120,000Rp). The hotel is on the right-hand side of the road coming from Bedugul, 700m before Munduk. Ask about the remote forest rooms. The name 'Sunset Bar' says everything you need to know.

Manah Liang Cottages   INN **$$**
(☑ 0362-700 5211; www.manahliang.com; r from 450,000Rp; ☜) About 800m east of Munduk,

MUNDUK'S WATERFALLS

Munduk's many waterfalls include the following three, which you can visit on a hike of four to six hours (note that the myriad local maps given out by guesthouses and hotels can be vague on details and it's easy to take a wrong turn). Fortunately, even unplanned detours are scenic. Clouds of mist from the water add to the already misty air; drips come off every leaf. There are a lot of often slippery and steep paths; rest up at tiny cafes perched above some of the falls.

Munduk Waterfall (Tanah Braak; 10,000Rp, parking 5000Rp) About 2km east of Munduk, look for signs to this waterfall along the road. Though the signs say the trail is 700m, it feels longer than that. This is the easiest waterfall to access without a map or guide.

Golden Valley Waterfall Fairly short but wide falls, watched over by a cute coffee stand.

Melanting Waterfall Over 25m, these are about 500m from Munduk Waterfall.

this country inn (whose name means 'feeling good') has traditional cottages overlooking the lush local terrain. The open-air bathrooms (with tubs) are as refreshing as the porches are relaxing. A short trail leads to a small waterfall. There are cooking classes and guided walks.

Villa Dua Bintang　　　　GUESTHOUSE $$
(📞0812 3700 5593, 0812 3709 3463; www.villaduabintang.com; Jl Batu Galih; r incl breakfast 800,000Rp; 🛜🛁) Hidden 500m down a tree-shaded lane that's off the main road, 1km east of Munduk. Four gorgeous rooms are elaborately built amid fruit trees and forest (two rooms are family-size). The scent of cloves and nutmeg hangs in the air from the porch. There's a cafe, and the family who owns it is lovely.

Meme Surung　　　　GUESTHOUSE $$
(📞0851 0001 2887; www.memesurung.com; r incl breakfast from 400,000Rp; 🛜) Two atmospheric old Dutch houses adjoin to form a compound of 11 rooms, immersed amid an English-style garden. The decor is traditional and simple; the view from the long wooden verandah is both the focus and joy here. It's located along the main strip of Munduk's township.

🍴 Eating

There are a couple of cute warungs (food stalls) in the village and a few stores with very basic supplies (including bug spray). Guesthouses have cafes: the restaurant at Puri Lumbung Cottages (p239) is the best option for nonguests.

Ngiring Ngewedang　　　　CAFE $
(📞0812 380 7010; www.ngiringngewedang.com; snacks 15,000-40,000Rp; ⏰10am-5pm) Stop in

at this coffeehouse, 5km east of Munduk; it grows its own coffee on the surrounding slopes and was completely rebuilt in 2016.

Don Biyu　　　　CAFE $
(📞0812 3709 3949; www.donbiyu.com; mains 26,000-80,000Rp; ⏰7.30am-10pm; 🛜) Catch up on your blog; enjoy good coffee; zone out before the sublime views; and choose from a mix of Western and interesting Asian fare. Dishes are served in mellow open-air pavilions. It also has six double rooms (600,000Rp), all with balconies and views. It's on the main road leading into Munduk.

ℹ️ Getting There & Away

Minibuses leave Ubung terminal in Denpasar for Munduk (25,000Rp) a few times a day. Driving to the north coast, the main road west of Munduk goes through a number of picturesque villages to Mayong (where you can head south to west Bali). The road then goes down to the sea at Seririt in north Bali.

GUNUNG BATUKAU AREA

📞0361

Gunung Batukau is Bali's second-highest mountain (2276m), the third of Bali's three major mountains and the holy peak of the island's western end. It's often overlooked, which is probably a good thing given what the vendor hordes have done to Gunung Agung.

You can climb its slippery slopes from one of the island's holiest and most underrated temples, Pura Luhur Batukau, or just revel in the ancient rice-terrace greenery around Jatiluwih.

◉ Sights & Activities

★ **Pura Luhur Batukau**   HINDU TEMPLE
(adult/child 20,000/10,000Rp; ⊘8am-6pm) On the slopes of Gunung Batukau, Pura Luhur Batukau was the state temple when Tabanan was an independent kingdom. It has a seven-roofed *meru* dedicated to Maha Dewa, the mountain's guardian spirit, as well as shrines for Bratan, Buyan and Tamblingan lakes. This is certainly the most spiritual temple you can easily visit in Bali.

The main *meru* in the inner courtyard have little doors shielding small ceremonial items. Outside the compound, the temple is surrounded by forest and the atmosphere is cool and misty; the chants of priests are backed by birds singing. Facing the temple, take a short walk around to the left to see a small white-water stream where the air resonates with tumbling water. Note the unusual fertility shrine.

There's a general lack of touts and other characters here – including hordes of tourists. Respect traditions and act appropriately while visiting temples. Sarong rental is included in the entrance price. Guides at the entrance offer worthwhile **two-hour jungle hikes** for 250,000Rp.

Gunung Batukau   HIKING
At Pura Luhur Batukau you are fairly well up the side of Gunung Batukau. For the trek to the top of the 2276m peak, you'll need a guide, which can be arranged at the temple ticket booth. Expect to pay more than 1,000,000Rp for a muddy and arduous journey that will take at least seven hours in one direction. Be sure to negotiate.

The rewards are potentially amazing views (depending on mist) alternating with thick dripping jungle, and the knowledge that you've taken a trail that is much less travelled than the ones on the eastern peaks. You can get a taste of the adventure on a two-hour mini-jaunt (250,000Rp for two).

Staying the night up the mountain might be possible but the assumption is that you will go up and back the same day. Talk to the guides ahead of time to see if you can make special arrangements to camp on the mountain.

DON'T MISS

JATILUWIH RICE FIELDS

At Jatiluwih, which means 'truly marvellous' (or 'real beautiful' depending on the translation), you will be rewarded with vistas of centuries-old rice terraces that exhaust your ability to describe green. Emerald ribbons curve around the hillsides, stepping back as they climb to the blue sky.

The terraces are part of Bali's emblematic – and Unesco-recognised – ancient rice-growing culture. You'll understand the nomination just viewing the panorama from the narrow, twisting 18km road, but getting out for a rice-field walk is even more rewarding, following the water as it runs through channels and bamboo pipes from one plot to the next. Much of the rice you'll see is traditional, rather than the hybrid versions grown elsewhere on the island. Look for heavy short husks of red rice.

Take some time, leave your driver behind and just find a place to sit and enjoy the views. It sounds like a cliché, but the longer you look the more you'll see. What at first seems like a vast palette of greens reveals itself to be rice at various stages of growth.

Note, however, that the terraces have become very popular and the road can be anything but tranquil. Worse, tour companies now operate ATV tours through the heart of the rice fields. Under threat by Unesco to have the site's status rescinded, the government has proclaimed a freeze on development, which is not a moment too soon after developers announced plans to bulldoze terraces for hotels.

There are cafes for refreshments along the route, including a rather garish collection about mid-drive. Your best bet is to browse a couple.

Because the road is sharply curved, vehicles are forced to drive slowly, which makes the Jatiluwih route a good one for bikes. There are toll booths for visitors (adult/child 20,000/15,000Rp per person, plus 5000Rp per car), which does *not* seem to be going to road maintenance – it's rough. Still the drive won't take more than an hour.

You can access the road in the west off the road to Pura Luhur Batukau from Tabanan, and in the east off the main road to Bedugul near Pacung. Drivers all know this road well and locals offer directions.

🛏 Sleeping

Two remote lodges are hidden away on the slopes of Gunung Batukau. You reach them via a spectacular small and twisting road that makes a long inverted V far up the mountain from Bajera and Pucuk on the main Tabanan–Gilimanuk road in west Bali.

★ Sarinbuana Eco Lodge   LODGE $$
(☑ 0361-743 5198; www.baliecolodge.com; Sarinbuana; bungalows 900,000-2,000,000Rp; 🛜) ⌀ These beautiful two-level bungalows are built on the side of a hill just a 10-minute walk from a protected rainforest preserve. Notable amenities include fridges, marble bathrooms and handmade soap. Think rustic luxe. There's even a treehouse. Food is organic.

There are cultural workshops, yoga classes and guided treks. The lodge has top-notch green cred and the organic Balinese restaurant is excellent.

Bali Mountain Retreat   LODGE $$
(☑ 0828 360 2645; www.balimountainretreat. com; r 270,000-900,000Rp; 🛜) ⌀ Luxurious rooms set in refined cottages are arrayed artistically at this hillside location. A pool and gardens mix with mannered architecture that combines new and old influences. Some rooms have large verandahs perfect for contemplating the views. Budget options include a bed in a vintage rice-storage barn. There are excellent treks.

❶ Getting There & Away

The only realistic way to explore the Gunung Batukau area is with your own transport.

There are two main approaches to the Gunung Batukau area. The easiest is via Tabanan: take the Pura Luhur Batukau road north 9km to a fork in the road, then take the left-hand turn (towards the temple) and go a further 5km to a junction near a school in Wangayagede village. Here you can continue straight to the temple or turn right (east) for the rice fields of Jatiluwih.

The other way is to approach from the east. On the main Denpasar–Singaraja road, look for a small road to the west, just south of the Pacung Indah hotel. Here you follow a series of small paved roads west until you reach the Jatiluwih rice fields. You'll get lost, but locals will quickly set you right and the scenery is superb anyway.

THE ANTOSARI ROAD
🗹 0361

Although most people cross the mountains via Candikuning or Kintamani, there is a very scenic third alternative that links Bali's south and north coasts. From the Denpasar–Gilimanuk road in west Bali, a road goes north from **Antosari** through the village of Pupuan and then drops to Seririt, west of Lovina in north Bali.

⊙ Sights & Activities

Starting through rice paddies, after 8km the road runs alongside a beautiful valley of rice terraces. Gorgeous gardens line the bluff and only enhance the already remarkable vistas.

Once you're deep in the foothills of Gunung Batukau, 20km north of Antosari, you'll smell the fragrant spice-growing village of **Sanda** before you see it. Look for the old wooden elevated rice barns that still feature in every house.

After another 8km north through coffee plantations, you'll reach **Pupuan**. A further 6km and you'll reach a highlight of the trip: the gorgeous **rice-growing valley** near Subuk. From here it is 6km or so to Mayong, where you can turn east to Munduk and on to Danau Bratan or go straight to Seririt.

🛏 Sleeping

Sanda Boutique Villas   LODGE $$
(☑ 0828 372 0055; www.sandavillas.com; bungalows incl breakfast from 750,000Rp; ❄🛜🏊) This boutique hotel offers a serene escape. Its large infinity pool seems to disappear into the rice terraces, while its eight bungalows are really quite luxe (not all have wi-fi). It's well run and the fusion cafe is excellent. The engaging owners will recommend walks among the coffee plantations and rice fields. It is just north of the village of Sanda.

Kebun Villas   LODGE $$
(☑ 0361-780 6068; www.kebunvilla.com; r from US$45; 🏊) Eight antique-filled cottages scattered down a hillside make the most of the sweeping views over rice fields in the valley. Getting to the pool area requires a hike down to the valley floor, but the pool is huge, and once there you may just linger all day.

North Bali

Best Places to Eat

➡ Damai (p252)

➡ Jasmine Kitchen (p251)

➡ Buda Bakery (p252)

➡ Global Village Kafe (p251)

➡ My Greek Taverna (p252)

Best Places to Sleep

➡ Matahari Beach Resort (p256)

➡ Damai (p251)

➡ Taman Selini Beach Bungalows (p256)

➡ Puri Ganesha Villas (p256)

➡ Taman Sari Bali Resort (p256)

Why Go?

The land on the other side, that's north Bali. Although one-sixth of the island's population lives here, this vast region is overlooked by many visitors who stay trapped in the south Bali–Ubud axis.

The big draw here is the incredible diving and snorkelling at nearby Pulau Menjangan. Arcing around a nearby bay, booming Pemuteran may be Bali's best beach escape. To the east is Lovina, a sleepy beach strip with cheap hotels and even cheaper sunset beer specials. All along the north coast are interesting little boutique hotels, while inland you'll find quiet treks to waterfalls.

Getting to north Bali for once lives up to the cliché: it's half the fun. Routes follow the thinly populated coastlines east and west, or you can go up and over the mountains by any number of routes, marvelling at crater lakes and maybe stopping for a misty trek on the way.

When to Go

➡ Most of north Bali doesn't have a high season in terms of visitors.

➡ The exceptions are Pemuteran, which is busy July, August and around Christmas and New Year; as are the diving and snorkelling sites around Menjangan, which can get overcrowded with schools of swimming visitors.

➡ Weather-wise north Bali is drier than the south. Days of perpetual sun are the norm year-round (most visitors get accommodation with air-con). The only real variation is when you venture back into the hills; mornings can be cool.

North Bali Highlights

1 Pulau Menjangan (p257) Plunging into the depths at Bali's best dive spot, or enjoying the show while snorkelling; all before discovering Bali's oldest temple on the namesake island.

2 Pemuteran (p254) Exploring underwater marvels while staying at this idyllic beach town.

3 Lovina (p247) Losing track of time, but not of your budget, at this laid-back, beachside town.

4 Air Terjun Singsing (p253) Hiking in the verdant hills of north Bali, especially to this plunging waterfall.

5 Singaraja (p245) Savouring Buleleng's rich culture at the museums of this historic royal city.

6 Bali Barat National Park (p259) Discovering, by foot or boat, Bali's national park, where there is wildlife-spotting amid mangroves, savannah and lush hillsides.

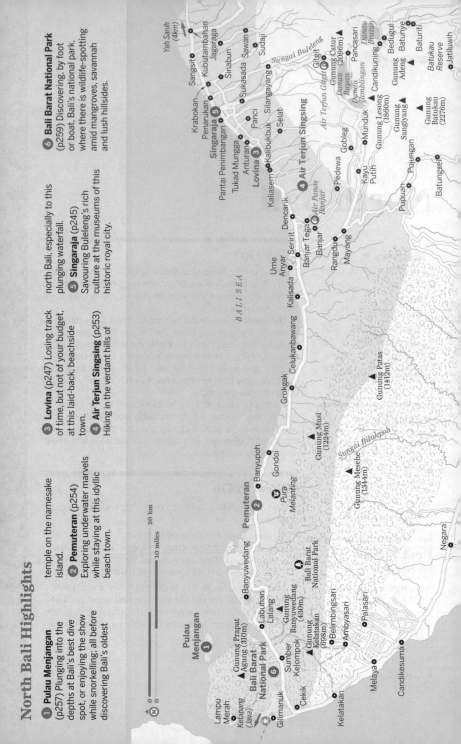

Yeh Sanih

☑ 0362

On the coast road to the beach and diving towns of east Bali, Yeh Sanih has famous hot springs. The drive continues along a great stretch of coast before passing into east Bali and on eventually to Tulamben.

◉ Sights & Activities

Between the springs and Pura Ponjok Batu, the road is often close to the sea. It's probably Bali's best stretch of pure coast driving, with waves crashing onto the breakwater and great views out to sea.

Symon Studios   GALLERY
(www.symonstudios.com; Jl Airsanih-Tejakula; ☺8am-6pm) Completely out of character for the Yeh Sanih area is a place run by Symon, the irrepressible American artist. It's bursting with a creativity that is, at times, vibrant, exotic and erotic. It's 5.7km east of Yeh Sanih on the Singaraja road.

Pura Ponjok Batu   HINDU TEMPLE
Boasting a commanding location between the sea and the road, Pura Ponjok Batu is some 7km east of Yeh Sanih. It has some very fine limestone carvings in the central temple area. Legend holds that it was built to provide some spiritual balance for Bali, what with all the temples in the south.

Air Sanih   SWIMMING
(Jl Airsanih-Tejakula; adult/child 8000/5000Rp; ☺8am-6pm) The freshwater springs of Air Sanih are channelled into large swimming pools before flowing into the sea. The pools are particularly picturesque at sunset, when throngs of locals bathe under blooming frangipani trees – most of the time they're alive with frolicking kids. It's about 15km east of Singaraja.

🛏 Sleeping

Cilik's Beach Garden   GUESTHOUSE $$
(☑0819 1570 0009; www.ciliksbeachgarden.com; Jl Airsanih-Tejakula; r incl breakfast from 0Q0, villas from €105; @) Coming here is like visiting your rich friends, albeit ones with good taste. These custom-built villas, 3km east of Yeh Sanih, are large and have extensive private gardens. Other accommodation is in stylish *lumbung* (rice barns with round roofs) set in a garden facing the ocean. The owners have even more remote villas further south on the coast. Good cafe.

ℹ Getting There & Away

Yeh Sanih is on the main road along the north coast. Frequent bemo (minibuses) and buses from Singaraja stop outside the springs (12,000Rp).

If heading to Tulamben or Amed, make certain you're on your way south from here by 4pm in order to arrive while there's still some light to avoid road hazards.

Singaraja

☑ 0362

With a population of more than 120,000 people, Singaraja (which means 'Lion King') is Bali's second-largest city and the capital of Buleleng Regency, which covers much of the north. With its tree-lined streets, surviving Dutch colonial buildings and charmingly sleepy waterfront area north of Jl Erlangga, it's worth exploring for a couple of hours. Most people stay in nearby Lovina.

Singaraja was the centre of Dutch power in Bali and remained the administrative centre for the Lesser Sunda Islands (Bali through to Timor) until 1953. It is one of the few places in Bali where there are visible traces of the Dutch period, as well as Chinese and Islamic influences. Today, Singaraja is a major educational and cultural centre, with two university campuses.

There's ongoing talk about building a new international airport in Singaraja. A toll road from the south has also been mooted.

◉ Sights

At the old harbour and waterfront, you can get a whisper of when Singaraja was Bali's main port before WWII. At the north end of Jl Hasanudin, you'll find a modern **pier** out over the water with a couple of simple cafes and some vendors.

Across the parking lot, look for some **old Dutch warehouses**. Nearby are the conspicuous **Yudha Mandala Tama monument** and the colourful Chinese temple, **Ling Gwan Kiong**. There are a few old canals here as well.

Walk up Jl Imam Bonjol and you'll see the art deco lines of late-colonial Dutch buildings. Note that east of the old port, there are plans to develop the waterfront with shops and restaurants.

Just 2km west of the centre, **Pantai Penimbangan** is a popular beach area. The sand may be a narrow ribbon but there are dozens of seafood cafes that draw throngs of locals, especially on weekend evenings.

Gedong Kirtya Library
LIBRARY

(☑ 0362-22645; Jl Veteran 23; ⊗ 8am-4pm Mon-Thu, 8am-1pm Fri) FREE This small historical library was established in 1928 by Dutch colonialists and named after the Sanskrit for 'to try'. It has a collection of *lontar* (dried palm leaf) books, as well as some even older written works in the form of inscribed copper plates called *prasasti*. Dutch publications, dating back to 1901, may interest students of the colonial period. It's on the same grounds as Museum Buleleng.

Museum Buleleng
MUSEUM

(Jl Veteran 23; ⊗ 9am-4pm Mon-Fri) FREE Museum Buleleng recalls the life of the last *radja* (rajah; prince) of Buleleng, Pandji Tisna, who is credited with developing tourism in Lovina to the west. Among the items here is the Royal (brand) typewriter he used during his unlucrative career as a travel writer before his death in 1978. It also traces the history of the region back to when there was no history.

Pura Jagat Natha
HINDU TEMPLE

(Jl Pramuka) Singaraja's main temple, the largest in northern Bali, is not usually open to foreigners. You can appreciate its size and admire the carved stone decorations from the outside.

LONTAR BOOKS

Lontar is made from the fan-shaped leaves of the *rontal* palm. The leaf is dried, soaked in water, cleaned, steamed, dried again, then flattened, dyed and eventually cut into strips. The strips are inscribed with words and pictures using a very sharp blade or point, then coated with a black stain which is wiped off – the black colour stays in the inscription. A hole in the middle of each *lontar* strip is threaded onto a string, with a carved bamboo 'cover' at each end to protect the 'pages', and the string is secured with a couple of *kepeng* (Chinese coins with a hole in the centre).

The Gedong Kirtya Library (p246) in Singaraja has the world's largest collection of *lontar* works.

✕ Eating

Cozy Resto
INDONESIAN $

(☑ 0362-28214; Jl Pantai Penimbangan; mains 20,000-50,000Rp; ⊗ 10am-10pm) One of the more established cafes at Pantai Penimbangan, Cozy has a long menu of Balinese, Indonesian and seafood dishes. Celebrating locals fill the open-air dining areas. Nearby, along the waterfront road, you'll find dozens more vendors and stalls with cheap and cheerful local fare.

Dapur Ibu
INDONESIAN $

(☑ 0362-24474; Jl Jen Achmed Yani; mains 10,000-20,000Rp; ⊗ 8am-10pm) A nice local cafe with a small garden off the street. The *nasi goreng* (fried rice) is fresh and excellent; wash it down with a fresh juice or bubble tea.

Istana Cake & Bakery
BAKERY $

(☑ 0362-21983; Jl Jen Achmed Yani; snacks from 3000Rp; ⊗ 8am-6pm) Fallen in love in Lovina? Get your wedding cake here. For lesser life moments like the munchies, choose from an array of tasty baked goods. There is a freezer full of ice-cream cakes and treats.

Hardy's Supermarket
SUPERMARKET

(☑ 0362-285806; Jl Pramuka; ⊗ 6am-10pm) For supplies and sundries, head to this large Hardy's Supermarket.

ℹ Information

MEDICAL SERVICES

Singaraja Public Hospital (☑ 0362-22046, 0362-22573; Jl Ngurah Rai 30; ⊗ 24hr) The largest hospital in northern Bali.

TOURIST INFORMATION

The **Buleleng Tourism Office** (Diparda; ☑ 0362-21342; Jl Kartini 6; ⊗ 8am-3.30pm Mon-Fri) has some OK maps and good information if you ask specifically about dance and other cultural events. It's 550m southeast of the Banyuasri bus station.

ℹ Getting There & Away

Singaraja is the main transport hub for the northern coast, with three bemo/bus terminals. From the Sangket terminal, 10km south of town on the main road, minibuses go sporadically to Denpasar (Ubung terminal; 40,000Rp) via Bedugul/Pancasari.

The **Banyuasri terminal**, on the western side of town, has buses heading to Gilimanuk (40,000Rp, two hours) and plenty of bemos to Lovina (10,000Rp). For Java, several companies have services, which include the ferry trip across the Bali Strait.

The **Penarukan terminal** (off Jl Surapati), 2km east of town, has bemos to Yeh Sanih (10,000Rp) and Amlapura (about 20,000Rp, three hours) via the coastal road; and also minibuses to Denpasar (Batubulan terminal; 40,000Rp, three hours) via Kintamani.

ⓘ Getting Around

Bemos link the three main bemo/bus terminals and cost about 7000Rp.

Around Singaraja

Interesting sites around Singaraja include some important temples, some with famous carvings.

◎ Sights

Pura Maduwe Karang　　　　HINDU TEMPLE
(Temple of the Land Owner; Kubutambahan) One of the most intriguing temples in north Bali, Pura Maduwe Karang is particularly notable for its sculptured panels, including the famous stone-carved **bicycle relief** that depicts a gentleman riding a bicycle with a lotus flower serving as the back wheel. It's on the base of the main plinth in the inner enclosure. The cyclist may be WOJ Nieuwenkamp, a Dutch artist who, in 1904, brought what was probably the first bicycle to Bali.

Like Pura Beji at Sangsit, this temple of dark stone is dedicated to agricultural spirits, but this one looks after nonirrigated land. The temple is easy to find in the village of Kubutambahan – seek the 34 carved figures from the Ramayana outside the walls. Kubutambahan is on the road between Singaraja and Amlapura, about 1km east of the turn-off to Kintamani.

Sangsit　　　　VILLAGE
About 6km northeast of Singaraja is an excellent example of the colourful architectural style of north Bali. Sangsit's **Pura Beji** is a temple for the *subak* (village association of rice-growers), dedicated to the goddess Dewi Sri, who looks after irrigated rice fields. The over the top sculptured panels along the front wall features cartoonlike demons and amazing *naga* (mythical snakelike creatures). The inside also has a variety of sculptures covering every available space. It's 500m off the main road towards the coast.

The **Pura Dalem** (Temple of the Dead) shows scenes of punishment in the afterlife, and other humorous, sometimes erotic, pictures. You'll find it in the rice fields, about 500m northeast of Pura Beji.

Sawan　　　　VILLAGE
Sawan, 7km inland from Jagaraga, is a centre for the manufacturing of gamelan gongs and instruments. You can see the gongs being cast and the intricately carved gamelan frames being fashioned. **Pura Batu Bolong** (Temple of the Hollow Stone) and its baths are also worth a look. Around Sawan there are cold-water **springs** believed to cure all sorts of illnesses.

Pura Dalem Jagaraga　　　　HINDU TEMPLE
(Jagaraga) In the village of Jagaraga, Pura Dalem is a small, interesting temple with delightful sculptured panels along its front wall. On the outer wall, look for a vintage car driving sedately past, a steamer at sea and even an aerial dogfight between early aircraft. It's about 8km east of Singaraja.

Air Terjun Gitgit　　　　WATERFALL
(Gitgit; adult/child 20,000/10,000Rp) Around 11km south of Singaraja, a well-signposted path goes 800m west from the main road to the touristy waterfall, Air Terjun Gitgit. The path is lined with souvenir stalls and guides to nowhere. The 40m waterfalls pound away and the mists are more refreshing than any air-con. Approximately 2km further up the hill, there's a multitiered waterfall about 600m off the western side of the main road. The path crosses a narrow bridge and follows the river through verdant jungle past several small sets of waterfalls.

Regular minibuses between Denpasar and Singaraja stop at Gitgit. The falls are also a major stop on organised tours of central and north Bali.

🛏 Sleeping

Villa Manuk　　　　VILLA $$
(☑0362-27080; www.villa-manuk.com; near Sawan; r incl breakfast from 600,000Rp; @🐾) In the lush hills near Sawan, this two-villa complex has a large natural-spring-fed pool. Guests enjoy rice-field views, walks to waterfalls, village life and absolute peace and quiet.

Lovina
☑0362

'Relaxed' is how people most often describe Lovina, and they are correct. This low-key, low-rise, low-priced beach resort is the polar opposite of Kuta. The waves are calm, the beach is thin and over-amped attractions nil.

Lovina

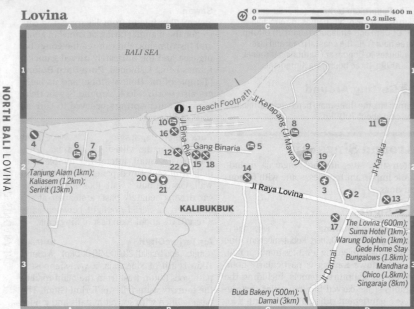

Lovina

⊙ Sights
1 Dolphin Monument	B1

⊕ Activities, Courses & Tours
2 Araminth Spa	D2
3 Sovina Shop	D2
4 Spice Dive	A2

⊜ Sleeping
5 Harris Homestay	C2
6 Homestay Purnama	A2
7 Lovina Beach Hotel	A2
8 Puri Bali Hotel	C2
9 Rambutan Boutique Hotel	C2
10 Sea Breeze Cabins	B2
11 Villa Taman Ganesha	D2

⊗ Eating
12 Akar	B2
13 Bakery Lovina	D2
14 Global Village Kafe	C2
15 Jasmine Kitchen	B2
16 My Greek Taverna	B2
17 Night Market	D3
Sea Breeze Café	(see 10)
18 Seyu	B2
Spice Beach Club	(see 4)
19 Warung Barclona	D2

⊙ Drinking & Nightlife
20 Kantin 21	B2
21 Pashaa	B2
22 Poco Lounge	B2

Lovina is sun-drenched, with patches of shade from palm trees. A highlight every afternoon at fishing villages like Anturan is watching *prahu* (traditional outrigger canoes) being prepared for the night's fishing; as sunset reddens the sky, the lights of the fishing boats appear as bright dots across the horizon.

The Lovina tourist area stretches over 8km, and consists of a string of coastal villages – Kaliasem, Kalibukbuk, Anturan and Tukad Mungga – collectively known as Lovina. The main focus is Kalibukbuk, 10.5km west of Singaraja and the heart of Lovina. Daytime traffic on the main road is loud and constant.

⊙ Sights & Activities

Beaches

The beaches are made up of washed-out grey and black volcanic sand, and while they're mostly clean near the hotel areas, they're not spectacular. Reefs protect the shore, calming the waves and keeping the water clear.

A paved **beach footpath** runs along the sand in Kalibukbuk and extends in a circuitous path along the seashore; it ranges from clean to grubby. Enjoy the postcard view to the east of the mountainous north Bali coast. Sunsets can be breathtaking.

The best beach areas include the main beach east of Kalibukbuk's elaborate **Dolphin Monument** (Jl Bina Ria), as well as the curving stretch a bit west. There's a **pier** popular for sunset watching at the end of Jl Mawar.

For a glitzy beach experience, walk west to Spice Beach Club (p252).

Dolphin Watching

Sunrise boat trips to see dolphins are Lovina's much-hyped tourist attraction, so much so that they have a monument in their honour.

Some days no dolphins are sighted, but most of the time at least a few surface.

Expect pressure from your hotel and touts selling dolphin trips. The price is fixed at 100,000/50,000Rp per adult/child by the boat-owners' cartel. Trips start at a non-holidaylike 6am and last about two hours. Note that the ocean can get pretty crowded with loud, roaring powerboats.

There's great debate about what all this means to the dolphins. Do they like being chased by boats? If not, why do they keep coming back? Maybe it's the fish, of which there are plenty off Lovina.

Diving & Snorkelling

Diving on the local reef is better at lower depths and night diving is popular. Many people stay here and dive Pulau Menjangan, a two-hour drive west.

Generally, the water is clear and some parts of the reef are quite good for snorkelling, though the coral has been damaged by bleaching and, in places, by dynamite fishing. The best place is to the west, a few hundred metres offshore from Billibo Beach Cottages. A two-hour boat trip will cost about 200,000Rp, including equipment.

Spice Dive   DIVING
(☑0851 0001 2666; www.balispicedive.com; off Jl Raya Lovina, Kalibukbuk; 2-tank dives from €50; ☉8am-9pm) Spice Dive is a large operation. It offers snorkelling trips and night dives (€60), plus popular Pulau Menjangan trips (snorkel/dive €55/80). It's based at the west end of the beach path, with Spice Beach Club. It also has an office on Jl Bina Ria.

Cycling

The roads south and west of Jl Raya Lovina are excellent for biking, with limited traffic and enjoyable rides amid the rice fields and into the hills for views.

It's easy to rent a bike from 20,000Rp per day; for a good selection, try Sovina Shop.

Sovina Shop   CYCLING
(☑0362-41402; Jl Ketapang; ☉10am-10pm) Sovina Shop has a good selection of bicycles for hire from 30,000Rp per day. Motorbikes are 50,000Rp per day.

Massages & Spas

Araminth Spa   SPA
(☑0362-41901; Jl Ketapang; massage per hr from 200,000Rp; ☉10am-9pm) Araminth Spa offers many types of therapies and massages, including Balinese and Ayurvedic, in a simple but soothing setting.

Ciego Massage   MASSAGE
(☑0877 6256 1660; Jl Raya Lovina, Anturan; 1hr massage from 80,000Rp; ☉10am-7pm) Highly skilled blind massage therapists provide no-nonsense muscle relief in a simple setting.

👉 Tours

⭐**Komang Dodik**   HIKING
(☑0877 6291 5128; lovina.tracking@gmail.com; hikes 350,000-600,000Rp) Komang Dodik leads hikes in the hills along the north coast. Trips can last from three to six hours. The highlight of most trips is a series of waterfalls, more than 20m high, in a jungle grotto. Routes can include coffee, clove and vanilla plantations. He also leads custom tours around the island.

🥾 Courses

⭐**Warung Bambu Pemaron**   COOKING
(☑0362-31455; www.warung-bambu.mahanara.com; Pemaron; classes for 1/2 people from 620,000/825,000Rp; ☉8am-1pm) Start with a trip to a large Singaraja food market and then, in a breezy setting amid rice fields east of Lovina, learn to cook up to nine classic Balinese dishes. Levels range from beginner to advanced, and there are vegetarian options. The staff are charming, and the fee includes transport within the area. When you're done, you get to feast on your labours.

🛏 Sleeping

Hotels are spread out along Jl Raya Lovina, and on the side roads going off to the beach. Overall, the choices tend to be more budget-focused; don't come here for a luxe experience. Be wary of hotels right on the main road due to traffic noise or those near the late-night Kalibukbuk bars.

During slow periods, all room prices are very negotiable; beware of touts who will literally lead you astray and quote prices that include a large kickback.

Anturan

A few tiny side tracks and one proper sealed road, Jl Kubu Gembong, lead to this lively little fishing village, which is a real travellers' hang-out. But it's a long way from Lovina's nightlife – expect to pay around 20,000Rp for transport the 3km back to Anturan from Kalibukbuk.

Mandhara Chico GUESTHOUSE $
(☑0812 360 3268; www.mandhara-chico-bali. com; off Jl Kubu Gembong; r with fan/air-con from 140,000/175,000Rp; ✳︎✿🌐🌊) This spiffy family-run guesthouse is right on a small strip of charcoal-sand beach. The 12 rooms are basic but tidy.

Gede Home Stay Bungalows HOMESTAY $
(☑0362-41526; www.gede-homestay.com; Jl Kubu Gembong; r incl breakfast 150,000–300,000Rp; ✳︎🌐) Don't forget to shake the sand off your feet as you enter this beachside eight-room homestay owned by a local fisherman. Cheap rooms have cold water while better ones have hot water and air-con.

Anturan to Kalibukbuk

Jl Pantai Banyualit has many modest hotels, although the beach is not very inspiring. There is a little park-like area by the water and the walk along the shore to Kalibukbuk is quick and scenic.

★**Villa Taman Ganesha** GUESTHOUSE $$
(☑0362-41272; www.taman-ganesha-lovina.com; Jl Kartika 45; r 550,000–700,000Rp; ✳︎🌐🌊) This lovely guesthouse is down a quiet lane lined with family compounds. The grounds are lush and fragrant with frangipani from around the world that have been collected by the owner, a landscape architect from Germany. The three units are private and comfortable. The beach is 400m away and it's a 10-minute walk along the sand to Kalibukbuk.

Suma Hotel GUESTHOUSE $$
(☑0362-41566; www.sumahotel.com; Jl Pantai Banyualit; r incl breakfast 350,000–600,000Rp;

✳︎@🌐🌊) Enjoy views of the sea from the upstairs rooms; the best of the 26 have air-con and hot water; large bungalows are quite nice as is the pool and cafe. An elaborate temple is nearby. Balconies and terraces have comfy wicker furniture for lounging.

Lovina BOUTIQUE HOTEL $$$
(☑0362-343 5800; www.thelovinabali.com; Jl Mas Lovina; ste from 1,900,000Rp; ✳︎🌐🌊) Clean, modern lines are the hallmark of this luxe beach resort, which is walkably close to the centre of Kalibukbuk. The 66 rooms are large, all with sitting areas and terraces or balconies. The furnishings are all in light colours, which adds to the contemporary feel. The pool is huge; guests can use bikes, kayaks and more.

Kalibukbuk

The 'centre' of Lovina is the village of Kalibukbuk. Mellow Jl Mawar is quieter and more pleasant than Jl Bina Ria. Small *gang* (alleys) lined with cheap accommodation lead off both streets.

★**Harris Homestay** HOMESTAY $
(☑0362-41152; Gang Binaria; s/d incl breakfast from 130,000/150,000Rp; 🌐) Sprightly, tidy and white, Harris avoids the weary look of some neighbouring cheapies. The charming family lives in the back; guests enjoy four bright, modern rooms up the front.

Sea Breeze Cabins GUESTHOUSE $
(☑0362-41138; off Jl Bina Ria; r incl breakfast 350,000–450,000Rp; ✳︎🌐🌊) One of the best choices in the heart of Kalibukbuk, the Sea Breeze has five bungalows and two rooms by the pool and the beach, some with sensational views from their verandahs. The only downside is that it can get noisy from nearby bars at night.

Puri Bali Hotel HOTEL $
(☑0362-41485; http://puribalihotel.wixsite.com/ lovina; Jl Mawar; r incl breakfast with fan/air-con from 200,000/350,000Rp; ✳︎🌐🌊) The pool area is set deep in a lush garden – you could easily hang out here all day and let any cares wander off to the ether. The 25 rooms are simple but comfortable.

Homestay Purnama HOMESTAY $
(☑0362-41043; Jl Raya Lovina; r from 150,000Rp; 🌐) One of the best deals on this stretch, Homestay Purnama has seven clean cold-water rooms, and the beach is only a

two-minute walk away. This is a family compound, and a friendly one at that.

Lovina Beach Hotel
HOTEL $

(☑0362-41005; www.lovinabeachhotel.com; Jl Raya Lovina; r incl breakfast 350,000-600,000Rp; ✸🖾🖾) This older, well-run beach hotel hasn't changed in years and neither have its prices. The 20 rooms, in a two-storey block, are clean if a bit frayed. Bungalows feature carving and Balinese details, the ones on the beach are a bargain. The grounds feel like a park.

Rambutan Boutique Hotel
HOTEL $$

(☑0362-41388; www.rambutan.org; Jl Mawar; s/d with fan from 280,000/350,000Rp, with air-con from 500,000/600,000Rp, villas from 1,650,000Rp; ✸@🖾🖾) The hotel, on 1 hectare of lush gardens, features two pools and a playground. The 30 rooms are decorated in Balinese style. The cheapest are fan-only. Villas are good deals; the largest are good for families and have kitchens.

Around Lovina

★ Damai
HOTEL $$$

(☑0362-41008; www.thedamai.com; Jl Damai; villas US$220-500; ✸🖾🖾) Set on a hillside behind Lovina, Damai has the kind of sweeping views you'd expect. Its 14 luxury villas mix antiques and a modern style accented with beautiful Balinese fabrics. The infinity pool seemingly spills onto a landscape of peanut fields, rice paddies and coconut palms. The spa is quite posh.

Larger villas have private pools and multiple rooms that flow from one to another. The restaurant is lauded for its organic fusion cuisine. Call for transport, or at the main junction in Kalibukbuk, go south on Jl Damai and follow the road for about 3km.

✗ Eating

Just about every hotel has a cafe or restaurant. Walk along the beach footpath to choose from a collection of basic places with cold beer, standard food and sunsets.

Anturan to Kalibukbuk

Warung Dolphin
SEAFOOD $

(☑0813 5327 6985; Jl Pantai Banyualit; mains from 40,000Rp; ⊙10am-10pm) Near the beach, this small cafe serves a fine grilled-seafood platter (which was probably caught by the guy next to you). There's live acoustic music many nights; a few other tasty cafes are nearby.

Bakery Lovina
CAFE $$

(☑0362-42225; Jl Raya Lovina; mains 80,000-150,000Rp; ⊙7am-7pm; ✸🖾) Enjoy Lovina's best cup of coffee amid groceries at this upmarket deli a short walk from the centre. The croissants and German breads are baked fresh daily, and there are good fresh meals, including European-style breakfasts. The lunch menu is long.

Kalibukbuk

★ Global Village Kafe
CAFE $

(☑0362-41928; Jl Raya Lovina; mains from 25,000Rp; ⊙8am-10pm; 🖾) Che Guevara, Mikhail Gorbachev and Nelson Mandela are just some of the figures depicted in the paintings lining the walls of this artsy cafe. The baked goods, fruit drinks, pizzas, breakfasts, Indo classics and much more are excellent. There are free book and DVD exchanges, plus a selection of local handicrafts. Profits here go to a foundation that funds local healthcare.

Akar
VEGETARIAN $

(☑0817 972 4717; Jl Bina Ria; mains 40,000-65,000Rp; ⊙7am-10pm; 🖾🖾) 🍃 The many shades of green at this vegetarian cafe aren't just for show. They reflect the earth-friendly ethics of the owners. Enjoy organic smoothies, house-made gelato, and fresh and tasty international dishes, such as char-grilled aubergine filled with feta and chilli.

Warung Barcelona
BALINESE $

(☑0362-41894; Jl Mawar; mains from 40,000Rp; ⊙8am-9pm; 🖾) Despite the vaguely Catalan name, this family-run restaurant has an ambitious and good Balinese menu. Choose a table on the open-air terrace and order *babi guling* (suckling pig). There are usually several seafood specials.

Night Market
BALINESE $

(Jl Raya Lovina; mains from 20,000Rp; ⊙5-11pm) Lovina's night market is a good choice for fresh and cheap local food. Each year it adds a few more interesting stands. Try the *piseng goreng* (fried bananas).

★ Jasmine Kitchen
THAI $$

(☑0362-41565; Gang Binaria; mains 45,000-80,000Rp; ⊙11am-10pm; 🖾) The Thai fare at this elegant two-level restaurant is excellent. The menu is long and authentic, and the staff are gracious. Try the homemade ice cream for dessert and enjoy it to the sounds of soft jazz. You can refill water bottles here for 2000Rp. The ground-floor coffee bar brews excellent drinks.

Seyu   JAPANESE $$
(✆0362-41050; www.seyulovina.com; Gang Bina-ria, Kalibukbuk; dishes from 50,000Rp; ⊗11am-10pm; ✆) This authentic Japanese place has a skilled sushi chef and a solid list of fresh nigiri and sashimi choices. The dining room is suitably spare and uncomplicated.

Sea Breeze Café   INDONESIAN $$
(✆0362-41138; off Jl Bina Ria, Kalibukbuk; mains from 45,000Rp; ⊗8am-10pm; ✆) Right by the beach, this breezy cafe is the best – and most intimate – of the beachside choices, especial-ly since a recent stylish makeover. The Indo-nesian and Western dishes are well-present-ed, as are the excellent breakfasts. The 'royal seafood platter' is like an entire fish market on a plate. The peanuts served with drinks are among Bali's best.

My Greek Taverna   GREEK $$
(✆0362-339 1503; Jl Bina Ria; mains 70,000-165,000Rp; ⊗5pm-midnight) Why go to Mykonos when you can go to Lovina? An expat Greek who's been on Bali for 40 years runs this au-thentic taverna. From the dolmades to the souvlaki to the moussaka, the dishes are spot on. Even better, service is smooth.

✕ Around Lovina

★Buda Bakery   BAKERY, CAFE $$
(✆0812 469 1779; off Jl Damai; mains 50,000-120,000Rp; ⊗8am-9pm) North Bali's best bak-ery has a huge array of breads, cakes and other treats produced fresh daily. However, the real reason to make the 10-minute walk here from Jl Raya Lovina is for the upstairs cafe, which does simple yet superlative In-donesian and Western fare. Note that the baked goods often sell out fast.

Spice Beach Club   INTERNATIONAL $$
(✆0851 0001 2666; www.spicebeachclubbali. com; off Jl Raya Lovina; mains 70,000-150,000Rp; ⊗kitchen 9-11am, bar to 12.30am; ✆) Mirrored shades are de rigueur at this stylish hang-out on a nice patch of beach. There's a whiff of Cannes about the rows of beach loungers backed by a pool. The menu ranges from burgers to seafood while the bar list is long. House music, lockers and showers are some of the amenities.

Tanjung Alam   SEAFOOD $$
(✆0362-41223; Jl Raya Lovina; meals 30,000-80,000Rp; ⊗9am-10pm; ✆) You'll see the fra-grant column of smoke rising through the palms before you find this entirely open-air waterfront restaurant where grilled seafood is king. Settle back at one of the tables in the long shady pavilions, let the gentle lapping of the nearby waves soothe you, and enjoy an affordable feast. It's 1.2km west of the centre.

★Damai   FUSION $$$
(✆0362-41008; www.thedamai.com; Jl Damai; 3-course meals from 470,000Rp; ⊗noon-2pm & 5-9pm, from 11am Sun; ✆) Enjoy the renowned organic restaurant at the boutique hotel in the hills behind Lovina. Tables enjoy views across the north coast. The changing menu draws its fresh ingredients from the hotel's organic farm and the local fishing fleet. Dishes are artful and the wine list one of the best in Bali. Sunday brunch is popular. Call for pick-up.

♟ Drinking & Nightlife

Many of Lovina's eateries are also fine for a drink, especially those on the beach. There's a clutch of similar cafes good for a sunset Bintang at the end of Jl Mawar. There's a compact nightlife zone in Kalibukbuk.

Pashaa   CLUB
(Jl Raya Lovina, Kalibukbuk; ⊗9pm-late) A small but high-concept club near the centre; DJs from around the island mix it up while bands play on and on.

Poco Lounge   BAR
(✆0362-41535; Jl Bina Ria, Kalibukbuk; ⊗2pm-2am; ✆) Cover bands perform nightly at this popular bar-cafe. Classic traveller fare is served at tables open to street life at the front and the river at the back.

Kantin 21   BAR
(✆0362-343 5635; Jl Raya Lovina, Kalibukbuk; ⊗11pm-late; ✆) The place to head for a night out on 'the town', this open-air venue has a long drinks list, nonstop 'thump, thump, thump', fresh juices and a few local snacks. On many nights, a local band plays after 9pm.

ℹ Getting There & Away

BUS & BEMO
To reach Lovina from south Bali by public trans-port, take a bus from Denpasar to the Sangket terminal in Singaraja. Once there take a bemo to Singaraja's Banyuasri terminal. Finally, get

another bemo to the Lovina area. This will take much of a day.

Regular bemos go from Singaraja's Banyuasri terminal to Kalibukbuk (about 7000Rp) – you can flag them down anywhere on the main road.

If you're coming by long-distance bus from the west, you can ask to be dropped off anywhere along the main road.

TOURIST SHUTTLE
Perama (☑ 0362-41161; www.peramatour.com; Jl Raya Lovina, Anturan) buses stop in Anturan. Passengers are then ferried to other points on the Lovina strip (15,000Rp). There's a daily bus to/from the south, including Kuta, Sanur and Ubud (all 125,000Rp).

ⓘ Getting Around

The Lovina strip is *very* spread out, but you can easily travel back and forth on bemos (7000Rp).

West of Lovina

The main road west of Lovina passes temples, farms and towns while it follows the thinly developed coast. You'll see many vineyards, where the grapes work overtime producing the sugar used in Bali's very sweet local vintages.

⊙ Sights

Air Terjun Singsing   WATERFALL
About 5km west of Lovina, a sign points to Air Terjun Singsing (Daybreak Waterfall), and 1km from the main road there's a warung on the left and a car park on the right. Walk past the warung and along the path for about 200m to the lower falls. The waterfall isn't huge, but the pool underneath is ideal for swimming, though not crystal-clear. The water, cooler than the sea, is very refreshing.

Clamber further up the hill to another, slightly bigger fall, **Singsing Dua**. It has a mud bath that is supposedly good for the skin (we'll let you decide about this). These falls also cascade into a deep swimming pool.

The area is thick with tropical forest and makes a nice day trip from Lovina. The falls are more spectacular in the wet season (October to March), and may be just a trickle at other times.

Brahma Vihara Arama   BUDDHIST MONASTERY
Bali's single Buddhist monastery is only vaguely Buddhist in appearance, with colourful decorations, a bright orange roof and statues of Buddha – it also has very Balinese decorative carvings and door guardians plus elaborately carved dark stones. It is quite a handsome structure in a commanding location, with views that reach down into the valley and across rice fields to the sea. You should wear long pants or a sarong, which can be hired for a small donation.

The monastery does not advertise any regular courses or programs, but visitors are more than welcome to meditate in special rooms. The temple is 3.3km off the main road – take the obvious turn-off in Dencarik.

⚡ Activities

Air Panas Banjar   HOT SPRINGS
(adult/child 10,000/5000Rp; ⊙ 8am-6pm) These hot springs percolate amid lush tropical plants. Eight fierce-faced carved stone *naga* pour water from a natural hot spring into the first bath, which then overflows (via the mouths of five more *naga*), into a second, larger pool. In a third pool, water pours from 3m-high spouts to give you a pummelling massage. The water is slightly sulphurous and pleasantly steamy (about 38°C).

You must wear a swimsuit and you shouldn't use soap in the pools, but you can use an adjacent outdoor shower. You can relax here for a few hours and have lunch at the cafe, or even stay the night.

From the bemo stop on the main road to the hot springs you can take an *ojek* (motorcycle that takes passengers); going back is a 2.4km downhill stroll.

🛏 Sleeping

Pondok Wisata Grya Sari   GUESTHOUSE $
(☑0362-92903; Jl Air Panas Banjar; r incl breakfast from 320,000Rp) In a verdant setting on a hillside 100m from Air Panas Banjar, the 12 rooms at Pondok Wisata Grya Sari have a timeless charm. The furniture and the decor haven't changed in decades, but more importantly nor has the great welcome. The setting is verdant and hikes into the surrounding densely grown countryside can be organised.

Seririt & Around

Seririt is a junction for roads that run south through the central mountains to Munduk or to Pupuan and west Bali via the beautiful Antosari road or an equally scenic road to Pulukan.

The **market** in the centre of town is renowned for its many stalls selling supplies for offerings. It also has ATMs.

Some 10km west of Seririt at Celukan-bawang you won't be able to miss a shock-ingly huge new power plant being built as a joint venture with China. Public details have been few, but it's designed to burn Chinese coal arriving on large ships at the new port.

🛏 Sleeping

Some 2km west of Seririt on Jl Singaraja–Gilimanuk, a smaller road, Jl Ume Anyar, runs north towards the narrow beaches and passes several secluded small resorts.

Mayo Resort   RESORT $$$
(📞 0811 380 0500; www.mayoresort.com; Jl Ume Anyar; r from 2,000,000Rp; ❄ 🛜 ☷) Rare for Bali, this small waterfront resort has a refreshing light-blue-and-white colour scheme. There are eight large units in a two-storey main building, each with a large terrace. And should you need it, there's a massage pavilion near the narrow beach. It is about 200m past Zen Resort Bali, 3km northwest of Seririt.

Zen Resort Bali   BOUTIQUE HOTEL $$$
(📞 0362-93578; www.zenresortbali.com; Jl Ume Anyar; r incl breakfast from US$150; ❄ 🛜 ☷) The name says it all, albeit very calmly. Yoga and a lavish spa figure prominently in the lifestyle at this resort devoted to your inter-nal and mental well-being. The 26 villas in bungalow-style units have a minimalist look designed to not tax the synapses, gardens are dotted with water features and the beach is 200m away. It's 600m off the main road.

Pemuteran

This popular oasis in the northwest corner of Bali has a number of artful resorts set on a little dogbone-shaped bay that's alive with lo-cal life such as kids playing soccer until dark. Pemuteran offers a real beach getaway. Most people dive or snorkel the underwater won-ders at nearby Pulau Menjangan while here.

The busy Singaraja–Gilimanuk road is the town's spine and ever more businesses aimed at visitors can be found along it. De-spite its popularity, Pemuteran's community and tourism businesses have forged a sus-tainable vision for development that should be a model for the rest of Bali.

◉ Sights

Pemuteran Beach   BEACH
The grey-brown sand is a little thin and defi-nitely not powdery but you can't beat the set-ting. The blue waters and surrounding green hills make for a beautiful scene, especially when crimson and orange join the colour palette at sunset. Strolling the beach is popu-lar, as you'd expect. The little fishing village is interesting; walk around to the eastern end of the dogbone to escape a lot of the develop-ment. Look for various traditional-style boats being built on the shore.

Proyek Penyu   HATCHERY
(Project Turtle; 📞 0362-93001; www.reefseenbali.com; Reef Seen; adult/child 25,000Rp/free; ⊘8am-5pm) 🐢 Pemuteran is home to the nonprofit Proyek Turtle, run by Reef Seen Divers' Re-sort. Turtle eggs and small turtles purchased from locals are looked after here until they're ready for ocean release. Thousands of turtles have been released since 1994. You can visit the small hatchery and make a donation to sponsor and release a tiny turtle. It's just off the main road, along the beach just east of Taman Selini Beach Bungalows.

Pulaki   VILLAGE
Pulaki is famous for its grape vines (Bali's Hattan Wines owns many), watermelons and for **Pura Pulaki**, a coastal temple that was completely rebuilt in the early 1980s, and is home to a large troop of monkeys. The area is also known for troops at a nearby army base. It's an easy walk from Pemuteran.

🏃 Activities

Extensive coral reefs are about 3km off-shore. Coral closer in is being restored as part of the Bio Rocks project. **Diving** and **snorkelling** are universally popular and are offered by dive shops and hotels. Snorkelling gear rents from 40,000Rp. The bay close in has a depth of under 15m, so shore diving is popular, especially at night.

★ Reef Seen Divers' Resort   DIVING
(📞 0362-93001; www.reefseenbali.com; 2-tank dives from 1,200,000Rp) Right on the beach in a large compound, Reef Seen is a PADI dive centre and has a full complement of class-es. It also offers **pony rides** on the beach for kids (from 200,000Rp for 30 minutes). Some dive packages include accommoda-tion at the dive complex. The company is active in local preservation efforts.

Garden of the Gods   DIVING
Out in Pemuteran Bay, you can make like Indiana Jones underwater at this intriguing dive site. More than 30 statues and sculp-tures have been erected on the sea floor

about 400m offshore. Shiva is at the centre and various Balinese gods and icons surround him.

Bali Diving Academy DIVING

(☎ 0361-270252; www.scubali.com; Beachfront, Taman Sari Bali Resort; Pulau Menjangan dives from 1,100,000Rp) The well-respected Bali-wide dive company has a shop right on the sand on the bay. It's near the Bio Rocks info booth. Ask about some of the lesser-known Menjangan dive sites.

Easy Divers DIVING

(☎ 0813 5319 8766; www.easy-divers.eu; Jl Singaraja-Gilimanuk; introductory dive from €55) Easy Divers' founder, Dusan Repic, has befriended many a diver new to Bali, and this shop is well recommended. It's on the main road near Taman Selini and Pondok Sari hotels.

🛌 Sleeping

Pemuteran has one of the nicest selections of beachside hotels in Bali plus a growing number of budget guesthouses. Many have a sense of style and all are low-key and relaxed, with easy access to the beach.

Some of the hotels are accessed directly off the main road, while others are off small roads that run either to the bay or south towards the mountains.

Double You Homestay GUESTHOUSE $

(☎ 0813 3842 7000; www.doubleyoubali.com; off Jl Singaraja-Gilimanuk; r incl breakfast from 360,000Rp; ❄ 🛜) On a small lane south of the main road, this stylish guesthouse is a good example of the many well-priced new accommodations springing up in Pemuteran. The four immaculate units are set in a flower-filled garden and have hot water and other comforts.

Bali Gecko Homestay GUESTHOUSE $

(☎ 0852 5301 5928; bali.gecko@ymail.com; Desa Pemuteran; r 300,000-400,000Rp; ❄ 🛜) About 500m west of Pemuteran's main strip and another 200m north off the main road, this family-run guesthouse is isolated. You can walk to a quiet part of the beach along a short trail or ascend a nearby hill for great views. The four rooms (some with air-con) are very simple.

Taruna GUESTHOUSE $

(☎ 0813 3853 6318; http://tarunapemuteran.com; Jl Singaraja-Gilimanuk; r incl breakfast fan/air-con 300,000-700,000Rp; ❄ 🛜 🏊) On the beach side of the main road and just a short walk from the sand, this professionally run place has nine well-designed rooms on a long, narrow site.

BIO ROCKS: GROWING A NEW REEF

Pemuteran is set among a fairly arid part of Bali where people have always had a hard-scrabble existence. In the early 1990s tourist operators began to take advantage of the excellent diving in the area. Locals who'd previously been scrambling to grow or catch something to eat began getting language and other training to welcome people to what would become a collection of resorts.

But there was one big problem: dynamite and cyanide fishing plus El Niño warming had bleached and damaged large parts of the reef.

A group of local hotels, dive-shop owners and community leaders hit upon a novel solution: grow a new reef using electricity. The idea had already been floated by scientists internationally, but Pemuteran was the first place to implement it on a wide – and hugely successful – scale.

Using local materials, the community built dozens of large metal cages that were placed out along the threatened reef. These were then hooked to very low-wattage generators on land (you can see the cables running ashore near the Taman Sari hotel). What had been a theory became a reality. The low current stimulated limestone formation on the cages which in turn quickly grew new coral. All told, Pemuteran's small bay is getting new coral (aka Bio Rocks) at five to six times the rate it would take to grow naturally.

The results are win-win all around. Locals and visitors are happy and so are the reefs; the project has gained international attention and awards. The collaborative local group, the Pemuteran Foundation (www.pemuteranfoundation.com/GBpag1pf.html), has an info booth with a sign reading 'Bio Rocks Reef Gardeners' on the beach by Pondok Sari. Info on their work is in most local resort lobbies. Note their list of rules for swimming in the bay, including not standing on coral, not taking coral and shells and not feeding the fish.

ⓘ ACCESSING PULAU MENJANGAN

With its great selection of lodgings, Pemuteran is the ideal base for diving and snorkelling Pulau Menjangan. Banyuwedang's harbour is just 7km west of town, so you have only a short ride before you're on a boat for the relaxing and pretty 30-minute journey to Menjangan. Dive shops and local hotels run snorkelling trips that cost US$35 to US$60; two-tank dive trips from US$80.

Some tours to Menjangan leave by boat right from Pemuteran Beach; this is best. Other trips involve a car ride and transfer at Banyuwedang.

★ Taman Selini Beach Bungalows   BOUTIQUE HOTEL $$
(☎0362-94746; www.tamanselini.com; Jl Singaraja-Gilimanuk; r incl breakfast 1,200,000-3,100,000Rp; ❄️🛜🏊) The 11 bungalows here recall an older, refined Bali, from the quaint thatched roofs down to the antique carved doors and detailed stonework. Rooms, which open onto a large garden running down to the beach, have four-poster beds and large outdoor bathrooms. The outdoor daybeds can be addictive. It's immediately east of Pondok Sari hotel, on the beach and off the main road.

★ Taman Sari Bali Resort   HOTEL $$
(☎0362-93264; www.tamansaribali.com; r incl breakfast from 550,000Rp, villas from 1,400,000Rp; ❄️@🛜🏊) Off a small lane, traditional-style rooms are set in gorgeous bungalows that feature intricate carvings and traditional artwork inside and out. The resort is located on a long stretch of quiet beach on the bay, and is part of the reef restoration project. Newer rooms are roomy and have views of the bay; a nearby compound holds large and lavish villas. Book ahead for beachside dinners.

Kubuku Ecolodge   GUESTHOUSE $$
(☎0362-343 7302; www.kubukuhotel.com; Jl Singaraja-Gilimanuk; r incl breakfast with fan/air-con from 350,000/450,000Rp; ❄️🛜) Modern Kubuku has a smallish pool with a bar and an inviting patch of lawn. The 14 comfortable rooms are decent value, and the restaurant serves tasty organic meals. The compound is down a lane on the mountain side of the main road.

Jubawa Homestay   GUESTHOUSE $$
(☎0362-94745; www.jubawa-pemuteran.com; r incl breakfast 400,000-800,000Rp; ❄️🛜🏊) One of Pemuteran's originals, Jubawa is a rather plush midrange choice. The 24 rooms are set in expansive gardens around a pool. The popular cafe-bar serves Balinese and Thai food. It's on the south side of the main road, near the large Matahari Beach Resort.

★ Matahari Beach Resort   RESORT $$$
(☎0362-92312; www.matahari-beach-resort.com; Jl Singaraja-Gilimanuk; r from 3,000,000Rp; ❄️🛜🏊) This lovely beachside resort, on the quieter east end of the bay, is set in spacious and verdant grounds. Widely spaced bungalows are works of traditional art. Common areas include a library and other luxuries. The spa is elegant and the beachside bar a good place for a pause as you explore the bay.

Puri Ganesha Villas   BOUTIQUE HOTEL $$$
(☎0362-94766; www.puriganesha.com; villas from US$550; ❄️@🛜) These four two-storey villas are on sweeping grounds; each has a unique style that mixes antiques with silks and relaxed comfort. Outside the air-con bedrooms, life is in the open air, including at your private pool. Dine in the small restaurant (it is a member of Slow Food Bali) or in your villa. It's located on the western point of the bay.

Pondok Sari   HOTEL $$$
(☎0362-94738; www.pondoksari.com; Jl Singaraja-Gilimanuk; r incl breakfast €70-210; ❄️🏊) There are 36 rooms here set in densely planted gardens that assure privacy. The pool is down by the beach; the cafe has sweet water views through the trees. Traditional Balinese details abound; bathrooms are open-air and a calling card for the stone-carvers. Deluxe units have elaborate stone tubs among other details. The resort is just off the main road.

Amertha Bali Villas   HOTEL $$$
(☎0362-94831; www.amerthabalivillas.com; Jl Singaraja-Gilimanuk; incl breakfast r 1,200,000-5,000,000Rp; ❄️🛜🏊) A slightly older resort with spacious grounds, the beachfront Amertha benefits from having large mature trees that give it that timeless tropical feel. Rooms are large; the 15 villas are sizeable, with a lot of natural wood and spacious covered patios. All have plunge pools.

✕ Eating

Joe's   INDONESIAN $
(☎0852 3739 0151; Jl Singaraja-Gilimanuk; mains from 40,000Rp; ⏱11am-midnight) The closest thing Pemuteran has to a party bar, Joe's has a dash of vintage style. Enjoy a seafood meal

DIVING & SNORKELLING PULAU MENJANGAN

Bali's best-known underwater attraction, Pulau Menjangan is ringed by over a dozen superb dive sites. The experience is excellent – iconic tropical fish, soft corals, great visibility (usually), caves and spectacular drop-offs. Lacy sea fans and various sponges provide both texture and myriad hiding spots for small fish that together form a colour chart for the sea. Few can resist the silly charms of parrotfish and clownfish. Among larger creatures, you may see whales, whale sharks and manta rays.

Of the named sites, most are close to shore and suitable for snorkellers or diving novices. But you can also venture out to where the depths turn black as the shallows drop off in dramatic cliffs, a magnet for experienced divers, who can choose from eight walls here.

This uninhabited island boasts what is thought to be Bali's oldest temple, **Pura Gili Kencana**, dating from the 14th century and about 300m from the pier. It has a huge Ganesha (elephant-headed Hindu deity) at the entrance. You can walk around the island in about an hour; unfortunately, the beaches often have trash problems.

Practicalities

Divers can customise their experience, although it often begins at an extraordinary 30m wall near the south side jetty. Snorkellers, however, may find themselves conveyed past the underwater beauty by guides who do this day-in and day-out and are just as happy to go home. This can happen with both top-end hotel-sponsored tours and the boats from Banyuwedang and Labuhan Lalang. Tips to maximise what will likely be a highlight of your Bali trip include the following:

➡ Boats often tie up to the jetty at Pulau Menjangan. The wall here – which rewards both divers and snorkellers – is directly out from the shore. Currents tend to flow gently southwest (the shore is on your right) so you can just literally go with the flow and enjoy the underwater spectacle. The richly rewarding north side of the island is another place where boats stop.

➡ For jetty stops, your guide may try to get you to swim back to the boat along the less-interesting bleached coral near the shore; this turns out to be for their convenience. Instead, suggest that the boat come down and pick you up when you're ready, thus avoiding the swim against the current followed by downtime at the jetty. The jetty wall extends far to the southwest and gets more pristine and spectacular as you go.

➡ North of the jetty, you can snorkel from shore and cover the sites in a big circle.

➡ Although the jetty area on the south side of the island is spectacular, most boat operators will take you there simply because it's the closest to the harbours and saves them fuel. The north side is also spectacular and is the best place to go midday. The coral is more varied here and there are turtles. **Mangrove Point** is an excellent snorkelling area.

➡ In the west, **Coral Gardens** is a fine spot. The **Anker Wreck**, a mysterious sunken ship, challenges even experts.

➡ Try to hover over some divers along the walls. Watching their bubbles sinuously rise in all their multihued silvery glory from the inky depths is just plain spectacular.

➡ Park fees add up: 200,000Rp per person, plus a diving/snorkelling fee 25,000/15,000Rp.

➡ If your guide really adds to your experience, tip accordingly.

➡ Friends of Menjangan (www.friendsofmenjangan.blogspot.com) has info. For updates, check its Facebook page.

Getting There & Away

The closest and most convenient dive operators are found at Pemuteran, where the hotels also arrange diving and snorkelling trips. Independent snorkellers can arrange trips from Banyuwedang and Labuhan Lalang. If you are day tripping from elsewhere on Bali, carefully find out how much time you'll be travelling each way. From Seminyak, congestion woes can make for seven or more hours on the road.

sitting around an old boat in the open-air dining room. Later, listen to diving tales great and small at the genial bar. It's in the middle of the main strip. A sign reads: 'Drinker of the month wins a bottle of whiskey'.

Bali Balance Café & Bistro   CAFE $
(☑ 0853 3745 5454; www.bali-balance.com; Jl Singaraja-Gilimanuk; mains from 30,000Rp; ⊙ 7.30am-7pm; 🛜) Excellent coffee, plus juices and tasty cakes, make this spotless cafe a good place for a pause any time. There's a short menu of sandwiches and salads, which can be enjoyed in the leafy back garden. It's on the hillside, roughly in the middle of the main strip.

La Casa Kita   PIZZA $$
(☑ 0852 3889 0253; Jl Gilimanuk-Seririk; mains 40,000-75,000Rp; ⊙ 10am-10pm) Grab a table and a cold Bintang on the outdoor lawn and choose from a menu with a classic holiday mix of thin-crust wood-fired pizzas plus Western and Indonesian dishes. It's on the main road across from Easy Divers.

ℹ Information

There are several ATMs on Pemuteran's main strip, which stretches along Jl Singaraja–Gilimanuk from the Matahari Beach Resort west to the lane down to the Taman Sari resort.

ℹ Getting There & Away

Pemuteran is served by buses on the Gilimanuk–Lovina–Singaraja run. To Pemuteran from Gilimanuk or Lovina, you should be able to negotiate a fare of around 20,000Rp. There's no stop, so just flag one down. It's a three- to four-hour drive from south Bali, either over the hills or around the west coast. A private car and driver costs 600,000Rp to either Ubud or Seminyak, among other destinations.

Banyuwedang

This mangrove-fringed cove just east of the national park is the main hub for boat trips to Pulau Menjangan.

🏃 Activities

If you are visiting Menjangan to dive or snorkel as part of a group, it's highly likely that you'll catch your boat at this bustling little harbour, which is 1.2km off Jl Singaraja–Gilimanuk.

You can also arrange your own snorkelling trips here; they typically take three hours, with one hour of that transit time.

You can leave from 8am to 2pm daily. Prices are fixed, reward groups and quickly add up: a boat (for one to 10 people) 525,000Rp; mandatory guide (for the group, many do little actual 'guiding') 200,000Rp; snorkel-set rental per person 40,000Rp; park-entrance fee per person 200,000Rp; diving/snorkelling fees 25,000/15,000Rp and insurance per person 4000Rp.

🛏 Sleeping

Mimpi Resort Menjangan   RESORT $$
(☑ 0362-94497, 0361-415020; www.mimpi.com; Pejarakan; incl breakfast r US$100-150, villas US$160-400; 🅿 @ 🛜 ≋) Near the docks for boats to Menjangan, this 54-unit resort extends down to a small, mangrove-fringed, white-sand beach. The rooms have an unadorned monochromatic motif with open-air bathrooms. Hot springs feed communal pools and private tubs in the villas. The grand villas, with a private pool and lagoon views, are a great tropical fantasy escape.

Menjangan   RESORT $$$
(☑ 0362-94700; www.themenjangan.com; Jl Raya Gilimanuk-Singaraja, Km 17; r/ste/villas incl breakfast from US$180/350/500; 🅿 🛜 ≋) Very close to Bali Barat National Park, this luxe resort is the perfect spot for those wanting to fully experience the national park. Spread over 382 hectares, it has two entities: the Monsoon Lodge has rooms set in the bush section; the Beach Villas overlook the mangroves and Pulau Menjangan. Activities include the resort's beach, horse riding, kayaking, hiking and more.

Labuhan Lalang

To catch a boat to visit or snorkel Pulau Menjangan, head to the jetty at this small harbour inside Bali Barat National Park. Prices should be the same as those at Banyuwedang. There are warungs and a pleasant beach 200m to the east.

◉ Sights

Makam Jayaprana   HINDU TEMPLE
A 20-minute walk up some stone stairs from the southern side of the road, a little west of Labuhan Lalang, will bring you to Jayaprana's grave. There are fine views to the north at the top.

Jayaprana, the foster son of a 17th-century king, planned to marry Leyonsari, a beautiful girl of humble origins. The king, however, also fell in love with Leyonsari and had Jayaprana killed. Leyonsari learned the truth of Jayaprana's death in a dream, and killed herself rather than marry the king. This Romeo and Juliet story is a common theme in Balinese folklore, and the grave is regarded as sacred, even though the ill-fated couple were not gods.

ℹ️ Information

Labuhan Lalang Information Office (Jl Singaraja-Gilimanuk; ⊙7am-7pm) Labuhan Lalang information office.

ℹ️ Getting There & Away

Buses making the run between Gilimanuk and Singaraja can be flagged down here.

Bali Barat National Park

☎ 0365

Most visitors to Bali's only national park, Bali Barat National Park (Taman Nasional Bali Barat), are struck by the mellifluous sounds emanating from the myriad birds darting among the rustling trees.

The park covers 190 sq km of the western tip of Bali. An additional 550 sq km is protected in the national park extension, as well as almost 70 sq km of coral reef and coastal waters. Together this represents a significant commitment to conservation on an island as densely populated as Bali.

It's a place where you can enjoy Bali's best diving at Pulau Menjangan, hike through forests and explore coastal mangroves.

Most of the natural vegetation in the park is not tropical rainforest, which requires year-round rain, but rather coastal savannah, with deciduous trees that become bare in the dry season. The southern slopes receive more rainfall, and so have more tropical vegetation, while the coastal lowlands have extensive mangroves.

There are more than 200 species of plants growing in the park. Local fauna includes black monkeys, leaf monkeys and macaques (seen in the afternoon along the main road near Sumber Kelompok); rusa, barking, sambar, Java and muncak (mouse) deer; and some wild pigs, squirrels, buffalo, iguanas, pythons and green snakes. There were once tigers, but the last confirmed sighting was in 1937 – and that one was shot. The birdlife is prolific, with many of Bali's 300 species found here, including the very rare Bali starling.

Just getting off the road a bit on one of the many trails transports you into the heart of nature. One discordant note: hikes in fuel

NORTH BALI BALI BARAT NATIONAL PARK

Bali Barat National Park

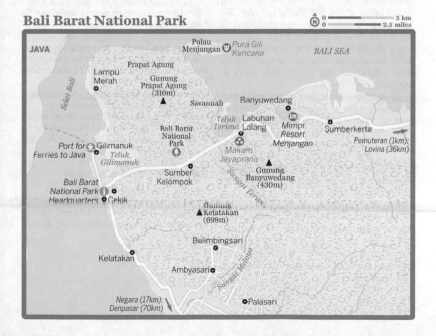

prices have seen lots of vendors along the road selling firewood taken from the forest.

🏃 Activities

By land, by boat or underwater, the park awaits exploration. However, you'll need a guide and negotiating a fee can be confounding. Virtually all costs are variable. You can arrange things at the park offices in Cekik or Labuhan Lalang.

Boat Trips

The best way to explore the mangroves of Teluk Gilimanuk (Gilimanuk Bay) or the west side of Prapat Agung is by chartering a boat. Let the fixed prices at nearby Banyuwedang be your guide to negotiating your price: a boat (for one to 10 people) 525,000Rp and mandatory guide (for the group, many do little actual 'guiding') 200,000Rp. Additionally, there is snorkel-set rental per person 40,000Rp; and park-entrance fees per person 200,000Rp, plus diving/snorkelling fees 25,000/15,000Rp.

Hiking

All hikers must be accompanied by an authorised guide. It's best to arrive the day before you want to hike and make arrangements at the park offices.

The set rates for guides in the park depend on the size of the group and the length of the hike – about 200,000Rp per hour for two people is extremely generous. Food (a small lunchbox) is included but transport is extra and all the prices are *very* negotiable. Early morning, say 6am, is the best time to start – it's cooler and you're more likely to see some wildlife.

If, once you're out, you have a good rapport with your guide, you might consider getting creative. Although you can try to customise your hike, the guides prefer to set itineraries, including some of the following sites.

From Sumber Kelompok, hikes head up **Gunung Kelatakan** (Mt Kelatakan; 698m), then down to the main road near Kelatakan village (six to seven hours). You may be able to get permission from park headquarters to stay overnight in the forest – if you don't have a tent, your guide can make a shelter from branches and leaves, which will be an adventure in itself. Clear streams abound in the dense woods.

A three- to four-hour hike will allow you to explore the **savannah** area along the coast northwest of Teluk Terima. You have a good chance of seeing monitor lizards, barking deer and black monkeys and a very rare chance of spotting a Bali starling. It includes a motorbike ride to the trailhead and a return trip by boat.

From a trail west of Labuhan Lalang, a three- to four-hour hike exploring **Teluk Terima** (Terima Bay) starts at the mangroves. You then partially follow Sungai Terima (Terima River) into the hills and walk back down to the road along the steps at Makam Jayaprana. You might see grey macaques, deer and black monkeys.

ℹ️ Information

DANGERS & ANNOYANCES

People claiming to be guides hang around the park offices. Their legitimacy can be as hard to discern as their fees. Proffered plastic-laminated rate guides are often works of fiction. Negotiate hard. For trekking, about 200,000Rp per hour for two people is extremely generous.

TOURIST INFORMATION

The **park headquarters** (📞 0365-61060; Jl Raya Cekik; ⊙6am-6pm) at Cekik displays a topographic model of the park area, and has a little information about plants and wildlife. The Labuhan Lalang Information Office is in a hut located in the parking area where boats leave for Pulau Menjangan.

You can arrange trekking guides and permits at either office; however, there are always a few characters hanging around, and determining who is an actual park official can be like spotting a Bali starling: difficult.

The main roads to Gilimanuk go through the national park, but you don't have to pay an entrance fee just to drive through. However, any activities in the park, such as hiking or diving Menjangan, require paying the 200,000Rp park fee plus any activity fees.

ℹ️ Getting There & Away

If you don't have transport, any Gilimanuk-bound bus or bemo from north or west Bali can drop you at park headquarters at Cekik (those from north Bali can drop you at Labuhan Lalang).

West Bali

Best Places to Eat

➡ Bali Silent Retreat (p265)

➡ Sushi Surf (p267)

➡ Warung Ment Tempeh (p270)

Best Places to Sleep

➡ Bali Silent Retreat (p265)

➡ Alila Villas Soori (p265)

➡ Gajah Mina (p266)

➡ Taman Wana Villas & Spa (p269)

➡ Puri Dajuma Cottages (p268)

Why Go?

Even as development from south Bali creeps ever further west (via hot spots like Canggu), Bali's true west, which is off the busy main road from Tabanan to Gilimanuk, remains mostly little visited. It's easy to find serenity amid its wild beaches, jungle and rice fields.

On the coast, surfers hit the breaks at Balian and Medewi. Some of Bali's most sacred sites are here, from the ever-thronged Pura Tanah Lot to the lily-pad-dappled beauty of Pura Taman Ayun and on to the wonderful isolation of Pura Rambut Siwi.

The tidy town of Tabanan is at the hub of Bali's Unesco-listed *subak*, the system of irrigation that ensures everybody gets a fair share of the water. On narrow back roads you can cruise beside rushing streams with bamboo arching overhead and fruit piling up below.

When to Go

➡ The best time to visit west Bali is during the dry season from April to September, although recent weather patterns have made the dry season wetter and the wet season drier. Hiking and trekking in Taman Nasional Bali Barat is much easier when it isn't muddy, and the waters of Pulau Menjangan are at their world-class best for diving on clear days.

➡ Along the coast, the west has yet to develop a peak season – although surfing is best in months without an 'r'. Yet even in busy months you'll still find the waves less crowded than you will further south.

West Bali Highlights

1 Balian Beach (p266)
Revelling in the cool beach vibe and pounding surf visuals in a place where surfer hang-outs and stylish digs rub shoulders.

2 Pantai Medewi (p267)
Nailing the long left break at this low-key haven.

3 Pura Taman Ayun (p263)
Finding your own tranquil corner at one of Bali's most evocative temples.

4 Pura Tanah Lot (p263)
Enjoying the morning spirituality of this tourist-filled temple before it gives way to the chaos of the afternoon.

5 Pura Rambu Siwi (p269)
Feeling the serenity at this historic and important seaside temple.

6 Cemagi (p263)
Substituting the seaside temple of Pura Gede Luhur Batu Ngaus for the Tanah Lot crowds.

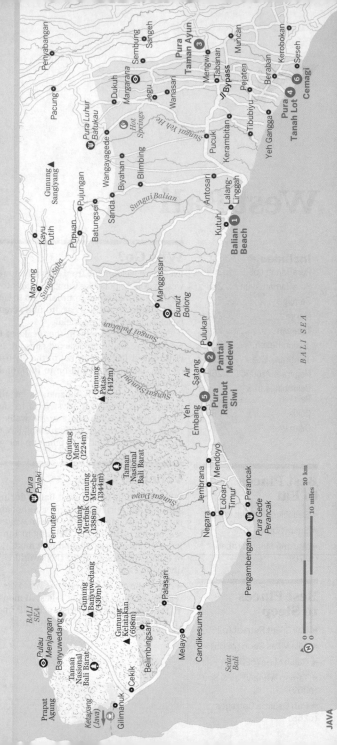

Pura Tanah Lot

Pura Tanah Lot (adult/child 60,000/30,000Rp, parking cars/motorbikes 5000/2000Rp; ⊘7am-7pm) is a hugely popular tourist destination. It does have cultural significance to the Balinese, but this can be hard to discern amid the crowds, clamour and chaos – especially for the over-hyped sunsets. It's the most visited and photographed temple in Bali; however, it has all the authenticity of a stage set – even the tower of rock that the temple sits upon is an artful reconstruction (the entire structure was crumbling) and more than one-third of the rock is artificial.

For the Balinese, Pura Tanah Lot is one of the most important and venerated sea temples. Like Pura Luhur Ulu Watu, at the tip of the southern Bukit Peninsula, and Pura Rambut Siwi to the west, it is closely associated with the Majapahit priest Nirartha. It's said that each of the sea temples was intended to be within sight of the next, so they formed a chain along Bali's southwestern coast – from Pura Tanah Lot you can usually see the clifftop site of Pura Ulu Watu far to the south, and the long sweep of seashore west to Perancak, near Negara.

But at Tanah Lot itself you may just see from one vendor to the next. To reach the temple, take the walkways that run from the vast parking lots through a mind-boggling sideshow of tatty souvenir shops down to the sea. Clamorous announcements screech from loudspeakers.

You can walk over to the temple itself at low tide, but non-Balinese people are not allowed to enter.

You won't be able to miss the looming Pan Pacific Nirwana resort with its water-sucking golf course. It has been controversial since the day it was built, because many feel its greater height shows the temple disrespect.

If coming from south Bali, take the coastal road west from Kerobokan and follow the signs. From other parts of Bali, turn off the Denpasar–Gilimanuk road near Kediri and follow the signs. During the pre- and post-sunset rush, traffic is awful with backups stretching for many kilometres.

Pura Taman Ayun

Don't miss one of the top temples on Bali, a serene place of enveloping calm. The huge royal water temple of **Pura Taman Ayun** (adult/child 20,000/10,000Rp; ⊘8am-6pm), surrounded by a wide, elegant moat, was the main temple of the Mengwi kingdom, which survived until 1891, when it was conquered by the neighbouring kingdoms of Tabanan and Badung. The large, spacious temple was built in 1634 and extensively renovated in 1937. It's a spacious place to wander around, away from crowds.

The first courtyard is a large, open, grassy expanse and the inner courtyard has a multitude of *meru* (multitiered shrines). Lotus blossoms fill the pools; the temple is part of the *subak* (complex rice-field irrigation system) sites recognised by Unesco in 2012. The market area immediately east of the temple has many good warungs (food stalls) for a simple lunch.

Cemagi

One of the waterfront areas being developed between Canggu and Tanah Lot, Cemagi is worth a visit for its picturesque temple and striking coastline.

⦿ Sights

Just north of Pura Gede Luhur Batu Ngaus is the black-sand **Pantai Mengening** beach.

Pura Gede Luhur Batu Ngaus　HINDU TEMPLE
Amid a growing number of villas, there is a dramatic outcrop of black lava rock jutting out into the pounding waves. Perched on top is the photogenic Pura Gede Luhur Batu Ngaus, which has all the classic elements of a Balinese temple and looks like a mini version of Tanah Lot, which is a further 3km northwest.

ENJOYING TANAH LOT

Why shouldn't you just skip Tanah Lot? Because it is an important spiritual site and the temple itself does have an innate beauty. The secret is to arrive before noon: you'll beat the crowds and the vendors will still be asleep. You'll actually hear birds chirping rather than buses idling and people carping. Besides, you can enjoy the sunset from many other places – like a beachfront bar south towards Seminyak.

Sleeping

Ombak Villa Cemagi VILLA $$$
(0851 0080 0800; www.ombak.co.id; Jl Pantai Mengening; villa from 3,6000,000Rp;) Typical of the luxe villas cloistered in the Cemagi area, Ombak offers lavish comfort at fairly good price, considering what you get. There are three large bedrooms, a grand pool, stylish sitting areas, a full kitchen and much more. A group can have an entire holiday without ever leaving, although the sunset views from the beach should entice.

Marga
 0361
Between the walls of traditional family compounds in the village of Marga, there are some beautifully shaded roads – but this town wasn't always so peaceful. On 20 November 1946, a much larger and better-armed Dutch force, fighting to regain Bali as a colony after the departure of the Japanese, surrounded a force of 96 independence fighters. The outcome was similar to the *puputan* (warrior's fight to the death) of 40 years earlier – Ngurah Rai, who led the resistance against the Dutch (and later had the airport named after him), was killed, along with every one of his men. There was, however, one important difference: this time the Dutch suffered heavy casualties as well, and this may have helped weaken their resolve to retake the rebellious colony.

Sights

Margarana MONUMENT
(Monumen Nasional Taman Pujaan Bangsa Margarana; off Jl Tunjuk Marga; donation 10,000Rp; 8am-5pm, museum to noon) Bali's role in Indonesia's independence struggle is commemorated at the Margarana, northwest of Marga village. Tourists seldom visit, but every Balinese

schoolchild comes here at least once, and a ceremony is held annually on 20 November. In a large compound stands a 17m-high pillar, and nearby is a **museum** with a few photos, homemade weapons and other artefacts from the conflict (Ngurah Rai's quoteworthy last letter includes the line: 'Freedom or death!'). Other than weekday-morning school groups, the site is quiet.

Behind the Margarana is a smaller compound with 1372 small stone memorials to those who gave their lives for the cause of independence – they're headstone markers in a **military cemetery**, though bodies are not actually buried here. Each memorial has a symbol indicating the hero's religion, mostly the Hindu swastika, but also Islamic crescent moons and even a few Christian crosses. Look for the memorials to 11 Japanese who stayed on after WWII and fought with the Balinese against the Dutch.

Getting There & Away

Even with your own transport, it's easy to get lost finding Marga and the memorial, so ask for directions. You can easily combine this trip with Pura Taman Ayun and the Jatiluwih rice terraces.

Tabanan

Tabanan, like most regional capitals in Bali, is a large, well-organised place. The verdant surrounding rice fields are emblematic of Bali's rice-growing traditions and are part of its Unesco recognition of this practice.

Sights

Mandala Mathika Subak MUSEUM
(Subak Museum; Jl Raya Kediri; adult/child 15,000/10,000Rp; 8am-5pm Sat-Thu, to 12.30pm Fri) You'll find this museum within a large complex devoted to Tabanan's *subak* organisations. It has displays about the

---

BALI'S UNESCO RECOGNITION

Playing a critical role in rural Bali life, the *subak* is a village association that deals with water, water rights and irrigation. With water passing through many, many scores of rice fields before it drains away for good, there is always the chance that growers near the source will be water-rich while those at the bottom could end up selling carved wooden critters at Tanah Lot. Regulating a system that apportions a fair share to everyone is a model of mutual cooperation and an insight into the Balinese character. (One of the strategies used is to put the last person on the water channel in control.)

This complex and vital social system was added to Unesco's World Heritage List in 2012. Specific sites singled out include much of the rice-growing region around Tabanan, Pura Taman Ayun, the Jatiluwih rice terraces and Danau Batur.

irrigation and cultivation of rice, and the intricate social systems that govern these. Staff will show you around; there is info on *subak*'s Unesco designation, an increasing number of placards in English and a good model showing the *subak* system in action. A new free booklet in English has a wealth of good content.

✖ Eating

Warung Nasi Ibu Agus
BALINESE $

(Jl Mawar, off Jl Dr Ir Soekarno; mains from 15,000Rp; ⊙ 7am-9pm) A *babi guling* restaurant off the main road has batches of fresh-roasted seasoned suckling pork throughout the day. It has a relaxed green-hued dining area.

Night Market
MARKET $

(Jl Gajah Mada; mains from 15,000Rp; ⊙ 5pm-midnight) Dozens of stalls offering freshly cooked food after dark.

Hardy's
SUPERMARKET

(☑ 0361-819850; ⊙ 8am-10pm) Hardy's is a huge, modern supermarket with groceries and sundries. Stock up for your villa here or get a fresh meal in the food court.

❶ Getting There & Away

Some bemos (small buses) and buses between Denpasar (Ubung terminal) and Gilimanuk stop at the terminal at the western end of Tabanan (10,000Rp).

The road to Pura Luhur Batukau and the beautiful rice terraces of Jatiluwih heads north from the centre of town.

South of Tabanan

Driving in the southern part of Tabanan district takes you though many charming villages and past a lot of vigorously growing rice. The fields are revered by many as the most productive in Bali.

◉ Sights

About 10km south of Tabanan is **Pejaten**, a centre for the production of traditional pottery, including elaborate ornamental roof tiles. Porcelain clay objects, which are made purely for decorative use, can be seen in a few workshops in the village. Check out the small showroom of **Pejaten Ceramic Art** (☑ 081 657 7073; ⊙ 9am-4pm Mon-Sat), one of several local producers. The trademark pale green pieces are lovely, and when you see the prices, you'll at least buy a toad. The

shop is close to the interesting daily **village market**.

A little west of Tabanan, a road goes 8km south via Gubug to the secluded coast at **Yeh Gangga**, where there's a good, usually quiet beach.

Further west of Tabanan on the main road, a road turns south to the coast via **Kerambitan**, a village noted for its dance troupe and musicians who perform across the south and in Ubud. Banyan trees shade beautiful old buildings, including the 17th-century palace **Puri Anyar Kerambitan** (☑ 0361-812668; Jl Raya Kerambitan; donation requested).

About 4km from southern Kerambitan is the small beachside village of **Tibubiyu**. For a lovely drive through huge bamboo, fruit trees, rice paddies and more, take the scenic road, Jl Meliling Kangin, northwest from Kerambitan to the main Tabanan–Gilimanuk road.

⮞ Sleeping

Soori Villas
VILLA $$$

(☑ 0361-894 6388; http://sooribali.com; Kelating; villas from 4,600,000Rp; ❄ ⊛ ⊛) This luxury villa compound on a (still) remote stretch of Bali's west coast has 46 very private villas, each with its own plunge pool. The accommodation has a modern minimalism and the setting is very private. The entire resort is getting a makeover during 2017. Canggu and Seminyak are 45 minutes to an hour away; the resort offers transport.

The compound is owned and designed by Singapore architect Soo K Chan and his wife, Ling Fu, who took over management of the resort in 2016 from Alila and reportedly have plans to launch their own brand.

North of Tabanan

The area north of Tabanan is a good spot to travel around with your own transport. There are some strictly B-grade attractions; the real appeal is just driving the fecund back roads where the bamboo arches temple-like over the road. And rice-field vistas await around almost every turn.

⮞ Sleeping

★ Bali Silent Retreat
BOUTIQUE HOTEL $

(☑ 0813 5348 6517; www.balisilentretreat.com; Penatahan; dm US$20, r US$40-120) Set amid gorgeous scenery, this place is just what its name says: somewhere to meditate, practise yoga, go on nature walks and more – all in total silence. The minimalist ethos stops at the food, however, which is organic and fabulous (per day US$30). It's 18km northwest of Tabanan.

Bali Homestay Program HOMESTAY $
(☑ 0817 067 1788; www.bali-homestay.com; Jegu; 2 nights all-inclusive s/d from US$185/330) 🍃 You can sample village life as part of this innovative program that places travellers in the homes of residents of the rice-growing village of Jegu, 9km north of Tabanan. The recommended full two-night package includes activities such as making offerings, village visits and cultural tours plus all meals. Book at least two weeks in advance.

Balian Beach

Ever more popular, Balian Beach is a rolling area of dunes and knolls overlooking pounding surf. It attracts both surfers and those looking to escape the bustle of south Bali.

You can wander between cafes and join other travellers for a beer, to watch the sunset and to talk surf. There are simple places to rent boards along the black-sand beach, while nonsurfers can simply enjoy bodysurfing the wild waves.

Balian Beach is right at the mouth of the wide Sungai Balian (Balian River). It is 800m south of the town of Lalang-Linggah, which is on the main road 10km west of Antosari.

🛏 Sleeping

⭐ **Surya Homestay** GUESTHOUSE $
(☑ 0813 3868 5643; wayan.suratni@gmail.com; r incl breakfast 200,000-300,000Rp) There are five rooms in bungalow-style units at this sweet little family-run place (Wayan and Putu are charmers), which is about 200m along a small lane from the main road. It's spotless, and rooms have cold water and fans. Ask about long-term rates.

Made's Homestay HOMESTAY $
(☑ 0812 396 3335; r 150,000-200,000Rp) Three basic bungalow-style units are surrounded by banana trees back from the beach. The rooms are basic, clean, large enough to hold numerous surfboards, and have cold-water showers.

Ayu Balian HOMESTAY $
(☑ 0812 399 353; Jl Pantai Balian; r incl breakfast 100,000-325,000Rp) The 15 rooms in this slightly shambolic two-storey cold-water block look down the road to the surf. The small cafe serves crowd-pleasing fare like Oreo shakes. The friendly owner Ayu is a genuine character.

⭐ **Gajah Mina** BOUTIQUE HOTEL $$
(☑ 0812 381 1630; www.gajahminaresort.com; villas incl breakfast US$100-170; ❋ 🛜 ≋) Designed by the French architect-owner, this 11-unit boutique hotel is close to the ocean. The private, walled bungalows march out to a dramatic outcrop of stone surrounded by surf. The grounds are vast and there are little trails for wandering and pavilions for relaxing. The on-site seafood restaurant, **Naga** (mains from 70,000Rp), overlooks its own little bowl of rice terraces.

Gubug Balian Beach GUESTHOUSE $$
(☑ 0812 3963 0605; gubugbalian@gmail.com; Jl Pantai Balian; r 350,000-720,000Rp; ❋ 🛜) On a spacious site close to the beach are 10 rooms, some of which have views down the lane to the surf. The cheapest rooms are fan and cold-water only.

Pondok Pisces GUESTHOUSE $$
(☑ 0813 3879 7722, 0361-780 1735; www.pondokpiscesbali.com; Jl Pantai Balian; r 420,000-1,100,000Rp; 🛜) You can certainly hear the sea at this tropical fantasy of thatched cottages and flower-filled gardens. There are 10 rooms; those on the upper floor have large terraces with surf views. In-house **Tom's Garden Cafe** (mains 40,000Rp to 80,000Rp) has grilled seafood and surf views.

Pondok Pitaya GUESTHOUSE $$
(☑ 0819 9984 9054; www.pondokpitaya.com; Jl Pantai Balian; r incl breakfast US$60-120; 🛜 ≋) With a spray-scented location right on wave-tossed Balian Beach, this complex features an eclectic range of rooms: from vintage Indonesian buildings (including a 1950 Javanese house and an 1860 Balinese alligator hunter's shack) to more modest accommodation. It's a great place for families as it has a popular pool. The **cafe** (mains from 35,000Rp to 120,000Rp) serves juices, organic fare and pizzas.

✕ Eating

Tékor Bali INTERNATIONAL $
(☏0815 5832 3330; tekorbali@hotmail.com; off Jl Pantai Balian; mains from 30,000Rp; ⊘7.30am-10pm; 🛜) Down a small lane 100m back from the beach, this inviting restaurant with a grassy lawn feels a bit like you've come to a mate's backyard for a barbecue. The menu is broad, with all the usual local and surf-er favourites, and the burgers are excellent. Cocktails are well made and there's cheap Bintang on tap.

Accommodation is available in two simple rooms (350,000Rp).

★ Sushi Surf JAPANESE $$
(☏0812 3709 0980; Jl Pantai Balian; mains from 40,000Rp; ⊘10am-10pm) *The* place for a sunset cocktail and bite of sushi. The surf action is arrayed out right in front of the quirky multilevel seating area. There are specials and a broad menu that goes beyond California rolls. It's run by the Pondok Pitaya people.

❶ Getting There & Away

Because the main west Bali road is usually jammed with traffic, Balian Beach is often at least a two-hour drive from Seminyak or the airport (55km). A car and driver will cost about 600,000Rp for a day trip. You can also get a bus (20,000Rp) going to Gilimanuk from Denpasar's Ubung terminal and be dropped off at the road entrance, which is 800m from the beach places.

Jembrana Coast

About 34km west of Tabanan you cross into Bali's most sparsely populated district, Jembrana. The main road follows the south coast most of the way to Negara. There's some beautiful scenery and little tourist development, with the exception of the surfing action at Medewi. At Pulukan you can turn north and enjoy a remote and scenic drive to north Bali.

Once capital of the region, Jembrana is the centre of the gamelan *jegog*, a gamelan using huge bamboo instruments that produces a low-pitched, resonant sound. Performances often feature gamelan groups engaging in a musical contest. Your best bet to hear this music is at a local festival. Have your driver or another local ask around to see if one is on while you're there.

Medewi

✓0365
On the main road, a large sign points down the short paved road (200m) to the surfing mecca of **Pantai Medewi** and its much-vaunted *long* left-hand wave. Rides of 200m to 400m are common.

The 'beach' is a stretch of huge, smooth grey rocks interspersed among round black pebbles. Think of it as free reflexology. Cattle graze by the shore, paying no heed to the spectators watching the action out on the water. There are a few guesthouses plus a couple of surf shops (board rental from 100,000Rp per day).

Medewi proper is a classic market town with shops selling all the essentials of west Bali life.

🛏 Sleeping

You'll find accommodation along short little Jl Pantai Medewi, which runs down to the surf break. Other lanes, about 2km in either direction of the main surf break, have isolated guesthouses. You'll want at least a motorbike for these.

Surf Villa Mukks GUESTHOUSE $
(☏0812 397 3431; www.surfvillamukks.com; Pulukan; r incl breakfast with fan/air-con 250,000/400,000Rp; ❄🛜) About 900m east of the Medewi surf break at Pulukan, this Japanese-owned guesthouse has modern rooms overlooking rice fields and distant surf. It's a chilled spot where some rooms have large bamboo blinds instead of doors. It rents boards and offers surf lessons.

Warung Gede & Homestay GUESTHOUSE $
(☏0812 397 6668; r from 150,000Rp) From the simple open-air cafe (open 6am to 10pm; meals from 20,000Rp) you can watch the breaks and enjoy basic Indonesian fare as well as good breakfasts. Rooms are surfer-simple: cold water and fans.

Mai Malu GUESTHOUSE $
(☏0819 1617 1045; maimalu.medewi@yahoo; off Tabanan-Gilimanuk Rd; r from 150,000Rp; 🛜) Near the highway on the Medewi side road, Mai Malu is a popular (and almost the only) hang-out. It serves crowd pleasing pizza, burgers and Indonesian meals in its modern, breezy upstairs eating area (mains from 35,000Rp). Rooms have the basics plus fans.

★ **Puri Dajuma Cottages**   HOTEL **$$**
(☎ 0361-813230, 0811 388 709; www.dajuma.com; cottages from 1,200,000Rp; ❋ @ 🛜 🛋) Coming from the east on the main road, you won't be able to miss this seaside resort, thanks to its prolific signage. Happily, the 20 cottages actually live up to the billing. Each has private garden, hammock, ocean view and walled outdoor bathroom. The Medewi surf break is 2km west.

ℹ️ Getting There & Away

Medewi Beach is 75km from the airport. A car and driver will cost about 650,000Rp for a day trip. You can also get a bus (25,000Rp) going to Gilimanuk from Denpasar's Ubung terminal and be dropped off at the road entrance.

Negara & Around

☑ 0365

Set amid the broad and fertile flatlands between the mountains and ocean, Negara is a tidy, prosperous town and a useful pit stop. Although it's a district capital, there's not much to see, until the town springs to life for the region's famous **bull races**. You can see bull-race practices Sunday mornings at a football field near Delod Berawan. To reach the area, turn off the main Gilimanuk–Denpasar road at Mendoyo and go south to the coast, which has a black-sand beach and irregular surf.

At the southern fringe of Negara, **Loloan Timur** is a largely Bugis community (originally from Sulawesi) that retains 300-year-old houses on stilts. Look for a few distinctive houses on stilts, some decorated with wooden fretwork.

Perancak is the site of Nirartha's arrival in Bali in 1546, commemorated by a limestone temple, **Pura Gede Perancak**. Ignore the sad little zoo nearby and go for a walk along the fishing harbour.

✖️ Eating

Hardy's Department Store   SUPERMARKET
(☎ 0365-40709; Jl Ngurah Rai; ⏱ 8am-10pm) Large supermarket with a food court in the heart of Negara. The best place to stock up on goods and supplies in west Bali.

ℹ️ Information

Jembrana Government Tourist Office
(☎ 0365-41060; Jl Dr Setia Budi 1, Negara; ⏱ 9am-3pm Mon-Fri)

ℹ️ Getting There & Away

Most bemos and minibuses from Denpasar (Ubung terminal) to Gilimanuk drop you in Negara (25,000Rp).

Belimbingsari & Palasari

Two fascinating religious towns, Belimbingsari and Palasari, north of the main road are worth a detour. Christian evangelism in Bali was discouraged by the secular Dutch, but sporadic missionary activity resulted in a number of converts, many of whom were rejected by their own communities. In 1939 they were encouraged to resettle in Christian communities in the wilds of west Bali.

Palasari is home to a Catholic community, which boasts the huge Sacred Heart Catholic Church, largely made from white stone and set on a large town square. It is really rather peaceful, and with the gently

---

BULL RACES

The Negara region is famous for bull races, known as *mekepung,* which culminate in the **Bupati Cup** in Negara on the Sunday before 17 August, Indonesia's Independence Day.

The racing animals are actually the normally docile water buffalo, which charge down a 2km stretch of road or beach pulling tiny chariots. Gaily clad riders stand or kneel on top of the chariots forcing the bullocks on. The winner is not necessarily first past the post – style also plays a part and points are awarded for the most elegant runner. There is much wagering on the results.

It must be noted that Bali's bull races have been criticised by animal-welfare experts as being inhumane because of the use of spiked prods and other methods to make the animals run faster.

Important races take place during the dry season on some Sunday mornings from July to October. Races and practices are held at several sites around Perancak on the coast and elsewhere, including Delod Berawan and Mertasari.

PURA RAMBU SIWI

Picturesquely situated on a clifftop overlooking a long, wide stretch of black-sand beach, the superb temple of **Pura Rambu Siwi**, shaded by flowering frangipani trees, is one of the important sea temples of west Bali. Like Pura Tanah Lot and Pura Ulu Watu, it was established in the 16th century by the priest Nirartha, who had a good eye for ocean scenery. Unlike Tanah Lot, it remains a peaceful and little-visited place: on non-ceremony days you'll just find a couple of lonely drink vendors.

Legend has it that when Nirartha first came here, he donated some of his hair to the local villagers. The hair is now kept in a box buried in a three-tiered *meru* (multitiered shrine), the name of which means 'Worship of the Hair'. Although the main *meru* is inaccessible, you can view it easily through the gate. The entire temple is reached by an imposing set of stone stairs from the parking area.

The caretaker rents sarongs for 2000Rp and is happy to show you around the temple and down to the beach. He will then open the guestbook and request a donation – a suitable sum is about 10,000Rp (regardless of the much higher amounts attributed to previous visitors). A path along the cliff leads to a staircase down to a small and even older temple, **Pura Penataran**.

The temple is located between Air Satang and Yeh Embang, 7km west of Medewi and 48km east of Gilimanuk. The broad 500m road to the site through lovely rice fields is well signposted; look for the turn-off near a cluster of warung on the Tabanan–Gilimanuk main road.

waving palms, it feels like old missionary Hawaii rather than Hindu Bali. The church does show Balinese touches in the spires, which resemble the *meru* (multiroofed shrines) in a Hindu temple, and features a facade with the same shape as a temple gate.

Nearby **Belimbingsari** was established as a Protestant community, and now has the largest Protestant church, Pura Gereja, in Bali, although it doesn't reach for the heavens the way the Palasari church does. Still, it's an amazing structure, with features rendered in a distinctly Balinese style – in place of a church bell there's a *kulkul* (hollow tree-trunk drum used to sound a warning) like those in a Hindu temple. The entrance is through a gate in the style of an *aling aling* (guard wall), and the attractive carved angels look very Balinese. Go on Sunday to see inside.

🛏 Sleeping

⭐ **Taman Wana Villas & Spa**   BOUTIQUE HOTEL ¥¥¥
(📞 0828 9712 3456, 0361-727770; www.bali-tama-nwana-villas.com; Palasari; r US$80-280; ❄ 🐕 ⊛)
For a near-religious experience you might consider staying at this remote boutique resort, a striking 2km drive through a jungle past the Palasari church. An architectural stunner, it has 27 rooms in unusual round structures, and 'posh' only begins to describe

the luxuries available at this cloistered refuge. Views are panoramic; get a room overlooking the rice fields.

ℹ Getting There & Away

The two villages are north of the main road, and the best way to see them is on a loop with your own transport. On the main road about 17km west from Negara, look for signs for the Taman Wana Villas. Follow these for 6.1km to Palasari. From the west, look for a turn for Belimbingsari, some 20km southeast of Cekik. A good road leads to the village. Between the two towns, only divine intervention will allow you to tackle the thicket of narrow but passable lanes unaided. Fortunately directional help is readily at hand.

Cekik

At the Cekik junction one road continues west to 3km to the Gilimanuk ferry port and another heads northeast towards north Bali. All buses and bemos to and from Gilimanuk pass through Cekik.

Archaeological excavations here during the 1960s yielded the oldest evidence of human life in Bali. Finds include burial mounds with funerary offerings, bronze jewellery, axes, adzes and earthenware vessels from around 1000 BC, give or take a few centuries. Look for some of this at the Museum Manusia Purbakala Gilimanuk in Gilimanuk.

On the southern side of the junction, the pagoda-like structure with a spiral stairway around the outside is a **war memorial**. It commemorates the landing of independence forces in Bali to oppose the Dutch, who were trying to reassert control of Indonesia after WWII.

Cekik is home to the park headquarters (p260) of the Taman Nasional Bali Barat; it's just off the main road near the junction.

Gilimanuk

Gilimanuk is the terminus for ferries that shuttle back and forth across the narrow strait to Java. Most travellers to or from Java can get an onward ferry or bus straight away, and won't hang around.

◉ Sights

Stop anywhere along the north shore of town to see the huge clash of waves and currents in the strait. It's dramatic and a good reason *not* to have that dodgy curry dish if you're about to board a ferry.

Museum Manusia
Purbakala Gilimanuk   MUSEUM
(Prehistoric People Museum; ☑ 0365-61328; Jl Rajawali; suggested donation 10,000Rp; ☺ hours vary) This part of Bali has been occupied for thousands of years. The Museum Manusia Purbakala Gilimanuk is centred on a family of skeletons, thought to be 4000 years old,

which were found locally in 2004. The bare bones, as it were, museum is 500m east of the ferry port.

✖ Eating

Warung Ment Tempeh   BALINESE $
(Terminal Lama; meals from 25,000Rp; ☺ 8am-10pm) An extended family runs several neighbouring iterations of this cafe, which serves a local dish Gilimanuk is known for: *betutu* chicken, a spicy form of steamed chicken that is redolent with herbs. It is located in the former bus terminal, about 500m south of the ferry port, 50m off the main road.

ℹ Information

There is a Bank BRI ATM, a post office and a police station on Jl Raya Gilimanuk.

ℹ Getting There & Away

Frequent buses run between Gilimanuk's large depot and Denpasar's Ubung terminal (30,000Rp, three hours), or along the north-coast road to Singaraja (30,000Rp). Smaller, slightly more comfortable minibuses serve both routes for 5000Rp more.

Car ferries to and from Ketapang on Java (30 minutes, adult/child 6000/4000Rp, motorbike/car 24,000/138,000Rp) run around the clock. Their safety record has been fair at best. The pedestrian terminal is 300m north of the large bus station.

Lombok

Best Places to Eat

➡ Laut Biru Bar & Restaurant (p297)

➡ Nugget's Corner (p293)

➡ Taliwang Irama (p275)

➡ Spice (p281)

➡ Coco Beach (p282)

Best Places to Sleep

➡ Rinjani Beach Eco Resort (p283)

➡ Qunci Villas (p281)

➡ Tugu Lombok (p283)

➡ Blongas Bay Lodge (p297)

➡ Pearl Beach (p277)

➡ Sempiak Villas (p296)

Why Go?

Long overshadowed by its superstar neighbour across the Lombok Strait there's a steady hum about Lombok that catches the ear of travellers looking for something different from Bali. Blessed with exquisite white-sand beaches, epic surf, a lush forested interior, and hiking trails through tobacco and rice fields, Lombok is fully loaded with equitorial allure. Oh, and you'll probably notice mighty Gunung Rinjani, Indonesia's second-highest volcano, its summit complete with hot springs and a dazzling crater lake.

And there's much more. Lombok's southern coastline is nature on a very grand scale: breathtaking turquoise bays, world-class surf breaks and massive headlands. Development on these splendid beaches is just around the corner, but until that moment comes, they are still natural wonders to explore over much-improved roads.

If you're going to the Gilis, a Lombok stopover is a must. It's easy to get around the Lombok–Gilis–Bali triangle.

When to Go

➡ Lombok is hot, sticky and tropical, with a marked rainy season (roughly late October and April). Climbing Gunung Rinjani can be more difficult than usual at this time.

➡ The driest months coincide with the peak tourist period in July and August. You'll need to balance crowds versus ideal weather.

➡ The rainy season offers an excellent time to catch a local festival, such as the spectacular rice-throwing event called Perang Topat (held at Pura Lingsar in November or December), Peresean stick-fighting competitions (in December) or the Narmada buffalo races (in April).

Lombok Highlights

1 Tanjung Desert
(p277) Taking the ride of your life on the temperamental break at Desert Point, Bangko-Bangko.

2 Gunung Rinjani (p287)
Tackling Lombok's incomparable sacred peak (and Indonesia's second-highest volcano), which lures trekkers with a challenging climb and surreal rewards.

3 Pantai Mawan
(p296) Setting eyes on this beach for the first time might must make you gasp. But go on, gasp again as you contemplate that there are a dozen more in south Lombok just like it.

4 Sembalun Valley
(p285) Beholding the idyllic mountain splendour from this high-mountain bowl that is Lombok's own Shangri-La.

5 Gili Gede (p277)
Wandering the filigreed southwest coast and discovering offshore islands which deserve the sobriquet 'the next Gilis'.

BALI SEA

Gili Meno
Gili Air
Gili Trawangan
Gondang
Tanjung
Sire
Teluk Nare
Bangsal
Pemenang
Teluk Nare/
Teluk Kade
Mangsit
Pusuk Pass
Gunung Sabiris (865m)
Senggigi
Pantai Senggigi
Endut
Cakranegara
Ampenan
Lingsar
Pura Lingsar
Mataram
Sweta Bertais
Kediri
Ubung
Selat Lombok
Gunung Pengsong
Gerung
Bali
Tanjung Desert
Teluk Terang
Panda-nan
Tanjung Empat
Gili Asahan
Gili Gede
Lembar
Bangko Bangko
Taun
Gunung Mareje (716m)
Selegang
Labuhan Poh
Tembowong
Sekotong
Pelangan
Kali Penunjak
Montongsapah
Keling
Selong Blanak
Blongas
Sepi
Teluk Mekaki
Blongas Bay
Pengantap
Mawi
Mawi
Tampa
Cathedrals
Magnet

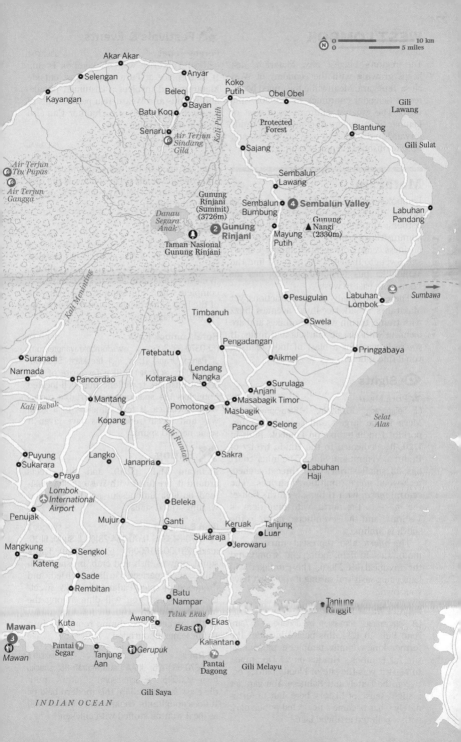

WEST LOMBOK

⏱ 0370

The region's biggest city, Mataram, just keeps growing with the economy of West Nusa Tenggara. Meanwhile the famed beach resort Senggigi continues in a 1990s time warp. The greatest allure is southwest of Lembar port, where the peninsula bends forward and back, the seas are placid, and bucolic offshore islands beckon.

Mataram

Lombok's capital is a blending sprawl of several (once separate) towns with fuzzy borders: Ampenan (the port); Mataram (the administrative centre); Cakranegara (the business centre, often called simply 'Cakra') and Sweta to the east, where you'll find the Mandalika bus terminal. It stretches for 12km from east to west.

There aren't many tourist attractions, yet Mataram's broad tree-lined avenues buzz with traffic, thrum with motorbikes and are teeming with classic markets and malls. If you're hungry for a blast of Indo realism, you'll find it here.

◉ Sights

★ Pura Meru   HINDU TEMPLE
(Jl Selaparang; 10,000Rp; ⊙ 8am-5pm) Pura Meru is the largest and second-most important Hindu temple on Lombok. Built in 1720, it's dedicated to the Hindu trinity of Brahma, Vishnu and Shiva. The inner court has 33 small shrines and three thatched, teak-wood *meru* (multitiered shrines). The central *meru*, with 11 tiers, is Shiva's house; the *meru* to the north, with nine tiers, is Vishnu's; and the seven-tiered *meru* to the south is Brahma's.

The *meru* also represent three sacred mountains, Rinjani, Agung and Bromo, and the mythical Mt Meru. The caretaker will lend you a sash and sarong if you don't have your own.

Mayura Water Palace   PARK
(Jl Selaparang; admission by donation; ⊙ 7am-7pm) Built in 1744, this palace includes the former king's family temple, a pilgrimage site for Lombok's Hindus on 24 December. In 1894 it was the site of bloody battles between the Dutch and Balinese. You can get a slight sense of history here, but unfortunately it has become a neglected public park with a polluted artificial lake.

✯ Festivals & Events

Perang Topat   CULTURAL
(⊙ Nov) This 'rice war' on Lombok is fun. It takes place at Pura Lingsar just outside Mataram and involves a costumed parade, and Hindus and Wektu Telu pelting balls of *ketupat* (sticky rice) at each other. Can also be held in December.

Peresean   CULTURAL
(⊙ Dec) Martial arts, Lombok-style. Competitors, stripped to the waist, spar with sticks and cowhide shields. The winner is the first to draw blood. It's held annually in Mataram late in the month.

🛏 Sleeping

Hotel Melati Viktor   GUESTHOUSE $
(⏱ 0370-633830; Jl Abimanyu 1; r incl breakfast 120,000-250,000Rp; ❄ 🞕) The high ceilings, 37 clean rooms and Balinese-style courtyard, complete with Hindu statues, make this one of the best-value places in town. The cheapest rooms have fans.

Hotel Lombok Raya   HOTEL $$
(⏱ 0370-632305; www.lombokrayahotel.com; Jl Panca Usaha 11; r incl breakfast 500,000-700,000Rp; ❄ 🞕 🞕) Still a favourite of old-school business travellers, this well-located hotel has 134 spacious, comfortable rooms with balconies. It feels timeless in a good way and recent renovations have given it some needed spunk.

🍴 Eating

Mataram Mall (p276), and the streets around it, are lined with Western-style fast-food outlets, Indonesian noodle bars and warungs (food stalls).

Ikan Bakar 99   SEAFOOD $
(⏱ 0370-643335, 0370-664 2819; Jl Subak III 10; mains 20,000-60,000Rp; ⊙ 11am-10pm) Think squid, prawns, fish and crab, brushed with chilli sauce, perfectly grilled or fried, and drenched in spicy Padang or sticky sweet-and-sour sauce. You will dine among the Mataram families who fill the long tables in the arched, tiled dining room. It's in a Balinese neighbourhood.

Mi Rasa   BAKERY $
(⏱ 0370-633096; Jl AA Gede Ngurah 88; snacks from 5000Rp; ⊙ 6am-10pm) Cakra's middle-class families adore this modern bakery. It does doughnuts, cookies and cakes as well as local wonton stuffed with chicken.

Mataram

Taliwang Irama (550m);
Lombok Handicraft
Centre (2km)

Kali Ancar

Rumah Sakit
Harapan Keluarga
(1.7km)

Pura
Meru

CAKRANEGARA

★ **Taliwang Irama**   INDONESIAN **$**

(☑ 0370-623163; Jl Ade Irma Suryani; mains from 20,000Rp; ☺ 11am-10pm) Excellent spicy Indonesian dishes lure in diners day in and day out. Eat in the plant-shaded courtyard or inside. As testament to the popularity, there are vendors out front. The chicken here seems even more tender and spicy than the average bird on Lombok.

🛍 Shopping

★ **Pasar Mandalika**   MARKET

(Bertais; ☺ 7am-5pm) There are no tourists at this vast market near the Mandalika bus terminal in Bertais, but it has everything else: fruit and veggies, fish (fresh and dried), baskets full of colourful, aromatic spices and grains, freshly butchered beef, palm sugar, pungent bricks of shrimp paste, and cheaper handicrafts than you will find anywhere else in west Lombok.

It's a great place to get localised after you've overdosed on the *bule* (slang for foreigner) circuit. Sundays are slow.

★ **Lombok Handicraft Centre**   ARTS & CRAFTS

(Jl Kerajinan, off Jl Diponegoro; ☺ 9am-6pm) At Sayang Sayang (2km north of Cakra), there's a wide range of small shops here; look for the arched sign over the narrow road which

Mataram

◉ **Top Sights**
1 Pura Meru D2

◉ **Sights**
2 Mayura Water Palace........................D2

🛏 **Sleeping**
3 Hotel Lombok Raya A2
4 Hotel Melati Viktor...........................B2

🍽 **Eating**
5 Ikan Bakar 99 ....B2
6 Mi Rasa...C2

🛍 **Shopping**
7 Mataram Mall A2
8 Pasar Cakranegara...........................D2

reads 'Handy Craft'. Browse crafts, including masks, textiles and ceramics from across Nusa Tenggara. This is a great place to stroll.

Pasar Cakranegara   MARKET

(cnr Jl AA Gede Ngurah & Jl Selaparang; ☺ 9am-6pm) Collection of quirky stalls, some of which sell good-quality ikat (traditional cloth), as well as an interesting food market. Think of it as a modern variation on a traditional market.

Mataram Mall
MALL

(Jl Selaparang; ⊙7am-9pm) A multistorey glitzy shopping mall with a supermarket, department stores, electronics and clothes shops, and some good restaurants.

ⓘ Information

MEDICAL SERVICES

Rumah Sakit Harapan Keluarga (✆0370-670000; www.harapankeluarga.co.id; Jl Ahmad Yani 9; ⊙24hr) The best private hospital on Lombok is just east of central Mataram and has English-speaking doctors.

ⓘ Getting There & Away

BUS & BEMO

The chaotic **Mandalika Terminal** (Jl Tuguh Faisal) is 3km from the centre and is a bus and bemo (minibus) hub. It's surrounded by the city's main market. Use the official ticket office to avoid touts. Yellow bemos shuttle to the centre (5000Rp).

Buses and bemos departing hourly from the Mandalika terminal include the following:

DESTINATION	FARE	DURATION
Airport (Damri Bus)	15,000Rp	45min
Kuta (no-change shuttle bus)	45,000Rp	1¼hr
Kuta (via Praya & Sengkol)	45,000Rp	2-3hr
Labuhan Lombok	35,000Rp	2½hr
Lembar	30,000Rp	45min
Senggigi (via Ampenan)	15,000Rp	1hr

TAXI

For a reliable metered taxi, use Blue Bird Lombok Taksi (p392).

BOAT

Should you want to sail to a far-flung Indonesian island from Lombok, you can make schedule inquiries and purchase tickets at the **local office** (✆0370-637212; Jl Industri 1; ⊙8am-noon & 1-3.30pm Mon-Thu & Sat, 8-11am Fri) for Pelni, the national shipping line.

Around Mataram

As well as Lombok's most important temple, sights around Mataram include the old port town of **Ampenan**. Although most people buzz through on their way to or from Senggigi, if you pause you'll discover a still-tangible sense of the Dutch colonial era in the tree-lined main street and the older buildings.

◉ Sights

★Pura Lingsar
HINDU TEMPLE

(off Jl Gora II; grounds free, temple admission by donation; ⊙7am-6pm) This large temple compound is the holiest in Lombok. Built in 1714 by King Anak Agung Ngurah, and nestled beautifully in lush rice fields, it's multidenominational, with a temple for Balinese Hindus (Pura Gaduh), and one for followers of Lombok's mystical take on Islam, the Wektu Telu religion.

It's just 6km northeast of Mataram in the village of Lingsar. Take a bemo from the Mandalika Terminal to Narmada, then another to Lingsar. Ask to be dropped off near the entrance to the temple complex.

Pura Gaduh has four shrines: one orientated to Gunung Rinjani (seat of the gods on Lombok), one to Gunung Agung (seat of the gods in Bali), and a double shrine representing the union between the two islands.

The Wektu Telu temple is noted for its enclosed and lily-covered pond devoted to Lord Vishnu, and for the holy eels, which can be enticed from their lair with hard-boiled eggs (available at stalls). It's considered good luck to feed them. You will be expected to rent a sash and/or sarong (or bring your own) to enter the shrines.

✸✸ Festivals & Events

Malean Sampi
CULTURAL

(⊙early Apr) Yoked buffalo race over waterlogged earth in Narmada, near Mataram on Lombok, their jockeys clinging tight. It's as dangerous, muddy and fun as it sounds.

ⓘ Getting There & Away

Having your own wheels is the best way to explore the area around Mataram. However, there are frequent bemos to Ampenan, where you can transfer to bemos to Senggigi.

Lembar

Lembar is Lombok's main port for ferries from Bali. The setting – think azure inlets ringed by soaring green hills – is stunning, but few folk stay beyond what their ferry transit requires.

Public ferries (child/adult/motorbike/car 29,000/44,000/123,000/879,000Rp, five to six hours) travel between the ferry port and Padangbai in Bali. Passenger tickets are sold near the pier and there are ATMs near the harbour entrance. Boats supposedly run 24 hours and leave about every 90 minutes, but the service can be unreliable – boats have caught on fire and run aground.

Bemo and bus connections are abundant and bemos run regularly to the Mandalika Terminal (15,000Rp). Taxis cost 80,000Rp to Mataram, and 150,000Rp to Senggigi.

Southwestern Peninsula

The sweeping coastline that stretches west of Lembar is blessed with boutique sleeps on deserted beaches and tranquil offshore islands. You can while away weeks here among the famous surf breaks, salty old mosques, friendly locals and relatively pristine islands. In fact, the buzz has started, calling the beautiful offshore islands 'the next Gilis'.

The only off-note on the landscape is the dull town of Sekotong, which you have to pass through on your way west. Otherwise, you follow the narrow coastal road along the contours of the peninsula, skirting white-sand beach after white-sand beach on your way to the village of Bangko Bangko and one of Asia's legendary surf breaks, Tanjung Desert (Desert Point), which has one of the world's longest left-hand barrels and a fantastic beach.

◉ Sights

Gili Gede   ISLAND
Of the dozen islands off the coast here, Gili Gede is a favourite. Although popular with day-tripping snorkellers and divers from across Lombok, the island itself is utterly serene and has a couple of isolated places to stay and unwind.

Gili Asahan   ISLAND
Gili Asahan is an idyllic spot: soothing winds gust, birds flutter and gather in the grass just before sunset, muted calls to prayer rumble, and the stars and moon light up the sky.

🏄 Activities

Tanjung Desert is legendary. However, non-expert surfers will find much to enjoy. As you make the drive along the coast, you'll see various water-sports vendors offering boat rides to the islands. Feel free to stop and negotiate a day out at the beaches at the offshore islands for a fee beginning at 400,000Rp. These trips can include snorkelling stops and other fun.

★ Tanjung Desert   SURFING
(Desert Point/Bangko-Bangko; access per person/vehicle 10,000/5000Rp) Often called 'the world's best wave', this famous break draws skilled surfers from around the world. Patience is a virtue as the conditions sometimes go calm for a time. But when the swells are coming in, you get very long, hollow waves that usually end in a barrel. Peak season is May to October.

🛏 Sleeping

There are a few hotels and resorts sprinkled along the northern coast of the peninsula, though the most atmospheric beaches and lodging are on the offshore islands. You'll eat where you sleep. Top-end places have dive operations.

Note that phone service at Tanjung Desert is dodgy and the area gets very crowded during peak surfing season (May to October), when you may not find room at the very basic inns. Several no-name warungs will let you crash for about 120,000Rp a night.

🛏 Mainland

Cocotino's   RESORT $$$
(📱0819 0797 2401; www.cocotinos-sekotong. com; Jl Raya Palangan Sekotong, Tanjung Empat; r/villa from US$100/275, ❄@🌐☕) This walled compound along the main road has an ocean-front location, a private beach and 36 high-quality bungalows (some with lovely outdoor bathrooms, some with sea views). It offers deals via its website. The setting is a sublime tropical idyll.

🛏 Islands

Madak Belo   BUNGALOW $
(📱0818 0554 9637; www.madak-belo.com; Gili Gede; r/bungalow from 250,000/500,000Rp, @) Here's a sensational French hippie-chic island paradise, with ooh-la-la views and three basic rooms upstairs in the main wooden and bamboo lodge. They share a bathroom and a bamboo lounge area strung with hammocks. It also has two private bungalows with queen beds and private bathrooms.

★ Pearl Beach   BUNGALOW $$
(📱0819 0724 7696; www.pearlbeach-resort.com; Gili Asahan; cottage/bungalow incl dinner from US$110; ☕) A private-island resort; cottages are simple, bamboo affairs with outdoor baths and a hammock on the porch. The 10 bungalows are chic, with polished concrete floors, soar-

ing ceilings, gorgeous outdoor baths, and fabulous daybed swings on the wooden porches. There's great diving, kayaks and more.

Kokomo Gili Gede RESORT **$$$**
(☑0819 0732 5135; http://kokomogiligede.com; Gili Gede; villas incl breakfast from 2,750,000Rp; ☞) The newest – and poshest – resort on the southwest Gilis, Kokomo has 15 large villas in a beautiful position right by the ocean. Units have fridges and other kitchen appliances. The decor picks up the stark white beauty of the sand. A stay here will be a long study in white, backed by the blue of the water.

Tanjung Desert

Desert Point Lodge BUNGALOW **$**
(☑0878 6585 5310; www.desertpointlodges.com; just east of Tanjung Desert; r from 350,000Rp) A solid choice near Tanjung Desert, with seven woven-bamboo and thatched bungalows with bamboo beds, hammocks on the porch and private baths attached. Surfing may be king here but you can also dive. Conditions, although a bit rough, are much more genteel than the shack-like places on the beach at the surf break.

Desert Point Bungalows BUNGALOW **$**
(☑0878 6585 5310; nurbaya_sari@yahoo.com; Tanjung Desert; r 300,000-400,000Rp) The most upscale place to stay right at Tanjung Desert (that's because there's a phone number you can try calling) has 10 rather shack-like bungalows. A generator provides power at certain times and there's a two-level surf-viewing platform.

✗ Eating

All the resorts have good restaurants where nonguests can enjoy meals.

At Tanjung Desert, you'll discover a strip of white sand and a row of flimsy bamboo cafes where you can scarf down simple meals, quaff cold beer and gaze out at the surf break. It's one of Lombok's highlights.

ⓘ Information

MONEY
The closest ATM is east in the ferry town of Lembar, 45km from Tanjung Desert.

ⓘ Getting There & Away

BEMO
Bemos run between Lembar and Pelangan (15,000Rp, 1½ hours) via Sekotong and Tem-

bowong every 30 minutes until 5pm. West of Pelangan transport is less regular, but the route is still served by infrequent bemos until Selegang. Private wheels are your best transport option.

CAR & MOTORCYCLE
Although winding, the road is in good shape almost until the end, when suddenly it switches to deeply rutted gravel and dirt. You can traverse it with a car or motorbike but you'll have to drive at a walking pace. After 2km you'll reach a fork; turn right for the fishing village of Bangko Bangko. Turn left for another 1km of road misery that ends at the oceanic wonders of Tanjung Desert. Your reward for enduring the horrible last 3km of road to Tanjung Desert? An entrance fee of 10,000Rp per person and 5000Rp per vehicle.

BOAT
You can take the slow public ferry from Bali to Lembar and then get ground transport or you can take the new fast boat service.

Gili Getaway (☑0813 3707 4147; http://gili getaway.com; one-way 250,000-675,000Rp) has service from Gili Gede to Gili T and Gili Air as well as Senggigi and Bali's Serangan Harbour.

TAXI BOAT
Taxi boats (per person 30,000Rp) shuttle from Tembowong on the mainland to Gili Gede. You'll see them near the Pertamina gas station. Chartered boats also connect Tembowong with the islands of Gili Gede and Gili Asahan (from 300,000Rp return).

Senggigi

Lombok's traditional tourist resort, Senggigi enjoys a fine location along a series of sweeping bays, with light-sand beaches sitting pretty below a backdrop of jungle-clad mountains and coconut palms. In the late afternoon a setting blood-red sun sinks into the surf next to the giant triangular cone of Bali's Gunung Agung.

Tourist numbers are relatively modest here and you'll find some excellent-value hotels and restaurants. Still, the tacky main strip could be more appealing, the noticeable influx of bar girls is sleazy, the influx of garish billboards is ugly and the resident beach hawkers can be over-persistent.

The Senggigi area spans 10km of coastal road; the upscale neighbourhood of Mangsit is 3km north of central Senggigi.

⊙ Sights

Pura Batu Bolong HINDU TEMPLE
(off Jl Raya Senggigi; admission by donation; ⊙7am-7pm) It's not the grandest, but Pura

Senggigi

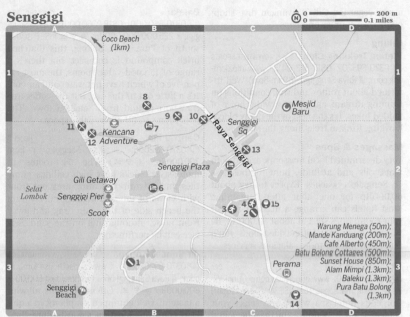

N 0 — 200 m / 0 — 0.1 miles

Coco Beach (1km)

Mesjid Baru

Senggigi Sq

JI Raya Senggigi

Kencana Adventure

Senggigi Plaza

Selat Lombok

Gili Getaway

Senggigi Pier

Scoot

Senggigi Beach

Perama

LOMBOK SENGGIGI

Warung Menega (50m);
Mande Kanduang (200m);
Cafe Alberto (450m);
Batu Bolong Cottages (500m);
Sunset House (850m);
Alam Mimpi (1.3km);
Baleku (1.3km);
Pura Batu Bolong (1.3km)

Senggigi

🟢 Activities, Courses & Tours
1 Blue Marlin	B3
2 Dream Divers	C2
3 Hallo Lombok Spa	C2
4 Rinjani Trekking Club	C2

🛏 Sleeping
5 Central Inn	C2
6 Santosa Villas	B2
7 Sonya Homestay	B2

🍽 Eating
8 Asmara	B1

🍸 Drinking & Nightlife
14 Hotel Lina	C3
15 Papaya Café	C2

🛍 Shopping
Asmara Collection	(see 8)

9 Banana Tree Cafe	B1
10 Cafe Tenda Cak Poer	B1
11 Office	A2
12 Spice	A2
13 Square	C2

Batu Bolong is Lombok's most appealing Hindu temple, and particularly lovely at sunset. Join an ever-welcoming Balinese community as they leave offerings at the 14 altars and pagodas that tumble down a rocky volcanic outcrop into the foaming sea about 2km south of central Senggigi. The rock underneath the temple has a natural hole, hence the name (*batu bolong* literally means 'rock with hole').

🏃 Activities

Snorkelling, Diving & Surfing
There's reasonable snorkelling off the point in Senggigi, 3km north of the town. You can rent gear (per day 50,000Rp) from several spots on the beach. Diving trips from Senggigi usually visit the Gili Islands.

Dream Divers   DIVING
(☏0370-693738; www.dreamdivers.com; JI Raya Senggigi; intro dives from 910,000Rp) The Senggigi office of the Gili diving original. Runs snorkelling trips out to the Gilis for 400,000Rp. It also organises activities such as Rinjani treks and runs dive courses.

Blue Marlin   DIVING
(☏0370-613 2424, 0370-693719; www.bluemarlin-dive.com; Holiday Resort Lombok, JI Raya Senggigi; single dive trips 490,000Rp) The local branch of

a well-regarded Gili Trawangan dive shop; offers dive courses and trips.

Hiking

Rinjani Trekking Club   ADVENTURE SPORTS
(☑0370-693202, 0817 573 0415; www.info2lom-bok.com; Jl Raya Senggigi; ⊙9am-8pm) Well informed about routes and trail conditions on Gunung Rinjani, and offers a wide choice of guided hikes. It's the best of the many places hawking Rinjani treks along the strip.

Massages & Spas

Very determined local masseurs, armed with mats, oils and attitude, hunt for business on Senggigi's beaches. Expect to pay about 60,000Rp for one hour after bargaining. Most hotels can arrange a masseur to visit your room; rates start at about 80,000Rp. Be warned, many of the streetside 'salons' you'll find are fronts for more salacious services.

★ Qamboja Spa   SPA
(☑0370-693800; www.quncivillas.com; Qunci Villas, Mangsit; massages from US$30; ⊙8am-10pm) Gorgeous hotel spa where you select your choice of oil depending on the effect and mood you require from your massage (uplifting, harmony...); types available include Thai, Balinese and shiatsu. They also offer yoga classes.

Hallo Lombok Spa   SPA
(☑0819 0797 6902; off Jl Raya Senggigi, Senggigi Plaza; massages from 70,000Rp; ⊙10am-9pm) An inexpensive spa with a range of scrubs, massages and treatments. The *lulur* (scrub) massage is a real treat and includes a body mask.

🛏 Sleeping

Senggigi's accommodation is very spread out. But even if you're located a few kilometres away (say, in Mangsit) you're not isolated as many restaurants offer free rides to diners and taxis are very inexpensive.

Check for off-season discounts. Note that many of Senggigi's places to stay feel like they've been unloved since the resort area's heyday in the 1990s.

🛏 Senggigi

Sonya Homestay   HOMESTAY $
(☑0813 3989 9878; Jl Raya Senggigi; r incl breakfast 100,000-200,000Rp; 🅿️🛜) A shady family-run enclave of nine very basic rooms (the cheapest are fan-only) with nice patios. It's off the road amid a small garden that is this guesthouse's best feature.

Baleku   GUESTHOUSE $
(☑0370-660 0001, 0818 0360 0001; Jl Raya Senggigi; r 225,000-300,000Rp; 🅿️🛜❄️) Set 300m south of Pura Batu Bolong, this thatched brick compound is compact, but there's a range of 15 good-value rooms, the most expensive of which have hot water and air-con. It's a little out of the way, but they offer free transport to and from Senggigi town. The pool seems to fill all available space.

Central Inn   HOTEL $
(☑0370-692006; Jl Raya Senggigi; r from 300,000Rp; 🅿️🛜❄️) The 54 rooms in motel-style blocks have high ceilings, shiny tiles and a bamboo seating area out front with views of the surrounding hills. It's on the beach side of the main drag and away from noise, although not on the sand. Service can be perfunctory.

★ Sunset House   HOTEL $$
(☑0370-692020; www.sunsethouse-lombok.com; Jl Raya Senggigi 66; r incl breakfast 600,000-800,000Rp; 🅿️🛜❄️) Offers 38 rooms, all with a tasteful, well-equipped simplicity, in a quiet ocean-front location towards Pura Batu Bolong (p278). Rooms on the upper floors have sweeping ocean views towards Bali. Wi-fi is only available in public areas. Good pool area and deck.

★ Alam Mimpi   HOTEL $$
(☑0370-617 0645; http://alammimpilombok.com; Jl Vincent Van Gogh; r incl breakfast 550,000Rp; 🅿️🛜❄️) South of the centre and inland, this modern compound actually makes the most of its quiet location. The 14 rooms surround a large pool and have balconies and terraces. The design is refreshingly modern and the upper-floor cafe has wide views. There's a shuttle to town and the beach.

Santosa Villas   RESORT $$
(☑0370-693090; http://santosalombok.com; Jl Raya Senggigi; r from 810,000Rp; 🅿️🛜❄️) The Santosa resort has comfortable accommodation ranging from 187 standard hotel rooms to high-end luxury villas set in large grounds on a curving beach with good views and a playground. It's smack in the centre of the Senggigi strip. It's a top pick among the surrounding mainstream resorts.

Batu Bolong Cottages   HOTEL $$
(☑0370-693198, 0370-693065; bbcresort_lombok@yahoo.com; Jl Raya Senggigi; r 400,000-800,000Rp; 🅿️🛜❄️) Charming two-level bungalow-style rooms by the sand are the best bets at this well-run hotel, which strad-

dles both sides of the road south of the centre. The beachfront rooms have quaint touches such as carved doors, and there's a low-key pool area. The rest of the rooms are in more standard two-storey blocks. Good breakfast.

Chandi Boutique Resort   RESORT $$$
(☑0370-692198; www.the-chandi.com; Batu Bolong; r from US$150; ✳🛜🌊) This stylish boutique hotel that still manages a lot of thatch is about 1km south of Pura Batu Bolong (p278). Each of the 15 rooms has an outdoor living room, and a hip modern interior with high ceilings and groovy outdoor bathrooms. The ample ocean-front perch is likely to absorb your daylight hours.

Mangsit

★ Qunci Villas   RESORT $$$
(☑0370-693800; www.quncivillas.com; Mangsit; r US$150-250; ✳🛜🌊) A spectacular, lovingly imagined property that comes close to a luxe experience. Everything, from the food to the lovely pool area to the spa, and especially the sea views (160m of beachfront), is magical. It has 78 rooms (including many villas) that, together with the other diversions here, give you little reason to leave.

Jeeva Klui   RESORT $$$
(☑0370-693035; www.jeevaklui.com; Jl Raya Klui Beach; r from US$200, villas from US$265; 🅿✳🛜🌊) This is why you came to the tropics: a palm-shaded, shimmering infinity pool and a lovely, almost private, beach, sheltered by a rocky outcrop. The 35 rooms and villas are evocatively thatched, and have bamboo columns and private porches. Villas are luxurious, private and have their own pools. It's one bay north of Mangsit.

✗ Eating

Senggigi

★ Cafe Tenda Cak Poer   INDONESIAN $
(Jl Raya Senggigi; mains 12,000-20,000Rp; ⊘6pm-late) Barely enclosed, this roadside warung wows the stool-sitting masses with hot-outta-the-wok Indo classics. Get the nasi goreng, made extra hot *(ekstra pedas)* and with extra garlic *(bawang putih ekstra),* and you'll be smiling through tears *and* sweating.

Asmara   INTERNATIONAL $
(☑0370-693619; www.asmara-group.com; Jl Raya Senggigi; mains 25,000-80,000Rp; ⊘8am-11pm;

🛜🏨) An ideal family choice, this place spans the culinary globe from tuna carpaccio to burgers to Lombok's own *Sate pusut* (minced-meat or fish sate). It also has a playground and kids' menu. Service and presentation are smooth.

Office   INTERNATIONAL $
(☑0370-693162; Jl Raya Senggigi, Pasar Seni; mains 25,000-70,000Rp; ⊘9am-10pm) This pub near the euphemistic 'art market' offers typical Indonesian and Western choices along with pool tables, ball games and barflies. It also has a Thai menu, which is the choice of those in the know. Tables on the sand near fishing boats are among Senggigi's best places for a relaxed sunset drink.

Mande Kanduang   INDONESIAN $
(Jl Raya Senggigi; mains from 15,000Rp; ⊘8am-11pm) The name means 'brother and sister' and that's just who's doing the work at this barely there, open-air roadside cafe. No-compromises Indonesian cooking is the order of the day here; the *kepalaq ikan kakap* (fish head stew) is much revered. Duck into the cooking area to see what else is bubbling away.

★ Spice   INTERNATIONAL $$
(☑0370-619 7373; www.spice-lombok.com; off Jl Raya Senggigi; mains from 70,000Rp; ⊘4pm-late) A much welcome addition to the humdrum Senggigi dining scene, Spice has airy quarters in the back of the euphemistically named Art Market. Tables at the sand are perfect for sunset drinks chosen from the long list. There are upscale pub snacks. Later, the upstairs stylish dining room catches the breezes. The cuisine features global island and beach flavours.

Square   INTERNATIONAL $$
(☑0370-693688; Jl Raya Senggigi; mains 40,000-150,000Rp; ⊘11am-11pm; 🛜) An upscale restaurant with beautifully crafted seating, and a menu that features Western and Indonesian fusion fare. The cooking is a cut above the local norm in terms of ambition. Many newcomers to Indonesia have been introduced to the cuisine by the tourist-friendly tasting menu. Get a table away from the road noise.

Banana Tree Cafe   INTERNATIONAL $$
(Jl Raya Senggigi; mains 40,000-120,000Rp; ⊘8am-10pm) One of the better choices in the centre, this refreshingly stylish cafe is set back from the road buzz and has a nice seating area to the rear. Its number-one appeal is the coffee bar operated by skilled baristas.

LOMBOK SENGGIGI

Food spans the globe, from Indo classics to Italian to seafood. It's all fresh and tasty, just like the juices.

Warung Menega SEAFOOD $$
(✆0370-692057; Jl Raya Senggigi, Pantai Batu Layar; meals 80,000-250,000Rp; ◷11am-11pm) If you fled Bali before experiencing the Jimbaran fish grills, you can make up for it at this beachside seafood barbecue. Choose from a daily catch of barracuda, squid, snapper, grouper, lobster, tuna and prawns – all of which are grilled over smouldering coconut husks and served on candlelit tables on the sand. Good sambal selection.

Cafe Alberto ITALIAN $$
(✆0370-693039; Jl Raya Senggigi; mains from 55,000Rp; ◷8am-11pm) A long-standing, beachside Italian kitchen, this place serves a variety of pasta dishes, but is known for its pizza. It offers free transport to and from your hotel. Best bet: wiggling your toes in the sand while sipping a cold one under the moonlight.

✖ North of Senggigi

★Coco Beach INDONESIAN $$
(✆0817 578 0055; Pantai Kerandangan; mains from 60,000Rp; ◷noon-10pm; ✔) This wonderful beachside restaurant has a blissfully secluded setting off the main road. It's pretty and stylish, with many choices for vegetarians. The nasi goreng is locally renowned and the seafood is the best in the area. It has a full bar and blends its own authentic *jamu* tonics (herbal medicines). It's about 2km north of central Senggigi.

🍷 Drinking & Nightlife

Not long ago, Senggigi's bar scene was pretty vanilla with most cafes and restaurants doing double duty. However, like something out of a Pattaya fever-dream, huge cinderblock buildings have now been built on the outskirts of the centre and feature arrays of 'karaoke' joints and massage parlours.

Few miss the chance to enjoy a sunset beverage at one of the many low-key places along the beach.

Hotel Lina BAR
(✆0370-693237; Jl Raya Senggigi; ◷8am-10pm) A small, aging hotel, Lina's seafront deck is a timeless spot for a sundowner. Happy hour starts at 4pm and ends an hour after dusk. You really can't get mellower than this and the view is unmatched.

Papaya Café BAR
(✆0370-693136; Jl Raya Senggigi; ◷8am-11pm) The decor here is slick, with exposed stone walls, rattan furniture and evocative Asmat art from Papua. There's a wide selection of imported liquor. By day the road noise intrudes but it dies down at night, especially when live bands drown it out.

🛍 Shopping

Asmara Collection ARTS & CRAFTS
(✆0370-693619; Jl Raya Senggigi; ◷8am-11pm) A cut above the rest, this store, next to the namesake restaurant, has well-selected tribal art, including richly detailed carvings and textiles from Sumba and Flores.

ℹ Getting There & Away

BEMO
Regular bemos travel between Senggigi and Ampenan's Kebon Roek terminal (5000Rp), where you can connect to Mataram (10,000Rp). Wave them down on the main drag.

BOAT
Fast boats to Bali leave from the large pier right in the centre of the beach. A ticket office is out on the pier.

Gili Getaway (✆0813 3707 4147; http://giligetaway.com; Senggigi Pier; one-way 200,000-250,000Rp) has useful service to Gili T and Gili Air as well as Gili Gede.

Perama (✆0370-693008; www.peramatour.com; Jl Raya Senggigi; ◷8am-8pm) has an economical shuttle-bus service that connects with the public ferry from Lembar to Padangbai, Bali (125,000Rp), from where there are onward shuttle-bus connections to Sanur, Kuta and Ubud (all 175,000Rp). These trips can take eight or more hours. It also offers a bus-and-boat connection to the Gilis for a reasonable 150,000Rp (two hours). It saves some hassle at Bangsal Harbour.

Scoot (✆0828 9701 5565; www.scootcruise.com; Senggigi Pier; one-way from 675,000Rp) has daily fast boats to Nusa Lembongan and Sanur on Bali.

For those going on adventures further into the Indonesian province Nusa Tenggara, **Kencana Adventure** (✆0370-693432; www.kencanaadventure.com; Jl Raya Senggigi; one-way deck/cabin from 1,450,000/4,500,000Rp) has an office where you can learn about heading east on a boat.

TAXI
A taxi to Lembar is 160,000Rp. Metered taxis to the airport in Praya cost about 160,000Rp and take an hour. There's no public bemo service north to Bangsal Harbour. A metered taxi costs about 100,000Rp.

ℹ️ Getting Around

Senggigi's central area is easy to negotiate on foot. If you're staying further from the centre, note that many restaurants offer a free lift for diners.

Motorbikes rent from 60,000Rp per day. Vehicle rental is competitive and ranges from 150,000Rp to 300,000Rp per day. A car and driver costs from 600,000Rp per day.

NORTH & CENTRAL LOMBOK

🎵 0370

Lush and fertile, Lombok's scenic interior is stitched together with rice terraces, lush forest, undulating tobacco fields and fruit and nut orchards, and is crowned by sacred Gunung Rinjani. Entwined in all this big nature are traditional Sasak settlements, some of which are known for their handicrafts. Public transport is not frequent or consistent enough to rely on, but the main roads are in good condition. With your own wheels you can explore black-sand fishing beaches, inland villages and waterfalls.

Bangsal to Bayan

Market towns and glimpses of coast are the norm on the run around the northwest coast of Lombok. The green slopes of Gunung Rinjani increasingly dominate the inland view and traffic blissfully fades away.

Sire

A hidden upmarket enclave, the Sire (or Sira) peninsula points out towards the three Gilis. It's blessed with gorgeous, broad white-sand beaches and good snorkelling offshore. Opulent resorts are now established here along-side a couple of fishing villages. Look out for the small **Hindu temple**, just beyond the Oberoi resort, which has shrines built into the coastal rocks and sublime ocean views.

🛏️ Sleeping

⭐ Rinjani Beach
Eco Resort   BOUTIQUE HOTEL $$
(🕿 0819 3677 5960; www.rinjanibeach.com; Karang Atas; bungalows 350,000-1,300,000Rp; ❄️ 🏊)
🍃 This gem has bamboo bungalows, each with its own theme; hammocks on private porches, and access to a pool on the black-sand beach. Two cheaper, smaller cold-water bungalows cater to budget travellers. There's also a restaurant, plus sea kayaks and mountain bikes. Waste water is treated and used to water the lush grounds. It's just along the coast from Sire.

⭐ Tugu Lombok   RESORT $$$
(🕿 0819 3799 5566, 0370-612 0111; www.tugu hotels.com; bungalows/villas incl breakfast from US$220/330; ❄️ 🛜 🏊) 🍃 An astonishing hotel, this larger-than-life amalgamation of luxury accommodation, eclectic design and spiritual Indonesian heritage sits on a wonderful white-sand beach. Room decor is a fantasy of Indonesian artistic heritage, while the exquisite spa is modelled on Java's Buddhist Borobudur. Smart green practices abound.

Oberoi Lombok   RESORT $$$
(🕿 0370-638444; www.oberoihotels.com; r from US$280, villas from US$500; ❄️ 🛜 🏊) For sheer get-away-from-it-all bliss the Oberoi simply excels. The hotel's core is a triple-level pool, which leads the eye to a lovely private beach. Indonesian rajah-style luxury is the look: sunken marble bathtubs, teak floors, antique furniture and oriental rugs. Service is flawless. There are 50 rooms and villas.

WEKTU TELU

Wektu Telu is a complex mixture of Hindu, Islamic and animist beliefs, though it's now officially classified as a sect of Islam. At its forefront is a physical concept of the Holy Trinity. The sun, moon and stars represent heaven, earth and water, while the head, body and limbs represent creativity, sensitivity and control.

As recently as 1965, the vast majority of Sasaks in northern Lombok were Wektu Telu, but under Suharto's 'New Order' government, indigenous religious beliefs were discouraged, and enormous pressure was placed on Wektu Telu to become Wektu Lima (Muslims who pray five times a day). But in the Wektu Telu heartland around Bayan, locals have been able to maintain their unique beliefs by differentiating their cultural traditions (Wektu Telu) from religion (Islam). Most do not fast for the full month of Ramadan, only attend the mosque for special occasions, and there's widespread consumption of *brem* (alcoholic rice wine).

LOMBOK DURING RAMADAN

Ramadan, the month of fasting, is the ninth month of the Muslim calendar. During daylight hours, many restaurants are closed in the capital and in conservative east and south Lombok (excepting Kuta and surrounding beach towns). Foreigners eating, drinking (especially alcohol) and smoking in public may attract a negative reaction in these areas. In Senggigi, resort areas and most of north Lombok, cultural attitudes are far less strict.

Gondang & Around

Just northeast of Gondang village, which is on the main Bansal–Bayan road, a 6km trail heads inland to Air Terjun Tiu Pupas, a 30m waterfall (per person 30,000Rp) that's only worth seeing in the wet season. Trails continue from here to other wet-season waterfalls, including Air Terjun Gangga, the most beautiful of all. A guide (about 80,000Rp) is useful to navigate the confusing trails in these parts.

Bayan

Wektu Telu, Lombok's animist-tinted form of Islam, was born in humble thatched mosques nestled in these Rinjani foothills. The best example is **Masjid Kuno Bayan Beleq**, next to the village of Beleq. Its low-slung roof, dirt floors and bamboo walls reportedly date from 1634, making this mosque the oldest on Lombok. Inside is a huge old drum which served as the call to prayer before PA systems.

Senaru

The scenic villages that make up Senaru merge into one along a steep road with sweeping volcano and sea views. Most visitors here are Gunung Rinjani–bound but beautiful walking trails and spectacular waterfalls beckon to those who aren't.

Senaru derives its name from *sinaru*, which means light. As you ascend the hill towards the sky and clouds, you'll see just why this makes sense.

◉ Sights

Air Terjun Sindang Gila   WATERFALL
(10,000Rp) This spectacular set of falls are a 20-minute walk from Senaru via a lovely forest and hillside trail. The hardy make for the creek, edge close and then get pounded by the hard, foaming cascade that explodes over black volcanic stone 40m above.

You do not need a guide to reach Air Terjun Sindang Gila; it is on a well-marked path.

Air Terjun Tiu Kelep   WATERFALL
A further 50 minutes or so uphill from the popular Air Terjun Sindang Gila is this waterfall with a swimming hole. The track is steep and guides are recommended (100,000Rp each; negotiable). Long-tailed macaques (locals call them kera) and the much rarer silvered leaf monkey sometimes appear.

Anyone lurking around the Air Terjun Sindang Gila ticket office is likely not an official guide. Avoid them. Legitimate guides are easy to find in town, especially in the small collection of shops by the entrance to Air Terjun Sindang Gila.

🏃 Activities

The main reason that people come to Senaru is for the trek up Gunung Rinjani. But if you have extra time, or aren't heading up the volcano, there are other worthy hikes here.

Guided walks and community tourism activities can be arranged at most guesthouses – they include a **rice-terrace and waterfalls walk** (per person 200,000Rp), which takes in Sindang Gila, rice paddies and an old bamboo mosque, and the **Senaru Panorama Walk** (per person 200,000Rp), which incorporates stunning views and insights into local traditions.

Note that trekking independently up Gunung Rinjani is not allowed.

Senaru Trekking   HIKING
(📱 0818 540 673; http://senarutrekking.com) 🌿
The monosyllabically named Jul is an excellent Rinjani guide. He offers 5% off his fees if you'll help him carry trash down from the mountain.

Rudy Trekker   HIKING
(📱 0818 0365 2874; www.rudytrekker.com) Rudy Trekker is a conscientious organisation based in Senaru. It has a variety of itineraries; most hikers prefer the three-day, two-night package starting from Sembalun Lawang. The office is near the entrance to Air Terjun Sindang Gila falls. It has a great list of what to pack displayed on the wall.

John's Adventures   HIKING
(📱 0817 578 8018; www.rinjanimaster.com) John's Adventures is a very experienced outfitter

that has toilet tents, thick sleeping mats, and itineraries that start from either Senaru or Sembalun. The Senaru office is 2km below the Gunung Rinjani Park Office.

Rinjani Trek Centre   TREKKING
(RTC; ☑0819 0741 1211; www.rinjanitrekcentre. com; ◷6am-4pm) The local guiding and mountaineering collective; a good stop for information and planning. It's located across from Pondok Senaru.

🛌 Sleeping

All of Senaru's accommodation options are strung along the 6.5km-long road that starts in Bayan and runs uphill via Batu Koq to the main Gunung Rinjani park office and Rinjani Trek Centre. Most are simple mountain lodges; the cool altitude means you won't need air-con.

Sinar Rinjani   LODGE $
(☑0818 540 673; www.sinarrinjani.com; r 200,000-350,000Rp; ❊⊗☎) The eight rooms here are huge and offer rain showers and king-sized beds; some have hot water and air-con. The rooftop restaurant has outstanding views. The lodge offers good trekking packages, and is 2.1km from the top of the road.

Pondok Senaru & Restaurant   LODGE $
(☑0818 0362 4129; pondoksenaru@yahoo.com; r 250,000-700,000Rp; ◷restaurant 7am-9pm; ❊☎) This place has 14 lovely little cottages (most fan-only) with terracotta-tiled roofs, and some well-equipped superior rooms with important niceties such as hot water. The restaurant, with tables perched on the edge of a rice-terraced valley, is a sublime place for a meal (mains 25,000Rp to 50,000Rp). It's at the entrance to Air Terjun Sindang Gila.

★ Rinjani Lighthouse   GUESTHOUSE $$
(☑0818 0548 5480; www.rinjanilighthouse.mm.st; r 350,000-900,000Rp; ☎) Set on a wide plateau just 200m from the Gunung Rinjani Park Office, this impressive guesthouse (with hot water) has thatched-roof bungalows in sizes ranging from double to family. There's also a restored old house that sleeps six. The owners are founts of Rinjani wisdom.

Rinjani Lodge   GUESTHOUSE $$
(☑0819 0738 4944; www.rinjanilodge.com; r 450,000-1,000,000Rp; ❊☎☇) A comfortable recent addition, the five bungalows here each have jaw-dropping views across north Lombok all the way to the ocean. Rooms are well furnished and both the restaurant and

the two pools enjoy the same vistas. In fact the local pack of grey monkeys enjoy them too. It's just down from the Air Terjun Sindang Gila entrance.

ℹ️ Getting There & Away
From Mandalika Terminal in Bertais (Mataram), catch a bus to Anyar (25,000Rp to 30,000Rp, 2½ hours). Bemos don't run from Anyar to Senaru, so you'll have to charter an *ojek* (motorcycle taxi; per person from 30,000Rp, depending on your luggage).

Sembalun Valley
☑0376
High on the eastern side of Gunung Rinjani is what could be the mythical Shangri-La: the beautiful Sembalun Valley. This high plateau (about 1200m) is ringed by volcanoes and peaks. It's a rich farming region where the golden foothills turn vivid green in the wet season. When the high clouds part, Rinjani takes front stage.

The valley has two main settlements, Sembalun Lawang and Sembalun Bumbung, tranquil bread baskets primarily concerned with growing cabbage, potatoes, strawberries and, above all, garlic – though trekking tourism brings in a little income, too.

🏃 Activities

Rinjani Information Centre   HIKING
(RIC; ☑0818 540 673; www.rinjaniinformation centre.com; Sembalun Lawang; ◷6am-6pm) A useful resource that also organises Rinjani treks. Well-informed English-speaking staff, and lots of fascinating panels on the local flora, fauna, geology and history. Camping

---

DON'T MISS

SEMBALUN VALLEY DRIVES
Any road you take in and around the Sembalun Valley is going to be spectacular. The drive north to Koko Putih, for instance, passes through some rich cashew forests. For a real treat do the nearly 60km route between Aikmel and Sembalun Lawang. The higher slopes on this road are dense with tropical rainforest. Stop anywhere to see an array of flowers and both black and grey monkeys. When you are on the south rim of the valley, the lookout views are sensational.

and trekking gear is available for hire. The office is right by a huge garlic statue on the main road and across from a very large mosque.

🛌 Sleeping

Maria Guesthouse GUESTHOUSE $
(☑0852 3956 1340; Sembalun Lawang; r from 250,000Rp; 🛜) Choose one of three large tin-roofed bungalows at the rear of a family compound. Digs are bright with vibrantly tiled floors; the family vibe is fun and the garden location calming.

Lembah Rinjani LODGE $
(☑0852 3954 3279, 0818 0365 2511; www.facebook.com/lembahrinjani/about; Sembalun Lawang; r 350,000-450,000Rp) This property has 15 basic, clean, tiled rooms with private porches and breathtaking mountain and sunrise views. There are shared bathrooms.

❶ Getting There & Away

From Mataram's Mandalika Terminal, take a bus to Aikmel (20,000Rp) and change there for a bemo to Sembalun Lawang (20,000Rp).

There's no public transport between Sembalun Lawang and Senaru, so you'll have to charter an *ojek*, for a potentially uncomfortable ride costing about 200,000Rp.

Gunung Rinjani

Lording over the northern half of Lombok, Gunung Rinjani (3726m) is Indonesia's second-tallest volcano. It's an astonishing peak, and sacred to Hindus and Sasaks who make pilgrimages to the summit and lake to leave offerings for the gods and spirits. To the Balinese, Rinjani is one of three sacred mountains, along with Bali's Agung and Java's Bromo. Sasaks ascend throughout the year around the full moon.

The mountain has climatic significance. Its peak attracts a steady stream of swirling rain clouds, while its ash emissions bring fertility to the island's rice fields and tobacco crops, feeding a tapestry of paddies, fields, and cashew and mango orchards.

Rinjani also attracts many trekkers who thrill to the otherworldly vistas. In fact, the volcano has become so popular that the number of annual trekkers has more than doubled to over 60,000 a year since 2013.

🏃 Activities

Treks to the rim, lake and peak should not be taken lightly, and guides are mandatory. Climbing Rinjani during the wet season (November to March) is usually completely forbidden due to the risk of landslide. June

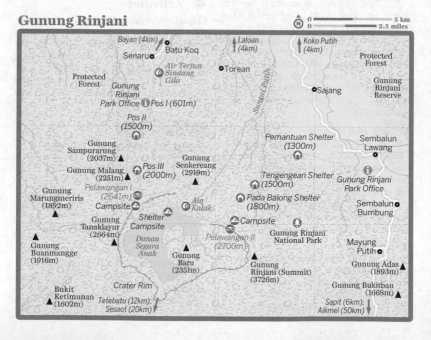

Gunung Rinjani

CLIMBING GUNUNG RINJANI

The recommended way to climb Gunung Rinjani is the five-day trek that starts at Senaru and finishes at Sembalun Lawang. Other possibilities include a summit attempt from Sembalun, which sits higher on the slope and can be done as a gruelling two-day return hike.

Day One: Senaru Pos I to Pos III (Five to Six Hours)

At the southern end of Senaru is the Gunung Rinjani Park Office (Pos I, 601m), where you register and pay the park fee. Just beyond the post, you'll head right when the trail forks. The trail climbs steadily through scrubby farmland for about half an hour to the official entrance of **Gunung Rinjani National Park** (Taman Nasional Gunung Rinjani). The wide trail climbs for another 2½ hours until you reach Pos II (1500m), where there's a shelter. Another 1½ hours' steady walk uphill brings you to Pos III (2000m), where there are two shelters in disrepair. Pos III is usually the place to camp at the end of the first day.

Day Two: Pos III to Danau Segara Anak & Aiq Kalak (Four Hours)

From Pos III, it takes about 1½ hours to reach the rim, **Pelawangan I** (2641m). Setting off very early promises a stunning sunrise. It's possible to camp at Pelawangan I, but level sites are limited, there's no water and it can be very blustery.

It takes about two hours to descend to **Danau Segara Anak**, one of the mountain lakes, and over to the hot springs, **Aiq Kalak**. The first hour is a very steep descent and involves a bit of bouldering. From the bottom of the crater wall it's an easy 30-minute walk across undulating terrain around the lake's edge. There are several places to camp, but most locals prefer to be near the hot springs to soak their weary bodies.

Day Three: Aiq Kalak to Pelawangan II (Three to Four Hours)

The trail starts beside the last shelter at the hot springs and heads away from the lake for about 100m before veering right. It then traverses the northern slope of the crater, and it's an easy one-hour walk along the grassy slopes before you hit a steep, unforgiving rise; from the lake it takes about three hours to reach the crater rim (2639m). At the rim, a sign points the way back to Danau Segara Anak. The trail forks here – straight on to Sembalun or along the rim to the campsite of **Pelawangan II** (2700m).

Day Four: Pelawangan II to Rinjani Summit (Five to Six Hours Return)

Gunung Rinjani's summit arcs above the campsite and looks deceptively close. You'll start the climb around 3am to reach it by sunrise. Depending on wind conditions, it may not be possible to attempt the summit at all, as the trail is along an exposed ridge.

It takes about 45 minutes to clamber up a steep, slippery and indistinct trail to the ridge that leads to Rinjani. Once on the ridge it's a relatively steady walk uphill. After about an hour heading towards a false peak, the real **summit of Rinjani** (3726m) looms. The trail then becomes increasingly steeper. About 350m before the summit, the scree is composed of loose, fist-sized rocks. This section can take about an hour. The views from the top are truly magnificent. In total it takes around three hours to reach the summit, and two to return.

Day Five: Pelawangan II to Sembalun Lawang (Six to Seven Hours)

After negotiating the peak, it's possible to reach Sembalun the same day. From the campsite, it's a steep descent to the village; you'll feel it in your knees. From the camp site, you head back along the crater rim. Shortly after the turn-off to Danau Segara Anak, there's a signposted right turn down to **Pada Balong** (also called Pos 3, 1800m). The trail is easy to follow; it takes around two hours to reach Pada Balong shelter.

The trail then undulates towards the **Sembalun Lawang** savannah, via Tengengean (or Pos 2, 1500m) shelter, beautifully situated in a river valley. It's another 30 minutes through long grass to lonely **Pemantuan** (or Pos 1, 1300m), and two more hours along a dirt track to Sembalun Lawang.

to August is the only time you are (almost) guaranteed minimal rain or clouds. Be prepared with layers and a fleece because it can get cold at the rim (and near-freezing at the summit) at any time of year.

Roughly the same trek packages and prices are offered by all operators, though some outfitters have a 'luxury' option. Typical itineraries include:

Crater Rim Two days – An up and back to see the caldera lake view round-trip from Senaru.

Rim & Lake Return Four Days – A return trip from either Senaru or Sembalun Lawang to the crater rim and then down into the caldera to the lake. Note that a three-day variation on this trip involves an exhausting and potentially dangerous 12-hour-plus marathon on the last day.

Senaru-Rim-Lake-Sembalan Lawang Five days – the classic trek takes in everything with little repetition and at a humane pace.

Trek prices get cheaper the larger the party. Costs (including food, equipment, guide, porters, park fee and transport back to Senaru) average US$100 per person per day, although this is very negotiable. Any posted prices are just an opening gambit.

Operators

The easiest way to organise a trip is through your accommodation. You will also find numerous independent operators.

In Senaru:

➡ John's Adventures (p284)

➡ Rudy Trekker (p284)

➡ Rinjani Trek Centre (p285)

➡ Senaru Trekking (p284)

In Sembalun Lawang:

➡ Rinjani Information Centre (p285)

Agencies in Kuta, Senggigi and beyond can organise Rinjani treks, too, with return transport from the point of origin.

Guides & Porters

Trekking independently is simply not allowed, and deeply unwise. People have died on Rinjani, with or without guides, and only the most skilled climbers should consider themselves qualified to undertake such a journey.

Guides and porters operate on loosely fixed fees, which are included in whatever trekking package you purchase. Tips of 20,000Rp to 50,000Rp per day are sufficient and can be paid at the end of the trip.

Entrance Fee & Equipment

Entrance to Gunung Rinjani National Park is 150,000Rp *per day* – you register and pay at the park offices near the trail heads in Senaru or Sembalun Lawang before your trek. Note that there are proposals to raise these fees even higher.

Sleeping bags and tents are essential and can be hired or included as part of a package. Decent footwear, warm clothing, wet-weather gear, gloves, cooking equipment and a torch are important (all can be hired if necessary). Expect to pay upwards of 100,000Rp a head per day for all your hired gear. Muscle balm (to ease aching legs) and a swimming costume (for the lake and hot springs) could also be packed. Discuss what to bring with your trekking organisation or guide.

Bring home your rubbish, including toilet tissue. Rinjani camps and trails are very litter-strewn.

Food & Supplies

Trek organisers usually arrange trekking food. Mataram is cheapest for supplies but many provisions are available in Senaru and Sembalun Lawang. Take more water than seems reasonable (dehydration can spur altitude sickness), extra batteries (as altitude can wreak havoc on those, as well) and a back-up lighter.

ⓘ Information

Gunung Rinjani National Park (Taman Nasional Gunung Rinjani; ☑0370-660 8874; www.rinjaninationalpark.com) The official website for the park has good maps, info and a useful section on reported scams by dodgy hiking operators.

Tetebatu
☑0376

Laced with Rinjani spring-fed streams and blessed with rich volcanic soil, Tetebatu is a Sasak breadbasket. The surrounding countryside is quilted with tobacco and rice fields, fruit orchards and cow pastures that fade into remnant monkey forest gushing with waterfalls. Tetebatu's sweet climate is ideal for long country walks (at 400m it's high enough to mute that hot, sticky coastal mercury). Dark nights come saturated with sound courtesy of a frog orchestra accompanied by countless gurgling brooks. Even insomniacs snore here.

◉ Sights

Tetebatu is spread out, with facilities on roads north and east (nicknamed 'waterfall road') of the central *ojek* stop, which happens to be the town's main intersection and a basis for all directions. You will always be in sight of selfie-perfect rice fields here.

Waterfall
WATERFALL

On the southern slopes of Rinjani, there is a waterfall which is accessible by private transport or a spectacular two-hour walk (one way) through rice fields from Tetebatu. If walking, hire a guide (about 200,000Rp) through your guesthouse. There's another very close by.

Taman Wisata Tetebatu
FOREST

(Monkey Forest) A shady 4km track leading from the main road, just north of the Tetebatu mosque, heads into this forest, where you'll find black monkeys and waterfalls – you'll need a guide, which you can arrange at your accommodation for around 200,000Rp.

Air Terjun Jukut
WATERFALL

A steep 2km hike from the car park at the end of the access road to Gunung Rinjani National Park leads to beautiful Air Terjun Jukut, an impressive 20m drop to a deep pool surrounded by lush forest.

Sapit
VILLAGE

On the southeastern slopes of Gunung Rinjani east of Tetebatu, Sapit is a tiny, very relaxed village with views across to Sumbawa. Tobacco-drying *open* (tall red-brick buildings) loom above the beautifully lush landscape. Sapit makes a delightful, peaceful rural base for a few days well off the tourist trail.

Kotaraja
VILLAGE

The nearest market town to Tetebatu is Kotaraja. Kotaraja is also host to a Sasak stick-fighting festival each August. The fights are both fierce and real, and end gracefully at the first sight of blood. Markets are held in Kotaraja on Monday and Wednesday mornings.

🛏 Sleeping & Eating

★ Tetebatu Mountain Resort
LODGE $

(☑ 0812 372 4040, 0819 1771 6440; r 300,000-500,000Rp; 🛜) These two-storey Sasak bungalows with 23 rooms in total are the best digs in town. There are separate bedrooms on both floors – perfect for travelling buddies – and a top-floor balcony with magical rice-field views.

Pondok Indah
Bungalows Tetebatu
BUNGALOW $

(☑ 0877 6172 2576; r from 250,000Rp) Two bi-level thatched bungalows are set amid beautiful rice fields. Although appearing romantically rustic, conditions are not: each has a bathroom, hardwood floors, outdoor seating areas with fabulous views and more. The decor is an eclectic mix of colours.

Hakiki Bungalows & Cafe
BUNGALOW $

(☑ 0818 0373 7407; www.hakiki-inn.com; r 150,000-425,000Rp; 🛜) A collection of seven bungalows in a blooming garden at the edge of the rice fields. You'll find it perched over the family rice plot about 600m from the intersection. There's even a honeymoon suite. Wi-fi is available in its cafe, which serves Indo classics, some nicely spicy.

Cendrawasih Cottages
COTTAGE $

(☑ 0878 6418 7063; r from 250,000Rp; ⊙ restaurant 8am-9pm) Sweet little *lumbung* (ricebarn) brick cottages with bamboo beds and private porches, nestled in the rice fields. Sit on floor cushions in the stunning stilted restaurant (mains 20,000Rp to 45,000Rp), which has Sasak, Indonesian and Western fare, and take in 360-degree rice-field views. It's about 500m east of the intersection.

ℹ Getting There & Around

All cross-island buses pass Pomotong (20,000Rp from Mandalika Terminal) on the main east–west highway. Get off here and you can hop an *ojek* (from 30,000Rp) to Tetebatu.

SOUTH LOMBOK
☑ 0370

Beaches just don't get much better: the water is warm, striped turquoise and curls into barrels, and the sand is silky and snow-white, framed by massive headlands and sheer cliffs. The south is noticeably drier than the rest of Lombok and more sparsely populated, with limited roads and public transport.

Southern Lombok's incredible coastline of giant bite-shaped bays is startling, its beauty immediate, undeniable and arresting. Yet this region has historically been the island's poorest, its sun-blasted soil parched and unproductive. These days those hills are also pocked with illegal, undocumented gold mines, which you'll see and hear grinding away as you head west to the surf beaches.

Praya

Sprawling Praya's claim to fame is as the location for Lombok's airport. It's also the main town in the south, with tree-lined streets and the odd crumbling Dutch colonial relic.

✱ Getting There & Away

Surrounded by rice fields and 5km south of Praya proper, the modern **Lombok International Airport** (LOP; www.lombok-airport. co.id) has become an attraction in its own right: on weekends you'll see vast crowds of locals sitting around watching and snacking. They're not waiting on anyone, rather they are hanging out for the day enjoying the spectacle of people flying in and out.

The airport is not huge, but has a full range of services such as ATMs (and convenience stores with ludicrous prices).

✱ Getting Around

Thanks to multilane roads, the airport is only 30 minutes' drive from both Mataram and Kuta and is well linked to the rest of the island.

Bus Damri operates hourly tourist buses; buy tickets in the arrivals area. Destinations: Mataram's Mandalika Terminal (25,000Rp) and Senggigi (35,000Rp).

Taxi The airport taxi cartel offers fixed-price rides to destinations that include: Kuta (100,000Rp, 30 minutes), Mataram (165,000Rp, 30 minutes), Senggigi (200,000Rp, one hour) and Bangsal (260,000Rp, 90 minutes), where you can access the Gili Islands.

Around Praya

Sukarara

The main street here is the domain of textile shops, where you can watch weavers work their old looms. **Dharma Setya** (☑0370-660 5204; Jl Sukarara; ⊙8am-5pm) has an incredible array of hand-woven Sasak textiles, including ikat and *songket* (handwoven silver- or gold-threaded cloth).

Penujak

Penujak is well known for its traditional *gerabah* pottery. Made from chocolatey terracotta-tinted local clay, it's hand-burnished and topped with braided bamboo. There are plates and cups on offer from the potters' humble home studios, most of which huddle around the eerie village cemetery.

Rembitan & Sade

The area from Sengkol down to Kuta is a centre for Sasak culture – traditional villages full of towering *lumbung* (rice barns). You may still see the odd *bale tani* (family house), a home made from bamboo, mud, and cow and buffalo dung.

Sade's **Sasak village** has been extensively renovated and has some fascinating *bale tani*. Further south, **Rembitan** has more of an authentic feel to it, boasts a cluster of houses and *lumbung* and the 100-year-old **Masjid Kuno**, an ancient thatched-roof mosque that is a pilgrimage destination for Lombok's Muslims. Both villages are worth a look but it's not possible to go without a guide (around 50,000Rp).

Kuta

☑0370

What could be a better gateway to the wonderful beaches of south Lombok? Imagine a crescent bay, turquoise in the shallows and deep blue further out. It licks a huge, white-sand beach, as wide as a football pitch and framed by headlands. Now imagine a coastline of nearly a dozen such bays, all backed by a rugged range of coastal hills spotted with lush patches of banana trees and tobacco fields, and you'll have a notion of Kuta's immediate appeal.

Kuta's original attraction was the limitless world-class breaks, and now even as developers lick their chops, the sets still keep rolling in. Meanwhile, the town itself is an appealing mix of guesthouses, cafes, restaurants and low-key places for a beer.

🏖 Beaches

Kuta's main beach can easily snare you and keep you from looking elsewhere. It's got ideal white sand and all those views. Plus the surf is just right for swimming. The waterfront is a slowly gentrifying place as landscaped areas gradually replace expans-

Kuta

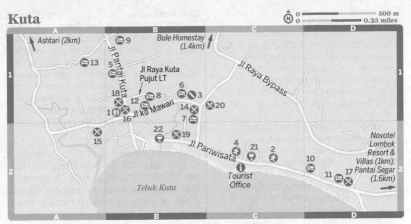

Kuta

🏃 Activities, Courses & Tours
1 Kimen Surf	B1
2 Mana Yoga Studio	C2
3 Scuba Froggy	B1
4 Whatsup? Lombok	C2

🛏 Sleeping
5 Bombara Bungalows	B1
6 Kuta Baru Hotel	B1
7 Lamancha Homestay	B1
8 Lara Homestay	B1
9 Mimpi Manis	B1
10 Puri Rinjani Bungalows	D2
11 Seger Reef Homestay	D2
12 Spot	B1
13 Yuli's Homestay	A1

🍽 Eating
14 DJ Coffee Corner	B1
15 Dwiki's	A2
16 El Bazar	B1
17 Full Moon Cafe	D2
18 Nugget's Corner	B1
19 Warung Bule	B2
20 Warung Flora	C1

🍸 Drinking & Nightlife
21 Sunset Bar	C2
22 Surfer's Bar	B2

es that used to be covered by bamboo huts. (Although a few bamboo joints have snuck back in to vend beer at night.) For now it's slightly bleak, but then again, there's that water...

🏃 Activities

There's a whole row of activity sales agents across the road from Lamancha Homestay (p292). They can set you up on anything from surf tours to snorkelling in obscure locations. Bargain hard.

Surfing

For surfing, stellar lefts and rights break on the reefs off Kuta Bay (Teluk Kuta) and east of Tanjung Aan (p294). Boatmen will take you out for around 200,000Rp. Seven kilometres east of Kuta is the fishing village of **Gerupuk**, where there's a series of reef breaks, both close to the shore and further

out, but they require a boat, at a negotiable 350,000Rp per day. Wise surfers buzz past Gerupuk and take the road to Ekas, where crowds are thin and surf is plentiful. West of Kuta you'll find **Mawan**, a stunning swimming beach, and **Mawi**, a popular surf paradise with world-class swells and a strong rip tide.

⭐ **Kimen Surf**   SURFING
(☎0370-655064; www.kuta-lombok.net; Jl ke Mawan; board rental per day 100,000Rp; lessons per person from 800,000Rp; ⏲9am-8pm) Swell forecasts, tips, kitesurfing, board rental, repairs and lessons. It runs guided excursions to breaks such as Gerupuk (500,000Rp).

Diving & Snorkelling

Scuba Froggy   DIVING
(☎0877 6510 6945; www.scubafroggy.com; Jl ke Mawan; discover dive US$65; ⏲9am-8pm) Runs

NYALE FESTIVAL

On the 19th day of the 10th month in the Sasak calendar (generally February or March), hundreds of Sasaks gather on the beach at Kuta, Lombok for a local version of poetry and big ceremonies and feasts involving the odd, worm-like *nyale* fish.

When night falls, fires are built and teens sit around competing in a Sasak poetry slam, where they spit rhyming couplets called *pantun* back and forth. At dawn the next day, the first of millions of *nyale* (which appear here annually) are caught, then teenage girls and boys take to the sea separately in decorated boats, and chase one another with lots of noise and laughter. The *nyale* are eaten raw or grilled, and are considered to be an aphrodisiac. A good catch is a sign that a bumper crop of rice is coming.

local trips to a dozen sites, most no deeper than 18m. From June to November, staff also run trips to the spectacular and challenging ocean pinnacles in Blongas Bay, famous for schooling hammerheads and mobula rays. Snorkelling trips are US$30. They also rent kayaks.

Other Activities

★**Mana Yoga Studio** YOGA
(www.manayogalombok.com; Jl Pariwisata; class 100,000Rp; ⊙9am-8pm) Open thatched pavilions are the location for yoga classes. Styles include vinyasa, yin/yang and surfers.

Whatsup? Lombok WATER SPORTS
(☑0878 6597 8701; http://whatsuplombok.com; Jl Pariwisata; rental 3hr 300,000Rp) South Kuta's bays are known for being excellent places for kitesurfing, standup paddling (SUP) and kayaking. At this shop you can rent gear, take lessons and join tours.

🛏 Sleeping

★**Lara Homestay** GUESTHOUSE $
(☑0370-615 4715; http://larahomestay.com; Jl Raya Kuta Pujut Lombok Tengah; r incl breakfast from 225,000Rp; ❄🛜) This excellent family-run guesthouse is on a quiet, palm-shaded back lane close to the heart of Kuta. Service could not be cheerier. Rooms in their multistorey main building are sparkling and very clean. The breakfasts are tasty.

Bule Homestay GUESTHOUSE $
(☑0819 1799 6256; Jl Raya Bypass; r 250,000-320,000Rp; ❄🛜) Although it's about 2km back from the beach near the junction of Jl Raya Kuta and Jl Raya Bypass, this nine-bungalow complex is worth consideration simply for the snappy way it's run. Dirt doesn't dare enter the small compound, where rooms gleam with a hospital white. It is surrounded by a wall that could have been in *The Flintstones*.

Lamancha Homestay HOMESTAY $
(☑0819 3313 0156, 0370-615 5186; r incl breakfast 175,000-300,000Rp; ❄🛜) A charming and expanding 10-room homestay offering a mix of somewhat frayed bamboo rooms with concrete floors, plus nicer air-con and fan-cooled non-bamboo rooms, draped with colourful tapestries and canopied beds. The management is endearing.

Spot GUESTHOUSE $
(☑0370-702 2100; www.thespotbungalows.com; Jl Pariwisata Kuta 1; r from US$24; ⊙cafe 7am-10pm; 🛜) You'll love the rustic thatched motif at this collection of nine bungalows set around a grassy plot (accessed via Jl ke Mawan). Everything is made from bamboo and thatch here – except the sheets.

Seger Reef Homestay INN $
(☑0370-615 5528; www.segerreef.com; Jl Raya Pantai Kuta; r incl breakfast 180,000-250,000Rp; 🛜) Twelve bright, spotless, family-owned bungalows across the street from the beach. Thatch is the theme here – it seems to cover every surface. Wi-fi is only available in the cafe.

Mimpi Manis B&B $
(☑0818 369 950; www.mimpimanis.com; off Jl Raya Kuta; dm 125,000Rp, r 220,000-400,000Rp; ❄🛜) An inviting B&B in a two-storey house with seven spotless rooms, some with air-con and showers. There are plenty of good books to browse and DVDs to borrow. It's 1km inland from the beach; the owners offer a free drop-off service to the beach and town, and arrange bike and motorbike rental. The dorm has five beds.

★**Bombara Bungalows** GUESTHOUSE $$
(☑0370-615 8056; bomborabungalows@yahoo.com; Jl Raya Kuta; r incl breakfast 400,000-650,000Rp; ❄🛜🏊) One of the best places for a low-cost stay in Kuta, these eight bungalows (some fan-cooled) are built around a lovely pool area. Coconut palms shade

loungers and the entire place feels like an escape from the hubbub of town. The staff understand the needs of surfers, and most everyone else.

★ **Kuta Baru Hotel** HOMESTAY $$
(☎ 0370-615 8645; Jl ke Mawan; r incl breakfast 250,000-1,000,000Rp; ❄ ☎ 🏊) One of Kuta's best homestays. There's a cute patio strung with the obligatory hammock, daily coffee service, sparkling tiles and an all-round good vibe. It's 110m east of the main intersection and has 20 rooms.

★ **Yuli's Homestay** HOMESTAY $$
(☎ 0819 1710 0983; www.yulishomestay.com; off Jl Raya Kuta; r incl breakfast 425,000-700,000Rp; ❄ ☎ 🏊) A popular choice, the 15 rooms here are immaculately clean, spacious and nicely furnished with huge beds and wardrobes. They also have big front terraces, and cold-water bathrooms. There's a guest kitchen, and a garden and large pool to enjoy.

Puri Rinjani Bungalows BUNGALOW $$
(☎ 0370-615 4849; Jl Raya Pantai Kuta; r from 450,000Rp; ❄ ☎ 🏊) A solid beachfront option that gets everything right: it's sparklingly clean, well-managed and has a lovely pool area. The 19 rooms are bright and airy and have nice, firm beds. There are even a few statues decorating the site.

Novotel Lombok Resort & Villas RESORT $$$
(☎ 0370-615 3333; www.novotel.com; r/villa from US$180/310; ❄ ☎ 🏊) One of the nicer beach resorts in Lombok, this appealing, Sasak-themed four-star resort spills onto a superb beach less than 3km east of the junction. The 102 rooms have high sloping roofs and modern interiors. There are two pools, a spa, resort-style restaurants, a swanky bar and a plethora of activities on offer.

✗ Eating

★ **Nugget's Corner** INDONESIAN $
(☎ 0878 9131 7431; Jl Pantai Kuta; mains from 25,000Rp; ☺ 8am-11pm; ✎) For a restaurant that seems cool and casual, this one has real drive. The vegan, veggie, and meaty mains are all prepared with attitude and authority. Flavours are bold and presentation is lovely. It's BYOB; the juices, smoothies and iced teas are superb. The dining room is open-air and bright.

Warung Flora INDONESIAN $
(☎ 0878 6530 0009; Jl Pariwisata; mains 20,000-80,000Rp; ☺ 11am-10.30pm) A total tropical

fantasy in bamboo and thatch. Sit under a palm tree while you dine on fresh fish caught by a local fisherman. The chef is his wife and together they create beautiful meals.

Full Moon Cafe CAFE $
(Jl Raya Pantai Kuta; mains from 30,000Rp; ☺ 8am-late; ☎) Right across from the beach, the 2nd-floor cafe here is like a tree house with killer ocean views. The menu has all the standards, from banana pancakes to various Indo rice creations and, yes, pizza! Come for the view and sunset, then hang out.

DJ Coffee Corner CAFE $
(Jl ke Mawan; treats from 15,000Rp; ☺ 8am-8pm; ❄) A switch from the thatch-and-bamboo cliche that dominates the local design palette: a sleek air-con coffee bar with a nice back garden. Get your real espresso fix here along with juices, light bites and baked goods.

El Bazar MEDITERRANEAN $$
(☎ 0819 9911 3026; Jl Raya Kuta; mains 30,000-150,000Rp; ☺ 8am-11pm) A small cafe that's big on flavour. Pass by the flowers at the entrance and you'll be entranced by authentic tastes from around the Mediterranean. Hearty soups, salads, luscious aubergine, Moroccan tagines and more.

Dwiki's PIZZA $$
(☎ 0859 3503 4489; Jl ke Mawan; mains 35,000-70,000Rp; ☺ 8am-11pm; ☎✎) A choice, relaxed spot for wood-fired thin-crust pizza in tiki-bar environs. And they deliver! Has lots of Indo standards, grilled seafood and an above average list of veggie options.

Warung Bule SEAFOOD $$
(☎ 0819 1799 6256; Jl Raya Pantai Kuta; mains 50,000-250,000Rp; ☺ 8am-10pm; ☎) Founded by the long-time executive chef at the Novotel, who delivers tropical seafood tastes at an affordable price. We like the tempura starter. His trio of lobster, prawns and mahi-mahi (a mild white fish) might have you cooing. It gets very busy in high season, so be prepared for a wait.

Ashtari VEGETARIAN $$
(☎ 0877 6549 7625; www.ashtarilombok.com; Jl ke Mawan; meals 25,000-80,000Rp; ☺ 7am-10pm; ✎) Perched on a mountaintop 2km west of town on the road to Mawan, this breezy, Moroccan-themed lounge-restaurant has spectacular vistas of pristine bays and rocky peninsulas that take turns spilling further

out to sea. Owned by a local property developer, it's a slick yoga-luxe sort of place.

🍷 Drinking & Nightlife

Surfer's Bar
BAR

(☑0878 6456 8195; www.facebook.com/surfers barkutalombok; ⊙9am-late) Tables are scattered across the sand at this thumping dive bar, which has frequent live music.

Sunset Bar
BAR

(☑0882 1907 1744; Jl Raya Pantai Kuta; ⊙8am-late) The local owners of this barely there shack of a bar have created a laid-back party vibe that draws in crowds each night. Guitars get strummed and it often morphs into a fully fledged jam. Hungry? Enjoy cheap Indo standards.

ℹ Information

DANGERS & ANNOYANCES

If you decide to rent a bicycle or motorbike, take care with whom you deal – arrangements are informal and no rental contracts are exchanged. There are reports of some visitors having motorbikes stolen, and then having to pay substantial sums of money as compensation to the owner. Renting a motorbike from your guesthouse is safest.

As you drive up the coastal road west and east of Kuta, watch your back – especially after dark. There have been reports of muggings in the area.

Throngs of vendors, many of them children, are relentless.

TOURIST INFORMATION

Tourist Office (Jl Pariwisata; ⊙8am-5pm) Located in a bright blue shipping container right on the beach, it offers tourist information for the Kuta area and the rest of Lombok.

ℹ Getting There & Away

You'll need at least three bemos to get here just from Mataram. Take one from Mataram's Mandalika Terminal to Praya (15,000Rp), another to Sengkol (5000Rp) and a third to Kuta (5000Rp).

Simpler are the daily tourist buses serving Mataram (125,000Rp), plus Senggigi and Lembar (both 150,000Rp).

A taxi to the airport costs 60,000Rp.

Ride-share cars are widely advertised around town. Destinations include: Bangsal for Gili Islands public boats (160,000Rp), Seminyak (Bali) via the public ferry (200,000Rp) and Senaru (400,000Rp).

East of Kuta

One of Kuta's joys is going exploring, looking for beaches. The filigreed coastline means that there's always a new discovery over the next knoll. Just east of Kuta are several excellent beaches.

◎ Sights

Tanjung Aan
BEACH

Some 5km east of Kuta, Tanjung Aan (aka A'an, Ann) is a spectacular sight: a giant horseshoe bay with two sweeping arcs of fine sand with the ends punctuated by waves crashing on the rocks. Swimming is good here and there's a little shade under trees and shelters, plus safe parking (for a small charge). Look for **Warung Turtle** at the east end of the beach. It wins plaudits for cheery service and cheap beer.

Pantai Segar
BEACH

(car/motobike 10,000/5000Rp) Pantai Segar, a lovely beach about 2km east of Kuta around the first headland, has unbelievably turquoise water, decent swimming (though no shade) and a break 200m offshore. There are two more beaches nearby, a decent cafe and vendors renting snorkelling gear. Come here for famous full moon parties.

Gerupuk

Just 1.6km past Tanjung Aan beach, Gerupuk is a fascinating little ramshackle coastal village where the thousand or so local souls earn their keep from fishing, seaweed harvesting and lobster exports. Oh, and guiding and ferrying surfers to the five exceptional surf breaks in its huge bay.

As you'll see from the nascent grand boulevards and vast earthworks between Tanjung Aan and Gerupuk, construction on the gigantic Mandalika resort complex is under way in fits and starts. Expect the area to change greatly in the next few years. Judging by the way the existing mangroves have been destroyed, concerns about environmental damage are well placed.

◎ Sights & Activities

To surf in the bay you'll need to hire a boat to ferry you from the fishing harbour, skirting the netted lobster farms, to the break (300,000Rp). The boatman will help you find the right wave and wait patiently. There are four waves inside and a left break outside on the point. All can get head high or bigger when the swell hits.

Pantai Bumbangku   BEACH
Follow a narrow track off the main road for 2.5km and you'll find a narrow and often deserted beach. The structures you see out in the bay are pearl farms.

🛏 Sleeping & Eating

Edo Homestay   INN $
(📞0818 0371 0521; Gerupuk; r incl breakfast 200,000-550,000Rp; ❄🛜🍴) Right in the village, this place offers 18 clean rooms (some fan-cooled). Most have colourful drapes and double beds; top-end rooms are in a villa. It has a decent restaurant and a surf shop too (boards per day 100,000Rp).

★ Bumbangku   BUNGALOW $$
(📞0852 3717 6168, 0370-620833; www.bumbangkulombok.com; r 250,000-750,000Rp; ❄) Bumbangku beach is across the bay from Gerupuk and is wonderfully remote – almost island-like. This relaxed resort has 25 rooms ranging from simple bamboo huts on stilts with outdoor baths and cold water to much nicer concrete rooms with hot water and air-con. It's 2km on a narrow lane off the main road.

Lakuen Beach Bungalows   BUNGALOW $$
(📞0877 6580 5081; Gerupuk; r 450,000-720,000Rp; ❄🛜🍴) At the west end of Gerupuk village, this five-bungalow compound offers commodious accommodation. It's close to the fishing port and about a 10-minute walk to the closest beach.

Surf Camp Lombok   SURF CAMP $$
(📞0819 1608 6876; www.surfcampindonesia.com; Gerupuk; 1 week from €650) Lodging at this fun surf resort at the eastern end of Gerupuk village is in a bamboo Borneo-style longhouse, albeit with lots of high-tech diversions. The beach setting feels lush and remote. All meals are included plus surf lessons, yoga and more. Rooms sleep four, except for one double. Recycling and other eco-friendly practices are embraced.

Ekas & Around

Ekas is an uncrowded find, where the breaks and soaring cliffs recall Bali's Ulu Watu – an almost-deserted Ulu Watu.

Ekas itself is a sleepy little village, but head south into the peninsula and you'll soon make the sorts of jaw-dropping discoveries that will have you tweeting like mad.

👁 Sights

Heaven Beach   BEACH
Ask directions to Heaven Beach for a real bit of sandy wonder. It's a stunning little pocket of white sand and surf about 4km from Ekas. Despite the omnipresent resort, you're free to access the shore: all Indonesian beaches are public.

Pantai Dagong   BEACH
What a sight! An utterly empty and seemingly endless white beach backed by azure breakers. To get here, drive south 6.5km from Ekas over the rough but passable road to Pantai Dagong.

🛏 Sleeping & Eating

Ekas Breaks   GUESTHOUSE $$
(📞0822 3791 6767; www.ekasbreaks.com/; r incl breakfast 600,000Rp; ❄🛜🍴) Some 2km from Ekas' surf breaks and beaches amid rolling land, this airy compound has 10 units. Some are in traditional *lumbung* style with thatched walls, others are in a modern style, with whitewashed walls and open bathrooms (we prefer those). The cafe makes a good mix of Western and Indo meals.

Heaven on the Planet   BOUTIQUE HOTEL $$$
(📞0812 375 1103, 0821 4424 4093; www.sanctuaryinlombok.com; Ekas Bay; per person all-inclusive US$120-240; ❄🛜🍴) The aptly named Heaven on the Planet has units scattered along a cliff's edge, from where you'll have spectacular bird's-eye views of the sea. Others are down at the idyllic beach. Each is utterly different. Heaven is primarily a posh and idiosyncratic surf resort, but kitesurfing, scuba diving and snorkelling are also possible. Meals are bountiful and creative.

West of Kuta

West of Kuta is a series of awesome beaches and ideal surf breaks. Developers are nosing around here, and land has changed hands, but for now it remains almost pristine and the region has a raw beauty. In anticipation of future developments, the road has been much improved. It meanders inland, skirting tobacco, sweet potato and rice fields in between turn-offs to the sand and glimpses of the gorgeous coast.

Mawun (Mawan)

◉ Sights

★ Pantai Mawan   BEACH

(Mawun; car/motorbike 10,000/5000Rp) How's this for a vision of sandy paradise? Some 8km west of Kuta and 600m off the main road, this half-moon cove is framed by soaring headlands with azure water and a swath of empty sand save a fishing village of a dozen thatched homes. It's a terrific swimming beach. There's paved parking, some modest cafes and large trees for shade. An upscale vendor rents loungers for a pricey 150,000Rp for all day.

Pantai Areguling   BEACH

(car/motorbike 10,000/5000Rp) Look for a steep track off the main coast road 6km west of Kuta. A rough 2km ride brings you to this broad bay with a wide beach of beige sand. It's a little scruffy and services are few but you can't beat the sense of space. Construction on the headland foreshadows changes to come.

🛏 Sleeping & Eating

Blue Monkey Villas   BUNGALOW $$

(☑ 0853 3775 6416; Pantai Areguling; r 500,000-1,000,000Rp; 🛜 ⛲) Set on a knoll above Areguling beach, this collection of traditional-style bungalows have sweeping views of the bay. The beach is a 500m walk down the hill. A simple cafe serves meals, where that view will compete with your food for your attention. At quiet times, service can be frayed but friendly.

Selong Blanak

Just when you think you've seen the most beautiful beaches Kuta has to offer, you reach this popular curving bay and beach. And it gets stiff competition in the fabulous sweepstakes from nearby Pantai Mawi.

◉ Sights

Pantai Selong Blanak   BEACH

(parking 10,000Rp) Behold the wide, sugar-white beach with water streaked a thousand shades of blue, ideal for swimming. You can rent surfboards (per day 100,000Rp) and arrange for a boat out to area breaks (three hours from 500,000Rp). The parking lot is just 400m off the main drag on a good road, the turn is 18km west of Kuta. The beach is popular with locals, loungers rent for 30,000Rp per day and there are lots of bamboo warung.

Pantai Mawi   BEACH

(car/motorbike 20,000/10,000Rp) This is a surf paradise: a stunning scene, with legendary barrels and several more beaches scattered around the great bay. Watch out for the strong rip tide. There's parking and vendors; surfboard rental is 50,000Rp for two hours. The turn for the beach is 16km west of Kuta, it's then a 3km drive down a rough road to the beach.

🛏 Sleeping & Eating

Sempiak Villas   RESORT $$$

(☑ 0821 4430 3337; www.sempiakvillas.com; villas from 1,300,000Rp; ❄ ⛲) Tucked away on the cliffs, this fabulous boutique resort is one of

---

A GRIM CATCH

Everyday fishing boats sail in and out of Tanjung Luar, a long-running fish market in southeast Lombok that has a bad reputation with environmental groups for the fishing of large species such as sharks, manta rays and dolphins.

While the meat is sold locally, the shark fins and manta gills are auctioned to buyers who ship their bounty to Hong Kong, where the items are considered delicacies.

Shark-fin buyers in Tanjung Luar confirm that few sharks remain in the sea around Lombok. In the 1990s fishermen didn't have to go far to hunt their take but these days they travel all the way to the Sumba strait between Australia and Indonesia, an important shark-migration channel.

Surveys by Project Aware (www.projectaware.org), a diving environmental group, found that mandatory government signs prohibiting dolphin catch as well as that of some shark species and sea turtles had been torn down.

Any real effect of Indonesia's declaration in 2014 of their waters being a protection zone for manta rays has yet to be seen.

the Kuta area's most upscale properties. The six villas are built into the hillside above the beach and feature antique wood; some have covered decks with stupendous views. It has a beach club for daytime frolic and dinners on the sand.

★ **Laut Biru Bar & Restaurant** SEAFOOD $$
(☑0821 4430 3339; mains 40,000-80,000Rp; ⊙8am-10pm; 🖥) At sea level, Laut Biru Cafe is open to all comers. They keep it simple here with muesli and yoghurt, eggs and toast for breakfast and Indo classics for lunch and dinner. It's a thatched-roof construction, with remixed world music floating through the room and patio.

Blongas & Around

Save a big 'Wow!' for this curving double bay with a sinuous strand of white ribbon that provides a brilliant line between the blue water and green hills. Nearby Bali has nothing even remotely like this beach and it's still yours for the exploring as development has barely touched this area.

⊙ Sights & Activities

Blongas Bay has two famed dive sites: **Magnet** and **Cathedrals**. Spotting conditions peak in mid-September when you may see schooling mobula rays in addition to hammerheads, which school around the pinnacle (a towering rock that breaks the surface of the ocean and is the heart of the dive sites) from June to November. It's not an easy dive, so you must be experienced and prepared for heavy currents.

Dive Zone DIVING
(☑0819 0785 2073, 0812 3924 1560; www.dive zone-lombok.com; Blongas Bay; 2 local boat dives from 1,500,000Rp) Dive Zone focuses on the local dive sites as well as the Gilis.

🛏 Sleeping

Blongas Bay Lodge BUNGALOW $$
(☑0370-645974; www.thelodge-lombok.com; bungalows 850,000-950,000Rp, meals 75,000Rp) This lodge offers spacious wooden bungalows with tiled roofs in a spacious, lovely coconut grove. It's fairly simple, which goes with the serene setting right on the water.

EAST LOMBOK
☑0376
All most travellers see of the east coast of Lombok is Labuhan Lombok, the port for ferries to Sumbawa. But the road around the northeast coast is pretty good, and can be traversed if you're hoping to complete a circumnavigation.

Labuhan Lombok

Labuhan Lombok (also known as Labuhan Kayangan or Tanjung Kayangan) is the port for ferries and boats to Sumbawa. The town centre of Labuhan Lombok, 3km west of the ferry terminal, is a scruffy place but it does have great views of Gunung Rinjani.

ⓘ Getting There & Away

BUS & BEMO
Regular buses and bemos buzz between Mandalika Terminal in Mataram and Labuhan Lombok; the journey takes 2½ hours (35,000Rp). Some buses will only drop you off at the port entrance road, from where you can catch another bemo to the ferry terminal. Don't walk – it's too far.

FERRY
Ferries run hourly, 24 hours a day, between Labuhan Lombok and Poto Tano, Sumbawa (passengers 19,000Rp, 1½ hours). Cars cost 466,000Rp, motorbikes 54,000Rp. Through buses to points east from Bali and Lombok include the ferry fare.

South of Labuhan Lombok

South of Labuhan Lombok, **Selong**, the capital of the east Lombok administrative district, has some dusty Dutch colonial buildings.

Tanjung Luar is one of Lombok's main fishing ports (and home to one of Indonesia's most egregious shark-finning operations) and has lots of Bugis-style houses on stilts. It's off the main road. From here, the road swings west to **Keruak**, where wooden boats are built, and continues past the turn to **Sukaraja**, a traditional Sasak village where you can buy woodcarvings. Just west of Keruak a road leads south via Jerowaru to Ekas and the spectacular southeastern peninsula.

Gili Islands

Includes ➡

Best Places to Eat

➡ Sasak Cafe (p313)

➡ Kayu Café (p307)

➡ Pituq Café (p307)

➡ Ruby's (p317)

➡ Kokomo (p307)

Best Places to Sleep

➡ Adeng Adeng (p312)

➡ Kebun Kupu Kupu (p312)

➡ Indigo Bungalows (p303)

➡ Pondok Santi Estate (p306)

➡ Wilson's Retreat (p306)

➡ Biba Beach Village (p316)

Why Go?

Picture three minuscule desert islands, fringed by white-sand beaches and coconut palms, sitting in a turquoise sea: the Gilis are a vision of paradise. These islets have exploded in popularity, and are booming like nowhere else in Indonesia – speedboats zip visitors direct from Bali and hip new hotels are massing.

It's not hard to understand the Gilis' unique appeal, for a serenity endures (no motorbikes or dogs!) and a palm-shaded languor. Still, despite a growing green conscience, all three islands are seeing a lot of development and, in peak season, can feel mobbed.

Each island has its own special character. Gili Trawangan (universally known as Gili T) is by far the most cosmopolitan; its bar and party scene is vibrant, its accommodation and restaurants are close to definitive tropical chic. Gili Air has the strongest local character, but also a perfect mix of buzz and bliss. Gili Meno is flirting with shoreline gentrification.

When to Go

➡ The wet season is approximately late October until late March. But even in the height of the rainy season, when it's lashing it down on Lombok or Bali, the Gilis can be dry and sunny.

➡ High season is between June and late August and again at Christmas, when rooms are very hard to find and prices surge (though great weather is almost guaranteed).

➡ The perfect months to visit are May and September. It's fairly dry, the crowds have abated and there's no cyclone season to worry about. Still, with the Gilis' popularity growing so quickly, it's always a good idea to book a room in advance.

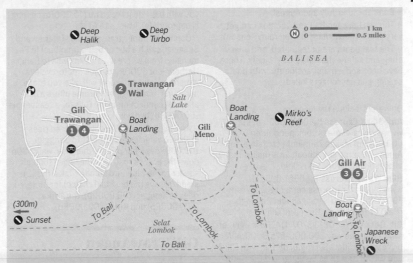

Gili Islands Highlights

1 Partying till Dawn (p309) Celebrating at Gili T's legendary raves and parties, which happen several nights a week at venues like Tir na Nog.

2 Trawangan Wall (p301) Swimming with all manner of fish at this popular dive spot near Gili T.

3 Gili Air (p314) Circling the island looking for your favourite beach.

4 Freediving (p301) Plumbing the depths on one breath, especially after you've taken lessons at one of Asia's best schools, Freedive Gili.

5 Great Eats (p318) Wandering the backstreets of Gili Air where you'll find excellent food, including Pura Vida.

🛈 Getting Around

CIDOMO

We cannot recommend using *cidomo* (horse-drawn carts) due to the significant questions about the treatment of the horses.

ISLAND-HOPPING

Recently introduced, public fast boats run almost hourly in daytime on a route linking Gili T, Gili Meno, Gili Air and Bangsal; they cost 85,000Rp. This makes it easy to hop from one Gili to another.

There's also a slow daily island-hopping boat service that loops between all three islands (15,000Rp to 50,000Rp). Check the latest timetable at the islands' docks. You can always charter boats between the islands (350,000Rp to 400,000Rp).

WALKING & CYCLING

The Gilis are flat and easy enough to get around by foot. Bicycles, available for hire on all three islands (per day 50,000Rp to 70,000Rp), can be a fun way to get around, but sandy stretches of path mean that you will spend time pushing your bike in the hot sun.

🛈 Getting There & Away

FROM BALI

Fast boats advertise swift connections (about two hours) between Bali and Gili Trawangan. They leave from several departure points in Bali, including Benoa Harbour, Sanur, Padangbai and Amed. Some go via Nusa Lembongan. Many dock at Teluk Nare/Teluk Kade on Lombok north of Senggigi before continuing on to Air and Trawangan (you'll have to transfer for Meno).

The website **Gili Bookings** (www.gilibookings. com) presents a range of boat operators and prices in response to your booking request. It's useful for getting an idea of the services offered, but it is not comprehensive and you may get a better price by buying direct from the operator.

Other considerations:

➡ Fares are not fixed, especially in quiet times – you should be able to get discounts on published fares.

➡ If you don't need transport to/from the boat, ask for a discount.

➡ The advertised times are illusionary. Boats are cancelled, unplanned stops are made or they simply run very late.

→ Book ahead in July and August.

→ The sea between Bali and Lombok can get very rough (particularly during rainy season).

→ The fast boats are unregulated, and operating and safety standards vary widely. There have been some major accidents, with boats sinking and passengers killed.

Operators include the following:

Amed Sea Express (✆0878 6306 4799; www.gili-sea-express.com; per person from 600,000Rp) Makes 75-minute crossings to Amed on a large speedboat. This makes many interesting itineraries possible.

Blue Water Express (✆0361-895 1111; www.bluewater-express.com; one way from 790,000Rp) From Serangan and Padangbai (Bali) to Teluk Kade, Gili T and Gili Air.

Gili Getaway (✆0813 3707 4147; www.giligetaway.com; one way 200,000-675,000Rp) Very professional; links Serangan on Bali with Gili T and Gili Air as well as Senggigi and Gili Gede.

Perama (✆0361-750808; www.peramatour.com; per person from 225,000Rp) Links Padangbai, the Gilis and Senggigi by a not-so-fast boat.

Scoot (www.scootcruise.com; one way from 700,000Rp) Boats link Sanur, Padangbai, Nusa Lembongan, Senggigi and the Gilis.

Semaya One (✆0361-877 8166; www.semaya-cruise.com; adult/child 650,000/550,000Rp) Network of services linking Sanur, Nusa Penida, Padangbai, Teluk Kade, Gili Air and Gili T.

FROM LOMBOK

Coming from Lombok, you can travel on one of the fast boats from Teluk Nare/Teluk Kade north of Senggigi. However, most people use the public boats that leave from Bangsal Harbour.

Boat tickets at Bangsal Harbour are sold at the port's large ticket office, which has posted prices and which is where you can also charter a boat. Buy a ticket elsewhere and you're getting played.

Public boats run to all three islands before 11am; after that you may only find one to Gili T or Gili Air. Public boats in both directions leave when the boat is full – about 30 people. When no public boat is running to your Gili, you may have to charter a boat (400,000Rp to 500,000Rp, carries up to 25 people).

One-way fares are 12,000Rp to Gili Air, 14,000Rp to Gili Meno and 15,000Rp to Gili Trawangan. Boats often pull up on the beaches; be prepared to wade ashore.

Public fast boats now run almost hourly in daytime on a route linking Gili T, Gili Meno, Gili Air and Bangsal; they cost 85,000Rp.

Although it had a bad reputation for years, **Bangsal Harbour** hassles are much reduced. Still, avoid touts and note that anyone who helps

you with bags deserves a tip (10,000Rp per bag is appropriate). There are ATMs.

Coming by public transport via Mataram and Senggigi, catch a bus or bemo (minibus) to Pemenang, from where it's a 1.2km walk to Bangsal Harbour – or 5000Rp by *ojek* (motorcycle taxi). A metered taxi to the port will take you to the harbour. From Senggigi, Perama offers a bus and boat connection to the Gilis for a reasonable 150,000Rp (two hours).

Arriving in Bangsal, you'll be offered rides in shared vehicles at the port. To Senggigi, 100,000Rp is a fair price. Otherwise, walk 500m down the access road past the huge tsunami shelter to the Blue Bird Lombok Taksi (p392) stand (always the best taxi choice) for metered rides to Senggigi (90,000Rp), the airport (200,000Rp) and Kuta (300,000Rp).

Gili Trawangan
✆0370

Gili Trawangan is a paradise of global repute, ranking alongside Bali and Borobudur as one of Indonesia's top destinations. Trawangan's heaving main drag, busy with bikes, horse carts and mobs of scantily clad visitors, can surprise those expecting some languid tropical retreat. Instead, a wall-to-wall roster of lounge bars, hip guesthouses, ambitious restaurants, convenience stores and dive schools clamour for attention.

And yet behind this glitzy facade, a bohemian character endures, with rickety warungs (food stalls) and reggae joints surviving between the cocktail tables, and quiet retreats dotting the much-less-busy north coast. Even as massive 200-plus-room hotels begin to colonise the gentrifying west coast, you can head just inland to a village laced with sandy lanes roamed by free-range roosters, fussing *ibu* (mothers) and wild-haired kids playing hopscotch. Here the call of the muezzin, not happy hour, defines the time of day.

🏖 Beaches

Gili T is ringed by the sort of powdery white sand people expect to find on Bali, but don't. It can be crowded along the bar-lined main part of the strip but walk just a bit north or south and east and you'll find some of Gili T's nicest beaches for swimming and snorkelling. You can find some solitude in parts of the west and north coasts, where it will be you and your towel on the sand – although water and Bintang vendors are never far away.

Note that at low tide large portions of the west and north coasts have rocks and coral near the surface, which makes trying to get off the shore deeply unpleasant. And the beach has eroded to oblivion on the northeast corner.

Many people simply enjoy the sensational views of Lombok and Gunung Rinjani as well as Bali and Gunung Agung.

🏃 Activities

Almost everything to do on Gili T will involve the water at some point.

Diving & Snorkelling

Trawangan is a major diving hot spot, with over a dozen professional scuba and freediving schools. Most dive schools and shops have good accommodation for clients who want to book a package.

There's fun snorkelling off the beach north of the boat landing – the coral isn't in the best shape here, but there are tons of fish. The reef is in much better shape off the northwest coast, but at low tide you'll have to scramble over some sharp dead coral (bring rubber booties) to access it. Snorkel gear rental averages 40,000Rp per day.

★ Lutwala Dive   DIVING
(✏ 0877 6549 2615; www.lutwala.com; divemaster courses 14,000,000Rp) A nitrox and five-star PADI centre owned by Fern Perry, who held the women's world record for deepest open-circuit dive (190m). A GIDA member, it also rents top-quality snorkelling gear.

Freedive Gili   DIVING
(✏ 0370-614 0503; www.freedivegili.com; beginner/advanced courses US$275/375) Freediving is a breath-hold technique that allows you to explore deeper depths than snorkelling (to 30m and beyond). Owned by an expert diver who has touched 90m on a single breath, Freedive Gili offers two-day beginner and three-day advanced courses. After a two-day course many students are able to get down to 20m on a single breath of air.

Trawangan Wall (15m)   DIVING
A noted spot for diving and snorkelling near Gili T.

Trawangan Dive   DIVING
(✏ 0370-614 9220; www.trawangandive.com; 5 guided nitrox boat dives from 2,700,000Rp) 🤿 A top, long-running dive shop and GIDA member with a fun (very large) pool-party vibe. Ask how you can join the regular beach

clean-ups. Also runs a paddle shop on-site, with stand up paddling (SUP) and kayak rentals and lessons.

Manta Dive   DIVING
(✏ 0370-614 3649; www.manta-dive.com; open-water courses 5,500,000Rp; 🐾) The biggest and still one of the best dive schools on the island, it has a large compound that spans the main road and a pool. It is a GIDA member and has special kids programs.

Blue Marlin Dive Centre   DIVING
(✏ 0370-613 2424; www.bluemarlindive.com; 10 dive nitrox package 5,100,000Rp) Gili T's original dive shop, and one of the best tech diving schools in the world. It's a GIDA member *and* home to one of Gili T's classic bars.

Big Bubble   DIVING
(✏ 0370-612 5020; www.bigbubblediving.com; fun dives day/night 490,000/600,000Rp) 🤿 The original engine behind the island's notable green crusading NGO, Gili Eco Trust, and a long-running dive school. It's a GIDA member. It's hidden behind a whitewashed cafe.

Surfing

Trawangan has a fast right reef break that can be surfed year-round (though it is temperamental) and at times swells overhead. Shop the backstreets for rentals as the much-hyped Surf Bar has outlandish prices for battered boards.

Walking & Cycling

Trawangan is perfect for exploring on foot or by bike. You can walk around the whole island in a couple of hours – if you finish at the hill on the southwestern corner (which

Gili Trawangan

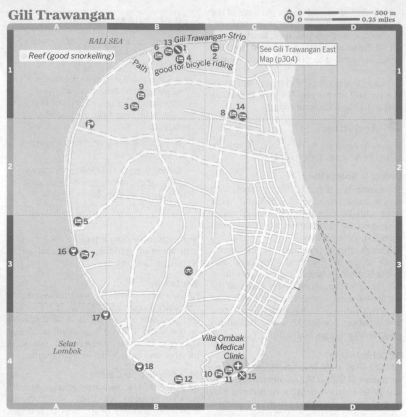

has the remains of an old Japanese gun placement circa WWII), you'll have terrific sunset views of Bali's Gunung Agung.

Bikes (per day from 50,000Rp to 100,000Rp; bargain hard) are a great way to get around. You'll find loads of rental outlets on the main strip. Beware of the bike-unfriendly north coast and know that the paths across the interior of the island are usually in good shape for cycling.

Sila   CYCLING
(☑0878 6562 3015; bike rentals per day from 50,000Rp) Has a huge range of bikes for rent, including two-seaters. Also does boat trips.

Yoga & Spas
Gili Yoga   YOGA
(☑0370-614 0503; www.giliyoga.com; per person from 100,000Rp) Runs daily vinyasa classes, and is part of Freedive Gili (p301).

Xqisit Spa   SPA
(☑0370-612 9405; www.exqisit.com; massages from 180,000Rp; ☺10am-10pm) A day spa on the waterfront with curtained-off treatment rooms for massage, and leather seats for mani-pedi or reflexology. Also has a coffee bar. The long list of services includes shiatsu and an 'extreme hangover recovery' massage treatment (700,000Rp) – talk about tapping into market demand!

🏃 Courses

Sweet & Spicy Cooking School   COOKING
(☑0877 6595 3052; www.facebook.com/gilicook ingschool; classes from 385,000Rp) Learn how to transform chillis and myriad other seasonings into spicy and flavourful Indonesian dishes at these entertaining daily cooking classes. As always, you get to eat your work.

Gili Trawangan

🛏 Sleeping

Gili T has more than 5000 rooms and an astonishing 675 registered places to stay, ranging from thatched huts to sleek, air-conditioned villas with private pools. Yet, in peak season the entire island is often booked out; reserve your room well ahead.

Many places are owned by local families with little or no experience of running hotels. Virtually all dive schools offer midrange accommodation; the cheapest digs are in the village.

⌂ Village

Madison Gili   BUNGALOW $
(📞 0878 6594 5554; www.madisongili.com; r from 350,000Rp; ✹🛜❄) Twelve bungalow-style units are crowded into a tight site around a pool. However, through clever design, each unit feels private. The rooms are comfortable and have extras like fridges. Staff are helpful. It's got a quiet back-lane location.

Pondok Gili Gecko   GUESTHOUSE $
(📞 0818 0573 2814; r incl breakfast from 350,000Rp; 🛜) An inviting guesthouse with a charming gecko motif. The four rooms are clean, and have ceiling fans and private tiled patios overlooking the garden.

Woodstock   BUNGALOW $$
(📞 0821 4765 5877; www.woodstockgili.com; r incl breakfast 500,000-1,000,000Rp; ✹🛜❄) Should the name surprise you given the vibe? Commune with the spirit of the Dead, Baez and Hendrix in 12 pristine rooms with tribal accents, private porches and outdoor baths, which surround a laid-back pool area.

★ Indigo Bungalows   GUESTHOUSE $$
(📞 0818 0371 0909; www.facebook.com/Indigo GiliT; r from 550,000Rp; ✹🛜❄) In the crowded Gili T midrange market, Indigo stands out for its attention to detail. The four rooms have hot water, patios and views of the pool or gardens. It's got a nice, quiet compound feel.

Oceane Paradise   COTTAGE $$
(📞 0812 3779 3533; r from 500,000Rp; ✹🛜) A terrific compound of nine wooden cottages with stylish outdoor bathrooms. One is family-sized.

Rumah Hantu   GUESTHOUSE $$
(📞 0819 1/10 2444; r from 450,000Rp; 🛜) A well-tended if simple collection of five thatch and bamboo rooms with high ceilings, in a garden plot. Management is welcoming and conscientious.

Alexyane Paradise   BUNGALOW $$
(📞 0878 6599 9645; r 300,000-900,000Rp; ✹🛜) Five great-quality dark-wood cottages with high ceilings, bamboo beds and lovely light-flooded outdoor baths. Nice wicker furniture on the porch.

Lumbung Cottages 2   BUNGALOW $$
(📞 0878 6589 0233; www.lumbungcottage.com; incl breakfast from 700,000Rp; ✹🛜❄) Eleven *lumbung* (rice-barn) cottages, set deep in the village, tucked up against the hillside, surrounding a black-bottom pool.

Gili Joglo   VILLA $$$
(📞 0813 5678 4741; www.gilijoglo.com; villas from 1,500,000Rp; ✹🛜) Three fabulous villas. One is crafted out of an antique *joglo* (traditional Javanese house) with polished concrete floors, two bedrooms and a massive indoor/outdoor great room. Though slightly smaller, we prefer the one built from two 1950s *gladaks* (middle-class homes). Rooms come with butler service.

Villa Nero   VILLA $$$
(📞 0819 0904 8000; www.thevillanero.com; villas incl breakfast from US$250; ✹🛜❄) One

GILI ISLANDS GILI TRAWANGAN

Gili Trawangan East

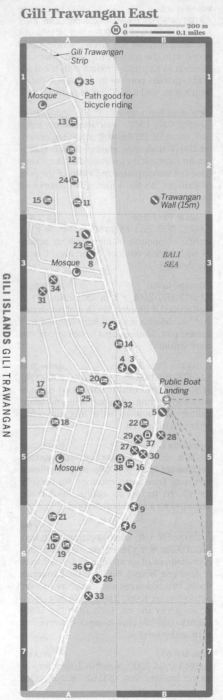

Gili Trawangan East

Activities, Courses & Tours
1	Big Bubble	A3
2	Blue Marlin Dive Centre	B5
3	Freedive Gili	B4
4	Gili Yoga	B4
5	Manta Dive	B5
6	Sila	B6
7	Sweet & Spicy Cooking School	A4
8	Trawangan Dive	A3
9	Xqisit Spa	B6

Sleeping
10	Alexyane Paradise	A6
11	Balé Sampan	A2
12	Blu d'aMare	A2
13	Danima Resort	A2
14	Gili Hostel	B4
15	Gili Joglo	A2
16	Le Petit Gili	B5
17	Lumbung Cottages 2	A4
18	Madison Gili	A5
19	Oceane Paradise	A6
20	Pondok Gili Gecko	A4
21	Rumah Hantu	A6
22	Sama Sama Bungalows	B5
23	Soundwaves	A3
24	Tanah Qita	A2
25	Villa Nero	A4

Eating
26	Beach House	A6
27	Green Cafe	B5
28	Kayu Café	B5
29	La Dolce Vita	B5
30	Pasar Malam	B5
31	Pituq Café	A3
32	Regina	B4
33	Scallywags	A6
34	Thai Garden	A3
	Warung Kiki Novi	(see 27)

Drinking & Nightlife
	Blue Marlin	(see 2)
35	La Moomba	A1
36	Tir na Nog	A6

Shopping
37	Abdi	B5
	Casa Vintage	(see 20)
38	Pasar Seni	B5

of the best-run and most luxurious places to stay on Gili T. Each of the 10 large units has hardwood floors across multiple rooms and a large lounging patio. The scheme is refreshingly minimalist, with accents of art and green plants. Among the many amenities: free bike use.

Main Strip

★ **Gili Hostel**   HOSTEL **$**
(☑ 0877 6526 7037; www.gilihostel.com; dm incl breakfast from 200,000Rp; ✳ 🛜 🏊) This co-ed dorm complex has a shaggy, bowed and peaked Torajan-style roof. The seven rooms each sleep seven, and have concrete floors, high ceilings, lockers and a sleeping loft. There's a rooftop bar with beanbags, sun loungers and hammocks, plus views of the treetops, the hills and the big party pool.

Le Petit Gili   GUESTHOUSE **$$**
(☑ 0878 6585 5545; www.facebook.com/LePetitGili; r 600,000-800,000Rp; ✳ 🛜) The three rooms here have a casual chic. The spaces are made cosy with natural woods and the odd antique. Big windows let the light in and let you look out at the views, which include the night market. Guests can use bikes and refill water bottles. Good ground-floor cafe.

Sama Sama Bungalows   BUNGALOW **$$**
(☑ 0370-612 1106; r incl breakfast 350,000-750,000Rp; ✳ 🛜) Just a few metres from where the fast boats drop you on the beach, the eight *lumbung* (rice-barn) units here are perfect if you want to be right in the very heart of the action.

Kokomo   VILLA **$$$**
(☑ 0370-613 4920; www.kokomogilit.com; r incl breakfast from 2,800,000Rp; ✳ 🛜 🏊) Offering beautifully finished and lavishly equipped modern accommodation, these 11 mini villas are set in a small complex at the quieter southern end of the main strip. All have private pools, contemporary decor and lovely indoor/outdoor living quarters. You can rent one, two or three bedrooms in your unit.

Pearl of Trawangan   RESORT **$$$**
(☑ 0813 3715 6999; www.pearloftrawangan.com; r incl breakfast from 1,600,000Rp; ✳ @ 🛜 🏊) Sinuous bamboo and thatch architecture echo the sinuous curves of the pool at this upscale property at the south end of the strip. There are tidy bungalows with 53 rooms on the inland side of the beach walk. Terraces boast very comfortable loungers. On the actual beach, there's a plush beach club.

Beachside

Tanah Qita   BUNGALOW **$$**
(☑ 0370-613 9159; 500,000-900,000Rp; ✳ 🛜) Tanah Qita ('Homeland') has large, immaculate *lumbung* units (with four-poster beds)

and smaller fan-cooled versions. The garden is a bucolic delight and you can escape the seaside crowds in the palm forests behind the rooms.

Soundwaves   BUNGALOW **$$**
(☑ 0819 3673 2404; www.soundwavesresort.com; r 400,000-1,200,000Rp; ✳ 🛜) The 13 rooms here are simple and clean with tiled floors. Some are set in wooden A-frames, others in a two-storey concrete building with staggered and recessed patios offering beach views from each room. Some rooms are fan-only.

Balé Sampan   HOTEL **$$**
(☑ 0812 3702 4048; www.balesampanbungalows.com; r incl breakfast garden/pool 910,000/1,000,000Rp; ✳ 🛜 🏊) On a nice wide-open stretch of beach. The 13 fine modern-edge rooms have stone baths and plush duvet covers. Other highlights include a freshwater pool and a proper English breakfast.

Blu d'aMare   BUNGALOW **$$$**
(☑ 0858 8866 2490; r from 1,500,000Rp; ✳ 🛜) At Blu d'aMare you can bed down in one of five lovely, 1920s Javanese houses (called *joglo*). Features include gorgeous old wood floors, queen beds, and freshwater showers in a sunken bath. It has a fine, Euro-accented cafe.

North, South & West Coasts

★ **Eden Cottages**   COTTAGE **$$**
(☑ 0819 1799 6151; www.edencottages.com; cottages 550,000-850,000Rp; ✳ 🏊) Six clean, thatched concrete bungalows wrapped around a pool, fringed by a garden and shaded by a coconut grove. Rooms have tasteful furnishings, stone baths, TV-DVD and (cold) fresh-water showers. The charming expat owner eschews wi-fi, which only increases the serenity.

Coconut Garden   BUNGALOW **$$**
(☑ 0819 0710 5769; www.coconutgardenresort.com; r incl breakfast from 750,000Rp; ✳ 🛜 🏊) An atmospheric spot with six bright and airy glass-box Javanese-style houses with tiled roofs connected to outdoor terrazzo baths. Expect plush linens, queen beds, a rolling lawn dotted with coco palms and small pool. It's on its own in a quiet inland quarter of the island and can be hard to find. Call ahead.

Alam Gili   HOTEL **$$**
(☑ 0370-613 0466; www.alamgili.com; r US$80-105; ✳ 🛜 🏊) A lush mature garden and a

quiet beach location are the main draws here. The nine rooms and villas in a small compound boast elegant lashings of old-school Balinese style. There's a small pool and a cafe on the beach.

★ Wilson's Retreat   RESORT $$$
(☑ 0370-612 0060; www.wilsons-retreat.com; r incl breakfast from 1,600,000Rp; ❋ 🛜 ❄) \Wilson's has 20 rooms plus four villas with private pools. Even though the setting is expansive, stylish and classy, it still manages some Gili languor. The excellent cafe overlooks a fine stretch of beach.

★ Pondok Santi Estate   RESORT $$$
(☑ 0370-714 0711; www.pondoksanti.com; r incl breakfast from US$200; ❋ 🛜 ❄) Ten gorgeous bungalows are set well apart on this old coconut plantation. Lawns now cover the grounds, and this is easily the classiest-looking resort on Gili T. The units have outdoor showers and rich, traditional wood decor. It's on a great beach and *just* close enough to the strip. Huge pool.

Five Elements   VILLA $$$
(☑ reservations 0361-870 9000; http://fiveelementsvillas.com; villa incl breakfast from 1,400,000Rp; ❋ 🛜 ❄) Widely spaced villas surround a 40m pool on a (still) lonely stretch of the west coast. The units are very comfortable and you can really feel like you've gotten away from it all here. Like other places on the west coast, this one is a hike if you want to have dinner on the strip.

Gili Teak Resort   BOUTIQUE HOTEL $$$
(☑ 0823 4018 4385; www.giliteak.com; r incl breakfast from 1,500,000Rp; ❋ 🛜 ❄) New Age bungalows have glass walls and a stylish, simple design that lets in lots of light. Terraces for each of the eight units have plush loungers plus there's a lovely seating area down by the ocean, all of which begs guests to settle back, relax and let the days drift by. The grounds are attractive, the cafe good.

Danima Resort   GUESTHOUSE $$$
(☑ 0878 6087 2506; www.giliresortdanima.com; r from 1,600,000Rp; ❋ 🛜 ❄) An intimate four-room boutique property. Nests are blessed with commodious king-sized beds, vaulted ceilings, tasteful lighting, rattan deck seating and rain showers. It has a romantic pool and beach area too.

Gili Eco Villas   VILLA $$$
(☑ 0361-847 6419; www.giliecovillas.com; r/villa from US$120/250; ❋ 🛜 ❄) 🍃 Nineteen classy rooms and villas, made from recycled teak salvaged from old Javanese colonial buildings, are set back from the beach on Trawangan's relaxed north coast. Comfort and style are combined with solid green principles (water is recycled, there's an organic vegetable garden, and solar and wind energy provide most of the power).

Kelapa Villas   VILLA $$$
(☑ 0812 375 6003; www.kelapavillas.com; villas from 1,700,000Rp; ❋ 🛜 ❄) Luxury development in an inland location with a selection

---

DANGERS & ANNOYANCES

➡ Although it's rare, some foreign women have experienced sexual harassment and even assault while on the Gilis – it's best not to walk home alone to the quieter parts of the islands.

➡ As tranquil as these seas appear, currents are strong in the channels between the islands. Do not try to swim between Gili Islands as it can be deadly.

➡ The drug trade remains endemic in Trawangan. You'll get offers of mushrooms, meth and other drugs. But remember, Indonesia has a strong anti-drugs policy; those found in possession of or taking drugs risk jail or worse.

➡ Tourists have been injured and killed by adulterated *arak* (colourless, distilled palm wine) on the Gilis; skip it.

➡ Bike riders (almost entirely tourists) regularly plough into and injure people on Gili T's main drag. *Cidomo* (horse-drawn carts) hauling construction goods are almost as bad.

➡ Police visit the Gilis sporadically. Immediately report thefts to the island *kepala desa* (village head), who will deal with the issue; staff at the dive schools will direct you to him.

➡ For trouble on Gili Trawangan, contact Satgas, the community organisation that runs island affairs, via your hotel or dive centre. Satgas tries to resolve problems and track down stolen property.

of 17 commodious villas, all with private pools, that offer style and space in abundance. There's a tennis court and a gym in the complex. Wi-fi does not cover all areas.

✕ Eating

In the evenings, numerous places on the main strip display and grill delicious fresh seafood. There's not much to distinguish them – pick by what looks good and how much chilli and garlic you like in your marinade.

Elsewhere on the strip, you'll find timeless beach bars with lots of Indo standards. There's also a growing number of high-concept cafes.

★ Pituq Café   VEGAN $
(☑0812 3677 5161; mains from 30,000Rp; 🍴) More lifestyle choice than food choice, this hippie-trail-to-Kerala place combines yoga, dreadlocks and exquisite vegan fare in a chilled-out open-air compound. Lounge around on raised platforms and discover the height Gili T's vegetables can reach when given a chance by the talents in the kitchen. Meditation classes daily (150,000Rp).

★ Pasar Malam   MARKET $
(mains 15,000-30,000Rp; ⊙6pm-midnight) Blooming every evening in front of Gili T's market, this night market is the place to indulge in ample local eats, including tangy noodle soup, savoury fried treats, scrumptious *ayam goreng* (fried chicken) and grilled fresh catch. Just wandering around the stalls looking at all the dishes vying for your attention will get you drooling. It's cleared away by day.

La Dolce Vita   ITALIAN $
(mains 20,000-40,000Rp; ⊙ 7.30am-5pm Tue-Sun; ❄) There comes that moment when another nasi goreng will just make you turn nasty. Don't delay, hop right on over to this expanded cafe that's not much bigger than one of its excellent espressos. Slices of authentic pizza and a whole range of pastries are joined by daily specials to sate the ravenous.

Warung Kiki Novi   INDONESIAN $
(mains from 15,000Rp; ⊙8am-10pm) Long-time islanders will tell you that this is the best place for *nasi campur* (rice with a choice of side dishes) in the Gilis, and they are right; this cheery dining room is the scene of budget-dining nirvana. Besides fine Indo mains there's a smattering of Western sandwiches and salads.

Green Cafe   INDONESIAN $
(☑0878 6335 4272; mains from 20,000Rp; ⊙6-11pm) Our favourite stall at the night market, Green Cafe is towards the back but you'll find it easily enough. Serves grilled mains, salads and an array of luscious desserts (which they cheerfully box to go). Waiters will help you through then line up for tips. During the day they have a cafe at the very back of the square.

★ Kayu Café   CAFE $$
(☑0878 6239 1308; mains 40,000-80,000Rp; ⊙8am-10pm; ❄🖥) There are two options here: the main cafe on the inland side of the strip has a lovely array of healthy baked goods, salads, sandwiches and the island's best juices, all served in air-con comfort. Across the road the beach cafe is all open air and exposed wood. Service on the sand can be slow – head inside to order.

★ Kokomo   INTERNATIONAL $$
(☑0370-613 4920; www.kokomogilit.com; mains 60,000-200,000Rp; ⊙8am-11pm; ❄🖥) One of the more formal dining spots on the island, Kokomo creates complex dishes with fresh local seafood and select imported meats. Lots of fresh salads, wonderful steaks and pasta – but for the ultimate treat, opt for a seafood or sashimi platter (with Atlantic salmon and yellowfin tuna). It's got a superb waterfront location.

Regina   PIZZA $$
(☑0877 6506 6255; mains 40,000-100,000Rp; ⊙5-11pm) The wood-fired oven rarely gets a break at this excellent Italian joint, just inland. At busy times there's a long line for takeaway pizzas, but a better option is to find a bamboo table in the garden and have some cold ones with the fine thin-crust pies. A sign announces: 'no pizza pineapple'. Ahh, the sound of authenticity...

Scallywags   INTERNATIONAL $$
(☑0370-614 5301; www.scallywagsresort.com; meals 40,000-180,000Rp; ⊙8am-10pm; 🖥) Offers casual yet stylish beach decor, polished glassware, switched on service and superb cocktails. The dinner menu features tasty seafood – fresh lobster, tuna steaks, snapper and swordfish – and a great salad bar. The seafood barbecue lures many right in.

Thai Garden   THAI $$
(☑0878 6453 1253; mains 50,000-120,000Rp; ⊙3-10pm) Who needs Bangkok when you have Gili T? The most authentic Thai food

DIVING THE GILIS

The Gili Islands are a superb dive destination as the marine life is plentiful and varied. Turtles and black- and white-tip reef sharks are common, and the macro life (small stuff) is excellent, with seahorses, pipefish and lots of crustaceans. Around the full moon, large schools of bumphead parrotfish appear to feast on coral spawn; at other times of year manta rays cruise past dive sites.

Though years of bomb fishing and an El Niño–induced bleaching damaged corals above 18m, the reefs are now well into a profound recovery and haven't looked this great in years. The Gilis also have their share of virgin coral.

Safety standards are reasonably high on the Gilis, but with the proliferation of new dive schools, several have formed the Gili Island Dive Association (GIDA), which comes together for monthly meetings on conservation and dive impact issues. They all mind a written list of standards that considers the safety of their divers, a limitation on number of divers per day and preservation of the sites to be paramount concerns, which is why we highly recommend diving with GIDA-associated shops (identifiable by a logo). All GIDA shops carry oxygen on their boats and have working radios. They also have a price agreement for fun dives, training and certification. Sample prices:

Introductory Dives 900,000Rp

Openwater Course 5,500,000Rp

Rescue Diver Course 5,000,000Rp

Some of the best dive sites include the following:

Deep Halik A canyon-like site ideally suited to drift diving. Black- and white-tip sharks are often seen at 28m to 30m.

Deep Turbo At around 30m, this site is ideally suited to nitrox diving. It has impressive sea fans and leopard sharks hidden in the crevasses.

Japanese Wreck For experienced divers only (it lies at 45m), this shipwreck of a Japanese patrol boat (c WWII) is another site ideal for tech divers.

Mirko's Reef Named for a beloved dive instructor who passed away, this canyon was never bombed and has vibrant, pristine soft and table coral formations.

Shark Point Perhaps the most exhilarating Gili dive: reef sharks and turtles are very regularly encountered, as well as schools of bumphead parrotfish and mantas.

Sunset (Manta Point) Some impressive table coral; sharks and large pelagics are frequently encountered.

this side of Phuket is served up in a cute little garden. The flavours are spot on thanks to regular imports of key spices. Here's the place to beat the Indo rice blues.

Pearl Beach Lounge INTERNATIONAL $$
(✆0370-613 7788; www.pearlbeachlounge.com; mains 60,000-200,000Rp; ⏰8am-11pm; 🛜)
The bamboo flows only a little less fluidly than the beer at this high-concept beachside lounge and restaurant. During the day, spending 100,000Rp on food and drink from the burger-filled menu gets you access to a pool and comfy beach loungers. At night the striking bamboo main pavilion comes alive, and more complex steak and seafood mains are on offer.

Beach House INTERNATIONAL $$
(✆0370-614 2352; www.beachhousegilit.com; mains 75,000-250,000Rp; ⏰11am-10pm; 🛜)
Boasts an elegant marina terrace, a wonderful nightly barbecue, a salad bar and fine wine. Among much competition, it's a contender for the best barbecued seafood around and is always popular. Book ahead.

🍷 Drinking & Nightlife

The island has oodles of beachside drinking dens, ranging from sleek lounge bars to simple shacks. Parties are held several nights a week, shifting between mainstay bars such as Tir na Nog and Rudy's Pub, and various other upstarts. The strip south of the Pasar Malam is the centre for raucous nightlife.

★ Casa Vintage Beach   LOUNGE
(⏰ 11am-10pm) While strains of Billie Holiday add mellifluous accents to the lapping surf, enjoy excellent Jamaican food (mains from 70,000Rp). Or just let the sand caress your toes as you hang low in a hammock. The Swedish-Jamaican owners make a mean carrot cake. Great sunsets; don't miss soul food Sundays.

Paradise Sunset Bar   BAR
(⏰ 10am-late) The name says it all. All types of seating can be found right on the beach. Large trees offer shade by day while the restful swish of the surf calms the soul. Sunsets are cinematic, drinks are good.

Exile   BAR
(📞 0819 0772 1858; ⏰ noon-late) This beach bar has a party vibe at all hours. It's locally owned and 20 minutes from the main strip on foot, or an easy bike ride. There is also a compound of 10 woven bamboo bungalows with rooms from 450,000Rp, just in case home seems too far.

La Moomba   BAR
(⏰ 10am-midnight) If you wish to chill on a luscious white beach, with bamboo lounges and reggae pumping from the tiki bar, head to La Moomba, Trawangan's best beach bar.

Tir na Nog   PUB
(📞 0370-613 9463; ⏰ 7am-2am Thu-Tue, to 4am Wed; 🛜) Known simply as 'the Irish', this hanger of hangovers has a sports-bar interior with big screens. It serves bar chow such as kebabs (mains 35,000Rp to 80,000Rp) in the heart of the bar zone. Its shoreside open-air bar is probably the busiest meeting spot on the island. Jovial mayhem reigns on Wednesday nights when the DJ takes over.

GREEN GILI

When you pay your hotel or diving bill on the Gilis you may be offered the chance to pay an 'Eco Tax' (50,000Rp per person). It's a voluntary donation, set up by the pioneering **Gili Eco Trust** (www.giliecotrust.com) to improve the island's environment.

It's a worthy cause. The environmental pressure on the Gilis as their popularity has grown is enormous. Intensive development and rubbish plus offshore reef damage from fishers using cyanide and dynamite to harvest fish have been just some of the problems. Up to 10,000 visitors and workers arrive on the islands each day.

Eco Trust has several initiatives to help:

➡ Distributing free reusable shopping bags to cut down on plastic-bag use, and encouraging restaurants to stop using plastic straws.

➡ An aggressive education campaign to get locals and business owners to recycle their rubbish. There are now over 1000 recycling bins on the islands.

➡ A long-term scheme to recycle virtually all the rubbish on the islands. Plans are being made for a recycling centre.

➡ Care of the islands' horses – vet clinics are offered and there are driver education programs in horse care.

➡ Biorock, a reef restoration program that now has over 120 installations around the islands.

There are many ways visitors to the Gilis can help, besides just paying the Eco Tax:

Clean up the beach Eco Trust and Trawangan Dive both organise weekly beach cleanups and more hands are always needed. Admire the white sand and azure waters as you do your own freelance beach clean-up. Toss anything you find in a recycling bin.

Report horse mistreatment Anyone seeing a *cidomo* (horse-drawn cart) driver mistreating a horse can get the number of the cart and report it to Eco Trust (📞 0370-625020 or 0813 3960 0553), which will follow up with the driver. Unfortunately, many transport carts with their heavy loads of construction supplies and Bintang have no cart numbers for reporting.

Build a reef For 10,000,000Rp you'll get two dives a day for two weeks, can help build a Biorock installation and get various specialist diving certifications. Eco Trust has details.

Blue Marlin BAR

(⊘8am-late) Of all the party bars, this upper-level venue has the largest dance floor and the meanest sound system – it pumps trance and tribal beats on Mondays.

🔒 Shopping

Gili Trawangan was once the domain of cheap knick-knack stalls and not much else, but a stream of refinement is rapidly taking root. Outlets of Bali boutiques are popping up along the main strip near the Pasar Malam.

★ Casa Vintage CLOTHING

(⊘9am-9pm) The best boutique on Gili T is tucked on a backstreet near the cafe Il Pirata. It's a treasure trove of vintage fashion sourced internationally, and displayed with grace. Browse chunky earrings, superb leather bags, baby-doll dresses, and John Lennon shades. It's a sibling of Casa Vintage Beach (p309) bar.

Abdi CLOTHING

(⊘10am-8pm) Forgot your favourite frock? Shop for flouncy beachwear at this stylish shop.

Pasar Seni MARKET

Everyday goods are sold at this small village marketplace.

ℹ️ Information

MEDICAL SERVICES

There's a **health clinic** (⊘24hr) just south of Hotel Vila Ombak.

MONEY

Gili T has abundant ATMs on the main strip and even on the west coast.

ℹ️ Getting There & Away

You can buy tickets and catch public and island-hopping boats at the public boat landing. While you wait for your ship to sail, note the amazing number of Bintang bottles arriving full and leaving empty. Several of the fast-boat companies have offices on Gili T.

The various fast boats run by private companies anchor all along the beach on the east side.

Gili Meno

📞 0370

Gili Meno is the smallest of the three Gili Islands and a good setting for your desert-island fantasy. Meno has a certain *Robinson Crusoe* charm, although new resorts under construction will mean Crusoe will want to don some Ray-Bans.

Most accommodation is strung out along the east coast, near the most picturesque beach. Inland you'll find scattered homesteads, coconut plantations and a salty lake. The once-lonely west coast is seeing some high-profile development, including an enormous beachside condo project called Bask (www.baskgilimeno.com) that is slated to have over 130 rooms when it opens in late 2017. It's got some powerful Australian backers and a high-profile pitchman, ex-*Baywatch* star David Hasselhoff (aka 'The Hoff'). The effect of this huge resort on little Gili Meno is likely to be profound.

🏖️ Beaches

Ringed by sand, Gili Meno has one of the best strips of beach in the Gilis at its southeast corner. The sand is wide and powdery white, while the swimming is excellent. The west coast is rockier with crushed coral, and a lot of rocks and coral near the surface at low tide. Meno's northeast also has nice sand, although erosion is a problem in parts. It takes around two hours to circumnavigate Meno on foot.

⊙ Sights

Gili Meno's large inland salt lake is home to imposing white egrets, which make it an intriguing natural attraction.

Turtle Sanctuary HATCHERY

(www.gilimenoturtles.com; donations accepted; ⊘office 9am-6pm; 🚻) Meno's turtle sanctuary consists of an assortment of pools and bathtubs on the beach, filled with baby green and loggerhead turtles. They're nurtured here until they're around eight months old, and then released. Some environmentalists say this is too long to keep turtles in captivity, yet the impact of the hatchery on turtle populations has been considerable.

With a simple snorkel you're all but guaranteed a sighting. You can also attend one of the regular releases.

🏃 Activities

Like the other Gilis, most of the fun here involves getting wet. Additionally, walking around the island is scenic and takes less than two hours.

Although you can rent bikes for 50,000Rp per day, you won't get far. The beach path from the southern tip right around up the

Gili Meno

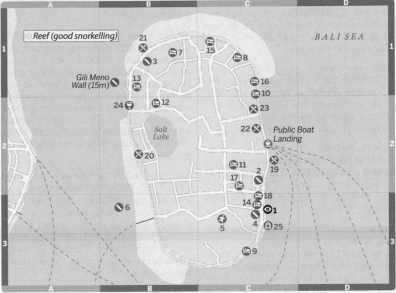

Gili Meno

◎ Sights
1	Turtle Sanctuary	C3

◉ Activities, Courses & Tours
2	Blue Marlin Dive	C2
3	Divine Divers	B1
4	Gili Meno Divers	C3
5	Mao Meno	C3
6	Meno Slope (21m)	B3

⊜ Sleeping
7	Adeng Adeng	B1
8	Ana Bungalow	C1
9	Biru Meno Beach Bungalows	C3
10	Gili Meno Eco Hostel	C1
11	Jepun Bungalows	C2
12	Kebun Kupu Kupu	B2
13	Mahamaya	B1

14	Mallias Bungalows	C3
15	Paul's Last Resort	C1
16	Seri Resort	C1
17	Tropicana Hideaways	C2
18	Villa Nautilus	C3

⊗ Eating
19	Rust Warung	C2
20	Sasak Cafe	B2
21	Webe Café	B1
22	Ya Ya Warung	C2
23	Zoraya Cafe	C2

⊜ Drinking & Nightlife
24	Diana Café	B2

⊜ Shopping
25	Art Shop Botol	C3

west coast to the top of the salt lake is a shadeless dry sand path that will have you walking your wheels. You can go for a little jaunt to the northwest coast on the good path along the north side of the lake, but again soft sand along the very north will stymie riding further.

Diving & Snorkelling

Snorkelling is good off the northeast coast, on the west coast towards the north, and also around the site of the vast new Bask

hotel on the west coast. Gear is available from 50,000Rp per day. Meno Slope (21m), off Gili Meno, and Gili Meno Wall (15m) are two top dive sites.

Blue Ocean   WATER SPORTS
(☑ 0813 3950 9859; boat tours 150,000Rp) The irrepressible Mr Dean offers snorkelling boat tours of the rich waters around the Gilis. Tours are two to three hours. He'll drop you at another island, so you can check out underwater delights as you island-hop.

Divine Divers DIVING

(📱0852 4057 0777; www.divinedivers.com; guided dives from 500,000Rp) This Meno-only dive shop is on a sweet slice of beach on the west coast. It has rooms, a pool and offers some good dive/stay packages.

Gili Meno Divers DIVING

(📱0878 6536 7551; www.gilimenodivers.com; Kontiki Cottages; introductory dives from 900,000Rp; ⊙9am-5pm) French and Indonesian owned; offers a range of courses including some good ones in underwater photography.

Blue Marlin Dive DIVING

(📱0370-639980; www.bluemarlindive.com; guided boat dives 490,000Rp) The Meno outlet of the Trawangan original, this is a well-respected mainstream dive shop. There are rooms here, too.

Yoga

Mao Meno YOGA

(📱0819 9937 8359; www.mao-meno.com; classes from 120,000Rp) Offers daily classes in styles that include ashtanga and vinyasa in a beautiful natural wood pavilion. It has simple cottages on its inland compound that rent from US$45 per night.

🛏 Sleeping

Meno leads the way in Gili growth and new properties are appearing – some rather posh. Prices have also climbed sharply as visitor numbers have increased. Also, as new developments are announced, older more modest guesthouses are literally wiped off the map, so confirm that the place you want to stay at is actually open.

Gili Meno Eco Hostel HOSTEL $

(📱0878 6249 2062; www.facebook.com/Gilimenoecohostel; dm/r from 90,000/200,000Rp; 🛜) 🍃 A fantasy in driftwood, this is the place you dream about when you're stuck in the snow waiting for a train. A volleyball court, groovy lounge, tree house, beach bar and more open onto the sand. Recycling and other ecofriendly practices are touted. But it's not for everyone: beds can be hammocks, there are no doors and service can be shambolic.

⭐**Kebun Kupu Kupu** GUESTHOUSE $$

(📱0819 0742 8165; www.kupumenoresort.com; r from 800,000Rp; ❄🛜🏊) Situated 300m from the beach, this collection of modern, sleek bungalows has a great pool, palm trees overhead and a quiet spot near the salt lake.

The French owners honour their heritage by serving excellent food (the crème brûlée is particularly good).

⭐**Adeng Adeng** BUNGALOW $$

(📱0818 0534 1019; www.adeng-adeng.com; r incl breakfast 750,000-2,000,000Rp; ❄🛜) 🍃 A creative five-unit guesthouse set among trees, just back from a fine stretch of sand. Its simple wooden bungalows have all the creature comforts and stylish outdoor terrazzo baths. The rambling tropical gardens are sprinkled with artisanal accents, and the cafe serves Thai-inspired fare. Good water conservation practices.

Biru Menu Beach Bungalows BUNGALOW $$

(📱0813 3975 8968; http://birumeno.com; r incl breakfast from 900,000Rp; ❄🛜) Attractive natural stone bungalows in a tree-shaded compound are the headline feature in this unassuming but welcoming resort on a beautiful stretch of beach. The beach is just over the shore path. The cafe has a wood-burning pizza oven.

Seri Resort RESORT $$

(📱0822 3759 6677; www.seriresortgilimeno.com; r 400,000-1,600,000Rp; ❄🛜🏊) It's a tough call, but we think this beachfront resort is just *that* much whiter than the surrounding sand. There is an interesting range of 75 rooms here, from budget huts that share bathrooms, to suites in three-storey blocks, to luxurious beach villas. Service is good, the atmosphere high end and there are activities including yoga.

Mallias Bungalows INN $$

(📱0878 6413 0719, 0819 1732 3327; www.malliasgili.com; r 500,000-1,500,000Rp; ❄🛜) This location right on Meno's best beach can't be beaten. The bungalows are simple – although some have air-con – really just bamboo and thatch. As such they are a good deal at the lower end of the price range. Then again, swinging on a hammock on your porch overlooking the beach is priceless.

Tropicana Hideaways BUNGALOW $$

(📱0878 6431 3828; www.tropicalhideawaysresort.com; r 400,000-900,000Rp; ❄🛜) A modest collection of five bungalows set in a sunny coconut-palm garden. Cottages are clean and basic; you'll find several similar places back here.

Ana Bungalow BUNGALOW $$

(📱0878 6169 6315; www.anawarung.com; r with fan/air-con from 400,000/600,000Rp; ❄🛜)

Four peaked-roof, thatch-and-bamboo bungalows with picture windows, and pebbled floors in the outdoor bathrooms. This family-run place has a cute used-book exchange on the beach next to its four lovely dining *berugas* (open-sided pavilions) lit with paper lanterns. Seafood dinners are excellent, as is the location.

Paul's Last Resort
BUNGALOW $$

(☑0878 6569 2272; r from 700,000Rp; ☜☒) This respectable collection of solid bungalows are in a good position. No one will be huffing and puffing at these units. It's comfortable and on a nice, white stretch of sand. If you need internet, check the wi-fi before you commit. The beachfront Ryan's Cafe has good sunset views.

Jepun Bungalows
BUNGALOW $$

(☑0819 1739 4736; www.jepunbungalows.com; r with fan/air-con 400,000/700,000Rp; ☒☜) Just 100m from the main beach path and harbour, with charming accommodation dotted around a garden. Choose from six lovely thatched *lumbung* (rice-barn) bungalows, or book the family house; all have bathrooms with fresh (hot) water and good-quality beds. Three have air-con.

Mahamaya
BOUTIQUE HOTEL $$$

(☑0888 715 5828, 0370-637616; www.mahamaya. co; r from 1,800,000Rp; ☒☜☒) 🏊 A blindingly whitewashed modern pearl with resort service and 14 rooms featuring attractive stone floors, rough-cut marble patios, and white- and washed-wood furnishings. The restaurant is good; have dinner at the water's edge at your own private table.

Villa Nautilus
VILLA $$$

(☑0370-642143; www.villanautilus.com; r incl breakfast from US$125; ☒☜☒) A comfortable, slightly rough-edged option, these five well-designed detached villas enjoy a grassy plot just off the beach. They're finished in contemporary style with natural wood, marble and limestone, and the hip bathrooms have fresh water. The deckchairs are addictive.

🍴 Eating

Almost all of Meno's restaurants have absorbing sea views, which is just as well as service can be slow everywhere.

Breakfast at one of the cafes on Meno's east coast is a sublime experience of turquoise water and Gunung Rinjani views.

★ Sasak Cafe
INDONESIAN $

(mains 25,000-80,000Rp; ⊙kitchen 7am-9pm, bar till late) Considering its out-of-the-way location, this bamboo-and-thatch, island-casual hang-out has tasty Indo standards, which literally take on a rosy glow when the sun sets. The tunes and the drinks flow late into the night.

Zoraya Cafe
CAFE $

(mains from 25,000Rp; ⊙8am-10pm) Little thatched platforms at the edge of the sea at this relaxed cafe allow you to enjoy a cheap Bintang and a simple meal while charter-boat skippers wander past and life drifts by around you.

Ya Ya Warung
INDONESIAN $

(dishes 15,000-30,000Rp; ⊙8am-10pm) Defining ramshackle. This food-stall-on-the-beach serves up Indonesian faves, curries, pancakes and plenty of pasta, along with the views you came to Meno to enjoy.

Webe Café
INDONESIAN $

(☑0821 4776 3187; mains from 25,000Rp; ⊙8am-10pm; ☜) A wonderful location for a meal, Webe Café has low tables sunk in the sand (and tables under shade), with the turquoise water just a metre away. It scores well for Sasak and Indonesian food such as *kelak kuning* (snapper in yellow spice); staff fire up a seafood barbecue most nights too. There are basic bungalows for rent (from 400,000Rp).

Rust Warung
INDONESIAN $

(☑0370-642324; mains 20,000-75,000Rp; ⊙8am-10pm) The most visible cog of the Rust empire (which includes Meno's one grocery) has a great waterfront position overlooking the beach. It's renowned for its grilled fish (with garlic or sweet-and-sour sauce), but also serves pizza and makes a very fine banana pancake any time of the day or night. Ask for the homemade sambal.

🍺 Drinking & Nightlife

Gili Meno is the kind of island where you stroll a white beach, then plop down under a bamboo thatched cover for a cold beer while your toes tickle the sand.

Diana Café
BAR

(⊙8am-9pm) If you find the pace of life on Meno too busy, head to this intoxicating little tiki bar. Diana couldn't be simpler: a wobbly looking bamboo-and-thatch bar, a few tables on the sand, a shack offering tattoos, a hammock or two, reggae on the stereo and a chill-out zone.

🛍 Shopping

★ Art Shop Botol   ARTS & CRAFTS
(⊙ hours vary) Art Shop Botol is a large hand-icrafts stall just south of Kontiki Meno hotel. Choose from masks, Sasak water baskets, wood carvings and gourds. It's run by an elderly shopkeeper with 11 children and countless grandchildren.

ℹ Information
Meno now has ATMs.

ℹ Getting There & Away
The public boat landing is an increasingly busy place. None of the fast boats from Bali directly serve Meno, although some provide connections. Otherwise, you can go to Gili Trawangan or Gili Air and take the regular interisland fast boat.

Gili Air
☑ 0370

Closest of the Gilis to Lombok, Gili Air falls between Gili T's sophistication and Meno's minimalist vibe, and is for many just right. The white-sand beaches here are arguably the best of the Gili bunch and there's just enough buzz to provide a dash of nightlife. Snorkelling is good right from the main strip – a lovely sandy lane dotted with bamboo bungalows and little restaurants where you can eat virtually on top of a turquoise sea.

Though tourism dominates Gili Air's economy, coconuts, fishing and creating the fake-distressed fishing-boat wood vital to any stylish Gili guesthouse are important income streams. Buzzy little strips have developed along the beaches in the southeast and the west, although the lanes are still more sandy than paved.

🏖 Beaches

The entire east side of the island has great beaches with powdery white sand and a gentle slope into beautiful turquoise water, with a foot-friendly sandy bottom. There are also good, private spots the rest of the way around Gili Air, but low-tide rocks and coral are a problem. For drinks and sunset, head north.

🏃 Activities

Diving & Snorkelling
The entire east coast has an offshore reef teeming with colourful fish; there's a drop-off about 100m to 200m out. Snorkelling gear is easily hired for about 50,000Rp per day. Air Wall (8m) is a popular dive site with a wall of coral.

The island has an excellent collection of dive shops which charge the standard Gili rates.

7 Seas   DIVING
(☑ 0370-663 2150; www.7seasdivegili.com; 4-day TEC diving packages 6,400,000Rp) ⌖ A vast dive shop with a range of accommodation and a good pool for training or just playing. A local leader in recycling.

Gili Air Divers   DIVING
(☑ 0878 6536 7551; www.giliairdivers.com; Sunrise Hotel; guided diving boat trip 490,000Rp; ⊙ 8am-8pm) ⌖ This French-Indo-owned dive shop is long on charm and skill.

Oceans 5   DIVING
(☑ 0813 3877 7144; www.oceans5dive.com; fun dives from 600,000Rp) ⌖ Has a 25m training pool, an in-house marine biologist and nice hotel rooms. Also offers a program of yoga diving, and emphasises sustainable diving practices to its guests.

Blue Marine Dive Centre   DIVING
(☑ 0812 377 0288; www.bluemarinedive.com; night dives 600,000Rp) ⌖ Has a nice location on the beautiful northeast corner of the island. Offers freediving courses. The owner is very active in reef preservation efforts.

Surfing
Directly off the southern tip of the island there's a long, peeling right-hand break that can get big at times.

Cycling
Bikes can be rented for 50,000Rp a day but large sections of the coastal path in the north and west are annoying, as long slogs of deep sand swallow the trail at times and mud after rains can be impassable. Inland lanes, however, are mostly concrete and very rideable. Some shops have bikes with huge tyres that actually aren't any easier to pedal.

Yoga & Spas
H2O Yoga   YOGA
(☑ 0877 6103 8836; www.h2oyogaandmedita tion.com; classes 100,000Rp, 3hr workshops

Gili Air

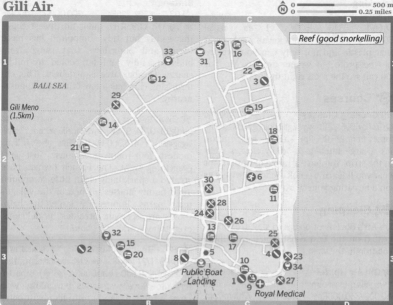

500 m
0.25 miles

Reef (good snorkelling)

BALI SEA

Gili Meno
(1.5km)

Public Boat
Landing

Royal Medical

Gili Air

Activities, Courses & Tours

Sleeping

Eating

Drinking & Nightlife

300,000Rp) This wonderful yoga and meditation retreat centre is set back from the beach on a well-signed path in the village. Top-quality classes are held in a lovely circular *beruga* (open-sided pavilion). Massage is also available. There are classes daily at 9am and 'candlelight yoga' at 5pm. Other sessions may be held at other times; call or stop in.

Harmony Spa   SPA
(☑ 0812 386 5883; massages from 150,000Rp; ☺ 9am-8pm) The beautiful north-coast location alone will make you feel renewed. Facials, body treatments and more are on offer. Call first.

Kayaking

Oriental Land   KAYAKING
(📞0878 6546 1505; 1-/2-hr rental 150,000/270,000Rp) Rent a kayak made from clear plastic and not only can you explore the reef-protected waters around Air, but you can see the reefs right under you.

🎓 Courses

Gili Cooking Classes   COOKING
(📞0877 6506 7210; www.gilicookingclasses.com; classes from 275,000Rp) This slick operation has a large kitchen for daily classes right on the strip. You have a range of options for what you'll learn to cook – choose wisely as you'll be eating your work.

🛏 Sleeping

Gili Air's dozens of places to stay are mostly located on the east coast. You'll find more isolation in the west.

⭐Gili Air Hostel   HOSTEL $
(www.giliairhostel.com; dm/r from 150,000/350,000Rp; ⊙reception 7.30am-7pm; ❄🛜) Beds at this fun hostel are in two- to seven-bed rooms, all of which share bathrooms. The decor defines cheery, and there's a cool bar, a huge frangipani tree and even a climbing wall.

Bintang Beach 2   BUNGALOW $
(📞0877 6522 2554; r 200,000-450,000Rp; ❄🛜) On Gili Air's quiet northwest coast, this sandy but tidy compound has basic rooms and bungalows that range from budget-friendly and fan-cooled to mildly snazzy. The bar area is a delight. This enterprising clan has a few other guesthouses nearby.

⭐Rival Village   GUESTHOUSE $$
(📞0819 0734 9148; www.facebook.com/rivalvillagegiliair; r 425,000-600,000Rp; ❄🛜) This modest four-room guesthouse just gets everything right. The French owners have created a sparklingly clean little compound amid family houses off one of the village's main paths. Rooms are large, the bathrooms are open-air, breakfast is delicious, everything works. *Très bon!*

⭐Biba Beach Village   BUNGALOW $$
(📞0819 1727 4648; www.bibabeach.com; rincl breakfast 800,000-1,600,000Rp; ❄🛜) Biba offers nine lovely, spacious bungalows with large verandahs, and grotto-like bathrooms that have walls inlaid with shells and coral. The gorgeous garden overlooks a great stretch of beach. Biba is also home to a good Italian restaurant. The best rooms have sea views.

SNORKELLING THE GILIS

Ringed by coral reefs, the Gilis offer superb snorkelling. Masks, snorkels and fins are widely available and can be hired for about 40,000Rp per day. It's important to check your mask fits properly: just press it gently to your face, let go and if it's a good fit the suction should hold it in place.

Snorkelling trips – many on glass-bottomed boats – are very popular. Typically, you'll pay about 200,000Rp per person or about 650,000Rp for the entire boat. Expect to leave at about 10am and visit three or more sites, with possibly a stop for lunch on another island. On Gili T there are many places selling these trips along the main strip; prices are very negotiable.

On Trawangan and Meno turtles very regularly appear on the reefs right off the beach. You'll likely drift with the current, so be prepared to walk back to the starting line. Over on Air, the walls off the east coast are good too.

It's not hard to escape the crowds. Each island has a less-developed side, usually where access to the water is obstructed by shallow patches of coral. Using rubber shoes makes it much easier to get into the water. Try not to stamp all over the coral but ease yourself in, and then swim, keeping your body as horizontal as possible.

Among the many reasons to snorkel in the Gilis are the high odds you'll encounter hawksbill and green sea turtles. Top overall snorkelling spots include the following:

➡ Gili Meno Wall

➡ The north end of Gili T's beach

➡ Gili Air Wall

Grand Sunset BUNGALOW $$
(☏ 0859 3610 3847; www.grandsunsetgiliair.com; r 800,000-1,200,000Rp; ✳ 🛜 ☷) These 24 sturdily built, bungalow-style rooms reflect the ethos of this modest resort: solid. Bathrooms are well designed and open-air, rooms have all the basic comforts, the pool is large and the beachside loungers have superb views. Plus there's the quietude that comes with the location on the sunset side of Air.

Krishna Sunset Bungalow GUESTHOUSE $$
(☏ 0877 6543 6703; r 300,000-600,000Rp) There's a '60s vibe at this chilled place with sweeping views of Lombok, other Gilis, Bali and the technicolour sunsets. You can cheerfully let another day slip past from the beach loungers. A top snorkelling location, Air Wall, is right off the beach.

Pelangi Cottages BUNGALOW $$
(☏ 0819 3316 8648; r incl breakfast 500,000-700,000Rp; ✳) Set on the north end of the island with coral reef out front, this place has 10 spacious but basic concrete and wood bungalows, friendly management, and quality mountain bikes for rent.

Youpy Bungalows BUNGALOW $$
(☏ 0819 1706 8153; r 450,000-800,000Rp; ✳ 🛜) Among the outcrop of driftwood-decorated beach cafes and guesthouses strung along the coast north of Blue Marine Dive Centre, Youpy has some of the best-quality bungalows. Bathrooms have colourful sand walls, the beds are big, and the ceilings are high.

7 Seas HOTEL $$
(☏ 0819 0700 3240; www.7seas-cottages.com; dm from 100,000Rp, r 450,000-950,000Rp; ✳ 🛜 ☷) Part of the 7 Seas dive empire, this is an attractive bungalow compound in a great location. Rooms are tidy and and have large balconies; cottages have soaring ceilings and thatch. There are also fan-cooled, bamboo, loft-like hostel rooms with lockers.

Segar Village BUNGALOW $$
(☏ 0819 1597 5043; www.segarvillages.blogspot. com; r 500,000-1,200,000Rp; ✳ 🛜) Eleven rather cute concrete, rock and coral bungalows with quirky touches and more than a little grace. Wraparound patios and soaring thatched ceilings are features and it's on the edge of a coconut grove just in front of a reef with resident sea turtles.

Sejuk Cottages BUNGALOW $$
(☏ 0370-636461; www.sejukcottages.com; r 450,000-1,000,000Rp; ✳ 🛜 ☷) Ten well-built, tastefully designed thatched *lumbung* (rice-barn) cottages, and pretty two- and three-storey cottages (some have rooftop living rooms) scattered around a fine tropical garden with a saltwater pool. Some rooms are fan-only, others have rooftop hammocks.

Vyaana Resort RESORT $$$
(☏ 0877 6538 8515; www.vyaanagiliair.com; r incl breakfast 1,600,000Rp; ✳ 🛜 ☷) This swathe of beach on the sunset side of Gili Air is still fairly quiet, and this bungalow compound is a fine place to enjoy it. The seven units are widely spaced for privacy and cute little artistic touches abound.

Villa Casa Mio BUNGALOW $$$
(☏ 0370-646160; www.casamiovillas.com; cottages incl breakfast from 1,400,000Rp; ✳ 🛜 ☷) Casa Mio has fine cottages with pretty garden bathrooms, as well as a riot of knick-knacks (from the artistic to the kitsch). Rooms have fridges, stereos and nice sun decks with loungers. It's on a great beach and the path here from the public dock is paved. There are several other good guesthouses nearby.

✖ Eating

Most places on Gili Air are locally owned and offer an unbeatable setting for a meal, with tables right over the water. Some of the most interesting new restaurants are opening on the backstreets of the village.

Eazy Gili Waroeng INDONESIAN $
(mains 25,000-40,000Rp; ⊙8am-10pm) In the buzzy main village, this spotless corner cafe serves up local fare aimed at visitors. It's the slightly Westernised face of the beloved Warung Muslim, immediately to the east. It also does breakfasts, sandwiches and superb *pisang goreng* (banana fritters).

★ Ruby's INDONESIAN $$
(☏ 0819 9913 7850; mains 40,000-160,000Rp; ⊙noon-11pm) One of the finest places to eat in the Gilis. Candles flicker atop bamboo tables at this back-lane eatery. The menu is short and there are daily specials; the secret here is the namesake genius in the kitchen. The calamari is perfectly light and crispy, the green curry is flavourful and nuanced, the burgers are simply superb. Great desserts.

Sunset Lounge SEAFOOD $$
(mains 40,000-120,000Rp; ⊙9am-11pm) More ambitious than your usual beachside bamboo hang-outs, Sunset offers a nightly seafood barbecue and an ever-changing line-up

of fresh fare. Good pasta shows what the Italians can do with *mie* (noodles). Come for drinks, stay for sunset and then have a moonlit meal. (On a bike, buzz over via the paved interior lanes.)

Le Cirque FRENCH, BAKERY $$
(☑ 0819 1601 0360; www.lecirque-giliair.com; mains 35,000-120,000Rp; ☺ 7am-10pm; 🛜 🚲) A clever French-accented culinary vision with a scrumptious bakery and tables spanning the path right up to the shore. The dinner menu is ambitious and there are nightly seafood specials. Kids get their own menu with tasty treats such as 'pizza circus'.

Scallywags Beach Club INTERNATIONAL $$
(☑ 0370-645301; www.scallywagsresort.com; mains 50,000-150,000Rp; ☺ 8am-10pm; 🛜) Set on Gili Air's softest and widest beach, there's elegant decor, upscale comfort food, great barbecue, homemade gelato and superb cocktails here. But the best feature is the alluring beach dotted with loungers. The choice of sambals is sublime.

Chill Out CAFE $$
(www.chilloutbungalows.com; mains 40,000-120,000Rp; ☺ 8am-11pm) Come for a swim and a sip with stunning views, and stay for dinner at a table on the sand. They put on a full nightly seafood barbecue and cook up some good pizzas in the wood-fired oven.

Warung Padang INDONESIAN
(☺ 8am-9pm) What's new is also old: a classic Padang-style eatery has opened deep in the village. As expected, you choose from the array of dishes and then settle back in the large and airy open-sided dining area. The selection is unfailingly fresh, and the spice levels are authentically assertive.

Siti Shop SUPERMARKET
(☺ 8am-8pm) A good general store in the village.

🍷 Drinking & Nightlife

Gili Air is usually a mellow place, but there are full-moon parties and things can rev up at the sunset bars in high season. Most people drink where they eat.

★ Pura Vida LOUNGE
(☺ 7.30am-10pm) A stylish bamboo bar with huge pillows right on the sand. Classy jazz plays over the sound system, and some nights there's live music. A wood-fired oven produces great thin-crust pizzas through the evening. Tops at sunset.

Lucky's Bar BAR
(☺ 10am-late) A great beach bar: lounge back on bamboo recliners and watch the sun set behind Gili Meno. There are frequent DJs and monthly full-moon parties.

Little Bar CAFE
(☺ 9am-late) Set on a sublime stretch of beach with technicolour sunsets, there is no better place for a sundowner than Little Bar. The menu includes snacks and veggie options.

Zipp Bar BAR
(☺ 9am-late) This large bar has an excellent booze selection (try the fresh-fruit cocktails) and tables dotted around a great beach. It hosts a beach party every full moon.

ℹ Information

MEDICAL SERVICES
Royal Medical (☑ 0878 6442 1212; ☺ phone service 24hr) has a simple clinic.

MONEY
There are ATMs along the southeast strip.

ℹ Getting There & Away

The public boat landing is busy. Gili Air's commerce and popularity mean that public boats fill rather quickly for the 15-minute ride to Bangsal. The ticket office has a fine, shady waiting area.

Understand Bali & Lombok

Bali & Lombok Today

Can you love a place to death? That's the question being asked more and more on Bali. As visitor numbers continue to soar like a kite over Sanur more than a few people are wondering if the island has finally reached the saturation point. From the ever-worse traffic to the proposal to fill in Benoa Bay (Teluk Benoa) for a tourist city, the ramifications of the island's popularity are all around.

Best on Film

Act of Killing (director Joshua Oppenheimer, 2013) A searing documentary about the 1965 slaughter of accused Communist sympathisers in Indonesia (including tens of thousands on Bali).

Cowboys in Paradise (director Amit Virmani, 2011) Enjoyable documentary about the scores of male gigolos working in south Bali.

Best in Print

Island of Bali (Miguel Covarrubias, 1937) The classic work about Bali and its civilisation.

Bali Soul Journals (Clare McAlaney, 2013) Written by a Bali expat and lavishly illustrated, it looks for Bali's soul today.

Bali Daze: Freefall Off the Tourist Trail (Cat Wheeler, 2011) Daily life in Ubud makes for an illuminating romp.

Secrets of Bali: Fresh Light on the Morning of the World (Jonathan Copeland and Ni Wayan Murni, 2010) A fun read about Bali and its people.

Eat, Pray, Love (Elizabeth Gilbert, 2007) This bestseller (and movie) lures believers to Bali every year.

Bye-Bye Bay

Right now, if you drive on the elevated toll road linking Sanur to Nusa Dua, you'll get sweeping views of the mangroves ringing the shallow bay. Five of Bali's polluted rivers empty through these forests and this ecosystem is vital for filtering out the trash and some of the pollutants.

The proposed Benoa Bay reclamation project would potentially devastate the bay and mangroves. A consortium backed by powerful Indonesian developers wants to build a network of 12 artificial islands (there's no word on where all the landfill would be obtained for this) in what's now the open waters you see from the toll road. A whole slew of projects would then follow, including a theme park, golf course and Formula One race course, plus countless condos, resorts and malls. Only a few channels would remain so that the river water could still flow out into the ocean, although it would no longer benefit much in the way of mangrove filtering.

After decades of being knocked around by developers and offering little protest, the Balinese are up in arms over the Benoa Bay project, which has touched a real nerve. First, there's the 70 Hindu holy sites that would be affected. Second, the island already had a nascent environmental movement as people are increasingly fed up with once pure rivers turning into toxic cesspools filled with trash. And third, there's a growing Bali nationalism that has been fueled by the perception that outsiders (primarily the well-connected from Jakarta) are getting rich off the island and leaving just a few crumbs for the locals.

Starting in 2015 and continuing right through 2016, protests have grown larger and louder. Anti-reclamation, pro-Balinese-pride banners from groups such as Tolak Reklamasi (Reject Reclamation), Bali Not for Sale (www.facebook.com/balinotforsale) and ForBali (www.forbali.

org) fly across the south. Rallies have drawn tens of thousands, including celebrities like the famous Indonesian punk band Superman is Dead.

Still, the project is moving towards groundbreaking. While there's widespread popular opposition, there has been no political opposition. The mangroves were unprotected by outgoing president Susilo Bambang Yudhoyono (SBY). His successor, the self-styled man of the people Joko Widodo, has stayed mum despite high-profile entreaties for him to restore the protections. Meanwhile, Bali's governor, Made Pastika, had been carving out quite a reputation as an environmentalist (he tried to ban plastic bags, for example), but on the landfill project he has essentially said that nothing should stop it. Then he announced he would not run for another term at the 2018 election.

With Bali's youth energised around this issue in a way not previously seen, expect it to remain hot for the foreseeable future, especially if work actually begins.

Jatiluwih Conundrum
In 2012 Unesco added Bali's ancient and truly amazing rice-field irrigation system (*subak*) to the World Heritage List. One key component of the listing are the Jatiluwih rice terraces north of Tabanan. These drop-dead gorgeous ribbons of green already drew a small number of day-trippers, but after Unesco put their stamp on the terraces, the road through this emerald wonderland was soon clogged with tourists. Ugly cafes soon sprang up, all jostling for the views, while tour groups on ATVs began rampaging across the fields. Developers announced plans to bulldoze terraces for hotels and it seemed that Jatiluwih would go the way of Canggu and Sideman, two places where unspoiled green vistas have been plowed under for profit.

But, then, in 2015, Unesco called time, suggesting that the coveted World Heritage Site designation could be snatched back. With inspections promised in 2016 and 2017, the normally ineffectual Bali central government managed to enact a building ban. Official worries are running high as they await the verdict of the Unesco inspectors.

Alcohol-Free Hangover
Nearly every tourist on Bali enjoys a drink. Thus proposals by religious conservatives in the Indonesian legislature in 2016 to ban alcohol across the nation caused a few minor strokes in Bali's tourism industry. Although the proposals were not passed, it's expected that they will resurface again. How Bali responds – both on the tourist industry side and on the cultural side (Bali's Hindus have no cultural taboo on drinking) – will be a major topic in the coming years.

POPULATION:
**BALI 4.3 MILLION,
LOMBOK 3.3 MILLION**

AREA: **BALI 5780 SQ KM,
LOMBOK 5435 SQ KM**

POPULATION PER SQ KM:
744

if Bali were 100 people

89 would be Balinese
7 would be other Indonesians
3 would be other nationalities
1 would be a tourist

belief systems
(% of population)

84 Hindu

1 Buddhist

3 Christian

12 Muslim

population per sq km

BALI   UK   USA

▮ ≈ 30 people

History

When Islam swept through Java in the 12th century, the kings of the Hindu Majapahit kingdom moved to Bali while the priest Nirartha established temples, including Rambut Siwi, Tanah Lot and Ulu Watu. In the 19th century, the Dutch formed alliances with local princes and eventually conquered the island. Westerners began celebrating Balinese arts in the 1930s; surfers arrived in the 1960s. As tourism has boomed, Bali's unique culture has proved to be remarkably resilient.

The First Balinese

The 14th-century epic poem *Sutasoma* has been given a sparkling new translation by Kate O'Brien. It follows the life of a Javanese prince as he becomes king and defeats the ultimate demon using the mystical beliefs that underpin Balinese faith today.

There are few traces of Stone Age people in Bali, although it's certain that the island was populated very early in prehistoric times – fossilised humanoid remains from neighbouring Java have been dated to as early as 250,000 years ago. The earliest human artefacts found in Bali are stone tools and earthenware vessels dug up near Cekik in west Bali, which are estimated to be 3000 years old. Discoveries continue, and you can see exhibits of bones that are estimated to be 4000 years old at the Museum Manusia Purbakala Gilimanuk. Artefacts indicate that the Bronze Age began in Bali before 300 BC.

Little is known of Bali during the period when Indian traders brought Hinduism to the Indonesian archipelago, although it is thought it was embraced on the island by the 7th century AD. The earliest written records are inscriptions on a stone pillar near Sanur, dating from around the 9th century; by that time, Bali had already developed many similarities to the island you find today. Rice, for example, was grown with the help of a complex irrigation system, probably very like the one employed now, and the Balinese had already begun to develop their rich cultural and artistic traditions.

If little is known about the earliest inhabitants of Bali, then even less is known about Lombok until about the 17th century. Early inhabitants are thought to have been Sasaks from a region encompassing today's India and Myanmar (Burma) as opposed to migrating Balinese.

TIMELINE	50 million BC	2000 BC	7th century
	A permanent gap in the earth's crust forms between Asia and Australia. The Wallace Line keeps Australian species from crossing to Bali until the invention of cheap Bintang specials.	A Balinese gentleman passes away. One of the first known inhabitants of the island, he rests peacefully until his bones are found and placed on display in Gilimanuk.	Indian traders bring Hinduism to Bali. Little is known about what was traded, although some speculate that they left with lots of wooden carvings of penises and bootleg lontar books.

Hindu Influence

Java began to spread its influence into Bali during the reign of King Airlangga (1019–42), or perhaps even earlier. At the age of 16, when his uncle lost the throne, Airlangga fled into the forests of western Java. He gradually gained support, won back the kingdom once ruled by his uncle and went on to become one of Java's greatest kings. Airlangga's mother had moved to Bali and remarried shortly after his birth, so when he gained the throne, there was an immediate link between Java and Bali. It was at this time that the courtly Javanese language known as Kawi came into use among the royalty of Bali, and the rock-cut memorials seen at Gunung Kawi, near Tampaksiring, provide a clear architectural link between Bali and 11th-century Java.

After Airlangga's death, Bali remained semi-independent until Kertanagara became king of the Singasari dynasty in Java two centuries later. Kertanagara conquered Bali in 1284, but the period of his greatest power lasted a mere eight years, until he was murdered and his kingdom collapsed. However, the great Majapahit dynasty was founded by his son, Vijaya (Wijaya). With Java in turmoil, Bali regained its autonomy, and the Pejeng dynasty rose to great power. Temples and relics of this period can still be found in Pejeng, near Ubud.

Oldest Sites

Goa Gajah, east of Ubud

Gunung Kawi, north of Ubud

Tirta Empul, north of Ubud

Stone Pillar, Sanur

HISTORY HINDU INFLUENCE

Exit Pejeng

In 1343, the legendary Majapahit prime minister, Gajah Mada, defeated the Pejeng king Dalem Bedaulu, and Bali was brought back under Javanese influence.

Although Gajah Mada brought much of the Indonesian archipelago under Majapahit control, this was the furthest extent of their power. The 'capital' of the dynasty was moved to Gelgel, in Bali, near modern Semarapura, around the late 14th century, and this was the base for the 'king of Bali', the Dewa Agung, for the next two centuries. The Gelgel dynasty in Bali, under Dalem Batur Enggong, extended its power eastwards to the neighbouring island of Lombok and even westwards across the strait to Java.

The collapse of the Majapahit dynasty into weak, decadent petty kingdoms opened the door for the spread of Islam from the trading states of the north coast into the heartland of Java. As the Hindu states fell, many of the intelligentsia fled to Bali. Notable among these was the priest Nirartha, who is credited with introducing many of the complexities of Balinese religion to the island, as well as establishing the chain of 'sea temples', which includes Pura Luhur Ulu Watu and Pura Tanah Lot. Court-supported artisans, artists, dancers, musicians and actors also fled

9th century	1019	12th century	1292
A stone carver creates an account in Sanskrit of now long-forgotten military victories. Bali's oldest dated artefact proves early Hindu influence and ends up hidden in Sanur.	A future king, Airlangga, is born in Bali. He lives in the jungles of Java until he gains political power and becomes king of the two islands, unifying both cultures.	Ten incredible 7m-high statues are carved from stone cliffs at Gunung Kawi, north of Ubud. Further monuments are created in nearby valleys.	Bali gains complete independence from Java with the death of Kertanagara, a powerful king who had ruled the two islands for eight years. Power shifts frequently between the islands.

ARTISTS IN CHARGE

The lasting wholesale change to Balinese life because of the mass exodus of Hindu elite from Javanese kingdoms in the 16th century cannot be overstated. It's as if all the subscribers to the opera were put in charge of a town – suddenly there would be a lot more opera. The Balinese had already shown a bent for creativity but once the formerly Javanese intelligentsia exerted control, music, dance, art and more flowered like the lotus blossoms in village ponds. High status was accorded to villages with the most creative talent, a tradition that continues today.

This flair for the liberal arts found a perfect match in the Hinduism that took full hold then. The complex and rich legends of good and evil spirits found ample opportunity to flourish, such as the legend of Jero Gede Macaling, the evil spirit of Nusa Penida.

to Bali at this time and the island experienced an explosion of cultural activity that has not stopped to this day.

Dutch Dealings

In 1597, Dutch seamen were among the first Europeans to appear in Bali. Setting a tradition that has prevailed to the present day, they fell in love with the island and when Cornelius de Houtman, the ship's captain, prepared to set sail from the island, two of his crew refused to come with him. At that time, Balinese prosperity and artistic activity, at least among the royalty, was at a peak, and the king who befriended de Houtman had 200 wives and a chariot pulled by two white buffalo, not to mention a retinue of 50 dwarfs, whose bodies had been bent to resemble the handle of a kris (traditional dagger). By the early 1600s, the Dutch had established trade treaties with Javanese princes and controlled much of the spice trade, but they were interested in profit, not culture, and barely gave Bali a second glance.

In 1710, the 'capital' of the Gelgel kingdom was shifted to nearby Klungkung (now called Semarapura), but local discontent was growing; lesser rulers were breaking away, and the Dutch began to move in, using the old strategy of divide and conquer. In 1846, the Dutch used Balinese salvage claims over shipwrecks as a pretext to land military forces in northern Bali, bringing the kingdoms of Buleleng and Jembrana under their control. Their cause was also aided by the various Balinese princes who had gained ruling interests on Lombok and were distracted from matters at home, unaware that the wily Dutch would use Lombok against Bali.

In 1894, the Dutch, the Balinese and the people of Lombok collided in battles that would set the course of history for the next several decades.

Locks of hair from Nirartha, the great priest who shaped Balinese Hinduism in the 16th century, are said to be buried at Pura Rambut Siwi, an evocative seaside temple in west Bali.

1343	1520	1546	1579
The legendary Majapahit prime minister, Gajah Mada, brings Bali back under Javanese control. For the next two centuries, the royal court is just south of today's Semarapura (Klungkung).	Java fully converts to Islam, leaving Bali in isolation as a Hindu island. Priests and artists move to Bali, concentrating and strengthening the island's culture against conversion.	The Hindu priest Nirartha arrives in Bali. He transforms religion and builds temples by the dozen including Rambut Siwi, Tanah Lot and Luhur Ulu Watu.	Sir Francis Drake, while looking for spice, is thought to be Bali's first European visitor.

With the north of Bali long under Dutch control and the conquest of Lombok successful, the south was never going to last long. Once again, it was disputes over the ransacking of wrecked ships that gave the Dutch an excuse to move in. In 1904, after a Chinese ship was wrecked off Sanur, Dutch demands that the rajah of Badung pay 3000 silver dollars in damages were rejected, and in 1906 Dutch warships appeared at Sanur.

Balinese Suicide

In 1906, the Dutch mounted a large invasion of Bali in order to subdue it once and for all. The Dutch forces landed despite Balinese opposition and, four days later, had marched 5km to the outskirts of Denpasar. On 20 September, the Dutch mounted a naval bombardment of Denpasar and began their final assault. The three princes of Badung realised that they were completely outnumbered and outgunned, and that defeat was inevitable. Surrender and exile, however, would have been the worst imaginable outcome, so they decided to take the honourable path of a suicidal *puputan* (a warrior's fight to the death). First the princes burned their palaces, and then, dressed in their finest jewellery and waving ceremonial golden kris, the rajah led the royalty, priests and courtiers out to face the modern weapons of the Dutch.

A Short History of Bali: Indonesia's Hindu Realm (2004), by Robert Pringle, is a thoughtful analysis of Bali's history from the Bronze Age to the present, with excellent sections on the 2002 bombings and ongoing environmental woes caused by tourism and development.

BALI LOSES LOMBOK

In 1894, the Dutch sent an army to back the Sasak people of eastern Lombok in a rebellion against the Balinese rajah who controlled Lombok with the support of the western Sasak. The rajah quickly capitulated, but the Balinese crown prince decided to fight on.

The Dutch camp at the Mayura Water Palace was attacked late at night by a combined force of Balinese and western Sasak, forcing the Dutch to take shelter in a temple compound. The Balinese also attacked another Dutch camp further east at Mataram, and soon, the entire Dutch army on Lombok was forced back to Ampenan where, according to one eyewitness, the soldiers 'were so nervous that they fired madly if so much as a leaf fell off a tree'. These battles resulted in enormous losses of men and arms for the Dutch.

Although the Balinese had won the first battles, they had begun to lose the war. They faced a continuing threat from the eastern Sasak, while the Dutch were soon supported with reinforcements from Java.

The Dutch attacked Mataram a month later, fighting street-to-street against Balinese and western Sasak soldiers and civilians. Rather than surrender, Balinese men, women and children opted for the suicidal *puputan* (a warrior's fight to the death) and were cut down by rifle and artillery fire.

In late November 1894, the Dutch attacked Sasari and, again, a large number of Balinese chose the *puputan*. With the downfall of the dynasty, the local population abandoned its struggle against the Dutch.

1580	1597	1795–1815	1830
The Portuguese also come looking for spice but in a foreshadowing of today's surfers, they wipe out on rocks at Ulu Watu and give up.	A Dutch expedition arrives off Kuta. A contemporary describes the skipper, Cornelius de Houtman, as a braggart and a scoundrel.	European wars mean that control of Indonesia nominally shifts from the Dutch to the French to the British and back to the Dutch.	The Balinese slave trade ends. For over two centuries, squabbling Balinese royal houses helped finance their wars by selling some of their most comely subjects.

The Dutch implored the Balinese to surrender rather than make their hopeless stand, but their pleas went unheeded and wave after wave of the Balinese nobility marched forward to their death, or turned their kris on themselves. In all, nearly 4000 Balinese died. The Dutch then marched northwest towards Tabanan and took the rajah of Tabanan prisoner – he also committed suicide rather than face the disgrace of exile.

The kingdoms of Karangasem (the royal family still lives in the palaces of Amlapura) and Gianyar had already capitulated to the Dutch and were allowed to retain some of their powers, but other kingdoms were defeated and their rulers exiled. Finally, in 1908, the rajah of Semarapura followed the lead of Badung, and once more the Dutch faced a *puputan*. As had happened at Cakranegara on Lombok, the beautiful palace at Semarapura, Taman Kertha Gosa, was largely destroyed.

With this last obstacle disposed of, all of Bali was under Dutch control and became part of the Dutch East Indies. There was little development of an exploitative plantation economy in Bali, and the common people noticed little difference between Dutch rule and the rule of the rajahs.

For much of the 19th century, the Dutch earned enormous amounts of money from the Balinese opium trade. Most of the colonial administrative budget went to promoting the opium industry, which was legal until the 1930s.

WWII

In 1942, the Japanese landed unopposed in Bali at Sanur (most Indonesians saw the Japanese, at first, as anticolonial liberators). The Japanese established headquarters in Denpasar and Singaraja, and their occupation became increasingly harsh for the Balinese. When the Japanese left in August 1945 after their defeat in WWII, the island was suffering from extreme poverty. The occupation had fostered several paramilitary, nationalist and anticolonial groups that were ready to fight the returning Dutch.

Independence

In August 1945, just days after the Japanese surrender, Sukarno, the most prominent member of the coterie of nationalist activists, proclaimed the nation's independence. It took four years to convince the Dutch that they were not going to get their great colony back. In a virtual repeat of the *puputan* nearly 50 years earlier, Balinese freedom fighters led by the charismatic Gusti Ngurah Rai (namesake of the Bali airport) were wiped out by the Dutch in the battle of Marga in west Bali on 20 November 1946. The Dutch finally recognised Indonesia's independence in 1949 – though Indonesians celebrate 17 August 1945 as their Independence Day.

Bali's airport is named for I Gusti Ngurah Rai, the national hero who died leading the resistance against the Dutch at Marga in 1946. The text of a letter he wrote in response to Dutch demands to surrender ends with 'Freedom or death!'

At first, Bali, Lombok and the rest of Indonesia's eastern islands were grouped together in the unwieldy province of Nusa Tenggara. In 1958 the central government recognised this folly and created three new governmental regions from the one, with Bali getting its own and Lombok becoming part of Nusa Tenggara Barat.

1856	1891–94	1908	1912
Mads Lange, a Danish trader, dies mysteriously in Kuta after earning a fortune selling goods to ships anchored off the beach. His death is blamed on poisoning by jealous rivals.	Years of failed Sasak rebellions in eastern Lombok finally take hold after a palace burning. With Dutch assistance the Balinese rulers are chased from the islands within three years.	The Balinese royalty commit suicide. Wearing their best dress and armed with 'show' daggers, they march into Dutch gunfire in a suicidal *puputan* (warrior's fight to the death) in Klungkung.	A German, Gregor Krause, photographs beautiful Balinese women topless. WWI intervenes, but in 1920 an 'art book' of photos appears and Dutch steamers docking in Singaraja now bring tourists.

Coup & Backlash

Independence was not an easy path for Indonesia to follow. When Sukarno assumed more direct control in 1959 after several violent rebellions, he proved to be as inept as a peacetime administrator as he was inspirational as a revolutionary leader. In the early 1960s, as Sukarno faltered, the army, communists and other groups struggled for supremacy. On 30 September 1965, an attempted coup – blamed on the Partai Komunis Indonesia (PKI; Communist Party) – led to Sukarno's downfall. General Suharto emerged as the leading figure in the armed forces, displaying great military and political skill in suppressing the coup. The PKI was outlawed and a wave of anticommunist massacres followed throughout Indonesia.

THE TOURIST CLASS

Beginning in the 1920s, the Dutch government realised that Bali's unique culture could be marketed internationally to the growing tourism industry. Relying heavily on images that emphasised the topless habits of Bali's women, Dutch marketing drew wealthy Western adventurers, who landed in the north at today's Singaraja and were whisked about the island on rigid three-day itineraries that featured canned cultural shows at a government-run tourist hotel in Denpasar. Accounts from the time are ripe with imagery of supposedly culture-seeking Europeans who really just wanted to see a boob or two. Such desires were often thwarted by Balinese women who covered up when they heard the Dutch jalopies approaching.

But some intrepid travellers arrived independently, often at the behest of members of the small colony of Western artists, such as Walter Spies in Ubud. Two of these visitors were Robert Koke and Louise Garret, an American couple who had worked in Hollywood before landing in Bali in 1936 as part of a global adventure. Horrified at the stuffy strictures imposed by the Dutch tourism authorities, the pair built a couple of bungalows out of palm leaves and other local materials on the otherwise deserted beach at Kuta, which at that point was home to only a few impoverished fishing families.

Word soon spread, and the Kokes were booked solid. Guests came for days, stayed for weeks and told their friends. At first, the Dutch dismissed the Kokes' Kuta Beach Hotel as 'dirty native huts', but soon realised that increased numbers of tourists were good for everyone. Other Westerners built their own thatched hotels, complete with the bungalows that were to become a Balinese cliché in the decades ahead.

WWII wiped out both tourism and the hotels (the Kokes barely escaped ahead of the Japanese), but once people began travelling again after the war, Bali's inherent appeal made its popularity a foregone conclusion.

In 1987, Louise Koke's long-forgotten story of the Kuta Beach Hotel was published as *Our Hotel in Bali*, illustrated with her incisive sketches and her husband's photographs.

1925	1936	1945	1946
The greatest modern Balinese dancer, Mario, first performs the Kebyar Duduk, his enduring creation. From a stooped position, he moves as if in a trance to the haunting melody of gamelan.	Americans Robert and Louise Koke build a hotel of thatched bungalows on then-deserted Kuta Beach. Gone is stuffy, starched tourism; replacing it is fun in the sun followed by a drink.	Following the Japanese surrender at the end of WWII, nationalists, Sukarno among them, proclaim independence from the Netherlands. It sets off an intense period of revolution.	Freedom fighter Ngurah Rai dies with the rest of his men at Marga. But this *puputan* slays the Dutch colonial spirit, and soon Indonesia is independent.

In Bali, the events had an added local significance as the main national political organisations, the Partai Nasional Indonesia (PNI; Nationalist Party) and the PKI, crystallised existing differences between traditionalists, who wanted to maintain the old caste system, and radicals, who saw the caste system as repressive and were urging land reform. After the failed coup, religious traditionalists in Bali led the witch-hunt for the 'godless communists'. Eventually, the military stepped in to control the anticommunist purge, but no one in Bali was untouched by the killings, estimated at between 50,000 and 100,000 out of a population of about two million, a percentage many times higher than on Java. Even as late as 2016, mass graves were still being discovered.

The 1963 Eruption

Amid the political turmoil, the most disastrous volcanic eruption in Bali in 100 years occurred in 1963. Gunung Agung blew its top in no uncertain manner, at a time of considerable prophetic and political importance.

Eka Dasa Rudra, the greatest of all Balinese sacrifices and an event that takes place only every 100 years on the Balinese calendar, was to culminate on 8 March 1963. It had been well over 100 Balinese years since the last Eka Dasa Rudra, but there was dispute among the priests as to the correct and most favourable date.

Naturally, Pura Besakih was a focal point for the festival, but Gunung Agung was acting strangely as final preparations were made in late February. Despite some qualms, political pressures forced the ceremonies forward, even as ominous rumblings continued.

On 17 March, Gunung Agung exploded. The catastrophic eruption killed more than 1000 people (some estimate 2000) and destroyed entire villages – 100,000 people lost their homes. Streams of lava and hot volcanic mud poured right down to the sea at several places, completely covering roads and isolating the eastern end of Bali for some time. Driving the main road near Tulamben you can still see some lava flows.

Suharto Comes & Goes

Following the failed coup in 1965 and its aftermath, Suharto established himself as president and took control of the government. Under his 'New Order' government, Indonesia looked to the West for its foreign and economic policies.

Politically, Suharto ensured that his political party, Golkar, with strong support from the army, became the dominant political force. Other political parties were banned or crippled. Regular elections maintained the appearance of a national democracy, but until 1999, Golkar won every election hands down. This period was also marked by great economic development in Bali and later on Lombok as social stability and mainte-

Kuta was never a part of mainstream Bali. During royal times, the region was a place of exile for malcontents and troublemakers. It was too arid for rice fields, the fishing was barely sustainable and the shore was covered with kilometres of useless sand...

A woman of many aliases, K'tut Tantri breezed into Bali from Hollywood in 1932. After the war, she joined the Indonesian Republicans in their postwar struggle against the Dutch. As Surabaya Sue, she broadcast from Surabaya in support of their cause. Her book, *Revolt in Paradise,* was published in 1960.

1949	1960s	1963	1965
South Pacific, the musical, opens on Broadway and the song 'Bali Hai' fixes a tropical cliché of Bali in the minds of millions (even though it's based on Fiji).	The lengthening of the airport runway for jets, reasonably affordable tickets and the opening of the Bali Beach Hotel in Sanur mark the start of mass tourism.	The sacred volcano Gunung Agung erupts, destroying a fair bit of east Bali, killing a thousand or more, leaving 100,000 homeless and sending out large lava flows.	Indonesia's long-running rivalry between communists and conservatives erupts after a supposed coup attempt by the former. The latter triumph and in the ensuing purges, tens of thousands are killed in Bali.

nance of a favourable investment climate took precedence over democracy. Huge resorts – often with investors in government – appeared in Sanur, Kuta and Nusa Dua during this time.

In early 1997, the good times ended as Southeast Asia suffered a severe economic crisis, and within the year, the Indonesian currency (the rupiah) had all but collapsed and the economy was on the brink of bankruptcy.

Unable to cope with the escalating crisis, Suharto resigned in 1998, after 32 years in power. His protégé, Dr Bacharuddin Jusuf Habibie, became president. Though initially dismissed as a Suharto crony, he made the first notable steps towards opening the door to real democracy, such as freeing the press from government supervision.

Peace Shattered & Democracy Dawns

In 1999, Indonesia's parliament met to elect a new president. The front-runner was Megawati Sukarnoputri, who was enormously popular in Bali, partly because of family connections (her paternal grandmother

Bali's history is reduced to miniature dramas with stilted dolls at the delightfully unhip Bajra Sandhi Monument in Denpasar. Meaning the 'Struggle of the People', the museum brings cartoon-like 3D veracity to important moments in the island's history.

THE BALI BOMBINGS

On Saturday 12 October 2002, two bombs exploded on Kuta's bustling Jl Legian. The first blew out the front of Paddy's Bar. A few seconds later, a far more powerful bomb obliterated the Sari Club.

The number of dead, including those unaccounted for, exceeded 200, although the exact number will probably never be known. Many injured Balinese made their way back to their villages, where, for lack of adequate medical treatment, they died.

Indonesian authorities eventually laid the blame for the blasts on Jemaah Islamiah, an Islamic terrorist group. Dozens were arrested and many were sentenced to jail, including three who received the death penalty. But most received relatively light terms, including Abu Bakar Bashir, a radical cleric who many thought was behind the explosions. His convictions on charges relating to the bombings were overturned by the Indonesian supreme court in 2006, enraging many in Bali and Australia. (In 2011 he was sent back to prison for 15 years after a new conviction on terrorism charges.)

On 1 October 2005, three suicide bombers blew themselves up: one in a restaurant on Kuta Square and two more at beachfront cafes in Jimbaran. It was again the work of Jemaah Islamiah, and although documents found later stated that the attacks were targeted at tourists, 15 of the 20 who died were Balinese and Javanese employees of the places bombed.

There was also justice as Umar Patek was convicted in 2012 of helping to assemble the 2002 Bali bombs and sentenced to 20 years in jail. But threats continue: in 2012 police on Bali shot dead five suspected terrorists and there have been occasional arrests of suspected terrorists through 2016.

1970	1972	1979	1998
A girl ekes out a living selling candy in Kuta. Surfers offer advice, she posts a menu, then she builds a hut and calls it Made's Warung. She prospers.	Filmmaker Alby Falzon brings a band of Australians to Bali for his surfing documentary *Morning on Earth*, which proves seminal for a generation of Australians who head to Kuta.	Australian Kim Bradley, impressed by the gnarly surfing style of locals, encourages them to start a club. Sixty do just that (good on an island where people fear the water).	Suharto, who always had close ties to Bali, resigns as president after 32 years. His family retains control of several Bali resorts, including the thirsty Pecatu Indah resort.

was Balinese) and partly because her party was essentially secular (the mostly Hindu Balinese are very concerned about any growth in Muslim fundamentalism). However, Abdurrahman Wahid, the moderate, intellectual head of Indonesia's largest Muslim organisation, emerged as president.

On Lombok, however, religious and political tensions spilled over in early 2000 when a sudden wave of attacks starting in Mataram burned Chinese and Christian businesses and homes across the island. The impact on tourism was immediate and severe, with some visitors also shunning Bali.

After 21 months of growing ethnic, religious and regional conflicts, parliament had enough ammunition to recall Wahid's mandate and hand the presidency to Megawati in 2001. In 2004 she was replaced by Indonesia's first democratically elected president, Susilo Bambang Yudhoyono (SBY). He had gained international recognition after he led the hunt for the 2002 Bali bombers.

The reign of SBY proved very successful. Indonesia's economy expanded at a rapid pace and he was easily reelected in 2009 for another five-year term during which the nation (and Bali in particular) enjoyed rising fortunes and political calm. In 2014, Joko Widodo, the governor of Jakarta, won the presidency. Seen as a man of the people, he enjoyed widespread support. Although this included Bali – where he won the popular vote – there was some concern on the island that Jokowi (as he's known) was the first Indonesian leader in several generations to have no blood and/or marriage ties to Bali.

In recent years, visitors have been big news on Bali. As fears sparked by the bombings faded, international arrivals have increased by 10% to 15% a year on average. Where a short time ago two million visitors was a big deal, now that number hovers well above four million. Tourism is literally taking over many aspects of Balinese life, especially economic ones.

Hotel Kerobokan (2009) is a lurid book detailing conditions inside Bali's notorious Kerobokan jail. Journalist Kathryn Bonella, who has written about noted former inmate Schapelle Corby, details the goings on behind the walls. The jail was nearly destroyed during riots in 2012.

2000	2002	2005	2015
Indonesian rioting spreads to Lombok and hundreds of Chinese, Christian and Balinese homes and businesses are looted and burned, particularly after a Muslim-sponsored rally to decry violence turns ugly.	Bombs in Kuta kill more than 200, many at the Sari Club. Bali's economy is crushed as tourists stay away and there is economic devastation across the island.	Three suicide bombers blow themselves up in Kuta and Jimbaran, killing 20 mostly Balinese and Javanese.	Bali tops four million foreign tourists for the year, a new record that continues many years of growth that averaged more than 15% a year.

Local Life & Religion

So many seem so relaxed on Bali. There is a gentleness to people that easily obscures their deep cultural heritage and belief systems. Balinese Hindus live lives deeply entwined in their belief systems. And on Bali in particular, religion plays a role in so much of what makes the island appealing to visitors: the art, the music, the offerings, the architecture, the temples and more.

Bali

Ask any traveller what they love about Bali and, most times, 'the people' will top their list. Since the 1920s, when the Dutch used images of bare-breasted Balinese women to lure tourists, Bali has embodied the mystique and glamour of an exotic paradise.

For all the romanticism, there is a harsher reality. For many Balinese, life remains a near hand-to-mouth existence, even as the island prospers due to tourism and the middle class grows. And the idea of culture can sometimes seem misplaced as overzealous touts test your patience in their efforts to make a living.

But there's also some truth to this idea of paradise. There is no other place in the world like Bali, not even in Indonesia. Being the only surviving Hindu island in the world's largest Muslim country, its distinctive culture is worn like a badge of honour by a fiercely proud people. After all, it's only in the last century that 4000 Balinese royalty, dressed in their finest, walked into the gunfire of the Dutch army rather than surrender and become colonial subjects.

True, development has changed the landscape and prompted endless debate about the displacement of an agricultural society by a tourism-services industry. And the upmarket spas, clubs, boutiques and restaurants in Seminyak and Kerobokan might have you mistaking hedonism, not Hinduism, for the local religion. But scratch the surface and you'll find that Bali's soul remains unchanged.

The island's creative heritage is everywhere you look, and the harmonious dedication to religion permeates every aspect of society, underpinning the strong sense of community. There are temples in every house, office and village, on mountains and beaches, in rice fields, trees, caves, cemeteries, lakes and rivers. Yet religious activity is not limited to places of worship. It can occur anywhere, sometimes smack-bang in the middle of peak-hour traffic.

A great resource on Balinese culture and life is www.murnis. com, the website for one of Ubud's original restaurants. Find explanations on everything from kids' names to what one wears to a ceremony, to how garments are woven; see the 'Culture' section.

Balinese Tolerance

The Balinese are famously tolerant of and hospitable towards other cultures, though they rarely travel themselves, such is the importance of their village and family ties, not to mention the financial cost. If anything, they're bemused by all the attention, which reinforces their pride; the general sense is, whatever we're doing, it must be right to entice millions of people to leave their homes for ours.

The Balinese are unfailingly friendly, love a chat and can get quite personal. English is widely spoken but they love to hear tourists attempt

Bahasa Indonesia or, better still, throw in a Balinese phrase such as *'sing ken ken'* (no worries); do this and you'll make a friend for life. They have a fantastic sense of humour and their easygoing nature is hard to ruffle. They generally find displays of temper distasteful and laugh at 'emotional' foreigners who are quick to anger.

Balinese culture keeps intimacy behind doors. Holding hands is not customary for couples in Bali, and is generally reserved for small children; however, linking arms for adults is the norm.

Lombok

While Lombok's culture and language is often likened to that of Bali, this does neither island justice. True, Lombok's language, animist rituals and music and dance are reminiscent of the Hindu and Buddhist kingdoms that once ruled Indonesia, and of its time under Balinese rule in the 18th century. But the majority of Lombok's Sasak tribes are Muslim – they have very distinct traditions, dress, food and architecture, and have fought hard to keep them. While the Sasak peasants in western Lombok lived in relative harmony under Balinese feudal control, the aristocracy in the east remained hostile and led the rebellion with the Dutch that finally ousted their Balinese lords in the late 1800s. To this day, the Sasaks take great joy in competing in heroic trials of strength, such as the stick-fighting matches held every August near Tetebatu.

WHAT'S IN A NAME

Far from being straightforward, Balinese names are as fluid as the tides. Everyone has a traditional name, but their other names often reflect events in each individual's life. They also help distinguish between people of the same name, which is perhaps nowhere more necessary than in Bali.

Traditional naming customs seem straightforward, with a predictable gender nonspecific pattern to names. The order of names, with variations for regions and caste, is:

First-born Wayan (Gede, Putu)

Second-born Made (Kadek, Nengah, Ngurah)

Third-born Nyoman (Komang)

Fourth-born Ketut (or just Tut, as in toot)

Subsequent children reuse the same set, but as many families now settle for just two children, you'll meet many Wayans and Mades.

Castes also play an important role in naming and have naming conventions that clearly denote status when added to the birth order name. Bali's system is much less complicated than India's.

Sudra Some 90% of Balinese are part of this, the peasant caste. Names are preceded by the title 'I' for a boy and 'Ni' for a girl.

Wesya The caste of bureaucrats and merchants. Gusti Bagus (male) and Gusti Ayu (female).

Ksatria A top caste, denoting royalty or warriors. I Gusti Ngurah (male) and I Gusti Ayu (female), with additional titles including Anak Agung, and Dewa.

Brahman The top of the heap: teachers and priests. Ida Bagus (male) and Ida Ayu (female).

Traditional names are followed by another given name – this is where parents can get creative. Some names reflect hopes for their child, as in I Nyoman Darma Putra, who's supposed to be 'dutiful' or 'good' (dharma). Others reflect modern influences, such as I Wayan Radio who was born in the 1970s, and Ni Made Atom who said her parents just liked the sound of this scientific term that also had a bomb named after it.

Many are tagged for their appearance. Nyoman Darma is often called Nyoman Kopi (coffee) for the darkness of his skin compared with that of his siblings. I Wayan Rama, named after the Ramayana epic, is called Wayan Gemuk (fat) to differentiate his physique from his slighter friend Wayan Kecil (small).

SMALL TALK

'Where do you stay?', 'Where do you come from?', 'Where are you going?'... You'll hear these questions over and over from your super-friendly Balinese hosts. While Westerners can find it intrusive, it's just Balinese small talk and a reflection of Bali's communal culture; they want to see where you fit in and change your status from stranger to friend.

Saying you're staying 'over there' or in a general area is fine, but expect follow-ups to get increasingly personal. 'Are you married?' Even if you're not, it's easiest to say you are. Next will be: 'Do you have children?'. The best answer is affirmative: never say you don't want any. 'Bclum' (not yet) is also an appropriate response, which will likely spark a giggle and an, 'Ah, still trying!'.

Lombok remains poorer and less developed than Bali, and is generally more conservative. Its Sasak culture is not as prominently displayed as Bali's Hinduism, but you'll see evidence of it, not least of which in the proud mosques that stand in every town.

On the Gilis, the local people practice a very moderate form of Islam.

Family Ties

Through their family temple, Balinese have an intense spiritual connection to their home. As many as five generations share a Balinese home, in-laws and all. Grandparents, cousins, aunties, uncles and various distant relatives all live together. When the sons marry, they don't move out – their wives move in. Similarly, when daughters marry, they live with their in-laws, assuming household and child-bearing duties. Because of this, Balinese consider a son more valuable than a daughter. Not only will his family look after them in their old age, but he will inherit the home and perform the necessary rites after they die to free their souls for reincarnation, so they do not become wandering ghosts.

A Woman's Work is Work

Men play a big role in village affairs and helping to care for children, and only men plant and tend to the rice fields. But women are the real workhorses in Bali, doing everything from manual labour jobs (you'll see them carrying baskets of wet cement or bricks on their heads) to running market stalls and almost every job in tourism. In fact, their traditional role of caring for people and preparing food means that women have established many successful shops and cafes.

In between all of these tasks, women also prepare daily offerings for the family temple and house, and often extra offerings for upcoming ceremonies; their hands are never idle. You can observe all of this and more when you stay at a classic Balinese homestay, where your room is in the family compound and everyday life goes on about you. Ubud has many homestays.

Religion

Hinduism

Bali's official religion is Hindu, but it's far too animistic to be considered in the same vein as Indian Hinduism. The Balinese worship the trinity of Brahma, Shiva and Vishnu, three aspects of the one (invisible) god, Sanghyang Widi, as well as the *dewa* (ancestral gods) and village founders. They also worship gods of earth, fire, water and mountains; gods of fertility, rice, technology and books; and demons who inhabit the world underneath the ocean. They share the Indian belief in karma and reincarnation, but much less emphasis is attached to other Indian customs.

Motorbikes are an invaluable part of daily life. They carry everything from towers of bananas and rice sacks headed to the market, to whole families in full ceremonial dress on their way to the temple, to young hotel clerks riding primly in their uniforms.

There is no 'untouchable caste', arranged marriages are very rare, and there are no child marriages.

Bali's unusual version of Hinduism was formed after the great Majapahit Hindu kingdom that once ruled Indonesia evacuated to Bali as Islam spread across the archipelago. While the Bali Aga (the 'original' Balinese) retreated to the hills in places such as east Bali's Tenganan to escape this new influence, the rest of the population simply adapted it for themselves, overlaying the Majapahit faith on their animist beliefs incorporated with Buddhist influences. A Balinese Hindu community can be found in west Lombok, a legacy of Bali's domination of its neighbour in the 19th century.

The most sacred site on the island is Gunung Agung, home to Pura Besakih and frequent ceremonies involving anywhere from hundreds to sometimes thousands of people. Smaller ceremonies are held across the island every day to appease the gods, placate the demons and ensure balance between dharma (good) and adharma (evil) forces.

Don't be surprised if on your very first day on Bali you witness or get caught up in a ceremony of some kind.

The ancient Hindu swastika seen all over Bali is a symbol of harmony with the universe. The German Nazis used a version where the arms were always bent in a clockwise direction.

SHOWING RESPECT

Bali has a well-deserved reputation for being mellow, which is all the more reason to respect your hosts, who are enormously forgiving of faux pas if you're making a sincere effort. Be aware and respectful of local sensibilities, and dress and act appropriately, especially in rural villages and at religious sites. When in doubt, let the words 'modest' and 'humble' guide you.

Dos & Don'ts

➡ You'll see shorts and short skirts everywhere on locals but overly revealing clothing is still frowned upon, as is wandering down the street shirtless quaffing a beer.

➡ Many women go topless on Bali's beaches, offending locals who are embarrassed by foreigners' gratuitous nudity.

➡ Don't touch anyone on the head; it's regarded as the abode of the soul and is therefore sacred.

➡ Do pass things with your right hand. Even better, use both hands. Just don't use only your left hand, as it's considered unclean.

➡ Beware of talking with hands on hips – a sign of contempt, anger or aggression (as displayed in traditional dance and opera).

➡ Beckon someone with the hand extended and using a downward waving motion. The Western method of beckoning is considered very rude.

➡ Don't make promises of gifts, books and photographs that are soon forgotten. Pity the poor local checking their mailbox or email inbox every day.

Religious Etiquette

➡ Cover shoulders and knees if visiting a temple or mosque; in Bali, a *selandong* (traditional scarf) or sash plus a sarong is usually provided for a small donation or as part of the entrance fee.

➡ Women are asked not to enter temples if they're menstruating, pregnant or have recently given birth. At these times women are thought to be *sebel* (ritually unclean).

➡ Don't put yourself higher than a priest, particularly at festivals (eg by scaling a wall to take photos).

➡ Take off your shoes before entering a mosque.

Islam

Islam is a minority religion in Bali; most followers are Javanese immigrants, Sasak people from Lombok or descendants of seafaring people from Sulawesi.

Most Muslims on Bali practise a moderate version of Islam, as in many other parts of Indonesia. They generally follow the Five Pillars of Islam; the pillars decree that there is no god but Allah and Muhammad is His prophet, and that believers should pray five times a day, give alms to the poor, fast during the month of Ramadan and make the pilgrimage to Mecca at least once in their lifetime. However, in contrast to other Islamic countries, Muslim women are not segregated, head coverings are not compulsory (although they are becoming more common) and polygamy is rare. A stricter version of Islam is beginning to spread from Lombok, which in turn is being influenced by ultra-conservative Sumbawa.

Wektu Telu

Believed to have originated in Bayan, north Lombok, Wektu Telu is an indigenous religion unique to Lombok. Now followed by a minority of Sasaks, it was the majority religion in northern Lombok until as recently as 1965, when Indonesia's incoming president Suharto decreed that all Indonesians must follow an official religion. Indigenous beliefs such as Wektu Telu were not recognised. Many followers thus state their official religion as Muslim, while practising Wektu traditions and rituals. Bayan remains a stronghold of Wektu Telu; you can spot believers by their *sapu puteq* (white headbands) and white flowing robes.

Wektu means 'result' in Sasak and *telu* means 'three', and it probably signifies the complex mix of Balinese Hinduism, Islam and animism that the religion is. The tenet is that all important aspects of life are underpinned by a trinity. Like orthodox Muslims, they believe in Allah and that Muhammad is Allah's prophet; however, they pray only three times a day and honour just three days of fasting for Ramadan. Followers of Wektu Telu bury their dead with their heads facing Mecca and all public buildings have a prayer corner facing Mecca, but they do not make pilgrimages there. Similar to Balinese Hinduism, they believe the spiritual world is firmly linked to the natural; Gunung Rinjani is the most revered site.

Black magic is still a potent force and spiritual healers known as *balian* are consulted in times of illness and strife. There are plenty of stories floating around about the power of this magic. Disputes between relatives or neighbours are often blamed on curses, as are tragic deaths.

Ceremonies & Rituals

Between the family temple, village temple and district temple, a Balinese person takes part in dozens of ceremonies every year, on top of their daily rituals. Most employers allow staff to return to their villages for these obligations, which consume a vast chunk of income and time (and although many bosses moan about this, they have little choice unless they wish for a staff revolt). For tourists, this means there are ample opportunities to witness ceremonial traditions.

Ceremonies are the unifying centre of a Balinese person's life and a source of much entertainment, socialisation and festivity. Each ceremony is carried out on an auspicious date determined by a priest and often involves banquets, dance, drama and musical performances to entice the gods to continue their protection against evil forces. The most important ceremonies are Nyepi, which includes a rare day of complete rest, and Galungan, a 10-day reunion with ancestral spirits to celebrate the victory of good over evil.

Under their karmic beliefs, the Balinese hold themselves responsible for any misfortune, which is attributed to an overload of *adharma* (evil). This calls for a *ngulapin* (cleansing) ritual to seek forgiveness and recover spiritual protection. A *ngulapin* requires an animal sacrifice and often involves a cockfight, satisfying the demons' thirst for blood.

Ceremonies are also held to overcome black magic and to cleanse a *sebel* (ritually unclean) spirit after childbirth or bereavement, or during menstruation or illness.

On top of all these ceremonies, there are 13 major rites of passage throughout every person's life. The most extravagant and expensive is the last – cremation.

Birth & Childhood

The Balinese believe babies are the reincarnation of ancestors, and they honour them as such. Offerings are made during pregnancy to ensure the mini-deity's well-being, and after birth, the placenta, umbilical cord, blood and afterbirth water – representing the child's four 'spirit' guardian brothers – are buried in the family compound.

Newborns are literally carried everywhere for the first three months, as they're not allowed to touch the 'impure' ground until after a purification ceremony. At 210 days (the first Balinese year), the baby is blessed in the ancestral temple and there is a huge feast. Later in life, birthdays lose their significance and many Balinese couldn't tell you their age.

A rite of passage to adulthood – and a prerequisite to marriage – is the tooth-filing ceremony at around 16 to 18 years. This is when a priest files a small part of the upper canines and upper incisors to flatten the teeth. Pointy fangs are, after all, distinguishing features of dogs and demons. Balinese claim the procedure doesn't hurt, likening the sensation to eating very cold ice: it's slightly uncomfortable, but not painful. Most tooth-filings happen in July and August.

Another important occasion for girls is their first menstrual period, which calls for a purification ceremony.

Marriage

Marriage defines a person's social status in Bali, making men automatic members of the *banjar* (local neighbourhood organisation). Balinese believe that when they come of age, it's their duty to marry and have children, including at least one son. Divorce is rare, as a divorced woman is cut off from her children.

The respectable way to marry, known as *mapadik*, is when the man's family visits the woman's family and proposes. But the Balinese like their fun and some prefer marriage by *ngrorod* (elopement or 'kidnapping'). After the couple returns to their village, the marriage is officially recognised and everybody has a grand celebration.

Marriage ceremonies include elaborate symbolism drawn from the island's rice-growing culture. The groom will carry food on his shoulders like a farmer while the bride will pretend to peddle produce, thus showing the couple's economic independence. Other actions need little explanation: the male digs a hole and the female places a seed inside for fertility, which comes after the male unsheathes his kris (knife) and pierces the female's unblemished woven mat of coconut leaves.

Death & Cremation

The body is considered little more than a shell for the soul, and upon death it is cremated in an elaborate ceremony befitting the ancestral spirit. It usually involves the whole community, and for important people, such as royalty, it can be a spectacular event involving thousands of people.

Because of the burdensome cost of even a modest cremation (estimated at around 7,000,000Rp), as well as the need to wait for an auspicious date, the deceased is often buried, sometimes for years, and disinterred for a mass cremation.

The Balinese tooth-filing ceremony closes with the recipient being given a delicious *jamu* (herbal tonic), made from freshly pressed turmeric, betel-leaf juice, lime juice and honey.

The Ubud tourist office (www.fabulousubud.com) is an excellent source for news of cremations and other Balinese ceremonies that occur at erratic intervals. Another good source is www.ubudnowandthen.com.

BALI PLAYS DEAD

Nyepi

This is Bali's biggest purification festival, designed to clean out all the bad spirits and begin the year anew. It falls around March or April according to the Hindu *caka* calendar, a lunar cycle similar to the Western calendar in terms of the length of the year. Starting at sunrise, the whole island literally shuts down for 24 hours. No planes may land or take off, no vehicles of any description may be operated, and no power sources may be used. Everyone, including tourists, must stay off the streets. The cultural reasoning behind Nyepi is to fool evil spirits into thinking Bali has been abandoned so they will go elsewhere.

For the Balinese, it's a day for meditation and introspection. For foreigners, the rules are more relaxed, so long as you respect the 'Day of Silence' by not leaving your residence or hotel. If you do sneak out, you will quickly be escorted back to your hotel by a stern *pecalang* (village police officer).

As daunting as it sounds, Nyepi is actually a fantastic time to be in Bali. Firstly, there's the inspired concept of being forced to do nothing. Catch up on some sleep, or if you must, read, sunbathe, write postcards, play board games...just don't do anything to tempt the demons! Secondly, there are colourful festivals the night before Nyepi.

Ogoh-Ogoh

In the weeks prior to Nyepi, huge and elaborate papier-mâché monsters called *ogoh-ogoh* are built in villages across the island. Involving everybody in the community, construction sites buzz with fevered activity around the clock. If you see a site where *ogoh-ogoh* are being constructed, there'll be a sign-up sheet for financial support. Contribute, say, 50,000Rp and you'll be a fully fledged sponsor and receive much street cred.

On Nyepi eve, large ceremonies all over Bali lure out the demons. Their rendezvous point is believed to be the main crossroads of each village, and this is where the priests perform exorcisms. Then the whole island erupts in mock 'anarchy', with people banging on *kulkuls* (hollow tree-trunk drums), drums and tins, letting off firecrackers and yelling '*megedi megedi!*' (get out!) to expel the demons. The truly grand finale is when the *ogoh-ogoh* all go up in flames. Any demons that survive this wild partying are believed to evacuate the village when confronted with the boring silence on the morrow.

Christians find unique parallels to Easter in all this, especially Ash Wednesday and Shrove Tuesday, with its wild Mardi Gras–like celebrations the world over.

In coming years, dates for Nyepi are 28 March 2017, 17 March 2018 and 7 March 2019.

The body is carried in a tall, incredibly artistic, multi-tiered pyre on the shoulders of a group of men. The tower's size depends on the deceased's importance. A rajah's or high priest's funeral may require hundreds of men to tote the 11-tiered structure.

Along the way, the group sets out to confuse the corpse so it cannot find its way back home; the corpse is considered an unclean link to the material world, and the soul must be liberated for its evolution to a higher state. The men shake the tower, run it around in circles, simulate war battles, hurl water at it and generally rough-handle it, making the trip anything but a stately funeral crawl.

At the cremation ground, the body is transferred to a funeral sarcophagus reflecting the deceased's caste. Finally, it all goes up in flames and the ashes are scattered in the ocean. The soul is then free to ascend to heaven and wait for the next incarnation, usually in the form of a grandchild.

In classic Balinese fashion, respectful visitors are welcome at cremations. It's always worth asking around or at your hotel to see if anyone knows of one going on. The Ubud tourist office is a good source too.

1. Ogoh-ogoh (p337) in a street parade **2.** Ceremonial offerings (p340) **3.** Rice paddies (p341)

Top Five Local Encounters

It's not the beaches, diving or even the nightlife that make Bali a destination like no other, it's the deep and rich culture that pervades every aspect of daily life. And even Lombok gets in on the action with its huge volcano.

Cremation

Balinese cremations (p336) are elaborate ceremonies that are memorable for anyone attending. When someone dies, their body may be temporarily buried while the relatives raise money for a proper – and fiery – send-off in a decorated tower.

Famous Subak

A key to the Balinese psyche is the *subak* system of rice-field irrigation (p341). Through collaborative arrangements, water that starts high in the mountains flows from one farmer's field to the next, with the last plot of land assured it won't be left dry.

Offerings

Throughout the day women leave offerings (p340) at the 10,000-plus temples on Bali, which, like the offerings, also come in many sizes. Offerings may be tiny, such as a few flower petals on a banana leaf, or large and elaborate creations.

Ogoh-Ogoh!

Huge monsters appear all over Bali in the weeks before Nyepi, the Day of Silence (p337). Built from papier-mâché, the elaborate figures stand up to 10m tall and take weeks to create. On Nyepi these 'evil spirits' are torched in ceremonies island-wide.

Sacred Mountain

Just as the Balinese have their sacred volcanos, the Sasak people of Lombok have Gunung Rinjani (p286). This volcano, the second-tallest mountain in Indonesia, occupies a vital part of their belief system, which also has elements of Islam.

Offerings

No matter where you stay, you'll witness women making daily offerings around their family temple and home, and in hotels, shops and other public places. You're also sure to see vibrant ceremonies, where whole villages turn out in ceremonial dress, and police close the roads for a spectacular procession that can stretch for hundreds of metres. Men play the gamelan while women elegantly balance magnificent tall offerings of fruit and cakes on their heads.

There's nothing manufactured about what you see. Dance and musical performances at hotels are among the few events 'staged' for tourists, but they do actually mirror the way Balinese traditionally welcome visitors, whom they refer to as *tamu* (guests). Otherwise, it's just the Balinese going about their daily life as they would without spectators.

Lombok

On Lombok, *adat* (tradition, customs and manners) underpins all aspects of daily life, especially regarding courtship, marriage and circumcision. Friday afternoon is the official time for worship, and government offices and many businesses close. Many, but not all, women wear headscarves, very few wear the veil, and large numbers work in tourism. Middle-class Muslim girls are often able to choose their own partners. Circumcision of Sasak boys normally occurs between the ages of six and 11 and calls for much celebration following a parade through their village.

The significant Balinese population on Lombok means you can often glimpse a Hindu ceremony while there; the minority Wektu Telu, Chinese and Buginese communities add to the diversity.

Village Life

Village life doesn't just take place in rural villages. Virtually every place on Bali is a village in its own way. Under its neon flash, chaos and otherworldly pleasures, even Kuta is a village; the locals meet, organise, cel-

---

Although illegal because it involves gambling, cockfighting is the top sport on Bali. It's easy to spot one when you know the main clue: lots of cars and motorbikes parked by the side of the road but no real sign of people. Or, just go to Pantai Masceti in east Bali where there is a huge cockfighting arena.

KEEPING TRACK OF TIME

Wondering what day of the week it is? You may have to consult a priest. The Balinese calendar is such a complex, intricate document that it only became publicly available some 60 years ago. Even today, most Balinese need a priest or *adat* leader to interpret it in order to determine the most auspicious day for any undertaking.

The calendar defines daily life. Whether it's building a new house, planting rice, having your teeth filed or getting married or cremated, no event has any chance of success if it does not occur on the proper date.

Three seemingly incompatible systems comprise the calendar (but this being Bali, that's a mere quibble): the 365-day Gregorian calendar, the 210-day *wuku* (or Pawukon) calendar, and the 12-month *caka* lunar calendar, which begins with Nyepi every March or April. In addition, certain weeks are dedicated to humans, others to animals and bamboo, and the calendar also lists forbidden activities for each week, such as getting married or cutting wood or bamboo.

Besides the date, each box on a calendar page contains the lunar month, the names of each of the 10 week 'days', attributes of a person born on that day according to Balinese astrology, and a symbol of either a full or new moon. Along the bottom of each month is a list of propitious days for specific activities, as well as the dates of *odalan* temple anniversaries – colourful festivals that visitors are welcome to attend.

In the old days, a priest consulted a *tika* – a piece of painted cloth or carved wood displaying the *wuku* cycle – which shows auspicious days represented by tiny geometric symbols. Today many people have their own calendars, but it's no wonder the priests are still in business!

ebrate, plan and make decisions as is done across the island. Central to this is the *banjar* (local neighbourhood organisation).

Local Rule Bali-Style

Within Bali's government, the more than 3500 *banjar* wield enormous power. Comprising the married men of a given area (somewhere between 50 and 500), a *banjar* controls most community activities, whether it's planning for a temple ceremony or making important land-use decisions. These decisions are reached by consensus, and woe to a member who shirks his duties. The penalty can be fines or worse: banishment from the *banjar*. (In Bali's highly socialised society where your community is your life and identity – which is why a standard greeting is 'Where do you come from?' – banishment is the equivalent of the death penalty.)

Although women and even children can belong to the *banjar*, only men attend the meetings where important decisions are made. Women, who often own the businesses in tourist areas, have to communicate through their husbands to exert their influence. One thing that outsiders in a neighbourhood quickly learn is that one does not cross the *banjar*. Entire streets of restaurants and bars have been closed by order of the *banjar* after it was determined that neighbourhood concerns over matters such as noise were not being addressed.

Rice Farming

Rice cultivation remains the backbone of rural Bali's strict communal society. Traditionally, each family makes just enough to satisfy their own needs and offerings to the gods, and perhaps a little to sell at market. The island's most popular deity is Dewi Sri, goddess of agriculture, fertility and success, and every stage of cultivation encompasses rituals to express gratitude and to prevent a poor crop, bad weather, pollution or theft by mice and birds.

Subak: Watering Bali

The complexities of tilling and irrigating terraces in mountainous terrain require that all villagers share the work and responsibility. Under a centuries-old system, the four mountain lakes and criss-crossing rivers irrigate fields via a network of canals, dams, bamboo pipes and tunnels bored through rock. More than 1200 *subak* (village irrigation associations) oversee this democratic supply of water, and every farmer must belong to his local *subak*, which in turn is the foundation of each village's powerful *banjar*.

Although Bali's civil make-up has changed with tourism, from a mostly homogenous island of farmers to a heterogeneous population with diverse activities and lifestyles, the collective responsibility rooted in rice farming continues to dictate the moral code behind daily life, even in the urban centres. *Subak*, a fascinating and democratic system, was placed on Unesco's World Heritage List in 2012.

LOCAL LIFE & RELIGION RICE FARMING

Huge decorated *penjor* (bamboo poles) appear in front of homes and line streets for ceremonies such as Galungan. Designs are as diverse as the artists who create them, but always feature the signature drooping top – in honour of the Barong's tail and the shape of Gunung Agung. The decorated tips, *samplan*, are exquisite.

Food & Drink

Bali is a splendid destination for food. The local cuisine, whether truly Balinese or influenced by the rest of Indonesia and Asia, draws from the bounty of fresh local foods and is rich with spices and flavours. Savour this fare at roadside warungs (simple local cafes) or top-end restaurants, and for tastes further afield, you can choose from restaurants offering some of the best dining in the region.

Balinese Cuisine

Cooking courses are popular and are great ways to learn about Balinese food and markets. Many are taught by chefs with reputations well beyond Bali. Recommended are Bumbu Bali Cooking School, in Tanjung Benoa, and Casa Luna Cooking School, in Ubud.

Food, glorious food – or should that be food, laborious food? Balinese cooking is a time-consuming activity, but no effort at all is required to enjoy the results. That part is one of the best things about travelling around Bali: the sheer variety and quality of the local cuisine will have your taste buds dancing all the way to the next warung.

The fragrant aromas of Balinese cooking will taunt you wherever you go. Even in your average village compound, the finest food is prepared fresh every day. Women go to their local marketplace first thing in the morning to buy whatever produce has been brought from the farms overnight. They cook enough to last all day, diligently roasting the coconut until the smoky sweetness kisses your nose, painstakingly grinding the spices to form the perfect *base* (paste) and perhaps even making fresh fragrant coconut oil for frying. The dishes are covered on a table or stored in a glass cabinet for family members to serve themselves throughout the day.

Six Flavours

Compared with that of other Indonesian islands, Balinese food is more pungent and lively, with a multitude of layers making up a complete dish. A meal will contain the six flavours (sweet, sour, spicy, salty, bitter and astringent), which promote health and vitality and stimulate the senses.

There's a predominance of ginger, chilli and coconut, as well as the beloved candlenut, often mistaken for the macadamia which is native to Australia. The biting combination of fresh galangal and turmeric is matched by the heat of raw chillies, the complex sweetness of palm sugar, tamarind and shrimp paste, and the clean, fresh flavours of lemon grass, musk lime, kaffir lime leaves and coriander seeds.

Every town of any size in Bali will have a *pasar malam* (night market), at which you can sample a vast range of fresh offerings from warungs and carts. Gianyar has a great one.

There are shades of south Indian, Malaysian and Chinese flavours, stemming from centuries of migration and trading with seafaring pioneers. Many ingredients were introduced in these times: the humble chilli was brought by the fearless Portuguese, the ubiquitous snake bean and bok choy by the Chinese, and the rice substitute cassava by the Dutch. In true Balinese style, village chefs selected the finest and most durable new ingredients and adapted them to local tastes and cooking styles.

Revered Rice

Rice is the staple dish in Bali and is revered as a gift of life from god. It is served generously with every meal – anything not served with rice is considered a *jaja* (snack). Rice acts as the medium for the various fragrant, spiced foods that accompany it, almost like condiments, with many dishes chopped finely to complement the dry, fluffy grains and for ease of eating with the hand. In Bali, a dish of steamed rice with mixed goodies is known as *nasi campur*. It's the island's undisputed 'signature' dish, eaten for breakfast, lunch and dinner.

There are as many variations of *nasi campur* as there are warungs. Just like a sandwich in the West can combine any number of fillings, each warung serves its own version according to budget, taste and whatever ingredients are fresh at the market. There are typically four or five dishes that make up a single serving, including a small portion of pork or chicken (small because meat is expensive), fish, tofu or tempeh (fermented soy-bean cake), egg, various vegetable dishes and crunchy *krupuk* (flavoured rice crackers). Beef seldom features because the Balinese believe cows are sacred. The 'side dishes' are arrayed around the centrepiece of rice and accompanied by the warung's signature sambal (paste made from chillies, garlic or shallots, and salt). The food is not usually served hot, because it would have been prepared during the morning.

The Food of Bali (1996), by Heinz von Holzen and Lother Arsana, brings to life everything from *cram cam* (clear chicken soup with shallots) to *bubuh injin* (black-rice pudding).

A Taste of Asia

Bali's multicultural population means many warungs serve pan-Indonesian and Asian cuisine, offering a taste of different foods from across the archipelago. Common menu items are often confused with being Balinese, such as nasi goreng (fried rice), *mie goreng* (fried noodles), the ever-popular gado gado, which is actually from Java, and *rendang sapi* (beef curry), which is from Sumatra. There are many restaurants serving Padang fare (which originates from Sumatra) in Bali, and Chinese food is common.

Breakfast

Many Balinese save their appetite for lunch. They might kick-start the day with a cup of rich, sweet black coffee and a few sweet *jaja* at the market: colourful temple cakes, glutinous rice cakes, boiled bananas in their peels, fried banana fritters and *kelopon* (sweet-centred rice balls). Popular fresh fruits include snake fruit, named after its scaly skin, and jackfruit, which is also delicious stewed with vegetables.

The famous *bubuh injin* (black-rice pudding with palm sugar, grated coconut and coconut milk), which most tourists find on restaurant dessert menus, is actually a breakfast dish and a fine way to start the day. A variation available at the morning market is the nutty *bubur kacang hijau* (green mung-bean pudding), fragrantly enriched with ginger and pandanus leaf and served warm with coconut milk.

MARKET LIFE

There's no better place to get acquainted with Balinese cuisine than the local market. But it's not for late sleepers. The best time to go is around 6am to 7am. If you're any later than 10am, the prime selections would have been snapped up and what's left would have begun to rot in the tropical climate.

Markets offer a glimpse of the variety and freshness of Balinese produce, often brought from the mountains within a day or two of being harvested, sometimes sooner. The atmosphere is lively and colourful with baskets loaded with fresh fruits, vegetables, flowers, spices, and varieties of red, black and white rice. There are trays of live chickens, dead chickens, freshly slaughtered pigs, sardines, eggs, colourful cakes, ready-made offerings and *base,* and stalls selling es cendol (colourful iced coconut drink), *bubur* (rice porridge) or *nasi campur* for breakfast. There's no refrigeration, so things come in small packages and what you see is for immediate sale. Bargaining is expected.

TRIOCEAN / SHUTTERSTOCK ©

1. *Babi guling* 2. *Nasi campur* 3. Bali stallholder 4. Bintang beer

Top Five Balinese Treats

Colourful, aromatic and fabulously flavourful, Bali's food (and drink) will have you coming back for more.

Babi Guling

What was once a dish reserved for special occasions is now one of Bali's favourite foods: *babi guling* (p346), a suckling pig filled with spices and roasted, is sold at scores of outlets.

Nasi Campur

Bali's equivalent of a national dish, this lunchtime staple (p346) defies description. At hundreds of warungs (food stalls) across the island you start with a plate and then select some rice (yellow? white? red?) and then the fun begins. Choose from an array of tempting meat, seafood and veggie dishes.

Sambal

There are as many variations on this staple condiment (p346) as there are versions of *nasi campur* and that's only fitting as it's the source of spicy heat in most Balinese foods. Chefs jealously guard their sambal recipes which are myriad.

Night Markets

Pasar malam (night markets) are popular sources for after-dark eats on Bali and Lombok. The best will have dozens of stalls and stands with staff cooking away like mad and offering a range of locally favourite dishes. Wander, browse and snack your way to joy.

Bintang

It's a marketer's dream: you don't say 'beer' on Bali, you say 'Bintang'. The beer that launched the branded singlet empire is a crisp, clean lager that refreshes on a hot day. Whether it's cooling off a fiery feast or making the sunset seem that much rosier, it goes down smoothly.

SAMBAL JOY

The Balinese certainly like a spicy kick with their meals. But where people get confused is when they assume Balinese food itself is spicy. Rather, the dishes are mild; locals relish a dollop of fiery sambal with every dish. Taste it to gauge the temperature before ploughing in. If you're averse to spicy food, request *tanpa* sambal (without chilli paste); better for most, though, is *tamba* (more) sambal!

One other note on sambal: if your request results in a bottle of the generically sweet commercial gloop, ask for 'Balinese sambal'. This latter request can open many more doors to eating joy because every Balinese cook has their own favourite way of creating sambal. If you add the many sambals adopted from other parts of Indonesia, especially neighbouring Lombok, you could get one of many variations, including:

Sambal bajak A Javanese sambal, this is a creamy tomato-based sauce that is redolent with crushed chillies, yet gets smoothed out with palm sugar and shallots and then fried. Very common.

Sambal balado Chillis, shallots, garlic and tomatoes are sauteed in oil for a literally hot sambal. Often fried up fresh on the spot.

Sambal matah A raw Balinese sambal made from thinly sliced shallots, tiny chilies, shrimp paste and lemongrass. Divine.

Sambal plecing A Lombok sambal, this one takes hot chillies and puts them in a tomato base, letting the heat sneak up on you.

Sambal taliwang Another Lombok sambal made with special peppers, garlic and shrimp paste. One of the few true culinary highlights of Bali's neighbour and a favourite on Bali, where spicy Lombok-style chicken is adored.

Lunch & Dinner

The household or warung cook usually finishes preparing the day's dishes mid-morning, so lunchtime happens around 11am when the food is freshest. This is the main meal of the day. Leftovers are eaten for dinner, or by tourists who awake late and do not get around to lunch until well after everyone else has had their fill. Dessert is a rarity; for special occasions, it consists of fresh fruit or gelato-style coconut ice cream.

The secret to a good *nasi campur* is often in the cook's own *base*, which flavours the pork, chicken or fish, and the sambal, which may add just the right amount of heat to the meal at one place, or set your mouth ablaze at another. The range of dishes is endless. Some local favourites include *babi kecap* (pork stewed in sweet soy sauce), *ayam goreng* (fried chicken), *urap* (steamed vegetables with coconut), *lawar* (salad of chopped coconut, garlic and chilli with pork or chicken meat and blood), fried tofu or tempeh in a sweet soy or chilli sauce, fried peanuts, salty fish or eggs, *perkedel* (fried corn cakes), and various satay made from chunks of goat meat, chicken and pork.

If you visit a homestay, like the many in Ubud, you'll see family members busily preparing food throughout the day.

Reason to Celebrate

Food is not just about enjoyment and sustenance. Like everything in Balinese life, it is an intrinsic part of the daily rituals and a major part of ceremonies to honour the gods. The menu varies according to the importance of the occasion. By far the most revered dish is *babi guling* (suckling pig), presented during rites-of-passage ceremonies such as a baby's three-month blessing, an adolescent's tooth filing, or a wedding.

Babi guling is the quintessential Bali experience. A whole pig is stuffed with chilli, turmeric, ginger, galangal, shallots, garlic, coriander seeds and aromatic leaves, basted in turmeric and coconut oil and skewered on a wooden spit over an open fire. Turned for hours, the meat takes on the flavour of the spices and the fire-pit, giving a rustic smoky flavour to the crispy crackling. Short of being invited to a ceremonial feast, you can enjoy *babi guling* at stands, warungs and cafes across Bali.

Bebek or *ayam betutu* (smoked duck or chicken) is another ceremonial favourite. The bird is stuffed with spices, wrapped in coconut bark and banana leaves, and cooked all day over smouldering rice husks and coconut husks. Ubud is the best place to enjoy smoked duck – head to Bebek Bengil (p175), which is actually the source for the many restaurants that offer *bebek betutu* if ordered in advance.

Often served at marriage ceremonies, *jukut ares* is a light, fragrant broth made from banana stem and usually containing chopped chicken or pork. The satay for special occasions, *sate lilit,* is a fragrant combination of good-quality minced fish, chicken or pork with lemon grass, galangal, shallots, chilli, palm sugar, kaffir lime and coconut milk. This is wrapped onto skewers and grilled.

Warungs

The most common place for dining out in Bali is a warung, the traditional street-side eatery. There's one every few metres in major towns, and several even in small villages. They are cheap, no-frills hang-outs with a relaxed atmosphere; you may find yourself sharing a table with strangers as you watch the world go by. The food is fresh and different at each, and is usually displayed in a glass cabinet at the entrance where you can create your own *nasi campur* or just order the house standard.

Both Seminyak and Kerobokan in particular are blessed with numerous warungs that are visitor-friendly, but many are on offer across Bali and half the fun is finding your own favourite.

Dining – or Not – Balinese Style

Eating is a solitary exercise in Bali and conversation is limited. Families rarely eat together; everyone makes up their own plate whenever they're hungry.

The Balinese eat with their right hand, which is used to give and receive all good things. The left hand deals with unpleasant sinister elements (such as ablutions). It's customary to wash your hands before eating, even if you use a spoon and fork; local restaurants always have a sink outside the restrooms. If you choose to eat the local way, use the bowl of water provided at the table to wash your hands after the meal, as licking your fingers is not appreciated.

Balinese are formal about behaviour and clothing, and it isn't polite to enter a restaurant or eat a meal half-naked, no matter how many sit-ups you've been doing or how many new piercings and tattoos you've acquired.

Cradle of Flavor (2006) is a mouth-watering treatise on Indonesian foods and cooking by James Oseland, the editor of *Saveur* magazine.

LOMBOK'S SASAK CUISINE

Lombok's Sasak people are predominantly Muslim, so Bali's porky plethora does not feature in their diet of fish, chicken, vegetables and rice. The fact that lombok means chilli in Bahasa Indonesia makes sense, because Sasaks like their food spicy; *ayam taliwang* (whole split chicken roasted over coconut husks served with tomato-chilli-lime dip) is one example.

Ares is a dish made with chilli, coconut juice and banana-palm pith; sometimes it's mixed with chicken or meat. *Sate pusut* is a delicious combination of minced fish, chicken or beef flavoured with coconut milk, garlic, chilli and other spices and wrapped around a lemon-grass stick and grilled.

If you wish to eat in front of a Balinese, it's polite to invite them to join you, even if you know they will say 'no', or even if you don't have anything to offer. If you're invited to a Balinese home for a meal, your hosts will no doubt insist you eat more, but you may always politely pass on second helpings or refuse food you don't find appealing.

Drinks

If there's a beach there's likely a beer vendor nearby to sell you a cold one while the sand tickles your toes. If you'd like something more posh, stylish and popular, beach venues can be found from Seminyak to Kerobokan and Canggu. No matter where you are, though, you're likely not too far from a typically mellow Bali cafe, where fresh juices, great coffee and various adult drinks will be on offer. Long after dark, luxe clubs and hip hang-outs can be found from Seminyak to Canggu. Go south to Kuta for legendary, raw-edged all-night partying.

For an exhaustive rundown of eating options in Bali, check out www.balieats. com. The listings are encyclopedic, continually updated and many have enthusiastic reviews.

Beer

Beer drinkers are well catered for in Bali thanks to Indonesia's ubiquitous crisp, clean national lager, Bintang. Bali Hai beer sounds promising, but isn't.

Wine

Wine connoisseurs had better have a fat wallet. The abundance of high-end eateries and hotels has made fine vino from the world's best regions widely available but it is whacked with hefty taxes. Medium-grade bottles from Australia go for US$50.

Of the local producers of wine, the least objectionable is Artisan Estate, which overcomes the import duties by bringing crushed grapes from Western Australia. Hatten Wine, based in north Bali, has gained quite a following among those who like its very sweet pink rosé. Two Islands also has a following.

Local Booze

At large social gatherings, Balinese men might indulge in *arak* (fermented wine made from rice or palms or...other materials) but generally they are not big drinkers. Watch out for adulterated *arak,* which is rare but can be poisonous (p382).

VEGETARIAN DREAMS

Bali is a dream come true for vegetarians. Tofu and tempeh are part of the staple diet, and many tasty local favourites just happen to be vegetarian. Try *nasi saur* (rice flavoured with toasted coconut and accompanied by tofu, tempeh, vegetables and sometimes egg), *urap* (a delightful blend of steamed vegetables mixed with grated coconut and spices), gado gado (tofu and tempeh mixed with steamed vegetables, boiled egg and peanut sauce) and *sayur hijau* (leafy green vegetables, usually *kangkung* – water spinach – flavoured with a tomato-chilli sauce).

In addition, the way *nasi campur* is served means it's easy to request no meat, instead enjoying an array of fresh stir-fries, salads, tofu and tempeh. When ordering curries and stir-fries such as *cap cay,* diners can usually choose meat, seafood or vegetarian.

Western-style vegetarian pasta and salads abound in most restaurants and many purely vegetarian eateries cater for vegans. Seminyak, Kerobokan and Canggu are good for meat-free fare while Ubud excels thanks to its yoga and healthy lifestyle ethos.

FAST FOOD BALI-STYLE

Usually the most authentic Balinese food is found street-side (although Denpasar and other areas have some sit-down places that are excellent). Locals of all stripes gather around simple food stalls in markets and on village streets, wave down *pedagang* (mobile traders) who ferry sweet and savoury snacks around by bicycle or motorcycle, and queue for *sate* or *bakso* (Chinese meatballs in a light soup) at the *kaki-lima* carts. *Kaki-lima* translates as something five-legged and refers to the three legs of the cart and the two of the vendor, who is usually Javanese.

One note on health: food cooked fresh from carts and stalls is usually fine but that which has been sitting around for a while can be dodgy at best or riddled with dubious preservatives.

Fresh Juice

Local nonalcoholic refreshments available from markets, street vendors, some warungs and many cafes are tasty and even a little psychedelic (in colour) – and without the hangover! One of Bali's most popular is *cendol*, an interesting mix of palm sugar, fresh coconut milk, crushed ice and various other random flavourings and floaties.

Coffee & Tea

Many Western eateries sell imported coffees and teas alongside local brands, some of which are very good.

The most expensive – and most overhyped – is Indonesia's peculiar kopi luwak (p189). Around 200,000Rp a cup, this coffee is named after the catlike civet *(luwak)* indigenous to Sulawesi, Sumatra and Java that feasts on ripe coffee cherries. Entrepreneurs initially collected the intact beans found in the civet's droppings and processed them to produce a supposedly extra-piquant brew. But now that interest in coffee *luwak* has exceeded all reason, trouble abounds, from fraudulent claims to documented animal mistreatment.

The Arts

Bali's vibrant arts scene makes the island so much more than just a tropical beach destination. In the paintings, sculpture, dance and music, you will see the natural artistic talent inherent in all Balinese, a legacy of their Majapahit heritage. The artistry displayed here will stay with you long after you've moved on from the island.

An Island of Artists

Colin McPhee's iconic book about Balinese dance and culture, *A House in Bali* (1946), has been made into an opera of the same name. It's the creation of Evan Ziporyn, a composer who spends much time in Ubud.

It's telling that there is no Balinese equivalent for the words 'art' or 'artist'. Until the tourist invasion, artistic expression was exclusively for religious and ritual purposes, and was almost exclusively done by men. Paintings and carvings were purely to decorate temples and shrines, while music, dance and theatrical performances were put on to entertain the gods who returned to Bali for important ceremonies. Artists did not strive to be different or individual as many do in the West; their work reflected a traditional style or a new idea, but not their own personality.

That changed in the late 1920s when foreign artists began to settle in Ubud; they went to learn from the Balinese and to share their knowledge, and helped to establish art as a commercial enterprise. Today, it's big business. Ubud remains the undisputed artistic centre of the island, and artists come from near and far to draw on its inspiration, from Japanese glass-blowers to European photographers and Javanese painters.

Galleries and craft shops are all over the island; the paintings, stone carvings and woodcarvings are stacked up on floors and will trip you up if you're not careful. Much of it is churned out quickly, and some is comically vulgar – put that 3m vision of a penis as Godzilla in your entryway, will you? – but there is also a great deal of extraordinary work.

Dance
Bali

There are more than a dozen different dances in Bali, each with rigid choreography, requiring high levels of discipline. Most performers have learned through painstaking practice with an expert. No visit is complete without enjoying this purely Balinese art form; you will be delighted by the many styles, from the formal artistry of the Legong to crowd-pleasing antics in the Barong. One thing Balinese dance is not is static. The best troupes, like Semara Ratih in Ubud, are continually innovating.

You can catch a quality dance performance at any place where there's a festival or celebration, and you'll find exceptional performances in and around Ubud. Performances are typically at night and last about 90 minutes, and you'll have a choice of eight or more performances a night.

With a little research and some good timing, you can attend performances that are part of temple ceremonies. Here you'll see the full beauty of Bali's dance and music heritage in the context of how it was meant to be seen. Performances can last several hours. Absorb the hypnotic music and the alluring moves of the performers as well as the rapt attention of the crowd. Music, theatre and dance courses are also available in Ubud.

With the short attention spans of tourists in mind, many hotels offer a smorgasbord of dances – a little Kecak, a taste of Barong and some Legong to round it off. These can be pretty abbreviated, with just a few musicians and a couple of dancers.

Kecak

Probably the best-known dance, for its spellbinding, hair-raising atmosphere, the Kecak features a 'choir' of men and boys who sit in concentric circles and slip into a trance as they chant and sing 'chak-a-chak a chak', imitating a troupe of monkeys. Sometimes called the 'vocal gamelan', this is the only music to accompany the dance re-enactment from the Hindu epic Ramayana, the familiar love story about Prince Rama and his Princess Sita.

The tourist version of Kecak was developed in the 1960s. This spectacular performance is easily found in Ubud (look for Krama Desa Ubud Kaja with its 80 shirtless men chanting hypnotically) and also at the Pura Luhur Ulu Watu.

Legong

Characterised by flashing eyes and quivering hands, this most graceful of Balinese dances is performed by young girls. Their talent is so revered that in old age, a classic dancer will be remembered as a 'great Legong'.

Peliatan's famous dance troupe, Gunung Sari, often seen in Ubud, is particularly noted for its Legong Keraton (Legong of the Palace). The very stylised and symbolic story involves two Legong girls dancing in

Balinese Dance, Drama and Music: A Guide to the Performing Arts of Bali, by I Wayan Dibia and Rucina Ballinger, is a lavishly illustrated and highly recommended in-depth guide to Bali's cultural performances.

THE ARTS DANCE

MONKEYS & MONSTERS

The Barong and Rangda dance rivals the Kecak as Bali's most popular performance for tourists. Again, it's a battle between good (the Barong) and bad (the Rangda).

The Barong is a good but mischievous and fun-loving shaggy dog-lion, with huge eyes and a mouth that clacks away to much dramatic effect. Because this character is the good protector of a village, the actors playing the Barong (who are utterly lost under layers of fur-clad costume) will emote a variety of winsome antics. But as is typical of Balinese dance, it is not all light-hearted – the Barong is a very sacred character indeed and you'll often see one in processions and rituals.

There's nothing sacred about the Barong's buddies. One or more monkeys attend to him and these characters often steal the show. Actors are given free rein to range wildly. The best aim a lot of high jinks at the audience, especially members who seem to be taking things a tad too seriously.

Meanwhile, the widow-witch Rangda is bad through and through. The Queen of Black Magic, the character's monstrous persona can include flames shooting out her ears, a tongue dripping fire, a mane of wild hair and large breasts.

The story features a duel between the Rangda and the Barong, whose supporters draw their kris (traditional dagger) and rush in to help. The long-tongued, sharp-fanged Rangda throws them into a trance, making them stab themselves. It's quite a spectacle. Thankfully, the Barong casts a spell that neutralises the power of the kris so it cannot harm them.

Playing around with all that powerful magic, good and bad, requires the presence of a *pemangku* (priest for temple rituals), who must end the dancers' trance and make a blood sacrifice using a chicken to propitiate the evil spirits.

In Ubud, Barong and Rangda dance troupes have many interpretations of the dance, everything from eerie performances that will give you the shivers (until the monkeys appear) to jokey versions that could be a variety show or Brit pantomime.

Barong masks are valued objects; you can find artful examples in the village of Mas, south of Ubud.

mirror image. They are elaborately made up and dressed in gold brocade, relating a story about a king who takes a maiden captive and consequently starts a war, in which he dies.

Sanghyang & Kekac Fire Dance

These dances were developed to drive out evil spirits from a village – Sanghyang is a divine spirit who temporarily inhabits an entranced dancer. The Sanghyang Dedari is performed by two young girls who dance a dreamlike version of the Legong in perfect symmetry while their eyes are firmly shut. Male and female choirs provide a background chant until the dancers slump to the ground. A *pemangku* (priest for temple rituals) blesses them with holy water and brings them out of the trance.

In the Sanghyang Jaran, a boy in a trance dances around and through a fire of coconut husks, riding a coconut palm 'hobby horse'. Variations of this are called the Kecak Fire Dance and are performed in Ubud almost daily.

Other Dances

The warrior dance, the Baris, is a male equivalent of the Legong – grace and femininity give way to an energetic and warlike spirit. The highly skilled Baris dancer must convey the thoughts and emotions of a warrior first preparing for action, and then meeting the enemy: chivalry, pride, anger, prowess and, finally, regret are illustrated.

In the Topeng, which means 'pressed against the face', as with a mask, the dancers imitate the character represented by the mask. This requires great expertise because the dancer cannot convey thoughts and meanings through facial expressions – the dance must tell all.

Lombok

Lombok has its own unique dances, but they are not widely marketed. Performances are staged in some top-end hotels and in Lenek village, known for its dance traditions. If you're in Senggigi in July, you might catch dance and *gendang beleq* (big drum) performances. The *gendang beleq*, a dramatic war dance also called the Oncer, is performed by men and boys who play a variety of unusual musical instruments for *adat* (traditional customs) festivals in central and eastern Lombok.

Music

Bali

Balinese music is based around an ensemble known as a gamelan, also called a *gong*. A *gong gede* (large orchestra) is the traditional form, with 35 to 40 musicians. The more ancient gamelan *selunding* is still occasionally played in Bali Aga villages such as Tenganan.

The popular modern form of a *gong gede* is *gong kebyar*, with up to 25 instruments. This melodic, sometimes upbeat and sometimes haunting percussion that often accompanies traditional dance is one of the most lasting impressions for tourists to Bali.

The prevalent voice in Balinese music is from the xylophone-like *gangsa*, which the player hits with a hammer, dampening the sound just after it's struck. The tempo and nature of the music is controlled by two *kendang* (drums), one male and one female. Other instruments are the deep *trompong* drums, small *kempli* gong and *cengceng* (cymbals) used in faster pieces. Not all instruments require great skill and making music is a common village activity.

Many shops in south Bali and Ubud sell the distinctive gongs, flutes, bamboo xylophones and bamboo chimes. Look online for downloads.

Women often bring offerings to a temple while dancing the Pendet, their eyes, heads and hands moving in spectacularly controlled and coordinated movements. Every flick of the wrist, hand and fingers is charged with meaning.

Preserving and performing rare and ancient Balinese dance and gamelan music is the mission of Mekar Bhuana (www.balimusicand-dance.com), a Denpasar-based cultural group. They sponsor performances and offer lessons.

Lombok

The *genggong*, a performance seen on Lombok, uses a simple set of instruments, including a bamboo flute, a *rebab* (two-stringed bowed lute) and knockers. Seven musicians accompany their music with dance movements and stylised hand gestures.

Wayang Kulit

Much more than sheer entertainment, *wayang kulit* has been Bali's candlelit cinema for centuries, embodying the sacred seriousness of classical Greek drama. (The word drama comes from the Greek *dromenon*, a religious ritual.) The performances are long and intense – lasting six hours or more and often not finishing before sunrise.

Originally used to bring ancestors back to this world, the shows feature painted buffalo-hide puppets believed to have great spiritual power, and the *dalang* (puppet master and storyteller) is an almost mystical figure. A person of considerable skill and even greater endurance, the *dalang* sits behind a screen and manipulates the puppets while telling the story, often in many dialects.

Stories are chiefly derived from the great Hindu epics, the Ramayana and, to a lesser extent, the Mahabharata.

You can find performances in Ubud, which are attenuated to a manageable two hours or less.

An *arja* drama is not unlike *wayang kulit* puppet shows in its melodramatic plots, its offstage sound effects and its cast of easily identifiable goodies (the refined *alus*) and baddies (the unrefined *kras*). It's performed outside and a small house is sometimes built on stage and set on fire at the climax!

Painting

Balinese painting is probably the art form most influenced by Western ideas and demand. Traditional paintings, faithfully depicting religious and mythological subjects, were for temple and palace decoration, and the set colours were made from soot, clay and pigs' bones. In the 1930s, Western artists introduced the concept of paintings as artistic creations that could also be sold for money. To target the tourist market, they encouraged deviance to scenes from everyday life and the use of the full palette of modern paints and tools. The range of themes, techniques, styles and materials expanded enormously, and women painters emerged for the first time.

INFLUENTIAL WESTERN ARTISTS

Besides Arie Smit (who died on Bali at age 99 in 2016), several other Western artists had a profound effect on Balinese art in the early and middle parts of the 20th century. In addition to honouring Balinese art, they provided a critical boost to its vitality at a time when it might have died out.

Walter Spies (1895–1942) A German artist, Spies first visited Bali in 1925 and moved to Ubud in 1927, establishing the image of Bali for Westerners that prevails today.

Rudolf Bonnet (1895–1978) Bonnet was a Dutch artist whose work concentrated on the human form and everyday Balinese life. Many classical Balinese paintings with themes of markets and cockfights are indebted to Bonnet.

Miguel Covarrubias (1904–57) *Island of Bali*, written by this Mexican artist, is still the classic introduction to the island and its culture.

Colin McPhee (1900–65) A Canadian musician, McPhee wrote *A House in Bali*. It remains one of the best written accounts of Bali, and his tales of music and house building are often highly amusing. His patronage of traditional dance and music cannot be overstated.

Adrien Jean Le Mayeur de Merpres (1880–1958) This Belgian artist arrived on Bali in 1932 and did much to establish the notions of sensual Balinese beauty, often based on his wife, the dancer Ni Polok. Their home is now an under-appreciated museum in Sanur.

A loose classification of styles is classical, or Kamasan, named for the village of Kamasan near Semarapura; Ubud style, developed in the 1930s under the influence of the Pita Maha; Batuan, which started at the same time in a nearby village; Young Artists, begun postwar in the 1960s, and influenced by Dutch artist Arie Smit; and finally, modern or academic, free in its creative topics, yet strongly and distinctively Balinese.

Where to See & Buy Paintings

There is a relatively small number of creative original painters in Bali, and an enormous number of imitators. Shops, especially in south Bali, are packed full of paintings in whatever style is popular at the time – some are quite good and a few are really excellent (and in many you'll swear you see the numbers used to guide the artists under the paint).

Top museums in Ubud, such as the Neka Art Museum (p152), Agung Rai Museum of Art (p154) and the Museum Puri Lukisan (p149), showcase the best of Balinese art and some of the European influences that have shaped it. There are more noted galleries as you go south of Ubud to Mas (p185).

Commercial galleries such as Ubud's Neka Gallery (p149) and Agung Rai Gallery (p155) offer high-quality works. Exploring the dizzying melange of galleries – high and low – makes for a fun afternoon or longer.

Treasures of Bali, by Richard Mann, is a beautifully illustrated guide to Bali's museums, big and small. It highlights the gems often overlooked by group tours.

Classical Painting

There are three basic types of classical painting – *langse, iders-iders* and calendars. *Langse* are large decorative hangings for palaces or temples that display *wayang* figures (which have an appearance similar to the figures used in shadow puppetry), rich floral designs and flame-and-mountain motifs. *Iders-iders* are scroll paintings hung along temple eaves. Calendars are, much as they were before, used to set dates for rituals and predict the future.

Langse paintings helped impart *adat* (traditional customs) to ordinary people in the same way that traditional dance and *wayang kulit* puppetry do. The stylised human figures depicted good and evil, with romantic heroes like Ramayana and Arjuna always painted with small, narrow eyes and fine features, while devils and warriors were prescribed round eyes, coarse features and facial hair. The paintings tell a story in a series of panels, rather like a comic strip, and often depict scenes from the Ramayana and Mahabharata. Other themes are the Kakawins poems, and demonic spirits from indigenous Balinese folklore – see the ceilings of the Kertha Gosa (Hall of Justice) in Semarapura for an example.

A good place to see classical painting in a modern context is at the Nyoman Gunarsa Museum near Semarapura, which was established to preserve and promote classical techniques.

The Pita Maha

In the 1930s, with few commissions from temples, painting was virtually dying out. European artists Rudolf Bonnet and Walter Spies, with their patron Cokorda Gede Agung Surapati, formed the Pita Maha (literally, Great Vitality) to take painting from a ritual-based activity to a commercial one. The cooperative had more than 100 members at its peak in the 1930s and led to the establishment of Museum Puri Lukisan in Ubud, the first museum dedicated to Balinese art.

The changes Bonnet and Spies inspired were revolutionary. Balinese artists such as the late I Gusti Nyoman Lempad, I Wayan Ketig, I Ketut Regig and Gus Made started exploring their own styles. Narrative tales were replaced by single scenes, and romantic legends by daily life: the harvest, markets, cockfights, offerings at a temple or a cremation. These paintings were known as Ubud style.

Meanwhile, painters from Batuan retained many features of classical painting. They depicted daily life, but across many scenes – a market, dance and rice harvest would all appear in a single work. This Batuan style is also noted for its inclusion of some very modern elements, such as sea scenes with the odd windsurfer.

The painting techniques also changed. Modern paint and materials were used and stiff formal poses gave way to realistic 3-D representations. More importantly, pictures were not just painted to fit a space in a palace or a temple.

In one way, the style remained unchanged – Balinese paintings are packed with detail. A painted Balinese forest, for example, has branches, leaves and a whole zoo of creatures reaching out to fill every tiny space.

This new artistic enthusiasm was interrupted by WWII and Indonesia's independence struggle, and stayed that way until the development of the Young Artists' style.

A carefully selected list of books about art, culture and Balinese writers, dancers and musicians can be found at www.ganeshabooksbali.com, the website for the excellent Ubud bookstore (with a branch in Sanur).

The Young Artists

Arie Smit was in Penestanan, just outside Ubud, in 1956, when he noticed an 11-year-old boy drawing in the dirt. Smit wondered what the boy could produce if he had the proper equipment. As the legend goes, the boy's father would not allow him to take up painting until Smit offered to pay somebody else to watch the family's ducks.

Other 'young artists' soon joined that first pupil, I Nyoman Cakra, but Smit did not actively teach them. He simply provided the equipment and encouragement, unleashing what was clearly a strong natural talent. Today this style of rural scenes painted in brilliant Technicolor is a staple of Balinese tourist art.

I Nyoman Cakra still lives in Penestanan, still paints, and cheerfully admits that he owes it all to Smit. Other Young Artists include I Ketut Tagen, I Nyoman Tjarka and I Nyoman Mujung.

TODAY'S BALINESE PAINTERS

Numerous Balinese artists are receiving international recognition for their work, which often has a strong theme of social justice and a questioning of modern values. Still, being Balinese and all, the works have a sly wit and even a wink to the viewer. Some names to watch for:

Nyoman Masriadi Born in Gianyar, Masriadi is easily the superstar of Bali's current crop of painters, and his works sell for upwards of a million dollars. He is renowned for his sharp-eyed observations of Indonesian society today and his thoroughly modern techniques and motifs.

Made Djirna Hailing from the comparatively wealthy tourist town of Ubud, Djirna has the perfect background for his works, which criticise the relationship between ostentatious money and modern Balinese religious ceremonies.

Agung Mangu Putra This painter from the deeply green hills west of Ubud finds inspiration in the Balinese being bypassed by the island's uneven economic boom. He decries the impact on his natural world.

Wayan Sudarna Putra An Ubud native, Putra uses satire and parody in his works, which cross media to question the absurdities of current Indonesian life and values.

Ketut Sana A resident of Keliki, a village near Ubud, Sana knew noted artists Gusti Nyoman Sudara Lempad and Wayan Gerudug when he was young. He started his impressionistic work by adapting scraps from their work.

Gede Suanda Sayur Sayur's works are often dark as he questions the pillaging of Bali's environment. He joined Putra to create an installation in a rice field near Ubud that featured huge white poles spelling out 'Not for sale'.

Top Five Arts Experiences

For such a little island, there's a lot of art on Bali. From works created by hand to performances using hands, Balinese art is all-encompassing.

Ikat

At an ikat factory you may find the frenetic clacking of dozens of ancient wooden looms hypnotic or cacophonous, but you'll likely find the results beautiful. Traditionally dyed threads are woven together to form beautiful and distinctly handmade patterns (p359).

Legong Dancing

The movements of the best Legong dancers (p351) seem impossibly robotic and rigidly controlled. Young girls and women dressed in tight-embroidered and gold-highlighted finery perform rigorous dances with precise movements of their eyes and virtually every muscle. Watch their hands as they create the flights of butterflies.

1. Ornamental relief carving **2.** Kecak performance at Pura Luhur Ulu Watu (p112) **3.** Legong dancers at Bali Arts Festival (p131)

Kecak Chanting

You'll be haunted for hours after you see a Kecak performance (p351). The sounds of dozens of men chanting and singing for more than an hour is bewitching and you may find you're slipping into a trance not unlike the performers. The sounds are rhythmic, the effect mesmerising.

Barong & Rangda

With a brightly coloured mask, Barongs (p350) are hard to miss in performance – and that's before you take in the rest of their huge shaggy costume. Representing good, Barongs clack their wooden mouths and generally do their best to steal the spotlight from their evil counterpart, Rangda.

Stone Carving

If Indiana Jones hired an artist it would be a Balinese carver. Using the island's soft volcanic stone, these craftspeople create elaborate designs that quickly age, so that a new temple soon looks like an ancient wonder (p361).

Other Styles

There are some other variants to the main Ubud and Young Artists' painting styles. The depiction of forests, flowers, butterflies, birds and other naturalistic themes, for example, sometimes called Pengosekan style, became popular in the 1960s. It can probably be traced back to Henri Rousseau, who was a significant influence on Walter Spies. An interesting development in this particular style is the depiction of underwater scenes, with colourful fish, coral gardens and sea creatures. Somewhere between the Pengosekan and Ubud styles sit the miniature landscape paintings that are popular commercially.

The new techniques also resulted in radically new versions of Rangda, Barong, Hanuman and other figures from Balinese and Hindu mythology. Scenes from folk tales and stories appeared, featuring dancers, nymphs and love stories, with an understated erotic appeal.

The magazine/comic *Bog Bog*, by Balinese cartoonists, is a satirical and humorous insight into the contrast between modern and traditional worlds in Bali. It's available in warungs (food stalls), bookshops and supermarkets or online at www.facebook.com/bogbogcartoon.

Crafts

Bali is a showroom for crafts from around Indonesia. The nicer tourist shops will sell puppets and batiks from Java, ikat garments from Sumba, Sumbawa and Flores, and textiles and woodcarvings from Bali, Lombok and Kalimantan. The kris, so important to a Balinese family, will often have been made in Java.

On Lombok, where there's never been much money, traditional handicrafts are practical items, but they are still skilfully made and beautifully finished. The finer examples of Lombok weaving, basketware and pottery are highly valued by collectors.

Textiles & Weaving

Bali

Textiles in Bali and Lombok are woven by women for ceremonies, as well as for gifts. They are often part of marriage dowries and cremations, where they join the deceased's soul as it passes to the afterlife.

The most common material in Bali is the sarong, which can be used as an article of clothing, a sheet or a towel, among other things. The cheap cottons, either plain or printed, are for everyday use, and are popular with tourists for beachwear.

For special occasions such as a temple ceremony, Balinese men and women use a *kamben* (a length of *songket* wrapped around the chest). The *songket* is silver- or gold-threaded cloth, handwoven using a floating weft technique, while another variety is the *endek* (like *songket,* but with pre-dyed weft threads).

The men pair the *kamben* with a shirt and the women pair it with a *kebaya* (long-sleeved lace blouse). A separate slim strip of cloth known as a *kain* (or known as *prada* when decorated with a gold-leaf pattern) is wound tightly around the hips and over the sarong like a belt to complete the outfit.

Where to Buy

Any market, especially in Denpasar, will have a good range of textiles. Often groups of stores will cluster on one street, such as Jl Sulawesi across from the main market in Denpasar and Jl Arjuna in Legian. Threads of Life (p181) in Ubud is a Fair Trade–certified textiles gallery that preserves traditional Balinese and Indonesian handweaving skills. Factories around Gianyar in east Bali and Blahbatuh southeast of Ubud have large showrooms. For exquisite work, seek out Gusti Ayu Made Mardiani's home and workshop Jepun Bali (p133) in south Denpasar.

OFFERINGS

Traditionally, many of Bali's most elaborate crafts have been ceremonial offerings not intended to last: *baten tegeh* (decorated pyramids of fruit, rice cakes and flowers); rice-flour cookies modelled into entire scenes with a deep symbolic significance and tiny sculptures; *lamak* (long, woven palm-leaf strips used as decorations in festivals and celebrations); stylised female figures known as *cili,* which are representations of Dewi Sri (the rice goddess); and intricately carved coconut-shell wall hangings.

Tourists in Bali may enjoy being welcomed as honoured guests, but the real VIPs are the gods, ancestors, spirits and demons. They are presented with these offerings throughout each day to show respect and gratitude, or perhaps to bribe a demon into being less mischievous. Marvel at the care and energy that goes into constructing huge funeral towers and exotic sarcophagi, all of which will go up in flames.

A gift to a higher being must look attractive, so each offering is a work of art. The most common is a palm-leaf tray little bigger than a saucer, artfully topped with flowers, food (especially rice, and modern touches such as Ritz crackers or individually wrapped lollies) and small change, crowned with a *saiban* (temple or shrine offering). More important shrines and occasions call for more elaborate offerings, which can include the colourful towers of fruits and cakes called *baten tegeh,* and even entire animals cooked and ready to eat, as in Bali's famous *babi guling* (suckling pig).

Once presented to the gods an offering cannot be used again, so new ones are made each day, usually by women. You'll see easy-to-assemble offerings for sale in markets, much as you'd find quick dinner items in Western supermarkets.

Offerings to the gods are placed on high levels and to the demons on the ground. Don't worry about stepping on these; given their ubiquity, it's almost impossible not to (just don't try to). In fact, at Bemo Corner in Kuta offerings are left at the shrine in the middle of the road and are quickly flattened by cars. Across the island, dogs with a taste for crackers hover around fresh offerings. Given the belief that gods or demons instantly derive the essence of an offering, the critters are really just getting leftovers.

Batik

Traditional batik sarongs, which fall somewhere between a cotton sarong and *kamben* for formality, are handmade in central Java. The dyeing process has been adapted by the Balinese to produce brightly coloured and patterned fabrics. Watch out for 'batik' that's been screenprinted: the colours will be washed out and the pattern is often only on one side (the dye in proper batik should colour both sides to reflect the belief that the body should feel what the eye sees).

Ikat

Ikat involves dyeing either the warp threads (those stretched on the loom) or weft threads (those woven across the warp) before the material is woven. The resulting pattern is geometric and slightly wavy. The colouring typically follows a similar tone – blues and greens; reds and browns; or yellows, reds and oranges. Gianyar, in east Bali, has a few factories where you can watch ikat sarongs being woven on a hand-and-foot-powered loom. A complete sarong takes about six hours to make.

Lombok

Lombok is renowned for traditional weaving on backstrap looms, the techniques handed down from mother to daughter. Abstract flower and animal motifs such as buffalo, dragons, crocodiles and snakes sometimes decorate this exquisite cloth. Several villages specialise in weaving cloth, while others concentrate on fine baskets and mats woven from *rotan* (hardy, pliable vine) or grass. You can visit factories around Cakranegara and Mataram that produce weft ikat on old hand-and-foot-operated looms.

Sukarara and Pringgasela are centres for traditional ikat and *songket* weaving (silver- or gold-threaded cloth, handwoven using floating weft technique). Sarongs, Sasak belts and clothing edged with brightly coloured embroidery are sold in small shops.

Woodcarving

Woodcarving in Bali has evolved from its traditional use for doors and columns, religious figures and theatrical masks to modern forms encompassing a wide range of styles. While Tegallalang and Jati, on the road north from Ubud, are noted woodcarving centres, along with the route from Mas through Peliatan, you can find pieces in any souvenir store. See beautiful work and possibly try your hand at creating some of your own at the workshop of Ida Bagus Anom Suryawan (p186) in Mas.

The common style of a slender, elongated figure reportedly first appeared after Walter Spies gave a woodcarver a long piece of wood and commissioned him to carve two sculptures from it. The carver couldn't bring himself to cut it in half, instead making a single figure of a tall, slim dancer.

Other typical works include classical religious figures, animal caricatures, life-size human skeletons, picture frames, and whole tree trunks carved into ghostly 'totem poles'. In Kuta there are various objects targeting beer drinkers: penis bottle openers (which are claimed to be Bali's bestselling souvenir) and signs to sit above your bar bearing made-to-order slogans.

Almost all carving is of local woods including *belalu* (quick-growing light wood) and the stronger fruit timbers such as jackfruit wood. Ebony from Sulawesi is also used. Sandalwood, with its delightful fragrance, is expensive and soft, and is used for some small, very detailed pieces, but beware of widespread fakery.

On Lombok, carving usually decorates functional items such as containers for tobacco and spices, and the handles of betel-nut crushers and knives. Materials include wood, horn and bone, and you'll see these used in the recent trend: primitive-style elongated masks. Cakranegara, Sindu, Labuapi and Senanti are centres for carving on the island.

Wooden articles lose moisture when moved to a drier environment. Avoid possible shrinkage – especially of your penis bottle opener – by

---

KRIS: SACRED BLADES

Usually adorned with an ornate, jewel-studded handle and a sinister-looking wavy blade, the kris is Bali's traditional, ceremonial dagger, dating back to the Majapahit era. A kris is often the most important of family heirlooms, a symbol of prestige and honour and a work of high-end art. Made by a master craftsperson, it's believed to have great spiritual power, sending out magical energy waves and thus requiring great care in its handling and use. Many owners will only clean the blade with waters from Sungai Pakerisan (Pakerisan River) in east Bali because it is thought to be the magical 'River of Kris'.

Balinese men will judge each other in a variation of 'show me your kris'. The size of the blade, the number owned, the quality, the artistry of the handles and much more will go into forming a judgement of a man and his kris. Handles are considered separately from a kris (the blade). As a man's fortunes allow, he will upgrade the handles in his collection. But the kris itself remains sacred – often you will see offerings beside ones on display. The undulations in the blade (called *lok*) have many meanings and there's always an odd number – three, for instance, means passion.

The Museum Negeri Propinsi Bali (p128) in Denpasar has a rich kris collection.

placing the carving in a plastic bag at home, and letting some air in for about one week every month for about four months.

Masks used in theatre and dance performances such as the Topeng require a specialised form of woodcarving. The mask master – always a man – must know the movements each performer uses so the character can be accurately depicted in the mask. These masks are believed to possess magical qualities and can even have the ability to stare down bad spirits.

Other masks, such as the Barong and Rangda, are brightly painted and decorated with real hair, enormous teeth and bulging eyes.

Puaya near Sukawati, south of Ubud, is a centre of mask carving. You can visit workshops there and see all manner of ceremonial art being created. The Museum Negeri Propinsi Bali in Denpasar has an extensive mask collection so you can get acquainted with different styles before buying.

Stone Carving

Traditionally for temple adornment, stone sculptures now make popular souvenirs ranging from frangipani reliefs to quirky ornaments that display the Balinese sense of humour: a frog clutching a leaf as an umbrella, or a weird demon on the side of a bell clasping his hands over his ears in mock offence.

At temples, you will see stone carving in set places. Door guardians are usually a protective personality such as Arjuna. Kala's monstrous face often peers out above the main entrance, his hands reaching to catch evil spirits. The side walls of a *pura dalem* (temple of the dead) might feature sculpted panels showing the horrors awaiting evildoers in the afterlife.

Among Bali's most ancient stone carvings are the scenes of people fleeing a great monster at Goa Gajah, the so-called 'Elephant Cave', believed to date to the 11th century. Inside the cave, a statue of Ganesha, the elephant-like god, gives the rock its name. Along the road through Muncan in east Bali you'll see roadside factories where huge temple decorations are carved in the open.

Much of the local work is made in Batubulan from grey volcanic stone called *paras,* so soft it can be scratched with a fingernail (which, according to legend, is how the giant Kebo Iwa created the Elephant Cave).

Pottery

Pejaten, near Tabanan, has a number of workshops producing ceramic figures and glazed ornamental roof tiles. Stunning collections of designer, contemporary glazed ceramics are produced at Jenggala Keramik in Jimbaran, which also hosts exhibitions of various Indonesian art and antiques.

Jewellery

Silversmiths and goldsmiths are traditionally members of the *pande* caste, which also incudes blacksmiths and other metalworkers. Bali is a major producer of fashion jewellery and produces variations on currently fashionable designs.

Very fine filigree work is a Balinese speciality, as is the use of tiny spots of silver to form a pattern or decorative texture – this is considered a very skilled technique because the heat must be perfectly controlled to weld the delicate wire or silver spots to the underlying silver without damaging it. Balinese work is nearly always handmade, rarely involving casting techniques.

Expat John Hardy built an empire worth hundreds of millions of dollars by adapting old Balinese silver designs along with his own beautiful innovations before he sold his company and started building bamboo buildings. Ubud has numerous creative silver jewellery shops, especially along upper Jl Hanoman.

Architecture

Design is part of Bali's spiritual heritage and creates the look of traditional homes, temples and even modern buildings, such as resorts. Bali style is timeless, whether it is centuries old or embodied in a new hip villa. And it's not static – Bali is the site of world-renowned architecture made with renewable materials like bamboo.

The various open-air *bale* in family compounds are where visitors are received. Typically, drinks and small cakes will be served and friendly conversations will ensue for possibly an hour or more before the purpose of a visit is discussed.

Architecture & Life

Architecture brings together the living and the dead, pays homage to the gods and wards off evil spirits, not to mention the torrential rain. As spiritual as it is functional, as mystical as it is beautiful, Balinese architecture has a life force of its own.

On an island bound by deep-rooted religious and cultural rituals, the priority of any design is appeasing the ancestral and village gods. This means reserving the holiest (northeast) location in every land space for the village temple, the same corner in every home for the family temple, and providing a comfortable, pleasing atmosphere to entice the gods back to Bali for ceremonies.

So while it exudes beauty, balance, age-old wisdom and functionality, a Balinese home is not a commodity designed with capital appreciation in mind; even while an increasing number of rice farmers sell their ancestral land to foreigners for villa developments, they're keeping the parcel on which their home stands.

Preserving the Cosmic Order

A village, a temple, a family compound, an individual structure – and even a single part of the structure – must all conform to the Balinese concept of cosmic order. It consists of three parts that represent the three worlds of the cosmos – *swah* (the world of gods), *bhwah* (world of humans) and *bhur* (world of demons). The concept also represents a three-part division of a person: *utama* (the head), *madia* (the body) and *nista* (the legs). The units of measurement used in traditional buildings are directly based on the anatomical dimensions of the head of the household, ensuring harmony between the dwelling and those who live in it.

The design is traditionally done by an *undagi* (a combination architect-priest); it must maintain harmony between god, man and nature under the concept of *Tri Hita Karana*. If it's not quite right, the universe may fall off balance and no end of misfortune and ill health will visit the community involved.

Building on the Bale

The basic element of Balinese architecture is the *bale,* a rectangular, open-sided pavilion with a steeply pitched roof of thatch. Both a family compound and a temple will comprise of a number of separate *bale* for specific functions, all surrounded by a high wall. The size and proportions of the *bale,* the number of columns and the position within the compound are all determined according to tradition and the owner's caste status.

The focus of a community is a large pavilion, called the *bale banjar,* used for meetings, debates and gamelan (traditional orchestra) practice, among many other activities. You'll find that large modern buildings such as restaurants and the lobby areas of resorts are often modelled on the larger *bale,* and they can be airy, spacious and very handsomely proportioned.

The Family Compound

The Balinese house looks inward – the outside is simply a high wall. Inside there is a garden and a separate small building or *bale* for each activity – one for cooking, one for washing and the toilet, and separate buildings for each 'bedroom'. In Bali's mild tropical climate people live

TYPICAL FAMILY COMPOUND

The following are elements commonly found in family compounds. Although there are variations, the designs are surprisingly similar, especially given they occur thousands of times across Bali.

Sanggah or Merajan Family temple, which is always at the *kaja–kangin* (sunrise in the direction of the mountains) corner of the courtyard. There will be shrines to the Hindu 'trinity' of Brahma, Shiva and Vishnu, and to *taksu* (the divine intermediary).

Umah Meten Sleeping pavilion for the family head.

Tugu Shrine to the god of evil spirits in the compound but at the far *kaja–kuah* (sunset in the direction of the mountains) corner; by employing the chief evil spirit as a guard, others will stay away.

Pengijeng Small shrine amid the compound's open space, dedicated to the spirit who is the guardian of the property.

Bale Tiang Sanga Guest pavilion, also known as the *bale duah*. Literally the family room, it's used as a gathering place, offering workplace or temporary quarters of lesser sons and their families before they establish their own home.

Natah Courtyard with frangipani or hibiscus shade trees, with always a few chickens pecking about, plus a fighting cock or two in a basket.

Bale Sakenam or Bale Dangin Working and sleeping pavilion; may be used for important family ceremonies.

Fruit Trees & Coconut Palms Serve both practical and decorative purposes. Fruit trees are often mixed with flowering trees such as hibiscus, and caged songbirds hang from the branches.

Vegetable Garden Small; usually just for a few spices such as lemongrass not grown on larger plots.

Bale Sakepat Sleeping pavilion for children; highly optional.

Paon Kitchen; always in the south, as that is the direction associated with Brahma, god of fire.

Lumbung Rice barn – the domain of both the precious grain and Dewi Sri, the rice goddess. It's elevated to discourage rice-eating pests.

Rice-Threshing Area Important for farmers to prepare rice for cooking or storage

Aling Aling Screen wall requiring visitors to turn a sharp left or right. This ensures both privacy from passers-by and protection from demons, which the Balinese believe cannot turn corners.

Candi Kurung Gate with a roof, resembling a mountain or tower split in half.

Apit Lawang or Pelinggah Gate shrines, which continually receive offerings to recharge the gate's ability to repel evil spirits.

Pigsty or garbage pit Always in the *kangin–kelod* (sunrise in the direction away from the mountains) corner, the compound's waste ends up here.

outside, so the 'living room' and 'dining room' will be open veranda areas, looking out into the garden. The whole complex is oriented on the *kaja–kelod* (towards the mountains–towards the sea) axis.

Homes from Head to...

Analogous to the human body, compounds have a head (the family temple with its ancestral shrine), arms (the sleeping and living areas), legs and feet (the kitchen and rice storage building), and even an anus (the garbage pit or pigsty). There may be an area outside the house compound where fruit trees are grown or a pig is kept.

TYPICAL TEMPLE ELEMENTS

No two temples on Bali are identical. Variations in style, size, importance, wealth, purpose and much more result in near infinite variety. But there are common themes and elements. Use this as a guide and see how many design elements you can find in each Balinese temple you visit.

Candi Bentar The intricately sculpted temple gateway, like a tower split down the middle and moved apart, symbolises that you are entering a sanctum. It can be quite grand, with auxiliary entrances on either side for daily use.

Kulkul Tower The warning-drum tower, from which a wooden split drum *(kulkul)* is sounded to announce events at the temple or warn of danger.

Bale A pavilion, usually open-sided, for temporary use or storage. It may include a *bale gong,* where the gamelan orchestra plays at festivals; a *paon,* or temporary kitchen, to prepare offerings; or a *wantilan,* a stage for dances or cockfights.

Kori Agung or Paduraksa The gateway to the inner courtyard is an intricately sculpted stone tower. Entry is through a doorway reached by steps in the middle of the tower and left open during festivals.

Raksa or Dwarapala Statues of fierce guardian figures who protect the doorway and deter evil spirits. Above the door will be the equally fierce face of a Bhoma, with hands outstretched against unwanted spirits.

Aling Aling If an evil spirit does get in, this low wall behind the entrance will keep it at bay, as evil spirits find it difficult to make sharp turns. Also found in family compounds.

Side Gate (Betelan) Most of the time (except during ceremonies), entry to the inner courtyard is through this side gate, which is always open.

Small Shrines (Gedong) These usually include shrines to Ngrurah Alit and Ngrurah Gede, who organise things and ensure the correct offerings are made.

Padma Stone Throne for the sun god Surya, placed in the most auspicious *kaja–kangin* (sunrise in the direction of the mountains) corner. It rests on the *badawang* (world turtle), which is held by two *naga* (mythical snakelike creatures).

Meru A multiroofed shrine. Usually there is an 11-roofed *meru* to Sanghyang Widi, the supreme Balinese deity, and a three-roofed *meru* to the holy mountain Gunung Agung. However, *meru* can take any odd number of steps in between, depending on where the intended god falls in the pecking order. The black thatching is made from sugar-palm fronds and is very expensive.

Small Shrines (Gedong) At the *kaja* end of the courtyard, these may include a shrine to the sacred mountain Gunung Batur; a Maospahit shrine to honour Bali's original Hindu settlers (Majapahit); and a shrine to the *taksu,* who acts as an interpreter for the gods. (Trance dancers or mediums may be used to convey the gods' wishes.)

Bale Piasan Open pavilions used to display temple offerings.

Gedong Pesimpangan A stone building dedicated to the village founder or a local deity.

Paruman or Pepelik Open pavilion in the inner courtyard, where the gods are supposed to assemble to watch the ceremonies of a temple festival.

There are several variations on the typical family compound. For example, the entrance is commonly on the *kuah* (sunset side), rather than the *kelod* (away from the mountains and towards the sea) side, but *never* on the *kangin* (sunrise) or *kaja* (in the direction of the mountains) side.

Traditional Balinese homes are found in every region of the island; Ubud remains an excellent place to see them simply because of the concentration of homes there. Many accept guests. South of Ubud, you can enjoy an in-depth tour of the Nyoman Suaka Home (p192) in Singapadu.

Temples

Every village in Bali has several temples, and every home has at least a simple house-temple. The Balinese word for temple is *pura*, from a Sanskrit word literally meaning 'a space surrounded by a wall'. Similar to a traditional Balinese home, a temple is walled in – so the shrines you see in rice fields or at 'magical' spots such as old trees are not real temples. Simple shrines or thrones often overlook crossroads, to protect passers-by.

All temples are built on a mountains–sea orientation, not north–south. The direction towards the mountains, *kaja,* is the end of the temple, where the holiest shrines are found. The temple's entrance is at the *kelod. Kangin* is more holy than the *kuah,* so many secondary shrines are on the *kangin* side. *Kaja* may be towards a particular mountain – Pura Besakih in east Bali is pointed directly towards Gunung Agung – or towards the mountains in general, which run east–west along the length of Bali.

Temple Types

There are three basic temple types found in most villages. The most important is the *pura puseh* (temple of origin), dedicated to the village founders and at the *kaja* end of the village. In the middle of the village is the *pura desa,* for the many spirits that protect the village community in daily life. At the *kelod* end of the village is the *pura dalem* (temple of the dead). The graveyard is also here, and the temple may include representations of Durga, the terrible side of Shiva's wife Parvati. Both Shiva and Parvati have a creative and destructive side; their destructive powers are honoured in the *pura dalem.*

Other temples include those dedicated to the spirits of irrigated agriculture. Because rice growing is so important in Bali, and the division of water for irrigation is handled with the utmost care, these *pura subak* or *pura ulun suwi* (temple of the rice-growers association) can be of considerable importance. Other temples may also honour dry-field agriculture, as well as the flooded rice paddies.

In addition to these 'local' temples, there are a lesser number of great temples. Often a kingdom would have three of these temples that sit at the very top of the temple pecking order: a main state temple in the heartland of the state (such as Pura Taman Ayun (p263) in Mengwi, western Bali); a mountain temple (such as Pura Besakih, eastern Bali); and a sea temple (such as Pura Luhur Ulu Watu (p112), southern Bali).

Every house in Bali has its house-temple, which is at the *kaja kangin* corner of the courtyard and has at least five shrines.

Temple Decoration

Temples and their decoration are closely linked on Bali. A temple gateway is not just erected; every square centimetre of it is carved in sculptural relief and a diminishing series of demon faces is placed above it as protection. Even then, it's not complete without several stone statues to act as guardians.

The level of decoration inside varies. Sometimes a temple is built with minimal decoration in the hope that sculpture can be added when more funds are available. The sculpture can also deteriorate after a few years

The gate to a traditional Balinese house is where the family gives cues as to its wealth. They range from the humble – grass thatch atop a gate of simple stones or clay – to the relatively grand, including bricks heavily ornamented with ornately carved stone and a tile roof.

Hard-wearing terracotta tiles have been the traditional roofing material since the Dutch era. Thatch in various forms or bamboo are now reserved for the most traditional and ceremonial sites.

because much of the stone used is soft and the tropical climate ages it very rapidly (that centuries-old temple you're looking at may in fact be less than 10 years old!). Sculptures are restored or replaced as resources permit – it's not uncommon to see a temple with old carvings, which are barely discernible, next to newly finished work.

Sculpture often appears in set places in Bali's temples. Door guardians – representations of legendary figures such as Arjuna or other protective personalities – flank the steps to the gateway. Above the main entrance to a temple, Kala's monstrous face often peers out, sometimes a number of times, and his hands reach out beside his head to catch any evil spirits foolish enough to try and sneak in.

Temple Design

Although overall temple architecture is similar in both northern and southern Bali, there are some important differences. The inner courtyards of southern temples usually house a number of *meru* (multitiered

TOP TEMPLE VISITS

Over 10,000 temples are found everywhere on Bali – from cliff tops and beaches to volcanoes – and are often beautiful places to experience. Visitors will find the following especially rewarding.

Directional Temples

Some temples are so important they are deemed to belong to the whole island rather than particular communities. There are nine *kahyangan jagat* (directional temples) including the following:

Pura Luhur Batukau (p241) One of Bali's most important temples is situated magically up the misty slopes of Gunung Batukau.

Pura Luhur Ulu Watu (p112) As important as it is popular, this temple has sweeping Indian Ocean views, sunset dance performances and monkeys.

Pura Goa Lawah (p207) See Bali's own Bat Cave at this cliff-side temple filled with the winged critters.

Sea Temples

The legendary 16th-century priest Nirartha founded a chain of temples to honour the sea gods. Each was intended to be within sight of the next, and several have dramatic locations on the south coast. They include the following:

Pura Rambu Siwi (p269) On a wild stretch of the west coast and not far from where Nirartha arrived in the 16th century. Locks of his hair are said to be buried in a shrine.

Pura Tanah Lot (p263) Sacred as the day begins, it becomes a temple of mass tourism at sunset.

Other Important Temples

Some temples have particular importance because of their location, spiritual function or architecture. The following reward visitors:

Pura Maduwe Karang (p247) An agricultural temple on the north coast, this is famous for its spirited bas-reliefs, including one of possibly Bali's first bicycle rider.

Pura Pusering Jagat (p185) One of the famous temples at Pejeng, near Ubud, which dates to the 14th-century empire that flourished here. It has an enormous bronze drum from that era.

Pura Taman Ayun (p263) This vast and imposing state temple was a centrepiece of the Mengwi empire and has been nominated for Unesco recognition.

Pura Tirta Empul (p187) The beautiful temple at Tampaksiring, with holy springs discovered in AD 962 and bathing pools at the source of Sungai Pakerisan.

THE POWER OF BAMBOO

Bali has always had natural cathedrals of bamboo. In the dense tropical forests of the east and west, soaring stalks arch together in ways that lift the soul. Now bamboo, one of the world's great renewable resources, is being used to create soaring and inspirational buildings whose sinuous designs are simply awe-inspiring.

Much credit for the current bamboo revolution goes to famed jeweller John Hardy, who had bamboo used in the revolutionary structures that formed the landmark **Green School** (Map p190; www.greenschool.org; Mambal) southwest of Ubud in 2007. People took one look at the fabulous fantasy of its bridge and came away inspired. Since then bamboo's use in buildings has taken off across Bali and there are some beautiful examples of its use that go far beyond the old bamboo hut cliche of *Gilligan's Island*. These include the following:

Fivelements (p185) A health resort, not far from the Green School.

Power of Now Oasis (p122) A striking beachside yoga studio in Sanur.

Hai Bar & Grill (p141) A beachside bar on Nusa Lembongan.

Sardine (p90) The lauded restaurant on its own rice field in Kerobokan.

Finn's Beach Club (p99) A high-style, upscale beach lounge and restaurant near Canggu.

Big Tree Farms (p188) A huge temple to chocolate that's also near the Green School.

shrines), together with other structures, whereas in the north, everything is grouped on a single pedestal. On the pedestal you'll find 'houses' for the deities to use on their earthly visits; they're also used to store religious relics.

While Balinese sculpture and painting were once exclusively used as architectural decoration for temples, you'll soon see that sculpture and painting have developed as separate art forms influencing the look of every aspect of the island. And the art of temple and shrine construction is as vibrant as ever: more than 500 new ones in all sizes are built every month.

The Birth of Bali Style

Tourism has given Balinese architecture unprecedented exposure and it seems that every visitor wants to take a slice of this island back home with them.

Shops all around Denpasar churn out prefabricated, knock-down *bale* for shipment to far-flung destinations: the Caribbean, London, Perth and Hong Kong. Furniture workshops in Denpasar and handicraft villages near Ubud are flat out making ornaments for domestic and export markets.

The craze stems back to the early 1970s, when Australian artist Donald Friend formed a partnership with Manado-born Wija Waworuntu, who had built the Tandjung Sari on Sanur beach a decade earlier. With a directive to design traditional, village style alternatives to the Western multistoreyed hotels, they brought two architects to Bali – Australian Peter Muller and the late Sri Lankan Geoffrey Bawa – who took traditional architecture and adapted it to Western standards of luxury.

Before long, the design sensation known as 'Bali Style' was born. Then, the term reflected Muller and Bawa's sensitive, low-key approach, giving precedence to culture over style, and respect for traditional principles and craftspeople, local renewable materials and age-old techniques. Today the development of a mass market has inevitably produced a much looser definition.

Look for carved wooden *garudas*, the winged bird that bears the god Wisnu, in the most surprising places – high up in pavilion rafters, at the base of columns, pretty much anywhere.

Contemporary Hotel Design

For centuries, foreign interlopers, such as the priest Nirartha, have played an intrinsic part in the island's myths and legends. These days, tourists are making an impact on the serenity of Balinese cosmology and its seamless translation into the island's traditional architecture. And while these visitors with large credit limits aren't changing the island's belief system – much – they are changing its look.

The rule that no building shall exceed the height of a coconut palm dates back to the 1960s when the 10-storey Bali Beach Hotel caused much consternation. However, soaring land prices in the south and ineffectual enforcement of building codes mean that this 'rule' is being increasingly challenged.

Most hotel designs on Bali and Lombok are purely functional or pastiches of traditional designs, but some of the finest hotels on the islands aspire to something greater. Notable examples in rough order of completion:

Tandjung Sari (p123) Located in Sanur, it is Wija Waworuntu's classic prototype for the Balinese boutique beach hotel.

Amandari (p172) The crowning achievement of architect Peter Muller, who also designed the two Oberois. Located near Ubud, the inclusion of traditional Balinese materials, crafts and construction techniques, as well as Balinese design principles, respects the island's approach to the world.

Oberoi (p81) The very first luxury hotel, located in Seminyak, and remains Muller's relaxed vision of a Balinese village. The *bale agung* (village assembly hall) and *bale banjar* form the basis for common areas.

Oberoi Lombok (p283) Both the most luxurious and the most traditionally styled hotel on Lombok.

Amankila (p211) In east Bali, Amankila adopts a garden strategy, with a carefully structured landscape of lotus ponds and floating pavilions that steps down an impossibly steep site.

Hotel Tugu Bali (p97) In Canggu, exemplifies the notion of instant age, the ability of materials in Bali to weather quickly and provide 'pleasing decay'.

When you stay in a hotel featuring *lumbung* design, you are really staying in a place derived from rice storage barns – the 2nd floor is meant to be airless and hot!

Four Seasons Resort (p172) A striking piece of aerial sculpture near Ubud, with a huge elliptical lotus pond sitting above a base structure that appears like an eroded and romantic ruin set within a spectacular river valley.

Alila Villas Uluwatu (p114) In far south Bali, Alila employs an artful contemporary style that's light and airy, conveying a sense of great luxury. Set amid hotel-tended rice fields, it embodies advanced green building principles.

Katamana (p89) The same architectural derring-do that makes neighbouring Potato Head much copied is on display at the club's hotel. However, here the details are lavish and artful. Designed by Indonesian Andra Martin, it's a lavish confection of Javanese bricks, Balinese stone and other indigenous materials.

Lombok Architecture

Traditional laws and practices govern Lombok's architecture. Construction must begin on a propitious day, always with an odd-numbered date, and the building's frame must be completed on that day. It would be bad luck to leave any of the important structural work until the following day.

A traditional Sasak village layout is a walled enclosure. There are three types of buildings: the *beruga* (open-sided pavilion), the *bale tani* (family house) and the *lumbung* (rice barn). The *beruga* and *bale tani* are both rectangular, with low walls and a steeply pitched thatched roof; of course, the *beruga* is much larger. A *bale tani* is made of bamboo on a base of compacted mud. It usually has no windows and the arrangement of rooms is very standardised. There is a *serambi* (open veranda) at the front and two rooms on two different levels inside – one for cooking and entertaining guests, the other for sleeping and storage. There are some picturesque traditional Sasak villages in Rembitan and Sade, near Kuta.

Environment

Bali has rich and varied natural environments which belie its relative small size. Volcanoes, beaches and reefs are just some of the prominent features. Along with this are an array of creatures, from ducks in the rice fields to one of the world's rarest birds. Still, with record tourism, the threats to these unique environments are many, but there's much each visitor can do to lessen their impact.

The Landscape

Bali is a small island, midway along the string of islands that makes up the Indonesian archipelago. It's adjacent to the most heavily populated island of Java, and immediately west of the chain of smaller islands comprising Nusa Tenggara, which includes Lombok.

The island is visually dramatic – a mountainous chain with a string of active volcanoes and several peaks around 2000m. The agricultural lands in Bali are south and north of the central mountains. The southern region is a wide, gently sloping area, where most of the country's abundant rice crop is grown. The northern coastal strip is narrower, rising rapidly into the foothills of the central range. It receives less rain, but coffee, copra, rice and cattle are farmed there. Bali also has beaches in all shapes, characters and colours. From hidden coves to dramatic sweeps, from lonely strands to party scenes, from pearly white to sparkling black.

Bali's arid, less-populated regions include the western mountain region, and the eastern and northeastern slopes of Gunung Agung. The Nusa Penida islands are dry, and cannot support intensive rice agriculture. The Bukit Peninsula is similarly dry, but with the growth of tourism, it's become very populous.

The Indonesian Ecotourism Centre (www.indecon.or.id) is devoted to highlighting responsible tourism; Bali Fokus (http://balifokus.asia) promotes sustainable community programs on Bali for recycling and reuse.

Volcanoes

Bali is volcanically active and extremely fertile. The two go hand-in-hand as eruptions contribute to the land's exceptional fertility, and high mountains provide the dependable rainfall that irrigates Bali's complex and amazingly beautiful patchwork of rice terraces. Of course, the volcanoes are a hazard as well – Bali has endured disastrous eruptions in the past, such as in 1963, and no doubt will again in the future. Gunung Agung, the 'Mother Mountain', is 3142m high and thickly wooded on its southern side. You can climb it or its steam-spewing neighbour, the comparatively diminutive 1717m Gunung Batur. The latter is a geographic spectacle, a snarling, active volcano rising from a lake that itself is set in a vast crater.

Animals & Plants

Since Bali is geologically young, most of its living things have migrated from elsewhere and true native wild animals are rare. This is not hard to imagine in the heavily populated and extravagantly fertile south of Bali, where the orderly rice terraces are so intensively cultivated they look more like a work of sculpture than a natural landscape.

In fact, rice fields cover only about 20% of the island's surface area, and there is a great variety of other environmental zones: the dry scrub of the northwest, the extreme northeast and the southern peninsula; patches of dense jungle in the river valleys; forests of bamboo; and harsh volcanic regions that are barren rock and volcanic tuff at higher altitudes.

Balinese Flora & Fauna (1999), published by Periplus, is a concise and beautifully illustrated guide to the animals and plants you'll see on your travels. The feature on the ecology of a rice field is excellent.

Wild Animals

Bali has lots and lots of lizards, and they come in all shapes and sizes. The small ones (onomatopoeically called *cecak*) that hang around light fittings in the evening, waiting for an unwary insect, are a familiar sight. Geckos are lizards often heard but less often seen. The loud and regularly repeated two-part cry 'geck-oh' is a nightly background noise that many visitors soon enjoy.

Bali has more than 300 species of birds, but the one that is truly native to the island is the Bali starling. Much more common are colourful birds such as the orange-banded thrush, numerous species of egrets, kingfishers, parrots, owls and many more.

Bali's only wilderness area, Bali Barat National Park (West Bali National Park), has a number of wild species, including grey and black monkeys (which you will also see in the mountains, Ubud and east Bali), *muncak* (barking deer), squirrels, bats and iguanas.

Marine Animals

There is a rich variety of coral, seaweed, fish and other marine life in the coastal waters off the islands; in fact Indonesia's entire marine territory has been declared a manta ray sanctuary. Much of the marine life can be appreciated by snorkellers, but you're only likely to see the larger marine animals while diving.

RESPONSIBLE TRAVEL

To visit Indonesia responsibly, try to tread lightly as you go, with respect for both the land and the diverse cultures of its people.

Watch your use of water Water demand outstrips supply in much of Indonesia – even at seemingly green places like Bali. Take your hotel up on its offer to save water by not washing your sheets and towels every day. At the high end you can also forgo your own private plunge pool, or a pool altogether.

Don't hit the bottle Those bottles of Aqua (a top local brand of bottled water, owned by Danone) are convenient but they add up. The zillions of such bottles tossed away each year are a serious blight. Since tap water is unsafe, ask your hotel if you can refill from their huge containers of drinking water. Some enlightened businesses already offer this service.

Support environmentally aware businesses The number of businesses committed to good environmental practices is growing fast in Indonesia.

Conserve power Turn off lights and air-con when not using them.

Bag the bags Refuse plastic bags, and say no to plastic straws too.

Leave the animals be Reconsider swimming with captive dolphins, riding elephants, and patronising attractions where wild animals are made to perform for crowds, interactions that have been identified by animal welfare experts as harmful to the animals. And don't try to pet, feed or otherwise interact with animals in the wild as it disrupts their natural behaviour and can make them sick.

BALI STARLING

Also known as the Bali myna, Rothschild's mynah, or locally as *jalak putih,* the Bali starling is perhaps Bali's only endemic bird (opinions differ – as other places are so close, who can tell?). It is striking white in colour, with black tips to the wings and tail, and a distinctive bright-blue mask. These natural good looks have caused the bird to be poached into virtual extinction. The wild population is thought to number under 100. In captivity, however, there are hundreds if not thousands.

Near Ubud, the Bali Bird Park (p192) has large aviaries where you can see Bali starlings. The park was one of the major supporters of efforts to reintroduce the birds into the wild. Efforts to reintroduce the species include a breeding program run by the NGO Friends of the National Parks Foundation (p146) on Nusa Penida.

Dolphins

Dolphins can be found right around the islands and have been made into an attraction off Lovina. But you're just as likely to see schools of dolphins if you take a fast boat between Bali and the Gilis.

Sharks

There are very occasional reports of large sharks, including great whites, throughout the region, although they are not considered a massive threat.

Fish

Smaller fish and corals can be found at a plethora of spots around the islands. Everybody's favourite first stop is Bali's Menjangan. Fish as large as whale sharks have been reported, but what thrills scores daily are the coloured beauty of an array of corals, sponges, lacy sea fans and much more. Starfish abound and you'll easily spot clownfish and other polychromatic characters.

Plants

Trees

Much of the island is cultivated. As with most things in Bali, trees have a spiritual and religious significance, and you'll often see them decorated with scarves and black-and-white chequered cloths (*poleng,* a cloth signifying spiritual energy) signifying their sacred status. The *waringin* (banyan tree) is the holiest Balinese tree and no important temple is complete without a stately one growing within its precincts. The banyan is an extensive, shady tree with an exotic feature: creepers that drop from its branches take root to propagate a new tree. *Jepun* (frangipani or plumeria trees), with their beautiful and sweet-smelling white flowers, are found everywhere.

Bali's forests cover 127,000 hectares, ranging from virgin land to tree farms to densely forested mountain villages. The total is constantly under threat from wood poaching for carved souvenirs and cooking fuel, and from development.

Bali has monsoonal rather than tropical rainforests, so it lacks the valuable rainforest hardwoods that require rain year-round. Nearly all the hardwood used for carving furniture and high-end artwork is imported from Sumatra and Kalimantan.

The plight of Bali's dogs and the irony of the important role they play in island life is captured by filmmakers Lawrence Blair and Dean Allan Tolhurst in *Bali: Island of the Dogs* (2010).

SEA TURTLES

Both green and hawksbill turtles inhabit the waters around Bali, and both species are supposedly protected by international laws that prohibit trade in anything made from sea turtles.

In Bali, however, green sea turtle meat *(penyu)* is a traditional and very popular delicacy, particularly for Balinese feasts. Bali is the site of the most intensive slaughter of green sea turtles in the world – no reliable figures are available, although in 1999 it was estimated that more than 30,000 are killed annually. It's easy to find the trade on the backstreets of waterside towns such as Benoa.

Still, some progress is being made, especially by groups like ProFauna (www.profauna. net), which is raising awareness on Bali about sea turtles and other animals across Indonesia.

A broad coalition of divers and journalists supports the SOS Sea Turtles (www. sos-seaturtles.ch) campaign, which spotlights turtle abuse in Bali. It has been instrumental in exposing the illegal poaching of turtles at Wakatobi National Park in Sulawesi for sale in Bali. This illegal trade is widespread and, like the drug trade, hard to prevent. Bali's Hindu Dharma, the body overseeing religious practice, has decreed that turtle meat is essential in only very vital ceremonies.

Some turtle hatcheries open to the public do a good job of educating locals about the need to protect turtles and think of them as living creatures (as opposed to satay), but these operations have their own complexities, and many environmentalists are opposed to them because they keep captive turtles. There are also hatcheries that are ostensibly conservationist, but in reality are run as commercial tourist attractions with little concern for the welfare of the turtles. Environmental groups recommend you do not visit certain hatcheries in Tangung Benoa and around Sanur.

Two that win praise are the Bali Sea Turtle Society (p52) in Kuta and Proyek Penyu (p254) in Pemuteran.

On Nusa Penida, volunteers can join the efforts of Green Lion Bali (p146), which runs a turtle hatchery.

A number of plants have great practical and economic significance. *Tiing* (bamboo) is grown in several varieties and is used for everything from satay sticks to hip and stylish resorts.

Flowers & Gardens

Balinese gardens are a delight. The soil and climate can support a huge range of plants, and the Balinese love of beauty and the abundance of cheap labour means that every space can be landscaped. The style is generally informal, with curved paths, a rich variety of plants and usually a water feature. Who can't be enchanted by a frangipani tree dropping a carpet of fragrant blossoms?

One hawksbill turtle that visited Bali was tracked the following year. He travelled to Java, Kalimantan, Australia (Perth and much of Queensland) and then back to Bali.

You can find almost every type of flower in Bali, but some are seasonal and others are restricted to the cooler mountain areas. Many of the flowers will be familiar to visitors – hibiscus, bougainvillea, poinsettia, oleander, jasmine, water lily and aster are commonly seen in the southern tourist areas.

Less-familiar flowers include Javanese *ixora (soka, angsoka),* with round clusters of red-orange flowers; *champak (cempaka),* a fragrant member of the magnolia family; flamboyant, the flower of the royal poinciana flame tree; *manori (maduri),* which has several traditional uses; and water convolvulus *(kangkung),* whose leaves are commonly used as a green vegetable. There are thousands of species of orchid.

Bali's climate means that gardens planted today look mature – complete with soaring shade trees – in just a couple of years. Good places to see Bali's plant bounty include Bali Botanical Garden (p236), Bali Orchid Garden (p121) and the many plant nurseries (north from Sanur and along the road to Denpasar).

Environmental Issues

Bali

Fast-growing populations, limited resources, pressure from the increasing number of visitors and lax or nonexistent environmental regulations mean that Bali is under great threat. And some of Bali's environmental worries are larger than the island: climate change is causing increased water levels that are damaging the coast and beaches.

Meanwhile, a fast-growing population in Bali has put pressure on limited resources. The tourist industry has attracted new residents, and there is a rapid growth in urban areas and of resorts and villas that encroach onto agricultural land. Concerns include:

Water Usage A major concern. Typical top-end hotels uses 1000 to 1500 litres of water a day per room, and the growing number of golf courses – the ones on the arid Bukit Peninsula in the Pecatu Indah development and at Nusa Dua, for example – put further pressure on an already stressed resource. The many huge new resorts on the Bukit's south coast are also massive water users.

Water pollution A major problem, both from deforestation brought on by firewood collecting in the mountains, and lack of proper treatment for the waste produced by the local population. Streams that run into the ocean at popular spots like Double Six Beach in Legian are very polluted, often with waste water from hotels. The vast mangroves along the south coast near Benoa Harbour are losing their ability to filter the water that drains here from much of the island and are themselves threatened with development.

Air pollution As anyone stuck behind a smoke-belching truck or bus on one of the main roads knows, south Bali's air is often smoggy. The view of south Bali from a hillside shows a brown blanket hanging in the air that could be LA in the 1960s.

Waste The problem is not just all those plastic bags and water bottles but the sheer volume of waste produced by the growing population – what to do with it? The Balinese look with sadness at the enormous amounts of waste – especially plastic – that have accumulated in their once pristine rivers.

On the upside, there is a nascent effort to grow rice and other foods organically. A sewage treatment program in the south is finally operating

Despite water shortages, villa construction and other loss of rice fields, Bali's rice production hit a record in 2013 (the last year with detailed records available) of 822,115 tonnes. With island consumption at 455,000 tonnes, that keeps Bali as a rice exporter.

THE WALLACE LINE

The 19th-century naturalist Sir Alfred Wallace (1822–1913) observed great differences in fauna between Bali and Lombok – as great as the differences between Africa and South America. In particular, there were no large mammals (elephants, rhinos, tigers etc) east of Bali, and very few carnivores. He postulated that during the ice ages, when sea levels were lower, animals could have moved by land from what is now mainland Asia all the way to Bali, but the deep Lombok Strait would always have been a barrier. He drew a line between Bali and Lombok, which he believed marked the biological division between Asia and Australia.

Plant life does not display such a sharp division, but there is a gradual transition from predominantly Asian rainforest species to mostly Australian plants, such as eucalypts and acacias, which are better suited to long, dry periods. This is associated with the lower rainfall as one moves east of Java. Environmental differences – including those in the natural vegetation – are now thought to provide a better explanation of the distribution of animal species than Wallace's theory about limits to their original migrations.

GROWING RICE

Rice cultivation has shaped the social landscape in Bali – the intricate organisation necessary for growing rice is a large factor in the strength of community life. Rice cultivation has also changed the environmental landscape – terraced rice fields trip down hillsides like steps for a giant, in shades of gold, brown and green, green and more green. Some date back 1000 years or more.

Subak, the village association that deals with water rights and irrigation, makes careful use of all the surface water. The fields are a complete ecological system, home for much more than just rice. In the early morning you'll often see the duck herders leading their flocks out for a day's paddle around a flooded rice field; the ducks eat various pests and leave fertiliser in their wake.

A harvested field with its leftover burnt rice stalks is soaked with water and repeatedly ploughed, often by two bullocks pulling a wooden plough. Once the field is muddy enough, a small corner is walled off and seedling rice is planted there. When it is a reasonable size, it's replanted, shoot by shoot, in the larger field. While the rice matures, there is time to practise the gamelan, watch the dancers or do a little woodcarving. Finally, the whole village turns out for the harvest – a period of solid hard work. While it's only men who plant the rice, everybody takes part in harvesting it.

In 1969, new high-yield rice varieties were introduced. These can be harvested a month sooner than the traditional variety and are resistant to many diseases. However, the new varieties also require more fertiliser and irrigation water, which strains the imperilled water supplies. More pesticides are also needed, causing the depletion of the frog and eel populations that depend on the insects for survival.

Although everyone agrees that the new rice doesn't taste as good as the traditional rice, the new strains now account for more than 90% of the rice grown in Bali. Small areas of traditional rice are still planted and harvested in traditional ways to placate the rice goddess, Dewi Sri. Temples and offerings to her dot every rice field.

Recently, a few farmers have been trying to grow organic rice and you may see it on menus in top restaurants and at better markets.

A study showed that the average occupied hotel room in south Bali accounted for 1000 to 1500 litres of water a day for use by its occupants and to service their needs. In contrast the average local required less than 120L a day for all needs.

in a few areas but businesses are objecting to the costs and refusing to connect.

In Pemuteran, artificial reef-growing programs have won universal praise. This is important as a study by the World Wide Fund for Nature found that less than 5% of Bali's reefs were fully healthy.

Lombok

On Lombok, environmental disaster in the gold rush town of Sekotong is ongoing. Gold mining using mercury in huge open-cast pits is causing enormous damage to once-pristine areas. Development in the south, especially around the beaches in the Kuta region, is accelerating with often enormous and unchecked environmental effects.

Coastal erosion is a problem here, just as it is on Bali. The Gilis are naturally concerned. On the plus side, the reefs around the Gilis have been quick to recover as tourism has spurred intense preservation efforts.

Survival
Guide

Directory A–Z

Accommodation

Bali has a huge range of great-value accommodation for any budget. If visiting in the peak periods of August and Christmas, book three or more months ahead.

Resorts Bali has some of the world's best resorts and at prices that would be a bargain elsewhere. You can be on the beach or nestled in a lush mountain valley.

Villas Enjoy a sybaritic escape and a private pool.

Hotels Many of Bali's hundreds of hotels are located near the action and offer good deals.

Homestays & guesthouses Bali's family-run accommodation is comfortable and puts you right in the middle of fascinating local life.

Booking Services

Websites such as homeaway. com and airbnb.com have hundreds of listings for Bali villas and private accommodation. However, many listed properties are not licensed, which makes for an unregulated market with all the associated pros and cons. Local agents include the following:

Bali Discovery (✆0361-286283; www.balidiscovery. com) The main local source for hotel deals (it's always worth comparing their rates to the major websites); also books villas.

Bali Private Villas (✆0361-844 4344; www.baliprivatevillas. com) Handles a variety of top-end villas.

Bali Ultimate Villas (✆0851 0057 1658; www.baliultimatevil-las.net) A villa agent that also offers wedding services.

Hotels

Pretty much every place to stay on Bali can arrange tours, car rental and other services. Laundry service is universally available, often cheap and sometimes free.

BUDGET HOTELS

The cheapest accommodation on Bali is in small places that are simple but clean and comfortable. Names often include the word 'losmen', 'homestay', 'inn' or *pondo*'.

Many are built in the style of a traditional Balinese home.

There are budget hotels all over Bali, and they vary widely in standards and price. Expect:

➡ Maybe air-con

➡ Maybe hot water

➡ Private bathroom with shower and Western-style toilet

➡ Often a pool

➡ Simple breakfast

➡ Carefree and cheery staff International budget chains are making a splashy entry into south Bali, but note that a tiny US$9 room quickly hits US$40 when you add various extras such as taxes and fees for items included elsewhere like internet and towels.

MIDRANGE HOTELS

Older midrange hotels are often constructed in Balinese bungalow style or in two-storey blocks and are set on spacious grounds with a pool. Many have a sense of style that is beguiling and may help postpone your departure. In addition to what you'll get at a budget hotel, expect:

➡ Balcony, porch or patio

➡ Satellite TV

➡ Small fridge

➡ Often wi-fi

Note that dozens of midrange chain hotels have appeared across south Bali. Rooms are often small and

---

SLEEPING PRICE RANGES

The following price ranges refer to a double room with a bathroom. Unless otherwise stated taxes are included in the price.

$ less than 450,000Rp (under US$35)

$$ 450,000–1,400,000Rp (US$35-100)

$$$ more than 1,400,000Rp (over US$100)

the sites cramped, although standards are reliable. But beware of properties far from the beach and nightlife.

TOP-END HOTELS

Top-end hotels and resorts in Bali are world-class. Service is refined and you can expect decor plucked from the pages of a glossy magazine, along with the following:

➡ Superb service

➡ Views – ocean, lush valleys and rice fields or private gardens

➡ Spa

➡ Maybe a private pool

➡ Not wanting to leave

Villas

Villas are scattered around south Bali and Ubud, and are now appearing in the east. They're often built in the middle of rice paddies, seemingly overnight. The villa boom has been quite controversial for environmental, aesthetic and economic reasons. Many skip collecting government taxes from guests, which has raised the ire of their luxury hotel competitors and brought threats of crackdowns.

Large villas can be bacchanalian retreats for groups of friends, such as those found in the Canggu area. Others are smaller, more intimate and part of larger developments – common in Seminyak and Kerobokan – or top-end hotels. Expect the following:

➡ Private garden

➡ Private pool

➡ Kitchen

➡ Air-con bedroom(s)

➡ Open-air common space

Villas will also potentially include:

➡ Your own staff (cook, driver, cleaner)

➡ Lush grounds

➡ Private beachfront

➡ Isolation (which can be good or bad)

Rates range from under US$200 per night for a modest villa to US$2000 per week and beyond for your own tropical estate. There are often deals, especially in the low season, and several couples sharing can make something grand affordable.

You can sometimes save quite a bit by waiting until the last minute, but during the high season the best villas book up far in advance.

VILLA RENTAL QUESTIONS

It's the Wild West out there. There are myriad agents, some excellent, others not. It is essential to be as clear

HOTELS TOO FAR

When booking a south Bali hotel room, be careful where you book. As tourist numbers on Bali have exploded, so have the number of chain hotels. The number of available rooms has doubled since 2005. The boom in building large hotels in Kuta, Legian, Seminyak, Kerobokan and now Canggu is changing the area's character in fundamental ways, especially as the many family-run, cheap and cheerful small inns are pushed out.

While some of these large new hotels are appearing in traditionally appealing areas of south Bali, not far from the beaches and nightlife, scores more are opening far from the areas visitors consider desirable. Many chains have properties in both good and unappealing areas and it is easy to get misled about a hotel's actual location, especially on booking websites. In the tradition of real estate agents everywhere, 'Seminyak' is now the address used for hotels far into Denpasar.

So when you see that great web bargain of a midrange room for US$40, carefully consider the following:

➡ Anything west of the Jl Legian–Jl Seminyak–Jl Kerobokan spine will be close to both beaches and nightlife.

➡ East of the spine and things begin to get inconvenient fast. There will be less to walk to, beaches can be far and cruising cabs hard to come by.

➡ Jl Ngurah Rai Bypass and Jl Sunset are both noisy major streets that lack charm and are main routes across. Many new chain hotels are located right on these traffic-choked thoroughfares.

➡ East of Jl Ngurah Rai Bypass and Jl Sunset and you are deep into suburban Denpasar, where it will be hard to find cabs or much else you'll be interested in.

➡ In Sanur, which is also getting an influx of chain hotels, Jl Ngurah Rai Bypass should be your absolute western border in your room hunt.

➡ With careful shopping, you can usually find great room deals in the most appealing parts of south Bali, and often you can end up at a small or family-run guesthouse with oodles more charm and character than a generic cheap hotel.

BOOK YOUR STAY ONLINE

For more accommodation reviews by Lonely Planet authors, check out http://lonelyplanet.com/hotels/. You'll find independent reviews, as well as recommendations on the best places to stay. Best of all, you can book online.

as possible about what you want when arranging a rental. Some things to keep in mind and ask about when renting a villa:

➡ How far is the villa from the beach and stores?

➡ Is a driver or car service included?

➡ If there is a cook, is food included?

➡ Is there an electricity surcharge?

➡ Are there extra cleaning fees?

➡ Is laundry included?

➡ What refunds apply on a standard 50% deposit?

➡ Is there wi-fi and is it free?

Long-Term Accommodation

For longer stays, you can find flats for US$300 to US$1200 a month and much more. Sources include:

➡ Facebook groups. There are scores with rentals on Bali; Bali Rooms for Rent (www.facebook.com/baliroomsforrent) is one large board. You can also try looking for groups with names like '[name of town] Housing'.

➡ Bali Advertiser (www.baliadvertiser.biz)

➡ Noticeboards in popular cafes such as Bali Bhudda in Ubud and Umalas plus the many Cafe Mokas. Bintang supermarkets in Seminyak and Ubud are also good.

➡ Word of mouth. Tell your new Bali friends you're looking, as everybody seems to know someone with a place for rent.

Village Stays

A good way to arrange a village stay is through the **JED** (Village Ecotourism Network; ☎0361-366 9951; www.jed.or.id; tours US$75-150) Village Ecotourism Network. Another good option is the **Bali Homestay Program** (☎0817 067 1788; www.bali-homestay.com; Jegu; 2 nights all-inclusive s/d from US$185/330) 🍃, north of Tabanan.

Customs Regulations

Indonesia's list of prohibited imports includes drugs, weapons, fresh fruit and anything remotely pornographic. Items allowed include:

➡ 200 cigarettes (or 50 cigars or 100g of tobacco)

➡ a 'reasonable amount' of perfume

➡ 1L of alcohol

Surfers with more than two or three boards may be charged a fee, and this can apply to other items if the officials suspect that you intend to sell them in Indonesia. There is no restriction on foreign currency, but the import or export of rupiah is limited to 5,000,000Rp. Greater amounts must be declared.

Electricity

Type C
220V/50Hz

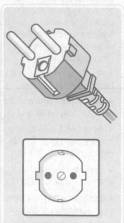

Type F
220V/50Hz

Climate
Denpasar

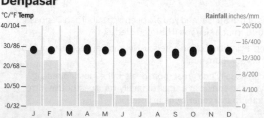

PRACTICALITIES

➡ Bali has a smoking ban that covers most tourist facilities, markets, shops, restaurants, hotels, taxis and more. In practice, adoption is uneven.

➡ Indonesia uses the metric system.

Embassies & Consulates

Foreign embassies are in Jakarta, the national capital. Most of the foreign representatives in Bali are consular agents (or honorary consuls) who can't offer the same services as a full consulate or embassy. A lost passport may mean a trip to an embassy in Jakarta.

The US, Australia and Japan have formal consulates in Bali (citizens from these countries make up half of all visitors).

Indonesian embassies and consulates abroad are listed on the website of Indonesia's Ministry of Foreign Affairs (www.kemlu.go.id). There is a handy search function under the 'Mission' menu item, which also gives contact details for other nation's embassies and contacts in Indonesia.

Australian Consulate (Map p130; ☑0361-241118; www.bali.indonesia.embassy.gov.au; Jl Tantular 32, Denpasar; ☺8am-4pm Mon-Fri) The Australian consulate has a consular sharing agreement with Canada.

Japanese Consulate (Map p130; ☑0361-227628; www.denpasar.id.emb-japan.go.jp; Jl Raya Puputan 170, Denpasar; ☺10am-3pm Mon-Fri)

US Consulate (☑0361-233605; https://id.usembassy.gov; Jl Hayam Wuruk 310, Renon, Denpasar; ☺9am-noon & 1-3.30pm Mon-Fri)

Etiquette

Indonesia is a pretty relaxed place, but there are a few rules of etiquette.

Body language Use both hands when handing somebody something. Don't show displays of affection in public, or talk with your hands on your hips (it's seen as a sign of aggression).

Clothing Avoid showing a lot of skin, although many local men wear shorts. Don't go topless if you're a woman at any pool or beach.

Photography Before taking photos of someone, ask – or mime – for approval.

Places of worship Be respectful in sacred places. Remove shoes and dress modestly when visiting temples and mosques.

Food & Drink

For an overview of Balinese cuisine, see p342.

Insurance

A travel-insurance policy to cover theft, loss and medical problems is essential. There is a wide variety of policies, most sold online; make certain your policy will cover speedy medical evacuation from anywhere in Indonesia.

Theft is a potential problem on Bali and elsewhere in Indonesia, so make sure that your policy covers expensive items adequately. Many policies have restrictions on laptops and expensive camera gear, and refunds are often for depreciated value, not replacement value.

Worldwide travel insurance is available at www.lonelyplanet.com/travel-insurance. You can buy, extend and claim online anytime – even if you're already on the road.

Internet Access

➡ Free wi-fi is common in cafes, restaurants, hotels and malls. Internet cafes are uncommon.

➡ Internet speeds are reasonably fast, especially in south Bali and Ubud.

➡ 3G data and faster is universal.

Language Courses

Many visitors to Bali like to learn at least the basics of Bahasa Indonesia. South Bali and Ubud have many tutors who advertise in the same places you'll find rental listings. Otherwise, the best place for courses in Bahasa Indonesia is the **Indonesia Australia Language Foundation** (IALF; ☑0361-225243; www.ialf.edu; Jl Raya Sesetan 190, Denpasar).

Legal Matters

The Indonesian government takes the smuggling, using and selling of drugs very seriously and the drug laws are unambiguous. If caught with drugs, you may have to wait for up to six months in jail before trial. As seen in high-profile cases involving foreigners, multiyear prison

EATING PRICE RANGES

The following price ranges represent the average cost of a main course or meal.

$ less than 60,000Rp (under US$6)

$$ 60,000–250,000Rp (US$6–25)

$$$ more than 250,000Rp (over US$25)

terms are common for people caught with illegal drugs, including marijuana. Those found guilty of dealing can be subject to the death penalty.

Gambling is illegal (although it's common, especially at cockfights), as is pornography.

Generally, you are unlikely to have any encounters with the police unless you are driving a rented car or motorcycle.

In Bali, there are police stations in all district capitals. If you have to report a crime or have other business at a police station, expect a lengthy and bureaucratic encounter. You should dress respectably, bring someone to help with translation, arrive early and be polite. You can also call the **Bali Tourist Police** (☎0361-224111) for advice.

Some police officers may expect to receive bribes, either to overlook some crime, misdemeanour or traffic infringement (whether actual or not), or to provide a service that they should provide anyway. Generally, it's easiest to pay up – and the sooner this happens, the less it will cost. Travellers may be told there's a 'fine' to pay on the spot, while others may offer to pay a 'fine' to clear things up. How much? Generally, 50,000Rp can work wonders and the officers are not proud. If things seem unreasonable, however, ask for the officer's name and write it down.

LGBT Travellers

Bali is a popular spot for LGBT travellers owing to the many ways it caters to a rainbow of visitors. There is a large gay and lesbian expat community and many own businesses that – if not gay-specific – are very gay-friendly. In south Bali and Ubud, couples have few concerns, beyond remembering that the Balinese are quite modest. Otherwise, there's a rollicking strip of very gay-friendly nightclubs in the heart of Seminyak, although there's no part of Bali any LGBT person should avoid.

Having said that, gay travellers in Bali (and Indonesia) should follow the same precautions as straight travellers: avoid public displays of affection. However, as the nation becomes more conservative, any form of closeness between people of the same sex may be unwise. On Lombok, LGBT travellers should refrain from public displays of affection (advice that also applies to straight couples).

Gay men in Indonesia are referred to as homo or gay; lesbians are lesbi. Indonesia's community of transvestite and transsexual *waria* – from the words *wanita* (woman) and *pria* (man) – has always had a very public profile; they are also known by the less polite term *banci*. Islamic groups proscribe homosexuality, but physical harassment is uncommon.

Resources

➡ GAYa Nusantara (www.gayanusantara.or.id) has a very useful website that covers local LGBT issues.

➡ Bali's gay organisation is Gaya Dewata (www.gayadewata.com).

Money

ATMs are common and it's easy to exchange money. Credit cards are accepted at more expensive establishments.

ATMs

There are ATMs all over Bali and in nonrural areas of Lombok. Notable exceptions include Nusa Lembongan. Most accept nonlocal ATM cards and major credit cards for cash advances.

➡ The exchange rates for ATM withdrawals are usually quite good, but check to see if your home bank will hit you with outrageous fees.

➡ Most ATMs allow a maximum withdrawal of one million rupiah.

➡ ATMs have stickers indicating whether they issue 50,000Rp or 100,000Rp notes (the former are easier to use for small transactions).

➡ Most ATMs return your card last instead of before dispensing cash, so it's easy to forget your card.

Credit Cards

Accepted at midrange and better hotels and resorts. More expensive restaurants and shops will also accept them, but there is often a surcharge of around 3%.

Money Changers

US dollars are by far the easiest currency to exchange. Try to have new US$100 bills.

STOPPING CHILD-SEX TOURISM

Strong laws exist in Indonesia to prosecute people seeking to sexually exploit local children, and many countries also have extraterritorial legislation which allows nationals to be prosecuted in their own country for these crimes.

Travellers can help stop child-sex tourism by reporting suspicious behaviour. Reports can be made to the **Anti Human Trafficking Unit** (☎021-721 8098) of the Indonesian police. If you know the nationality of the individual, you can contact their embassy directly.

Humantrafficking.org (www.humantrafficking.org) is an international group with numerous links to groups working to prevent human exploitation in Indonesia.

Follow these steps to avoid getting ripped off when exchanging money:

→ Find out the going exchange rate online. Know that anyone offering a better rate or claiming to charge no fees or commissions will need to make a profit through other means.

→ Stick to banks, airport exchange counters or large and reputable operations such as the Central Kuta Money Exchange (www.centralkutabali.com), which has locations across south Bali and Ubud.

→ Avoid exchange stalls down alleys or in otherwise dubious locations (that sounds obvious but scores of tourists are ripped off daily).

→ Common exchange scams include rigged calculators, sleight-of-hand schemes, 'mistakes' on the posted rates, and demands that you hand over your money before you have counted the money on offer.

→ Use an ATM to obtain rupiah.

Tipping

→ Tipping a set percentage is not expected in Bali, but if the service is good, it's appropriate to leave at least 5000Rp or 10% or more.

→ Hand cash directly to individuals (taxi drivers, porters, people giving you a massage, bringing you a beer at the beach etc) to recognise their service; 5000Rp to 10,000Rp or 10% to 20% of the total fee is generous.

→ Most midrange and all top-end hotels and restaurants add 21% to the bill for tax and service (called 'plus plus').

Opening Hours

Typical opening hours are as follows:

Banks 8am to 2pm Monday to Thursday, 8am to noon Friday, 8am to 11am Saturday

---

RUPIAH REDENOMINATION

Indonesia has plans to redenominate the rupiah by removing three digits from the currency, although the timing of this has been debated for years. For example, the 20,000Rp note would become the 20Rp note. The exchange value of the new notes would remain the same. Changing the national currency is likely to be a very complex process.

Government offices 8am to 3pm Monday to Thursday, 8am to noon Friday (although these are not standardised)

Post offices 8am to 2pm Monday to Friday, longer in tourist centres

Restaurants & cafes 8am to 10pm daily

Shops & services catering to visitors 9am to 8pm or later daily

Post

Every substantial town has a *kantor pos* (post office). In tourist centres, there are also postal agencies, which provide postal services and are often open long hours. Sending postcards and normal-sized letters (ie under 20g) by airmail is cheap, but not very fast.

From Bali mail delivery takes two weeks to the US and Australia, and three weeks to the UK and the rest of Europe.

Most post offices will properly wrap parcels over 20g for shipping for a small fee. Don't use the post for anything you'd miss.

International express companies like DHL, Fedex and UPS operate on Bali and offer reliable, fast and expensive service.

Public Holidays

The following holidays are celebrated throughout Indonesia. Many of the dates change according to the phase of the moon (not by month) or by religious calendar, so the following are estimates only.

Tahun Baru Masehi (New Year's Day) 1 January

Tahun Baru Imlek (Chinese New Year) Late January to early February

Wafat Yesus Kristus (Good Friday) Late March or early April

Hari Buruh (Labour Day) 1 May

Hari Waisak (Buddha's birth, enlightenment and death) May

Kenaikan Yesus Kristus (Ascension of Christ) May

Hari Proklamasi Kemerdekaan (Independence Day) 17 August

Hari Natal (Christmas Day) 25 December

The following Islamic holidays are celebrated by Bali's large Muslim population; in addition, many Indonesians travel to Bali at these times. Dates change each year.

Isra Miraj Nabi Muhammad (Ascension of the Prophet Muhammad) Around April

Idul Fitri (Also known as Lebaran) This two-day national public holiday marks the end of Ramadan; avoid travel due to crowds. Around June.

Idul Adha (Islamic feast of the sacrifice) Around September

Muharram (Islamic New Year) Around September

Maulud Nabi Muhammad (Birthday of the Prophet Muhammad) Around December

Safe Travel

It's important to note that compared to many places in the world Bali is fairly safe. There are some hassles from the avaricious, but most visitors face many more dangers at home. There have been some high-profile cases of visitors being injured or killed on Bali, but in many cases these tragedies have been inflamed by media sensationalism.

Boat travel carries risks. Take precautions (p388).

Alcohol Poisoning

Outside of reputable bars and resorts, avoid *arak*, the locally produced fermented booze made from rice or palm. Deaths and injuries happen – especially on Bali and the Gilis – when unscrupulous vendors stretch stocks with poisonous chemicals.

Drugs

Numerous high-profile drug cases on Bali and Lombok should be enough to dissuade anyone from having anything to do with illicit drugs. As little as two ecstasy tabs or a bit of pot have resulted in huge fines and multiyear jail sentences in Bali's notorious jail in Kerobokan. Try smuggling and you may pay with your life. Kuta is filled with cops posing as dealers.

Hawkers & Touts

Many visitors regard hawkers and touts as *the* number one annoyance in Bali (and in tourist areas of Lombok). Visitors are frequently, and often constantly, hassled to buy things. The worst places for this are Jl Legian in Kuta,

Kuta Beach, the Gunung Batur area and the temples at Besakih and Tanah Lot. And the cry of 'Transport?!?' – that's everywhere. Many touts employ fake, irritating Australian accents ('Oi! Mate!').

Use the following tips to deflect attention:

➡ Completely ignore touts/hawkers

➡ Don't make any eye contact

➡ A polite *tidak* (no) actually encourages them

➡ Never ask the price or comment on the quality of their goods unless you're interested in buying Keep in mind, though, that ultimately they're just people trying to make a living, and if you don't want to buy anything, you are wasting their time trying to be polite.

Orphanages

Bali has a number of 'fake' orphanages designed to extract money from well-meaning tourists. If you are considering donating anything to an orphanage, carefully research its reputation online. Orphanages using cab drivers as hawkers are especially suspect.

Swimming

Kuta Beach and those to the north and south are subject to heavy surf and strong currents – always swim between the flags. Trained lifeguards are on duty, but only at Kuta, Legian, Seminyak, Nusa Dua, Sanur and (sometimes) Senggigi. Other beaches can have strong currents, even when protected by reefs.

Be careful when swimming over coral, and never walk on it. It can be very sharp and coral cuts are easily infected. In addition, you are damaging a fragile environment.

Water pollution is a problem, especially after rain. Swim far away from any open streams you see flowing into the surf, including the often foul and smelly ones at Double Six Beach and Seminyak Beach. The seawater around Kuta is commonly contaminated by run-off from built-up areas.

Theft

Violent crime is uncommon, but bag-snatching from motorbikes, pickpocketing and theft from rooms and parked cars occurs. Take the same precautions you would in any urban area. Other common-sense tips:

➡ Secure money before leaving an ATM (and don't forget your card!).

➡ Don't leave valuables on a beach while swimming.

➡ Use front desk/in-room safes.

Traffic & Footpaths

Apart from the dangers of driving in Bali, the traffic in most tourist areas is often annoying and frequently dangerous to pedestrians. Footpaths can be rough, even unusable; gaps in the pavement are a top cause of injury. Carry a torch (flashlight) at night.

Scams

It's hard to say when an 'accepted' practice such as overcharging becomes an unacceptable rip-off, but be warned that there are people in Bali (not always Balinese) who will try to rip you off.

Most Balinese would never perpetrate a scam, but it seems that very few would warn a foreigner when one is happening. Be suspicious if you notice that bystanders are uncommunicative and perhaps uneasy, and one person is doing all the talking.

CAR CON

Locals (often working in pairs) discover a 'serious problem' with your car or motorcycle – it's blowing smoke, leaking oil or petrol, a wheel is wobbling or a tyre is flat (problems that one of the pair creates while the other distracts you). Coincidentally, a brother/cousin/friend nearby can help, and soon, they're demanding an outrageous sum for their trouble.

WRONG NUMBER?

Bali's landline phone numbers (those with area codes that include ☎0361, across the south and Ubud) are being changed on an ongoing basis. To accommodate more lines, a digit is being added to the start of the existing six- or seven-digit phone number. So ☎0361-761 xxxx might become ☎0361-4761 xxxx. You'll hear a recording first in Bahasa Indonesia and then in English, telling you what digit to add to the changed number.

CASH SCHEMES

Many travellers are ripped off by money changers who use sleight of hand and rigged calculators. Always count your money at least twice in front of the money changer, and don't let them touch the money again after you've finally counted it. The best defence is to use a bank-affiliated currency exchange or ATMs (although there has been a rash of fake card skimmers attached to ATMs, so check authenticity).

Telephone
Mobile Phones

➡ Data speeds of 3G and faster are common across Bali. Any modern mobile phone will work.

➡ SIM cards come with cheap rates for calling other countries, starting at US$0.20 per minute.

➡ SIM cards are widely available and easily topped up with credit.

➡ Watch out for vendors who sell SIM cards to visitors for 50,000Rp or more. If they don't come with at least 45,000Rp in credit you are being ripped off. Go elsewhere.

➡ Data plans average about 200,000Rp for 3.5GB of data.

➡ Telkomsel, a major carrier, often has reps selling SIM cards in the airport arrivals area just before

---

the 'duty-free' shop. They cost 50,000Rp, and come with credit, plus they offer good data deals. This is an easy way to get set up, but make sure you're not dealing with a faux vendor charging outlandish rates.

Phone Codes

The international access code can be any of three versions; try all three.

Indonesia country code	☎62
International call prefix	☎001/008/017
Police	☎110
Fire	☎113
Medical Emergency	☎119

Time

Bali is on Waktu Indonesian Tengah or WIT (Central Indonesian Standard Time), which is eight hours ahead of Greenwich Mean Time/Universal Time or two hours behind Australian Eastern Standard Time. Java is another hour behind Bali.

Not allowing for daylight-saving time elsewhere, when it's noon in Bali, it's 11pm the previous day in New York, 8pm in Los Angeles, 4am in London, and 2pm in Sydney and Melbourne.

Toilets

Western-style toilets are almost universally common in tourist areas. During the day, look for a cafe or hotel and smile (public toilets only exist at some major sights).

Tourist Information

The tourist office in **Ubud** (Fabulous Ubud; Map p150; ☎0361-973285; www.fabulousubud.com; Jl Raya Ubud; ☺8am-8pm; 🛜) is an excellent source of information on cultural events. Otherwise the tourist offices in Bali are not useful.

Some of the best information is found in the many free publications and websites aimed at tourists and expats. There are also numerous Facebook groups, although some are simply forums for the intolerant.

Bali Advertiser (www.baliadvertiser.biz) Has excellent columns with info for visitors including 'Greenspeak' by journalist Cat Wheeler and 'Bali Explorer' by legendary travel writer Bill Dalton.

Bali Discovery (www.balidiscovery.com) The weekly online news report by Jack Daniels is a must-read of events in Bali.

The Beat Bali (http://thebeatbali.com) Useful website and biweekly publication with extensive entertainment and cultural listings.

The Yak (www.theyakmag.com) Glossy, cheeky mag celebrating the expat swells of Seminyak and Ubud.

Ubud Now and Then (http://ubudnowandthen.com) Run by famous photographer Rio Helmi and other luminaries; has Ubud-centric info and features as well as excellent Bali-wide cultural listings.

RENEWING YOUR VISA

You can renew a 30-day Visa on Arrival once (but not a Visa Free). The procedures are complex:

➡ At least seven days before your visa expires, go to an immigration office. These can usually be found in larger cities and regional capitals. The best one for south Bali is the **immigrasi office** (Immigration Office; ☎0361-935 1038; Jl Raya Taman Jimbaran; ☺8am-4pm Mon-Fri) near Jimbaran.

➡ Bring your passport, a photocopy of your passport and a copy of your ticket out of Indonesia (which should be for a date during the renewal period).

➡ Wear modest clothes (eg men may be required to wear long pants).

➡ Pay a fee of 250,000Rp.

➡ You may have to return to the office twice over a three- to five-day period for fingerprinting, photos and other procedures.

One way to avoid the renewal hassle is to use a visa agent such as **ChannelOne** (Map p76; ☎0878 6204 3224; www.channel1.biz; Jl Sunset 100X, Kerobokan) on Bali, who for a fee will do most of the bureaucratic work for you.

Fines for overstaying your visa expiration date are 300,000Rp per day and include additional hassles.

Travellers with Disabilities

Indonesia has very little supportive legislation or special programs for people with disabilities, and it's a difficult destination for those with limited mobility.

Very few buildings have disabled access, and even international chain hotels often don't have proper facilities.

Pavements are riddled with potholes, loose manholes, parked motorcycles and all sorts of street life, and are very rarely level for long until the next set of steps. Even the able bodied walk on roads rather than negotiate the hassle of the pavement (sidewalk).

Public transport is difficult; cars with a driver can easily be hired at cheap rates. Guides are found readily in tourist areas and, though not usual, they could be hired as helpers if needed.

Bali, with its wide range of tourist services and facilities, is the most favourable destination for travellers with disabilities, although this does not mean it is easy.

Visas

Visas are easy to obtain but can be a hassle if you hope to stay longer than 30 days.

Social Visas

If you have a good reason for staying longer (eg study or family reasons), you can apply for a *sosial/budaya* (social/cultural) visa. You will need an application form from an Indonesian embassy or consulate, and a letter of introduction or promise of sponsorship from a reputable person or school in Indonesia. It's initially valid for three months, but it can be extended for one month at a time at an immigration office within Indonesia for a maximum of six months. There are fees for the application and for extending the visa.

Visa Types

The three main visas types for visitors:

Visa in Advance Visitors can apply for a visa before they arrive in Indonesia. Typically this is a visitor's visa, which is valid for 30 or 60 days. Details vary by country; contact your nearest Indonesian embassy or consulate to determine processing fees and times. Note: this is the only way to obtain a 60-day visitor visa, even if you qualify for Visa on Arrival (VOA).

Visa on Arrival Citizens of most countries may apply for a 30-day visa when they arrive at major airports and harbours. The cost is US$35; be sure to have the exact amount in US currency. VOA renewals for 30 days are possible.

Visa Free Citizens of most countries can receive a 30-day visa for free upon arrival. But note that this visa cannot be extended.

If you have obtained one of the coveted 60-day visas in advance, be sure the immigration official at the airport gives you a 60-day tourist card.

For further info on Indonesia's visa situation, contact an Indonesian embassy.

Volunteering

There's a plethora of opportunities to lend a hand in Bali. Information sources include the Bali Advertiser (www. baliadvertiser.biz), under 'Community Groups', and Bali Spirit (www.balispirit.com/ngos). There are also Ubud organisations helping Bali's dogs (p182).

Local Organisations

The following organisations need donations, supplies and often volunteers. Check their websites to see their current status.

Amicorp Community Centre (www.amicorpcommunitycentre. com) This organisation is building a community centre in the village of Les in northeast Bali; tours and programs including culinary classes, permaculture training, Balinese gamelan and dance workshops.

Bali Children's Project (www. balichildrensproject.org) Funds education and offers English and computer training.

East Bali Poverty Project (0361-410071; www.eastbalipovertyproject.org) Works to help children in the impoverished mountain villages of east Bali.

Friends of the National Parks Foundation (www.fnpf.org) Has volunteer programs on Nusa Penida aimed at wildlife conservation.

Gus Bali (www.gus-bali.org) Works to raise environmental awareness on Bali and runs beach clean-up projects that anyone can join.

IDEP (Indonesian Development of Education & Permaculture; 0812 4658 5137; www.idepfoundation.org) Has projects across Indonesia; works on environmental projects, disaster planning and community improvement.

JED (Village Ecotourism Network; 0361-366 9951; www. jed.or.id; tours US$75-150) Organises highly regarded tours of small villages, some overnight. Often needs volunteers to improve its services and work with the villagers.

ROLE Foundation (www. rolefoundation.org) Works to improve well-being and self-reliance in underprivileged Bali communities; has environmental projects.

Smile Foundation of Bali (www. senyumbali.org) Organises surgery to correct facial deformities; operates the **Smile Shop** (Map p150; 0361-233758; www.senyumbali.org; Jl Sriwedari; 10am-4pm Tue-Sun) in Ubud to raise money.

Yayasan Rama Sesana (www. yrsbali.org) Dedicated to improving reproductive health for women across Bali.

Yayasan Bumi Sehat (www.bumisehatfoundation.org) Operates an internationally recognised clinic and gives reproductive services to disadvantaged women in Ubud; accepts donated time from medical professionals. Founder Robin Lim has had international recognition.

YKIP (www.ykip.org) Established after the 2002 bombings, it organises and funds health and education projects for Bali's children.

Women Travellers

Bali

Bali is generally safer for women than many areas of the world, and with the usual care and common sense, women should feel secure travelling alone.

Lombok

Traditionally, women on Lombok and the Gilis are treated with respect, but in the touristy areas, harassment of single foreign women may occur. Would-be guides/boyfriends/gigolos are often persistent in their approaches, and can be aggressive when ignored or rejected. Clothes that aren't too revealing are a good idea – beachwear should be reserved for the beach. Two or more women together are less likely to experience problems, and women accompanied by a man are unlikely to be harassed.

Transport

GETTING THERE & AWAY

Most visitors to Bali will arrive by air. Island-hoppers can catch frequent ferries between eastern Java and Bali, between Bali and Lombok, and between Lombok and Sumbawa.

Flights, tours and rail tickets can be booked online at www.lonelyplanet.com/bookings.

Air

Although Jakarta, the national capital, is the gateway airport to Indonesia, there are also many direct international flights to Bali.

Airports & Airlines

BALI AIRPORT

Ngurah Rai International Airport (http://bali-airport.com), just south of Kuta, is the only airport in Bali. It is sometimes referred to inter-nationally as Denpasar or on some internet flight-booking sites as Bali.

Bali's current airport terminal opened in 2013. Unfortunately, it has many problems:

➔ Outrageous food and drink prices, even by airport standards.

➔ A serpentine layout that forces departing passengers to walk a very long narrow path amid shops.

➔ Long lines at immigration and customs. Immigration officials may offer passengers a chance to cut the queue for an unsanctioned fee of 750,000Rp.

➔ Nonoperating escalators.

➔ Touts offering dubious accommodation and transport services in the arrivals area.

International airlines flying to and from Bali have myriad flights to Australia and Asian capitals. The present runway is too short for planes flying nonstop to/from Europe.

Domestic airlines serving Bali from other parts of Indonesia change frequently.

Air Asia (www.airasia.com) Serves Jakarta as well as Bangkok, Kuala Lumpur, Singapore and Australian cities.

Cathay Pacific Airways (www.cathaypacific.com) Serves Hong Kong.

China Airlines (www.china-airlines.com) Serves Taipei.

Emirates (www.emirates.com) Has good connections from Europe via Dubai.

Eva Air (www.evaair.com) Serves Taipei.

Garuda Indonesia (www.garuda-indonesia.com) Serves Australia, Japan, Korea, London and Singapore direct, plus cities across Indonesia.

Jetstar (www.jetstar.com) Serves Australia.

KLM (www.klm.com) Serves Amsterdam via Singapore.

CLIMATE CHANGE & TRAVEL

Every form of transport that relies on carbon-based fuel generates CO_2, the main cause of human-induced climate change. Modern travel is dependent on aeroplanes, which might use less fuel per kilometre per person than most cars but travel much greater distances. The altitude at which aircraft emit gases (including CO_2) and particles also contributes to their climate change impact. Many websites offer 'carbon calculators' that allow people to estimate the carbon emissions generated by their journey and, for those who wish to do so, to offset the impact of the greenhouse gases emitted with con-tributions to portfolios of climate-friendly initiatives throughout the world. Lonely Planet offsets the carbon footprint of all staff and author travel.

DEPARTURE TAX

Departure tax is included in the price of a ticket.

Korean Air (www.koreanair.com) Serves Seoul.

Lion Air (www.lionair.co.id) Serves cities across Indonesia and Kuala Lumpur.

Malaysia Airlines (www.mas.com.my) Serves Kuala Lumpur.

Qatar Airways (www.qatarairways.com) Serves Doha nonstop with good connections to Europe.

Singapore Airlines (www.singaporeair.com) Serves Singapore several times daily.

Thai Airways International (www.thaiair.com) Serves Bangkok.

Virgin Australia (www.virginaustralia.com) Serves Australia.

LOMBOK AIRPORT

Lombok International Airport (LOP; www.lombok-airport.co.id) Near Praya, this airport is ever more busy. There is good service to Bali and Java, with fewer services going east into Nusa Tenggara. Flights also serve the international hubs of Singapore and Kuala Lumpur. You'll find travel agents for airline tickets in Kuta, Mataram and Senggigi.

Land

Any trip to Bali over land will require a ferry crossing.

Bus

The ferry crossing from Bali is included in the services offered by numerous bus companies, many of which travel overnight to Java. It's advisable to buy your ticket at least one day in advance from a travel agent or at the terminals in Denpasar (Ubang) or Mengwi. Note that flying can be almost as cheap as the bus.

Fares vary between operators; it's worth paying extra for a decent seat (all have air-con). Destinations include Yogyakarta (350,000Rp, 16 hours) and Jakarta (500,000Rp, 24 hours). You can also get buses from Singaraja in north Bali.

Train

Bali doesn't have trains but the **State Railway Company** (Map p130; ☑0361-227131; Jl Diponegoro 150/B4; ☺8am-3pm Mon-Fri, 9am-2pm Sat & Sun) does have an office in Denpasar. From here buses leave for eastern Java where they link with trains at Banyuwangi for Surabaya, Yogyakarta and Jakarta, among other destinations. Fares and times are comparable to the bus, but the air-conditioned trains are more comfortable, even in economy class. Note: Google Translate works well on the website.

Sea

Pelni (www.pelni.co.id), the national shipping line, operates large boats on infrequent long-distance runs throughout Indonesia. For Bali, Pelni ships stop at the harbour in Benoa. Schedules and fares are found on the website. You can enquire and book at the **Pelni ticket office** (Map p58; ☑0361-763963; www.pelni.co.id; Jl Raya Kuta 299; ☺8am-noon & 1-4pm Mon-Fri, 8am-1pm Sat) in Tuban.

Java

You can reach Java, just west of Bali, via the ferries that run between Gilimanuk in west Bali and Ketapang (Java), and then take a bus all the way to Jakarta.

Sumbawa

Ferries travel between Labuhan Lombok on Lombok and Poto Tano on Sumbawa frequently throughout the day.

Lombok

Public car ferries travel slowly between Padangbai and Lembar on Lombok. There are also fast boats from various ports in Bali to the Gilis and Lombok.

GETTING AROUND

The best way to get around is with your own transport whether you drive, hire a driver or cycle. This gives you the flexibility to explore places that are otherwise inaccessible.

Car Rent a small 4WD for under US$30 a day or get a car and driver for US$60 a day.

Motorbike Rent one for as little as US$5 a day.

Public transport Bemos (small vans) provide very cheap transport on fixed routes but most locals have switched to motorbikes.

Tourist shuttle bus Combine economy with convenience.

Taxi Fairly cheap, but only use Bluebird Taxis to avoid scams.

Bemo

Bemos are normally a minibus or van with a row of low seats down each side and

MENGWI BUS TERMINAL

The Mengwi bus terminal is 12km northwest of Denpasar, just off the main road to west Bali. Many long-distance buses to/from Denpasar's Ubung bus terminal also stop here.

When travelling to/from south Bali, you can save time using this terminal compared to Denpasar. Metered taxis are available and fares should be 150,000Rp to 200,000Rp.

which carry about 12 people in very cramped conditions. They were once the dominant form of public transport in Bali, but widespread motorbike ownership (which can be cheaper than daily bemo use) has caused the system to wither. Expect to find that getting to many places is both time-consuming and inconvenient. It's uncommon to see visitors on bemos in Bali.

Fares

Bemos operate on a standard route for a set (but unwritten) fare. The minimum is about 5000Rp. If you get into an empty bemo, always make it clear that you do not want to charter it.

Terminals & Routes

Every town has at least one terminal (terminal bis) for all forms of public transport. There are often several terminals in larger towns. Terminals can be confusing, but most bemos and buses have signs, and if you're in doubt, people will usually help you.

To travel from one part of Bali to another, it is often

TRAVELLING SAFELY BY BOAT

Fast boats linking Bali, Nusa Lembongan, Lombok and the Gili Islands have proliferated, especially as the latter places have become more popular. But safety regulations are nonexistent and accidents continue to happen. In 2016 two tourists were killed when a fast boat to the Gilis exploded.

Crews on these boats may have little or no training: in one accident, the skipper admitted that he panicked and had no recollection of what happened to his passengers. And rescue is far from assured: a volunteer rescue group in east Bali reported that they had no radio.

Conditions are often rough in the waters off Bali. Although the islands are in close proximity and are easily seen from each other, the ocean between can get more turbulent than is safe for the small speedboats zipping across it.

With these facts in mind, it is essential that you take responsibility for your own safety because no one else will. Consider the following points:

Bigger is better It may add half an hour or more to your journey, but a larger boat will simply deal with the open ocean better than the over-powered small speedboats. Also, trips on small boats can be unpleasant because of the ceaseless pounding through the waves and the fumes coming from the screaming outboard motors. Avoid anything under 30 seats except between Nusa Lembongan and Nusa Penida.

Check for safety equipment Make certain your boat has life preservers and that you know how to locate and use them. In an emergency, don't expect a panicked crew to hand them out. Also, check for lifeboats. Some promotional materials show boats with automatically inflating lifeboats that have later been removed to make room for more passengers.

Avoid overcrowding Some boats leave with more people than seats and with aisles jammed with stacked luggage. Passengers are forced to sit on cabin roofs in unsafe conditions. If this happens, don't use the boat.

Look for exits Cabins may have only one narrow entrance, making them death traps in an accident. Sitting at the open back may seem safer but fuel explosions regularly injure passengers at the back of boats.

Avoid fly-by-nighters Taking a fishing boat and jamming too many engines on the rear in order to cash in on booming tourism is a recipe for disaster.

Don't ride on the roof It looks like carefree fun but travellers are regularly bounced off when boats hit swells and crews may be inept at rescue. Rough seas can drench passengers and ruin their belongings.

The ferry isn't safer One of the big Padangbai–Bangsal, Lombok car ferries caught fire and sank in 2014. A Gilimanuk, Bali–Java ferry capsized and sank in 2016.

Use common sense There are good operators on the waters around Bali but the line-up changes constantly. If a service seems sketchy before you board, go with a different operator. Try to get a refund but don't risk your safety for the cost of a ticket.

necessary to go via one or more terminals. For example, to get from Sanur to Ubud by bemo, you go to the Kereneng terminal in Denpasar, transfer to the Batubulan terminal, and then take a third bemo to Ubud. This is circuitous and time-consuming, two of the reasons so few visitors take bemos in Bali.

Bicycle

Increasingly, people are touring the island by *sepeda* (bike) and many visitors are using bikes around towns and for day trips.

There are plenty of bicycles for rent in the tourist areas, but many are in poor condition. Ask at your accommodation. Prices are from 30,000Rp per day.

Bus
Public Bus
BALI

Larger minibuses and full-size buses ply the longer routes, particularly on routes linking Denpasar, Singaraja and Gilimanuk. They operate out of the same terminals as bemos. However, with everybody riding motorbikes, there are long delays waiting for buses to fill up at terminals before departing.

LOMBOK

Mandalika Terminal (Jl Tuguh Faisal) is 3km east of central Mataram; other regional terminals are in Praya, Anyar and Pancor (near Selong). You may have to go via one or more of these terminals to get from one part of Lombok to another. Fixed fares should be displayed. Public transport becomes scarce in the late afternoon and normally ceases after dark.

Tourist Bus
BALI

Tourist buses are economical and convenient ways to get around. You'll see signs offer-

Trans-Sarbagita (Map p54; Jl Imam Bonjol; fare 3500Rp; ⏱5am-9pm) runs large, air-con commuter buses like you find in major cities the world over. It is suited more to locals due to long wait times and unreliable schedules; however, it's handy if you're heading along any of the following four routes: the bypass linking Sanur to Nusa Dua; Denpasar to Jimbaran; Tabanan to Bandara; or Mahendradata to Lebih via Sanur.

ing services in major tourist areas. Typically a tourist bus is an eight- to 20-passenger vehicle. Service is not as quick as with your own car and driver but it's far easier than trying for public bemos and buses.

Kura-Kura Bus (Map p54; ☎0361-370 0244; www.kura2bus.com; Jl Ngurah Rai Bypass, Ground Fl, DFS Galleria; rides 20,000-80,000Rp, day pass from 150,000Rp; 🛜) This innovative Japanese-owned tourist bus service covers important areas of south Bali and Ubud. Buses have wi-fi and run during daylight hours and early evening, and frequencies range from 20 minutes to over two hours. Check schedules online or with the app. There are eight lines and the hub is the DFS Galleria duty-free mall.

Perama (☎0361-751170; www.peramatour.com) The major tourist bus operator. It has offices or agents in Kuta, Sanur, Ubud, Lovina, Padangbai and Candidasa as well as Gili T and Senggigi on Lombok.

Advantages of tourist buses:

➡ Fares are reasonable (eg Kuta to Lovina is 125,000Rp).

➡ They have air-con.

➡ You can meet other travellers.

Disadvantages of tourist buses:

➡ Stops are often outside the centre, requiring another shuttle or taxi.

➡ Buses may not provide a direct service – stopping, say, at Ubud between Kuta and Padangbai.

➡ Popular spots like Bingin and Seminyak are not served.

➡ Three or more people can hire a car and driver for less.

LOMBOK

There are tourist shuttle-bus services between the main tourist centres in Lombok (Senggigi and Kuta) and most tourist centres in south Bali and the Gilis. Typically these combine a minibus with public ferries. Tickets can be booked directly or at a travel agent. These schemes are heavily marketed.

Car & Motorcycle

Renting a car or motorbike can open up Bali for exploration – and can also leave you counting the minutes until you return it; there can be harrowing driving conditions on the islands at certain times and south Bali traffic is often awful. But it gives you the freedom to explore myriad back roads and lets you set your own schedule.

Most people don't rent a car for their entire visit but rather get one for a few days of meandering.

Driving Licences
CAR LICENCES

If you plan to drive a car, you're supposed to have an International Driving Permit (IDP). You can obtain one from your national motoring organisation if you have a normal driving licence. Bring your home licence as well. Without an IDP, add 50,000Rp to any fine you'll have to pay if stopped by the police (although you'll have to pay this fine several times to exceed the cost and hassle of getting the mostly useless IDP).

MOTORCYCLE LICENCES

If you have a motorcycle licence at home, get your IDP endorsed for motorcycles too; with this you will have no problems. Otherwise you have to get a local licence – something of an adventure.

Officially, there's a 2,000,000Rp fine for riding without a proper licence, and your motorcycle can be impounded. Unofficially, you may be hit with a substantial 'on-the-spot' payment (50,000Rp seems average) and allowed to continue on your way. Also, if you have an accident without a licence your insurance company might refuse coverage.

To get a local motorcycle licence in Bali (valid for a year), go to the **Poltabes Denpasar** (Map p190; ☎0361-142 7352; Jl Gunung Sanhyang; ☺8am-1pm Mon-Sat), which is northwest of Kerobokan on the way to Denpasar. Bring your passport, a photocopy of your passport (just the page with your photo on it) and a passport photo. Then follow these steps:

➡ Ignore the mobbed hall filled with jostling permit seekers.

➡ Look helpless and ask uniformed officials 'motorcycle licence?'.

➡ Be directed to cheery English-speaking officials and pay 250,000Rp.

➡ Take the required written test (in English, with the answers provided on a sample test).

➡ Get your permit. Sure it costs more than in the hall of chaos, but who can argue with the service?

Fuel

Bensin (petrol) is sold by the government-owned Pertamina company, and costs a cheap (it's subsidised) 6500Rp per litre. Bali has scads of petrol stations. On Lombok there are stations in major towns. Motorbike fuel is often sold from roadside stands out of Absolut vodka bottles.

Hire

Very few agencies in Bali will allow you to take their rental cars or motorcycles to Lombok.

CAR

The most popular rental vehicle is a small 4WD – they're compact and are well suited to exploring back roads. Automatic transmissions are unheard of.

Rental and travel agencies in tourist centres rent vehicles quite cheaply. A small 4WD costs a negotiable 50,000Rp per day, with unlimited kilometres and very limited insurance. Extra days often cost much less than the first day.

There's no reason to book rental cars in advance or with a tour package; doing so will almost certainly cost more than arranging it locally. Any place you stay can set you up with a car, as can the ever-present touts in the street.

MOTORCYCLE

Motorbikes are a popular way of getting around – locals ride pillion almost from birth. A family of five all riding cheerfully along on one motorbike is called a Bali minivan.

Rentals cost 50,000Rp a day, less by the week. This should include minimal insurance for the motorcycle but not for any other person or property. Many have racks for surfboards.

Think carefully before renting a motorbike. It is dangerous and every year visitors go home with lasting damage – this is no place to learn to ride. Helmet use is mandatory.

Insurance

Rental agencies and owners usually insist that the vehicle itself is insured, and minimal insurance should be included in the basic rental deal – often with an excess of as much as US$100 for a motorcycle and US$500 for a car (ie the customer pays the first US$100/500 of any claim).

Check to see what your own vehicle, health and travel insurance covers, especially if you are renting a motorbike.

Road Conditions

Bali traffic can be horrendous in the south, up to Ubud, and as far as Padangbai to the east and Gilimanuk to the west. Finding your way around the main tourist sites can be a challenge because roads are only sometimes signposted and maps are unreliable. Off the main routes, roads can be rough but they are usually surfaced.

Avoid driving at night or at dusk. Many bicycles, carts

and vehicles do not have proper lights, and street lighting is limited.

Road Rules

Visiting drivers commonly complain about crazy Balinese drivers, but often it's because the visitors don't understand the local conventions of road use. For instance, the constant use of horns doesn't mean 'Get the @£*&% out of my way!'; rather, it is a very Balinese way of saying 'Hi, I'm here.'

➡ Watch your front – it's your responsibility to avoid anything that gets in front of your vehicle. In effect, a car, motorcycle or anything else pulling out in front of you has right of way.

➡ Often drivers won't even look to see what's coming when they turn left at a junction – they listen for the horn.

➡ Use your horn to warn anything in front that you're there, especially if you're about to overtake.

➡ Drive on the left side of the road.

Traffic Police

Some police will stop drivers on very slender pretexts. If a cop sees your front wheel half an inch over the faded line at a stop sign, if the chin-strap of your helmet isn't fastened, or if you don't observe one of the ever-changing and poorly signposted one-way traffic restrictions, you may be waved down.

The cop will ask to see your licence and the vehicle's registration papers, and they'll also tell you what a serious offence you've committed. Stay cool and don't argue. Don't offer a bribe. Eventually they'll suggest that you can pay them some amount of money to deal with the matter. If it's a very large amount, tell them politely that you don't have that much. These matters can be settled for something between 10,000Rp and 100,000Rp, although it will be more if you argue.

Hitching

Hitchhiking is almost unseen on Bali, and as it can never be entirely safe, we do not recommend it. Travellers who hitch should understand that they are taking a small but potentially serious risk. Instead, consider taking an *ojek* (a motorcycle that takes passengers).

Local Transport

Dokar

Small *dokar* (pony carts) are still seen in parts of Denpasar and Kuta, but they're uncommon. Treatment of the horses is a major concern and there is no good reason to go for an expensive tourist ride.

Ojek

Around towns and along roads, you can always get a lift by *ojek* (a motorcycle or motorbike that takes a paying passenger). Formal *ojek* are less common now that anyone with a motorbike can

---

HIRING A VEHICLE & DRIVER

An excellent way to travel anywhere around Bali is by hired vehicle, allowing you to leave the driving and inherent frustrations to others. If you're part of a group, it can make sound economic sense as well. This is also possible on Lombok but less common.

It's easy to arrange a charter: just listen for one of the frequent offers of 'transport?' in the streets around the tourist centres. Approach a driver yourself or ask at your hotel, which is often a good method, because it increases accountability. Also consider the following:

➡ Although great drivers are everywhere, it helps to talk with a few.

➡ Get recommendations from other travellers.

➡ You should like the driver and their English should be sufficient for you to communicate your wishes.

➡ Costs for a full day should average 500,000Rp to 800,000Rp.

➡ The vehicle, usually a late-model Toyota Kijang seating up to seven, should be clean.

➡ Agree on a route beforehand.

➡ Make it clear if you want to avoid tourist-trap restaurants and shops (smart drivers understand that tips depend on following your wishes).

➡ On the road, buy the driver lunch (they'll want to eat elsewhere, so give them 20,000Rp) and offer snacks and drinks.

➡ Many drivers find ways to make your day delightful in unexpected ways. Tip accordingly.

be a freelance *ojek* (stand by the side of the road, look like you need a ride and people will stop and offer). They're OK on quiet country roads, but a risky option in the big towns. *Ojek* are more common on Lombok.

Fares are negotiable, but about 30,000Rp for 5km is fairly standard.

Taxi

BALI

Metered taxis are common in south Bali and Denpasar (but not Ubud). They are essential for getting around and you can usually flag one down in busy areas. They're often a lot less hassle than haggling with drivers offering 'transport!'

➔ The best taxi company by far is **Blue Bird Taxi** (☑0361-701111; www.bluebirdgroup.com), which uses blue vehicles with a light on the roof bearing a stylised bluebird. Drivers speak reasonable English and use the meter at all times. Many expats will use no other firm. Blue Bird has a slick app that summons a taxi to your location just like Uber. Watch out for myriad fakes – there are many. Look for 'Blue Bird' over the windscreen and the phone number.

➔ Taxis are fairly cheap: Kuta to Seminyak can be only 80,000Rp.

➔ Avoid any taxis where the driver won't use a meter, even after dark when they claim that only fixed fares apply.

➔ Other taxi scams include lack of change, 'broken' meter, fare-raising detours, and offers for tours, massages, prostitutes etc.

LOMBOK

Reliable metered taxis operated by **Blue Bird Lombok Taksi** (☑0370-627000; www.bluebirdgroup.com) are found in west Lombok.

Tours

Standardised organised tours are a convenient and popular way to visit a few places in Bali. There are dozens and dozens of operators who provide a similar product and service. Much more interesting are specialised tour companies that can take you far off the beaten track, offer memorable experiences and otherwise show you a different side of Bali. You can also easily arrange your own custom tour.

Standard Day Tours

Tours are typically in white minibuses with air-con, which pick you up from and drop you off at your hotel. Prices range from 100,000Rp to 500,000Rp for what are essentially similar tours, so it pays to shop around. Consider the following:

➔ Will lunch be at a huge tourist buffet or somewhere more interesting?

➔ How much time will be spent at tourist shops?

➔ Will there be a qualified English-speaking guide?

➔ Are early morning pick-ups for the convenience of the company, which will then dump you at a central point to wait for another bus?

Specialist Tours

Many Bali tour operators offer experiences that vary from the norm. These can include cultural experiences hard for the casual visitor to find, such as cremations or trips to remote villages where life has hardly changed in decades. Often you'll avoid the clichéd tourist minibus and travel in unusual vehicles or in high comfort.

Bali Discovery Tours (☑0361-286283; www.balidiscovery.com; prices vary) Personalised and customisable tours across Bali.

Hanafi (Map p54; ☑0821 4538 9646; www.hanafi.net; Jl Pantai Kuta) This legendary tour guide operates from Kuta. Customises trips of all kinds whether for families or couples. Gay friendly too.

JED (Village Ecotourism Network; ☑0361-366 9951; www.jed.or.id; tours US$75-150) Community-based, organises highly regarded tours of small villages, some overnight.

Suta Tours (☑0361-462666, 0361-466783; www.sutatour.com; prices vary) Arranges the standard tours and also trips to cremation ceremonies and special temple festivals, market tours and other custom plans.

Health

Treatment for minor injuries and common traveller's health problems is easily accessed in Bali. For serious conditions, you will need to leave the island.

Travellers tend to worry about contracting infectious diseases when in the tropics, but infections are a rare cause of serious illness or death in travellers. Pre-existing medical conditions, such as heart disease, and accidental injury (especially traffic accidents) account for most life-threatening problems. Becoming ill in some way is relatively common, however; ailments you may suffer include gastro, overexposure to the sun and other typical traveller woes.

It's important to note certain precautions you should take on Bali, especially in regard to rabies, mosquito bites and the tropical sun.

The advice we provide is a general guide only and does not replace the advice of a doctor trained in travel medicine.

BEFORE YOU GO

Make sure all medications are packed in their original, clearly labelled containers. A signed and dated letter from your physician describing your medical conditions and medications (including generic names) is also a good idea. If you are carrying syringes or needles, be sure to have a physician's letter documenting their medical necessity. If you have a heart condition ensure you bring a copy of an electrocardiogram taken just prior to travelling.

If you take any regular medication bring double your needs in case of loss or theft. You can buy many medications over the counter without a doctor's prescription, but it can be difficult to find some of the newer drugs, particularly the latest antidepressant drugs, blood-pressure medications and contraceptive pills.

Insurance

Unless you are definitely sure that your health coverage at home will cover you in Bali, you should take out travel insurance; bring a copy of the policy as evidence that you're covered. It's a good idea to get a policy that pays for medical evacuation if necessary (which can cost US$100,000).

Some policies specifically exclude 'dangerous activities', which can include scuba diving, renting a local motorcycle and even trekking. Be aware that a locally acquired motorcycle licence isn't valid under some policies.

Worldwide travel insurance is available at www.lonelyplanet.com/bookings. You can buy, extend and claim online anytime – even if you're already on the road.

HEALTH ADVISORIES

It's usually a good idea to consult your government's travel-health website before departure, if one is available.

Australia (www.smarttraveller.gov.au)

UK (www.gov.uk/foreign-travel-advice)

USA (www.travel.state.gov)

There is a wealth of travel health advice on the internet.

World Health Organization (www.who.int/ith) Publishes a superb book called *International Travel & Health*, which is revised annually and is available online at no cost.

Centers for Disease Control & Prevention (www.cdc.gov) Good general information.

Recommended Vaccinations

Specialised travel-medicine clinics are your best source of information; they stock all available vaccines and will be able to give specific recommendations for you and your trip.

Your doctor may also recommend the following:

➜ Tetanus Single booster
➜ Hepatitis A
➜ Typhoid
➜ Rabies

Required Vaccinations

The only vaccine required by international regulations is yellow fever. Proof of vaccination will only be required if you have visited a country in the yellow-fever zone (primarily some parts of Africa and South America) within the six days prior to entering Southeast Asia.

Medical Checklist

Recommended items for a convenient personal medical kit (other items can be easily obtained on Bali if needed):

➜ antibacterial cream (eg muciprocin)

➜ antihistamine – there are many options (eg cetirizine for daytime and promethazine for night)

➜ antiseptic (eg Betadine)

➜ contraceptives

➜ DEET-based insect repellent

➜ first-aid items such as scissors, bandages, thermometer (but not a mercury one) and tweezers

➜ ibuprofen or another anti-inflammatory

➜ steroid cream for allergic/itchy rashes (eg 1% to 2% hydrocortisone)

➜ sunscreen and hat

➜ throat lozenges

➜ thrush (vaginal yeast infection) treatment (eg clotrimazole pessaries or diflucan tablet)

IN BALI & LOMBOK

Availability & Cost of Health Care

In south Bali and Ubud there are clinics catering to tourists, and just about any hotel can put you in touch with an English-speaking doctor.

International Medical Clinics

For serious conditions, foreigners are best served in the costly private clinic **BIMC** (Map p54; ☑0361-300 0911, 0361-761263; www.bimcbali.com; Jl Ngurah Rai 100X; ⏱24hr), which caters mainly to tourists and expats. Confirm that your health and/or travel insurance will cover you. In cases where your medical condition is considered serious you may be evacuated by air ambulance to Singapore or beyond; this is where proper insurance is vital because these flights can cost more than US$50,000.

BIMC is on the bypass road just east of Kuta near the Bali Galleria. It's a modern Australian-run clinic that can do tests, hotel visits and arrange medical evacuation. Visits can cost US$100 or more. It has a branch in Nusa Dua.

Hospitals

There are two facilities in Denpasar that offer a good standard of care. Both are more affordable than the international clinics.

BaliMed Hospital (☑0361-484748; www.balimedhospital.co.id; Jl Mahendradatta 57) On the Kerobokan side of Denpasar, this private hospital has a range

---

AVOIDING MOSQUITO BITES

Travellers are advised to prevent mosquito bites by taking these steps:

➜ Use a DEET-containing insect repellent on exposed skin. Wash this off at night, as long as you are sleeping under a mosquito net. Natural repellents such as citronella can be effective, but must be applied more frequently than products containing DEET.

➜ Sleep under a mosquito net impregnated with permethrin.

➜ Choose accommodation with screens and fans (if not air-conditioned).

➜ Impregnate clothing with permethrin in high-risk areas.

➜ Wear long sleeves and trousers in light colours.

➜ Use mosquito coils.

➜ Spray your room with insect repellent before going out for your evening meal.

If you are going to an area where there is a malaria problem, consult with a clinic about the various prescription drugs you can use to reduce the odds that you'll get it.

of medical services. A basic consultation is 220,000Rp.

RSUP Sanglah Hospital
(Rumah Sakit Umum Propinsi Sanglah; Map p130; ☎0361-227911; www.sanglahhospitalbali.com; Jl Diponegoro; ⊙24hr) The city's general hospital has English-speaking staff and an ER. It's the best hospital on the island, although standards are not the same as at those in first-world countries. It has a special wing for well-insured foreigners, **Paviliun Amerta Wing International** (Map p130; ☎0361-257477, 0361-740 5474).

Pharmacies

Many drugs requiring a prescription in the West are available over the counter in Indonesia, including powerful antibiotics.

The **Kimia Farma** (www.kimiafarma.co.id) chain is recommended. It has many locations, charges fair prices and has helpful staff. The Guardian chain of pharmacies has appeared in tourist areas, but the selection is small and prices can be shocking even to visitors from high-priced countries. Elsewhere you need to be more careful as fake medications and poorly stored or out-of-date drugs are common.

Infectious Diseases

Bird Flu

Otherwise known as avian influenza, the H5N1 virus remains a risk to be aware of when travelling in Southeast Asia. It has claimed more than 100 victims in Indonesia. Most cases have been in Java.

Dengue Fever

This mosquito-borne disease is a major problem on Bali; the number of reported cases in 2016 was 80% higher than 2015's already high figure. As there is no vaccine

---

---

available it can only be prevented by avoiding mosquito bites. The mosquito that carries dengue bites day and night, so use insect avoidance measures at all times. Symptoms include high fever, severe headache and body ache (dengue was previously known as 'breakbone fever'). Some people develop a rash and experience diarrhoea. It's vital to see a doctor to be diagnosed and monitored.

Hepatitis A

A problem throughout the region, this food- and waterborne virus infects the liver, causing jaundice (yellow skin and eyes), nausea and lethargy. There's no specific treatment for hepatitis A; you just need to allow time for the liver to heal. All travellers to Southeast Asia should be vaccinated against hepatitis A.

Hepatitis B

The only sexually transmitted disease that can be prevented by vaccination, hepatitis B is spread by body fluids.

HIV

HIV is a major problem in many Asian countries, and Bali has one of the highest rates of HIV infection in Indonesia. The main risk for most travellers is sexual contact with locals, prostitutes and other travellers.

The risk of sexual transmission of the HIV virus can be dramatically reduced by the use of a *kondom* (condom). These are available from supermarkets, street stalls and drugstores in tourist areas, and from the

---

apotik (pharmacy) in almost any town. Don't buy a cheap brand.

Malaria

The risk of contracting malaria is greatest in rural areas of Indonesia. Generally malaria is not a concern on Bali or in the main touristed areas of Lombok. Consider precautions if you are going into remote areas or on side trips beyond Bali.

Two strategies should be combined to prevent malaria: mosquito avoidance (p394) and antimalarial medications. Most people who catch malaria are taking inadequate or no antimalarial medication.

Rabies

Rabies is a disease spread by the bite or lick of an infected animal, most commonly a dog or monkey. Once you are exposed, it is uniformly fatal if you don't get the vaccine very promptly. Bali has had a major outbreak dating to 2008 and people continue to die each year.

To minimise your risk, consider getting the rabies vaccine, which consists of three injections. A booster after one year will then provide 10 years' protection. This may be worth considering given Bali's rabies outbreak. The vaccines are often unavailable on Bali, so get them before you go.

Also, be careful to avoid animal bites. Especially watch children closely.

Having the pre-travel vaccination means the post-bite treatment is greatly simplified. If you are bitten or scratched, gently wash the wound with soap and water, and apply an iodine-based antiseptic. It is a good idea to also consult a doctor.

Those not vaccinated will need to receive rabies immunoglobulin as soon as possible. Clean the wound immediately and do not delay seeking medical attention. Note that Bali is known to run out of rabies immunoglobulin, so be prepared to go to Singapore immediately for medical treatment.

Typhoid

This serious bacterial infection is spread via food and water. Its symptoms are a high and slowly progressive fever, headache and possibly a dry cough and stomach pain. It is diagnosed by blood tests and treated with antibiotics. Vaccinations are 80% effective and should be given one month before travelling to an infected area.

Traveller's Diarrhoea

Traveller's diarrhoea (aka Bali belly) is by far the most common problem affecting travellers – between 30% and 50% of people will suffer from it within two weeks of starting their trip. In over 80% of cases, traveller's diarrhoea is caused by bacteria (there are numerous potential culprits), and therefore responds promptly to treatment with antibiotics.

Traveller's diarrhoea is defined as the passage of more than three watery bowel actions within 24 hours, plus at least one other symptom such as fever, cramps, nausea, vomiting or feeling generally unwell.

Treatment

Loperamide is just a 'stopper' and doesn't get to the cause of the problem. However, it can be helpful, for example, if you have to go on a long bus ride. Don't take Loperamide if you have a fever or blood in your stools. Seek medical attention quickly if you do not respond to an appropriate antibiotic.

➡ Stay well hydrated; rehydration solutions such as Gastrolyte are the best for this.

➡ Antibiotics such as Norfloxacin, Ciprofloxacin or Azithromycin will kill the bacteria quickly.

Giardiasis

Giardia lamblia is a parasite that is relatively common in travellers. Symptoms include nausea, bloating, excess gas, fatigue and intermittent diarrhoea. The parasite will eventually go away if left untreated but this can take months. The treatment of choice is Tinidazole, with Metronidazole being a second-line option.

Environmental Hazards

Diving

Divers and surfers should seek specialised advice before they travel to ensure their medical kit contains treatment for coral cuts and tropical ear infections, as well as the standard problems. Divers should ensure their insurance covers them for decompression illness – get specialised dive insurance if necessary.

Divers should note that there is a **decompression chamber** in Sanur, which is a fast-boat ride from Nusa Lembongan. Getting here from north Bali can take three to four hours.

Heat

Bali is hot and humid throughout the year. It takes most people at least two weeks to adapt to the hot climate. Swelling of the feet and ankles is common, as are muscle cramps caused by excessive sweating. Prevent these by avoiding dehydration and excessive activity in the heat. Be careful to avoid the following conditions:

Heat exhaustion Symptoms include weakness, headache, irritability, nausea or vomiting, sweaty skin, a fast, weak pulse and a normal or slightly elevated body temperature. Treatment involves getting out of the heat and/or sun, fanning the victim and applying cool wet cloths to the skin, laying the victim flat with their legs raised, and rehydrating with water containing one-quarter of a teaspoon of salt per litre. Recovery is usually rapid and it is common to feel weak for some days afterwards.

Heatstroke A serious medical emergency. Symptoms come on suddenly and include weakness, nausea, a hot dry body with a body temperature of over 41°C, dizziness, confusion, loss of coordination, fits and eventually collapse and loss of consciousness. Seek urgent medical help and commence cooling by

---

WATER

Tap water in Bali is never safe to drink.

Widely available and cheap, bottled water is generally safe but check the seal is intact when purchasing. Look for places that allow you to refill containers, thus cutting down on landfill.

Most ice in restaurants is fine if it is uniform in size and made at a central plant (standard for large cities and tourist areas). Avoid ice that is chipped off larger blocks (more common in rural areas).

Avoid fresh juices outside of tourist restaurants and cafes.

getting the person out of the heat, removing their clothes, fanning them and applying cool wet cloths or ice to their body, especially to hot spots such as the groin and armpits.

Prickly heat A common skin rash in the tropics, caused by sweat being trapped under the skin. The result is an itchy rash of tiny lumps. Treat by moving out of the heat into an air-conditioned area for a few hours and by having cool showers.

Bites & Stings

During your time in Indonesia, you may make some unwanted friends.

Bedbugs These don't carry disease but their bites are very itchy. They live in the cracks of furniture and walls and then migrate to the bed at night to feed on you as you sleep. You can treat the itch with an antihistamine.

Jellyfish Most are not dangerous, just irritating. Stings can be extremely painful but rarely fatal. First aid for jellyfish stings involves pouring vinegar onto the affected area to neutralise the poison. Do not rub sand or water onto the stings. Take painkillers, and anyone who feels ill in any

way after being stung should seek medical advice.

Ticks Contracted after walking in rural areas, ticks are commonly found behind the ears, on the belly and in armpits. If you have had a tick bite and experience symptoms such as a rash at the site of the bite or elsewhere, fever or muscle aches, you should see a doctor.

Skin Problems

Fungal rashes There are two common fungal rashes that affect travellers. The first occurs in moist areas that get less air such as the groin, armpits and between the toes. It starts as a red patch that slowly spreads and is usually itchy. Treatment involves keeping the skin dry, avoiding chafing and using an antifungal cream such as Clotrimazole or Lamisil. *Tinea versicolor* is also common – this fungus causes small, light-coloured patches, most commonly on the back, chest and shoulders. Consult a doctor.

Cuts & scratches These can easily get infected in tropical climates so take meticulous care of any cuts and scratches. Immediately wash all wounds in clean water and apply antiseptic.

If you develop signs of infection see a doctor. Divers and surfers should be careful with coral cuts because they become easily infected.

Sunburn

Even on a cloudy day sunburn can occur rapidly, especially near the equator. Don't end up like the dopey tourists you see roasted pink on Kuta Beach. Instead:

➡ Use a strong sunscreen (at least SPF 30).

➡ Reapply sunscreen after a swim.

➡ Wear a wide-brimmed hat and sunglasses.

➡ Avoid baking in the sun during the hottest part of the day (10am to 2pm).

Women's Health

In the tourist areas and large cities, sanitary napkins and tampons are easily found. This becomes more difficult the more rural you go. Birth-control options may be limited so bring adequate supplies of your own form of contraception.

Language

Indonesian, or Bahasa Indonesia as it's known to the locals, is the official language of Indonesia. It has approximately 220 million speakers, although it's the mother tongue for only about 20 million. Most people in Bali and on Lombok also speak their own indigenous languages, Balinese and Sasak respectively. The average traveller needn't worry about learning Balinese or Sasak, but it can be fun to learn a few words, which is why we've included a few in this chapter. For practical purposes, it probably makes better sense to concentrate your efforts on learning Bahasa Indonesia.

Indonesian pronunciation is easy to master. Each letter always represents the same sound and most letters are pronounced the same as their English counterparts, with c pronounced as the 'ch' in 'chat'. Note also that kh is a throaty sound (like the 'ch' in Scottish loch), and that the ng combination, which is found in English at the end or in the middle of words such as 'ringing', also appears at the beginning of words in Indonesian.

Syllables generally carry equal emphasis – the main exception is the unstressed e in words such as besar (big) – but the rule of thumb is to stress the second-last syllable.

In written Indonesian there are some inconsistent spellings of place names. Compound names are written as one word or two, eg Airsanih or Air Sanih, Padangbai or Padang Bai. Words starting with 'Ker' sometimes lose the e, eg Kerobokan/Krobokan. Some Dutch variant spellings also remain in use, with tj instead of the modern c (eg Tjampuhan/Campuan), and oe instead of u (eg Soekarno/Sukarno).

Pronouns, particularly 'you', are rarely used in Indonesian. Anda is the egalitarian form used to overcome the plethora of words for 'you'.

WANT MORE?

For in-depth language information and handy phrases, check out Lonely Planet's *Indonesian Phrasebook*. You'll find it at **shop.lonelyplanet.com**.

BASICS

Hello.	Salam.
Goodbye. (if leaving)	Selamat tinggal.
Goodbye. (if staying)	Selamat jalan.
How are you?	Apa kabar?
I'm fine, and you?	Kabar baik, Anda bagaimana?
Excuse me.	Permisi.
Sorry.	Maaf.
Please.	Silahkan.
Thank you.	Terima kasih.
You're welcome.	Kembali.
Yes./No.	Ya./Tidak.
Mr/Sir	Bapak
Ms/Mrs/Madam	Ibu
Miss	Nona
What's your name?	Siapa nama Anda?
My name is ...	Nama saya ...
Do you speak English?	Bisa berbicara Bahasa Inggris?
I don't understand.	Saya tidak mengerti.

ACCOMMODATION

Do you have any rooms available?	Ada kamar kosong?
How much is it per night/person?	Berapa satu malam/orang?
Is breakfast included?	Apakah harganya termasuk makan pagi?
I'd like to share a dorm.	Saya mau satu tempat tidur di asrama.
campsite	tempat kemah
guesthouse	losmen
hotel	hotel
youth hostel	pemuda
a ... room	kamar ...
single	untuk satu orang
double	untuk dua orang

air-conditioned	dengan AC
bathroom	kamar mandi
cot	velbet
window	jendela

DIRECTIONS

Where is ...?	Di mana ...?
What's the address?	Alamatnya di mana?
Could you write it down, please?	Anda bisa tolong tuliskan?
Can you show me (on the map)?	Anda bisa tolong tunjukkan pada saya (di peta)?

at the corner	di sudut
at the traffic lights	di lampu merah
behind	di belakang
in front of	di depan
far (from)	jauh (dari)
left	kiri
near (to)	dekat (dengan)
next to	di samping
opposite	di seberang
right	kanan
straight ahead	lurus

EATING & DRINKING

What would you recommend?	Apa yang Anda rekomendasikan?
What's in that dish?	Hidangan ituisinya apa?
That was delicious.	Ini enak sekali.
Cheers!	Bersulang!
Bring the bill/check, please.	Tolong bawa kuitansi.

I don't eat ...	Saya tidak mau makan ...
dairy products	susu dan keju
fish	ikan
(red) meat	daging (merah)
peanuts	kacang tanah
seafood	makanan laut

a table ...	meja ...
at (eight) o'clock	pada jam (delapan)
for (two) people	untuk (dua) orang

KEY PATTERNS

To get by in Indonesian, mix and match these simple patterns with words of your choice:

When's (the next bus)?
Jam berapa (bis yang berikutnya)?

Where's (the station)?
Di mana (stasiun)?

How much is it (per night)?
Berapa (satu malam)?

I'm looking for (a hotel).
Saya cari (hotel).

Do you have (a local map)?
Ada (peta daerah)?

Is there (a toilet)?
Ada (kamar kecil)?

Can I (enter)?
Boleh saya (masuk)?

Do I need (a visa)?
Saya harus pakai (visa)?

I have (a reservation).
Saya sudah punya booking).

I need (assistance).
Saya perlu (dibantu).

I'd like (the menu).
Saya minta (daftar makanan).

I'd like (to hire a car).
Saya mau (sewa mobil).

Could you (help me)?
Bisa Anda (bantu) saya?

Key Words

baby food (formula)	susu kaleng
bar	bar
bottle	botol
bowl	mangkuk
breakfast	sarapan
cafe	kafe
children's menu	menu untuk anak-anak
cold	dingin
dinner	makan malam
dish	piring
drink list	daftar minuman
food	makanan
food stall	warung
fork	garpu
glass	gelas
highchair	kursi tinggi
hot (warm)	panas
knife	pisau

SIGNS

Buka	Open
Dilarang	Prohibited
Kamar Kecil	Toilets
Keluar	Exit
Masuk	Entrance
Pria	Men
Tutup	Closed
Wanitai	Women

lunch	makan siang
menu	daftar makanan
market	pasar
napkin	tisu
plate	piring
restaurant	rumah makan
salad	selada
soup	sop
spicy	pedas
spoon	sendok
vegetarian food	makanan tanpa daging
with	dengan
without	tanpa

Meat & Fish

beef	daging sapi
carp	ikan mas
chicken	ayam
duck	bebek
fish	ikan
lamb	daging anak domba
mackerel	tenggiri
meat	daging
pork	daging babi
shrimp/prawn	udang
tuna	cakalang
turkey	kalkun

Fruit & Vegetables

apple	apel
banana	pisang
beans	kacang
cabbage	kol
carrot	wortel
cauliflower	blumkol
cucumber	timun
dates	kurma
eggplant	terung
fruit	buah
grapes	buah anggur
lemon	jeruk asam
orange	jeruk manis
pineapple	nenas
potato	kentang
raisins	kismis
spinach	bayam
vegetable	sayur-mayur
watermelon	semangka

Other

bread	roti
butter	mentega
cheese	keju
chilli	cabai
chilli sauce	sambal
egg	telur
honey	madu
jam	selai
noodles	mie
oil	minyak
pepper	lada
rice	nasi
salt	garam
soy sauce	kecap
sugar	gula
vinegar	cuka

Drinks

beer	bir
coconut milk	santan
coffee	kopi
juice	jus
milk	susu
palm sap wine	tuak
red wine	anggur merah
soft drink	minuman ringan
tea	teh
water	air
white wine	anggur putih
yogurt	susu masam kental

EMERGENCIES

Help!	*Tolong saya!*
I'm lost.	*Saya tersesat.*
Leave me alone!	*Jangan ganggu saya!*
There's been an accident.	*Ada kecelakaan.*
Can I use your phone?	*Boleh saya pakai telpon genggamnya?*
Call a doctor!	*Panggil dokter!*
Call the police!	*Panggil polisi!*
I'm ill.	*Saya sakit.*
It hurts here.	*Sakitnya di sini.*
I'm allergic to (antibiotics).	*Saya alergi (antibiotik).*

SHOPPING & SERVICES

I'd like to buy ...	*Saya mau beli ...*
I'm just looking.	*Saya lihat-lihat saja.*
May I look at it?	*Boleh saya lihat?*
I don't like it.	*Saya tidak suka.*
How much is it?	*Berapa harganya?*
It's too expensive.	*Itu terlalu mahal.*
Can you lower the price?	*Boleh kurang?*
There's a mistake in the bill.	*Ada kesalahan dalam kuitansi ini.*
credit card	*kartu kredit*
foreign exchange office	*kantor penukaran mata uang asing*
internet cafe	*warnet*
mobile/cell phone	*hanpon*
post office	*kantor pos*
signature	*tanda tangan*
tourist office	*kantor pariwisata*

TIME & DATES

What time is it?	*Jam berapa sekarang?*
It's (10) o'clock.	*Jam (sepuluh).*
It's half past (six).	*Setengah (tujuh).*

QUESTION WORDS

How?	*Bagaimana?*
What?	*Apa?*
When?	*Kapan?*
Where?	*Di mana?*
Which?	*Yang mana?*
Who?	*Siapa?*
Why?	*Kenapa?*

in the morning	*pagi*
in the afternoon	*siang*
in the evening	*malam*
today	*hari ini*
tomorrow	*besok*
yesterday	*kemarin*
Monday	*hari Senin*
Tuesday	*hari Selasa*
Wednesday	*hari Rabu*
Thursday	*hari Kamis*
Friday	*hari Jumat*
Saturday	*hari Sabtu*
Sunday	*hari Minggu*
January	*Januari*
February	*Februari*
March	*Maret*
April	*April*
May	*Mei*
June	*Juni*
July	*Juli*
August	*Agustus*
September	*September*
October	*Oktober*
November	*Nopember*
December	*Desember*

TRANSPORT

Public Transport

bicycle-rickshaw	*becak*
boat (general)	*kapal*
boat (local)	*perahu*
bus	*bis*
minibus	*bemo*
motorcycle-rickshaw	*bajaj*
motorcycle-taxi	*ojek*
plane	*pesawat*
taxi	*taksi*
train	*kereta api*

I want to go to ...	*Saya mau ke ...*
How much to ...?	*Ongkos ke ... berapa?*
At what time does it leave?	*Jam berapa berangkat?*
At what time does it arrive at ...?	*Jam berapa sampai di ...?*
Does it stop at ...?	*Di ... berhenti?*

NUMBERS

1	satu
2	dua
3	tiga
4	empat
5	lima
6	enam
7	tujuh
8	delapan
9	sembilan
10	sepuluh
20	duapuluh
30	tigapuluh
40	empatpuluh
50	limapuluh
60	enampuluh
70	tujuhpuluh
80	delapanpuluh
90	sembilanpuluh
100	seratus
1000	seribu

What's the next stop?	Apa nama halte berikutnya?
Please tell me when we get to ...	Tolong, beritahu waktu kita sampai di ...
Please stop here.	Tolong, berhenti di sini.
the first	pertama
the last	terakhir
the next	yang berikutnya
a ... ticket	tiket ...
1st-class	kelas satu
2nd-class	kelas dua
one-way	sekali jalan
return	pulang pergi
aisle seat	tempat duduk dekat gang
cancelled	dibatalkan
delayed	terlambat
platform	peron
ticket office	loket tiket
timetable	jadwal
train station	stasiun kereta api
window seat	tempat duduk dekat jendela

Driving & Cycling

I'd like to hire a ...	Saya mau sewa ...
4WD	gardan ganda
bicycle	sepeda
car	mobil
motorcycle	sepeda motor
child seat	kursi anak untuk di mobil
diesel	solar
helmet	helem
mechanic	montir
petrol/gas	bensin
pump (bicycle)	pompa sepeda
service station	pompa bensin
Is this the road to ...?	Apakah jalan ini ke ...?
(How long) Can I park here?	(Berapa lama) Saya boleh parkir di sini?
The car/motocycle has broken down.	Mobil/Motor mogok.
I have a flat tyre.	Ban saya kempes.
I've run out of petrol.	Saya kehabisan bensin.

LOCAL LANGUAGES

Balinese

How are you?	Kenken kabare?
What's your name?	Sire wastene?
My name is ...	Adan tiange ...
I don't understand.	Tiang sing ngerti.
How much is this?	Ji kude niki?
Thank you.	Matur suksma.
What do you call this in Balinese?	Ne ape adane di Bali?
Which is the way to ...?	Kije jalan lakar kel ...?

Sasak

What's your name?	Saik aranm side?
My name is ...	Arankah aku ...
I don't understand.	Endek ngerti.
How much is this?	Pire ajin sak iyak?
Thank you.	Tampak asih.
What do you call this in Sasak?	Ape aran sak iyak elek bahase Sasek?
Which is the way to ...?	Lamun lek ..., embe eak langantah?

GLOSSARY

adat – tradition, customs and manners

adharma – evil

aling aling – gateway backed by a small wall

alus – identifiable 'goodies' in an *arja* drama

anak-anak – children

angker – evil power

apotik – pharmacy

arja – refined operatic form of Balinese theatre; also a dance-drama, comparable to Western opera

Arjuna – a hero of the *Mahabharata* epic and a popular temple gate guardian image

bahasa – language; Bahasa Indonesia is the national language of Indonesia

bale – an open-sided pavilion with a steeply pitched thatched roof

bale banjar – communal meeting place of a *banjar*; a house for meetings and *gamelan* practice

bale tani – family house in Lombok; see also *serambi*

balian – faith healer and herbal doctor

banjar – local division of a village consisting of all the married adult males

banyan – a type of ficus tree, often considered holy; see also *waringin*

bapak – father; also a polite form of address to any older man; also *pak*

Barong – mythical lion-dog creature

baten tegeh – decorated pyramids of fruit, rice cakes and flowers

batik – process of colouring fabric by coating part of the cloth with wax, dyeing it and melting the wax out; the waxed part is not coloured, and repeated waxing and dyeing builds up a pattern

batu bolong – rock with a hole

belalu – quick-growing, light wood

bemo – popular local transport in Bali and on Lombok; usually a small minibus but can be a small pick-up in rural areas

bensin – petrol (gasoline)

beruga – communal meeting hall in Bali; open-sided pavilion on Lombok

bhur – world of demons

bhwah – world of humans

Brahma – the creator; one of the trinity of Hindu gods

Brahmana – the caste of priests and the highest of the Balinese castes; all priests are Brahmanas, but not all Brahmanas are priests

bu – mother; shortened form of *ibu*

bukit – hill; also the name of Bali's southern peninsula

bulau – month

candi – shrine, originally of Javanese design; also known as *prasada*

candi bentar – entrance gates to a temple

cendrawasih – birds of paradise

cengceng – cymbals

cidomo – horse cart with car wheels (Lombok)

cili – representations of Dewi Sri, the rice goddess

dalang – puppet master and storyteller in a *wayang kulit* performance

Dalem Bedaulu – legendary last ruler of the Pejeng dynasty

danau – lake

desa – village

dewa – deity or supernatural spirit

dewi – goddess

Dewi Sri – goddess of rice

dharma – good

dokar – horse cart; known as a *cidomo* on Lombok

Durga – goddess of death and destruction, and consort of Shiva

dusun – small village

endek – elegant fabric, like *songket*, with pre-dyed weft threads

Gajah Mada – famous *Majapahit* prime minister who defeated the last great king of Bali and extended *Majapahit* power over the island

Galungan – great Balinese festival; an annual event in the 210-day Balinese *wuku* calendar

gamelan – traditional Balinese orchestra, with mostly percussion instruments like large xylophones and gongs; may have one to more than two dozen musicians; also used to refer to individual instruments such as drums; also called a *gong*

Ganesha – Shiva's elephant-headed son

gang – alley or footpath

Garuda – mythical man-bird creature, vehicle of Vishnu; modern symbol of Indonesia and the national airline

gedong – shrine

genggong – musical performance seen in Lombok

gili – small island (Lombok)

goa – cave; also spelt *gua*

gong – see *gamelan*

gong gede – large orchestra; traditional form of the *gamelan* with 35 to 40 musicians

gong kebyar – modern, popular form of a *gong gede*, with up to 25 instruments

gua – cave; also spelt *goa*

gunung – mountain

gunung api – volcano

gusti – polite title for members of the *Wesia* caste

Hanuman – monkey god who plays a major part in the *Ramayana*

homestay – small, family-run accommodation; see also losmen

ibu – mother; also a polite form of address to any older woman

Ida Bagus – honourable title for a male Brahmana

ikat – cloth where a pattern is produced by dyeing the individual threads before weaving

jalak putih – local name for Bali starling

jalan – road or street; abbreviated to Jl

jepun – frangipani or plumeria trees

Jl – *jalan;* road or street

kahyangan jagat – directional temples

kain – a length of material wrapped tightly around the hips and waist, over a sarong

kain poleng – black-and-white chequered cloth

kaja – in the direction of the mountains; see also *kelod*

kaja-kangin – corner of the courtyard

kaki lima – mobile food carts

kala – demonic face often seen over temple gateways

kamben – a length of *songket* wrapped around the chest for formal occasions

kampung – village or neighbourhood

kangin – sunrise

kantor – office

kantor imigrasi – immigration office

kantor pos – post office

Kawi – classical Javanese; the language of poetry

kebyar – a type of dance

Kecak – traditional Balinese dance; tells a tale from the *Ramayana* about Prince Rama and Princess Sita

kelod – in the direction away from the mountains and towards the sea; see also *kaja*

kempli – gong

kendang – drums

kepala desa – village head

kori agung – gateway to the second courtyard in a temple

kras – identifiable 'baddies' in an *arja* drama

kris – traditional dagger

kuah – sunset side

kulkul – hollow tree-trunk

drum used to sound a warning or call meetings

labuhan – harbour; also called *pelabuhan*

laki-laki – boy

lamak – long, woven palm-leaf strips used as decorations in festivals and celebrations

langse – rectangular decorative hangings used in palaces or temples

Legong – classic Balinese dance

legong – young girls who perform the *Legong*

lontar – specially prepared palm leaves

losmen – small Balinese hotel, often family-run

lulur – body mask

lumbung – rice barn with a round roof; an architectural symbol of Lombok

Mahabharata – one of the great Hindu holy books, the epic poem tells of the battle between the Pandavas and the Kauravas

Majapahit – last great Hindu dynasty on Java

mekepung – traditional water buffalo races

meru – multi-tiered shrines in temples; the name comes from the Hindu holy mountain Mahameru

mobil – car

moksa – freedom from earthly desires

muncak – barking deer

naga – mythical snake-like creature

nusa – island; also called *pulau*

Nusa Tenggara Barat (NTB) – West Nusa Tenggara; a province of Indonesia comprising the islands of Lombok and Sumbawa

nyale – worm-like fish caught off Kuta, Lombok

Nyepi – major annual festival in the Hindu *saka* calendar, this is a day of complete stillness after a night of chasing out evil spirits

ogoh-ogoh – huge monster dolls used in the *Nyepi* festival

ojek – motorcycle that carries paying passengers

open – tall red-brick buildings

padi – growing rice plant

padmasana – temple shrine resembling a vacant chair

pak – father; shortened form of *bapak*

pantai – beach

paras – a soft, grey volcanic stone used in stone carving

pasar – market

pasar malam – night market

pecalang – village or *banjar* police

pedagang – mobile traders

pemangku – temple guardians and priests for temple rituals

perempuan – girl

plus plus – a combined tax and service charge of 21% added by midrange and top-end accommodation and restaurants

pondok – simple lodging or hut

prada – cloth highlighted with gold leaf, or gold or silver paint and thread

prahu – traditional Indonesian boat with outriggers

prasasti – inscribed copper plates

propinsi – province; Indonesia has 27 *propinsi* – Bali is a *propinsi*, Lombok and its neighbouring island of Sumbawa comprise propinsi Nusa Tenggara Barat (NTB)

pulau – island; also called *nusa*

puputan – warrior's fight to the death; an honourable but suicidal option when faced with an unbeatable enemy

pura – temple

pura dalem – temple of the dead

pura desa – village temple for everyday functions

pura puseh – temple of the village founders or fathers, honouring the village's origins

pura subak – temple of the rice growers' association

puri – palace

pusit kota – used on road signs to indicate the centre of town

rajah – lord or prince

Ramadan – Muslim month of fasting

Ramayana – one of the great Hindu holy books; these stories form the keystone of many Balinese dances and tales

Rangda – widow-witch who represents evil in Balinese theatre and dance

raya – main road, eg Jl Raya Ubud means 'the main road of Ubud'

RRI – Radio Republik Indonesia; Indonesia's national radio broadcaster

rumah makan – restaurant, literally 'eating place'

saiban – temple or shrine offering

Sasak – native of Lombok; also the language

sate – satay

sawah – rice field; see also *subak*

selat – strait

sepeda – bicycle

Shiva – the creator and destroyer; one of the three great Hindu gods

songket – silver- or gold-threaded cloth, handwoven using a floating weft technique

stupas – domes for housing Buddha relics

subak – village association that organises rice terraces and shares out water for irrigation

Sudra – common caste to which the majority of Balinese belong

sungai – river

swah – world of gods

tahun – year

taksu – divine interpreter for the gods

tanjung – cape or point

teluk – gulf or bay

tika – piece of printed cloth or carved wood displaying the Pawukon cycle

tirta – water

toya – water

undagi – designer of a building, usually an architect-priest

Vishnu – the preserver; one of the three great Hindu gods

wantilan – large *bale* pavilion used for meetings,

performances and cockfights; community hall

waria – female impersonator, transvestite or transgendered person; combination of the words *wanita* and *pria*

waringin – large shady tree with drooping branches which root to produce new trees; see banyan

wartel – public telephone office; contraction of *warung telekomunikasi*

warung – food stall

wayang kulit – leather puppet used in shadow puppet plays; see also *dalang*

Wektu Telu – religion peculiar to Lombok; originated in Bayan and combines many tenets of Islam and aspects of other faiths

wuku – Balinese calendar made up of 10 different weeks, between one and 10 days long, all running concurrently; see also *saka*

yeh – water; also river

yoni – female symbol of the Hindu god Shiva

Behind the Scenes

SEND US YOUR FEEDBACK

We love to hear from travellers – your comments keep us on our toes and help make our books better. Our well-travelled team reads every word on what you loved or loathed about this book. Although we cannot reply individually to your submissions, we always guarantee that your feedback goes straight to the appropriate authors, in time for the next edition. Each person who sends us information is thanked in the next edition – the most useful submissions are rewarded with a selection of digital PDF chapters.

Visit **lonelyplanet.com/contact** to submit your updates and suggestions or to ask for help. Our award-winning website also features inspirational travel stories, news and discussions.

Note: We may edit, reproduce and incorporate your comments in Lonely Planet products such as guidebooks, websites and digital products, so let us know if you don't want your comments reproduced or your name acknowledged. For a copy of our privacy policy visit lonelyplanet.com/privacy.

OUR READERS

Many thanks to the travellers who used the last edition and wrote to us with helpful hints, useful advice and interesting anecdotes:

Ana Tiganescu, Ed Cox, George Nelis, Germma Marjaya, Johannes Feddersen, Kate Larson, Kirsty Spence, Krissi Hall, Kristian Folkman, Marek Porzycki, Marina Abate, Maxime Smits, Meaghan Philpott, Mim Nelson-Gillett, Peter Neundorfer, Rudi Peeters, Sarah Westelinck, Todd Robins, Valeria Parrini, Vincent Janssen

WRITER THANKS
Ryan Ver Berkmoes
Many thanks to friends like Patticakes, Ibu Cat, Hanafi, Stuart, Suzanne, Rucina, Neal, Jenny and Phillip, Ani, Nicoline, Eliot Cohen, Pascal and Pika and many more including Samuel L Bronkowitz. Huge thanks to Amy, the rest of the family and Charlie, who never once ate my shoes. Love to Alexis Ver Berkmoes, we'll always have Bali (Lada Warung or not).

ACKNOWLEDGEMENTS

Climate map data adapted from Peel MC, Finlayson BL & McMahon TA (2007) 'Updated World Map of the Köppen-Geiger Climate Classification', Hydrology and Earth System Sciences, 11, 163344.

Cover photograph: woman carrying flowers through rice paddies, Martin Puddy/Getty ©

THIS BOOK

This 16th edition of Lonely Planet's *Bali & Lombok* guidebook was researched and written by Ryan Ver Berkmoes, who also wrote the previous edition, and curated by Kate Morgan. This guidebook was produced by the following:

Destination Editors Sarah Reid, Dora Whitaker
Product Editor Kate Kiely
Senior Cartographer Julie Sheridan
Book Designer Katherine Marsh
Assisting Editors Janet Austin, Judith Bamber, Melanie Dankel, Kate James, Gabrielle Innes, Kellie Langdon, Kate Mathews, Anne Mulvaney, Fionnuala Twomey, Simon Williamson, Gabrielle Stefanos
Cartographer Julie Dodkins
Cover Researcher Naomi Parker
Thanks to Andi Jones, Lauren Keith, Claire Naylor, Karyn Noble, Lauren O'Connell

Index

Map Pages **000**
Photo Pages **000**

LONELY PLANET IN THE WILD

Send your 'Lonely Planet in the Wild' photos to social@lonelyplanet.com
We share the best on our Facebook page every week!